T0304304

REFLECTION WITHOUT RULES

Reflection without Rules offers a comprehensive, pointed exploration of the methodological tradition in economics and the breakdown of the received view within the philosophy of science. Professor Hands investigates the increased role of naturalistic and sociological approaches in methodological debates and examines the roles of pragmatism, discourse, and situatedness in discussions of scientific knowledge before turning to a systematic exploration of more recent developments in economic methodology. The treatment emphasizes the changes taking place in science theory and its relationship to the movement away from a rules-based view of economic methodology. The work will be of interest to all economists concerned with methodological issues as well as philosophers and others studying the relationships between economics and contemporary science theory.

D. Wade Hands is Professor of Economics at the University of Puget Sound in Tacoma, Washington. He is a frequent contributor to the literature on economic methodology and the history of economic thought. Professor Hands is the author of *Testing Rationality and Progress* (1993), *Introductory Mathematical Economics* (1991), and one of the editors (with John Davis and Uskali Mäki) of *The Handbook of Economic Methodology* (1998). He is currently an Associate Editor of the *Journal of the History of Economic Thought.*

Reflection without Rules

ECONOMIC METHODOLOGY AND
CONTEMPORARY SCIENCE THEORY

D. WADE HANDS
University of Puget Sound

CAMBRIDGE
UNIVERSITY PRESS

CAMBRIDGE
UNIVERSITY PRESS

32 Avenue of the Americas, New York NY 10013-2473, USA

Cambridge University Press is part of the University of Cambridge.

It furthers the University's mission by disseminating knowledge in the pursuit of education, learning and research at the highest international levels of excellence.

www.cambridge.org
Information on this title: www.cambridge.org/9780521497152

First published 2001
Reprinted 2012

A catalogue record for this publication is available from the British Library

Library of Congress Cataloguing in Publication data

Hands, D.Wade
   Reflection without rules: economic methodology and contemporary science theory / D.Wade Hands.
     p. cm.
   ISBN 0 521 49715 9 hardback
   ISBN 0 521 79796 9 paperback
   1. Economics – Methodology. 2. Science – Methodology. I. Title.
HB131.H358   2001
330'.01–dc21   00-041418

ISBN 978-0-521-49715-2 Hardback
ISBN 978-0-521-79796-2 Paperback

To My Students: Past, Present, and Future.

The writing style which is most natural for you is bound to echo speech you heard when a child. English was the novelist Joseph Conrad's third language, and much that seems piquant in his use of English was no doubt colored by his first language which was Polish. And lucky indeed is the writer who has grown up in Ireland, for the English spoken there is so amusing and musical. I myself grew up in . . . Indiana, where common speech sounds like a band saw cutting galvanized tin, and employs a vocabulary as unornamental as a monkey wrench.

[Kurt Vonnegut, 1981, pp. 78–9]

CONTENTS

PREFACE

This book was conceived during a long walk on a sunny North Carolina beach with Bruce Caldwell and Uskali Mäki in the late summer of 1993. It had a very long and – from the author's point of view – often a rather difficult gestation period. While the basic idea seemed (and still seems) quite straightforward – write an interpretative survey of recent work in economic methodology and the various developments within contemporary science theory that are relevant to it – at various points the execution of the task felt overwhelming. One problem was, of course, the "moving target" nature of the subject matter; there were many times where the relevant literature was literally appearing in print at a faster rate than I could read it, much less synthesize, or write about it. Another difficulty stemmed from the fact that my own views about the composition of the "relevant" science theory kept changing and, in particular, expanding during the evolution of the project. Finally, of course, there is always the issue of that nebulous adjective "interpretative," and how it should be, well, interpreted. Although the finished product is undoubtedly a compromise on these and other issues, it is a well-deliberated compromise; I have tried to present a vast amount of literature in a way that is informative, balanced, and fair.

A complete list of all the individuals that I have talked to about these matters would include the majority of the people that I have come into professional contact with during the last twenty years. So with apologies in advance to all of those who I have forgotten to mention, let me just name: Roger Backhouse, Jack Birner, Mark Blaug, Pete Boettke, Stephan Böhm, Larry Boland, Bill Brown, Bruce Caldwell, Doug Cannon, Nancy Cartwright, Bob Coats, Harry Collins, Allin Cottrell, John Davis, Neil De Marchi, Michel De Vroey, Art Diamond, Ross Emmett, Milton Fisk, Steve Fuller, Ron Giere, Doug Goodman,

Craufurd Goodwin, Scott Gordon, Bert Hamminga, Daniel Hammond, Dan Hausman, Jim Henderson, Abe Hirsch, Geoff Hodgson, Kevin Hoover, David Hull, Maarten Janssen, Albert Jolink, Bill Keith, Harold Kincaid, Martyn Kingston, Philip Kitcher, Arjo Klamer, Judy Klein, Noretta Koertge, Roger Koppl, Maurice Lagueux, Larry Larson, Don Lavoie, Tony Lawson, Axel Leijonhufvud, Rob Leonard, Tim Leonard, Paul Loeb, Helen Longino, Steven Lukes, David Magnus, Uskali Mäki, Bruce Mann, Tom Mayer, Deirdre McCloskey, Steve Medema, Philip Mirowski, Mary Morgan, Fred Moseley, Robert Nadeau, Alan Nelson, John Pheby, Andy Pickering, Mark Risjord, Abu Rizvi, Richard Rorty, Alex Rosenberg, Paul Roth, David Ruccio, Malcolm Rutherford, Andrea Salanti, Warren Samuels, Margaret Schabas, Esther-Mirjam Sent, Jeremy Shearmur, Ross Singleton, Kate Stirling, Steve Turner, Mike Veseth, Roy Weintraub, Michael White, Jim Wible, and Nancy Wulwick. From this list I would particularly like to thank Bruce Caldwell, John Davis, Uskali Mäki, and Philip Mirowski, who provided valuable comments on various parts of (in Phil's case all of) the manuscript; I certainly appreciate (although probably did not pay enough attention to) their advice.

I would like to thank the University of Puget Sound (UPS) for consistently supporting me in my research on this book and throughout my career. Over the last two decades, UPS has basically given me every research award, travel grant, and professional growth opportunity that it had available to offer its faculty. In addition, I would like to thank my colleagues in the UPS Economics Department, who have not only supported – but actually encouraged – my (rather strange) interdisciplinary research. I realize that not every economist doing work in the history and philosophy of economics has the advantage of congenial colleagues and a supportive departmental environment. I know how rare it is and I truly do appreciate it. I also am indebted to the various audiences who provided useful comments, at the untold conferences and universities, in many different countries, where the ideas in this book were originally presented. I also would like to thank the anonymous readers for Cambridge University Press as well as all of the other anonymous referees who have provided valuable comments on parts of this manuscript and the various projects that have led up to it. Thanks also go to the people at Cambridge University Press, particularly Scott Parris, and their prompt, efficient, and understanding support throughout this entire project.

Finally, the book contains some material that appeared in earlier papers and I would like to thank the publishers of the following journals and edited volumes for their kind permission to reproduce portions of this material.

"The Structuralist View of Economic Theories: A Review Essay," *Economics and Philosophy*, 1, 1985, 303–35.

"The Logical Structure of Pure Exchange Economics: Another Alternative," *Theory and Decision*, 19, 1985, 259–78.

"The Problem of Excess Content: Economics, Novelty, and a Long Popperian Tale," in *Appraising Economic Theories: Studies in the Methodology of Scientific Research Programs*, M. Blaug and N. De Marchi (eds.), Aldershot: Edward Elgar, 1991, 58–75.

"Blurred Boundaries: Recent Changes in the Relationship Between Economics and the Philosophy of Natural Science," *Studies in History and Philosophy of Science*, 25, 1994, 751–72.

"Conjectures and Reputations: The Sociology of Scientific Knowledge and the History of Economic Thought," *History of Political Economy*, 29, 1997, 695–739.

"Rorty, Richard" and "Positivism" in *The Handbook of Economic Methodology*, J. B. Davis, D. W. Hands, and U. Mäki (eds.), Cheltenham: Edward Elgar, 1998.

"Empirical Realism as Meta-Method: Tony Lawson on Neoclassical Economics" in *Critical Realism in Economics: Development and Debate*, Steve Fleetwood (ed.), London: Routledge, 1999, 169–85.

1

Introduction

Those who can, do science; those who can't prattle about its methodology.

[Samuelson 1992, p. 240]

If we were to believe many economic methodologists, particularly those attempting to impress philosophers of science, you would think that all methodologists sit around "appraising" the work of economists. I have a vision of these guys sitting around in priestly robes ... passing judgment on people such as Becker, Arrow, Samuelson, Friedman, Keynes, etc. On what basis do they criticize such economists? Do they accuse economists of being unscientific? Who cares?

[Boland 1997, p. 152]

Back in 1982, a brief but brusque exchange, touching on the relations between Philosophy and Economics, took place between James Tobin, the liberal, Nobel Laureate, Yale economist, and Robert Nozick, the conservative Harvard philosopher. In the course of a debate . . . Tobin exclaimed at Nozick: "There's nothing more dangerous than a philosopher who's learned a little bit of economics." To which Nozick immediately responded: "Unless it's an economist who hasn't learned any philosophy."

[Hutchison 1996, p. 187]

This book has three separate but interrelated goals. The first is to provide a *survey of recent developments in the field of economic methodology.*

1

The second goal is to *survey contemporary science theory* as it relates to economics and economic methodology. I say contemporary "science theory" in order to include fields like the sociology of scientific knowledge and the rhetoric of science as well as the more traditional fields of philosophy of science and epistemology. Both of these surveys are frankly interpretative, but the survey of economic methodology is perhaps less interpretative than the discussion of science theory. I have tried to touch on most of the major debates within economic methodology; I felt no such compulsion when it came to contemporary philosophy of science and science studies. Although these two surveys constitute the preponderance of the text, they really do not need much introduction; their execution requires a great amount of time and detail, but their motivation is pretty straightforward. This is not the case for the third aspect of the book.

The third goal is to convince the reader that we *should change the subject* (or perhaps I should say that we *should recognize the subject has changed*, since the change is already underway). The traditional subject of economic methodology has been *applied philosophy of science*; economists have simply borrowed various arguments from the philosophy of natural science and then applied (or tried to apply) those arguments to economics – most commonly focusing on the issue of whether economics is (or is not), or what it would need to do to become, a legitimate empirical science. This view – what I have elsewhere (Hands 1994a) called the "shelf of scientific philosophy" view of economic methodology – is, I hope to show the reader, no longer a good place to invest our intellectual resources. Note the word "show"; I will attempt to persuade the reader by titillation rather than regulation; I am not trying to outlaw the production of literature that takes the traditional approach to economic methodology (I have certainly been involved in such work myself). My effort will be on the demand side, an effort to tempt readers away from familiar habits of thought by pointing out the difficulties with those habits and also by letting them try out some of the other approaches that are (increasingly) available. Consistent with the naturalistic perspective I will be presenting, this is not an edict from above, but rather a simple attempt to get the reader into a new intellectual vehicle by giving them a "free" mechanical inspection of their old one, a list of many happy new owners (some of whom aren't aware they traded), and a test drive in a few of the new models with the most innovative features. I realize of course that most readers are just looking – reading this book as a survey of the literature (which most of it is) – and not seriously shopping for either model: new or old.

1.1 Economic Methodology

There are, of course, many ways to characterize the field of economic methodology. One way to think about methodology is to view it as the study of "methods": the practical techniques employed by successful economists in the execution of their day-to-day professional activities. This type of methodology has appropriately been called lower-case-m methodology (McCloskey 1985a, p. 25); it is essential to professional success, usually acquired tacitly, or by rote, in the context of actually working on specific economic research projects: initially under the guidance of one's research supervisor or thesis director, and then later through interaction with one's colleagues, department chair, and various journal editors. It is the source of answers to day-to-day questions like: Is an R^2 this low OK for this kind of model? Is it reasonable to assume the Jacobian matrix has this strange sign pattern? or, It's OK to drop all of the data from the first two quarters of 1929, right? As important as such questions might be, lower-case-m methodology is *not* what most economists mean when they use the term Economic Methodology. One will not find such discussions in existing surveys of the methodological literature such as Blaug (1980, 1992) or Caldwell (1982, 1994a); it is not generally what one will see published in journals like *Economics and Philosophy* or *The Journal of Economic Methodology*, which specialize in methodological research; and, whereas one might overhear such topics discussed by Nobel laureates, it is not what they write about when they write about "Methodology."

Methodology has traditionally focused on the issue of *scientific knowledge* and whether economics in general, or a particular economic theory, is or is not, scientific knowledge. Methodology has traditionally been about the methodological *appraisal* of economic theory: the job of deciding whether an economic theory is a success or failure with respect to the rigorous standards of the scientific method. This view of methodology, of course, carries us immediately into the field of the philosophy of natural science; if one wants to appraise an economic theory with respect to *the scientific method*, then one needs to know what the scientific method is (and is not) and that specification has traditionally been the responsibility of the philosophy of science. In the words of William Whewell over 150 years ago: "The Philosophy of Science . . . would imply nothing less than a complete insight into the essence and conditions of all real knowledge, and an exposition of the best methods for the discovery of new truths" (quoted by Hacking 1996, p. 38). This methodological perspective leads us directly into the traditional "shelf of scientific philosophy" view of economic methodology. We want to have *rules* for what is and is not good science so that we can methodologically appraise economics (or some part of economics) and the best source for these rules is the philosophy of science. Now, it may be the case that the particular subject matter and/or character of economics requires (or allows) the rules to be tweaked a bit in order to accommodate the specific concerns of the economic scientist, but the point of departure clearly remains the shelf of (natural) scientific philosophy.

This way of thinking about economic methodology is certainly consistent with the Enlightenment view of scientific knowledge that has been handed down from Bacon, Descartes, and other philosophers. The view that knowledge of the causal structure of the world could be obtained with certainty if the proper method were followed, and even though philosophers have differed radically about what that proper method actually is, the idea that it – the scientific method – is the secret of epistemic success is common to all the various philosophical approaches. If a social science like economics is to be a science and have certain access to the causal structure of the social and economic world, then it, too, will need to abide by the rules of the proper scientific method. The argument is that science *progresses* in a way that no other human activity progresses, and if economics is to partake in such (even potential) progress, then it had better follow the scientific method. This is, of course, a very difficult assignment for a social science such as economics, which has traditionally been concerned with agency, subjective valuations, individual interests, and intentionality: but according to the traditional view this is a problem for economics and not a problem for the scientific method. The scientific gauntlet has been thrown down; it is up to the economics profession to show it can meet the cognitive challenge. Either economists need to demonstrate that their theoretical concepts pass rigorous scientific muster, or to make a convincing case for some kind of partial special-exemption that allows economics to *be* scientific while playing the epistemic game by slightly different rules. Almost all of the traditional work in economic methodology has fallen into one of these two general categories. Chapter 2 will discuss many of these traditional approaches to economic methodology, while Chapter 7 will examine the more recent literature (some of which is relatively traditional in this sense, and some of which is not).

1.2 Contemporary Science Theory

Science theory went through a major transformation during the latter half of the twentieth century. Perhaps "transformation" is not the best word to describe the process, as transformation suggests that the changes actually culminated in a new well-formed consensus about the structure and character of scientific knowledge. Not so. What happened was a major upheaval with no clear victor emerging (as yet) from amongst the rubble. There was a mainstream view in (at least Anglo-American) philosophy of science during the middle of the twentieth century – as we will see, it was variously called the Received View, or Legend, or (less appropriately) Positivism – and it began to unravel during the 1960s and 1970s. There is not as yet a clear replacement for this mainstream view.

What has become increasingly clear during the last few years is that in order to even be included within the (large) set of contenders, a particular approach to scientific knowledge must be able to address a set of specific and fairly well-defined issues; these are essentially the issues that sunk the former consensus and, consequently, they need to be addressed by any competing approach. They are, in no particular order: underdetermination, theory-ladenness, the social nature of science, relativism, antifoundationalism, and naturalism (all defined and discussed in detail in the chapters that follow). Although it is possible for a particular approach to effectively avoid a direct assault on a few of these issues, such dodges will only be acceptable if they are counterbalanced by exceptional success with respect to most of the others. These issues and concerns constitute the *problem situation* for contemporary science theory. Explaining how these issues came to be the main issues, how various approaches have attempted to deal with them, and how all of this involves (and affects) economics, constitutes the main task of Chapters 3–6.

Because the following chapters examine these issues in what some readers (particularly economists) will consider to be excruciating detail, it does not seem to be particularly useful to jump into the philosophical debate in this brief introduction. This said, I would in fact like to make at least a clumsy pass at one of these particular issues: foundationalism (and antifoundationalism). My reasons for introducing this topic at this point are twofold. First, it is fairly easy to see what the issue is and how it relates to the standard *rules* approach to economic methodology. And, second, it is an issue that begins to play a role very early in the literature on economic methodology (early in Chapter 2).

One way to characterize the problem of the proper scientific method is to focus on the question of *justified* belief. If properly applied, what the scientific method should do is to guarantee that beliefs that have been dutifully processed via the method will be justified. *Foundationalism* is the traditional approach to such justification. Suppose we could identify a set of *basic* beliefs that were "directly" justified – they were self-justified, or incorrigible, and did not rely on any other beliefs for their justification – once we had such basic beliefs we could then "indirectly" infer the justification of other, higher level, beliefs derived from these basic beliefs. These basic beliefs are the *foundations* of knowledge, and the various epistemological frameworks built on such incorrigible foundations are *foundationalist* approaches to knowledge. Of course, foundationalism comes in a variety of different hues; the two most influential in the history of philosophy are *empiricism* (where sense data serve as foundations) and *rationalism* (where reason serves as the foundation). We will find that empiricist foundationalism has constituted the epistemological backdrop for most of mainstream philosophy of science (until quite recently), and that wrestling with the tensions between empiricist foundationism and the practice of economic science has been one of the main concerns of those writing in the field of economic methodology. The unraveling of empiricist foundationalism is one of the main developments leading to the substantial changes that have taken place within contemporary science theory.

1.3 Changing the Subject

The disarray within contemporary science theory poses an interesting problem for the traditional shelf-of-philosophy approach to economic methodology. Although I will argue that the shelf-approach has always been problematic, one does not need to accept this conclusion in order to see that it is *particularly problematic today*, given the current malaise within the philosophy of science and science theory more generally. If philosophers and others within science theory can't agree about the constitution of the scientific method (or even whether asking about a scientific "method" makes any sense), doesn't it seem a little dubious for economists to continue blithely taking things off the shelf and attempting to apply them to economics? The people who have traditionally claimed to be most knowledgeable about the subject of knowledge are currently in disarray on almost every substantive issue; they no longer provide (assuming they ever did) a reliable tool for discussing the relationship between economics and scientific knowledge. The old view of economic methodology as a rule-giving meta-discourse derived from the philosophy of natural science, a methodology that sought to prescribe the correct scientific practice for economists, is entirely discredited by these philosophical (and other) developments. In this (narrow) sense I am in agreement with the recent pronouncements of the "death of economic methodology" by economists such as D. McCloskey (1985a/1998, 1994) and Roy Weintraub (1989).

The difference between me and the aforementioned critics is that I find the revolt against borrowed rules to be liberating, not a death knell: not the end of economic methodology but a chance to change the subject, to reformat the debate, in a more viable and interesting direction. Although the narrow borrowed-rule-giving economic methodology is effectively dead, I believe this is a very fertile and productive period for work in a new more broadly defined field of economic methodology. If economic methodology is defined as the *interpenetration of economics and science theory*, then economic methodology is not only alive, but alive and well. The developments in contemporary science theory open the door not only to new ways of thinking about economics, and economics as knowledge, but also about how economic ideas might be used to help us understand scientific knowledge more generally. Economic methodology is dead; long live economic methodology.

It is important to note that I am not just making a normative claim – arguing that we should adopt a new broader definition of economic methodology – I also will be arguing, in fact mostly arguing, descriptively; the change has already taken place (although many of those who have changed the subject are not aware that they have done so). All I am really asking readers to do is to *recognize* the change that has taken place within the field (and within science theory more generally), and, once it is recognized, to perhaps allow their methodological imaginations to wander a bit more widely than they have in the past. I am advocating the displacement and redirection of the current methodological problematic, but much of my advocacy amounts to little more than pointing out the displacement and redirection that has already occurred. I spend very little time arguing directly against borrowed-rules economic methodology – although once in a while I do attack particular approaches to such rules (old habits die hard) – mostly I will just try to make a new way of thinking and a new vocabulary seem inviting by showing all of the things that have been, and might be, done with them. I will detail the problems within contemporary science theory, but even there I will focus more on redescription than direct attack.

One of my themes throughout is that economics was in some sense *always* involved in science theory – that there never was a pristine shelf of science theory that existed independently of what the contributors to the shelf thought about production, distribution, markets, economic life, and economic theory. I make an ongoing argument that our views about the epistemic order are (and have always been) inexorably intertwined with our views about the economic order. Although I think this is an extremely important point – and one that undermines the traditional view of economic methodology independently of the disarray within contemporary science theory – I also want to stress that even if one does not buy this part of my story, it seems undeniable (at least by the end of Chapter 8) that economics is inexorably intertwined with science theory today. As we will see, the problems of contemporary science theory open the door to economics in significantly new ways; I would say to foreground that which had previously been backgrounded, but in significantly new ways in any case.

As a final point, I would like to note that none of this needs to bring discomfort to those who hold a relatively traditional view of scientific knowledge. One could choose a radical reading of the recent developments within science theory, but it is not necessary. Suppose science does have the unique key to discovering the way that nature really is; such a supposition doesn't alleviate the current problem within the philosophy of science. Science may very well be the unique path to objective truth about the world, but we do not currently know why that is the case or how in any detailed way to differentiate those activities that do the epistemic right thing from those that do not. Sure, we have some rough ideas – conduct empirical tests, be objective, control variables – but there no longer exists a generally accepted philosophical Received View that spells this out in any great detail. This could very well just be a problem *for the philosophy of science* and *not at all a problem for science*, but it still means we should be extremely skeptical about using philosopher's epistemic stories to "appraise" the scientific status of any field: natural or social. In fact, as we will see, the recent "naturalist" turn in science theory (discussed in detail in Chapter 4) considers contemporary *science* to be the starting point for the study of scientific knowledge. Antifoundationalism is not inconsistent with the basic Enlightenment commitment to science as a uniquely worthy form of life, and naturalist versions of antifoundationalism actually elevate science over the traditional foundationalist discourse of philosophers. Does this relief also apply to those with a relatively traditional view of economic knowledge? Perhaps, but it is not entirely clear; we shall see.

1.4 A Reader's Guide

I want to close this introduction with a chapter-by-chapter reader's guide, but before undertaking that task I would like to make a few general remarks about audience, tone, what is and is not included, and such. These remarks are not presented in any particular order of importance.

First, while I certainly hope this book is interesting and useful to philosophers and students of philosophy, people in science studies and students of science studies, and a wide range of general readers, the fact is that it is written primarily with economists and economics students in mind. Most of the people who read and write economic methodology – and, consequently, most of the people who would find a survey useful (and those whom I would want to convince to change the subject) – are economists. They have been trained in economic theory and econometrics and they know what professional life in economics is all about (if they forget, it only takes a moment's conversation with their colleagues or teachers to refresh their memory). Most people interested in economic methodology (or students of economic methodology) do not need a survey of economic theory or a discussion of what economists do and think – they already know those things – what they need is a survey of what is happening elsewhere in intellectual life (particularly in science theory), which might help them in their reflections concerning economics. To this end, the book, although written primarily with economists in mind, does *not* contain very much economics. There are numerous examples scattered throughout the book, but there is not, as is often the case with methodology books written by philosophers, any detailed case studies or attempts to give an elaborate discussion of some particular aspect of economic theory. In other words, the book assumes the reader has more background in economics than in science theory. The book *concerns* economics; it *explains* science theory. The absence of detailed case studies is certainly not because I think such studies are uninteresting or not useful; I have written detailed case studies in the history of economic thought, including contemporary economic thought, and intend to produce many more in the future. It is just that the main purpose of this particular work is to discuss economic methodology and contemporary science theory in the way that best serves the interests of the representative reader: a reader who generally has a pretty good idea what economics is, but would like to know (a lot) more about science theory.

Second, the focus is on *disciplinary* economics – the economics of academic economists and those trained by them – and not ersatz economics, better business bureau economics, or folk economics. *It concerns what students think economics is after they take an economics class, not before.* This is certainly not to suggest that these other forms of economics are not interesting – in fact, I think the relationship between these other forms of economics and disciplinary economics is extremely interesting – it is just that work in economic methodology generally concerns disciplinary economics. It is important to note that, although the focus is on disciplinary economics, it is not exclusively on mainstream disciplinary economics. The book contains substantial discussion of various aspects of heterodox economics – Marxist, Institutionalist, Austrian, and others – as well as mainstream views that are no longer mainstream (say, Mill or Ricardo). Heterodox economists have generally been the disciplinary economists most interested in and most sensitive to methodological issues, and the attention they receive in the following chapters reflects the attention they have given to methodological subjects.

Third, many worthy subjects do not get discussed in the following chapters. Most of the examples of economic theorizing come from microeconomics, general equilibrium theory, and macroeconomics, and while these are clearly the theoretical heart of the discipline, there are other relevant areas within contemporary economics that end up getting short shrift; econometrics and experimental economics come immediately to mind. Econometrics and experimental economics are areas where there has been increased methodological discussion during the last few years and perhaps the framework presented here will serve as an inspiration for additional work in these areas. Another missing subject is any discussion of the growing literature on "ethics and economics"; the book contains a lot of philosophy, but for the most part it is epistemology-based philosophy and not moral philosophy. This, too, is an important subject for additional research.

Fourth, the following chapters do not discuss many of the economists who have made substantial contributions to the methodological literature. Because the book is primarily concerned with recent developments, the discussion of the methodological classics in Chapter 2 focuses mainly on the big names – the "greatest hits" – and neglects many of the economists who had very interesting things to say on methodological topics. There is not any serious discussion of the methodological ideas of economists like Fritz Machlup, Joseph Schumpeter, Tjalling Koopmans, or Wesley C. Mitchell. All I can say is that space considerations and the focus on recent changes precluded the methodological work of such economists. If it is any consolation to readers troubled by the neglect of one (or all) these figures, I would like to note that the book also does not seriously discuss the methodological writings of Frank Knight, a figure that I personally find extremely interesting. I too share the pain of "space considerations."

Finally, there is always the question of when to stop. In writing a survey of a body of literature that continues to grow, one must at some point stop trying to include all of the relevant new material. In my case, that point was reached sometime during the first few months of 1999. Although a few things published after that date make their way into the following chapters, that was the point at which I stopped trying to include everything that I thought might be relevant. In particular, Cartwright (1999b); Favretti, Sandri, and Scazzieri (1999); Friedman (1999); Fuller (2000); Garnett (1999); Goldman (1999); Hacking (1999); and Motterlini (1999) are among the works that appeared too late to be integrated into the text.

With that bit of background out of the way, I now move to the chapter-by-chapter reader's guide.

Chapter 2 surveys the traditional methodological literature. It starts with the work of John Stuart Mill and the Millian tradition in the nineteenth century; proceeds systematically through the work of Lionel Robbins, Terence Hutchison, and certain Austrians early in the twentieth century; and ends with the post-World War II classics by Milton Friedman and Paul Samuelson. This chapter provides a thumbnail sketch of the literature that was called "economic methodology" for most of the twentieth century (at least prior to the last few decades).

Chapter 3 documents the demise of the Received View within the philosophy of science and the literature that surrounded that event. The first section provides a rather detailed discussion of Logical Positivism, Logical Empiricism, and Popperian falsificationism. The second section focuses on the work of W. V. O. Quine, Thomas Kuhn, and related subjects. It examines the two core difficulties identified by Quine and Kuhn – theory-ladenness and underdetermination – and discusses how these problems contributed to the breakdown of the Received View. The chapter also examines a body of literature I call "first round responses" to the problems of the Received View: particularly the work of Imre Lakatos and certain developments within scientific realism.

Chapter 4 discusses some of the many faces of naturalism. The naturalistic turn is examined, with a particular emphasis on Quine's contribution to it, as well as the two main frameworks within naturalized epistemology: evolutionary epistemology and those based on cognitive science. Here, as elsewhere, I emphasize the role of economics and economic ideas on the development of these various philosophical approaches.

Chapter 5 examines the sociological turn in contemporary science theory. The first section traces the sociological approach from its early Marxist roots through the literature on Mertonian functionalism. The second section examines the rise of the sociology of scientific knowledge and the associated tensions within science theory, particularly with respect to the issues of relativism and reflexivity. The final section considers the importance of economics in the sociological literature.

Chapter 6 considers a number of the philosophical (and metaphilosophical) ideas that have influenced contemporary discourse about scientific knowledge, but fall outside the realm of both the philosophy and sociology of science. Over half of the chapter focuses on pragmatism – classical as well as contemporary neopragmatism – but subjects such as postmodernism, the rhetoric of science, and feminist epistemology, are also examined. The relationship between these ideas and economics is emphasized throughout.

Chapter 7 is the longest chapter, and it surveys the recent literature on economic methodology. This chapter basically covers the explosion of work that has occurred in the field since the early 1970s. All of the various twists and turns of the Popperian (and Lakatosian) tradition in economic methodology are discussed, along with recent versions of the Millian approach (Hausman and Cartwright), two important brands of philosophical realism (Lawson and Mäki), the folk-psychological interpretation of economics (Rosenberg), as well as a number of other recent methodological approaches.

Chapter 8 examines the expanding literature where economics is used as a resource in the study of scientific knowledge. This is a rapidly growing field of research, with contributions coming from both philosophers and economists. This literature is extremely important to the overall theme, because it essentially inverts the shelf of scientific philosophy view of economic methodology; this literature takes economics as the shelf, with philosophers and others interested in the growth of scientific knowledge borrowing from the economic shelf.

Chapter 9 provides a summary and some concluding reflections.

2

The Methodological Tradition in Economics

In the definition which we have attempted to frame of the science of Political Economy, we have characterized it as essentially an *abstract* science, and its method as the method *a priori.*

[Mill 1874, p. 143]

I have been increasingly moved to wonder whether my job is a job or a racket, whether economists, and particularly economic theorists, may not be in the position that Cicero ... ascribed to the augurs of Rome – that they should cover their faces or burst into laughter when they met on the street.

[Knight 1956, p. 252]

By the time I had come to work on my doctoral dissertation, I had somehow absorbed Popperian falsificationism without ever reading Popper. Some of it I acquired from Milton Friedman's classic essay "The Methodology of Positive Economics" (1953), which, without mentioning Popper, presents a sort of vulgar, Mickey Mouse Popperianism.

[Blaug 1994a, p. 22]

This chapter will survey the field of economic methodology as it existed in the Anglo-American literature prior to the revival of the last few decades. Although I realize that any attempt to "survey" such a wide-ranging and diverse literature in such a brief amount of space will undoubtedly do an injustice to many authors and many ideas, I hope the injustices are mitigated by the contents of the remaining chapters.[1] The various positions that are introduced here will resurface again and again in later chapters: sometimes as fodder for opposing views, sometimes as reinterpretations, and sometimes as exemplars of particular methodological positions. For example, almost half of this chapter focuses on the Millian tradition: views about economic methodology grounded in the mid-nineteenth-century writings of John Stuart Mill. Three separate subsections are dedicated to the Millian method: the first to Mill's own writings, the second to his nineteenth-century interpreters, and the third to the early twentieth-century authors who were influenced by his approach. Although this discussion only carries the Millian tradition up to the interwar period, the thread is picked up in earnest again in Chapter 7, where various recent reinterpretations of the Millian approach are examined in detail (the work of Daniel Hausman and Nancy Cartwright in particular, along with non-Millian authors, such as Tony Lawson, who also emphasize "tendency laws"). Similar claims can be made regarding the other views surveyed in this chapter. Hutchison's approach (Section 2.2.1) is informed by the positivism and falsificationism discussed in Chapter 3, and his view is examined again in Chapter 7; Friedman's methodology (Section 2.2.2) is alluded to in numerous places and discussed in detail again in Chapter 6; Samuelson's operationalism (Section 2.2.3) is also an example of philosophical positions explored in Chapters 3 and 4. In summary, this chapter merely introduces the main characters of the traditional methodological cast; it does not constitute their only appearance on stage. Later chapters will examine the significant changes that have taken place in methodological research during the last few years, but familiarity with these traditional views is an important prerequisite for understanding these recent changes.

2.1 The Millian Tradition in Economic Methodology

I begin my discussion of the methodological tradition with the work of John Stuart Mill (1806–73). This is certainly not to suggest that methodological writing, even English-language methodological writing, did not exist before Mill. There was, of course, an extensive methodological literature that preceded the publication of the *Wealth of Nations* in 1776, and there were also numerous methodological commentaries on Smith's treatise as well as most of the major works in early nineteenth-century British political economy.[2] Mill is chosen because his work rep-

[1] And the fact that several excellent surveys of these topics are currently available within the methodological literature: Blaug (1980/1992) and Caldwell (1982/1994a) for example.
[2] See Redman (1997) for a recent discussion of this literature.

resents the clearest point of departure for the mainstream methodological tradition discussed in this chapter. He assumed the existence of a body of literature that constituted legitimate "political economy"; he had an explicit philosophical image of natural science and reflected his discussion of political economy off of that scientific image; and he articulated many of the key philosophical issues that repeatedly reemerged in later methodological discussion.

John Stuart Mill was in his mid-twenties when he first formulated his views regarding the method of political economy. His essay "On the Definition of Political Economy" (Mill 1874) – written in 1830–31 and first published in 1836 – still represents one of the most carefully thought-out and articulate documents in the philosophy of economic science. His basic theme – economics *should be, and is,* a science, but its method is *not exactly* the same as the method of the physical sciences – became the dominant view for the next one hundred or so years, and remains one of a handful of views currently competing within the methodological arena.

The first section takes a rather direct approach to Mill's own writings on the method of political economy. Although a massive interpretative literature has emerged on Mill during the last few decades,[3] I will neglect these reinterpretations (some will be discussed in Chapter 7) and simply provide my own reading of Mill's original texts (primarily 1874 and 1884). The second section will examine a few of the other nineteenth-century authors who wrote broadly from within the Millian methodological tradition, particularly John E. Cairnes (1875) and John Neville Keynes (1917). The third section will examine Lionel Robbins's (1932) twentieth-century rendition of the Millian approach, while the final section will discuss the methodology of the Austrian school. The Austrian tradition is not in fact Millian, but, for reasons that will become apparent as the story goes along, it often gets lumped in together with the Millian *a priorist* approach to economic methodology.

2.1.1 John Stuart Mill and the Method A Priori

As John Stuart Mill's famous autobiography (Mill 1961) makes clear, he was a man who struggled to reconcile numerous tensions within his overall system of ideas – the Enlightenment rationality of his father and Jeremy Bentham contrasted with the elegiac sensitivities of Harriet Taylor and the romantic poets, the laissez-faire political economy of

---

[3] Including Cartwright (1989a, 1994b, 1995a), De Marchi (1983, 1986, 1988b), Hausman (1981b, 1992, 1995), Hirsch (1992, 1995), Hirsch and De Marchi (1990), Hollander (1983, 1985), Hollander and Peart (1999), Oakley (1994), Peart (1995), Redman (1997), Schabas (1995), Schwartz (1972), and Whitaker (1975).

Smith and Ricardo with the utopian socialism of Comte and Saint-Simon – but perhaps his greatest challenge was the reconciliation of *empiricist epistemology* and (Ricardian) *economic theory*. Mill was a radical empiricist – the only source of knowledge was sense experience; knowledge was obtained inductively; and scientific laws were simply empirical event regularities – and yet he never surrendered the Ricardian economics of his youth: an economic theory with a tight deductive structure, based on a minimal number of rationally derived assumptions, and exhibiting a less-than-stellar empirical track record. How can economics be scientific, if science is characterized in such narrowly empiricist and inductivist terms? This is Mill's methodological problem, and it is a problem that remains, with various vernacular upgrades, as one of the core problems in the current methodological literature.

Mill's most important work in epistemology and the philosophy of science was *A System of Logic* (1884) originally published in 1843. The first five books of *Logic* laid out his general philosophical position, while the sixth and final book discussed the "logic of the moral sciences," including, of course, economics. Although there are minor changes from his early "On the Definition" essay, the main argument remains the same from 1830 to 1831 to the eighth edition of *Logic*.[4] Mill offers a radical empiricist view of science and then argues for a special dispensation to social sciences such as economics; a dispensation that is based in part on the absence of experimental-laboratory control in the social sciences, and in part on the features of their particular domain of inquiry. In fact, it can be argued that the first five books of *Logic* were merely a set-up for Book Six; Mill never lost sight of the special case of economics in the act of formulating the general case of scientific knowledge. As one recent commentator put it, "Mill's principal reason for writing the *System of Logic* was to build a solid foundation for studying society and politics" (Redman 1997, p. 324).

Mill begins *Logic* with a distinction between truths that are "known directly" and those that are know by "inference" (1884, p. 19); logic is exclusively concerned with the latter. How, or if, our intuitions, sensations, and feelings hook up to the world is the subject of the (separate) field of metaphysics; the study of logic only concerns how we make inferences, that is, how we move from those things known directly to those that are known only indirectly.

> The object of logic ... is to ascertain how we come by that portion of our knowledge (much the greatest portion) which is

---

[4] In fact, at the key point in the *Logic's* discussion of economics (1884, pp. 624–5), Mill's "argument" consists of a long quote from his earlier essay (1874, pp. 137–40).

not intuitive: and by what criterion we can, in matters not self-
evident, distinguish between things proved and things not
proved, between what is worthy and what is not worthy of belief.
(Mill 1884, p. 27)

For Mill, sensations are both the bedrock of knowledge and the stuff
of inference. To say that the sensations I perceive from my computer
screen come from an independent external object (the computer) is to
say that I *believe* such a computer exists; the legitimacy of this belief
(from direct perception alone) is an issue for metaphysics, not logic.
Logic merely provides a mechanism for reliably inferring certain additional beliefs from these initial (directly perceived) beliefs. Knowledge
is thus built up by inference from direct sensations.

It may, therefore, safely be laid down as a truth both obvious in
itself, and admitted by all whom it is at present necessary to take
into consideration, that, of the outward world, we know and can
know absolutely nothing, except the sensations which we experience from it. (Mill 1884, p. 56)

From the viewpoint of contemporary philosophy, such a position represents a (radical) version of empiricist foundationalism.

Although Mill's tone is absolutist about the foundations of knowledge,
he seems more open to contingency when it comes to the *definition* of
particular sciences. He argues that particular sciences should be defined
by the practitioners of those fields, and that changes in scientific theory
over time are likely to cause changes in the definitions of these various
special sciences (such a view is suggestive of the "naturalism" discussed
in later chapters).

What is true of the definition of any term of science, is of course
true of the definitions of a science itself; and accordingly . . . the
definition of a science must necessarily be progressive and provisional. Any extension of knowledge or alteration in the current
opinions respecting the subject-matter, may lead to a change
more or less extensive in the particulars included in the science;
and its composition being thus altered, it may easily happen that
a different set of characteristics will be found better adapted as
differentiae for defining its name. (Mill 1884, p. 110)

Although Mill spends a lot of time on the subject of deduction (syllogism), it always remains of secondary importance. For Mill, all inference
is inductive inference. Because nothing is contained in the conclusion of
a deductive argument that was not already contained in the argument's

premises (deduction is nonampliative) all real inference must be inductive (ampliative). We do not obtain knowledge by deducing "Socrates is
mortal" from the statements "All men are mortal" and "Socrates is a
man"; the only knowledge involved in such a syllogism was acquired in
the inductive process that allowed us to go from the observations of particular men to "All men are mortal" (or from information about Socrates
to "Socrates is a man"). Remember, for Mill all knowledge comes from
observation, and *one does not observe universals*; one only observes particulars. Deduction from universal laws is only as good as the inductive
inferences from particular observations that allowed us to establish the
universal laws in the first place.

> All inference is from particulars to particulars: General propo-
> sitions are merely registers of such inferences already made, . . .
> The major premise of a syllogism, . . . the real logical antecedent,
> or premise, being the particular facts from which the general
> proposition was collected by induction. Those facts, and the indi-
> vidual instances which supplied them, may have been forgotten:
> but a record remains, not indeed descriptive of the facts them-
> selves, but showing how those cases may be distinguished,
> respecting which, the facts, when known, were considered to
> warrant a given inference. . . . a conclusion from the forgotten
> facts. (Mill 1884, p. 146)

It is useful to keep this argument in mind for later when Mill asserts that
economics is a deductive science.

The important distinction for Mill is not induction versus deduction –
in a sense, there is no such thing as deductive inference – but rather
between sciences that *can be made deductive* and those which *must
remain experimental* (Mill 1884, p. 165). He argues that Newtonian
mechanics is an example of the former and chemistry an example of the
latter. In Newtonian mechanics, there are universal laws that can be
mathematically formalized and used for deductions about specific cases,
while chemistry is (or was in Mill's day) still restricted to a case-by-case
experimental method. Mill finds the key to the deductive-experimental
difference in the *law of composition of causes*: the law that "the joint
effect of several causes is identical with the sum of their separate effects"
(Mill 1884, p. 267). In mechanics, there may be many different causes in
operation ($A_1, A_2, \ldots A_n$) but the result of their joint action is the same
as the sum of their independent actions (think of forces as vector addition). In chemistry, by contrast, there is no such law of the composition;
one can not add up the independent properties of oxygen and the independent properties of hydrogen and get the properties of water: or to

use Mill's own example "the taste of sugar of lead is not the sum of the tastes of its component elements" (Mill 1884, p. 267). Sciences such as chemistry that breach the principle of the composition of causes are called *heteropathic* (Mill 1884, p. 269).

Not only does Mill make the distinction between sciences that obey the law of composition of causes and those that do not, he makes a further distinction *within* these two sets. Within the heteropathic sciences there are some (like chemistry) where the experimental method works quite effectively – cases where the process can be reversed and the causes recovered (one can recover hydrogen and oxygen from water) – and others (like the laws of the mind) that do not respond to the experimental method. By contrast, within the sciences that *are* subject to the composition of causes there are also two major divisions: *deductive* (*a priori*) and *experimental* (*a posteriori*). The deductive sciences are those where the various individual causes within the combination are sufficiently identified to allow for deduction based on the individual causes, whereas the experimental sciences (within the class of sciences where the composition of causes is in effect) are those where only the ensemble of causes can be identified.

> The law of an effect . . . is a result of the laws of the separate causes on the combination of which it depends, and is, therefore, in itself capable of being deduced from these laws. This is called the method *a priori*. The other, *a posteriori* method, professes to proceed according to the canons of experimental inquiry. Considering the whole assemblage of concurrent causes . . . as one single cause, it attempts to ascertain the causes in the ordinary manner, by comparison of instances. (Mill 1884, p. 320)

Mill goes on to identify two different versions of the method *a posteriori* on the basis of whether a reproducible experiment is available or whether the only option is pure observation (correlations found in observed cases). He offers the palliative impact of mercury on the human body as a particular example that might be examined in any (or all) of the three (composition) ways: deduction (deduce the impact from laws of mercury and laws of the body), experiment (give mercury to patients and observe results), and pure observation (observe various patients and correlate their recovery with the presence of mercury). Figure 2.1 depicts all of the different versions of the scientific method according to Mill; the top shows the three options that are available when the law of composition of causes is in effect and the bottom shows the two (heteropathic) cases where the composition of causes does not hold.

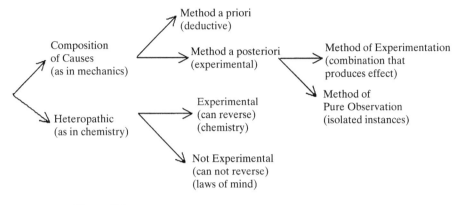

Figure 2.1

Mill warns that when dealing with the composition of causes it is always possible that various causes will offset or cancel each other out; each cause exerts a direct influence, but the observed result depends on the particular combination and thus will depend on the specific magnitude and direction of the various components. For this reason, Mill argues that laws of causation should always be considered *tendency laws*: "All laws of causation, in consequence of their liability to be counteracted, require to be stated in words affirmative of tendencies only, and not of actual results" (Mill 1884, p. 319). The tendency law characterization allows Mill to assert that laws are either true or false, and not that they are sometimes true and sometimes false depending on whether or not countervailing forces are in effect. For example, Mill would not say that a body moves in a particular manner unless prevented by some counteracting cause, but rather that "it *tends* to move in that manner even when counteracted" (Mill 1884, p. 319); it is not that countervailing forces produce exceptions to Newton's law, but rather "that all heavy bodies *tend* to fall; and to this there is no exception" (Mill 1884, 320).

So Mill clearly offers a number of different scientific "methods" depending on the specific characteristics of the science in question, but where do the social sciences, and in particular economics, fit into his schema? In simplest terms, economics is an example of the topmost sequence in the above diagram; it is the deductive (method *a priori*) version of the law of the composition of causes.

Economic phenomena are subject to the law of the composition of causes because social phenomena are simply the sum of the actions of the individuals in the society. Mill is a *methodological individualist* par excellence.

> The laws of the phenomena of society are, and can be, nothing but the laws of the actions and passions of human beings united together in the social state. Men, however, in a state of society are still men; their actions and passions are obedient to the laws of individual human nature. Men are not, when brought together, converted into another kind of substance, with different properties; as hydrogen and oxygen are different from water, . . . Human beings in society have no properties but those which are derived from, and may be resolved into, the laws of the nature of individual man. In social phenomena the composition of causes is the universal law. (Mill 1884, p. 608)

The *deductive* character of economics derives from two main features of the discipline. First, Mill argues that economics, like the other social and moral sciences, does not have the luxury of controlled experiments. Mill uses the example of free trade between nations to emphasize the point. He admits that a "decisive experiment" in trade theory would be desirable, but in order to conduct such an experiment we "must find two nations alike in every other aspect, or at least possessed, in a degree exactly equal, of everything which conduces to national opulence, and adopting exactly the same policy in all their other affairs, but differing in this only, that one of them adopts a system of commercial restrictions, and the other adopt free trade" (Mill 1874, p. 148).[5] Because the experimental (*a posteriori*) method is not available in the social domain, the deductive (*a priori*) method is the only method available to economic science. Economics is a deductive science and only a deductive science.

> But we can go farther than to affirm that the method *a priori* is a legitimate mode of philosophical investigation in the moral sciences; we contend that it is the only mode. We affirm that the method *a posteriori*, or that of specific experience, is altogether inefficacious in those sciences, as a means of arriving at any considerable body of valuable truth; . . . (Mill 1874, p. 145)

Although economics must (by default) be *a priori*, this does not necessarily put it at an epistemic disadvantage. There are particular features

---

[5] We will discover in the next chapter that this problem is just one example of a more general problem associated with empirical testing of scientific theories (the Duhem-Quine underdetermination problem), and that it is not unique to the social sciences.

of the economic domain that make it distinctively amenable to the deductive approach; these features constitute a second reason for Mill's defense of the *a priori* method in economics. The most important of these features is that the economic domain is restricted to just one particular type of phenomena: that which is directly associated with *the pursuit of wealth*. Although many different causes are involved in economic phenomena – and any given effect comes about as the result of the composition of these (often complex) causes – all of these different causes ultimately flow "solely from the desire for wealth" (Mill 1874, p. 138). Economics is thus, in effect, a single cause science; its domain of inquiry is only such phenomena that arises from the pursuit of wealth and economic science is defined solely by the laws associated with that pursuit.

> What is now commonly understood by the term "Political Economy" is not the science of speculative politics, but a branch of that science. It does not treat of the whole of man's nature as modified by the social state, nor of the whole conduct of man in society. It is concerned with him *solely as a being who desires to possess wealth*, and who is capable of judging of the comparative efficiency of means for obtaining that end. It predicts only such of the phenomena of the social state as take place in consequence of the pursuit of wealth. (Mill 1874, p. 137)

This is, of course, an abstraction – the pursuit of wealth is obviously not the only factor operative in our economic lives – but it is a necessary abstraction that defines the science of economics.

> Political Economy considers mankind as occupied solely in acquiring and consuming wealth; and aims at showing what is the course of action to which mankind, living in a state of society, would be impelled, if that motive, . . . were absolute ruler of all their actions. . . . Not that any political economist was ever so absurd as to suppose that mankind are really thus constituted, but because this is the mode in which science must necessarily proceed. (Mill 1874, pp. 138–9)

Economics is thus an *abstract* science and its method is the deductive method *a priori*. Economists start from assumed premises about the behavior of economic agents engaged in activities related to the pursuit of wealth and then deduce various conclusions on the basis of that behavior. The result is a science such as *geometry*, which is true in the abstract but will only be true in concrete cases with inclusion of the proper specific allowances (Mill 1874, p. 145).[6] This situation is (negatively) the result of the lack of experimentation, and (positively) because all of the relevant phenomena can ultimately be reduced to the effect of a single cause: the pursuit of wealth.

Although it is the case that economics is "true only in the abstract," it is decidedly not the case that economics is thereby rendered otiose for practical and policy purposes. Like geometry, economics is abstract, but it is also quite useful as a guide for practical activities: building bridges in the case of geometry, and deciding trade policy in the case of economics. Such applications actually reintroduce the *a posteriori* back into economic science; in order to apply economics it is necessary to *verify* which particular causes (and countervailing forces) are in effect. In Mill's words, the *a posteriori* method is important in economics "not as a means of discovering truth, but of verifying it, and reducing to the lowest point that uncertainty ... arising from the complexity of every particular case, and from the difficulty (not to say impossibility) of our being assured *a priori* that we have taken into account all the material circumstances" (Mill 1874, pp. 152–3). Concrete cases and real-world applications require knowledge about specific conditions and disturbing causes, and that in turn requires empirical verification, since the "discrepancy between our anticipations and the actual fact is often the only circumstance which would have drawn our attention to some important disturbing cause which we had overlooked" (Mill 1874, p. 154). Notice that Mill is not arguing for the empirical testing of the core presuppositions of economic theory (as many later methodologists will endorse) but rather the empirical examination of the details of the specific case in order to discover which particular factors, particularly disturbing causes, are in effect. It is an abstract *a priori* method, that employs *a posteriori* empirical verification in the context of concrete applications.

In saying this, of course, we should not forget the (rather radical) empiricism that undergirds Mill's entire philosophical project. Although Mill does assert that economics is based on the deductive method *a priori*, we also must remember that for him *there is no such thing* as *a priori* knowledge. All knowledge is *a posteriori*: grounded in, and inductively inferred from, direct observation. The universals that economists take as *a priori* for the purposes of economic analysis, constitute knowledge only to the extent that they are (or were at some point) grounded

---

[6] Remember, for Mill, geometry, like all other mathematics, ultimately starts from observation and constitutes knowledge only to the extent that its axioms were (at one point) derived by induction from empirical observations. This is a much stronger form of empiricism than the empiricism endorsed by the logical positivists discussed in the next chapter (it also predates the disruptive impact of non-Euclidean geometry).

in particular empirical observations and generalized on the basis of valid inductive inference. The economist's *a priori* method involves syllogistic reasoning, and for Mill, "where syllogism is used, the syllogism is not the correct analysis of that process of reasoning . . . which is, on the contrary . . . an inference from particulars to particulars; authorized by a previous inference from particulars to generals, and . . . therefore, of Induction" (Mill 1884, p. 148). Economists employ the *a priori* method, but economic science constitutes *knowledge* because of the empirical grounding – including introspection as a type of empirical ground – and the logic of the inductive inferences that lie behind the general laws about the actions of humans in the pursuit of wealth. We will see that this is not what many (most) later methodologists mean by *a priori*.

Mill argues that much of the confusion regarding economics – specifically Ricardian economics – comes about because the "best teachers" of economics have rendered "it perfect as an abstract science" (Mill 1874, p. 149), and such an abstract science does not necessarily coincide with the interests of the "practical man." Not only must economics be abstract because of the lack of experimental control, the complexity of economic events makes verification of specific concrete cases particularly difficult; the result is that economists have elaborated an abstract deductive science of *tendency laws*. Although these tendency laws are useful for the analysis of concrete problems, the resulting science is at best *inexact*; they will be capable of identifying the underlying causal tendencies, but it may be very difficult to identify the myriad of countervailing forces necessary to refine the law so that it can be applied to specific concrete cases. The practical man thinks of economic laws as riddled with exceptions, when in fact they should think of economic laws as exceptionless, but inexact, statements about tendencies; such laws can provide insight into concrete cases, but, by necessity, must remain at a relatively abstract level.

Mill's own discussion of the falling rate of profit and the movement of the economy toward the stationary state in Book Six of his *Principles of Political Economy* (1909) represents a good example of how such abstract tendency laws relate to the concrete concerns of the practical man. Mill argues, following Ricardo, that the combination of Malthusian population theory and the differential fertility of agricultural land will produce a tendency for the rate of profit to fall in a capitalist economy. The causal story is that profit leads to investment, which increases the demand for labor, which in turn increases wages above the subsistence level. In the long run, higher wages will cause (via Malthus) population to increase, which will increase the demand for food, which will in turn bring less fertile land into cultivation. Moving to less fertile land (via

Ricardian rent and profit theory) will cause rents to rise and the rate of profit to fall. For Mill, this is a (true) tendency law; there are many countervailing forces to this tendency (which Mill discusses in detail), but the countervailing forces do not mean that the law of the falling rate of profit is subject to exceptions. The law says there is a *tendency* for the rate of profit to fall in a capitalist economy, and as a law about tendencies it is exceptionless. The deduction of the law follows from the desire to pursue wealth (economics), the laws of population theory, and the differential fertility of the soil (viewed as natural laws); and is epistemically grounded in the inferences that originally justified these laws from particular observations. The law of the tendency of the rate of profit to fall does have certain practical implications – like supporting the repeal of the Corn (and Poor) Laws – but it is too inexact to predict (even qualitatively) what the rate of profit will be in any particular capitalist economy at any particular point in time. The practical man may desire more, but such abstract tendency laws are really the best that economics has (or will have) to offer. Economics is clearly a science and produces knowledge, but it is a particular type of science, and the type of (inexact) knowledge that it produces is not the same as the knowledge available in the (exact) physical sciences.

2.1.2 The Millian Tradition in the Nineteenth Century

Mill was certainly not alone in defending Ricardian political economy as an inexact deductive science. Nassau Senior's *An Outline of the Science of Political Economy* (1936) was published the same year as Mill's own "Outline" and endorsed a similar view. Senior argued that the science of political economy ultimately rested on four "general propositions": (1) that "every man desires to obtain additional wealth with as little sacrifice as possible," (2) that population is limited by the available resources, (3) that capital enhances the productivity of labor, and (4) that agriculture exhibits diminishing returns (Senior 1836, p. 26). Senior's defense of the first (pursuit of wealth) assumption was characteristically Millian: "In short, it [the pursuit of wealth] is in Political Economy what gravitation is in Physics . . . the ultimate fact beyond which reasoning can not go, and of which almost every other proposition is merely an illustration" (Senior 1936, p. 28).

Despite Mill's methodological defense and the British government's acceptance of many Ricardian policy proposals, all was not well within the Ricardian camp. During the fifty years following the publication of the *Principles* (1817), the Ricardian program came under attack from a wide range of critics and on a wide range of different issues. One problem was the available empirical evidence; the data seemed to be so much at

odds with the theory's predictions that even Mill's numerous methodological hedges (inexactness, tendencies only, . . .) were not sufficient to
allay all of the suspicions regarding the adequacy of the Ricardian framework.[7] Second, the Ricardian program was assailed by a cacophony of
critical voices exhorting political economists to adopt a more empirical,
inductive, and *a posteriori*, approach to their science. This methodological attack came from at least three (related but not coordinated) directions: a general methodological critique by scientists and historians
of natural science like William Whewell (1794–1866); the alternative
methodological approach offered by the German historical school of
Bruno Hildenbrand (1812–78), Wilhelm Roscher (1817–94), Karl Knies
(1821–98), and Gustav von Schmoller (1838–1917); and the sustained
criticism of English historists like Walter Bagehot (1826–77), William
Cunningham (1849–1919), John K. Ingram (1823–1907), Richard Jones
(1790–1855), Cliffe Leslie (1825–82), and others.[8] This latter group of
English historists was particularly damaging to the Ricardian program;
they "questioned the scientific status of political economy and the
purpose of the subject; they protested against the narrowness of its
scope; and they complained of the excessive reliance on the abstract-
deductive method of reasoning" (Coats 1992, p. 221). All three of these
critical literatures endorsed an approach to economics that was more historical, more directly empirical, less general, less abstract, and less dependent on the key assumption of the pursuit of wealth; in other words,
they expressly rejected Mill's arguments regarding the inexact deductive
science of economics.

John Cairnes's *The Character and Logical Method of Political
Economy* (1875), first published in 1857, offered a forceful counterof-
fensive to these critical assaults. Cairnes was able to simultaneously shore
up the weak points in the Millian philosophical fortification and to "dis-
credit the empirical objections of Ricardo's critics" (Blaug 1958, p. 216).
According to Cairnes, political economy provides humanity with a
unique intellectual resource, and the "writer who has employed this
particular resource most freely and with the most effect is Ricardo;
nor could a more decisive proof be given of the ignorance generally
prevailing on the subject of Political Economy than is furnished by the

---

[7] There is a substantial debate within the historical literature regarding the degree to which
Ricardian theory did (or did not) make empirical predictions, and did (or did not) agree
with the available empirical evidence. See Blaug (1958) and De Marchi (1970), for example.

[8] Because there is an extensive literature on all three of these topics, I just mention De
Marchi and Sturges (1973), Henderson (1990, 1998), and Hollander (1983) on Whewell,
and Coats (1992) and Koot (1987) on the British historists; the German historical school
will appear again during the discussion of the *Methodenstreit* (in Section 2.1.4).

flippant attacks which have been made upon this eminent thinker from so many quarters on this account" (Cairnes 1875, p. 93).

Although Cairnes's approach was broadly Millian – economics is an inexact deductive science of tendency laws – he deviated from Mill on a number of specific points. Although individually each of these deviations seems to be relatively minor, they add up to a substantive revision of the Millian method; Millian method circa 1857 was different from – and in certain respects provided a more robust defense of Ricardian economics than – the Millian method of 1836.

Although Mill often spoke of economics as a "hypothetical" science, Cairnes is much more insistent about the importance of the discipline's hypothetical character. Unlike Mill, Cairnes makes a strict demarcation between sciences that are "hypothetical" and sciences that are "positive." His distinction between "hypothetical" and "positive" roughly accords with Mill's distinction between "deductive" and "experimental" (see Figure 2.1 above). The "physical sciences which have advanced so far as to admit of deductive reasoning must be considered hypothetical" (Cairnes 1875, p. 61). Deducing concrete results from abstract laws is only possible if countervailing forces are not significant (or cancel each other out), that is under the *hypothesis* that all of the relevant causes have been identified. In Cairnes's own words:

> The conclusions, e.g., of a mechanician or of an astronomer, though correctly deduced from premises representing concrete realities, may have nothing accurately to correspond with them in nature. The mechanician may have overlooked the disturbing influence of friction. The astronomer may have been ignorant of the existence of some planet, . . . The conclusions of each, therefore, when applied to the facts, can only be said to be true *in the absence of disturbing causes*; which is, in other words, to say that they are true on *the hypothesis* that the premises include all of the causes affecting the result. (Cairnes 1875, p. 61, emphasis in original)

The sciences that "have not advanced far enough to admit of deductive reasoning" are stuck with laws that are simply "generalized statements of observed phenomena," and "represent not hypothetical but positive truth" (Cairnes 1875, p. 62). Political economy is a "hypothetical" science, but this is simply because *it is sufficiently advanced* to have reached the deductive stage. The conclusions of economic science "will correspond with facts *only in the absence of disturbing causes*, which is, in other words, to say that they represent not positive but hypothetical truth" (Cairnes 1875, p. 64, emphasis in original). This is certainly a Millian view, but it is not exactly the view of Mill. In particular, what might be called Mill's epistemic graciousness seems to be gone; it is not simply that there are different scientific methods for different domains of inquiry; now some sciences are *advanced* and others are left behind (political economy, of course, makes the grade).

Another difference is that although Cairnes agrees with Mill that experimentation is not available in economics, he views this as a *strength* and not just a dissimilarity with physics. Economists are concerned with activities associated with the pursuit of wealth, but such activities vary widely among different people depending on their context, culture, individual characteristics, and so on – economics deals with complex phenomena that are not amenable to experimental inquiry. If the physical sciences were in this situation, then scientific inquiry would never get off the ground, as the ultimate physical causes – gravity, energy, and so on – are unobservable; before science the physical universe is just a "mighty maze" (Cairnes 1875, p. 81). But economics is different (actually lucky), because economists do have immediate access to the causal forces behind economic phenomena: "certain mental feelings and certain animal propensities in human beings" (Cairnes 1875, p. 87).

> *The economist starts with a knowledge of ultimate causes. . . .* He is already, at the outset of his enterprise, in the position which the physicist only attains after ages of laborious research. (Cairnes 1875, p. 87)

Not only are some sciences advanced enough to be deductive, there is one particularly lucky deductive science that has immediate access to the ultimate causes within its domain. Economics is not just good science, it seems to be blessed science.

Cairnes also discusses the role of *verification* in economics, and, like Mill, he considers it to be a way of determining which countervailing or disturbing forces are in effect in particular concrete cases. But there is a difference here as well. For Mill, the deductive aspect (of even a deductive science like economics) is always secondary; empirical verification takes place at the very end of the process, but much more important is the induction from specific empirical facts that initially provided the laws employed in the deduction. For Mill, science is wholly empirical; it starts with particular facts and ends with particular facts; deduction is just a convenient middle step. Not so for Cairnes. Because we know the relevant causes with certainty, the *only* role for empirical evidence is in verification at the end of the process.

What the precedents of physical science, rightly understood, teach the economist is to regard deduction as his principle resource; the facts furnished by observation and experience being employed, so far as circumstances permit, as the means of verifying the conclusions thus obtained, as well as, where discrepancies are found to occur between facts and his theoretical reasonings, for ascertaining the nature of the disturbing causes to which such discrepancies are due. It is in this way, and *in this way only*, that the appeal to experience is made in those physical sciences which have reached the deductive stage – that is to say, which in the logical character of their problems present any real analogy to economic science. (Cairnes 1875, pp. 96–7, emphasis added)

It is easy to see how Cairnes's seemingly minor modifications of Mill's methodological approach would go a long way in the direction of insulating Ricardian economics from the attacks of historists and other critics; it is less clear that Cairnes's view consistently maintains John Stuart Mill's strong version of empiricism. Perhaps the only way to save the Ricardian baby from drowning in the empiricist bathwater was simply to throw out the bathwater (or at least drain off enough to eliminate the danger). As Mark Blaug put it many years ago:

In the last analysis, Cairnes' defense of Ricardo seems to emanate from a desire to stem the tide of ... empiricism which was sweeping over contemporary economic thinking. Bad theory was better than no theory at all. And as he surveyed the scene he saw no satisfactory substitute for the general approach of Ricardo and his followers. (Blaug 1958, p. 220)

The last nineteenth-century patron to be examined – John Neville Keynes – could no longer claim to be in the position of having "no satisfactory substitute" for Ricardian economics. Neville Keynes, the father of John Maynard Keynes, was not only writing after the neoclassical revolution of the 1870s – his *Scope and Method of Political Economy* (1917) was initially published in 1890, the same year as the first edition of the *Principles of Economics* (1949) by his friend Alfred Marshall. Keynes was writing after the rise of neoclassicism; after, and in response to, the German *Methodenstreit* (discussed below); and with a self-consciously Marshallian perspective on both economic theory and method (particularly the relationship between neoclassicism and the Ricardian school). In Phyllis Deane's words, Keynes's book "was accepted by a majority of

reviewers as being the definitive methodological text for the new political economy (in Britain identified with Marshall's *Principles*), and as
ending the long and tedious *Methodenstreit*" (Deane 1983, pp. 3–4). So
how could the "definitive methodological text" for Marshallian economics be in the same methodological tradition as the work of strict
Ricardians like Mill and Cairnes? The answer lies in the catholicity and
subtlety of Keynes's text.

Keynes begins by summarizing the methodological tradition of Mill,
Senior, Cairnes, and others: "Fundamentally they are in agreement in
regarding political economy as a science that is in its scope positive as
distinguished from ethical or practical, and in its method abstract
and deductive" (Keynes 1917, p. 12). According to Keynes, this (Millian)
methodological tradition is characterized as: (1) sharply distinguishing
between positive science and normative evaluation, (2) isolating
the study of wealth from all other aspects of society, (3) deductive
or *a priori* and not experimental, (4) abstract, (5) hypothetical (a science of tendencies only), and (6) observation enters as verification (at
the end).

Keynes viewed the first of these six characteristics – economics is a
positive and not a normative science – as an extremely important distinction (it is often cited as his main methodological contribution). The
separation of the positive and the normative was a subset of Keynes's
more general tripartite distinction between *positive science, normative
science,* and *art.* Positive science concerned the study of fact (what is);
normative science concerned the study of norms and rules (what ought
to be); and art focused on policy application (what can be achieved). In
his own (often quoted) words:

> As the terms are here used, a *positive science* may be defined as
> a body of systematized knowledge concerning what is, a *norma-
> tive* or *regulative science* as a body of systematized knowledge
> relating to criteria of what ought to be, and concerned therefore
> with the ideal as distinguished from the actual; and *art* as a
> system of rules for the attainment of a given end. The object of
> a positive science is the establishment of *infirmities*, of a nor-
> mative science the determination of *ideals*, of an art the formu-
> lation of *precepts*. (Keynes 1917, pp. 34–5)[9]

---

[9] It is important to note that Keynes is concerned with *normative science*; Keynes, like Mill,
considered (at least certain types of) ethical questions to be scientific questions. It is not
until the logical positivism of the early twentieth century (discussed in Chapter 3) that all
consideration of the "normative" gets barred from scientific inquiry. This is important to
remember when reading contemporary authors who claim to endorse Keynes's distinction

Keynes used taxation as an example of how one might apply this tri-partite distinction. Positive economics concerns the incidence of a tax; normative economics focuses on which group should bear the tax burden; and the policy arts address the details of practical implementation of the tax (Keynes 1917, pp. 32–3).

For Keynes, the major methodological debates in economics simply involved confusing these three categories (particularly the positive and the normative). "The main point to notice is that the endeavour to merge questions of what ought to be with questions of what is tends to confuse, not only economic discussions themselves, but also discussions about economic method" (Keynes 1917, p. 63). Keynes's general message was that the (Millian) method characterized by these six propositions was basically fine – it captured what the best (classical and neoclassical) economists actually did as well as what proper economic scientists should do – economists just needed to be a bit more tidy in the way they conceptualized their problems. The issue was more about conceptual housekeeping than about substantive methodological disagreement. Those familiar with Alfred Marshall's view of the "disagreement" between classicals (particularly Ricardo) and neoclassicals (particularly Jevons) will recognize Keynes's position as a kind of meta-Marshallianism: settling the methodological debates between Millians (*a priori*) and historists (*a posteriori*) in the same "neither side is really wrong, we should combine the best of both" way that Marshall "settled" the debate between classical (cost determined) and neoclassical (demand determined) price theory.

> If pure induction is inadequate, pure deduction is equally inadequate. The mistake of setting up these methods in mutual opposition, as if the employment of either of them excluded the employment of the other, is uniformly very common. As a matter of fact, it is only the unprejudiced combination of the two methods that any complete development of economic science is possible. (Keynes 1917, 172)

Although Keynes's methodology talks the Marshallian compromising party line, it also seems to be meta-Marshallian in a deeper and more subtle way. Although Marshall talked about, and perhaps was even committed to, a compromise position, the fact is that his price theory "reconciled" classical and early neoclassical value theory by eliminating the

between positive science and normative ethics. For Keynes (unlike many contemporary authors) it is not a distinction between positive science and normative nonsense, it is just a distinction between two different types of scientific knowledge.

classical labor theory of value; the result of the reconciliation was a price theory that looked a lot more like one of the reconciled groups (neo-classical) than the other (classical). So, too, for Keynes's methodology; Keynes reconciled the *a priori*-deductivist approach and the *a posteriori*-inductivist approach in a way that deflected much of the historists' criticism of the deductive method. Keynes's methodological reconciliation ended up looking a lot more like the method of Mill or Cairnes than that of the German or British historical school.

Keynes defined science "as a connected and systematized body of truths possessing generality of form," and, thus, truth "lacking generality cannot constitute a science" (Keynes 1917, p. 150). In other words, science requires *general laws*. But, enter Mill and Cairnes, how can such general laws be obtained in an nonexperimental science such as economics? Certainly not from any *a posteriori* method; instead, the economist must rely on "deduction from elementary principles of human nature" (Keynes 1917, p. 211).

> In so far as the method of specific experience fails to afford reliable knowledge of economic laws, recourse must be had to a method, whose essence consists in the preliminary determination of the principal forces in operation, and the deduction of their consequences under various conditions. For an *a posteriori* argument depending entirely upon the examination of concrete facts in all the complexity of their actual presentation, is substituted an *a priori* argument depending upon knowledge of the general characteristics displayed by men in their economic dealings with one another. (Keynes 1917, p. 216)

This *a priori* method will, of course, result in a "hypothetical science" (Keynes 1917, p. 217), that will, because of countervailing causes, be concerned with "tendencies only" (Keynes 1917, p. 218), and will always involve "a process of abstraction, necessitating a frequent recurrence of the qualification *ceteris paribus*" (Keynes 1917, p. 218). Empirical *verification* is certainly required, but as with Cairnes, it comes in at the end and is only to determine which disturbing causes were in effect. If the empirical results do not come out as the theory predicts, one should *not* reject the theory; economics is complex business with many disturbing causes. One must be concerned about negative empirical evidence:

> But we should not hastily draw negative conclusions, or suppose theories overthrown, because instances of their operation are not patent to observation. For the complexity of the actual eco-

nomic world, which in the first place makes it necessary to have recourse to the deductive method, may also render it difficult to determine whether or not the actual effects of any given agency really correspond with the results of our deductive calculations. (Keynes 1917, p. 233)

It seems that when Keynes reconciles Cairnes and the historists, he gets, well, Cairnes. The methodology that Mill and Cairnes had used to defend Ricardian economics evidently works just as well in the defense of Marshallian price theory.

Before leaving this subject, it is useful to say a bit more about the positive and normative distinction that Keynes popularized in economic methodology. This distinction can be traced back to David Hume, and for that reason is often called "Hume's guillotine" or "Hume's fork." Hume's purpose was to block any effort to develop systematic nonmoral foundations for moral theory; if one can not deduce "ought" from "is" then one is effectively blocked from arriving at ethically normative or evaluative conclusions from premises involving what is the case. No amount of evidence about how the world is will be able, by itself, to tell us how it should be. In Hume's own words from *A Treatise of Human Nature* (1888, Book III, Part I, Section I):

> In every system of morality, which I have hitherto met with, I have always remark'd that the author proceeds for some time in the ordinary way of reasoning, and establishes the being of God, or makes observations concerning human affairs; when of a sudden I am supriz'd to find, that instead of the usual copulations of propositions, *is*, and, *is not*, I meet with no proposition that is not connected with an *ought*, or an *ought not*. This change is imperceptible; but is, however, of the last consequence. For as *ought*, or *ought not*, expresses some new relation of affirmation, 'tis necessary that it should be observ'd and explain'd; and at the same time that a reason should be given, for what seems altogether inconceivable, how this new relation can be a deduction from others, which are entirely different from it. (Hume 1888, p. 469, emphasis in original)[10]

Although the "is-ought" distinction is still regularly wielded about in the methodological literature, it is useful to keep in mind a number of

---

[10] The exact meaning of this passage has been the subject of a long and ongoing debate within ethical philosophy. The literature is massive, but a good place to start is with various papers in Chappell (1968). See Blaug (1998) and Machlup (1969) for general discussions regarding the positive and normative distinction in economics.

features of Keynes's version that seem to be absent from most contemporary appearances of the distinction. First, for Keynes the distinction between positive and normative differentiated two different types of science, not science and nonsense. Second, whereas positive and normative were mutually exclusive for Keynes, they were not exhaustive of all types of meaningful propositions. Third, the term "positive" meant something different, and generally something more comprehensive, in the nineteenth than it does in the twentieth century. And finally, and perhaps most important for the discussion in later chapters, the term "normative" means *ethically* normative and not *epistemically* normative. Although one may not be able to derive ethical norms from empirical observations, many contemporary philosophers argue that one can (in fact must) derive epistemological norms from empirical observations of what scientists actually do or have done. While this final point is a topic of much debate within the philosophy of science (related to the "naturalism" discussed in Chapter 4), at this juncture the lesson is simply that there are many different types of "norms" and not all involve ethics.

2.1.3 Robbins on the Nature and Significance of Economics

The final variation of the Millian approach discussed in this chapter carries us into the early twentieth century. Lionel Robbins's *An Essay on the Nature and Significance of Economic Science* (1932/1952) represented (at least until quite recently) the highwater mark of the Millian methodological tradition. For many years, Robbins's book was proffered as the (inadequate) standard against which newcomers would invariably contrast their improved methodological wares.

Although Robbins was influenced by the Austrians discussed in the next section, and (at least on one important issue) by the logical positivists discussed in the next chapter, his overall methodology remained essentially within the Millian tradition. Like Cairnes in particular, Robbins responded to the absence of controlled experiments and the dearth of historical data capable of generalization by grounding economics on the indisputable facts of direct introspective experience. For Robbins, the postulates of economics are not the fallible implications of some long inferential train; they rest on that which is immediate and obvious.

> These are not postulates the existence of whose counterpoint in reality admits of extensive dispute once their nature is fully realized. We do not need controlled experiments to establish their

> validity: they are so much the stuff of our everyday experience
> that they have only to be stated to be recognized as obvious.
> (Robbins 1952, p. 79)[11]

Again like Cairnes, this makes economics actually more (not less) scientifically reliable than the natural sciences

> In Economics, as we have seen, the ultimate constituents of
> our fundamental generalizations are known to us by immediate
> acquaintance. In the natural sciences they are known only infer-
> entially. This is much less reason to doubt the counterpart in
> reality of the assumption of individual preferences than that of
> the assumption of the electron. (Robbins 1952, p. 105)

The criticisms raised by the inductivists and the historists (and by
the 1930s, the Institutionalists) were all basically beside the point once
one understood the indisputable foundations of economic science. For
Robbins, such criticisms should not be considered epistemologically
serious; they were, for the most part, (ineffective) cloaking devices for
a *political* attack on orthodox economics (Robbins 1952, p. 82). The
bottom line for Robbins was basically that the Millian methodological
tradition was just fine and there really wasn't any reason for "a fuss."

> Stated in this way, surely the case for the point of view underly-
> ing the so-called "orthodox" conception of the science since the
> time of Senior and Cairnes is overwhelmingly convincing. It is
> difficult to see why there should have been such a fuss, why
> anybody should have thought it worth while calling the whole
> position in question. (Robbins 1952, p. 82)

Despite Robbins's commitment to a generally Millian interpretation
of economic science, there were a few places where his position differed
substantially from that of John Stuart Mill. Perhaps the most significant
concerns the *definition* of economic science. Robbins flatly rejected Mill's
definition of economics as the science of wealth, or as later Marshallians
would put it, the science of material welfare. Robbins argued that many
things are "material" without being "economic" (say a set of blueprints
or a pile of worthless rocks), while many other things are clearly "economic" without being "material" (say labor services or the right of first

---

[11] It is interesting to note that this often-quoted statement of Robbins's view does not
appear until the 2nd edition, published in 1935. The subject of why Robbins made the
changes he did in the 2nd edition (after only three years) certainly warrants additional
research.

refusal). What makes something the subject of economic analysis is its *scarcity*: the fact that it has multiple uses, and that using it in one way necessarily implies that it is not available to be used in other ways. Economics is about choice, opportunity costs, and trade-offs.

> Economics is the science which studies human behaviour as a relationship between ends and scarce means which have alternative uses. (Robbins 1952, p. 16)

Notice this definition not only has nothing to do with "material wealth," it has nothing particularly to do with markets or capitalism. Robinson Crusoe, a premodern village, or a central planner, must make decisions involving scarce resources which have alternative uses and thus engage in *economic* activity. Economics is the study of the relationship between (any) ends and the scarce means for achieving those ends. This definition, while it is still popular in introductory textbooks, is really a definition that reduces all of economics to a particular kind of microeconomics; it excludes not only Institutionalism and various historical approaches, but also macro, growth theory, econometrics, and all of classical economics, including (most importantly for Mill) the economics of David Ricardo. Being part of the Millian methodological tradition clearly is not the same thing as defending a position that John Stuart Mill would himself accept.

Another place where Robbins shifted the focus of (previously mainstream) economics concerns *interpersonal utility comparisons*. It was a standard late nineteenth-century utilitarian argument – endorsed by most Marshallians – that because of the diminishing marginal utility of money income, a transfer of income from the rich to the poor would necessarily increase social welfare (the sum of individual utilities). Robbins aggressively denied that such a conclusion could be reached on the basis of economic *science*. Economics starts with the preference orders (or utility functions) of individuals, but these are subjective preferences (or utilities) that can not be compared between any two individuals. I have my subjective preferences and you have yours, but we can not compare (add or subtract) mine and yours. For Robbins, these comparisons do not involve observables and are therefore not subject to scientific investigation:

> *There is no means of testing the magnitude of A's satisfaction as compared with B's.* . . . Introspection does not enable A to measure what is going on in B's mind, nor B to measure what is going on in A's. There is no way of comparing the satisfactions

of different people. (Robbins 1952, pp. 139–40, emphasis in original)[12]

For Robbins, those who make intrepid claims about the social welfare impact of redistributive taxation are simply confusing *positive* and *normative* economics. Such arguments belong in ethical philosophy and can not be decided by positive science: "Economics deals with ascertainable facts; ethics with valuations and obligations." Evidently Mill's science of utilitarian ethics is no longer a science at all.

In closing this section, it is important to point out one rather subtle but very important change that takes place in the Millian methodological tradition as we moved from Mill to Cairnes to Keynes to Robbins in the last three sections. Although I have mentioned many differences in detail, there is one more general change that takes place almost imperceptibly as we move from one author to another. The change is the movement from *characterizing the method of economics as it contrasts with the different methods of other sciences* in Mill, to specifying *rules for the proper conduct of any science, and thus economics*, in Robbins. For Mill, chemistry is a science, mathematics is a science, utilitarian ethics is a science, and economics is a science; all knowledge comes through the senses, different sciences just have different ways of obtaining such knowledge. For Mill, the issue is not about demarcating science, or even good science, from nonsense; the Enlightenment won; the only issue is deciding who (which discipline) gets what from among the spoils. As we move through the end of the nineteenth century and into the twentieth, things begin to change; the optimism fades. Mainstream economics is attacked – British historicists, German historicists, Marxists, Institutionalists – and almost all of the critics seem to be launching their attacks from a position that claims to be fortified by better science. Demarcation and rules become the order of the day. Although Robbins is certainly not as strict or rule-oriented as most of the methodologists discussed in later chapters, the tone has clearly started to change. Economic science is *not* to be confused with economic history, or normative ethics, or metaphysics, or politics, or a variety of other nonscientific inquires; economic science *does not* make interpersonal utility comparisons; and methodology is starting to be about *rules*.

---

[12] It is interesting, though getting ahead of our story a bit, that Robbins employs what is an essentially positivist notion of scientific meaningfulness (discussed in the next chapter) here in his critique of interpersonal utility comparisons, when earlier in the same book (Robbins 1952, pp. 87–90), he rejects the "behaviorist" argument that purposive or intentional behavior should be excluded from human science because it involves things (goals, purposes) that are not empirically observable. See Davis (1994, pp. 50–7).

2.1.4 Austrian Economic Methodology

Although Robbins was influenced by certain Austrian ideas, his methodology does not offer a very smooth transition into the Austrian literature discussed in this section. Unfortunately, a more effective segue is not really available. The problem is the rather enigmatic relationship that exists between the Millian and Austrian methodological traditions. On the one hand, Austrian methodology is frequently presented as a special case of Millian *a priorism*, and, yet, on the other hand, the Austrian tradition is both antiempiricist (and, thus, deeply at odds with Mill's fundamental philosophical commitments) and earnestly marginalist in its economics (and, thus, equally at odds with Mill's commitment to classical economics). As we will see in later chapters, the tendency to view these two methodological approaches as fundamentally similar undoubtedly owes more to the influence of mid-twentieth century positivism than to any deep philosophical common ground, but, nonetheless, it still provides the main rationale for adding the Austrian position to this section on Millian methodology.

Austrian methodology is far more difficult to summarize than the methodological writings of Mill, Robbins, or the other authors in this section. Like the work of these authors, the Austrian view is subject to a variety of different interpretations, but the Austrian situation is compounded by the fact that there are so many different economists, with so many different points of view, that can all be (and would probably want to be) classified as "Austrian." The sheer bulk of the literature and the range of diversity within the program combine to make it effectively impossible to examine all, or even the majority, of the work in the Austrian methodological tradition. My approach will be to briefly consider the founder of the Austrian school, Carl Menger, and then turn to the methodological writings of the two most important figures in twentieth-century Austrian economics: Ludwig von Mises and Friedrich von Hayek. Although the resulting discussion is not a thorough examination of Austrian methodology, it should provide a useful introduction as well as an effective guide for those wishing to delve deeper into the subject.

Carl Menger (1840–1921) was both the architect of the Austrian school and one of the economists sharing responsibility for the early development of neoclassical economics. Menger's *Principles of Economics* (1976), Leon Walras's *Elements of Pure Economics* (1954), and William Stanley Jevons's *Theory of Political Economy* (1879) all appeared in the early 1870s and are generally considered to be the three most important books in what ultimately came to be called the neoclassical (or marginalist) revolution. The works of Menger, Walras, and Jevons do have much in common, but there are also significant differences (Jaffé 1976), and Menger's economics in particular differed substantially from that of Jevons and Walras. One difference was that both Jevons and Walras relied heavily on differential calculus (and thought it was essential for the argument), while Menger avoided the use of advanced mathematics entirely, but the differences run much deeper than simply the use of calculus. Menger advocated a "subjectivist neoclassicism" (Greenfield and Salerno 1983) – that emphasized the subjective goal-directed actions of individual economic agents – a view that continues to characterize the "Austrian" approach to economic theory, but one that ultimately came to be overshadowed by the (now dominant) Walrasian research program.

Although Menger has been the subject of a massive interpretative literature, the customary reading is that while Menger had many intellectual influences (see various papers in Caldwell 1990), his underlying philosophical position is best described as a version of Aristotelian essentialist realism.[13] It is important to emphasize Menger's Aristotelianism, since it represents a radically different point of departure than the empiricism of John Stuart Mill. Although Mill and Menger both end up advocating a deductive *a priori* approach to economics, and although their general approach to theorizing (as opposed to their actual economic theories) may be indistinguishable to the casual observer, they are in fact starting from entirely different philosophical positions (Cartwright 1994b). This tension – the tension between an empiricist-inspired deductivism (the Millian tradition) and the openly antiempiricist deductivism of certain Austrians – has manifested itself in many different ways during the last hundred years of methodological debate.[14]

Although the *Methodenstreit* within the German historical school probably pushed Menger into a rather exaggerated version of his view, it is also clear that his position within the debate reflected his overall methodological convictions. The actual debate between Menger and Gustav Schmoller was remarkably short-lived. It began in 1883 with Schmoller's harsh review of Menger's *Untersuchungen* (translated as *Problems of Economics and Sociology* 1963), and ended in 1884 with

---

[13] See, for example, Cartwright (1994b), Hutchison (1973), Kauder (1957), Klant (1984, pp. 66–71) Clive Lawson (1996), Mäki (1990a, 1990b, 1992c, 1997), Mirowski (1988, pp. 22–5; 1989a, pp. 260–2), Oakley (1997), and Smith (1990).

[14] Lionel Robbins seems to be a good example of this tension; it is never entirely clear (particularly in the 2nd edition of his *Essay*) which side of this philosophical fence he is on, and this foundational bipolarity seems to open the door to a number of different criticisms.

Menger's equally strident reply, a reply that took the form of a pamphlet written as letters to a friend. Although the formal exchange between the two individuals ended with Menger's reply, the *Methodenstreit* dragged on throughout Menger's life and ultimately had a profound impact on both the teaching of economics in Germany and the Austrian attitude about the importance of methodology.

> It is necessary to realise fully the passion which this controversy aroused, and what the break with the ruling school in Germany meant to Menger and his followers, if we are to understand why the problem of the adequate methods remained the dominating concern of most of Menger's later life. Schmoller, indeed, went so far as to declare publicly that members of the "abstract" school were unfit to fill a teaching position in a German university, and his influence was quite sufficient to make this equivalent to a complete exclusion of all adherents to Menger's doctrines from academic positions in Germany. (Hayek 1934, p. 407)

The standard interpretation of the *Methodenstreit* reduces the entire debate to a disagreement about whether deduction or induction represents the (only) proper method for obtaining economic knowledge. Menger is viewed as a radical deductivist who wanted to deduce all of economic theory from a few basic propositions about economic behavior, while the German historical school is viewed as an equally radical, inductivist sect that wanted to abandon theory altogether in favor of the endless accumulation of empirical and historical data. This portrait of Menger suggests that he was not at all interested in either empirical evidence or the structure of social institutions, while this interpretation of Schmoller makes him into an interminable fact finder: an "inductivist" who never gets around to actually making any inductive inferences. This standard caricature really does an injustice to both sides of the debate. Although sorting out the literature on the *Methodenstreit* is clearly beyond the current project, it should at least be noted in passing that neither side actually advocated a view that was anywhere near as simplistic as that suggested by the standard interpretation. Even recognizing that the heat of the fray often pushes authors into simplistic positions, the arguments of both sides were substantially more complex (and much more philosophically interesting) than merely quarreling over whether pure deduction or pure induction constitutes the proper method of economic science.[15]

---

[15] There is surprisingly little English language literature on the *Methodenstreit*, given that it lurked in the background of most late nineteenth- and early twentieth-century methodological writing. As we saw in the previous discussion of Keynes and Robbins, a common

The methodological position of one of Menger's most influential followers, the third-generation Austrian economist Ludwig von Mises (1881–1973), does though come fairly close to the caricature version of Menger's position in the *Methodenstreit*.[16] While Mises's view represents a radical departure from the methodological mainstream in economics – a mainstream that despite its diversity tends to be generally empiricist and methodologically monist (social and natural science should practice the same "scientific method") – his view is often presented as the paradigm case of Austrian methodology (see, for example, Hutchison 1981). Perhaps commentators equate Austrian methodology with Mises's interpretation because extreme positions make easier targets, or perhaps it is simply because of the vehemence with which Mises advocated the same (rather radical) methodological position throughout his career.

Mises (1949, 1978) called his approach to economic methodology "praxeology." The philosophical origins of praxeology are Kantian: just as Kant answered the question of how our concepts and experiences match up to the objective features of the external world by turning the question upside down – making the objective world match up to our concepts and experiential framework – Mises, too, relied on the essential features of the human subjective constitution to ground his concept of knowledge.[17] For Kant, there were certain basic principles and judgments that formed the basis of our knowledge – things such as the rules of logic, the idea that every event has a cause, and the fact that objects exist – that are so fundamental to our understanding that without them no meaningful experience would be possible at all; because knowledge of such principles is necessary (a precondition) for understanding at all, they can not come from outside, from empirical observation, but must be *synthetic a priori true*. For Mises, economic knowledge also has a (unique) necessary precondition – a synthetic *a priori* true proposition necessary for the possibility of meaningful experience – it is that *human beings act* (engage in intentional or purposive behavior).

> The a priori knowledge of praxeology is entirely different – categorically different – from mathematics. . . . The starting point

approach was to use it as a kind of ominous threat; "Listen to my, more moderate, methodology, so we do not fall into extreme (and unproductive) views like *those*." Certain later Austrians even seemed to take such a stance (see Böhm-Bawerk 1890, for example). Some of the more contemporary literature on the *Methodenstreit* includes Barkai (1996), Bostaph (1978), Frisby (1976), Hutchison (1973), and Mäki (1997).

[16] Menger is considered to be a first-generation Austrian; his younger colleagues, such as Wieser and Böhm-Bawerk, constituted the second generation, making Mises a member of the third generation.

[17] See Barrotta (1996) and Parsons (1997b) for a recent exchange concerning the connection between Mises and Kant.

of all praxeological thinking is not arbitrarily chosen axioms, but a self-evident proposition, fully, clearly and necessarily present in every human mind. . . . The characteristic feature of man is precisely that he consciously acts. Man is Homo agens, the acting animal. . . . To act means: to strive after ends, that is, to choose a goal and to resort to means in order to attain that goal sought. (Mises 1978, pp. 4–5)

Knowledge of the fact that humans act purposefully is not only a precondition for all knowledge of human behavior, it is knowledge that we possess, in part, because of our self-knowledge regarding our own actions.

What we know about our own actions and about those of other people is conditioned by our familiarity with the category of action that we owe to a process of self-examination and intro-spection as well as of understanding of other people's conduct. To question this insight is no less impossible than to question the fact that we are alive. (Mises 1978, p. 71)[18]

This postulate – that agents act and thereby engage in purposeful, intentional, goal-directed behavior – is the starting point for the entire Misesian research program in economics. All legitimate economic theory follows as a deduction from this core *a priori* presupposition.

Praxeology is a priori. All its theorems are products of deduc-tive reasoning that starts from the category of action. . . . Every theorem of praxeology is deduced by logical reasoning from the category of action. It partakes of the apodictic certainty pro-

---

[18] The claim that our understanding of the actions of others comes from sharing a common interpretive framework opens the door to *Verstehen* or hermeneutic approaches to the social sciences: approaches often considered to be the polar opposite of an economic approach to human behavior.

The economist *qua* acting individual "understands" intent by virtue of person-ally engaging in purposeful action. A consequence of this *Verstehen*, or "inter-pretive understanding," is that one imputes meaning to the action or object on the basis of analogy with one's own pattern of purposeful action. (Greenfield and Salerno 1983, p. 49)

This has led to a fairly extensive literature on the relationship between economics, partic-ularly Austrian economics, and the triad of *Verstehen*, hermeneutics, and interpretation. See Bacharach (1989), Gordon (1991, Ch. 14), Greenfield and Salerno (1983), Hayek (1973), Klant (1984, pp. 76–82), Lavoie (1990, 1991b), and Lewin (1996) for a wide range of dif-ferent views on the subject. See Winch (1990) for a classic statement of the interpretive view of social science and Rosenberg (1995a) for a recent survey of the subject.

vided by logical reasoning that starts from an a priori category. (Mises 1978, p. 44)

The Misesian approach has at least three important methodological implications: *methodological individualism, methodological dualism, and a priorism* (Boettke 1998). It is useful to examine each of these in turn.

Methodological individualism is a common position in the philosophy of economics; it was advocated by Mill, Robbins, and most of the others discussed above (and below as well). Although the philosophical literature is replete with numerous specific versions of methodological individualism (see Kincaid 1996, for example), the Misesian variant is based on the simple presupposition that only individuals act: "The collective has no existence and reality but in the actions of individuals" (Kincaid 1996, p. 81). This means (as with Robbins) that all of economics is microeconomics, and although macroeconomic regularities might sometimes be of interest to economists and policy makers, macroeconomic constructs such as the consumption function are totally devoid of any real explanatory power. As Walter Block explains in a reply to a paper on Austrian methodology by the philosopher Robert Nozick (1977):

> For the claim of the Austrians is that although *microeconomics* is correct in its own terms, able to trace phenomena back to the causal agents (individual decisions), macroeconomics includes only artificial constructs which, apart from the individual choices upon which they are very indirectly based, have no causal explanatory power on their own. There are, to be sure, statistical correlations between various of the macroeconomic aggregates. But cut off from the *purposes* of human actors, the only causal agent in economics, they are powerless to form part of a causal genetic chain. (Block 1980, p. 407)

Although individualism is a common view among those writing on economic methodology, Mises's second affirmation – methodological dualism – is quite uncommon. Methodological dualism is the position that the human and social sciences are fundamentally different in character than the natural sciences: that there is not a single scientific method, but rather two different methods, one suitable for studying humans in society and another for studying nonhuman nature. Of course, dualism (two different methods) is a subset of methodological pluralism: the view that there are many different ways of obtaining knowledge depending on the subject at hand. Mill, who was firmly monistic with respect to epistemology (all knowledge was grounded in empirical evidence), was methodologically pluralistic – different sciences have different specific methods for obtaining knowledge in their particular domain – but such pluralism is relatively rare among those writing on economic methodology (and later authors in the Millian tradition played down this aspect of Mill's view). Mises's dualism follows immediately from his definition of *human action*. Humans act teleologically – they engage in purposeful goal-directed behavior – rocks and trees do not. Perhaps at one point in our history, when lightning bolts were viewed as a result of purposeful behavior by angry gods, humans explained natural phenomena in teleological terms, but modern science has replaced such concepts with the laws of nature. Whereas modern science may have accomplished a lot with the materialistic point of view, Mises argues that it is not possible to reduce the goal-directed action of humans to physiology or brain chemistry, and our knowledge of human beings must therefore remain grounded in praxeology, not natural science (Mises 1978, pp. 28–34).[19] There are two different ways to do science; economics is not, can not be, and should not try to be, physics.[20]

Finally there is the issue of Mises's version of *a priorism* and in particular its relation to the empirical testing of economic theories. For Mises, economics is not subject to empirical tests; the fundamental presuppositions of praxeology are *a priori* true, and, therefore, assuming the deduction is done correctly, the conclusions of deductive arguments based on those premises are true as well. There really isn't any room (or reason) for "empirical testing" of substantive economic theory. In fact the entire notion of testing involves a basic inconsistency (or misunderstanding) of the category of human action. As Bruce Caldwell explains.

> The fundamental postulate of human action is that all action is rational. Praxeologists assert that this postulate is know to be true with apodictic certainty; that is, it is a priori true. Mises argues that since attacks on the postulate require purposeful human action, attempts to refute it necessarily involve inconsistency. (Caldwell 1984b, p. 364)

[19] Mises anticipates, and critiques, the "eliminative materialist" claims discussed below (at the end of Chapter 4).

[20] According to Mises, attempts to try to do economics like physics lead to undesirable political consequences. The desire to make the social sciences universal – a tendency that Mises rightly identifies with logical positivism (see Chapter 3) – stems, he argues, from a "dictatorial complex" to "see themselves in the role of the dictator – the *duce*, the *Führer*, the production tsar – in whose hands all other specimens of mankind are mere pawns" (Mises 1978, pp. 40–1).

Of course, like many of those in the Millian tradition, Mises would certainly agree that empirical evidence can be useful in deciding about the applicability or relevance of a certain result for a particular problem or in a specific context, but these are questions about history not about economic theory. Again Walter Block:

> Clearly, for the Austrians, economic *theory* is completely devoid of any empirical role, while it is necessary, although not sufficient, for an understanding of economic *history*. Experience is also vitally important in determining the *applicability* of apodictically certain economic theory. . . . note how different here is the employment of the term "empirical" from its ordinary use in economics. The Austrians use it to denote the applicability of *a prioristic* economic law to reality . . . ; on the part of establishment economists, empirical work is done in order to "test" the truth of economic hypotheses. (Block 1980, pp. 419–20)[21]

Needless to say, this contemplated lack of concern over empirical testing of fundamental economic theory will become a significant bone of contention in the later methodological literature. All of the non-Austrian authors discussed in the rest of this chapter will use the issue of empirical testing as their main point of attack as well as a conduit for the presentation of their own methodological views.

The Nobel laureate Friedrich Hayek (1899–1992) was a fourth-generation Austrian working in the Mengerian tradition, and although his methodological views certainly overlap with those of Mises (his friend and teacher), there are also substantial differences. Hayek is clearly a methodological individualist, but he substantially softens both the dualism and the *a priorism* of Mises.[22] This softening occurs in a number of different ways.

One of Hayek's most important moves is to distinguish "scientism" from "science" and direct his attack against the former, not the latter.

---

[21] It is useful to note that Mises's attitude about empirical testing seems to be much easier to defend now that problems like theory-ladenness and underdetermination (discussed in detail in Chapter 3) are generally accepted within the philosophical literature (see Caldwell 1984b and Boettke 1998). Of course, this does not vindicate Mises's position, but it does legitimize many of his criticisms of empiricism and positivism in ways that would have been inconceivable only a few decades ago.

[22] There is some debate about when (or if) Hayek made the "transformation" from Mises's methodological views. Bruce Caldwell (1988) has argued that there was a transformation that began around the time of Hayek's "Economics and Knowledge" (1937), but the transformation had less to do with Mises than with Hayek's growing discomfort with equilibrium analysis for dealing with important questions like the coordination of knowledge. See Caldwell (1992a, 1992b, 1998a) and Hutchison (1981, Ch. 7, 1992a).

According to Hayek, scientism "involves a mechanical and uncritical application of habits of thought to fields different from those in which they have been formed" (Hayek 1979, p. 24) and this uncritical application is the problem, not science (or even the philosophy of science): "It need scarcely be emphasized that nothing we shall have to say is aimed against the methods of Science in their proper sphere or is intended to throw the slightest doubt on their value" (Hayek 1979, p. 23). Hayek seems to be much more sensitive to the fact that he is living, writing, and attempting to persuade readers, in the age of science; although Mises is never explicit about it, one gets the feeling that he could just as well do without science entirely (or at least without the whole scientific form of life). In many ways, Mises is a nineteenth-century humanist, idealist-inspired, philosopher. Hayek, although sharing many of Mises's views on politics and economics, seems much more (earnestly or rhetorically) resigned to empirical science as the hegemonic form of intellectual life; meaning has clearly left the stage; the task is to salvage as many of its best features as possible, and that task may be best accomplished by conciliation with the powers that be.

For Hayek, the aim of a social science such as economics "is to explain the unintended or undesigned results of the actions of many men" (Hayek 1979, p. 41). Such social science must start with human action, the subjective goal-directed action of individual agents, but it is much more. Social science must study the coordination of those individual actions into social phenomena and structures that were not the goal of any individual agent: "To grasp how the independent action of many men can produce coherent wholes, persistent structures of relationships which serve important human purposes without having been designed for that end" (Hayek 1979, p. 141). Hayek calls this approach the "compositive" method, and attributes it originally to Menger (Hayek 1979, pp. 65–6).[23] An example of the compositive method might be Menger's discussion of money in Chapter 8 of his *Principles* (1976); establishing money, a means of exchange, is not the purpose of any individual's action, and yet money emerges as an unintended consequence of that individually self-interested behavior. Those who embrace scientism not only do not practice the compositive method, it has become a "constant source of irritation of the scientistically minded" (Hayek 1979, p. 146). The

---

[23] As we will see (in Chapter 7), the philosopher Karl Popper also characterized social science as the study of the unintended consequences of individual rational action. Although it is clear that such ideas go back at least to Bernard Mandeville, Adam Ferguson, and Adam Smith, Hayek suggests that Popper got the idea of unintended consequences directly from him (Hayek 1967c, p. 100). See Caldwell (1991a, 1992a, 1992b, 1998a) and Hutchison (1981, Ch. 7, 1992a) for different views of the Popper-Hayek connection.

scientistically minded view institutions as conscious consequences (not unintended consequences) of human design; as it is generally not, at least postmonarchy, the design of a single individual, it must be the result of a conscious group mind. The result is a "collectivist prejudice inherent in the scientistic approach" (Hayek 1979, p. 65); this methodological collectivism (Hayek 1979, p. 93) is closely related to various types of political and economic collectivism, which in turn leads to economic planning, social engineering, and Stalin's "engineers of the soul" (Hayek 1979, p. 166).

In his later methodological work, particularly (1967a) and (1967b), Hayek emphasizes that while economics is capable of making certain types of empirical predictions, the complex nature of economic phenomena prevents economists from making anything more than generic, or what Hayek calls "pattern" predictions. These pattern predictions are associated with a particular type of scientific explanation: "explanations of the principle." The complexity of economic phenomena, for example, prevents economists from predicting what any particular consumer will buy, but it is possible to predict the general pattern of an individual's consumption and how it is likely to change in response to taxes or subsidies. What an economist is explaining in such theoretical exercises is the general principle at work behind the scenes of the observed pattern of economic behavior. In Hayek's own words:

> Though we may never know as much about certain complex phenomena as we can know about simple phenomena, we may partly pierce the boundary by deliberately cultivating a technique which aims at more limited objectives – the explanation not of individual events but merely of the appearance of certain patterns or orders. Whether we call these mere explanations of the principle or mere pattern predictions or higher-level theories does not matter. Once we explicitly recognize that the understanding of the general mechanism which produces patterns of a certain kind is not merely a tool for specific predictions but important in its own right, and that it may provide important guides to action (or sometimes indications of the desirability of no action), we may indeed find that this limited knowledge is most valuable. (Hayek 1967b, p. 40)

Again, this is certainly an Austrian argument, but is not as radically *a priorist* as the Misesian version of the Austrian method. Unfortunately, Hayek and his methodological followers often do get caught in what seems to be a rather debilitating crossfire. Critics outside the Austrian school often ignore such moderate views and characterize Austrian methodology solely in terms of Mises's most radical statements; by contrast, many of those sympathetic to Austrian economics seem to view Hayek's methodological moderation as a potentially dangerous slippery slope (with Walrasian or Keynesian economics waiting at the bottom). The result is that Hayek's Austrian methodology, an Austrian view that is more moderate and in many respects philosophically rather contemporary, gets much less attention than Mises's praxeology.

2.2 Variations on Positivist Themes

Positivist philosophy of science will not be discussed in detail until the next chapter, but this section continues the theme of examining the "greatest hits" of economic methodology by discussing the methodological writings of three influential economists – Terence Hutchison, Milton Friedman, and Paul Samuelson – who were all, in one way or another, influenced by positivist ideas. These economists clearly represent the "big three" of twentieth-century methodological writing (at least prior to the explosion of literature during the last few decades), and for those of us who are middle-aged American-educated professional economists, they (particularly Friedman and Samuelson) represent the sum total of what we learned about "economic methodology" in graduate school. This section will examine the methodological writings of these three economists as relatively free-standing arguments about the proper way to conduct the science of economics – the methodological rules – without any serious consideration of the underlying positivist philosophy. While this may appear to be an unusual approach – discussing the application of positivist ideas before discussing positivism – it actually works quite well in the case of these authors. Although all three were broadly influenced by positivist ideas, none of them actually employed the positivist philosophical language or literature in a very precise or systematic way. Hutchison's work is by far the most philosophically astute, and yet even he fuses logical positivism and elements of Karl Popper's philosophy in a way that makes his position (particularly the early work discussed in this section) more of a free-standing economic methodology than a particular "application" of either logical positivism or Karl Popper's philosophy. Friedman's methodological writings are basically aphilosophical, written by a practicing economist for practicing economists, with minimal donnish ornamentation; and, although Samuelson does endorse "operationalism," a particular version of the positivist tradition, he constructs his own specific version of the operationalist approach. So, yes, the discussion of positivism can safely be deferred until the next chapter.

2.2.1 Hutchison on the Significance
of the Basic Postulates

Terence Hutchison was only twenty-six years old when *The Significance and Basic Postulates of Economic Theory* (1938) appeared in print.[24] While the book was many things – including the economic profession's first systematic introduction to the philosophical ideas of Karl Popper and Logical Positivism – it was most poignantly an attack on the *a priorist* praxeology of Ludwig von Mises. As Hutchison put it years later in the preface to the 1960 edition, his critique was originally aimed at "the dogmatic and extreme *a priorism* of Professor Mises, which was much more influential in the thirties" (1960, p. xxi). Over the years, Hutchison's exemplar for methodological malpractice shifted a bit toward (or at least to include) Marx and Marxian economics, but in 1938 the target was clearly Mises.

Hutchison was aggressively committed to the position that economics should be (and praxeology was not) a *Science* in the image of the natural sciences. Economics should be above the political and ideological fray: a science clearly differentiated from metaphysical speculation and whose propositions were systematically disciplined by objective empirical facts.

> If there is any object in pursuing an activity one calls "scientific," and if the word "science" is not simply to be a comprehensive cloak for quackery, prejudice, and propaganda, then there must be a definite objective criterion for distinguishing propositions which may be material for science from those that are not, and there must be some effective barrier for excluding expressions of ethical or political passion, poetic emotion or metaphysical speculation from being mixed in with so-called "science." (Hutchison 1960, p. 10)

Gone from Hutchison's view of scientific inquiry is the "moral science" of Mill and the "normative science" of Keynes; gone is the plurality of disparate scientific endeavors each with its own discipline-specific characteristics. For Hutchison, only one unique and narrowly defined type of intellectual activity should be allowed to sit at the captain's table of science, and an "effective barrier for excluding" all others should be strictly enforced. He drew a demarcational line in the sand; on one side was a relatively homogeneous set of activities that had earned the right to be designated "Science" and on the other side was basically

[24] See Caldwell (1998b) and Coats (1983a) for a general discussion of Hutchison's work and Coats (1983b) for a bibliography of his writings (prior to 1983).

everything else: metaphysics, religion, ideology, ethics, poetics, praxeology, and all the other intellectual activities that, however interesting and passion-inspiring they might be, remain epistemically trifling.

Hutchison's criterion for demarcating the scientific and empirically meaningful from the non-scientific and meaningless resides in the *empirical testability* (*potential falsifiability*) of the proposition in question.

> We suggest that the economic scientist is transgressing the frontiers of his subject whenever he resorts to, or advances as possessing some empirical content, propositions which, whatever emotional associations they may arouse, can never conceivably be brought to any intersubjective empirical test, and of which one can never conceivably say that they are confirmed or falsified, or which cannot be deduced from propositions of which that can conceivably be said. (Hutchison 1960, p. 10)

If the proposition is subject to "intersubjective empirical test" – if it is subject to potential refutation by the empirical evidence – then it is "scientific"; if not, then it is not. As Hutchison put it in his reply to Frank Knight (1940): "Scientific propositions in question must be testable. . . . The difference between the propositions about snakes of the scientific zoologist and those of the sufferer from delirium tremens is just that" (Hutchison 1941, p. 738).

As the discussion in the next chapter will make clear, Hutchison's demarcation criterion seems to amalgamate at least three different ways that philosophers have tried to differentiate the scientific or cognitively meaningful from that which is nonscience or cognitively meaningless: the logical positivist criterion of cognitive meaningfulness, the logical empiricist criterion of empirical testability, and the falsificationist demarcation criterion of Karl Popper. In later work, Hutchison became more attuned to the subtle distinctions between these three criteria – and sided with Popperian falsificationism – but in 1938 he was not concerned with such philosophical nuances (nor, frankly, were the relevant philosophers yet clear about the distinctions themselves). In *Significance*, Hutchison was making a simple, if rather doctrinaire, point; economics should be a *Science* and science involves propositions that can be empirically tested. Theorizing based exclusively on propositions that are not subject to empirical test, such as the "synthetic *a priori* true" propositions of Misesian praxeology, is simply not science and has no place in scientific economics. As Hutchison restated the argument fifty years after the publication of *Significance* (adding the

Marxists to the *a priorist* roll),[25] the argument is simultaneously epistemological and political.

> A priorism rejects fundamentally the falsifiability principle
> (FP) and all empirical testing. . . . Long supported in economics
> by Misesians . . . a priorism has now found support among
> Marxians . . . Misesians and Marxians presumably claim author-
> ity, and reject all testing and falsifiability, for quite different,
> perhaps flatly contradictory, fundamental axioms. . . . The polit-
> ical implications are alarmingly hostile to freedom of econo-
> mists, or of any group or authority, claiming infallibility, or
> "apodictic certainty," for selected axioms, and conclusions
> deduced from them that are claimed to possess significant eco-
> nomic content, but for which testing, and falsifiability are com-
> prehensively rejected. The FP, on the other hand, is a truly
> libertarian principle because, in demanding testing and falsifia-
> bility, it is based on human fallibility and denies the infallibility
> claimed by the a priorists, Misesian, and Marxian. (Hutchison
> 1988, p. 176, note 3)

Although empirical testability was necessary for scientific economics,
Hutchison realized that economic science would also contain nonempirical propositions; in fact, he insisted that "pure theory" was entirely
deductive and not empirical at all. According to Hutchison, pure theory
simply involved the (deductive) drawing out of the implications of
various analytical presuppositions. Quoting the positivist philosopher
Moritz Schlick, Hutchison called such exercises "a game with symbols"
(Hutchison 1960, p. 33). It is a game that is quite useful because it allows
us to ferret out the various implications of our analytical definitions, but
since they are "neither confirmable nor contradictable by an empirical
synthetic proposition, propositions of pure theory cannot tell us anything
new in the sense of telling us new facts about the world" (Hutchison
1960, p. 34). Hutchison claimed – a claim harshly criticized in the later
literature – that such propositions were necessarily "tautological" (i.e.,
true by the definitions of the terms).[26] Whether or not "tautological" is

[25] Perhaps Hollis and Nell (1975), in particular.
[26] The critical reviews of Hutchison (1938) – particularly Klappholz and Agassi (1959),
Knight (1940), and Machlup (1955) – constitute some of the most important methodological literature of the middle of the twentieth century. Although many of the issues raised
by these critics were unappreciated (or misunderstood) at the time, recent methodological debates have given us a new respect for many of the arguments raised in these papers.

the proper term, it is clear that Hutchison saw a role for pure theory, but it is also clear that he viewed pure theory as merely a useful accouterment to the main project of empirical economic science.

Although Hutchison admitted the usefulness of (nonempirical) pure theory, he did not consider the main "laws" of economics to be of such analytical character. The laws of economics were testable empirical propositions. The primary law of economic motivation – the assumption of rational economic man – was not simply an *a priori* proposition; it was a testable empirical proposition about human behavior.

> It is . . . an empirical generalisation capable of being tested empirically and of being falsified, possessing therefore *some* empirical content, however insignificant this may be. It is not simply an empirically empty definition, which is what is sometimes offered as a "Fundamental principle" of economic conduct. (Hutchison 1960, p. 114, emphasis in original)

Hutchison not only considered general principles like the rationality assumption to be testable, he also considered more specific restrictions such as the law of diminishing marginal utility (Gossen's law) to be testable as well. According to Hutchison, the problem is not with such "laws" but with the way that economists have traditionally thought about them.

> If one conceives of Gossen's Law as an empirical generalisation one can, when one wants to, go to the facts of economic behaviour to test it. On the other hand, simply to rely on dogmatic assertion even when supported by phrases like "inner feelings of necessity" and "*a priori* facts," is to commit scientific suicide. (Hutchison 1960, p. 135)

The bottom line for Hutchison (at least in *Significance*) seemed to be that there was not really anything much wrong with the practice of economics along the lines of Cairnes's "hypothetical" method or Keynes's positive economics; the problem was mostly in how economists thought (and defended) the propositions of economic theory. Hutchison, of course, thought that some economics (Mises, Marx, etc.) was clearly bad science, but for the most part the mainstream economic tradition from Mill through Marshall seemed to be defensible on the basis of Hutchison's scientific demarcation criterion. This attitude changed in Hutchison's later work (see 1992b, in particular). Here, Marx and Mises remain villains, but now the "formalist-abstractionist" mathematical theorists that dominated Anglo-American economics in the latter half of the twentieth century also become the subject of rebuke. Economics is no longer about policy or "the real world" but a game to be played for the respect of (only) other professional economists. According to Hutchison, the result is an "abstractionist-mathematical blight" (Hutchison 1992b, p. 102) that has divorced economics from both social engagement and the rules of proper scientific method. In recent work, Hutchison has even blamed certain economic methodologists for many of these troubling developments. Evidently those writing on economic methodology during the 1960s and 1970s were influenced by the "ultra permissive attitude" of the "flower children" (Hutchison 1992b, p. 48) and were thus unable (or unwilling) to keep the economics profession's feet to the scientific fire. But, of course, consideration of such accusations would carry us way ahead in our story. For now, let us "drop out" of such recent debates and return to the second of the three main characters in mid-twentieth-century economic methodology: Milton Friedman.

2.2.2 Friedman on the Methodology of Positive Economics

Milton Friedman's essay on "The Methodology of Positive Economics" (1953) is clearly the best-known work in twentieth-century economic methodology. It was "a marketing masterpiece" (Caldwell 1982, p. 173) that is cited in almost every economics textbook and it remains, almost a half-century after its publication, "the only essay on methodology that a large number, perhaps majority, of economists have ever read" (Hausman 1992, p. 162).

Unlike Hutchison, Friedman was not writing so much in response to a debate about the philosophical foundations of economics but rather in response to certain contemporary debates regarding the theoretical and empirical practices of the economics profession. There were, of course, many such debates – recall this was a period of great change in economics, marked by the rise of Keynesian macroeconomics, Walrasian general equilibrium theory, mathematical economics, and econometrics, as well as by the decline of various indigenous American strains of economic theorizing – but I will limit my comments to three controversies that seemed to bear most directly on Friedman's methodological views.

First, and the issue that gets the most press in the methodological literature, was the debate over the appropriateness of "marginal analysis" in the study of labor markets and the theory of the firm. Richard Lester (1946) and others (Hall and Hitch 1939) had made the case (in part based on survey data from business managers) that firms do not actually maximize expected returns as assumed in the standard marginalist framework.[27] Second, and related to the marginalist controversy, was the "imperfect competition revolution" – initiated by Chamberlin (1933) and Robinson (1933) – which offered a major challenge to the assumption of perfectly competitive markets that had dominated economic analysis since the time of Adam Smith. Third, and most relevant in light of later developments in economic theory, was the so-called measurement without theory debate between representatives of the Cowles Commission (Koopmans 1947 and 1949) and the Chicago school of economics (Vining 1949a and 1949b).[28] This debate was ostensibly about the proper role of "theory" and "empirical observation" in the analysis of business cycles (Burns and Mitchell 1946), but actually reflected a much deeper schism between the members of the Chicago economics department (including Friedman) and the members of the Cowles Commission who were physically (but not intellectually, methodologically, or politically) housed at the University of Chicago from 1939 to 1955.[29] The stable equilibrium that Friedman sought to negotiate among, and in response to, these (and other) disruptive forces was a type of Marshallian, partial equilibrium, small-number-of-equations, micro and monetary economics that would steer a theoretical middle ground between the abstract Walrasian theorizing of Cowles on one hand, and the more-broadly-social theorizing of certain Institutionalists on the other. This equilibrium also needed to sustain the use of the available empirical evidence and statistical techniques without being forced into the Procrustean bed of Cowlesian structural equation econometrics; allow for the use of certain Keynesian-based theoretical constructs (like the IS-LM model) without buying into Keynesian-interventionist policy or political philosophy; and preserve both the two-hundred-year-old framework of economic analysis based on competitive markets, and the neoclassical assumption of rational maximizing agents. Keeping all of these balls in the air at the same time was not an easy job.

Friedman's main argument in "The Methodology of Positive Economics" was that for the purposes of positive (as opposed to normative) economics, *the truth of the assumptions of a theory do not matter all.* The only thing that matters in deciding among various economic theo-

[27] See Machlup (1946) and Stigler (1947) for other responses to this literature.
[28] The papers associated with the "measurement without theory" debate are reprinted in Volume II of Caldwell (1993); also see Mirowski (1989b). Daniel Hammond's (1993) interview with Friedman provides some insight into the factors that Friedman himself (at least with hindsight) felt were most important in the development of his methodology.
[29] See Mirowski and Hands (1998) for a discussion of Friedman's involvement in the disagreements between the Cowles Commission and the Chicago economics department during this period.

ries is which one is most successful in making empirical *predictions*. The theory that makes the most accurate predictions in the relevant domain is the best theory, and if it employs "unrealistic" assumptions this should not in any way detract from its success as a positive scientific theory.

> Viewed as a body of substantive hypotheses, theory is to be judged by its predictive power for the class of phenomena which it is in tended to "explain." Only factual evidence can show whether it is "right" or "wrong" or, better, tentatively "accepted" as valid, or "rejected." . . . the only relevant test of the *validity* of a hypothesis is comparison of its predictions with experience. (Friedman 1953, pp. 8–9, emphasis in original)

While only predictions matter, Friedman does argue that some predictions are more important than others. Predicting a *novel fact* – evidence not yet observed – is the key determinant of a successful economic theory. In Friedman's own words, the "ultimate goal of a positive science is the development of a 'theory' or 'hypothesis' that yields valid and meaningful . . . predictions about phenomena not yet observed" (Friedman 1953, p. 7). Now, since economics often predicts things that happened in the past, whether that past is nineteenth-century economic history or this morning's stock market, Friedman also makes it clear that "novel" does not necessarily mean "in the future," but rather "unknown" to the economist proposing the theory in question: "they may be about phenomena that have occurred but observations on which have not yet been made or are not known to the person making the prediction" (Friedman 1953, p. 9). It is useful to note that Friedman has consistently maintained the importance of novel facts throughout his career – from his critique of Lange in 1946 ("the ability to deduce facts that have not yet been observed," p. 631) to the Friedman and Schwartz response to Hendry and Ericsson in 1991 ("any hypothesis must be tested with data or nonquatitative evidence other than that used in deriving the regression or available when the regression was derived," p. 49) – it is certainly not an argument that just appeared in the 1953 methodological essay.[30]

Of course, if prediction is all that matters, novel or otherwise, then the "realism" of the assumptions are entirely irrelevant to the importance of an economic theory.[31] To use two of Friedman's own examples, objects

---

[30] We will discover in Chapters 3 and 7 that novel facts are also important for other methodological approaches.

[31] Mäki (1989, 1992b, and elsewhere) has, I think correctly, argued that "realisticness" is a much better term for what Friedman is interested in than "realism," but I will follow tradition and continue to use the term realism. See Section 7.3.2 below for more discussion of Mäki's argument.

fall *as if* they were falling in a vacuum and the leaves on a tree arrange themselves *as if* they were trying to maximize the sunlight they receive; these assumptions – the presence of a vacuum and leaves acting rationally – are highly unrealistic, and yet scientific theories based on such unrealistic assumptions yield highly reliable (and often novel) empirical predictions. According to Friedman, "the relevant question to ask about the 'assumptions' of a theory is not whether they are descriptively 'realistic,' for they never are, but whether they are sufficiently good approximations for the purpose in hand" (1953, p. 15), and "in general, the more significant the theory, the more unrealistic the assumptions" (1953, p. 14). Such arguments about the irrelevance of unreal assumptions led Paul Samuelson to characterize Friedman's methodological position as the *F-twist* (a label that has stuck in the literature): "A theory is vindicable if (some of) its consequences are empirically valid to a useful degree of approximation; the (empirical) unrealism of the theory 'itself,' or of its 'assumptions,' is quite irrelevant to its validity and worth" (Samuelson 1963, p. 232).

Friedman's position on the importance of prediction and the irrelevance of unrealistic assumptions both have important implications for the theoretical debates in which he, and the economics profession more generally, was embroiled at the time and for the next few decades. The sole criteria of predictive accuracy bore directly on his debates with Cowles and other Keynesians, since their many-equation big econometric macro-models didn't seem to perform predictively any better than the small, often single-equation, models of Friedman and other monetarists. The irrelevance of unreal assumptions had an obvious impact on the "marginalist controversy" and debates about the appropriateness of the assumption of perfect competition. If models assuming profit maximization and perfect competition were more predictively successful than the available alternatives (which Friedman certainly assumed), then the purported unrealism of their assumptions was entirely irrelevant to their scientific usefulness; and, perhaps even more important, one could just drop the entire irrelevant debate about whether such assumptions were unrealistic or not and get on with actually doing economics (i.e., making economic predictions). Friedman made these implications quite clear in his original essay.

> The abstract methodological issues we have been discussing have a direct bearing on the perennial criticism of "orthodox" economic theory as "unrealistic" as well as the attempts that have been made to reformulate theory to meet this charge. . . . As we have seen, criticism of this type is largely beside the point

unless supplemented by evidence that a hypothesis differing in one or another of these respects from the theory being criticized yields better predictions for as wide a range of phenomena. (Friedman 1953, pp. 30–1)

This message – essentially "don't criticize until you have a theory that predicts better" – seems to have been greeted with a sense of *liberation* by the economics profession. Economists "could now get on with the job of exploring and applying their models without bothering with objections to the realism of their assumptions" (Hausman 1992, p. 164, note 18).

Friedman's essay has generated a massive critical and interpretative literature.[32] The first round of these debates was dubbed the "assumptions controversy" and contributions to it have proceeded relatively unimpeded since its beginnings in the mid-1950s until the current time. There also have been other subdebates that have emerged along the way (some of these will be discussed in Chapters 6 and 7) and Friedman's position has consistently served as a foil for, or as the backdrop to, authors presenting other methodological views. Although it has died down in recent years, there were a few decades where almost everything written about economic methodology seemed to start with Friedman's essay. Given the extent of the debate, I will not attempt to summarize the literature on the assumptions controversy; instead, I will just pick two authors – Musgrave (1981) and Hausman (1992) – that have made particularly influential remarks regarding Friedman's essay.[33]

Alan Musgrave's (1981) rather simple, but very important, point, is that not all assumptions play the same role in economic (or for that matter any scientific) theory. Friedman just talks about "assumptions" without specifying exactly what type of assumptions he is talking about. Musgrave simply argues that for certain types of assumptions, Friedman is right – they don't matter – but for other types of assumptions, they do. He divides the "assumptions" in economics into three main types:

---

[32] The preponderance of this literature has been critical (Mayer 1993 and 1995 are exceptions). This creates a rather quizzical situation where many, perhaps even most, practicing economists endorse Friedman's view (at least in a pro forma way), while almost all of the commentary written on the paper is quite critical. This reflects in part *who* has written on the subject of economic methodology in the latter half of the twentieth century, but there are undoubtedly other factors as well. At this juncture, I only want to point out how different this is from say, Mill.

[33] Other key contributions to the assumptions controversy include Bear and Orr (1967), Klappholz and Agassi (1959), Koopmans (1957), Mäki (1989, 1992b, 2000a), Melitz (1965), Nagel (1963), Rotwein (1959), Samuelson (1963), and Wong (1973). See Hausman (1992, p. 163, n. 17) or Redman (1991, p. 99, n. 4) for a more complete list.

negligibility, domain, and heuristic. Musgrave discusses each of these types, but also notes that his threefold classification does not exhaust all of the various types of assumptions that appear in Friedman's paper.

Negligibility assumptions simply specify that some factor x is negligible; in other words things act as if x were the case. The way to think about negligibility assumptions is not that such factors are absent, but rather that they are "irrelevant for the phenomena to be explained" (Musgrave 1981, p. 380). Musgrave gives the example of a "no government sector" assumption in a macro-model, but perhaps a better example would be the assumption of perfect competition in the analysis of short-run (qualitative) comparative statics. An increase in demand will increase the price of the good whether the firm is competitive or a monopoly; the assumption that the market is competitive is irrelevant for this particular phenomena. Musgrave argues that Friedman is basically correct about negligibility assumptions – some of the things that Friedman says about them are not exactly right – but Friedman is correct that the realism of such assumptions is irrelevant to the validity or usefulness of an economic theory.

Musgrave's second type of assumption is a domain assumption; it specifies that a theory works (perhaps only works) in some particular domain. To pursue the macro example; a domain assumption that there is "no government sector" would say that the theory works (perhaps only works) in an economy without a government sector. Musgrave argues, contra Friedman, that such assumptions do matter. In particular, if one converts a falsified negligibility assumption into a domain assumption, one decreases the testability of the theory.

Finally, heuristic assumptions are assumptions that are initially assumed to be negligible, but eventually, at a later stage, will be weakened to see if they have any impact. Continuing with the example of "no governmental sector"; as a heuristic assumption, it would say "let's assume for the moment that there is no government sector, but later we will relax the assumption and see if it has an impact on the results." Heuristic assumptions, according to Musgrave, are extremely important in a scientific theory such as economics where the "logico-mathematical machinery is so complicated that a *method of successive approximation* has to be used" (Musgrave 1981, p. 383, emphasis in original). Because of the tentative nature of such assumptions, they are involved more in the process of theory refinement than in empirical prediction.

Musgrave concludes his analysis of Friedman's essay with the following summary of his position.

I have claimed that the so-called "assumptions" of economic theories (and of other scientific theories) play at least three different roles within those theories, and are assertions of (at least)
three different types. I have argued that Friedman overlooked
these distinctions, and was led thereby to the mistaken thesis
that "the more significant the theory, the more unrealistic the
assumptions" (Musgrave 1981, p. 385)[34]

Daniel Hausman has been a prolific contributor to the recent methodological literature (his work will be examined in more detail in Chapter
7) and has made critical remarks about Friedman's methodology in a
number of different contexts. The criticism that I will discuss in this
section is the criticism he raises in Chapter 9 of *The Inexact and Separate Science of Economics* (1992). Here, Hausman makes the argument
that Friedman's claims about the realism of assumptions do not stand up
even if one accepts empirical prediction as the sole criterion for scientific success: Hausman's criticism should (for reasons that will be obvious
in a moment) be called the "used car argument." He begins by summarizing Friedman's argument in the following way:

1. A good hypothesis provides valid and meaningful predictions
   concerning the class of phenomena it is intended to explain
   (premise).
2. The only test of whether an hypothesis is a good hypothesis is
   whether it provides valid and meaningful predictions
   concerning the class of phenomena it is intended to explain
   (invalidly from 1).
3. Any other facts about an hypothesis, including whether its
   assumptions are realistic, are irrelevant to its scientific assessment (trivially from 2). (Hausman 1992, p. 166)

The main problem with the argument is that is it not a valid "argument"
at all: Statement 2 is not true and it does not follow from statement 1.
Hausman uses the following analogous argument to make his point:

1′. A good used car drives reliably (over-simplified premise).
2′. The only test of whether a used car is a good used car is whether
   it drives reliably (invalidly from 1′).

---

[34] Mäki (2000a) presents a number of criticisms of Musgrave's interpretation of the
assumptions controversy.

3'. Anything one discovers by opening the hood and checking the separate components of a used car is irrelevant to its assessment (trivially from 2'). (Hausman 1992, p. 166)

The problem is of course that with a used car or an economic model the relevant issue is how well it will perform in the future and in other circumstances. Theory should be a guide – even if we focus on empirical prediction – to new circumstances and new situations, and for those forward-looking applications examining the parts (the assumptions) matter. In fact, though Hausman does not make this point, Friedman's emphasis on novel facts gives away his commitment to successful future performance, but Friedman never closes the circle. Friedman seems to be making the implicit assumption that success in one novel situation improves the probability of success in additional and/or future novel situations that we might have an interest in, but there is no obvious reason for this to be the case. Such issues actually carry the discussion beyond Friedman's essay and into debates about "realism" and "instrumentalism" in the philosophy of science: a discussion that must wait until the next chapter. At this point I just want to note that Hausman's criticism of Friedman seems to be correct – even if one is only interested in prediction, the assumptions still matter.

2.2.3 Samuelson and Operationalism in Economics

Paul Samuelson had a profound impact on the shape and structure of postwar economics. Not only was he an economist with arresting technical abilities, he was also the second individual (and first American) to receive the Nobel Prize in economic science, and, he was also, more than any other individual, responsible for the structure and content of economics education in postwar America. During the 1950s and 1960s, the teaching of college-level economics in the United States stabilized around two key texts: Samuelson's *Economics* (1948a) at the undergraduate-introductory level and Samuelson's *Foundations of Economic Analysis* (1947) at the graduate level. Although these two books were ultimately replaced in their respective markets by more user-friendly spin-offs from other authors, they nonetheless effectively defined (and to a lesser extent continue to define) the teaching of "modern scientific" economics in both form and content. In terms of pedagogical form *Economics* gave us the framework for the two-part, micro and macro, introductory sequence familiar to many (even noneconomist) readers from their own undergraduate education, whereas *Foundations* sent the clear signal that students should not even think about graduate work in economics until they have jumped through the appropriate mathematical hoops (demonstrating competency in at least multivariate calculus, real analysis, and linear algebra). With respect to theoretical content, both texts affirmed the "neoclassical synthesis" of Walrasian microeconomics and Keynesian macroeconomics; at the introductory level, the micro was a bit more Marshallian with its focus on single markets and firms, but even there the tone was firmly Walrasian.

Samuelson clearly demonstrated technical brilliance in economic theory and he certainly had an important impact on the teaching of college-level economics, but even these two factors together are not sufficient to account for his wide-ranging influence on economics and the image of the economics profession. Another contributing factor was undoubtedly Samuelson's reputation as "Mr. Science" (Pearce and Hoover 1995, p. 184); it was actually "Samuelson, and not Friedman, who by both word and deed was responsible for the twentieth century self-image of the neoclassical economist as 'scientist'" (Mirowski 1989c, p. 182). Samuelson offered the economics profession, and those in government and business associated with the profession, an image of scientific economics that was above the political fray, neither extreme right nor extreme left (neither Mises nor Marx), but an objective disinterested instrument of scientific analysis that could be used to reconcile and harmonize the various conflicting interests in postwar economic life. As Pearce and Hoover put it in a recent study of Samuelson's introductory text:

> His *Economics* is above all a harmonist book. The core model continues in its sanctified role as the Prince of Peace among competing economic doctrines. The foundations of the peaceable kingdom are, above all, in *scientific* economics. ... Science, for Samuelson, is not just a matter of naive realism; it also relies on a neutral and generally applicable analytical framework. (Pearce and Hoover 1995, p. 198, emphasis in original)

While these motivations seem similar to the motivations of Hutchison and J. N. Keynes discussed above, in Samuelson's case (and in the post-Hiroshima era) they manifest themselves in a fundamentally different set of methodological recommendations.

Samuelson's stated economic methodology is *operationalist* and *descriptivist*, and although both of these philosophical positions will be examined in more detail in the next chapter, Samuelson was fairly clear what he meant by both terms. Consider operationalism first.

Although operationalist ideas go back at least to the nineteenth century, operationalism was firmly established as a reputable philosophical position by the publication of Percy Bridgman's *The Logic of*

Modern Physics in 1927.[35] Bridgman was a practicing physicist (Nobel Laureate in 1946) who wrote widely on operationalist philosophical ideas and their implications for contemporary physical theory. The first reference to Bridgman's operationalism in economics seems to have been in Henry Schultz's *Theory and Measurement of Demand* (1938), but, since operationalist ideas were widely discussed during the 1930s and 1940s (in psychology as well as philosophy and physics), it is not clear whether Samuelson picked up these ideas from Schultz during his undergraduate years at Chicago, or from elsewhere on the intellectual landscape.[36]

The core operationalist idea is that a question has *meaning* only if there exist a set of operations that will provide a definitive answer to it. Correspondingly, a concept or term is *operationally meaningful* if it can be characterized by a particular set of operations, and the meaning of a concept or term is *defined by* that set of operations. Bridgman himself used the concept of "length" as an example.

> What do we mean by the length of an object? We evidently know what we mean by length if we can tell what the length of any and every object is, and for the physicist nothing more is required. To find the length of an object, we have to perform certain physical operations. The concept of length is therefore fixed when the operations by which length is measured are fixed: that is, the concept of length involves as much as and nothing more than the set of operations by which length is determined. In general, we mean by any concept nothing more than a set of operations; *the concept is synonymous with the corresponding set of operations.* (Bridgman 1927, p. 5, emphasis in original)

Samuelson's *Foundations* was based on his 1941 doctoral dissertation, which carried the subtitle "The Operational Significance of Economic Theory," and from the very first page of the book he makes it clear that he is exclusively concerned with (and also that he thinks that not enough previous economists have been concerned with) "the derivation of *operationally meaningful* theorems" (Samuelson 1947, p. 3, emphasis in original). For Samuelson, a theorem is operational if it can be empirically tested; a meaningful theorem is "simply a hypothesis about empirical

---

[35] Although it is clear that Bridgman disliked the term "operationalism" and felt that in some ways he had "created a Frankenstein" (Green 1992, p. 310).

[36] Unlike most of the economists discussed in this chapter, it also is less clear what specific intellectual concerns motivated Samuelson's methodological commitments. I personally suspect that it was a series of deeply disturbing run-ins with Frank Knight during Samuelson's years at Chicago, but this is purely speculation on my part.

data which could conceivably be refuted, if only under ideal conditions" (1947, p. 4). Although this is not exactly Bridgman's operationalism, it is certainly operationalist in spirit.[37]

A second feature of Samuelson's methodological position (also shared with Bridgman) is a *descriptivist* view of scientific theories; scientific theories *merely describe* the empirical evidence and do not go beyond the evidence to *explain* any deeper, underlying, or hidden causes of the phenomena. On this view, science can indeed provide explanations, but such explanations are independent of the cognitive content of the scientific theories involved; scientific explanations are nothing more than convenient redescriptions of the empirical evidence motivated by convenience or other pragmatic concerns. We will see in the next chapter that such descriptivism was representative of early (but not later) logical positivism, but it is a position that Samuelson has consistently maintained throughout his career. As he responds to critics in 1965:

> There has been no successful demolition of my view that science consists of *descriptions* of empirical regularities; nor of my insistence that *what is called an explanation in science can always be regarded as a description at a different level* – usually a superior description in that it successfully fits a wide range of empirical regularities. (Samuelson 1965, p. 1171, emphasis added)

To see how the operationalist methodology is involved in Samuelson's own economic research, it is useful to elaborate on the general project of the *Foundations of Economic Analysis*. For that elaboration, it is useful to consider a specific example.

Consider the problem of maximizing a function of two variables x_1 and x_2 where the objective function f also depends on the parameter β. The problem is thus:

$$\underset{\{x\}}{\text{Max}}\ f(x, \beta)$$

where $x = (x_1, x_2)$ and $f(x, \beta) = f(x_1, x_2, \beta)$.

Assuming the objective function is sufficiently differentiable and the solution $x^* = (x_1^*, x_2^*)$ is in the interior of the domain, it must satisfy the following first- and second-order conditions:

[37] As with Friedman, most of the methodological literature has been quite critical of Samuelson's operationalism (and it has come from a wide range of different perspectives). A nonexhaustive list includes: Cohen (1995), Gordon (1955), Hausman (1992, pp. 156–8), Lewin (1996), Machlup (1964, 1966), Massey (1965), Mirowski (1989c, 1998a), and Wong (1973, 1978).

(1st) $f_1(x^*) = 0$ (2nd) $f_{11}(x^*) < 0$ $f_{22}(x^*) < 0$

$f_2(x^*) = 0$ $f_{11}(x^*)f_{22}(x^*) - [f_{12}(x^*)]^2 > 0$

Where $f_i(x^*) = \partial f(x^*, \beta)/\partial x_i$ and $f_{ij}(x^*) = \partial^2 f(x^*, \beta)/\partial x_i \partial x_j$ for i, j = 1, 2.

Under the conditions of the implicit function theorem (guaranteed by the second-order conditions) the 1st order conditions can be "solved" for the solutions x* as (differentiable) functions of the parameter β. Thus we can write the solution as x*(β) = [x₁*(β), x₂*(β)]. *Qualitative comparative statics* involve determining the impact that a change in the parameter β will have on the solution vector x*; in other words, it involves finding (if possible) the signs of the terms dx₁*/dβ and dx₂*/dβ. Because these signs could, at least conceivably, be empirically determined, these qualitative comparative statics results are, in Samuelson's words "operationally meaningful theorems." One of the main themes of *Foundations* is that this type of operationally meaningful comparative statics results can (often) be obtained from the "maximization hypothesis": essentially the assumption that the problem satisfied the above 1st and 2nd order conditions.

To see how this works, consider a case where the parameter β has a positive impact on the partial derivative of f with respect to x_1 and does not have any impact on the partial derivative of f with respect to x_2. In other words, consider the case where

$$f_{1\beta} = \partial^2 f/\partial x_1 \partial \beta > 0 \quad \text{and} \quad f_{2\beta} = \partial^2 f/\partial x_2 \partial \beta = 0.$$

Substituting the solution vector x*(β) back into the above 1st order conditions gives us the following identities:

$$f_1[x_1^*(\beta), x_2^*(\beta), \beta] \equiv 0,$$
$$f_2[x_1^*(\beta), x_2^*(\beta)] \equiv 0.$$

Differentiating these identities with respect to β we have the following linear system of two equations and two unknowns (the two desired comparative statics terms).

$$f_{11}(x^*)dx_1^*\big/d\beta + f_{12}(x^*)dx_2^*\big/d\beta + f_{1\beta} = 0,$$
$$f_{21}(x^*)dx_1^*\big/d\beta + f_{22}(x^*)dx_2^*\big/d\beta = 0.$$

In Matrix form this system becomes:

$$\begin{bmatrix} f_{11}(x^*) & f_{12}(x^*) \\ f_{21}(x^*) & f_{22}(x^*) \end{bmatrix} \begin{bmatrix} dx_1^*\big/d\beta \\ dx_2^*\big/d\beta \end{bmatrix} = \begin{bmatrix} -f_{1\beta} \\ 0 \end{bmatrix}.$$

Solving, and using the information supplied by the second-order conditions we have:

$$\frac{dx_1^*}{d\beta} = \frac{-f_{1\beta}f_{22}}{f_{11}(x^*)f_{22}(x^*) - [f_{12}(x^*)]^2} > 0,$$

$$\frac{dx_2^*}{d\beta} = \frac{f_{1\beta}f_{21}}{f_{11}(x^*)f_{22}(x^*) - [f_{12}(x^*)]^2} = ?.$$

Notice that the restrictions of the "maximization hypothesis" (first- and second-order conditions) are not sufficient to sign the second comparative statics term – the impact of a change in the parameter on the optimal value of the second variable – but they *are* sufficient to sign the first comparative statics term. For this model, the maximization hypothesis implies that an increase in the parameter β will cause (be followed by) an increase in optimal value of the first variable. Since such a result could conceivably be tested, this is, according to Samuelson, an operationally meaningful theorem derived from the maximization hypothesis. A large part of *Foundations* consists of deriving such comparative statics results for a wide range of economic models.

Another part of *Foundations* consists of deriving similar comparative statics results for (nonoptimization based) dynamic models characterized by systems of differential equations. For example, a two variable dynamic model analogous to the above maximization problem might be:

$$\dot{x}_1 = f_1(x_1, x_2, \beta),$$
$$\dot{x}_2 = f_2(x_1, x_2),$$

where dots over variables indicate time derivatives and the equilibrium $x^*(\beta) = [x_1^*(\beta), x_2^*(\beta)]$ is where there is no change in either variable: where $\dot{x}_1 = f_1(x^*) = 0$ and $\dot{x}_2 = f_2(x^*) = 0$.

According to Samuelson's *correspondence principle*, "there exists an intimate formal dependence between comparative statics and dynamics" (Samuelson, 1947, p. 284); in other words, the hypothesis that the equilibrium position is dynamically *stable* can (often) be used to generate comparative statics results in such dynamic economic models. The assumption of stability in dynamic models plays roughly the same role in these models that the second-order conditions play in optimization models. Actually, comparative statics results are generally more difficult to obtain in dynamic models, because the relevant matrices are almost never symmetric, but that is a technical point. The main argument is that meaningful (comparative statics) theorems can be obtained in two ways:

from the first- and second-order conditions for optimization problems, and from stability conditions for dynamic models. Most of the microeconomic models discussed in *Foundations* employ the former, while most of the macroeconomic models employ the latter; but according to Samuelson, they are both built on exactly the same "foundations": the same *"general theory which underlies the particular theories and unifies them with respect to those central features"* (Samuelson 1947, p. 3, emphasis in original).

Another example of operationalism at work in Samuelson's economics, and the one that gets mentioned most frequently in methodological discussions, is the *revealed preference* theory of consumer choice (Samuelson 1938a, 1948b, 1950, 1953).

> Since the emphasis of my *Foundations of Economic Analysis* on "operationally meaningful" theorems has been brought up, it gives me the opportunity to use my strength against a friendly critic. The doctrines of revealed preference provide the most literal example of a theory that has been stripped down to its bare implications for empirical realism: Occam's Razor has cut away every zipper, collar ... and fig leaf. (Samuelson 1964, p. 738)

Samuelson offered revealed preference theory as an "operational" replacement for the standard utility-maximization-based theory of consumer choice. The standard theory had come under attack because the various concepts of utility and preference (cardinal as well as ordinal) were all fundamentally mentalistic and subjective: as Samuelson put it in his Nobel lecture, "Prior to the mid-1930s, utility theory showed signs of degenerating into a sterile tautology ... utility or satisfaction could scarcely be defined, let alone be measured" (Samuelson 1972, p. 255). His stated goal in revealed preference theory was to provide a vehicle for the scientific, thus operationally meaningful, reconstitution of the neoclassical theory of consumer choice: a "theory of consumer's behaviour freed from any vestigial traces of the utility concept" (Samuelson 1938a, p. 71).[38] Revealed preference theory approached this task by replacing the concept of utility with a set of "operations," which would allow the agent to empirically "reveal" their preferences.

In the first revealed preference paper (1938a), Samuelson employed three postulates (none involving utility) to deduce the main results of

---

[38] Although the original revealed preference paper (1938a) was clearly operationalist in spirit, the term "operational" did not actually appear in the paper; the term did appear though, in another Samuelson paper published the same year (1938b) on the operationally meaningful implications of the standard utility theory.

consumer choice theory.[39] Two of the assumptions were common to the theory of utility maximization (and shown to be redundant in Samuelson, 1938c), but the third was the key assumption that ultimately came to be called the *Weak Axiom of Revealed Preference*:

$$\sum_{i=1}^{n} p_i x_i' \leq \sum_{i=1}^{n} p_i x_i \Rightarrow \sum_{i=1}^{n} p_i' x_i > \sum_{i=1}^{n} p_i' x_i', \qquad \text{(WARP)}$$

where $x = (x_1, \ldots, x_n)$ is the bundle of good purchased at the price vector $p = (p_1, \ldots, p_n)$ and $x' = (x'_1, \ldots, x'_n)$ is the bundle of goods purchased at the prices $p' = (p'_1, \ldots, p'_n)$. Since x' was affordable at p, but was not purchased, x was "revealed preferred" to x'; thus when x' was purchased at p', it must have been because the "preferred" bundle was not afford-able. This assumption allowed Samuelson to deduce most of the impli-cations of consumer choice theory while totally avoiding the concept of utility: "The whole theory of consumer's behavior can thus be based upon operationally meaningful foundations in terms of revealed prefer-ence" (Samuelson 1948b, p. 157).

A fairly extensive literature has developed around the question of whether Samuelson was successful in the methodological project of revealed preference – whether he did in fact remove "the last vestiges" of utility; whether WARP is operational (or empirical in any other sense); whether there is a logical problem associated with saying that two theories are identical and yet one is more empirical than the other; whether Samuelson the theorist practiced what Samuelson the method-ologist preached, and so on.[40]

Although it is certainly not necessary to go into this critical litera-ture in any detail, it is useful to examine one issue involving the opera-tionalism-WARP nexus, since it relates directly to various themes that will emerge in later chapters. The issue is that Samuelson seemed to change the methodological target in the period between the publication of the original paper in 1938 and (say) the late 1940s. In the beginning the goal was clearly to *purge* the mentalistic concept of utility and *replace it* with something that was scientifically more acceptable (something more operationally meaningful). The chemical equivalent of this move would seem to be the movement from phlogiston to oxygen; one just gets rid of the scientifically inadequate concept and replaces it with a

---

[39] One missing result was the symmetry of the Slutsky matrix ("integrability conditions"); this result does follow from Houthakker's (1950) stronger revealed preference condition (termed the Strong Axiom of Revealed Preference by Samuelson 1950).

[40] Most of the critical references in note 37 are concerned with the issue of whether revealed preference theory is the operationalist success story that Samuelson has consis-tently claimed.

scientifically adequate one. The claim that Samuelson was interested in totally eliminating the concept of utility is of course supported by the "free from any vestigial traces" (Samuelson 1938a, p. 71) language, but it also is supported by the fact that Samuelson did *not* use the word *preference* (or any surrogate for it) in the original paper (or in *Foundations*). The term revealed *preference* doesn't appear until his 1948 paper. In the early work the project was not to "reveal" preferences – any more than oxygen is a way to "reveal" phlogiston – the project was to replace the concepts of utility and preference entirely. In language that will be introduced more carefully in the next two chapters, Samuelson circa 1938 was (only) concerned with observable *behavior* and eliminating (not revealing) *unobservable intentional* concepts from the theory of consumer choice. The problem for the consistency of his methodological position is that later he did change to talking about *revealing* preferences. By the 1948 and 1950 papers, his position seems to be that subjective intentional concepts are perfectly acceptable in economic science. WARP no longer seems to be a replacement for the concept of preference but instead is just a convenient tool for empirically discovering this elusive, but evidently explanatory, intentional phenomenon; as Hendrik Houthakker put it, "the stone the builder rejected in 1938 seemed to have become the cornerstone in 1950" (Houthakker 1983, p. 63). By his Nobel lecture, Samuelson seems to be completely back on (and claims never to have left) the utility bandwagon: "From the beginning I was concerned to find out what *refutable* hypotheses on the observable facts on price and quantity demanded were implied by the assumption that the consumer spends his limited income at given prices in order to maximize his ordinal utility . . ." (Samuelson 1972, p. 256).

It is interesting, though admittedly getting a bit ahead in our story, that precisely the same movement seemed to take place with respect to operational concepts in psychology during this same period. Bridgman's operationalist ideas were originally introduced into psychology by Stevens (1939) and others in order to eliminate the mentalistic notions that had been psychology's traditional conceptual fodder. What happened over time though, as with Samuelson, was that the new and ostensibly more operational concepts ended up being used to defend and put a new scientific sheen on the traditional concepts, rather than as a replacement for them. Christopher Green discusses the psychological work of Edward Tolman in this regard.

> Whereas Bridgman offered operations as *replacements for* the metaphysical concepts which supposedly had led to the crisis in physics, Tolman took operations to *measure expressions of* these

metaphysical concepts which similarly bedeviled psychology. Tolman, in effect, turned operationalism inside-out. Where Bridgman sought to rid science of metaphysical concepts. Tolman sought to legitimize them by attaching them to related physical operations. This inversion of operationalism would prove to be crucial to the theoretical path followed by psychology through the next few decades. (Green 1992, p. 300, emphasis in original)

Although the impact on economics was not nearly as great as it was on psychology, it does seem that Samuelson also turned operationalism inside-out. This – like Mill's Ricardian-empiricist tension, Cairnes's attempts to rebuff the attacks on Ricardian economics, Keynes's Marshallianism, the political economy-methodology connection in the work of Robbins, the Austrians and Hutchison, and Friedman's efforts to keep a number of different balls in the air – should start to erode the view of methodology as simply taking (relatively pristine) ideas off the shelf of scientific philosophy. It seems that politics, context, and contingency are deeply involved in the selection process, and as we will begin to see in the next chapter, also what finds its way onto the philosophical shelf.

3

The Breakdown of the Received View within the Philosophy of Science

If it is true that there are but two kinds of people in the world – the logical positivists and the god-damned English professors – then I suppose I am a logical positivist.

[Glymour 1980, ix]

... is a positivist, i.e., one of those who always thinks of "science" with a capital S ... and use it in a context which conveys instructions pronounced in the awe-inspired tone chiefly familiar in public prayer. This emotional pronouncement of value judgments condemning emotion and value judgments seems to the reviewer a symptom of a defective sense of humor.

[Knight 1940, p. 151]

Everybody knows nowadays that logical positivism is dead. But nobody seems to suspect that there may be a question to be asked here – the question "Who is responsible?" ... I fear that I must admit responsibility.

[Popper 1976b, p. 88]

Once, in those dear dead days, almost, but not quite beyond recall, there was a view of science that commanded widespread popular and academic assent. This view deserves a name. I shall call it "Legend." ... So much for the dear dead days. Since the 1950s the mists have begun to fall. Legend's lustre has dimmed. While it may continue to figure in textbooks and journalistic expositions, numerous intelligent critics now view Legend as smug, uninformed, unhistorical, and analytically shallow.

[Kitcher 1993, pp. 3–5]

The last half of the previous chapter examined a number of economists whose methodological writings were broadly informed by "positivist" philosophy of science. This chapter will consider positivist philosophical ideas in much greater detail. The main subject will be the so-called Received View (a term popularized by Frederick Suppe [1977]), the dominant framework within Anglo-American philosophy of science during the 1950s and 1960s and the main heir to the positivist tradition.[1] While the discussion will begin with Vienna Circle positivism in the 1930s, and end with some of the program's recent descendants, the main focus will be the factors that contributed to the demise of the Received View during the last few decades. In general, I will try to stick rather closely to the philosophical literature, but there is one place where the discussion will deviate from standard philosophical parlance. The philosophical literature usually identifies the Received View exclusively with "logical empiricism" – the philosophical program that was both the immediate descendant and the final incarnation of the logical positivism of the 1930s – but I will use the term for a rather loose amalgam of logical empiricism and the falsificationism of Karl Popper. The "logical empiricism plus falsificationism" definition will be used, since it corresponds to the way the term Received View is most frequently employed within economic methodology.

One disclaimer seems to be in order before embarking on this discussion of the Received View. The disclaimer is that this chapter certainly does not constitute a comprehensive examination of logical positivism, the Received View, or the arguments leading to its decline; it is an interpretative discussion that emphasizes only a few main issues. There are standard, and quite reliable, sources that cover the field in much more detail than what is offered here.[2] My main purpose is to provide a general overview that focuses on two issues that will be emphasized repeatedly in the following chapters (theory-ladenness and underdetermination). It is also important to keep in mind that the ultimate topic is economic methodology, and that not all aspects of the Received View and its

---

[1] Philip Kitcher (1993) refers to this mainstream view as *Legend*, but his characterization is a bit more general than the positivist-inspired Received View. I will stick with the term Received View in this chapter, since positivism is the main focus, employing the term Legend in later chapters where the target is more general.

[2] For example, Achinstein and Barker (1969) and Ayer (1946 and 1959) are standard sources for logical positivism; Hempel (1965 and 1966) and Nagel (1961) are paradigmatic statements of the Received View; and Suppe (1977) and Laudan et al. (1986) summarize the criticisms that contributed to its decline. Caldwell (1982/1994) contains the most detailed discussion of the Received View available within the economics literature.

critique have played (or should play) an equal role in methodological discourse about economics.

3.1 The Received View within the Philosophy of Science

The Received View is most clearly identified with the logical empiricist program in the philosophy of science, and logical empiricism in turn descended from the logical positivism of the Vienna Circle. The first section will discuss the main features of these two philosophical programs as well as the associated variant of falsificationism. The final subsection (3.1.4) will examine the ways in which the Received View had started to unravel from internal tensions and criticisms long before the critiques of Quine, Kuhn, and the others that will be discussed later in the chapter.

3.1.1 Logical Positivism

The philosophical movement called "logical positivism" was once viewed as a fresh and liberating voice on the intellectual landscape; it was a movement that commanded respect from the very beginning, grew steadily in influence, and by mid-century effectively conditioned the discourse in almost every area of scholarly inquiry. But not anymore. Positivism is now perceived almost universally as a villain, a wrong move that is responsible for much of what is wrong in nearly every intellectual discipline; the term "positivism" is now exclusively a "philosophical Boo-adjective" (Hutchison 1981, p. 204). The descent of positivism began when it was attacked (and effectively routed) by a coalition of forces in 1970s philosophy of natural science; immediately thereafter it began a precipitous slide from its position of prominence in almost every other area of inquiry. In order to understand this descent, it is necessary to go back to the very beginning of the positivist program. What exactly then is/was the philosophy of logical positivism?

Historically, logical positivism began with Moritz Schlick's Thursday evening discussion groups in Vienna in the late 1920s; intellectually, it began with the crisis that Einstein's theory of relativity initiated in German philosophy during the decade or so following its publication in 1905. Einstein's theory induced a rupture in physics – a body of scientific theorizing previously considered to be the exemplar of timeless and incorrigible knowledge – that could not effectively be sutured by any of the reigning philosophical characterizations of scientific knowledge.

The term "logical positivism" was used by Blumberg and Feigel (1931) to label the general philosophical perspective that emerged from Schlick's Vienna Circle seminar and those associated with it. A list of the main participants in the Vienna Circle includes names such as Rudolph Carnap, Herbert Feigl, Philipp Frank, Hans Hahn, Victor Kraft, Karl Menger, and Otto Neurath, although many others who passed through or were associated with the seminar at various points.[3] Some, such as Ludwig Wittgenstein, played an important role in the development of the Circle's philosophical position while having very little direct contact with the actual seminar. Others, such as Hans Reichenbach in Berlin, Alfred Tarski in Poland, and Bertrand Russell in England, were associated with the general positivist movement, but had varying degrees of direct contact with Schlick's immediate group. The movement was popularized initially by A. J. Ayer in England and by C. W. Morris in the United States, and later by the members of the Vienna Circle who immigrated to these two countries during World War II.

The philosophy of the Vienna Circle was never presented in a single canonical text, but the pamphlet "The Scientific Conception of the World: The Vienna Circle (*Wissenschaftliche Weltauffassung, Der Wiener Kreis*)" achieved near-canonical status. This pamphlet, written primarily by Hahn, Neurath, and Carnap, was originally presented to Schlick in October of 1929 when he returned from a visiting position in the United States. The pamphlet was considered by many members of the Circle to be the manifesto of the logical positivist program.

The name "logical positivism" is actually a fairly descriptive appellation for the Vienna Circle's philosophical program, since the members actively sought to combine aspects of *logicism* and *positivism*. In particular, the program combined Frege and Russell's conception of logic with the classical empiricist/positivist epistemology of Hume, Comte, and Mach. As noted above, empiricists like John Stuart Mill had argued for the reduction of even mathematics and logic to empirical science. Although the logical positivists also considered mathematical inquiries to be a type of genuine knowledge, they did not follow Mill in grounding such knowledge in empirical observation. For the logical positivists, mathematics and logic were knowledge, but they were strictly *a priori*, and not the type of *a*

---

[3] In fact, what came to be known as the "Vienna Circle" was not a single seminar. In addition to Schlick's Thursday evening group, there also were meetings organized by Victor Kraft and Edgar Zilsel, as well as Karl Menger's famous mathematical colloquium. Menger's colloquium is particularly important for the history of modern economic thought, not only because it was organized by Carl Menger's son, but also because of the role it played in the early history of mathematical general equilibrium theory (see Arrow and Debreu 1954, pp. 287–9; Arrow and Hahn 1971, pp. 8–11; Menger 1973; Wald 1951; Weintraub 1983 and Ch. 6 of 1985). Leonard (1995a, 1998) examines the interwoven themes of Vienna circle philosophy, Karl Menger's ethical theories, certain developments in the visual arts, and mathematical economics.

posteriori knowledge produced by empirical science. Mathematical and logical propositions were *analytic*; they were (when validly derived) true in all possible worlds, and therefore represented a type of genuine, but purely *a priori*, knowledge. According to the logical positivists the only other type of genuine knowledge was produced by empirical science. Science, unlike mathematics, was factual and empirical; its propositions were *synthetic* and true only under certain empirical conditions. For the Vienna Circle, these two categories *exhausted knowledge*: the synthetic factual truth of empirical science, and the purely formal analytic truth of logic and mathematics. The logical positivist position was summarized nicely by Carnap in his intellectual autobiography.

> In this way, the distinction between logical and factual truth, which had always been regarded in our discussions in the Vienna Circle as important and fundamental, was at last vindicated. In this distinction we had seen the way out of the difficulty which had prevented the older empiricism from giving a satisfactory account of the nature of knowledge in logic and mathematics. Since empiricism had always asserted that *all* knowledge is based on experience, this assertion had to include knowledge in mathematics. . . . Our solution, . . . consisted in asserting the thesis of empiricism only for factual truth. By contrast, the truths in logic and mathematics are not in need of confirmation by observations, because they do not state anything about the world of facts, they hold for any possible combination of facts. (Carnap 1963, p. 65, emphasis in original)

Because the only valid form of synthetic knowledge was empirical science, the logical positivists followed the young Wittgenstein (1922) in arguing that all "metaphysical" propositions – statements such as those originating in theology, religion, or idealistic philosophy – were simply "meaningless." The commitment to this criterion of (non)significance, "the meaningless of all nonempirical (synthetic) propositions" became the single most important demarcation criterion for logical positivism, radically dividing those who were, and those who were not, positivists.[4] This strict demarcation led many logical positivists into a kind of "onto-phobia," a fear of talking about anything that purported to go beyond, or get behind, that which was immediately apparent to the human senses.

[4] One example of the elimination of ostensibly meaningless propositions from economic science was discussed above: the elimination of interpersonal utility comparisons from welfare economics and consumer choice theory by Robbins (1932/1952) and others – although even here the issues are not as simple as they might seem (see Cooter and Rapoport 1984; Davis 1990a; and Ch. 7 of Walsh 1996).

The logical positivist position on metaphysics is stated boldly in the early paper by Blumberg and Feigel (1931).

> Logical positivism goes beyond the earlier positivistic and pragmatic rejection of metaphysics as superfluous which applied the principle of Occam's razor. For the new positivism, metaphysical propositions are, strictly speaking, meaningless, since a proposition has meaning only when we know under what conditions it is true or false. (p. 293)

This view of metaphysics forced the logical positivists to redefine the proper role of the discipline of philosophy. Much of what had previously been called "philosophy" was now considered to be meaningless metaphysical speculation, and yet it was also clear that the kind of analysis produced by the Vienna Circle was something quite different from the knowledge produced by empirical science. If all meaningful discourse is either analytic formalism or empirical science, then what is the role of the philosopher of science (and what is the "cognitive significance" of his/her discourse)? The logical positivist response was to redefine the job of the philosopher, to turn philosophy into a kind of conceptual cleanup operation: to clean up various conceptual messes by pointing out what was, and was not, meaningful discourse. "In other words, the philosopher is reduced, or elevated, to the position of a park keeper whose business it is to see that no one commits an intellectual nuisance; the nuisance in question being that of lapsing into metaphysics" (Ayer 1990, p. 5); or, even more colorfully, the purpose of the new philosophy was "to rid ourselves of intellectual cramps" (Ayer 1990, p. 59). This view of philosophy, as a type of conceptual analysis that decides what is and what is not meaningful, also carried over to the later Received View and other philosophical positions that were less strict in their definition of cognitive significance.

Although everyone associated with the logical positivist movement agreed that metaphysics was meaningless, and that empirical science was meaningful,[5] there was substantially less agreement regarding exactly how

---

[5] Although even here the logical positivists were not entirely of one mind. Two polar cases were Schlick and Neurath. For Schlick, there was an independent "empirical criterion of meaningfulness" and since science lived up to this standard it was meaningful, and since theology did not, it was not. As we will see, Neurath took a much more "naturalistic" line (this sense of "naturalism" will be discussed in the last section of this chapter and throughout the chapters that follow), arguing that to put anything, even a philosophical criterion of meaningfulness, above empirical science smacks of metaphysics and represents a step backward toward a prelogical positivist way of philosophizing. In the language of "foundationalism" and "antifoundationalism," Schlick was a very foundationalist logical positivist, while Neurath was a much more naturalist and antifoundationalist positivist. See Uebel (1992) and Cartwright, Cat, Fleck, and Uebel (1997) for book-length discussions of these issues.

the empirical content (and thus meaningfulness) came to manifest itself within science. There was, over time, a substantial disagreement among the various members of the Vienna Circle regarding the details of the empirical transmission mechanism involved in science. One manifestation of this disagreement was the so-called protocol sentence debate, or the debate over "physicalism"; this debate not only generated disagreement among various members of the Vienna Circle, it also caused at least one member – Carnap – to substantially modify his position over time. Although many positivist philosophical disputes would carry us too far afield, the protocol sentence debate (a debate over the exact empirical nature, and thus meaningfulness, of science) had such a significant impact on later developments within the philosophy of science (and thus economic methodology) that it is useful to examine it in some detail.

It is perhaps best to introduce the protocol sentence debate by characterizing Carnap's position in *Der Logische Aufbau der Welt* (1928): the definitive statement of the early Vienna Circle view of scientific knowledge. The argument in the *Aufbau* was based on a version of empiricist foundationalism; the idea was to start with sentences about observable empirical phenomena – the incorrigible foundations for knowledge – then via induction, generalize these observation sentences to obtain scientific theories. In this way, scientific theories were purely descriptive, they could always be translated back, without loss of meaningful content, into statements about observables. Scientific theories were merely redescriptions of empirical observations expressed in terms of some phenomenal observation language, the *protocol language*. The sentences that formed the empirical basis for science were thus *protocol sentences* – sentences expressed in the phenomenal protocol language – and these protocol sentences formed the ultimate foundations for science; all scientific discourse was either expressed in terms of these protocol sentences, or could be translated into them by so-called correspondence rules. This protocol language was an integral part of the *verifiability criterion of meaningfulness*; for a sentence to be meaningful it must be "in principle verifiable," that is, it must be possible to specify, at least in principle, the conditions under which the sentence would be true; "observational evidence can be described which, if actually obtained, would conclusively establish the truth of the sentence" (Hempel 1965, p. 103). The protocol language provides the discursive context for the application of this criterion of meaningfulness; it provided the conduit by which such empirical verification could take place.[6] Carnap summarizes his early view in the following way:

---

[6] This empiricist reading of logical positivism, and Carnap in particular, has recently been challenged by a more Kantian interpretation (see Coffa 1991 and Friedman 1992, 1993).

We assumed that there was a certain rock bottom of knowledge, the knowledge of the immediately given, which was indubitable. Every other kind of knowledge was supposed to be firmly supported by this basis and therefore likewise decidable with certainty. This was the picture which I had given in *Logischer Aufbau*; . . . This conception led to Wittgenstein's principle of verifiability, which says that it is in principle possible to obtain either a definite verification or a definite refutation for any meaningful sentence. (Carnap 1963, p. 51)

Not all members of the Vienna Circle were equally comfortable with this criterion of meaningfulness. Otto Neurath was critical of it, at least in part, because it seemed to exclude many of the concepts employed in the social sciences. Neurath, interested in social science and sympathetic to Marxist ideas, was extremely concerned with the social and political implications of the logical positivist program.[7] For Neurath the basic motivation for the program was to help create a better world by eliminating the conservative influence of traditional metaphysical ideas; Neurath wanted "to render scientific philosophy 'useful for Marxism'" (Uebel 1992, p. 78).[8]

"Bourgeoisie against the proletariat" also means "metaphysics against science." Neurath was sure that the fight for the proletarian interests is both a fight against metaphysics and a fight for a scientific approach. And vice versa. (Cartwright, Cat, Fleck, and Uebel 1996, p. 76)[9]

Neurath's approach to the language of science was called *physicalism*. He argued that "there is no fundamental difference in the subject matter between the natural sciences and the psychological and sociological disciplines, because human individuals and societies are basically nothing

[7] Neurath even wrote on a number of economic topics (see Uebel 1998 and Cartwright, Cat, Fleck, and Uebel 1996). See Jolink (1999) for an interesting discussion of Neurath's influence on Terence Hutchison's methodological ideas.

[8] The impact of Neurath's political economy on his philosophy of science has been examined in a number of recent works, including: Cartwright, Cat, Fleck, and Uebel (1996), Cat, Cartwright, and Chang (1996), O'Neill (1995), Reisch (1997a, 1997b), and Uebel (1992). I will return to this issue in the discussion of "unified science" at the end of this section. Recent research also suggests that Neurath's politics contributed to the antipositivism of many Austrian economists including Mises and Hayek (see Caldwell 1997 and O'Neill 1995, 1997).

[9] Or as Joseph Agassi (1998, p. 84) put it, for Neurath:

upper-class thinking = metaphysics = idealism = pessimist historicism = evil
working-class thinking = science = materialism = optimist historicism = goodness

other than more or less complex physical systems" (Hempel 1969, p. 167). All science, natural and social (and thus all meaningful discourse), traffics in the same physicalist vocabulary – "a thing-language where one speaks of material things and ascribes observable properties to them" (Suppe 1977, p. 14) – because, according to the scientific conception of the world, such observable physical things (events in space and time) exhaust the contents of the world (to attempt to go any deeper would be to sink into metaphysical speculation).

There are two important points to make about Neurath's notion of a physicalist vocabulary. First, it is *broad*, and, second, it is *revisable*. Regarding breadth, Neurath had a very wide-ranging conception of the types of things that could be described within the physicalist idiom. According to Neurath, physicalism was not just the language of physics; it included the language of physics, but it also included much more. "Neurath's 'physicalism' did not require the reduction of different forms of scientific discourse to that of physics, but only that they be so formulated as to allow an actual or possible 'disconfirmation' by events in space and time" (Cartwright, Cat, Fleck, and Uebel 1996, pp. 95–6). This meant that almost anything that could be expressed in the language of science, any science, natural or social, was considered to be meaningful discourse. This breadth was, of course, consistent with Neurath's social objectives; the language of the behavioristic and social sciences was, thus, capable of providing perfectly legitimate scientific knowledge. "Neurath's theory of science allowed different disciplines to engage in autonomous concept formation without reducing them to physics" (Cartwright, Cat, Fleck, and Uebel 1996, p. 96). Metaphysics and religion were out, but almost all of modern (even social) science was in.[10]

Neurath's physicalist language was also revisable; the empirical basis of science was open to revision, and had in fact been revised continuously during the course of scientific development. This commitment to the revisability of the empirical basis of science – what could be called protocol fallibilism – was often illustrated by Neurath's famous "boat" metaphor:[11]

> We possess no fixed point which may be made the fulcrum for
> moving the earth; and in like manner we have no absolutely firm

[10] Neurath even proposed an "*index verborum prohibitorum*" that would list all of the words that should be prohibited because they were "dangerous" or "dubious" (i.e., non-scientific). Reisch (1997b) discusses Neurath's index and provides a partial list of the prohibited words; as one might expect the list includes things like "essence" and "soul," but less obviously it also includes "observation" and "explanation."

[11] Evidently there were at least five different versions of the "boat" metaphor in Neurath's work and the first one appeared in a 1913 article on the "Problems of War Economics" (see Cartwright, Cat, Fleck, and Uebel 1996, p. 91).

ground upon which to establish the sciences. Our actual situation is as if we were on board ship on an open sea and were required to change various parts of the ship during the voyage. (Neurath 1937, p. 276)

By the early 1930s, Carnap had started to move away from the commitments of the *Aufbau*, and had begun to move in the direction of Neurath's physicalism. Although there were undoubtedly many reasons for this change, Neurath's sustained argumentation (and related arguments made by Karl Popper) was certainly an important factor.[12] These changes coincided with Carnap's movement from the relatively strict "verifiability" criterion of significance to a more liberal principle of "confirmability," further undermining the empiricist foundationalism that was defended in the *Aufbau*. Carnap discusses these changes in his autobiography.

> Under the influence of some philosophers, especially Mach and Russell, I regarded in the *Logischer Aufbau* a phenomenalistic language as the best for a philosophical analysis of knowledge. I believed that the task of philosophy consists in reducing all knowledge to a basis of certainty. Since the most certain knowledge is that of the immediately given, whereas knowledge of material things is derivative and less certain, it seemed that the philosopher must employ a language which uses sense-data as a basis. In the Vienna discussions my attitude changed gradually toward a preference for the physicalistic language. (Carnap 1963, p. 50)

Carnap's movement toward physicalism and a more liberal criterion of meaning did not come as a single one-shot change of mind in the 1930s but rather took place continuously over a period of years. These changes in his position received varying degrees of acceptance by other members of the Vienna Circle and their associates. Schlick, for instance, died in 1936, but in the last few years of his life he was quite critical of the liberalizing tone that had begun to characterize Carnap's position. Although I will not document all of these changes, two brief comments are in order regarding these later developments in the logical positivist program.

First, Carnap's revised view never obtained the kind of committed following that he had enjoyed with the *Aufbau*. By the mid-1930s, the Vienna Circle had become less cohesive intellectually and more scattered geographically; these changes began to undermine the unity that

---

[12] The social and political situation also seemed to play a role; Carnap readily admits that it was the "left wing of the Circle" that "came to the conclusion that we had to look for a more liberal criterion of significance than verifiability" (Carnap 1963, p. 57).

characterized the Circle's public persona during the early years. This situation was further exacerbated by the authors themselves; Neurath continued to maintain his physicalist position, but his arguments were often loose and unsystematic, whereas Carnap, who was very systematic and structured in any particular book or paper, seemed to change his mind over time. The second point is that despite the fact that Carnap moved in the direction of Neurath's physicalism, he never fully adopted it. Carnap's view became more liberal over time – at one point amounting to a version of "operationalism" – but he never endorsed the exact same view of physicalism that Neurath had pushed so aggressively in the early years of the Vienna Circle.[13]

Implicit in this discussion of Neurath's physicalism is a final aspect of logical positivism that needs to be discussed before moving on to Logical Empiricism: the issue of "unified science." The Vienna Circle always considered "unified science" to be an important goal for scientific philosophy as well as for the practice of science itself. As Carnap, Hahn, and Neurath stated in their *Der Wiener Kreis* pamphlet:

> The scientific world conception is characterised not so much by theses of its own, but rather by its basic attitude, its points of view and direction of research. The goal ahead is *unified science*. The endeavour is to link and harmonise the achievements of individual investigators in their various fields of science. (Carnap, Hahn, and Neurath 1929, pp. 7–8, emphasis in original)

Although all of the members of the Vienna Circle were interested in unified science, it was Neurath who prosecuted the unification project most earnestly; unification not only had a special interest for Neurath, it also had a special meaning. Given his social concerns and his fairly liberal definition of cognitive significance (physicalism), Neurath's version of "unification" did not eliminate the special (particularly social) sciences:

---

[13] The issue of "operationalism" is quite interesting. Many logical positivists referred to Bridgman's (1927, 1938) operationalism – either as a variant of Carnap's criterion of verifiability or confirmability (or even as a type of correspondence rule) – but the remarks were usually offered in passing. Operationalism was certainly not a major theme in the logical positivist program, and later logical empiricists like Hempel were openly critical of Bridgman's position (see Ch. 6 of Hempel 1965). Despite this, when *social scientists* were introducing logical positivist ideas to their colleagues, the positivist criterion of meaning was *equated* with Bridgman's notion of operationally meaningful. A good example of this is Stevens (1939). Koch (1992) presents a detailed critique of the way that logical positivism and operationalism were interpreted by psychologists in the 1930s and 1940s; these remarks mirror some of the criticism of Samuelson discussed in the previous chapter (particularly Cohen 1995).

either by reduction to physics or by a narrow application of the criterion of cognitive significance. For Neurath, the unification took the form of an "encyclopedia," where the output of the various special sciences would be clearly displayed in a common physicalist language; this common idiom would, according to Neurath, best accommodate the effective and coordinated employment of these various sciences to the success of his social and political goals. The hierarchical picture of science "would be replaced by the orchestration of different instruments, each distinct but brought together to accomplish something bigger than any could do individually" (Galison 1998, p. 55).

> Neurath's social plans of this period provide new foci for the political role of unified science, in two ways. First, science serves as a weapon against metaphysics. This idea was widely shared among the members of the Vienna Circle, yet there was a difference. Whereas for most others the motivation for fighting metaphysics was chiefly epistemological, for Neurath it was strongly political. (Cat, Cartwright, and Chang 1996, p. 367)

In order to promote (his version of) the unification of the sciences Neurath became editor-in-chief of the *International Encyclopedia of Unified Science*, a project initiated in 1938. This series included works as diverse as John Dewey's *Theory of Valuation* and Thomas Kuhn's *The Structure of Scientific Revolutions*: works that one would not necessarily associate with either logical positivism or the Vienna Circle.

Although the relationship between Neurath's view of unification and his political economy is well established within the philosophical literature, some recent commentators have pushed the economic connection even farther. Cartwright, Cat, Fleck, and Uebel (1996) relate Neurath's unity of science project directly to the *Methodenstreit* between Gustav Schmoller and Carl Menger. Schmoller had served as Neurath's thesis examiner and it is clear that the "unity of science" offered a possible solution to this controversy, while simultaneously satisfying Neurath's own social and political interests.

> Neurath founded the Unity of Science Movement in 1934. For Neurath – a social scientist – the drive for unity was rooted in the great debates between Carl Menger and his thesis examiner, Gustav Schmoller, about the nature of political economy. . . . In this setting, unity of science necessarily meant unity of the social and natural sciences. For Neurath it meant both more and less: he did not look for a sweeping philosophical union of two

great domains of human thought, but rather for the practical unification of the rich variety of special disciplines in all their detail. (Cartwright, Cat, Fleck, and Uebel 1996, p. 167)[14]

All of this interplay between political economy and the core ideas of logical positivism puts an interesting spin on the standard shelf-of-scientific philosophy view of economic methodology that following positivist (or falsificationist) dictums allows, or perhaps is necessary for, economics to be purely "objective" and rise above the melee of political-economic controversy. Such a stance seems rather ironic, given that the same positivist dictums that ostensibly allow economics to transcend the political fray were themselves forged in the cauldron of, and thus conditioned by, political-economic debate and methodological controversy.

3.1.2 Logical Empiricism

Logical empiricism was the dominant approach in post-World War II Anglo-American philosophy of science. A few of the influential contributors to the program were Richard Braithwaite, Carl Hempel, and Ernest Nagel (one could also include certain parts of Carnap's later work). Although there were disagreements among members of the Vienna Circle, it is important to recognize that logical positivism was always a much more cohesive and programmatic approach than the logical empiricism that followed it. Logical positivism had a particular time and place of origin, and the members of the Vienna Circle were deeply committed to, and made a concerted effort to present, a unified "scientific view of the world"; despite some in-house disagreements, logical positivism was in fact a distinct philosophical "school." Logical empiricism, by contrast, never became a truly self-conscious philosophical "school"; it was simply what one did if one was a professional philosopher of science in the 1950s. In a very real sense, logical empiricism (or the Received View more generally) did not become recognized as, or recognize itself as, a particular "view" until it came under attack in the late 1960s.

The first topic to consider is actually a continuation of the previous discussion of logical positivism; it is the *gradual breakdown of the theory/observation distinction.* The liberalization of the notion of cognitive significance that occurred with the move from the phenomenalistic protocol language of the *Aufbau* to a more physicalistic observation lan-

---

[14] It is interesting that a view that is now so uncontroversial – that Neurath's view of unified science (and science generally) was greatly influenced by his political economy – was considered to be so controversial when suggested earlier by Austrian economists such as Mises (1978, p. 131).

guage, and the corresponding movement from verifiability to confirmability, continued with the Received View. According to logical positivism, scientific theories are formulated in a "theoretical vocabulary" and connected to (reduced to) the "observational vocabulary" of the protocol language by "correspondence rules." These correspondence rules guaranteed the cognitive significance of the theoretical terms by transmitting this cognitive significance up from the observation language. By the 1950s, not only had the nature of the observation language changed, but the core distinction between "the theoretical" and "the observational" had become blurred. The terms "observational" and "theoretical" continued to be employed of course, but it became increasingly difficult to demarcate these two components of the language of science in any substantive or consistent way. As Hempel explains the situation:

> Furthermore, there remains no satisfactory general way of dividing all conceivable systems of theoretical terms into two classes: those that are scientifically significant and those that are not; those that have experiential import and those that lack it. Rather, experiential, or operational, significance appears as capable of gradations.... experiential significance presents itself as capable of degrees, and any attempt to set up a dichotomy allowing only experientially meaningful and experientially meaningless concept systems appears as too crude to be adequate for a logical analysis of scientific concepts and theories. (Hempel 1965, pp. 131–2)

The second important aspect of logical empiricism is closely related to the blurring of the observational/theoretical distinction; it is the question of *the cognitive status of scientific theories*. In the rather tight framework of early logical positivism, scientific theories were merely descriptive – they were merely convenient ways of describing empirical regularities. As discussed above, the correspondence rules allowed the theoretical terms to be translated, without loss of cognitive content, into the observation language. Questions were raised about the translation-correspondence rules, and about the nature of the observation-protocol language, but because scientific theories were not considered to be anything more than, or contain anything other than, the observations on which they were based, there was not really any serious discussion about the "cognitive status of scientific theories." As the distinction between theory and observation became more blurred, and the protocol language (via physicalism) became more dependent on the theoretical languages of current scientific practice, the issue of the cognitive status of scientific theories emerged as an independent and substantive issue.

Logical empiricism offered two fundamentally different arguments about the cognitive status of scientific theories. One response was the *instrumentalist view of theories* and the other was the *realist view of theories*. In its simplest form, "instrumentalism" says that scientific theories are merely instruments for making empirical predictions; by contrast, the simplest version of scientific "realism" says that scientific theories contain statements that can actually be true or false.[15] Because instrumentalism converts scientific theories into mere tools, and because not all tools are equally well suited to any particular job, instrumentalism shifts the question of the "status" of scientific theories from "cognitive significance" to heuristic effectiveness. Realism, by contrast, argues that the theoretical terms in a scientific theory actually "refer" to real but unobservable entities and their properties. Instrumentalism dissolves (rather than solves) the problem of the cognitive status of scientific theories by eliminating such theories from the list of things that might possess cognitive significance, whereas realism shifts the responsibility for cognitive significance onto the theoretical terms themselves. Either one of these two views is broadly consistent with the other significant features of logical empiricism. Many different versions of these two interpretations were offered during the heyday of the Received View, and new strains of both views have emerged in the later philosophical literature (and economic methodology). This is only a brief introduction to the realism/instrumentalism debate, but it will suffice, as many of the later strains are discussed below.

The third relevant aspect of logical empiricism is the change from an inductive to a *hypothetico-deductive* view of the structure of scientific theories. The logical empiricists did not continue the early Vienna Circle view of scientific theories: theories as being built up inductively from (theory-neutral) protocol statements. Philosophers such as Hempel and Nagel defended an alternative, deductive, relationship between scientific laws (theoretical generalizations) and the empirical evidence that supported them. According to logical empiricism, only the deductive consequences of a scientific theory were relevant to its empirical support. Wesley Salmon provides a succinct statement of this approach:

> Schematically, the hypothetico-deductive method works as follows: From a general hypothesis and particular statements of initial conditions, a particular predictive statement is deduced. The statements of initial conditions, at least for the time, are accepted as true; the hypothesis is the statement whose truth is

---

[15] The canonical logical empiricist statement of these two views is contained in Chapter 6 of Nagel (1961).

at issue. By observation we determine whether the predictive statement turned out to be true. If the predictive consequence is false, the hypothesis is disconfirmed. If observation reveals that the predictive statement is true, we say the hypothesis is confirmed. . . . A hypothesis that is sufficiently confirmed is accepted, at least tentatively. (Salmon 1966, p. 18)

One reason for adopting the hypothetico-deductive method was to avoid the inveterate "problem of induction." This problem, originally articulated by David Hume, is the philosophical problem of *justifying induction*. In terms of the popular ornithological example: how is it that we are justified – or are we justified – in concluding that "all ravens are black" after observing some finite but large number of black (and only black) ravens? This problem has been a significant issue for the empiricist view of science. Simply put, the empiricist notion of a scientific law is that of a generalization based on empirical observations; as such, they require an ampliative inference, a jump from individual observations to the properties of "all" such systems. Justifying this type of ampliative inference is the Humean problem of induction. It is fairly clear how the hypothetico-deductive method might help circumvent this problem, since, according to this view, scientific theories are "based on" empirical observations (deductively), but not literally "built up from" those observations (inductively). There was a rather extensive (and inconclusive) debate within logical empiricism regarding the degree to which the hypothetico-deductive method was actually successful in avoiding the problem of induction,[16] but perhaps more important for our purposes is how this method relates to the fourth important aspect of the logical empiricist program, the so-called deductive-nomological (or D-N) model of *scientific explanation*.

According to classical empiricism and early logical positivism, scientific theories *do not explain at all*; the scientific domain is the domain of empirical observation and the purpose of a scientific theory is to reliably describe those empirical observations.[17] The commonsense view of science that science should "explain" what we observe in the world by uncovering deep, underlying, not directly observable, causal mechanisms, is a view that is alien to strict empiricism; in "science there are no 'depths'; there is surface everywhere" (Carnap, Hahn, and Neurath 1929, p. 8). And, yet, even the logical positivists agreed that science does

---

[16] Salmon (1966, pp. 17–21) argues rather convincingly that the hypothetico-deductive method does not succeed in avoiding the problem of induction.

[17] Recall Samuelson's defense of just such a descriptivist or anti-explanatory view (particularly in Samuelson [1965]).

explain what we see in the world; not only does science explain, but one of the most persuasive arguments for adopting the scientific view is how much better science explains what we see in the world than the explanations offered by earlier philosophical and religious views. One of the major moves, and the thing that is probably still considered to be the greatest accomplishment of logical empiricism, was to provide a model of scientific *explanation* that is broadly consistent with an empiricist view of scientific theories.

The logical empiricist's answer to the problem of scientific explanation is the deductive-nomological (or D-N) model, initially presented by Hempel and Oppenheim in 1948.[18] According to the D-N model, a particular observed event (say entity x exhibiting property y) is "explained" by subsuming the event under a general law (say x is an instance of z, and all zs exhibit property y). An economic example might be to explain why a particular firm x raised the price of its product; the explanation might be that firm x is a monopoly that has experienced an increase in marginal cost, and that all monopolistic firms will raise the price of their product when they experience an increase in marginal cost. In a D-N explanation, the phenomena to be explained (the explanandum) is deduced (the "deductive" part of the D-N) from the explanans, the explanation of the phenomena, which is composed of initial conditions and at least one general law (the "nomological" part of the D-N). Schematically then, a D-N explanation will take the following general form.

$$C_1, C_2, \ldots C_n$$
$$L_1, L_2, \ldots L_m \qquad \text{(explanans)}$$
$$\text{------------}$$
$$E \qquad \text{(explanandum)}$$

where each C_i represents a sentence that describes an initial condition, and each L_i represents a general law.

Converting the previous economic example into this schematic form we have:

C_1 = x is a monopoly firm
C_2 = marginal cost increased
C_3 = no other relevant variables changed (ceteris paribus condition)
L_1 = All monopoly firms raise their price when marginal cost increases (ceteris paribus)

Therefore firm x raised its price.

[18] There is some debate about whether the model originated with Karl Popper or not (see Hands 1991a).

In the original Hempel and Oppenheim paper, the general law(s) as well as the initial conditions had to be true; in later versions, the restrictions on the general laws were weakened to conditions such as "confirmed," or "corroborated," or "not known to be false." Hempel also expanded the original D-N model to cover certain types of statistical explanations where the relevant law holds only with a certain (known) probability. It is fair to say that during the 1950s and early 1960s the topic of scientific explanation, with the D-N model always at the center of the debate, became one of the (or probably "the") most discussed topics in the philosophy of science. Supporters of the D-N model argued that it was broadly applicable to many types of explanations outside of the natural sciences: including history, certain types of functional explanations in the social and biological sciences, and the "rational choice" models of microeconomics.[19] Critics attacked the D-N model from the inside (suggesting minor changes but keeping the core arguments about deduction and general laws) as well as from the outside (arguing that the entire approach was flawed and suggesting alternative models of explanation). As it currently stands, the D-N model has been harshly criticized, but no other alternative model has gained enough support among philosophers of science to be seriously regarded as a viable replacement. The D-N model remains the standard, if highly criticized, characterization of scientific explanation.[20]

In closing this discussion of the D-N model, I would like to point out two ways in which this model of scientific explanation connects up with other aspects of logical empiricism discussed above. First, notice that the D-N model works equally well with either the instrumentalist or realist interpretation of scientific theories; the D-N model seems to be neutral on the issue of the cognitive status of scientific theories (at least neutral between the two positions advocated by logical empiricists). Second, notice the relationship between the D-N model and the hypothetico-deductive method; the D-N model makes the deductive form of scientific explanations exactly the same as the hypothetico-deductive approach to the relationship between theory and data. This leads to logical empiricism's *symmetry thesis*. The symmetry thesis says that explanation (D-N) and prediction (hypothetico-deductive method) have the same form; explanations come after events, and predictions come

---

[19] Economics was discussed briefly in the original Hempel and Oppenheim paper, but Hempel (1962) is a more detailed attempt to subsume rational choice explanations under the D-N rubric (see Ayer 1967, for a similar argument).

[20] The definitive history of the debate over the D-N model is Salmon (1989); Salmon even provides a "chronological bibliography" of the relevant literature. A number of the more important papers are reprinted in Pitt (1988).

before, but the basic deductive form is the same. "Testing" and "explaining" are two sides of the same scientific coin.

Although there are many other aspects of logical empiricism that might be considered – the distinction between the "context of discovery" and the "context of justification," for instance – these four main issues are sufficient for the purpose at hand. The next task is to examine the "falsificationist" answer to the questions raised by logical empiricism. I have included Karl Popper's falsificationism as part of the Received View, even though, as noted above, most equate the Received View exclusively with logical empiricism.

3.1.3 Popperian Falsificationism

Karl Popper was mentioned briefly in Chapter 2 in the context of Terence Hutchison's methodological writings. Despite Hutchison's influence, there was very little inkling at mid-century that Popper would end up being the dominant philosophical name in post-World War II economic methodology. The fact that Popper did eventually attain such status among economists is particularly curious given that he never achieved a similar standing among his cohort group within the philosophy of natural science.

The philosophical position that is most commonly associated with Popper's name (in either economic methodology or the philosophy of science) is *falsificationism*. According to the standard rendition, Popper first presented his falsificationist approach in *Logik der Forschung*[21] in 1934, and the rest of his life's work was dedicated to defending, and expanding upon, that original presentation. Over the years, a number of commentators (particularly Popperians) have challenged this standard reading of Popper's career; some have disputed the claim that Popper ever advocated the strict falsificationist view, and others have argued that falsificationism was just one, early and relatively minor, aspect of his more general philosophical program. In the last few years, this debate over the "real" Popper (or at least what is most interesting and useful in the Popperian tradition) has spilled over into the literature on economic methodology. Given the recency of this controversy, it will be deferred until the discussion of "recent developments" in Chapter 7. The topic in this chapter is simply *falsificationism*. The purpose is merely to introduce the standard falsificationist reading of Popper's philosophy so that it can be compared directly to logical empiricism, and also to help us understand the many later developments that build on, or critique, the falsificationist view.

---

[21] English translation, *The Logic of Scientific Discovery* (Popper 1968), hereafter abbreviated *LSD*.

Karl Popper's falsificationism evolved out of his contact with, and criticism of, the views of the Vienna Circle. Popper was a young philosopher in Vienna in the early years of logical positivism and positivism provided the intellectual backdrop – or, as Popper would say, "the philosophical problem situation" – for the development of his own approach (Hacohen 1998). It was Herbert Feigel, an early member of the Vienna Circle, who originally convinced Popper to write the book that ultimately became *Logik der Forschung*, and although Popper was never invited to present a paper in Schlick's seminar, he did present his work in other forums associated with the Vienna Circle (Popper 1976b, pp. 82–5).

Popper's main problem with early logical positivism was its commitment to induction. The intuition behind his argument is simply that while no amount of empirical evidence will ever prove that a general theory is true (Hume's problem of induction), even a single piece of evidence can prove that a theory is false. To continue the earlier ornithological example: no matter how many black ravens are observed it is not possible to prove that *all* ravens are black; on the other hand, a single observation of a nonblack raven will in fact refute, or falsify, the claim that all ravens are black. For Popper, the logic of science is *modus tollens* ($A \Rightarrow B$ and $\sim B \therefore \sim A$) rather than *modus ponens* ($A \Rightarrow B$ and $A \therefore B$) and the empirical method of science is falsification (or attempted falsification) rather than induction. The problem of induction simply dissolves as a philosophical problem since science does not proceed by the inductive method. As Popper summarized the argument in his autobiography:

> This way of looking at knowledge made it possible for me to reformulate Hume's *problem of induction*. In this objective reformulation the problem of induction is no longer a problem of our beliefs – or of the rationality of our beliefs – but a problem of the logical relationship between singular statements (descriptions of "observable" singular facts) and universal theories.
>
> *In this form, the problem of induction becomes soluble*; there is no induction, because universal theories are not deducible from singular statements. But they may be refuted by singular statements, since they may clash with descriptions of observable facts. . . . Thus *there is no induction*: we never argue from facts to theories, unless by way of refutation or "falsification." (Popper 1976b, p. 86, emphasis in original)

Popper used the idea of falsification to establish his own *demarcation criterion* between science and nonscience. Popper viewed this demarcation criterion (employed in economics by Hutchison) as a replacement for the logical positivist criterion of cognitive significance. The logical positivists wanted to demarcate that which was "meaningful" from that which was "meaningless," but Popper found this distinction problematic. One of the main problems for Popper was that he wanted to preserve certain types of metaphysical propositions as meaningful,[22] even though they were not part of empirical science. As a result, Popper focused on the demarcation of "science from nonscience" rather than "meaningful from meaningless." His demarcation criterion was based on the "potential falsifiability" of the proposition in question; for a theory to be scientific it needs to be at least potentially falsifiable, that is, there must exist at least one empirical observation statement that is in conflict with it.

If the only role for empirical evidence is to falsify scientific theories, rather than to confirm them, then it would seem that the only legitimate activity for scientists would be to reject, that is to throw out, scientific theories: or at least to try to throw out scientific theories by attempting to falsify them. But what does this say about the theories that are left? More specifically, what if there are two scientific theories in the same domain, both are potentially falsifiable, and both have passed the same number of tests; which do we choose? Popper's response to this practical problem – the problem of choosing between two falsifiable, but unfalsified, theories – was his theory of *corroboration* (or testability). Popper argued that the most preferred theory is the one that is least likely, the one that sticks its empirical neck out the most. For Popper, the empirical content of a scientific theory is the number of potential falsifiers the theory has – for example, a tautology has no empirical content because it has no potential falsifiers, whereas a very general physical law has a very large number of potential falsifiers and, therefore, high empirical content – thus, the more empirical content a theory has, the more *bold* the theory is, and the more significant its survival should be. A theory that has survived severe tests is considered to be corroborated, and the theory that has passed the most severe tests, the boldest nonfalsified theory, is the most corroborated (has the highest degree of corroboration) and is the most preferred theory.[23]

> As for my *degree of corroboration*, the idea was to sum up, in a short formula, a *report* of the manner in which a theory has passed – or not passed – its tests, including an evaluation of the severity of the tests: only tests undertaken in a *critical* spirit – attempted refutations – should count. . . . A decisive point about the degree of corroboration was that, because it increased with

---

[22] Including his own philosophical arguments, a traditional problem for logical positivism.
[23] Popper's position on corroboration, bold theories, and severe tests is related to his views on "ad hocness" and "novel facts." These issues will be discussed below.

the severity of tests, it could be high only for *theories with a high degree of testability or content.* But this meant that degree of corroboration was linked to *improbability* rather than *probability*: ... (Popper 1976b, pp. 103–4, emphasis in original)

Popper's view of science, the method of bold conjecture and severe test, is built on a foundation of "fallibilist realism" or "conjectural realism."[24] For Popper, there exists a knowable objective world, and finding out the truth about that world is the aim of science; the problem is that we never know when it is that we have actually found the truth. The method of conjectures and refutations is a method of error elimination that gets us closer to the truth,[25] but we can never be certain that we have actually found it, and, worse still, what we have found is always subject to revision. The empirical evidence has an important role to play in Popperian falsificationism, but its role is far less canonical than the role that it plays in logical positivism. Truth, too, has an important role, but it is very different from the role it plays in many other philosophical approaches, including early logical positivism. For Popper truth is a "regulative idea"; it is that which we are striving for, and hopefully getting closer to – and as such it is an indispensable notion – and yet we must always recognize our fallibilism; we never really know that we have actually found the truth we seek.

> Thus the very idea of error – and of fallibility – involves the idea of an objective truth as the standard of which we may fall short. (It is in this sense that the idea of truth is a *regulative* idea.) ... We accept the idea that the task of science is the search for truth, that is, for true theories (even though as Xenophanes pointed out we may never get them, or know them *as true* if we get them). (Popper 1965, p. 229)

The final topic to be discussed before leaving this introduction to Popperian philosophy of science is his view of the empirical basis of science. For Popper, the empirical basis of science is *fallible, conventional, and theory-laden.*

The first and second of these, the fallibility and conventionalism of the empirical basis, follow quite naturally from Popper's general fallibilist position. The empirical basis of science, the collection empirical "basic

---

[24] Popper also calls his position "modified essentialism" (Popper 1972). Musgrave (1993, Ch. 15) and Worrall (1982) are reliable secondary sources on the question of Popper's brand of realism.

[25] Popper's notion of "getting closer to the truth" or "truthlikeness" (verisimilitude) will be discussed in more detail below in Chapter 7 (also see Hands 1991b).

statements" that are accepted by the scientific community and used in the empirical testing of scientific theories, is not infallible; it is subject to revision. For Popper, unlike classical empiricism or most members of the early Vienna Circle (not Neurath), observation statements in the protocol language do not provide an incorrigible foundation for scientific knowledge; protocol sentences can be, and generally will be, revised during the progress of science.

> The empirical basis of objective science has thus nothing "absolute" about it. Science does not rest upon solid bedrock. The bold structure of its theories rises, as it were, above the swamp. It is like a building erected on piles. The piles are driven down from above into the swamp, but not down to any natural or "given" base; and if we stop driving the piles deeper, it is not because we have reached firm ground. We simply stop when we are satisfied that the piles are firm enough to carry the structure, at least for the time being. (Popper 1968, p. 111)

Popper's conventionalism regarding the empirical basis of science is his response to this admitted fallibility, and potential variability, of the protocol language. For Popper, giving up the classical empiricist notion of an incorrigible observation language meant that we must make a *decision* about what is, and what is not, to be accepted as part of the empirical basis; for Popper, the empirical basis is accepted by convention.[26] An attempted falsification of a theory is a confrontation between the theory (which is being questioned) and an empirical basic statement (which is accepted by convention) and as such the outcome is the result of a human decision.

> We need not say that the theory is "false," but we may say instead that it is contradicted by a certain set of accepted basic statements. Nor need we say of basic statements that they are "true" or "false," for we may interpret their acceptance as the result of a conventional decision, and the accepted statements as results of this decision. (Popper 1968, p. 274)

[26] Although Popper admits to being a "conventionalist about the empirical basis" of science, he does not accept the other aspects of what he considers to be the "conventionalist" view of scientific knowledge.

> It is the central idea of the conventionalist, and also his starting point, that no theory is unambiguously determined by experience; a point with which I agree. He believes that he must therefore choose the "simplest" theory. But since the conventionalist does not treat his theories as falsifiable systems but rather as conventional stipulations, he obviously means by "simplicity" something different from degree of falsifiability. (Popper 1968, p. 144)

Popper not only considered statements about the empirical basis to be fallible and accepted by convention, he also considered them to be *theory-laden*. For Popper, all observations are observations in light of theories; we have certain theoretical expectations given by our particular context (our "problem situation") and the act of "observation" is never independent of these background theories. There is for Popper no "natural" distinction between theory and observation; for the purpose of testing a particular theory we "accept," by convention, certain basic observation statements, but these observation statements are themselves the result of interpreting the world in light of theories; we "make" observations, we do not "have" them (Popper 1972, p. 342). There are no immaculate perceptions.

> [O]bservations, and even more so observation statements and statements of experimental results, are always *interpretations* of the facts observed; that they are *interpretations in the light of theories*. (Popper 1968, p. 107, note 3, emphasis in the original)

As will become clear in following sections, theory-ladenness is one of the issues that most clearly differentiates contemporary discussions about scientific knowledge from those of the Received View. Popper did tend to emphasize this issue more in his later work than in the 1st edition of *LSD* (the previous quote was from a note added to the second edition), but the basic recognition of the problem of theory-ladenness was in Popper's work from the very beginning.

3.1.4 Self-Sewn Seeds of Destruction

The next section will discuss two problems – underdetermination and theory-ladenness – that have played an important role in undermining the hegemony of the Received View. The arguments will be presented through the work of the two most recognized advocates of each position – W. V. Quine on underdetermination and Thomas Kuhn on theory-ladenness. Before turning to these "definitive critiques," though, it is useful to review the story thus far; in particular, it is useful to recognize the extent to which developments within logical positivism, logical empiricism, and Popperian falsificationism had already begun to undermine the basic vision of the Received View long before the philosophical clinchers introduced (or at least popularized) by Quine and Kuhn.

Although there are many different debates within the Received View that helped to undermine it,[27] I want to focus on just one of these: the

---

[27] One such case is the undermining of the logical empiricist notion of confirmation by the so-called paradoxes of confirmation. Perhaps the most famous of these paradoxes was the "grue" paradox of Nelson Goodman (1955), but there were others including Hempel's own raven paradox (1965, Ch. 1).

problem of the empirical basis or observation language. Recall that both logical positivism and logical empiricism are *empiricist* philosophical positions. Although all versions of empiricism claim that knowledge starts with observation, and that sense experience is the foundation for knowledge, more radical versions like Hume and some logical positivists claim that knowledge ends with observation as well: that science is observation, wholly observation, and nothing but observation (to talk about anything deeper or behind observation is to participate in metaphysical speculation). If this core notion regarding sense experience is to be cashed out into a framework for discussing and justifying scientific theories, then there needs to be a way of going from the (foundational) sense experiences to sentences that can be built up, or used to test, the more general sentences contained in scientific theories; we need an objective theory-neutral protocol language that maps into sense experience in a simple and reliable way. Without this reliable rock-bottom linkage between sense experience and the language of scientific theories, the entire empiricist project of knowledge as a particular kind of justified belief begins to unravel. The protocol sentence debate, the adoption of a version of a physicalist observation language, the eventual blurring of the distinction between theory and observation among logical empiricists, and Popper's arguments about the fallibility, the conventional nature, and theory-ladenness of the empirical basis, *all undermined this core empiricist project*. Empiricist foundationalism was suffering from a number of self-inflicted wounds long before the critiques of Quine, Kuhn, and others began to take effect; by the late 1960s, there was little more than the rhetorical impact of repeated assertion to hold together the empiricist program of the Received View. As Ronald Giere phrased it in an interview with Werner Callebaut: "internally, logical empiricism was getting squishier and squishier" (Callebaut 1993, p. 39).

The point about the self-undermining of what was originally the logical positivist position is driven home by the following quote from Carnap's autobiography; in it, Carnap is discussing one of the conversations he had with Albert Einstein late in Einstein's life.

> On one occasion Einstein said that he wished to raise an objection against positivism concerning the question of the reality of the physical world. I said that there was no real difference between our views on this question. But he insisted that he had to make an important point here. Then he criticized the view, going back to Ernst Mach, that sense data are the only reality, or more generally, any view which presumes something as an absolutely certain basis of all knowledge. I explained that we had

abandoned these earlier positivistic views, that we did no longer believe in a "rock bottom basis of knowledge"; and I mentioned Neurath's simile that our task is to reconstruct the ship while it is floating on the ocean. He emphatically agreed with this metaphor and this view. But then he added that, *if positivism were now liberalized to such an extent, there would no longer be any difference between our conception and any other philosophical view.* (Carnap 1963, p. 38, emphasis added)

3.2 The Attack on the Received View

The critical attack that finally precipitated the downfall of the Received View took place across a number of different fronts, and by a wide range of different critics. A list of the most influential critics would include names such as Paul Feyerabend, N. R. Hanson, Thomas Kuhn, Michael Polanyi, W. V. Quine, and Stephen Toulmin. Rather than attempting to say a little something about each of these authors, I will focus on just two – Quine and Kuhn – and just two core criticisms – underdetermination and theory-ladenness. Although this limitation is motivated by space considerations, it is justified by the fact that excellent histories are available elsewhere, and the fact that underdetermination and theory-ladenness are driving forces behind the story that unfolds in the following chapters.

3.2.1 Quine and the Problems of Empiricism

Willard Van Orman Quine is one of the most influential philosophers of the late twentieth century. His philosophical views were influenced by logical positivism as well as American pragmatism. In addition to his role in undermining logical positivism and the Received View (the focus of this section), he also played a substantial role in the movement toward naturalized epistemology (Chapter 4) and the revival of philosophical pragmatism (Chapter 6). In addition to the aspects of Quine's philosophy that will be examined here and in the following chapters, he also is associated with the thesis of "ontological relativity," advocacy of the "radical indeterminacy of translation," and a number of other important ideas that have profoundly influenced the course of recent philosophical debate. Quine, like Kuhn, is often cited as the father of a number of quite radical ideas in contemporary philosophy of science (and philosophy more generally), even though, again like Kuhn, he commonly disavows these radical readings of his work.

Quine's "Two Dogmas of Empiricism" is one of the most cited and interrogated papers in post-World War II philosophy. By 1980, when it was reprinted in the second edition of *From a Logical Point of View*, it had already been anthologized twenty-five times (Quine, 1980a, viii). The paper is credited with establishing the so-called Duhem-Quine under-determination thesis as a fundamental (perhaps household) concept in contemporary philosophy, as well as driving one of the final nails in the coffin of logical positivism.

In a nutshell, the Duhem-Quine[28] *underdetermination thesis* asserts that any scientific theory can be immunized against refuting empirical evidence, that is, that no test is truly definitive. The problem is that no theory is ever tested in isolation. In order to conduct an empirical test a number of auxiliary hypotheses must be made – auxiliary hypotheses about the empirical evidence, the testing technique, the values of constants, the boundary conditions, the role of ceteris paribus, and a host of other assumptions and restrictions – and when contradictory evidence is found it is not clear whether the problem is with one (or many) of these auxiliary hypotheses or with the theory itself. To continue the earlier raven example, the observation of a white raven could just as well suggest that birds exist that are similar to ravens in general appearance but are white rather than black, or that in the process of spray-painting the local bridge the painters accidentally sprayed a raven nest, as to suggest that there really are nonblack ravens. Logically underdetermination is the problem of "where to aim the arrow of *modus tollens*"; if T is the theory in question, A represents the set of auxiliary hypotheses, and e is the empirical evidence, then a standard test would be $T \wedge A \Rightarrow e$, but then $\sim e \Rightarrow \sim (T \wedge A)$ rather than simply $\sim T$. A negative test result simply indicates there is an *inconsistency* between the evidence e, and one (or more) elements of the *test system* $T \wedge A$. Because there are always a large (perhaps infinite) number of different ways of modifying the test system to make it consistent with the relevant evidence, an alternative characterization of the underdetermination thesis is that observation will always support a large (perhaps infinite) number of empirically equivalent theoretical hypotheses.

As one, historically interesting, economic example of the Duhem-Quine problem consider the various attempts to test the neoclassical theory of demand.[29] The standard "empirical" implications of neoclassical demand theory include the symmetry of (compensated) Slutsky matrix, the homogeneity (of degree zero) of individual (and aggregate) demand functions, and Walras's Law ("adding up" or Engel aggrega-

---

[28] There is substantial disagreement about whether Quine, or Duhem (1954), or neither should be given credit for the underdetermination thesis (see Ariew 1984). Quine cites Duhem in note 17 of "Two Dogmas" (Quine 1980b, p. 41).

[29] See Gilbert (1991) and Keuzenkamp (1994) for critical discussion of testing neoclassical demand theory.

tion).[30] Over the last seventy years, repeated attempts have been made to "test" one or more of these empirical implications, and while the results of these tests have almost always been contrary to the theory of demand, the theory remains a respected (perhaps the most respected) component of microeconomic science. One of the early efforts to test demand theory was Henry Schultz's *Theory and Measurement of Demand* (1938). Schultz tested the Slutsky symmetry conditions (among other things) for a broad range of (primarily) agricultural commodities and found that the symmetry conditions almost never held. Although he insisted repeatedly that the empirical evidence should provide a definitive "test" for the theory of demand (or as he said at the time "rationality"), he did not actually advocate the rejection of the theory when it was falsified by the empirical evidence. Instead of abandoning the theory, Schultz offered a number of different reasons why the empirical tests were less than perfect: reasons ranging from problems of aggregation to the reliability of the empirical data. In Duhem-Quine terms, such factors were simply auxiliary hypotheses that were presumed to hold in the initial test system, but that, after the fact, Schultz argued did not actually hold (Schultz 1938, pp. 600–64).

Over forty years later, and after much improvement in both data collection and econometric technique, Deaton and Muelbauer similarly found demand theory to be in conflict with the available data.

> We have looked at different models, each embodying different approximations, and these have been fitted to different data sets from several countries, but *the same conclusions have repeatedly emerged. Demand functions fitted to aggregate time series data are not homogeneous and probably not symmetric.* (Deaton and Muelbauer 1980, p. 78)

And yet, after all of these negative empirical results, Deaton and Muelbauer conclude, much as Schultz had concluded earlier, that other problems (problems in the auxiliary hypotheses) must be responsible and not the theory itself.

> We do not believe that, at this stage, it is necessary to abandon the axioms of choice in the face of the results of this chapter. Ultimately, of course, given sufficiently convincing evidence, we should be prepared to do so. But ... it is clear that there are many more obvious misspecifications that should be corrected first. (Deaton and Muelbauer 1980, p. 82)

---

[30] These standard results are available in any microeconomics textbook (see Chs. 2 and 3 of Mas-Colell, Whinston, and Green 1995, for example).

Demand theory is just one of many examples that could be used to demonstrate the Duhem-Quine problem at work in economics.[31] Rather than offering other economic examples, or considering examples from other areas of science, let us return to Quine's "Two Dogmas" and give a more careful examination of his argument for underdetermination.

The "two dogmas" of empiricism that Quine considered were *reductionism* and the *analytic-synthetic distinction*. Both of these topics were introduced in the previous section on logical positivism – the analytic-synthetic distinction was discussed explicitly, and reductionism was implicitly considered in the section on the verificationist theory of meaning. Consider reductionism first.

By "reductionism," Quine basically means the empiricist criterion of meaningfulness: "The belief that each meaningful statement is equivalent to some logical construct upon terms which refer to immediate experience" (Quine 1980b, p. 20). Although there are many different aspects to his argument, they essentially reduce to Carnap's problem with the verificationist theory of meaning and the protocol sentence debate. Quine argues that classical empiricists such as Hume and Locke asserted the *radical reduction* of science to sense data: that every "meaningful statement is held to be translatable into a statement (true or false) about immediate experience" (Quine 1980b, p. 38). Although these early empiricists asserted the reductionist position, it was in fact *just* that, an assertion, a dogma of empiricism. It was the early Carnap who actually "took serious steps toward carrying out the reduction" (Quine 1980b, p. 39). But, as documented above, Carnap's project ultimately failed and the legacy of later positivism and logical empiricism became a version of a physicalist vocabulary that involved the theoretical language of science in an ineliminable way and a much weaker confirmationist theory or meaning (or a falsificationist theory of demarcation and a conventionalist view of the empirical basis for Popper). For Quine, the proper metaphor for the empirical practice of science was Neurath's boat, not the dogma of reductionism. Our scientific view of the world is part of our general "web of belief" that must be revised incrementally as we proceed; it is not that individual observation statements map directly into sensory experience as suggested by radical reductionism, but rather that

---

[31] A number of authors have applied the Duhem-Quine thesis to particular areas within economics; for example Cross (1982) applied it to macroeconomics, Hands (1983) to perfect competition, Smith (1989) to experimental economics, and Leonard (1997) to the recent debate over minimum wages. Also see Cross (1998) and Sawyer, Beed, and Sankey (1997) for a general discussion. As a historical point, De Marchi (1983, p. 174) suggests that John Stuart Mill became aware of the problem through the early nineteenth-century work of the Scottish philosopher Dugald Stewart, and Schabas (1990, p. 73) indicates that Jevons discussed what we now call the Duhem-Quine thesis in his *Principles of Science* (1877).

our web of mutually interlocking scientific beliefs must be revised in response to the impinges of experience. The exact portion of the web to be revised – in the idiom used above, whether it be the particular theory, the auxiliary hypotheses, or the observation itself – depends upon context and pragmatic considerations that are above and beyond any simple empiricist dogma of reductionism.

> The totality of our so-called knowledge or beliefs, . . . is a man-made fabric which impinges on experience only along the edges. Or, to change the figure, total science is like a field of force whose boundary conditions are experience. A conflict with experience at the periphery occasions readjustments in the interior of the field. . . . Having reevaluated one statement we must reevaluate some others, which may be statements logically connected with the first or may be the statements of logical connections themselves. But the total field is so *underdetermined* by its boundary conditions, experience, that there is much latitude of choice as to what statements to reevaluate in the light of any single contrary experience. No particular experiences are linked with any particular statements in the interior of the field, except indirectly through considerations of equilibrium affecting the field as a whole. (Quine 1980b, pp. 42–3, emphasis added)

This underdetermination thesis is related to Quine's *holism* – that it is always an ensemble of theories and a web of belief that confronts experience, rather than a single theory confronting a single observation statement. There has been a substantial debate about the differences (if any) between the underdetermination thesis and Quine's holism;[32] although that debate is not really germane to the following discussion, it is probably useful to be clear about how I will use the two terms. I will use "underdetermination" (or the Duhem-Quine problem) as a problem associated with the empirical testing of scientific theories – that decisions must always be made about how (what part of the test system) to modify in response to (particularly negative) empirical observations – and I will use "holism" to describe the more general, but closely related, proposition that our scientific beliefs are held together as an interrelated web (that no theory stands alone) and that no part is immune to potential revision.[33]

---

[32] See Hoefer and Rosenberg (1994), for instance.

[33] This use of the terms "holism" and "underdetermination" differs a bit from Quine's own attempt to clarify the distinction in Quine (1975). In that paper, Quine used "holism" for both the testing problem and the interrelatedness of our scientific beliefs, while "underdetermination" referred to the fact (an implication of holism) that "all possible observations are insufficient to determine theory uniquely" (Quine 1975, p. 313); also see Rosenberg and Hoefer (1994).

The above quote also suggests Quine's related argument against the second dogma of empiricism, the "analytic-synthetic distinction." Notice that among the things that might be revised in response to experience Quine explicitly includes "statements logically connected with the first or may be the statements of logical connections themselves" (Quine 1980b, p. 42). Remember that according to logical positivism there are only two types of meaningful propositions, synthetic propositions that must satisfy the verificationist criterion of meaning, and analytical propositions which say nothing about the world, but are true by definition. Quine dissolves this rigid separation between what is analytic and what is synthetic. On the one hand, analytic propositions that claim to be "true by definition" can not actually be defined without reference to other, synthetic, propositions – on the other hand, as the above quote suggests, all aspects of our knowledge are subject to revision by experience, including the logical and mathematical propositions that positivists considered to be purely analytic. In the same way that later logical positivists and logical empiricists blurred the rigid distinction between what was considered observational and what was considered theoretical, Quine blurred the earlier distinction between the purely analytical and the purely synthetic.

> If this view is right, it is misleading to speak of the empirical content of an individual statement. . . . Furthermore it becomes folly to seek a boundary between synthetic statements, which hold contingently on experience, and analytic statements, which hold come what may. Any statement can be held true come what may, if we make drastic enough adjustments elsewhere in the system. Even a statement very close to the periphery can be held true in the face of recalcitrant experience by pleading hallucination or by amending certain statements of the kind called logical laws. . . . No statement is immune to revision. (Quine 1980b, p. 43)

This brings us back to the issue of theory-ladenness and for that topic we need to examine the work of another extremely influential voice, that of Thomas S. Kuhn.

My distinction seems to be consistent with the way that the terms are used most frequently in contemporary philosophy of science. It is also consistent with Boylan and O'Gorman's useful distinction between what they call "meaning holism" (my holism) and "testing holism" (underdetermination or the Duhem-Quine problem); see Boylan and O'Gorman (1995, pp. 74–82).

3.2.2 *Kuhn and* The Structure of Scientific Revolutions

Although Quine's "Two Dogmas" contributed to the ultimate demise of positivist-inspired philosophy of science, its impact was nowhere near as great as that of Thomas Kuhn's *The Structure of Scientific Revolutions* in 1962. This book not only helped close the door on the Received View, it also initiated a profound change in the relationship between the history and the philosophy of science, helped to create the field of contemporary sociology of scientific knowledge, and made "paradigm" an academic household word. "There can be no one active today in philosophy, history, or sociology of science whose approach to the problem of scientific rationality has not been shaped by the Gestalt switch Kuhn wrought on our perspective on science" (Laudan 1984, p. xii). "After Kuhn, philosophy of science would never be the same" (Callebaut 1993, p. 12).[34]

Although the central thesis of *The Structure of Scientific Revolutions* is probably familiar to most readers, a brief summary still seems to be in order. Kuhn's basic approach, unlike the *a priori* approach of much traditional philosophy of science, was to examine the historical development of science, in an attempt to discover how great scientific achievements, scientific revolutions in particular, had actually taken place. What Kuhn found, rather than a process of incremental development where scientific knowledge grew slowly through the steady accumulation of empirical evidence and inductive generalization (or the corroboration of potentially falsifiable conjectures), was that the actual development of great science had occurred through a series of substantive revolutionary transformations where the old accepted scientific theory was totally abandoned and replaced by an entirely different theoretical framework or "paradigm."

The fact of revolutionary transformation was not Kuhn's most radical discovery though; his most radical discovery was *how* the revolutionary transformation took place. These transformations did not occur as the result of a single "crucial test" (as a falsificationist might predict); in fact, scientists would often hold on to the old paradigm in the face of massive contrary evidence. Most of the history of science, Kuhn discovered, was "normal science," that is scientific work *within* a given paradigm – what Kuhn called "paradigm articulation" – and within the context of normal science the existing framework was simply accepted without question. In

---

[34] Economists were relatively quick to "apply" Kuhn to their own field; early applications include Bronfenbrenner (1971), Coats (1969), Karsten (1973), and Stanfield (1974). Deborah Redman provides a "partial bibliography" of the "Kuhn and economics" literature (as of 1991) that contains thirty-one entries (Redman 1991, p. 96, note 1). Gutting (1980) reprinted a number of the early responses to, and applications of, Kuhn's *Structure*.

fact, if a scientist were to discover an "anomaly," an empirical result that seemed to be inconsistent with the reigning paradigm, it was generally the scientist, and/or his/her laboratory, that was indicted, not the paradigm itself. There were of course revolutions in science, paradigms were overthrown, but these changes came as the result of a very long process involving the accumulation of a large number of empirical anomalies and unsolved puzzles; often it took the demise of the older generation of scientists and the rise of a younger generation to actually precipitate the change to a new paradigm. Kuhn's examination of a number of different episodes in the history of great science suggested that scientific revolutions were not a particularly rational affair (at least not rational in the way that scientific rationality had traditionally been defined). For Kuhn, the change to a new paradigm was a social change, a change in the dominant beliefs of the members of the relevant scientific community, and as such it was not the type of change that could be explained in terms of any simple "rules" of proper scientific method (positivist or falsificationist). The type of transformation that took place during a scientific revolution was (more like a political revolution) the result of contingent circumstances and the specific (social) context of the scientific community; the proper tool for understanding such change was not traditional epistemology, but a version of Gestalt psychology. Paradigm shifts involve a radical transformation in the way a scientist perceives his or her domain of inquiry: a transformation that fundamentally alters the scientific "world" in which the scientist lives.[35]

> Led by a new paradigm, scientists adopt new instruments and look in new places. Even more important, during revolutions scientists see new and different things when looking with familiar instruments and places they have looked before. It is rather as if the professional community had been suddenly transported to another planet where familiar objects are seen in a different light and are joined by unfamiliar ones as well. Of course, nothing of quite that sort does occur: there is no geographical transplantation; outside the laboratory everyday affairs usually continue as before. Nevertheless, paradigm changes do cause scientists to see the world of their research-engagement differently. In so far as their only recourse to that

---

[35] Actually, Kuhn is always careful not to make the potentially idealist move and say that "the world" is different; rather it is simply the way that the scientist "sees" the world that is transformed by the change in paradigm. "Confronting the same constellation of objects as before and knowing that he does so, he nevertheless finds them transformed through and through in many of their details" (Kuhn 1970a, p. 122). As we will see later, many of Kuhn's followers have a more radical reading of such changes.

world is through what they see and do, we may want to say that after a revolution scientists are responding to a different world. (Kuhn 1970a, p. 111)

It is important to emphasize how strongly Kuhn's view supports the "theory-ladenness" of observations. For Kuhn scientists do not just "see," they "see as," and it is the paradigm,[36] their shared conceptual framework, that determines what is seen as what. The paradigm provides the lens, or interpretative framework, by which various aspects of the world are observed. As Philip Kitcher (1993, p. 133) so cleverly phrased it, there are no "out-of-theory" experiences. Viewed through the spectacles of the Ptolemaic system the morning sun rises; viewed from the Copernican perspective, we roll under it. Kuhn's work is replete with psychological examples which undermine any simple one-to-one relationship between the object and what is observed (the rabbit-duck case where a single object is seen in two different ways, and the inverted lens case where two people see different things the same way) as well as frequent discussion of the problems of radical translation. The theory-ladenness, or paradigm dependency, of observations leads to the "incommensurability" of different scientific theories. If there is no theory-neutral observation vocabulary, and each theory determines its own domain of observation, then there is no way to compare the theory before a scientific revolution to the theory that comes after it – scientific theories are thus "incommensurable." Although the rather radical incommensurability thesis in *Structure* was softened a bit in Kuhn's later work – where some translation is possible between theories but such translation is always imperfect and never point-by-point – the basic argument was retained.

> The point-by-point comparison of two successive theories demands a language into which at least the empirical consequences of both can be translated without loss or change. That such a language lies ready to hand has been widely assumed since at least the seventeenth century.... Philosophers have now abandoned hope of achieving any such ideal, but many of them continue to assume that theories can be compared by recourse to a basic vocabulary consisting entirely of words which are attached to nature in ways that are unproblematic and, to the extent necessary, independent of theory.... I have argued at

[36] Many critics argued that Kuhn used the term "paradigm" to cover a variety of different concepts in *The Structure of Scientific Revolutions* (Masterman 1970, found twenty-one different uses of the term). In response, Kuhn (1970b, 1977b) adopted the term "disciplinary matrix" for some of his previous uses, and "exemplar" for others. It is not necessary to pursue these distinctions in the current discussion.

length that no such vocabulary is available. In the transition from one theory to the next words change their meanings or conditions of applicability in subtle ways. Though most of the same signs are used before and after a revolution – e.g., force, mass, element, compound, cell – the ways in which some of them attach to nature has somehow changed. Successive theories are thus, we say, incommensurable. (Kuhn 1970b, pp. 266–7)

It is also important to emphasize the fundamentally *social* nature of theory-ladenness (and Kuhn's view of science more generally). It is not just that an individual "holds" a paradigm that influences what is and is not observed, the paradigm is one aspect of the shared professional culture of the scientific community and, more than anything else, defines membership in that community; the paradigm is taught, and learned, and one comes to hold it as the result of a process of social acculturation. Although Kuhn discussed the social nature of paradigms in the first edition of *Structure*, it received even greater attention in his later work.

If I were writing my book again now, I would therefore begin by discussing the community structure of science, and I would not rely exclusively on shared subject matter in doing so. Community structure is a topic about which we have very little information at present, but it has recently become a major concern for sociologists, and historians are now increasingly concerned with it as well. (Kuhn 1970b, p. 252)

And again, even more strongly, a few years before his death in 1996:

Understanding the process of evolution has in recent years seemed increasingly to require conceiving the gene pool, not as the mere aggregate of the genes of individual organisms, but as itself a sort of individual of which the members of the species are parts. I am persuaded that this example contains important clues to the sense in which science is intrinsically a community activity. . . . the traditional view of science as, at least in principle, a one-person game, will prove, I am quite sure, to have been an especially harmful mistake. (Kuhn 1993, p. 329)

Another point to emphasize is how much Kuhn's view accommodates an inversion of the methodological positions discussed in Chapter 2. Almost all of these authors had a clear view of how "science" should be, and was, practiced. These authors seldom reflected on the character of *natural* science in their writings on economic methodology; science was believed to be empirical in roughly the same way that positivist philosophy of science said that it was empirical. *The* question for these authors was whether economics, or any other social science, could adhere to this same scientific method or whether economics required a different/ separate/special methodology. For most authors writing on economic methodology before the latter half of the twentieth century, natural science came first; it was the solid, and epistemologically privileged, standard by which economics must be judged. Kuhn opened the door for a possible reversal of this relationship. For Kuhn, there was no firm and fast scientific method that was responsible for the privileged status of natural science (or less radically: there might be such a method but philosophers of science certainly hadn't identified it), but in order to understand what did go on in the natural sciences one needed to apply sociology or social psychology. Despite the fact that Kuhn often made disparaging remarks about social science, on the basis of his view understanding the social context of science was a prerequisite to understanding science. Thus, one implication of Kuhn's work, and for many later interpreters the most important implication of his work, was that social science came first; it became the stable ground on which one must stand to analyze the less stable, or at least less understood, practice of natural science. This shift, inherent in Kuhn's work (but not endorsed by him) has helped precipitate a major change in the relationship between the philosophy of natural science and those concerned with the methodology of particular social sciences such as economics. This issue will resurface many times in later chapters.

The critics of Kuhn have accused him of many things, but the two most frequently cited are "idealism" and "relativism." Considering idealism first, it is quite easy to see why Kuhn is accused of such a position. In simplest caricature, idealism says that reality is, in some sense, a product of consciousness, and it does seem that the scientist's world is determined by the paradigm they hold and thus by consciousness. Although Kuhn clearly rejected the idealist label, he did not defend himself against this accusation in any systematic way. The issue has been systematically discussed, and Kuhn exonerated, in Paul Hoyningen-Huene's *Reconstructing Scientific Revolutions* (1993). Hoyningen-Huene makes three arguments to defend Kuhn against the accusation of idealism (on pp. 267–70). First, the phenomenal world of Kuhn's scientists is a reshaping of the world-in-itself that commits him to a version of (ontological, but not scientific) realism. Second, if it is an idealism, it is not the traditional individualist idealism, but rather some sort of social idealism, since it is the culture of the scientific community that influences what scientists observe and not individual consciousness. Finally, the world-in-itself offers "resistances" to the moves of scientists; there are anomalies, in fact persistent anomalies, and these anomalies originate in a world that exists outside of the paradigm.

Kuhn has said much more about "relativism" – the position that there are no good reasons for preferring one scientific theory over another (thus making theory choice a purely arbitrary affair)[37] – and his response has been to categorically deny any such relativistic implications from his work. His denial is based on a type of pragmatic or generic naturalism;[38] there are standards in science, but they are the standards of actual scientists, and they can only be examined historically. To say that science is "irrational" or that there are no good (nonrelativist) reasons for choosing one theory over another because the type of choice that we observe actual scientists making does not comply with some philosopher's notion of correct scientific practice is "vaguely obscene," and it opens "the door to cloud-cuckoo land" (Kuhn 1970b, p. 264). Of course there are standards in science, scientists employ them all the time; just because they are not what philosophers think scientists should do reflects much more on the philosophy of science than on the historical practice of scientists.

> My critics respond to my views on this subject with charges of irrationality, relativism, and the defense of mob rule. These are all labels which I categorically reject, even when they are used in my defense. . . . To say that, in matters of theory-choice, the force of logic and observation cannot in principle be compelling is neither to discard logic and observation nor to suggest that there are not good reasons for favoring one theory over another. To say that trained scientists are, in such matters, the highest

[37] One needs to be very careful with the term "relativism." For example, in Chapter 5 we will consider certain sociologists of science (many who claim to draw their inspiration from Kuhn) who are often accused of being "relativists" because they explain the holding of scientific beliefs by scientists in the same way that one would explain why any member of a particular culture comes to hold the beliefs that they do. Such sociologists would not say that there are "no good reasons" why scientists hold beliefs, but they would say that there are not special "scientific" or "cognitive" or "epistemically privileged" reasons for holding scientific beliefs – that scientific beliefs are the result of the same social forces that determine what one believes about any other aspect of culture: such as chastity, witches, inflation, or which fork to eat your salad with. When the label "relativism" is used in contemporary philosophy or science studies (and it seems to be used a lot recently), it usually means "there are not good, traditional, epistemological, reasons for preferring one theory over another."

[38] Naturalism will be discussed in more detail below.

court of appeal is neither to defend mob rule nor to suggest that scientists could have decided to accept any theory at all. (Kuhn 1907b, p. 234)

One thing that has provided ammunition for those who accuse Kuhn of "relativism" (and/or "irrationalism") is Kuhn's unwillingness to employ the veracious language of traditional philosophy of science. Kuhn rejects the idea of science getting closer to the truth, while simultaneously holding on to the notion of a mind-independent world that resists our efforts to engage it, as well as the claim that there are good reasons why one theory might be better than another.

> I begin with the question of science's zeroing in on, getting closer and closer to, the truth. That claims to that effect are meaningless is a consequence of incommensurability.... There is, for example, no way, even in an enriched Newtonian vocabulary, to convey the Aristotelian propositions.... It follows that no shared metric is available to compare our assertions about force and motion with Aristotle's and thus to provide a basis for a claim that ours (or, for that matter, his) are closer to the truth.... A lexicon or lexical structure is the long-term product of tribal experience in the natural and social worlds, but its logical status, like that of word-meanings in general, is that of convention. Each lexicon makes possible a corresponding form of life within which the truth or falsity of propositions may be both claimed and rationally justified, but the justification of lexicons or of lexical change can only be pragmatic. (Kuhn 1993, pp. 330–1)

Although Kuhn's "relativism" and the various issues that surround it will reappear in various places (and in other guises) below, for now let us end this brief introduction to Kuhn's view of science and try to recap the main themes from the last two sections.

3.2.3 Two Core Difficulties: Theory-ladenness and Underdetermination

Theory-ladenness and underdetermination will be recurrent themes in the following discussion. I will argue repeatedly that these two problems, or more accurately trying to avoid the issues raised by these two problems, have been fundamental to the development of late twentieth century philosophy of science. These two issues have so profoundly disturbed the temporary equilibrium engendered by the Received View, that the impact has spread backward, up the path of intellectual genealogy, to the point where our core epistemological presuppositions have been profoundly challenged. All of this, I will argue, has had an equally significant impact on methodological discourse in/about economics. And finally that the way forward is not "more of the same," not continuing to offer ever more clever suggestions for circumventing these problems in foundationalist methodology, but rather to simply "change the subject," to accept these foibles and move forward on a new, redefined, type of methodological discourse.

Whereas I am quite confident that the above discussion will provide a sufficient background for the arguments that follow, I also think a note of circumspection is in order. The above story – that Quine was the main source for the problem of underdetermination and that Kuhn was the main source for theory-ladenness (although certain positivists and Popper clearly recognized the latter problem) – is *extremely simplified*. Both of these problems are much messier than the above discussion suggests. The rest of this section will focus on some of these complexities.

First, although it is fair to say that Quine is more responsible for drawing our attention to underdetermination than Kuhn is, and that Kuhn is more responsible for emphasizing theory-ladenness than Quine is, both authors in fact emphasize both problems. Quine's work on radical translation and his general holism both recognize the problem of theory-ladenness (in some sense a more radical version than Kuhn's). At the same time, Kuhn's discussion of the way that anomalies are absorbed by normal science clearly recognizes the Duhem-Quine underdetermination problem.

Second, these are only two of the many authors that have contributed to the general recognition of these problems. The underdetermination problem was clearly recognized by philosophers such as Neurath and Popper, whereas theory-ladenness was a major theme in the work of Feyerabend (1975),[39] Hansen (1958), Polanyi (1958), and a host of others. Both of these problems also emerge in the later work of Wittgenstein (1953), and there is even a growing literature emphasizing the similarities between Kuhn's position and that of Carnap in his later work.[40] These influential tunes were clearly not solo compositions.

Third, it is important to emphasize that there is not just one problem of "underdetermination" or just one problem of "theory-ladenness"; these terms actually identify two rather broad families of problems,

---

[39] The incommensurability problem is often referred to as the Kuhn-Feyerabend incommensurability problem in the same way that underdetermination is referred to as the Duhem-Quine underdetermination problem.

[40] See Boyd (1983), Earman (1993), Irzik and Grünberg (1995), and Reisch (1991) for example.

families whose members certainly bear a strong family resemblance, but also exhibit their own unique personal characteristics. The distinction between Quine's holism and the Duhem-Quine thesis on empirical testing was emphasized above, and yet both of these ideas are clearly members of the same family of underdetermination problems. Many different schemes have been offered for identifying various members of the underdetermination family. For instance, Boylan and O'Gorman (1995, pp. 76–80) individuate four separate Quinean "holistic" theses; first, they make the distinction between "meaning holism" (roughly what I have called "holism") and "testing holism" (roughly what I have called underdetermination), and then they further subdivide this latter category into "weak," "stronger," and "radical" versions.

Finally, the situation is complicated still further by the fact that underdetermination and theory-ladenness are so conceptually intertwined. There seems to be very little difference between saying that the theory is "underdetermined" by the data, and saying that the data is "overdetermined" by (or laden with) the theory. Both problems ultimately reduce to "arguments about the underdetermination of belief by encounters with nature" (Kitcher 1992, p. 93) and, as such, they are both "underdetermination" problems of a very general sort. For instance, Kitcher identifies five separate members of the family of problems that "muffle the impact of our encounters with nature"; his five members are, "shifting standards," "theory-ladenness of observations," "assessment of experiments," "social-embedding," and "effects of authority" (1992, pp. 94–5). His "theory-ladenness" category is roughly what I have called theory-ladenness, and his "assessment of experiments" category is roughly what I have called underdetermination. Thus, not only are there many different concepts that are members of the two core families of underdetermination and theory-ladenness, many philosophers consider these two families to be simply households within an identifiable larger family of conceptual problems.

Despite all of these potential complications, I still believe that the family resemblance among the members of the underdetermination and theory-ladenness families as I have identified them are sufficiently distinct to be tractable and useful in understanding the evolution of the philosophy of science and economic methodology. As I said, these concepts will be recurrent themes in the chapters that follow; they are the main problems that eroded the hegemony of empiricist foundationalism in epistemology, philosophy of science, and economic methodology. Quine and Kuhn were major contributors to that erosion, although there were many others, some of which would swear unflinching allegiance to the position they helped undermine.

3.3 First Round Responses

The next two sections will briefly examine two sets of responses to the problems raised by Quine, Kuhn, and others who attacked the Received View. The first section examines what I call "quasi-historical" responses; although there are a number of different positions that might be considered in this section, only Imre Lakatos will be discussed in any detail. The second section considers various realist and empiricist responses; again only a few of many possible views will be examined.

3.3.1 Lakatos and the Quasi-Historical Move

One of the impacts of Kuhn's *Structure* was to open a brief period of rapprochement between historians and philosophers of science.[41] Kuhn was, after all, a *historian* of science, not a philosopher of science, and yet it was quite clear that his historical work had broad and quite negative implications for the Received View of scientific knowledge. Contrary to the *a priorism* that had traditionally characterized the philosophy of science, Kuhn argued that one should examine the *actual history of science* in order to understand the nature of scientific knowledge. To make matters worse, what he found when he examined the actual history was something quite different than what one would expect based on mid-twentieth-century mainstream philosophy of science. Something had to give.

This section will discuss one particular quasi-historical response to the problems raised by Kuhn. The strategy behind this response might be characterized as a type of plea bargaining; the idea was to accept most of what Kuhn said about the actual history of science but minimize the normative damage done by that acceptance. The goal was to find a new demarcation criterion and new methodological rules that would be more consistent with the actual history of science, but could be justified in traditional ways and avoid the relativism and irrationalism often associated with Kuhn. This plea-bargaining strategy initiated what some have called the "historical turn" within the philosophy of science, a situation where philosophers fully admitted the presence of paradigms, normal science, and theory-ladenness, while simultaneously directing their professional energies toward discovering a new epistemologically justified set of methodological rules that would be (at least broadly) consistent with the history of science.[42]

---

[41] See Nickles (1995), for a discussion of this post-Kuhnian relationship.

[42] I will use the term "quasi-historical" for this particular literature, rather than the more common term "historical," because I want to separate this specific first-round response from the more general trend toward historical (and sociological) approaches to the study

The only first-round quasi-historical response that I will examine in any detail is Imre Lakatos's "methodology of scientific research programs" (MSRP).[43] Lakatos was a Hungarian émigré who left Hungary, like so many others, in 1956. Trained in mathematics, science, and philosophy, he had been politically active in his youth, once serving as a secretary in the Hungarian Ministry of Education (Larvor 1998, pp. 1–7). He became a student of Popper's, and while he made important contributions to the philosophy of mathematics (Lakatos 1976), we will focus our attention here on his philosophy of science (the MSRP). Lakatos's ultimate goal was to smooth out the Kuhn-initiated rift between the history and philosophy of science, more specifically, to meld Popperian falsificationism and Kuhnian historicism. He wanted the best of both worlds: a normative philosophy of science that could be used to "appraise" scientific theories but also to have those norms be consistent with the "best gambits" (Lakatos 1971, p. 111) from the history of science. Although Lakatos's approach does represent (as he put it) a way "for the philosopher of science to learn from the historian of science and vice versa" (Lakatos 1971, p. 111), the MSRP might also be interpreted as a kind of jujitsu move that allowed him to turn the (Kuhnian) enemy's attack into a victory for Popperian philosophical program.

The first move in Lakatos's approach was to shift attention away from individual "scientific theories" to a series of theories contained in a "scientific research program." A scientific research program is defined as a loose ensemble of a "hard core," a "protective belt," and a set of "positive and negative heuristics." The hard core contains the fundamental metaphysical presuppositions of the research program; it defines the program and (as the term "hard core" suggests) its elements are irrefutable by the empirical evidence. The hard core propositions remain fixed during the program's development, and to reject the hard core, is to abandon the program itself. The protective belt contains the auxiliary hypotheses, the empirical conventions, and other theoretical structures of the program; it is where all of the "action" takes place, where all of

of scientific knowledge. The normative role of the history of science certainly expanded after Kuhn, but this general expansion is separate from the more specific (plea-bargaining) approach being considered here, and the term "historical" does not effectively capture this difference.

[43] An early version was presented in Lakatos (1968), but the main statement is Lakatos (1970); the most careful defense of his general philosophical approach was given in Lakatos (1971). Another one of these first-round quasi-historical responses was Laudan (1977). Space considerations, and Lakatos's importance in economics, precludes a detailed discussion of Laudan (1977) or any of the other quasi-historical approaches. Laudan has since denounced his own first-round response (see Laudan 1986), unfortunately, Lakatos's untimely death makes it impossible for us to know if he would have done the same.

the changes occur as the program moves through time. The protective belt forms a buffer zone between the hard core and the empirical evidence, a buffer zone that continually changes as the program moves forward in response to changes in the empirical evidence. The positive and negative heuristics provide information about what should (positive) and should not (negative) be pursued during the development of the program; appropriate and inappropriate questions (and answers) are defined by the program's heuristics. Such a model seems to be roughly consistent with Kuhn's view of science; most activity within a scientific research program occurs within the protective belt and leaves the hard core untouched (it is normal science), while a scientific revolution replaces the hard core itself.

A scientific research program is appraised only with hindsight; after a particular change in the protective belt has taken place we can appraise whether the change was or was not "progressive." For Lakatos, a series of theories is "theoretically progressive" if each new theory "has some excess empirical content over its predecessor, that is, if it predicts some novel, hitherto unexpected fact" (Lakatos 1970, p. 118); such a series is "empirically progressive" if "some of this excess content is also corroborated, that is, if each new theory leads us to the actual discovery of some *new* fact" (1970, p. 118, emphasis in original). Lakatos calls a research program "progressive" if it "is both theoretically and empirically progressive, and *degenerating* if it is not" (1970, p. 118, emphasis in original). Finally, Lakatos's demarcation criterion is based on his notion of theoretical progress; a research program is "scientific" if it is "at least theoretically progressive" (1970, p. 118) and, if not, then it is rejected as "pseudoscientific" (1970, p. 118).

Notice that, whereas Lakatos's concept of scientific progress does not require the falsifiability of the hard core, nor does the protective belt need to contain bold conjectures that have been subjected to severe tests, his notion of empirical content is thoroughly Popperian. First, the empirical content of a theory is its set of potential falsifiers and these potential falsifiers are empirical basic statements accepted by convention. Second, Lakatos employs Popper's notion of a *novel fact*, an idea that grew out of Popper's requirement of "independent testability." Popper recognized that it was always possible to patch up a theory in order to avoid any particular piece of falsifying evidence – all ravens are black except the white one you just showed me – and that real progress in science should rule out such ad hoc theory adjustments. His solution was the requirement of independent testability: that in order to constitute progress the new theory "must have new and testable consequences (preferably consequences of a *new kind*); it must lead to the prediction of phenomena which have not so far been observed" (Popper 1965, p. 241, emphasis in original).[44]

There are at least three points to be made regarding Lakatos's use of novelty as the sole criterion for progress in science (and since that definition of progress is used to demarcate science from pseudoscience, novel facts are, for Lakatos, the sole criterion for what is and what is not "science"). First, there is not a generally accepted definition of "novel fact," even among members of the Popperian school.[45] The intuition seems to be fine – the theory should predict something we don't already know – but when one tries to hone that intuition into something specific enough to actually dissect historical episodes in the development of science serious problems always emerge. As Clark Glymour characterized Lakatos's discussion of novel facts, it "is at once suggestive and obscure" (1980, p. 99). Second, even though Lakatos was following Popper, and the Popperian literature on novel facts seems to have a life of its own, the idea that novel facts are particularly significant in science is a very old (certainly pre-Popperian) idea. William Whewell's notion of the "consilience of inductions" in the early nineteenth century, Jevons's (1877) discussion of "prophetic triumphs," as well as the 150-year-long debate over the "so-called rule of predesignation" (Laudan 1984, p. 36), were all, in one way or another, arguments in favor of the unique epistemic benefits associated with predicting novel facts.[46] Third, although

---

[44] This paragraph is only the tip of the iceberg regarding the multiple interrelationships among the various concepts of testability, independent testability, ad hocness, non-ad hocness, progress, and novelty in the Popperian philosophical tradition. Because these issues (particularly novelty) will be examined in more detail below (Chapter 7) this brief introduction will be sufficient for now. Also see Hands (1985a, 1988, and 1991b).

[45] Murphy (1989) considered six different definitions of novel fact, whereas I discussed five (Hands 1991c), and undoubtedly there are definitions we both missed.

[46] The role of economists in this discussion is quite interesting. While Jevons is sometimes cited on the pronovel facts side, Keynes and Mill are almost always listed among the critics (for instance, Popper 1965, pp. 247–8 and Lakatos 1970, pp. 123–4). Keynes is fairly clear on the matter in *A Treatise on Probability*:

> The peculiar virtue of prediction or predesignation is altogether imaginary. The number of instances examined and the analogy between them are the essential points, and the questions as to whether a particular hypothesis happens to be propounded before or after their examination is quite irrelevant. (Keynes 1962, p. 305)

Although a number of economists have commented about Keynes's discussion in the *Treatise* (Lawson 1985 and O'Donnell 1990, for instance), and economists have joined into the debate about how novel facts should be characterized (Kahn, Landsburg, and Stockman 1992, for example), these discussions remain unconnected with the methodological literature that tries to apply Lakatos to economics (Chapter 7).

there is a longstanding debate about the unique importance of novel facts both inside and outside of the Popper/Lakatosian literature, there isn't a clear consensus on the matter among contemporary commentators. Many simply conclude that novel facts do not have any special cognitive virtues. For example, Gerald Doppelt argues:

> In the case of the rule of predesignation, after 150 years of inquiry and debate, there isn't even any empirical evidence that it is or is not an effective means to the associated cognitive aim of true, simple, and general theories. (Doppelt 1990, p. 13)

These remarks are echoed by the historian of science Stephen Brush:

> Perhaps the only definite conclusion so far is that scientists do not usually give any more weight to *novel* predictions – predictions of previously unknown phenomena – than to deductions of known facts. Novelty per se does not count for much in deciding whether a theory is valid, though it may be quite important in publicizing a theory and persuading scientists to take it seriously. (Brush 1993, p. 566)

Thus, the followers of Lakatos seem to be in the predicament of hanging both "progress" and "science" on the hook of novel facts, when they do not have an agreement regarding the definition of novel facts, and, although the concept has a long history, philosophers in general do not even agree that novel facts are cognitively important, much less the sole factor demarcating science from pseudoscience. Lakatos will be discussed later in the context of economic methodology, but the point here is simply that while Lakatos's quasi-historical response to the issues raised by Kuhnian turn was extremely important and innovative, ultimately it did not end up being successful in staving off the critical onslaught. The idea that one could find a set of universal methodological rules for the proper conduct of science that were grounded in solid foundationalist epistemology was under severe attack from many different directions, and Lakatos's jujitsu move did almost nothing to slow the enemy's advance.

3.3.2 Realist and Empiricist Moves

Another first-round response to demise of the Received View has been the growth of *scientific realism*. Whereas realist responses also might be categorized as a version of plea bargaining, since they do admit (often start from) the problems of the Received View, the authors of these responses are generally much less historical than the quasi-historical response of philosophers such as Lakatos. There were (and are) many different versions of realism, and here as with other topics, my discussion will be neither exhaustive nor complete, and will focus only on versions that will surface in later chapters. In addition to examining a few different versions of realism, I will also, at the end of this section, discuss one empiricist (or contemporary positivist) response: the constructive empiricism of Bas van Fraassen. This choice is again based on the recent economic literature.

The discussion will start with some generic characteristics of the realist position, focusing in particular on realism as a response to underdetermination, theory-ladenness, and the related problems of the Received View. I will then briefly examine two particular versions of realism, what I call "referential realism" (Richard Boyd, in particular) and the "transcendental realism" of Roy Bhaskar. Referential realism has been widely discussed within the philosophy of natural science, while transcendental realism is more often a subject for economists and philosophers of social science. I will end this brief discussion of realism by mentioning a few of the other versions of realism that are available in the contemporary literature.

If one were forced to characterize post-Enlightenment epistemology and philosophy of science as one big fight between just two contestants – I'm not suggesting this is the best way to think about the history of epistemology, but *if* one were forced to think in such terms – then it would be a fight between "empiricism" and "realism." In its crudest form, empiricism says that all knowledge is about observables, sense experience, and that scientific theories, if they are to be justified as knowledge, are nothing more than ways of systematizing patterns within the observable domain. For empiricism, the core notion of cause is simply a constant conjunction of observable events, and any attempt to get behind, or uncover the hidden essence, of such observations or their regularities is just "metaphysics" and should be left behind with the rest of our prescientific prejudices. Empiricism avoids the skeptic's claim that there may be a gap between experience and reality by making reality identical to experience. The details and the degree of commitment of course varies among specific empiricist programs – we have already seen how these ideas were softened during the evolution of positivism and the Received View – but nonetheless these core propositions remain at the heart of empiricism. Scientific realism, also distilled down to its crudest form, says that scientific knowledge goes beyond, that is it transcends, the observable domain; that there really are underlying causal mechanisms or capacities that generate the empirical regularities that we observe and that it is the task of science to discover these (initially) hidden causes and capacities. Many realists go one step further to argue that not only do such unobservables exist, and not only is it science's job to uncover them, but that most of what mature science says about such unobservables is basically true. Again, details and the degree of commitment varies among realists, but these remain key propositions.[47]

Now, it seems likely that attacks on the foundations of empiricism and the empiricist characterization of scientific knowledge – attacks such as underdetermination and theory-ladenness – would help score points for the "other side," that is, scientific realism. The issues raised by Kuhn, Quine, and others – issues that seem to cut deeply into the empiricist view of science – do, at least on first gloss, appear to leave the realist world of hidden causal mechanisms entirely intact. Remember, Quine spoke of the "two dogmas" of empiricism, and "dogmas" sound a lot like untestable metaphysical beliefs, whereas Kuhn and others emphasized theory-ladenness, a stake through the heart of the core empiricist notion of observation. Realism is less frightened of metaphysics and significantly less whetted to the importance of observation; it is not unreasonable to expect that realism would be able to take advantage of its major competitor's recent woes. Certainly some realists argue in exactly this way. Richard Boyd, for instance, an author discussed in more detail below, characterizes the situation in the following way:

> [A]ll of the fundamental methods by which knowledge is obtained are profoundly theory-dependent: principles of classification, methods for assessing projectability and for assessing

---

[47] There are many ways of cutting up, or differentiating, various types of realism. One useful schema is given in Nola (1988). Nola distinguishes three different forms of realism.

1. Ontological Realism (asserting the existence of a world that is independent of knowing subjects).
2. Referential or Semantic Realism (asserting that some nonobservational terms refer and some sentences that contain such nonobservables are true).
3. Epistemological Realism (asserting that we are warranted to believe in, or it is known, that (1) and (2) are the case).

Nola actually offers nine different forms of realism – each of the above categories is subdivided into three different (weak, middle, and strongest) versions – I have blended all three intracategory versions in my definitions. It is important to note that ontological realism says nothing about the truth, or even the possibility of the truth, of scientific theories; it is, thus, a very weak form of realism and it is held by many authors who consider themselves to be opponents of "realism" (most of the sociologists of science discussed in Chapter 5 for instance). It should also be noted that some very strong realists (the eliminative materialists discussed in Chapter 4, for instance) do not subscribe to epistemological realism; true beliefs are still beliefs, and for these authors "belief" is not a term that refers to something that exists in the world. Also see Mäki (1998b) for a discussion of the various versions of realism.

the quality and evidential import of observations, standards for assessing explanatory power, etc.

Scientific realism has gained considerable credibility as a result of the recognition of these facts about scientific practice. It seems possible to argue that inductive inferences in science *about observables* are reliable only because they are guided by methodological principles which reflect previously acquired (approximate) knowledge of unobservable real essences. . . . philosophical examination of the methods of actual science has led, in the last few decades, to the confirmation of what might have been Locke's worst nightmare. (Boyd 1991, p. 133, emphasis in original)

Nancy Cartwright, a different kind of realist, says much the same thing about the status "observables" in the empiricist story about scientific knowledge.

But what about this decontaminated data base? Where is it in our experience? It is a philosophical construction, a piece of metaphysics, a way to interpret the world. . . . My experiences are of people and houses and pinchings and aspirins, all things which I understand, in large part, in terms of their natures. I do not have any raw experience of a house as a patchwork of colors. . . . Sense data, or *the given*, are metaphysical constructs which, unlike natures, play no role in testable scientific claims. (Cartwright 1992, pp. 60–1, emphasis in original)

After this brief introduction to the question of why realism might be (or at least view itself as) a response the problems of underdetermination and theory-ladenness, let us examine two specific realist programs, both of which claim to draw inspiration from the crisis within empiricist philosophy of science.

The first view is the referential realism of Richard Boyd (1973, 1983, 1991, 1992). Boyd was a student of Hilary Putnam, also a very important figure in the development of contemporary scientific realism, and Boyd's arguments have much in common with those of (early) Putnam.[48] Boyd's realism has four basic components:

    a. Theoretical terms potentially refer.
    b. Scientific theories are often confirmed as approximately true as a result of standard methodological practice.

---

[48] Putnam has changed his viewpoint from that exhibited in his earlier realist work (1975 and 1983, for instance), and now seems to be more sympathetic to pragmatism (see 1994 and 1995, for instance).

c. The historical progress of mature science entails increasingly accurate approximations to the truth.
d. Ontological realism: there exists a reality independent of our theorizing about it (Boyd 1983, p. 45).

Boyd's argument in support of his brand of scientific realism is based on the "inference to the best explanation" (IBE) and it relies on the fact that science is both theory-dependent and instrumentally successful. The argument is that the best explanation for the instrumental success of science is that its theory-dependent structures actually refer, that scientific theories are (at least approximately) true. In Boyd's own words: "realism provides the only acceptable explanation for the current instrumental reliability of scientific methodology" (Boyd 1983, p. 88). Or, as Putnam summarizes the argument:

> According to Boyd (and to me in the Locke lectures), metaphysical realism can be reformulated as an overarching empirical theory about the success of science, namely the (meta) theory that the success of the theories of the mature physical sciences is explained by the fact that the terms used in those theories typically *refer* (refer to subsets of the Totally of All Objects, that is) and that the statements that constitute the basic assumptions of those theories are typically *approximately* true. (Putnam 1994, p. 303)

Although the type of argumentation involved in the IBE has a long history – it is in some ways a version of the "abductive" method of the pragmatist Charles S. Peirce (discussed in Chapter 6), and it was first applied to the question of realism by H. von Helmholtz in the nineteenth century (Hacking 1983, p. 52) – it is also important to emphasize that Boyd's defense of scientific realism is clearly a post-crisis-of-the-Received-View development.[49] Notice that Boyd accepts theory-ladenness and related problems as well as the necessity of examining the actual history of science in (or as background to) his program; Boyd's scientific realism is clearly a product of (or at least relies on) the difficulties that have been documented elsewhere in this chapter.

Although the IBE argument is abductive, the intuition behind the argument is the same as the so-called no-miracles argument for scientific realism. The "no miracles" argument is basically that the success of science would be simply miraculous if scientific theories were not true. John Worrall provides a clear statement of the "no miracles" position.

---

[49] For one of the many critiques of the IBE defense of realism, see Day and Kincaid (1994).

It would be a miracle, a coincidence on a near cosmic scale, if a theory made as many correct empirical predictions as, say, the general theory of relativity or the photon theory of light *without* what that theory says about the fundamental structure of the universe being correct or "essentially" or "basically" correct. But we shouldn't accept miracles, not at any rate if there is a non-miraculous alternative. If what these theories say is going on "behind" the phenomena is indeed true or "approximately true" then it is no wonder that they get the phenomena right. So it is plausible to conclude that presently accepted theories are indeed "essentially" correct. (Worrall 1989, p. 101, emphasis in original)

Probably the simplest way to characterize Boyd's scientific realism is to say that it is a (the most) sophisticated defense of this general "no miracles" argument. Although many philosophers (even some realists[50]) have criticized Boyd's realism, I will not attempt to document any of these criticisms; the point was simply to introduce Boyd's realism and link it to the problems of the Received View.

The second version of realism that I would like to consider is the "transcendental realism" of Roy Bhaskar.[51] Bhaskar's realism has a more ontological focus than the representational realism of Boyd. Boyd of course accepted ontological realism, but his main point is about the representational success and approximate truth of the theories of mature science. Bhaskar is a fallibilist about the truth of any particular scientific theory, and concentrates instead on the transcendental question of what conditions would be required for the very possibility of scientific knowledge.

---

[50] Ian Hacking (1983), Rom Harré (1986), and Richard Miller (1987), to name just a few.

[51] See Bhaskar (1978, 1987, 1989, and 1991) and Collier (1994). Bhaskar's realism has been applied to economics by Tony Lawson (1989a, 1989b, 1994a, 1995, 1997a, and elsewhere), William Jackson (1995), and many others. Although this economics literature will not be discussed until Chapter 7, it is important to point out that Bhaskar is being considered here *because of his importance in economics and the philosophy of social science more generally*; Bhaskar, unlike Boyd, is seldom cited in the (purely) philosophical literature. More influential philosophers such as Nancy Cartwright (1989a) often state positions that have much in common with Bhaskar's realism and yet there does not seem to be any recognition of the commonalty (from either side).

Bhaskar originally used the term "transcendental realism" for his general (realist) philosophy of science, and "critical naturalism" for the application of his view to the human sciences; later interpreters/supporters combined these two expressions and adopted the term "critical realism" for his general approach (natural or social science). Even though Bhaskar now accepts the term critical realism (Bhaskar 1989, p. 190), I will continue to use transcendental realism in this section on his general philosophy of science, and use critical realism in Chapter 7 in the discussion of economics.

Bhaskar begins by uncovering some fundamental tensions within the positivist-inspired view of scientific knowledge. Any theory of knowledge, Bhaskar argues, presupposes some (perhaps implicit) ontological commitment regarding the objects of that knowledge. Empiricist epistemology inspires an implicit ontology of *empirical realism*, which makes the objects of scientific investigation the same as the objects of experience. Since those things that can be observed, the objects of experience, are most often empirical event regularities, event regularities become the objects of (the only objects of) scientific inquiry. Bhaskar refers to this as the *epistemic fallacy*: the fallacy of reducing matters of ontology (existence or being) to matters of epistemology (knowledge).

The epistemic fallacy generates an *ontological tension* (Bhaskar 1989, p. 18) in at least two ways. First, it generates a tension between the standard philosophical characterization of scientific knowledge and the ontological presuppositions of practicing scientists. Practicing scientists actually look for the underlying, hidden, causal mechanisms that generate the empirical regularities they observe, and consider these underlying causes, not the empirical regularities, to be the proper objects of scientific inquiry. A second, related, tension emerges within the experimental practice of science. Successful experimental practice always entails structuring the environment so that the effect of a single causal mechanism can be isolated; it requires the artificial structuring of the experimental context so as to eliminate or neutralize the impact of all other causal mechanisms other than the one under examination. The empirical regularities that are supposed to be at the heart of science can only be observed in the closed environment of experimental systems, that is, there is nothing "natural" about the domain of natural science. The necessity of experimental closure doubly vindicates realism. On the one hand, the "facts" of science are clearly a social product; the observable facts of science "are real; but they are historically specific social realities" (Bhaskar 1989, p. 61). This means that if, as empiricism suggests, the "laws of nature" are factual regularities then "we are logically committed to the absurdities that scientists, in their experimental activity, cause and even change the laws of nature!" (Bhaskar 1989, pp. 15–16). On the other hand, in order to apply science outside the environment of the laboratory one must presuppose the same causal mechanisms that were empirically revealed in the closed experimental context will continue to act in the more complex open environment outside the lab, again suggesting that something must be going on other than the constant conjunction of empirical events. All of this adds up to an extremely problematic situation for empiricist philosophy of science; Bhaskar offers transcendental realism as a solution to these problems.

Transcendental realism starts with an ontological distinction between the underlying causal mechanisms (generative structures, capacities, causal powers, etc.) and the observable patterns of events (empirical regularities). These underlying causal mechanisms are the *intransitive* objects of scientific inquiry, whereas the empirical regularities are the *transitive* products of scientific inquiry. These causal laws are *tendencies* that may or may not exhibit themselves empirically in any particular situation. In the complex and open world outside the experimental context there are many causal forces at work, many tendencies, and that which becomes empirically manifest is coproduced by the interaction of these multiple causal factors. Within the closed experimental environment the empirical manifestations are more likely to be observed, but that is the purpose of experimental context; the "experimental activity can be explained as an attempt to intervene in order to *close* the system, in order, in other words, to insulate a particular mechanism of interest by holding off all other potentially counteracting mechanisms" (Lawson 1994, p. 268, emphasis in original). The process of scientific development is the process of uncovering ever deeper layers of these causal forces; the intransitive domain of these causal forces exists independently of our scientific investigation, but the scientific investigation itself is a transitive and historically contingent social process. Transcendental realism simultaneously sustains the claims that: (1) the object of science is to uncover nonobservable causal laws that exist independently of our theorizing about them, and (2) that science is socially produced and its empirical domain does not exist independently of our theorizing.

> Now I have argued ... that constant conjunctions are not in general spontaneously available in nature but rather have to be worked for in the laboratories of science, so that causal laws and the other objects of experimental investigation must, if that activity is to be rendered intelligible, be regarded as ontologically independent of the patterns of events and the activities of human beings alike; and that, conversely, the concepts and descriptions under which we bring them must, if *inter alia* scientific development is to be possible, be seen as part of the irreducibly social process of science. Thus experiences (and the facts they ground), and the constant conjunctions of events that form the empirical grounds for causal laws, are social products. But the objects to which they afford us access, such as causal laws, exist and act quite independently of us. (Bhaskar 1989, p. 51)

Bhaskar's transcendental realism has particularly strong implications for the human/social sciences. For one thing, social systems are inherently open systems making useful empirical regularities particularly difficult to find. This means that human science will be much more concerned with explanation than prediction. For another thing, the social nature of fact production is even more significant in the social sciences where the (social) process of science is more clearly, and more inseparably, intertwined with the (social) object domain. For Bhaskar, the human sciences are clearly "sciences," but they have their own unique characteristics and he does not in any way support their reduction to biology or physics. Bhaskar's general characterization of social science shares a strong affinity with the tendency law view of the Millian tradition discussed in Chapter 2.

> To sum up, then, society is not given in, but presupposed by, experience. But it is precisely its peculiar ontological status, its transcendentally real character, that makes it a possible object of knowledge for us. Such knowledge is non-natural but still scientific.
>
> As for the law-like statements of the social sciences, they designate tendencies operating at a single level of the social structure only. Because they are defined only for one relatively autonomous component of the social structure and because they act in systems that are always open, they designate tendencies (such as for the rates of profit on capitalist enterprises to be equalized) which may never be manifested. (Bhaskar 1989, p. 87)

The social science implications of Bhaskar's transcendental realism will be examined in more detail in Chapter 7, where I discuss the recent economic applications of his work. Before moving on to some other forms of realism though, let me make a brief comment regarding Bhaskar's political (or political economic) position; a position that is suggested by his choice of example in the above quote (equal rates of profit among capitalist firms). As with Neurath and many other philosophers of science (including Popper although it is not really clear from the above discussion of falsificationism), their social/political values are deeply intertwined with their epistemic values and beliefs about (even natural) scientific knowledge. Bhaskar comes out of the Marxist intellectual tradition, and he clearly views transcendental realism as a solution to various problems within that tradition as well as a solution to problems within the philosophy of natural science.[52] He considers transcendental realism to be a view

---

[52] For differing Marxist views on how successful he is in this endeavor, see Gunn (1989) and Lovering (1990).

of scientific knowledge, unlike positivism and its derivatives, that is consistent with the broader goal of human emancipation. This explicit political focus may help explain the attention that Bhaskar has received from certain social scientists and the (non)attention his program has received among philosophers of natural science.

We have now examined two versions of contemporary realism in some detail: the representational realism of Boyd and the transcendental realism of Bhaskar. These two are but a small sample of the different realisms that currently exist within the philosophical literature. Although space considerations preclude a detailed examination of any of these other realisms, I would like to briefly mention a few that seem to be of particular interest (some of which will make an appearance in later chapters). Ian Hacking (1983) has defended a view (experimental realism) that supports a version of representational realism about the entities that appear in science, but not about scientific theories themselves. Hacking attempts to reconcile our basic realist intuitions with the type of complex case studies that emerge from a close examination of the experimental practice of science. His perspective has influenced many of the authors that will be discussed in Chapters 4 and 5. Nancy Cartwright (1983, 1989a, 1992) has severely criticized traditional empiricist view of laws and defended a realist interpretation of nature's "capacities"; her realism has some elements in common with Bhaskar and others with Hacking. Because she has applied her arguments to economics, her work will be discussed in Chapter 7. Rom Harré (1986) has defended a realism that makes "science not just an epistemological but also a moral achievement" (Harré 1986, p. 1). Whereas Harré emphasizes the community of science, he finds that community's shared moral values to be its most important virtue. Popper's conjectural realism was considered above, but the original version has run into difficulties (most associated with his concept of verisimilitude) and has been modified in a number of ways by later Popperian philosophers.[53] One of the many topics considered in the next chapter is "evolutionary epistemology," and, whereas there are many different versions of this general view, all of them are, in one way or another, sympathetic to scientific realism. The recent work of Philip Kitcher (1993), discussed in Chapter 8, is also a defense of a particular version of scientific realism (a version that is close to Boyd's). Finally, even some of the sociological approaches discussed in Chapter 5 – most of which claim to be antirealist – actually support a version of realism: a type of social realism.

---

[53] There is even a post-Lakatosian version that ties realism up with the prediction of novel facts (see Musgrave 1988 and Worrall 1989).

The last topic in this section will be a brief consideration of a contemporary empiricist view, perhaps one should say a version of post-positivist positivism. Unlike realism, there are not many such views, but one author has received quite a bit of attention in the philosophical literature and has also made an appearance in economic methodology. The approach in question is the "constructive empiricism" of Bas van Fraassen (1980).

Van Fraassen's *The Scientific Image* (1980) is an empiricist response to the realist response to the demise of the Received View. Van Fraassen accepts theory-ladenness, underdetermination, and the other criticisms of positivist-inspired philosophy of science – logical positivism "had a rather spectacular crash" (van Fraassen 1980, p. 2) – but he also rejects – radically rejects – the claim that positivism's crash provides an argument in favor of the realist view of science. According to van Fraassen, scientific realism is the position that science aims to give us "a literally true story of what the world is like" (van Fraassen 1980, p. 8). As an alternative to such realism, van Fraassen offers *empirical adequacy*, not truth (literal or otherwise), as the proper goal of science. Empirical adequacy is a purely *descriptive* characteristic of a scientific theory; a theory is empirically adequate if "what it says about the observable things and events in this world, is true – exactly if it 'saves the phenomena'" (van Fraassen 1980, p. 12). Notice: It is "what it says" about observables that must be true, not that "it," the scientific theory itself, is true. Van Fraassen's constructive empiricism is wholly within the empiricist philosophical tradition; science is about accurately describing empirical observations, not about uncovering hidden causal mechanism or finding literally true theories that go beyond the observable domain.

Although empirical adequacy is solely about description, van Fraassen freely admits that scientific theories do, as a practical matter, go beyond empirical description: in fact, they are even used to provide scientific explanations. For van Fraassen, this is simply the difference between the epistemic and the pragmatic dimensions of science. Empirical adequacy is an epistemic criterion, but theory acceptance is based on a much broader set of evaluative standards that include pragmatic considerations. The pragmatic virtues that a theory might have include simplicity, elegance, usefulness, and the ability to provide scientific explanations. Such things are part of applied science; they "are specifically human concerns, a function of our interests and pleasures, which make some theories more valuable or appealing to us than others" (van Fraassen 1980, p. 87). There are two important points to note about this separation (and purification) of the epistemic from the pragmatic and applied. First, it pushes most of Kuhn's sociological insights (and thus most of the "irrationalism" he found) onto the pragmatic domain of applied science where its epistemic damage is minimized. Second, van Fraassen's view of scientific explanation carries us back, well past the Received View, to the early logical positivist view of science as pure description.

Because theory-ladenness is normally interpreted to be a critique, perhaps a devastating critique, of the empiricist view of scientific knowledge, van Fraassen spends a lot of time ferreting out exactly what he means by "observable" and "empirical."[54] At the heart of his argument is the distinction between "seeing" and "seeing that." Essentially, observation is about "seeing," while empirical description is about "seeing that," and it is the latter, not the former, that is theory-laden. The example that van Fraassen uses (1980, p. 15) involves exposing "Stone Age" people to a tennis ball. If you throw the ball into their field of sight they certainly do not "see that" it is a tennis ball (one needs to share our cultural/theoretical world to see it that way), but they do "see" the ball. In van Fraassen's words: "To say that he does not see the same things and events as we do, however, is just silly; it is a pun which trades on the ambiguity between seeing and seeing that" (1980, p. 15). The epistemic dimension is the observable (seeing) while actual science involves the theory-laden domain of empirical description (seeing that). As Boylan and O'Gorman describe van Fraassen's view: "Scientific description, in so far as it is describing that, is theory-laden, whereas observation, as distinct from observing that, is not theory-laden" (1995, pp. 146–7). Needless to say, the issue of whether van Fraassen is actually successful in his attempt to hold empiricism and theory-ladenness in a single vision is still (at best) an open question. One application of constructive empiricism to economics will be considered in Chapter 7.

3.4 Setting the Stage for the Naturalistic Turn

This chapter has covered a lot of ground. We moved from the Vienna Circle through the Received View and falsificationism, on to the critiques of Quine and Kuhn, and continued on through the first round responses to those critiques: the quasi-historical approach of Lakatos, various contemporary realisms, and finally the constructive empiricism of van Fraassen. The themes of theory-ladenness and

---

[54] Because radical empiricism and theory-ladenness seem so *prima facie* inconsistent, it is useful to quote van Fraassen himself.

> All our language is thoroughly theory-infected. If we could cleanse our language of theory-laden terms, . . . we would end up with nothing useful. The way we talk, and scientists talk, is guided by the pictures provided by previously accepted theories. . . . Hygienic reconstructions of language such as the positivists envisaged are simply not on. (van Fraassen 1980, p. 14)

underdetermination were traced throughout; not only did they emerge in the sections on Quine and Kuhn where they are quite familiar, but earlier, in Neurath's physicalism and Popper's conventionalist view of the empirical basis; so, too, in the later literature, where these two themes emerged as issues that must be dealt with, in some way, before any new variant of normative philosophy of science can go forward.

We have reached the end of this long segue. The next move in the philosophy of science and science studies is transitional; it is not a new set of moves in the same old foundationalist game (like Lakatos, van Fraassen, and certain versions of realism) *but a completely new game.* The new game is *naturalism* and it will be the guiding theme in many of the remaining chapters. Philosophy of science has taken *the naturalistic turn* (or perhaps return) and it is a change that has fundamentally altered the relationship between the special sciences (including economics) and the philosophy of science. At its core (and we will find there are many specific versions), naturalism "claims that whatever exists or happens in the world is susceptible to explanation by natural scientific methods; it denies that there is or could be anything which lies in principle beyond the scope of scientific explanation" (Callebaut 1993, p. xv). Contemporary naturalism is a leveling, and a redefinition, of the traditional relationship between philosophy and science. According to the traditional relationship philosophy comes first; philosophy *justifies* scientific knowledge by elaborating the foundations for knowledge and specifying a set of rules, the scientific method, which guarantee the justification is transmitted to the theoretical artifacts of science. Philosophy sits in judgment; it is the high court of knowledge claims, or, in Habermas's apt phrase, it is the "usher" (1987, p. 298) for our cognitive life. This chapter has documented the failure (or at least quagmire) of this traditional view. The many versions of naturalism are now the standard responses to this failure of foundationalist philosophy of science.

Because naturalism will be examined in detail below, all I want to do in the closing paragraphs of this chapter is to suggest a few of the ways that the naturalistic turn was anticipated by some of the authors discussed above. Although the naturalistic turn is normally considered to be of recent vintage (or at least its substantive impact is of recent vintage), the seeds of the idea began to germinate much earlier than this recent, and fecund, harvest. I will not mention Quine at this point, since he is a major figure in the naturalistic movement and his naturalism will be examined in detail in Chapter 4; I also will not mention Popper, because there is further discussion of the Popperian tradition below.

One member of the Vienna Circle who had a decidedly naturalistic bent was Neurath. For Neurath, science was the measure of all things –

witness his support of a physicalist vocabulary based on the best scientific practice rather than the phenomenalistic vocabulary of traditional empiricism – and to try to "ground" science by epistemology was to put something higher than science itself (and thus kowtow to metaphysics). For Neurath, science is just fine – there are no philosophical problems with/about science; there is only the need to spread the scientific world view and overcome occult metaphysics. Neurath was "the first positivist to articulate a doctrine of what we might call dogmatic relativism: Even though there are no standards extrinsic to the actual practice of science that can stand in judgment of it (relativism), science is (dogmatically) asserted to be overwhelmingly superior to any other system of beliefs (like metaphysics or religion) and indeed can stand in judgment of them" (Coffa 1991, p. 364).

Another author with broadly naturalistic sympathies is Thomas Kuhn. Remember what Kuhn said regarding the charge of "irrationality" – to say science was "irrational" because it didn't do what philosophers thought it should do was "vaguely obscene," and opened "the door to cloud-cuckoo land" (Kuhn 1970b, p. 264). For Kuhn, his historical studies uncovered what had actually happened in great science and such science was the most rational of all human activities; if these facts do not fit one's definition of rationality, then it reflects negatively on one's definition of rationality, not on science. "No process essential to scientific development can be labeled 'irrational' without vast violence to the term" (Kuhn 1970b, p. 235). As Giere put it in an interview with Werner Callebaut: "For me now the most important thing is Kuhn's naturalism, the idea that the central task of the philosophy of science is to develop a theoretical understanding of how science actually works – not to show that science is 'justified' or 'rational' or 'progressive'" (Callebaut 1993, p. 42).

Kuhn and Neurath are just two of the many authors who, in one way or another, anticipated the recent naturalistic turn, a turn to which we now, well, . . . turn.

4

The Naturalistic Turn

Principles of Evidence and Theories of method are not to be constructed *a priori*. The laws of our rational faculty, like those of every other natural agency, are only learned by seeing the agent at work. The earlier achievements of science were made without the conscious observance of any scientific method; and we should never have known by what process truth is to be ascertained, if we had not ascertained many truths.

[J. S. Mill 1884, p. 579]

I hold that knowledge, mind, and meaning are part of the same world that they have to do with, and that they are to be studied in the same empirical spirit that animates natural science. There is no place for a prior philosophy.

[Quine 1969a, p. 26]

[K]nowledge and belief, reference, meaning, and truth, and reasoning, explaining and learning, are each the focus of eroded confidence in "the grand old paradigm," a framework derived mainly from Logical Empiricism, whose roots, in turn, reach back to Hume, Locke, and Descartes. . . . it is not that there has been a decisive refutation of "the grand old paradigm." Paradigms rarely fall with decisive refutations; rather, they become enfeebled and slowly lose adherents. . . . But many of us sense that working within "the grand old paradigm" is not very rewarding. By contrast, there is considerable promise in a naturalistic approach, . . . Epistemology

conceived in this spirit is what W. V. Quine has called
naturalized epistemology.

[Patricia Churchland 1987, p. 546]

The history of philosophy is often characterized as a series of substantive "turns"; examples include the rationalist turn during the seventeenth
century, the idealist turn in eighteenth-century German philosophy,
and the logistic turn that gave analytical philosophy its impetus early in
the twentieth century. There are clear indications that epistemology,
and perhaps philosophy more generally, is currently engaged in one
such substantive turn: the *naturalistic turn*. This naturalistic movement
will be described in detail below, but at this point let me just say that
it is a turn away from *a priori* philosophy and toward a philosophical
vision that is informed by contemporary scientific practice. According
to this view, the theory of knowledge should employ the same scientific
tools we use to investigate any other aspect of nature; epistemology so
informed is *naturalized epistemology*. We will see that such naturalization can take many forms and that there is much debate about whether
these (or which of these) naturalized epistemologies should be given the
rights of, or have fulfilled the obligations of, more traditional approaches
to the theory of knowledge.

Before embarking on a serious look at naturalized epistemology I
would like to make one point about how words such as "naturalized" or
"naturalism" will, and more important, will *not* be used in this chapter
(and in the chapters that follow). They will not be used as synonyms for
"methodological monism": the thesis that the social sciences can and
should employ the same scientific method as the natural sciences. There
is a long tradition in the philosophy of social science, dating back to at
least Condorcet, which equates the word *naturalism* with methodological monism: the claim is that since there is only one natural world
(even though it contains both human and nonhuman objects) there is
only one appropriate way to investigate it: the method of natural science.
The discussion in Chapter 2 demonstrated that naturalism in this sense,
as methodological monism, has been a major (perhaps the major) theme
in the history of economic methodology. Despite this, and despite the
fact that the two uses are clearly related – both consider human knowers
to be an aspect of the natural world (Kincaid 1996, p. 21) – I will use the
word "naturalism" in the way that it is used in the contemporary literature on naturalized epistemology, and reserve the term "methodological
monism" for the thesis that the social sciences should follow in the
methodological footsteps of the natural sciences.

4.1 Naturalizing Epistemology

This section will examine the general topic of naturalized epistemology. The discussion will be fairly thorough, but it will be restricted to the general idea of naturalized epistemology, and not to specific examples of naturalization. The idea of naturalized epistemology is one thing, but the particular approach that one takes to naturalization (or as I will say later, what one chooses as a naturalizing base) is a separate issue. This section will focus exclusively on the general idea, whereas the other three sections of this chapter (as well as various parts of later chapters) will focus on particular approaches to naturalization.

There are two subsections to the general discussion. The first examines the general notion of naturalization and situates it relative to more traditional approaches to the theory of knowledge. This discussion will take for granted the breakdown of the Received View and the problems of theory-ladenness and underdetermination that were discussed in Chapter 3. The second subsection will examine the paper that effectively launched (or at least relaunched) the entire naturalistic program: Quine's "Epistemology Naturalized" (1969b). Quine was an important figure in Chapter 3 when the genealogy of theory-ladenness and underdetermination were being discussed, and he is also important here in the discussion of the naturalistic turn (he is perhaps even more important here since he is responsible for coining the term "naturalized epistemology").

4.1.1 Naturalizing Knowledge

The traditional vision of the relationship between philosophy and science (at least since Descartes) has been based on *epistemology* as "first philosophy." According to this traditional view there exists a hierarchy of intellectual ideas and philosophy comes in at the very beginning; philosophy, epistemology in particular, has the responsibility for laying the foundations, or the groundwork, for empirical science. The job of epistemology is to answer the question "what is knowledge?" To answer this question it is necessary to inquire into the fundamental category(ies) of knowledge: that is to understand the "nature" of knowledge. The right tool for this investigation, so the traditional argument goes, is the "philosophical method" (in particular, it is not the method of empirical science). This philosophical method is the method of rational and logical analysis, the *a priori* method of armchair philosophical reflection.

According to this traditional view, *philosophy of science* is simply applied epistemology; once the job of first philosophy has been done and the fundamental categories of "knowledge" have been analyzed, the final step is to instantiate that first philosophy in the rules of scientific method. These methodological rules are normative, they describe what scientists ought to do to produce the type of knowledge that epistemology justifies. The traditional view of *economic methodology* places it one step further removed from first philosophy; first the epistemology, then the scientific method, then the application of the scientific method to the particular social science of economics. While the Kuhnian revolution challenged this traditional hierarchy by introducing a normative role for the history of science and emphasizing the social nature of the knowledge production process, the basic vision of epistemology as first philosophy has remained deeply ingrained within our general intellectual framework. It was so ingrained that until very recently any other way of thinking about the relationship between science and epistemology seemed to be simply unconscionable, flying squarely in the face of philosophical common sense.

But, as documented in Chapter 3, the philosophical mainstream is under duress. Problems such as theory-ladenness and underdetermination have not only led to the breakdown of the Received View, they seem to be sufficient to undermine our long-held faith in the entire philosophical project of first philosophy and the related hierarchical division of knowledge studies. So given this situation, given the current epistemic malaise, where do we turn? What approach to knowledge might escape these difficulties and how might the philosophy-science boundary be renegotiated? Enter the naturalistic turn.

To help motivate the basic argument for naturalism consider two "orders" of questions/topics/issues. First-order questions have to do with things that are empirical, causal, and scientific. First-order questions range from relatively sophisticated scientific topics such as the structure of the chromosome to something as simple as predicting the boiling point of water. Second-order questions are the questions that have traditionally been considered to be meta-questions: topics that stand above the first-order questions. Second-order questions concern issues that are foundational, justificatory, legitimative, rationalizing, and epistemological. First-order questions are answered by science, while second-order questions are answered by philosophy.[1] An economic example of a first-order question might be the impact of a particular Central Bank policy on interest rates and investment spending, whereas an associated second-order question might be the methodological justification for the particular macroeconomic model that is used to answer the first-order

---

[1] These two categories obviously form an incomplete disjunction; they do not exhaust the set of all possible classes of questions that might be asked.

question about monetary policy; first-order questions are answered by economists, whereas second-order questions have traditionally been answered by those writing in the field of economic methodology.

The traditional approach was of course to consider second-order questions first, and then to use the answers to these second-order questions to help with, give some guidance to, the activities associated with the first-order questions; decide what knowledge is first, then use this information to help with science. The simplest possible way to characterize *naturalism* is to say that it *inverts the traditional approach to these two sets of questions*. A naturalist approach *starts with first order questions and uses the answer to those first-order questions to help with, to give some guidance to, questions of the second order.* Naturalists start with science (*a posteriori*) and use it to assist with philosophy (previously *a priori*). Although such naturalism may fly in the face of philosophical conventional wisdom, it also seems to have a certain disarming charm; once one adjusts to thinking in naturalistic terms, it seems to be a rather obvious, and prima facie appropriate, strategic move in a contemporary context where the value of science is, for the most part, simply a given, and the philosophy that is supposed to ground that science is in much more disarray than science itself. One wants to stand on the firmest available ground, and currently the ground beneath our best scientific practice seems to be much less squishy than that which supports empiricist epistemology.[2]

The remainder of this chapter will examine a number of *different approaches* to the naturalization of epistemology, but before we turn to these particulars, it is useful to raise a few concerns about naturalism in general. Although all of the various approaches to naturalization deal with these issues in their own way, all of these concerns are applicable to naturalism in general and not unique to any particular naturalistic framework. I will discuss four such issues.

The first involves the distinction between *reformist* and *revolutionary* naturalized epistemology.[3] The reformist brand of naturalism employs science to reform epistemology; the traditional epistemological questions remain the same, science just provides a new set of answers/solutions.[4] Revolutionary naturalized epistemology seeks to change the

---

[2] Since many of the contributors to this naturalistic movement will be discussed (and cited) in the pages that follow, I will only mention two general volumes at this point. Papineau (1993) is a general discussion of naturalism in philosophy and Kornblith (1985b) is an important book of readings. Schmitt (1985) provides a thirty-page bibliography of the literature on naturalized epistemology.

[3] This terminology comes from Ch. 6 of Haack (1993).

[4] There are, of course, various degrees of reform from relatively minor to almost revolutionary.

subject entirely. According to the revolutionary vision, the old epistemological questions are faulty and should be replaced by an entirely different set of questions.[5] The majority of the authors discussed in this
chapter will take a reformist position; the old questions are basically fine,
but the answers need to be reformed. By contrast, some of the authors
discussed in later chapters (particularly 5 and 6) will take a more
revolutionary stance. We will also discover that, while it is relatively easy
to say that a particular individual or school is "more" reformist than revolutionary, or vice versa, the issue is seldom black and white; certain
authors even seem to maintain a position of cultivated ambiguity regarding this particular topic.

The second issue (all four of these issues are interrelated) is the
question of *what one naturalizes "on."* Naturalism always entails the
rejection of a priori philosophical theorizing and its replacement by a
naturalistic frame of reference, but what does one mean by "naturalistic"? Naturalists seem to fall into basically two camps on this issue. One
camp, the *generic science* camp, would naturalize on empirical science
broadly defined, that is, on our generally accepted empirical beliefs. The
generic naturalist holds everything, including our epistemological beliefs
up to the tribunal of experience;[6] the result is an empiricism without the
traditional epistemological justification of that position. According to
this view, epistemology requires the input of our generally accepted
empirical beliefs (including the best scientific theories) but is not based
on, or limited to, any particular scientific theory. The second approach,
specific science naturalism, reduces epistemological questions to some
particular scientific theory.[7] If one uses the language of a "naturalizing

---

[5] We will see that there is sometimes a third approach – call it *debunking* naturalized epistemology. Here the focus is neither reformist nor revolutionary but purely critical. Science
is used to show how the old approach fails, but no immediate replacement is offered. If
reformists put new facades on old buildings, and revolutionaries level the old buildings in
order to build new ones, then debunkers simply level and then admire their work. Perhaps
to be more fair to the debunkers, one could say that their work involves a division of labor;
before anyone can construct anything new the old needs to be removed and there is no
reason for the demolition crew and the construction crew to be composed of the same
people or employ the same tools.

[6] Different authors and schools interpret the relevant "experience" in different ways. In
some cases, experience means basically the brute empirical sense data of classical empiricism, whereas for others, pragmatists in particular, it is viewed more broadly.

[7] There is a third, or middle, ground here. The most general case is to base epistemology
on "experience" broadly defined (generic naturalism), while the least general case is to
base it on a specific scientific theory (specific naturalism), but there is an intermediate case
where one bases it on contemporary science – not experience in general but also not just
one scientific theory. Many authors in the generic camp seem to prefer the most general
(experience) view, while others seem to lean more toward the middle ground of generic

base," then generic naturalism considers all of our accepted scientific beliefs to be its "base," whereas specific naturalism would pick one particular branch of contemporary science as its (at least primary) "base." I will focus almost exclusively on specific science naturalism, since it has been the main focus of the recent naturalistic turn and also because it appears to be most relevant to economic methodology. The main question for such naturalism is "what science do you want to naturalize on"? The cases of specific naturalism examined in this chapter will reduce epistemology to, or base it on, cognitive psychology (Section 2) and evolutionary biology (Section 3). If knowledge is about acquiring reliable beliefs, then epistemology should start from our best psychological theories about how humans actually acquire beliefs; by contrast, if science is about adapting more effectively to the constraints of nature, then one should start from the biological perspective of evolutionary adaptation. In certain cases, it is unclear whether a particular author or school is endorsing a generic or a specific version of naturalism, but in most cases it is unambiguously the latter (less ambiguous, at least, than the issue of reform versus revolution).

The third issue (again interrelated) is perhaps the most divisive of the four issues I consider here. This is the issue of *prescription* versus *description*. Since science describes (and perhaps predicts and/or explains) nature, it seems reasonable to argue that a naturalistic analysis could describe scientific knowledge, but this would seem to be separate from the normative project, the traditional epistemic project, of advising science about what it "ought" to do in order to obtain justified or reliable knowledge. Traditional epistemology was normative; naturalized epistemologies are, the argument goes, only (or at best) descriptive. The rigid distinction between "is" and "ought," the proposition that "one cannot deduce ought from is," was termed "Hume's guillotine" in Chapter 2 and it has played an extremely important role in the history of economic methodology. This issue about, or many would say problem with, naturalism, is simply the application of Hume's guillotine to naturalized epistemology.[8] Scientific analysis of knowledge production can describe, and perhaps even predict or explain, the production of knowledge, but it cannot tell us how knowledge ought to be produced; "is" doesn't imply an epistemic ought any more than it implies an ethical

contemporary science. Since most of my attention will be on naturalists who want to reduce epistemology to some specific science, I will not try to ferret out the distinction between these two different versions of generic naturalism.
[8] G. E. Moore (1903) referred to the problem of mixing is and ought as the "naturalistic fallacy." Of course, Moore was concerned with naturalized ethics rather than naturalized epistemology, but the problem of naturalistic prescription is the same in both cases.

ought. Because this is a very important issue, probably the most important issue, in the literature on naturalized epistemology, and because several responses to this issue will be examined in the following sections, I will not elaborate on the problem at this point. The only passing comment I will make concerns the relationship between the first of the above topics – revolution versus reform – and this third topic of prescription versus description. Naturalism's (possible) lack of normative bite is most problematic for those of the reformist persuasion: for in this case the naturalist program is supposed to help with the traditional questions of normative epistemology, and if it can only describe, there will certainly be a problem completing that normative task. For the revolutionaries, this is not much of a problem, since the traditional normative project should be abandoned for something else, perhaps just description, anyway.

The fourth and final issue that I will introduce at this point involves *circularity*. Suppose that one follows a naturalist approach, and just to elucidate the problem most clearly, suppose that one endorses a naturalistic view that is reformist (issue 1), specific (issue 2), and normative (issue 3). So one used a particular scientific theory (say, theory A) to help us understand the traditional epistemological problem of demarcating justified from unjustified belief and the resulting theory provides prescriptive information about how science ought to be practiced. Okay so far. Now apply this normative philosophy of science (derived, remember, from the insights of scientific theory A) to theory A. Such an application certainly seems to entail a (potentially vicious) type of circularity. How can one justify the practices of a certain scientific community when the standards for epistemic justification were based on the theoretical practices of that same community? If the science we are trying to appraise is the whole of scientific knowledge, then of course the same circularity problem applies to a more generic approach as well.[9] This issue, like the other three, has been given a variety of answers, or circumventions, by various different naturalistic authors, and it is also an issue that will reemerge in a number of places in the following discussion. With this very brief introduction to these four issues, I will now turn to Quine's particular version of naturalized epistemology.

4.1.2 Quine's Naturalism

Although naturalistic ideas have a long history in Western thought, the germinal contribution to contemporary naturalism is clearly

---

[9] This problem is often called the problem of "reflexivity" when it occurs in social science and the social study of science. This issue will be discussed in detail in Chapter 5.

Quine's "Epistemology Naturalized" (1969b). Like the "Two Dogmas" paper discussed in Chapter 3, this paper had a profound (if lagged) effect on an entire generation of philosophers. Ronald Giere tells his own story about its impact in an interview.

> In retrospect, Quine's criticisms began in the early 1950s. I remember reading Quine (1951) as an undergraduate. It did not seem to me as powerful a critique as it in fact was. Then there was his "Epistemology Naturalized" (1969b). At that time the program of naturalized epistemology seemed to me so obviously circular that I could not take it seriously. . . . It was only in the late 1970s, when I independently became convinced that the traditional epistemological project in the philosophy of science was fundamentally misconceived, that I began to appreciate what Quine had been saying. (Giere in Callebaut 1993, p. 64)

Although Quine's original paper is a bit of a montage, it is still possible to separate out three distinctive (or at least distinguishable) aspects of his argument. The first aspect is purely critical; Quine claims, based on the critique of positivism by himself and others (theory-ladenness, underdetermination, indeterminacy of translation, etc.), that traditional epistemology is bankrupt and that it needs to be replaced by something new and totally different. The second aspect of the paper is his positive proposal to substitute naturalized epistemology for the traditional theory of knowledge. This second part is clearly the paper's most defining (and enduring) feature. Finally, Quine offers a specific proposal about the particular science that the new epistemology should be naturalized "on." Although almost all commentators agree with Quine's critical point, and many accept the general idea of a naturalized alternative, Quine's own naturalizing base is only one (and now not even the most popular) of many available alternatives.

Since the critique of positivism by Quine and others was the topic of the previous chapter, it is not necessary to review the critical part of Quine's argument; let us just accept for the time being the critique of the Received View and Quine's radical reading of that critique (that a totally different epistemological vision is required). By contrast, the second part of his argument – Quine's plea for a naturalized epistemology – deserves some attention.

Quine makes the argument that what we want is "simply to understand the link between observation and science" and "we are well advised to use any available information, including that provided by the very science whose link with observation we are seeking to understand" (Quine 1969b, p. 76). For Quine, this does not introduce a problem of circularity, because the issue is "understanding" and not epistemic justification. For Quine, the bankruptcy of the traditional approach makes it clear that we must give up all pretense to first philosophy and the traditional epistemic project; all that remains is to understand the relationship between science and observation. As Quine expressed it in a *Festschrift* for Carl Hempel:

> I see philosophy not as an *a priori* propaedeutic or groundwork for science, but as continuous with science. I see philosophy as science as in the same boat – a boat which, to revert to Neurath's figure as I so often do, we can rebuild only at sea while staying afloat in it. There is no external vantage point, no first philosophy. All scientific findings, all scientific conjectures that are at present plausible, are therefore in my view as welcome for use in philosophy as elsewhere. (Quine 1969c, pp. 126–7)

Traditionally, epistemology sustained science – science was privileged/special because it was justified by epistemology. Quine reversed this relationship – science is the most stable component in our web of belief and thus its services should be available to help us make sense of, and stabilize, the other components of the web: including epistemology. As Quine put it more recently: our scientific knowledge has "outpaced knowledge about knowledge" (Quine 1995, p. 2); in other words, the theory of knowledge occupies a more leaky part of Neurath's boat than science itself.

Most philosophers interpret Quine's argument to give up first philosophy and utilize science as an argument for abandoning normative epistemology altogether in favor of purely *descriptive* inquiry. Since the issue is no longer epistemic justification – the vehicle of inquiry is science, and science describes the world – naturalized epistemology should abandon its normative pretensions and focus exclusively on describing the knowledge production process. In terms of the naturalistic issues discussed in the previous section, Quine is advocating a revolutionary (not reformist) naturalism that is descriptive (not prescriptive).

> Quine's proposal . . . is asking us to set aside the entire framework of justification-centered epistemology. That is what is new in Quine's proposals. Quine is asking us to put in its place a purely descriptive, causal-nomological science of human cognition. . . . Epistemology is to go out of the business of justification. . . . Quine is urging us to replace a normative theory of cognition with a descriptive science. (Kim 1988, pp. 388–9)

The mention of "theory of cognition" in the above quote brings us to the third aspect of Quine's program, the particular science that he proposes to naturalize on. Quine's naturalizing base is psychology, particularly behaviorist psychology.[10] "Epistemology, or something like it, simply falls into place *as a chapter of psychology* and hence of natural science" (Quine 1969b, p. 82, emphasis added). Thus, his generic proposal for replacing traditional epistemology with a naturalized alternative rests on, or at least is bolstered by, a very specific proposal about what kind of science should be involved in the process of naturalizing the theory of knowledge. We want to understand the relationship between a scientist's theory and his or her data – that is, a relationship between stimulus (data input) and response (theoretical output) – and that is a question for psychology.[11] The "conspicuous difference between old epistemology and the epistemological enterprise in this new psychological setting is that we can now make free use of empirical psychology" (Quine 1969b, p. 83). Thus, Quine's naturalized epistemology is not only revolutionary and descriptive; it is also specific.

Quine's paper has generated a massive, and critical, secondary literature that I will not attempt to summarize, or even cite. The ultimate interest remains economics, and while it may not be apparent to most readers what the connection between Quine's naturalized epistemology and economic science is at this point, let me simply assert that there is such a connection (actually there are many) and promise that it will emerge as we proceed. Although I will not try to survey the derivative literature, there are a few controversial issues that need to be discussed before we move on to the second generation literature on naturalization in the next section. I will quickly mention five points of controversy and/or importance regarding Quine's version of naturalism.

The first point is the most common criticism of Quine's position; it is the issue of *whether description is really enough.* In fact, it is clear that most philosophers are *not* willing to accept that epistemology should be eliminated and replaced entirely by descriptive inquiry; to do so would

[10] The behaviorism of Quine's early work on naturalized epistemology seems to have been replaced with a more generic perspective in his later work. He now talks about evolutionary biology, cognitive psychology, and his naturalistic inquiry proceeding "in disregard for disciplinary boundaries" (1995, p. 16).
[11] Actually, Quine is a bit fuzzy about whether this is about an individual scientist and his or her data (psychology) or about the scientific community and its data (social psychology or sociology). One can find arguments for both stories in Quine (1969b); on the one hand, he says "psychology," but on the other hand, his notion of observation involves the fundamentally social concept of a speech community. As we will see this issue of whether the relevant human science is psychology, social psychology, or sociology becomes an important bone of contention in the later literature.

amount to a kind of professional mass suicide where philosophers simply close up shop and turn (what's left of) their work over to practicing scientists. Whereas most philosophers now admit that it is time for a new approach – and perhaps even something that is naturalistic – the vast majority of, even naturalistic, philosophers support a more reformist approach where science helps with traditional questions in the theory of knowledge. Most recognize that the resulting epistemology will not be as stridently normative as the traditional view, but they nonetheless want to retain a modicum of normative bite. Although there are many different answers to the question of how one might actually accomplish this, the goal remains the majority view (at least among philosophers[12]). Larry Laudan exemplifies this attitude:

> Is's and ought's, on this view, are on opposite sides of a great epistemic divide. Some naturalists give up the candle at this point. Quine, for one, seems to accept that there is little if any place for normative considerations in a suitably naturalized epistemology. I daresay that Quine regards his relegation of epistemology to a sub-branch of "descriptive psychology" as a matter of boldly biting the naturalistic bullet; but in my view, the abandonment of a prescriptive and critical function for epistemology – if that is what Quine's view entails – is more akin to using that bullet to shoot yourself in the foot. (Laudan 1990, pp. 45–6)

The second question is the more exegetical issue of *whether Quine really did give up on the normative*, that is, whether mere description really "is what Quine's view entails." Certainly Quine talks about giving up first philosophy and substituting something new for the traditional epistemological vision, and there certainly is some evidence that he wanted to substitute description for prescription, but this may not be the only way to interpret his position (even in the original paper). Although Quine explicitly rejects first philosophy and traditional epistemology, it can be argued that there is some ambivalence about whether or not he wants to abandon any semblance of epistemology-like inquiry. It is clear what he wants to get rid of; it is less clear what he would put in its place. Quine frequently talks about "something like" epistemology (1969b, p. 82) and the "epistemological enterprise" in a "new setting" (1969b, p. 83) and he does call the new program naturalized "epistemology" and not something totally different (naturalized gavagai perhaps). Although it is

---

[12] As we will see in the next chapter, this is not always the case among sociologists of science.

still standard to read Quine as strictly revolutionary and descriptive, these ambiguities have led some authors to suggest that he at least leaves the door open for the more reformist project of using science (first-order issues) to help with certain second-order (normative) issues.[13] The result is that both the reformists and revolutionaries pay homage to Quine as the original architect of their approach.

The third issue is one that has been raised repeatedly in the secondary literature and is perhaps the most obvious of five issues I will consider. Even if we accept Quine's naturalistic program in general, why must we accept his specific naturalizing base, his commitment to behavioral psychology? *Why not naturalize on some other science?* The two possibilities discussed in the rest of this chapter are cognitive psychology and evolutionary biology, but as we will see there are many other options for a naturalizing base[14] (even some interesting possibilities for economics). One can clearly accept Quine's argument about the bankruptcy of traditional epistemology and the need for a naturalistic alternative (reformist or revolutionary) and not agree with his choice about the naturalizing base. This of course opens up the possibility of a very large number of different naturalisms, all claiming Quine as their intellectual grandparent and yet all quite different. It also opens up a (confusing) space for work that claims to criticize "naturalism" in epistemology, when in fact the relevant difficulty is not with naturalism in general, but rather with the particular science (or branch of science) that is being used as the naturalizing base.

Fourth, Quine seems to *invert the traditional hierarchy* among the three fields of philosophy, natural science, and social science. As Quine says:

[13] The normative element seems to be more present in his later work. For example, in his Ferrater Mora Lectures, Quine says:

> A normative domain within epistemology survives the conversion to naturalism, contrary to widespread belief, and it is concerned with the art of guessing, or framing hypotheses. . . . Normative epistemology is the art or technology not only of science, in the austere sense of the word, but of rational beliefs more generally. Literature has burgeoned in this domain, and I do not see how the shift from phenomenalism to naturalism would conflict with it. (Quine 1995, pp. 49–50)

This version of naturalism – epistemology as therapy, or as a helpful uncle – is normative, but it is a long way from the traditional view of normative epistemology. It is interesting from the perspective of economics that Quine lists "game theory" and "decision theory" as examples of this "burgeoning" normative literature.

[14] As Kim puts it hyperbolically: "if normative epistemology is not a possible inquiry, why shouldn't the would-be epistemologist turn to, say, hydrodynamics or ornithology rather than psychology" (Kim 1988, p. 391).

> The old epistemology aspired to contain, in a sense, natural science; it would construct it somehow from sense data. Epistemology in its new setting, conversely, is contained in natural science, as a chapter of psychology. (Quine 1969b, p. 83)

But the old view not only contained natural science within epistemology, it also contained human sciences such as psychology within natural science. The traditional hierarchy was philosophy, then natural science, then human science; for Quine it was human science (psychology), then natural science, then philosophy. In fact, things are not quite so crisp or distinct for Quine – since all three (philosophy, natural science, and psychology) are inexorably intertwined in our web of belief – the point is not to endorse a (new) rigid hierarchy but rather simply that the old hierarchy is fundamentally disturbed. When one combines the possibility that a human science might be considered the most solid ground (the most anchored region of the web), with physics next most solid, and finally epistemology as the least firm – with the preceding argument about naturalizing on other (particularly human) sciences – one quickly ends up with a plethora of possibilities that are radically at odds with both the traditional approach to the philosophy of science and most of what has been written in the field of economic methodology.

The final point relates this discussion of Quine to the discussion of the Received View in the previous chapter. At the end of Chapter 3, there was brief mention of how Kuhn, Neurath, and others anticipated the naturalistic turn. This discussion of Quine should drive home that earlier point. Quine's repeated reference to Neurath's boat is not a coincidence, and it is also not a coincidence that the author of the underdetermination thesis is also the author of "Epistemology Naturalized." The Received View wasn't felled with a single blow, and the naturalistic turn was wide and slow, but many of the same interests, forces, and individuals were at work in both events.

4.2 Psychology and the Cognitive Approach to Knowledge

This section will examine the literature on psychological approaches to naturalized epistemology. The literature is often, and rightly, considered to be a "second-generation" version of Quinean naturalism. These psychological approaches take Quine's basic naturalistic framework but employ later, postbehaviorist, developments in psychology in their analysis of the knowledge acquisition process. The first subsection will examine the work of Alvin Goldman and others who employ contemporary cognitive psychology in the project of naturalization. The second subsection is shorter and it examines Herbert Simon's impact on the literature of naturalized epistemology. The discussion of Simon is clearly motivated by his connection with economics.

Before turning to the specific research programs of Goldman and others it is important to understand how and why the so-called cognitive revolution in psychology impacted the discussion of naturalized epistemology in the way that it did. To this end, consider the following three questions:[15]

1. How ought we to arrive at our beliefs?
2. How do we arrive at our beliefs?
3. Are the processes by which we actually do arrive at our beliefs the ones that we ought to use to arrive at our beliefs?

The traditional view was to strictly separate questions 1 and 2; question 1 was to be answered (exclusively) by philosophy, while question 2 was to be answered (exclusively) by psychology. Quine's naturalism asserted that the first question could not be answered independently of the second question: that epistemology "simply falls into place as a chapter of psychology" (Quine 1969b, p. 82). According to the revolutionary/descriptive reading of Quine he wanted to replace question 1 with question 2; a more reform-minded naturalist might simply assert that the two questions are fundamentally inseparable. We will see that most of the second-generation naturalists, who are generally reformists, see the naturalistic turn primarily as the search for an answer to the third question.

Notice a strict behaviorist would have little or nothing to say about *any* of these questions. After all, behaviorism sees the human mind as a black box, as something that generates certain responses to certain stimuli, and not as something that even has anything that might meaningfully be called "beliefs." For a strict behaviorist, purely mentalistic phenomena such as beliefs and desires are simply occult notions left over from our prescientific worldview, concepts that will be eliminated by the systematic progress of scientific psychology.[16] Thus, it was very difficult to link question 1 and question 2 in the heyday of behaviorism, when the prevailing orthodoxy effectively denied the existence (or at least scientific respectability) of any beliefs, wrong or right. Serendipitously for (but perhaps not independently of) naturalized epistemology, the dominance of strict behaviorism did not last forever.

During the late 1950s and early 1960s, "a quiet revolution in thought took place in scientific psychology" (Baars 1986, p. 141); this change was

---

[15] This follows Kornblith, 1985a.

[16] The final section of this chapter will discuss a contemporary rendition of this view.

the development of cognitive science and the ensuing cognitive revolution. Although the term "cognitive science" actually encompasses a variety of fields including artificial intelligence (AI) and cognitive neuroscience as well as cognitive psychology, the revolution's impact on the discipline of psychology was quite profound. The cognitive revolution reintroduced into psychological discourse (or at least allowed the psychologist to talk sensibly about) concepts like belief, meaning, desire, and intentionality. Although cognitive psychology after the revolution was still self-consciously scientific – it was not a return to Freud or other rationalistic approaches – it did allow the cognitive scientist to relate observed behavior to various types of "unobservable explanatory constructs" (Baars 1986, p. 144) involving the language of mentalistic phenomena. The goal was to predict and explain human behavior, and given the empirical verifiability (or falsifiability) of the hypotheses involved, there was not any particular prohibition against positing various types of mental phenomena or activities to facilitate the scientific project of prediction and explanation. The cognitive revolution was theoretically liberating, because it suspended the prohibition on nonobservables and allowed for much greater latitude in psychological theorizing.[17]

Although there were a number of factors that contributed to the cognitive revolution, the most important was undoubtedly the development of the digital computer and the associated practice of thinking about the human mind as a type of information processing unit. Other factors included a number of influential experimental developments and (at least among philosophers) Chomsky's influential critique of Skinner's work on verbal behavior (Chomsky 1959). These changes and the ensuing cognitive revolution opened the door for an investigation into the relationship between the beliefs that humans actually acquire and the beliefs that would promote the acquisition of knowledge.

> Yet perhaps none of these internal philosophical developments was as important for the revival of epistemological naturalism as the contemporaneous changes that occurred within psychology itself. Against the background of the (behaviorist)

---

[17] Simon will be discussed below, but it is interesting to note that when he was asked in an interview how it was that he managed to avoid the constraints of behaviorism, he replied:

> I guess one very obvious thing was I was never trained in that paradigm. I never had a formal course in psychology. So I didn't know what you weren't supposed to do. I knew about behaviorism, I'd read about such things – not with great belief, but I knew it existed. But I was exposed to a number of other traditions in biology and in the social sciences where people were very much more relaxed about the variety of things they took as data and the variety of ways in which they looked at it. (Simon 1986, p. 371)

psychology dominant in the 1940s and 1950s, epistemological talk of psychological mechanisms would have appeared not only contrary to Fregean gospel but also quaint. After Noam Chomsky's subsequent development of his ideas about innate knowledge, cognitive psychology began to provide an idiom for discussing epistemological issues. (Kitcher 1992, p. 61)

4.2.1 Cognitive Science and Epistemology

Knowledge has traditionally been defined as "justified true belief." Although this definition has a long, and highly contested history, two examples offered by Edmund Gettier (1963) became the rallying point for an entire generation of, particularly naturalist, critics of this traditional view. The so-called Gettier-examples – or more often "Gettier-type" examples, since his particular examples became the prototype for a large (potentially infinite) number of such counterexamples – are basically cases of *failed knowledge*; that is to say, they are cases of (clearly) justified true belief that is (equally clearly) not knowledge.[18] The Gettier-examples show that justified true belief is not sufficient for knowledge, and have, thus, become a point of entry for a wide-ranging critique of the traditional definition and approach.

The most obvious place to start an examination of the traditional view of knowledge is with the notion of justification. What do we (should we) mean by the "justified" in "justified true belief"? The history of philosophy has provided two main approaches to answering this question: foundationalism and coherence. As explained above, foundationalism is based on the idea that knowledge has the character of an edifice, that knowledge is built up systematically from more fundamental beliefs. Justification, according to this view, requires that some beliefs be taken as "foundations of knowledge," as beliefs that are independently secure and not in need of further justification. We have seen that empiricist foundationalism – where sense data are the incorrigible foundations for knowledge – formed the epistemological backbone of mainstream philosophy of science. Although the foundationalism examined above has been empiricist, this is certainly not the only possible form that founda-

---

[18] Nozick paraphrases one of Gettier's examples.

> Two people are in my office and I am justified on the basis of much evidence in believing the first owns a Ford car; though he (now) does not, the second person (a stranger to me) owns one. I believe truly and justifiably that someone (or other) in my office owns a Ford car, but I do not know someone does. Concluded Gettier, knowledge is not simply justified true belief. (Nozick 1981, p. 173)

Nozick offers his own "tracking" solution to this problem.

tionalism can take; there are many other versions, including rationalism and revelation-based religious approaches. The coherence theory is based on the idea that beliefs are justified if they "hang together," if they cohere, with already accepted beliefs. The emphasis in coherence theories is on the consistency of the system and the way that the various components of the system mutually support each other within the tapestry of knowledge. Like foundationalism, there are many different versions of coherence theory.

Both of these traditional theories of knowledge are termed "internalist," because they base the justification of any particular belief on other beliefs. In the case of foundationalism, a belief is justified if it has been built up from other (foundational) beliefs, and according to the coherence view a belief is justified if it is mutually supported by other beliefs. Much of the work in naturalized epistemology attempts to solve the problems of the traditional view (including the Gettier examples) by moving away from (either version of) the internalist approach to an *externalist* view of knowledge. The core notion of externalism is that beliefs might be justified by means of something that the agent does not have cognitive access to, in other words, justified by something "external" to the individual (in particular, it is not justified by other beliefs). This approach constitutes a radical shift from the traditional internalist view of knowledge and is probably best conveyed by looking at actual examples of such approaches. The most influential of these has been the work of Alvin Goldman.

Goldman's work on naturalized epistemology can be divided into two (interrelated) parts: one part more dominant in his earlier research and the other part being emphasized more recently. His early and most influential research – summarized in *Epistemology and Cognition* (1986) – applies cognitive science directly to the problems of epistemology. This work is individualistic in orientation; it is concerned with the process of reliable belief formation by individual scientists.[19] Because of the emphasis on the reliability of the belief formation processes, Goldman's approach is called *reliabilism*. The second aspect of Goldman's work has emerged more recently and focuses on the social aspects of scientific knowledge. Goldman considers this later work to be "social epistemology"; the integration of the (cognitive science-based) naturalized epistemology and the recognition (by Kuhn and others) that science is a fundamentally social endeavor. Because it is not possible to discuss Goldman's entire epistemic project (and the many reactions to it), I will

---

[19] Actually, Goldman is concerned with reliable belief formation in cognitive agents, not just scientists, but I will focus exclusively on scientists.

simply describe the basic reliabilist approach and then discuss two of his later social arguments that relate directly to economics.[20]

Goldman's work is an example of what has been called the "cognitive turn" (Thagard 1993, p. 50) in the philosophy of science: application of the results of the cognitive revolution to the field of epistemology. Goldman refers to this approach as *"the cognitive science of science"* (1993, p. 33). Naturalism is the general framework; naturalizing on cognitive science is one way to naturalize; and Goldman's own program is one particular example of the cognitive approach.[21] The mainstay of all cognitive approaches is that human beings are information-processing systems. This information processing involves mental representations of various features of the external world. Processing of information in the context of prior beliefs and representations produces new acquired beliefs. The question, thus, becomes when, or how, does that acquired belief possess cognitive virtue. Notice that the justification of particular beliefs, the cognitively virtuous ones, is not based on how those beliefs relate to other beliefs (as with internalist approaches like foundationalism or coherence) but on the type of information processing that produced them; the standards do not apply to a particular scientific theory but to the "activity of the cognizers" (Goldman 1986, p. 125) that produced it. Notice that this version of naturalism, unlike the standard interpretation of Quine's view, is *normative*; it is concerned with how reasoning and belief formation *ought* to proceed and not just how they do in fact proceed. Although it is normative, its externalism and naturalism make it sufficiently different from the standard approach to normative epistemology that Goldman calls the field "epistemics" rather than (even naturalized) epistemology.

The main cognitive virtue that Goldman considers is *reliability*. In simplest terms reliability is the ability to produce a high ratio of true to false beliefs. There is no single standard for passing the reliabilist criterion; very high truth ratios are desirable, but $>.5$ is probably sufficient (Goldman 1986, p. 105). For Goldman, reliably produced belief is justified belief, and knowledge is reliably produced (thus justified) true belief. A belief-producing process is reliable if it produces a high ratio of true beliefs, and a reliable belief-producing process is thus one that is justified. Because reliability is not the only cognitive virtue – others include things like "power" (problem-solving ability) and "speed" (how quickly

---

[20] At this point, I will not discuss Goldman's work that directly applies economic analysis (Cox and Goldman 1994; Goldman and Shaked 1991), because it forms part of the "economics of scientific knowledge" discussed in Chapter 8.

[21] In fact, there are other versions of reliabilism, but I will simply identify reliabilism with Goldman's approach.

beliefs are processed) – and these virtues do not always pull or work in the same direction (any more than power and speed work in the same direction in other aspects of life, like, say, in a golf shot), it is often necessary to trade off one, or some, of these virtues against the others. This leads to the question of the costs and benefits of additional reliability, a move that potentially opens the door for economic analysis.

Goldman's view of knowledge makes him a scientific realist "of sorts" (Goldman 1986, p. 17). He certainly believes that statements are true or false independently of our knowledge or theorizing (he is a veristic realist[22]), but he is skeptical of the notion of getting closer to the truth in the correspondence sense. He uses the term "correspondence$_1$" for the standard view that the world is structured in such a way that language can correctly mirror it: "that truth consists in language or thought mirroring a precategorized world" (Goldman 1986, p. 152). He prefers "correspondence$_2$," which is correspondence in the sense of "fittingness" (Goldman 1986, p. 152). According to this weaker form of correspondence, statements are true or false on the basis of the way the world is, but it does not require the direct mirroring of the world by language. Goldman often uses the clothes analogy to explicate this second, weaker, notion of correspondence and truth; some clothes fit and some clothes do not fit, and whether they do or not depends on the way the world (person) is, but one would not say that clothes mirror the person in the sense of correspondence$_1$. This notion of correspondence and truth is fundamentally realist, but it also allows for a certain element of social construction; it tries to walk a middle ground between realism and the issues associated with the social aspects of science raised by Kuhn and others. Giere discusses the connection between Kuhn and the cognitive approach:

> Kuhn's official theory is the stage theory. But in fact, I think what he is groping toward is a cognitive theory. He picked Gestalt psychology because that was the best thing around in the late 1950s. He did not pick behaviorism, and that was smart because it was lousy! So in that sense he was striving for a cognitive theory; and there are all kinds of cognitive things in the theory. But he was writing before cognitive science had been invented. (Giere in Callebaut 1993, p. 352)

Goldman clearly recognized the social dimension of knowledge in *Epistemology and Cognition* but the main focus of that work was on the individual; social epistemology has only surfaced as a central issue in his

---

[22] In Mäki's (1989) terms.

more recent research. When "social" problem solving was mentioned in his earlier work (Goldman 1986, pp. 136–8), it was accommodated, Goldman claimed, by focusing on the "products" of science, rather than the internal states of the individual scientists, but then these products were simply reduced to the categories of cognitive science: "even the evaluation of products in the social arena may be illuminated by reference to human psychology" (Goldman 1986, p. 138). In later work, the focus has been more earnestly social; along with the "primary individual epistemics," he also includes "social epistemics" (Goldman, 1987) as a separate topic. The focus is still on belief, or as he would say, on belief states, but in social epistemics the interesting belief states are those of "a community, group, or culture" (Goldman 1987, p. 110).

Goldman's basic approach to social epistemics does not differ from his approach to individual epistemics; both are not only naturalistic, they are also normative and reformist (perhaps radical reformist). He argues that the same type of veristic standards discussed earlier, reliability, and so on, can be applied directly to social groups as well.

> There are, indeed, a number of distinct truth-linked standards, any or all of which can be used to appraise social institutions as practices. Five different standards can usefully be distinguished: (1) reliability, (2) power, (3) fecundity, (4) speed, and (5) efficiency. (Goldman 1987, p. 128)

Because these various standards must be traded off against each other and the benefits of a gain in one (or a subset) must be weighed against the cost of a loss in another (or a subset), Goldman admits that his version of social epistemology might involve economic analysis. "The economics of information is certainly an important topic in the theory of information, and should not be omitted from the agenda of social epistemics" (Goldman 1987, p. 129). This is just the first of many examples that we will discover where economics is employed (or at least it is suggested that it should be employed) in the philosophical examination of scientific knowledge. Goldman's particular approach to social epistemics sets the stage for Philip Kitcher's approach (discussed in Chapter 8).

Although Goldman's social epistemics opens the door to an economic analysis of the efficiency of various substitutions between/among the various veristic standards that he considers relevant, this is not the only way that economics has entered his more recent work. Goldman is also concerned with applied ethics and social welfare.

> Most modern moral theories, especially those in the utilitarian tradition, assign an important place to the concepts of happiness,

utility, welfare, or well-being. Morally good actions or social policies are widely thought to be ones that promote the general welfare, or encourage an appropriate distribution of welfare. The exact nature of happiness, welfare, or well-being, however, needs detailed investigation, and this is a topic to which cognitive psychology is making interesting contributions. (Goldman 1993, p. 134)

Goldman is interested in this topic in part because it involves the application of cognitive science to yet another area of philosophy (ethics), but this is not the only motivation. This work on cognitive science and utility also relates to naturalized epistemology. To see how this works, consider Goldman's analysis of interpersonal utility comparisons in Goldman (1995). In this paper, he presents the standard criticisms of interpersonal utility (IU), but also argues, like many economists do, that standards like Pareto optimality that are devised to guide policy in the absence of IU comparisons are far too weak to serve as the basis for any interesting social analysis. His goal is to find a way of justifying IU comparisons; he cites Harsanyi (1955), but wants to go much further than Harsanyi's commonsense defense. For Goldman, this is an epistemological issue: How do we get reliable or justified access to the mental states of others?

> The epistemological problem facing IU comparisons under experientialism is straightforward. If anyone tries to compare the hedonic states of persons A and B, there seems to be no sound epistemic route to both of their states. (Goldman 1995, p. 717)

And this epistemological issue, like any other, can be examined from a naturalized (and cognitive) framework. Goldman's actual solution involves a particular approach – simulation theory (or empathetic methodology) – that, although quite new in its current cognitive science guise, goes back to Adam Smith (sympathy) and various *verstehen* approaches to the social sciences.[23] The simulation theory is basically a way of making inferences about the mental states of other agents (or possibly decision-making systems) by mirroring (or simulating) their decision-making mechanisms in ours; feed their initial information into our system and simulate their processing. Now, such simulations could be quite wrong, but they can be appraised, and it is possible that such simulations are *reliable* in Goldman's sense. If so, the combination of the

---

[23] See Gordon (1986, 1992), Harris (1992), and Goldman (1992).

simulation and reliabilism can produce IU judgments that do qualify, according to Goldman, as knowledge.

> On this theory of knowledge, it is certainly possible that IU propositions should be known to be true (or false). For example, certain uses of the simulation heuristic might be reliable ways of arriving at IU beliefs. I say "certain uses" because it is obvious that ill-informed or sloppy simulation has no chance of being generally reliable. . . . But well-informed and sensitive use of the simulation heuristic may indeed be reliable. So the possibility of knowing IU propositions by means of simulation, seems to be genuine. (Goldman 1995, pp. 720–1)

Because examples like this where there is radical interpenetration of economic issues/concepts and those of naturalized epistemology will be the topic of a more careful analysis in later chapters, I will not attempt to ferret out all (or any) of the possible implications here, but just for a moment think of how Goldman's argument might impact economics, and how *very different* the whole project is from the traditional/shelf relationship between economics and philosophy of science. If one believes Goldman's story (and there are of course a myriad of potential criticisms) then interpersonal utility comparisons would be perfectly justified in economic science. The justification would come from a naturalized epistemology that is based on the information-processing approach to the human mind, consistent with recent developments in cognitive science, and still basically normative. In effect, Goldman offers a contemporary naturalized epistemology-based solution to John Stuart Mill's core philosophical problem of reconciling empiricist epistemology, utilitarian ethics, and economics; and it even draws inspiration from Adam Smith's notion of sympathetic understanding.

Although my discussion of Goldman has barely scratched the surface of his extensive philosophical project, enough has been said to get a rough feel for his particular version of naturalized epistemology. The concept of reliabilism should be fairly clear, as should his distinction between individual and social epistemics. There are other second-generation naturalists, but Goldman is one of the most influential and his work has generated an extensive derivative (third-generation?) literature. It also should be clear that there are a number of ways in which such naturalistic approaches can, and do, touch the science of economics. It is now time to consider one economist who has influenced the direction of the naturalistic turn.

4.2.2 H. A. Simon and Human Knowledge

Most economists realize that Herbert Simon is not only a Nobel Prize-winning economist but also a very important contributor to the fields of artificial intelligence and cognitive science. Perhaps less well known to economists is the way in which Simon's theory of satisficing and bounded rationality has influenced the field of naturalized episte-mology. This section will briefly examine Simon's important relationship to this philosophical literature.[24]

When Simon started working on his first book, *Administrative Behavior* (1945), he did not intend to write the germinal contribution in organizational theory and administrative science; the book started out more traditionally, as a work in the foundations of social science under the influence of Rudolf Carnap. The finished work, although it did not employ the terms "satisficing" and "bounded rationality" that later came to be the rigid designators of Simon's position, did basically lay out the intellectual project that was to guide the rest of his professional life. Simon's argument was that the perfect rationality of neoclassical eco-nomics did not, and could not, describe the behavior of real human agents. Economic rationality requires agents to know far more than any real agents could ever know; it requires them to have perfect knowledge of all available choices and all relevant information, and in addition, to have the capacity to compute and execute the optimal choice. For Simon, real human agents have neither the information nor the computational capability to make such perfectly rational choices. In contrast to this "economic man," Simon characterized the "administrative man" who made choices in an environment of limited information and limited computational capacity; a person who found solutions that were "good enough" or "satisfactory" (later satisficing) for the situation at hand, and who employed "rules of thumb" or "heuristics" to facilitate his or her decision making in a less than perfect environment. The type of ratio-nality exhibited by agents who perform in this way came to be called "bounded rationality," and for Simon this was the basic insight that guided his "whole scientific output" (Simon 1991, p. 88).[25]

---

[24] Another economist that will not be discussed but is worthy of more serious research in this regard is Friedrich Hayek. Hayek's seldom-discussed 1952 book on *The Sensory Order* utilized the earlier work of Herman Helmholtz and Johannes Müller. It is now clear (see Meyering 1989 and Barry Smith 1997) that these authors (particularly Helmholtz) advo-cated a view of human knowledge and perception that was not only naturalistic but was also a precursor to many recent developments in cognitive science. See Birner (1999), Caldwell (1997, p. 1875), and Ch. 5 of Mirowski (1999).

[25] Bounded Rationality has experienced a powerful resurgence in recent economic theory (Conlisk 1996; Rubinstein 1998; Sargent 1993), but the way the term is employed in these

The link between bounded rationality and his later work in the field of artificial intelligence (AI) is fairly direct. As Simon explains in the Introduction to the second edition of *Administrative Behavior* (1957a):

> This description of administrative man is essentially a development and formalization of the description in . . . *Administrative Behavior*. But how do we know that it is a *correct* description – more accurate, for example, than the model of economic man? . . . Formalization of the theory over the past several years . . . has made a sharper test possible. For within the past six months, Allen Newell and I have succeeded in describing in detail a decision-making mechanism capable of exhibiting certain complex human problem-solving behavior. . . . In fact, we are now able to simulate such complex human behavior, using this decision-making program, with the aid of an ordinary electronic computer. . . . I do not regard the description of human rationality in Chapters IV and V as hypothetical, but as now having been verified in its main features. (Simon 1957a, pp. xxvi–xxvii)

As Esther-Mirjam Sent explains in a recent discussion of Simon:

> The concepts Simon developed in bounded rationality served as a springboard to his interpretation of artificial intelligence. Simon's bounded rationality program, . . . offered an open window into the workings of the human mind. The same ideas of "heuristic' or "rule-bound" search, "satisficing" behavior, and "goal, sub-goal" strategy that shaped Simon's theory of bounded rationality also became key concepts in his problem-space approach to reproducing human-style reasoning . . . Simon's bounded rationality program embodied ideas for programming a computer how to think. An understanding of the "real" processes at work behind human decision-making allowed Simon to build computers that replicated these processes and to serve his interest in finding out how people made decisions. (Sent 1997, p. 334)

The path-breaking work in AI and cybernetics that established Simon's reputation in his later life, was started as an effort to test – and according to Simon did successfully – the theory of bounded rationality.

recent applications often differs substantially from Simon's original formulation (see Mirowski 1998b and Sent 1997a, 1998a, 1998b).

Expert systems that matched and often exceeded the decision-making performance of human professionals (in chess and elsewhere) were systems designed in the spirit of bounded rationality; such systems searched selectively, employed rules of thumb, and stopped when a satisfactory solution had been found (Newell and Simon, 1972). Thus, bounded rationality, satisficing, artificial intelligence, cognitive science, and the general characterization of the human mind as an information processor are all aspects of the single elaborate research project initiated in part as an effort to find a realistic alternative to the rational economic man of neoclassical economics.

While Simon clearly played an important role in the development of the cognitive science/AI perspective that underwrites the naturalized epistemologies of Goldman and others, his influence does not stop with this important, but background, work. Simon's own research has moved beyond the relatively well-structured problems of his early work to the solution of problems that are much more complex and have a much less rigid structure. One such ill-structured problem is *the problem of scientific discovery*. If it is possible to model the complex decision making that takes place in games, government, business, and industry, then an obvious next step would seem to be to model the type of decision making involved in the process of scientific discovery (and from a purely naturalistic perspective, solve one of the fundamental problems in the philosophy of science). These so-called discovery programs are "aimed at studying the process of scientific discovery by constructing computer programs that are capable of making discoveries and that simulate, at a grosser or finer level of approximation, the paths that have been followed by distinguished scientists on their roads to important discoveries" (Kulkarni and Simon 1988, p. 139).[26] A number of philosophers, including Clark Glymour (1980) and Ronald Giere (1988, 1992, 1999), have directly applied Simon's work on scientific discovery as well as his general notion of satisficing to the philosophy of science. As Giere summarizes Simon's role in the philosophical literature:

> Clark Glymour was among the first philosophers of science to grasp the possibility of deploying methods and results from the cognitive science, particularly artificial intelligence, to the philosophy of science itself. (Herbert Simon, who I definitely would

---

[26] This particular paper (and it is just one of many) uses the computer program KEKADA to "model as concretely as possible the heuristics Hans Krebs employed in his discovery of the urea cycle" (Kulkarni and Simon 1988, p. 173). See Langley, Simon, Bradshaw, and Zytkow (1987) for other examples, and Simon (1992) for a general discussion of the relationship between discovery programs and Simon's earlier work.

wish to claim as a philosopher of science, must surely have been first). (Giere 1992, p. xxvii)

The next step in the project would seem to be to attempt to account for the social nature of science by viewing scientific communities from the perspective of "distributed artificial intelligence" (DAI). Paul Thagard has made important contributions to this literature.

> DAI is a relatively new branch of the field of artificial intelligence that is concerned with how problems can be solved by networks of intelligent computers that communicate with each other. Although I assume the cognitivist view that individual scientists are information processors, I shall argue that the view of a scientific community as a network of information processors is not reductionist and does not eliminate or subordinate the role of sociologists or social historians in understanding science. I shall also show that a DAI approach provides a helpful perspective on the interesting social question of the cognitive division of labor. (Thagard 1993, p. 49)

It seems that we have now come full circle. Simon started with a problem in economic methodology, the problem of finding a scientifically satisfactory theory of economic rationality; his search for a more adequate economic theory led him to bounded rationality and then into cognitive science and AI. This work contributed to the cognitive revolution that facilitated the development of versions of naturalized epistemology that characterize the individual scientist as a type of information processor. These epistemics now challenge the epistemological mainstream that has existed since at least the time of Descartes and Bacon. But Kuhn and others have made it clear that understanding the individual scientist is not enough: science is fundamentally social. Now we have philosophers using DAI in an attempt to understand science as a cognitive *and* social endeavor, and they are suggesting there are benefits to a "cognitive division of labor" (which sounds a lot like an economic approach to scientific knowledge). But all this is getting us ahead of our story. It is now time to move away from cognitive science for a while and look at a different (but related) approach to naturalized epistemology, that which employs evolutionary notions from biological science.

4.3 Encouragement from Darwin: Evolutionary Epistemology

This section will discuss an alternative version of naturalized epistemology – evolutionary epistemology – a version where the naturalizing base is evolutionary biology.[27] In simplest possible terms, evolutionary epistemology argues that there is an interesting and exploitable relationship between the process of biological evolution and the development of human knowledge. Evolution, not psychology or information processing, is the operative metaphor for this second version of naturalized epistemology.

This section is divided into two parts. The first subsection introduces the general notion of evolutionary epistemology and briefly examines the work of two influential contributors. Although this first subsection is designed to convey the general spirit of the evolutionary approach, it will barely scratch the surface of this diverse and rapidly expanding field.[28] The second subsection is concerned with one (small) subset of the available evolutionary approaches; those claiming to have an explicitly Popperian lineage. The motivation for giving separate consideration to these Popperian perspectives is the direct connection that such evolutionary views have to economics and economic methodology: first, Popper's general influence on economic methodology, and, second, economic ideas such as the "invisible hand" and the "marketplace of scientific ideas" appear most explicitly in the Popperian version of the evolutionary approach.

4.3.1 Biology and Human Knowledge

As Michael Bradie points out in his survey (1986) of evolutionary epistemology, the field actually contains two distinct but related subprograms: a more biological program, that uses evolutionary theory to explain the development of particular cognitive structures in humans and animals (brains, sensory systems, etc.), and a more epistemologically oriented program, that uses evolutionary theory to account for the growth of scientific knowledge. He calls the first program "the evolution of cognitive mechanisms program (EEM)," and the second program "the evolution of theories program (EET)" (Bradie 1986 and 1998). EEM involves the direct embedding of the cognitive into the biological,

---

[27] Perhaps "alternative" is too strong, since evolutionary and cognitive approaches are often complements rather than substitutes. Some authors (Kitcher 1992, and Rosenberg 1996, for instance) even argue as if evolutionary concepts were essential to every naturalized epistemology. Although one can undoubtedly find at least a trace of biology in every naturalist view, it is equally clear that some approaches are much more explicit about the role of, and focus almost exclusively on, evolutionary biology; these are the versions of naturalism that I will call evolutionary epistemology.

[28] The Cziko and Campbell (1990) bibliography of evolutionary epistemology runs forty pages (subsuming the earlier bibliographies in Campbell 1974 and Campbell, Heyes, Cecilia, and Callebaut 1987); it is continually revised, and at the time of this writing the revised version runs over 1,100 entries.

whereas EET involved the use of formal analogy between the two perspectives. EEM is mostly descriptive, whereas EET is (or can be) both descriptive and prescriptive. I will briefly discuss each of these in turn, starting with the EEM program, since it seems to relate most directly to the cognitive approach of Goldman and others, and then turning to EET, which has the most direct contact with economics and the sociological approaches examined in the next chapter.

It is not immediately apparent how or why EEM – a theory about the evolution of insect tympana and human cerebral cortexes – would have anything directly to do with the naturalized epistemology discussed in this chapter. Actually, the relationship between contemporary[29] EEM and naturalized epistemology is rather subtle; to help clarify it, recall how knowledge is characterized in cognitive approaches such as Goldman's reliabilism. According to reliabilism, science is an efficient information processing system, one that constantly updates its priors in ways that generate high truth ratios (traded off against speed, power, etc.); it gives us an increasingly reliable handle on the world. The problem, it is argued, is that whereas science might be reliable, it has no way to explain how the representational systems of science (like theories) "hook up to the world" (Churchland and Churchland 1983). To use an older philosophical parlance (one that most contemporary naturalists would reject) reliabilism may give us an instrumentalist defense of scientific practice, but it does not seem to give us a realist one. Even if the world exists and science produces increasingly reliable representations of it, we still do not know that we have solid contact, that is, how, or if, those representations "hook up." A naturalist can not seek comfort in foundations – we are always afloat in Neurath's boat, constantly revising and updating our beliefs – but even if our method of updating is reliable, how is it that we are honing in on (or there even exist) accurate representations?

Enter evolutionary biology and a version of proof (or perhaps persuasion) by contradiction. Suppose not; suppose that our most reliable representations were way off, that we were radically unhooked – then of course we wouldn't be here. EEM tells us that our cognitive mechanisms – our eyes, our brains, our inference algorithms – have been selected for *referential competence*. We are organisms, and organisms are calibrated by nature (Churchland and Churchland 1983, p. 13); if we hadn't been

---

[29] I say "contemporary EEM" because the program has a long history going back into the late nineteenth century and including important work by Konrad Lorenz in the twentieth (see Campbell 1960; Danailov and Tögel 1990; Lorenz 1977; Munz 1993; or references Cziko and Campbell 1990, bibliography). Despite this history, I will focus exclusively on the contemporary version of EEM.

initially close we wouldn't be here to be asking the question. As Philip Kitcher summarizes the argument:

> A promising and popular defense . . . is to find "encouragement in Darwin." If our initial cognitive equipment were as unfortunate as the skeptic portrays it as being, then, the suggestion runs, our ancestors would have been eliminated by natural selection. They weren't, so it wasn't. In this way, we can appeal to Darwinian evolutionary theory to support the idea that our initial ways of classifying stimuli must correspond to objective regularities in nature, and our modes of reasoning must work reliably in producing accurate representations. (Kitcher 1992, p. 91)

The contact points between EET and philosophy of science (and economics) are not nearly as narrow as the contact points are for EEM. Versions of EET compete with not only other version of naturalism, but more traditional approaches to the philosophy of science as well. There are many different versions of EET, but they all share the common theme that scientific theories get "selected" by nature through a process that is similar to the process by which nature selects species and their characteristics. There is "survival of the fittest" (or at least fitter) among scientific theories much as with living organisms; those that survive are more fit, and, at least in some versions, are more likely to be true, than those that are not selectively retained. This is clearly a naturalized vision of the growth of knowledge; it explains the evolution of science in terms of the science of evolution. These evolutionary versions of naturalism could be revolutionary in their epistemic purpose, but they usually are not; they are usually offered as a version of scientific realism, or more specifically, a way of "saving" scientific realism from the relativism of Kuhn and other critics, and are thus reformist in their naturalistic spirit.[30]

---

[30] It is important to note that evolutionary epistemology (particularly EET) has generated a massive critical literature, some of it directed at the general idea of evolutionary epistemology, and some – actually more – at specific approaches to the topic. Although there is not room to discuss this critical literature in any serious way, let me in passing point out two of the standard arguments. One is that science is more Lamarkian than Darwinian; mutations are not random and variations are not blind. The second is that fitness is not the same (or at least evolutionary epistemologists haven't explained how it is the same) as truth. Almost every author in the field (including the Popperians discussed in the next section) proffers a response to these two criticisms, but at this point none seems to be entirely satisfactory. Bradie (1986), Kitcher (1992), O'Hear (1987), and Sterelny (1994) discuss these and other criticisms.

The person most often given credit for introducing the term "evolutionary epistemology" is psychologist/philosopher Donald Campbell (1960, 1974, 1990), and his extensive work in, and sustained advocacy for, the evolutionary approach has been crucial to the program's ongoing development. Although a few of the details have changed over the thirty-plus years that Campbell promoted his "blind-variation-and-selective-retention" model of human thought and knowledge, his basic argument remained the same: the right stuff gets selected in both our cognitive mechanisms (EEM) and our scientific theories (EET).[31] "Campbell is among the hard-liners in evolutionary epistemology in arguing for the applicability of a 'blind-selection-and-retention' model to explain not only the evolution of all biological structures (and not merely cognitive ones) but also the growth of scientific knowledge which is more properly viewed as part of the . . . EET program" (Bradie 1986, p. 406). I will not examine Campbell's ideas in any detail, since much of his work has been integrated into the Popperian evolutionary approach discussed in the next section.[32]

Another, epistemologically weaker, version of evolutionary epistemology is offered by David Hull (1988).[33] Hull provides a "selectionist" model that, although based on evolutionary ideas, is only weakly (or non) prescriptive, and can be applied outside the strictly scientific domain. As he characterizes his own project.

> In this book I do not attempt to answer any traditional problems in epistemology. . . . Instead I set out a general analysis of selection processes that is equally applicable to biological, social, and conceptual development. Selection processes have several features that are worthy of pointing out, but one of them is not that they guarantee the generation of perfectly adapted organisms or infallibly true statements. . . . If urging the use of successful methods amounts to epistemology, then my concerns are "epistemological," but only in the most anemic sense of the term. (Hull 1988, p. 13)

[31] It is interesting that a large portion of Campbell's influential 1960 paper is a critique of the work of Herbert Simon and his associates. The reason is of course that Simon requires heuristics and efficient algorithms, whereas Campbell would have *blind* variation and selective retention. Campbell eventually concluded that his view was not really that different from Simon's; his argument was basically that heuristics can be the unit of selection.

[32] Campbell discussed the few ways that his view differed from Popper's in Campbell (1988).

[33] Despite the fact that Hull's work is almost always included in discussions of evolutionary epistemology (Bradie 1986; Munz 1993; Sterelny 1994, for example), he himself does not actually use the term, ostensibly because it is too often associated with traditional (foundationalist) approaches to scientific knowledge.

Hull's model of the scientific process is, in many respects, a Darwinized version of Kuhn's view. Like Kuhn, it is the social structure of science that matters, not the cognitive profiles of the individual scientists: but unlike Kuhn, there is a detailed discussion of exactly how, through an evolutionary selection process, the collective goals of science actually come to be manifested. For Hull, the replicators (genes in biology) are scientific theories, beliefs about the goals of science, accumulated data, and all of the related intellectual materials of science; the scientists themselves are the "interactors" (organisms in biology) that carry the replicators into the environment of science. The evolution of scientific knowledge is viewed as a selection process whereby replicators increase or decrease their relative frequency, relative to other replicators. This selection process takes place within the community of science and the ultimate outcome, the replicators that survive, is a product of the structure and characteristics of that community. Hull emphasizes that scientists have a wide range of goals and interests – intellectual, professional, career, social/political, and so forth – but the structure of the scientific community is such that the collective goals of the growth of scientific knowledge is almost always achieved. As he says: "One of the chief messages of this book is that factionalism, social cohesion, and professional interests need not frustrate the traditional goal of knowledge acquisition" (Hull 1988, p. 26). Not only "need not" such interests frustrate knowledge acquisition, in places Hull argues for an even stronger thesis, that "some of the behavior that appears to be the most improper actually facilitates the manifest goals of science ... the least productive scientists tend to behave the most admirably, while those who make the greatest contribution just as frequently behave the most deplorably" (Hull 1988, p. 32). Even though Hull does not refer to economics explicitly, this argument is essentially the *invisible hand* story from economics – given the right institutional structure, self-interested and ostensibly antisocial behavior on the part of individuals will lead to the socially optimal collective outcome.[34] Hull basically argues that the social structure of science provides an effective framework for the selective retention of replicators that accomplish science's collective goals. The reason that this is a Darwinized version of Kuhn and not a full-blown (prescriptive) evolutionary epistemology is that Hull says little or nothing about how the goals of science connect up with truth or representation. Within the community of science, theories (replicators) come and go, and for Kuhn (at least the standard reading of Kuhn) the process was

---

[34] Hull later came to be more explicit about the economic connection and the role of the invisible hand (Hull 1997). See Wray (2000) and Ylikoski (1996) for criticisms of Hull's use of the invisible hand concept.

irrational. For Hull, the process is much more rational, analogous to the selective process at work in biological evolution; the structure of science is such that what emerges is consistent with the collective goals of the scientific community, even though individual scientists may be pursuing goals that seem to be at odds with the collective interest. Hull reconciles the behavior of the individual scientist with the notion of science as a collectively held paradigm, but he does not address, or at least does not systematically address, the traditional epistemological question of how those paradigms hook up with the world. Such epistemic issues get more attention in the Popperian tradition examined in the next section.

4.3.2 Popperian Evolutionary Epistemology

There was very little in the discussion of falsificationism in Chapter 3 to suggest that Popper took an evolutionary, or even a naturalistic, approach to the philosophy of science. The method of bold conjecture and severe test seemed to have originated entirely from traditional philosophical analysis; it was based on logical and rational inquiry, and, while Popper seemed to believe that was actually practiced by the best scientists, it was not derived directly from the history of science, nor was it dependent on any particular scientific theory as a starting point. Although Popper's conjectural realism and his conventionalism about the empirical basis may have technically freed him from the charge of foundationalism, most philosophers (even some supporters) continue to interpret falsificationism as merely an alternative answer to the questions posed by, and based on the same philosophical tradition as, positivism. Although this nonevolutionary characterization may be accurate for Popper's early work such as the *Logic of Scientific Discovery* (1934, 1959) it seems much less appropriate for his later work such as *Objective Knowledge* (1972). It is clear that Popper adopted some version (or versions) of evolutionary epistemology in his later writings, and, while he personally considered this evolutionary turn to be just an extension of his original approach, it is possible, with hindsight, to read it as a variant of naturalized philosophy of science.[35] The problem with trying to discuss "Popper's" version of evolutionary epistemology is that, while his writings on the topic were highly suggestive, his position was

---

[35] It should be noted that most Popperians do not consider this (or any other) change to be a "turn" at all, but rather to be simply the natural unfolding and clarification of the ideas originally present in Popper's *Logik der Forschung* (1934). Whether it represents a change in Popper's view or merely the further elaboration of his original idea is an exegetical issue that is not really relevant to the current discussion. The fact is that Popper started to explicitly characterize his position as an evolutionary approach to knowledge sometime in the 1960s and Popper (1972) is the first serious presentation of this evolutionary view.

never presented in the form of a single coherent thesis; Popper (1972) is a collection of essays, and his other writings on the topic are spread out over a number of different works, for different audiences, and never seem to take on any finished final form. Fortunately, other philosophers have provided more systematic renditions of the Popperian approach to evolutionary epistemology. I will first examine the evolutionary perspective of Munz (1993) and then turn briefly to Bartley and Radnitzky, two Popperian authors who directly involve economics in their evolutionary vision of the growth of scientific knowledge.

Munz (1993) offers systematic presentation of "philosophical Darwinism,"[36] an evolutionary perspective that he claims adds "very little to the Popperian schema" (Munz 1993, p. 219). Despite the clear debt to Popper, Munz also considers – and in some cases even integrates – many of the philosophical developments that have been discussed in the last two chapters: Kuhn's theory-ladenness and social emphasis, Quine's underdetermination and naturalistic focus, the cognitive turn, and so on. Like most evolutionary visions of the growth of scientific knowledge, Munz sees knowledge acquisition as continuous with biological evolution. He sees organisms as "embodied theories" and linguistically expressed theories as "disembodied organisms." Both evolve through a process of chance mutation and selective retention. In the case of biological organisms (embodied) those that survive "represent a comparatively truthful description of at least their immediate environment, and their survival vouchsafed that kind of truthfulness" (Munz 1993, p. 169); this process is natural and automatic, and the sorting out is "done by differential birth and death rates" (Munz 1993, p. 169). In the case of scientific theories (disembodied) the process is slightly different, but works in essentially the same way. Following Popper he says:

> We learn and pick up information . . . by selecting it from an abundance of conjectures which are guesses and stabs in the dark. In this form, the theory is directly opposed to the view that we pick up information by observing, the world and by being, so to speak, instructed by it. The "knower" makes proposals, and

---

[36] Munz denies supporting "evolutionary epistemology." He says:

> It has . . . become customary to refer to the cognitive consequences of biology as evolutionary epistemology – that is, as a theory of knowledge which solves many or most traditional problems of epistemology with the help of the theory of evolution. There is no consensus about and not even a clear understanding of what is meant by evolutionary epistemology. The subject is frequently mentioned, but none of the many references to it have much in common. (Munz 1993, p. 205)

> these proposals are scrutinised by reality. The process is, of
> course, not automatic. The scrutiny is the result of conscious crit-
> icism carried out by the proposer or by other people in the light
> of their experience of the world. (Munz 1993, p. 144)

To connect this process of selection for fitness to the notion of discovering true theories, Munz employs Popper's notion of "verisimilitude"
or truthlikeness. "The notion that knowledge acquisition progresses by
this method of selection from a large number of proposals allows us to
see this progress as yielding more and more verisimilitude" (Munz 1993,
p. 179).

Although Munz admits that "adaptation," "fitness," and "truth" are
not normally considered to be exactly the same things, he argues that
this is because of problems associated with our traditional notion of
truth: a "correspondence" between a sentence and the facts. Munz finds
this traditional notion problematic: "A sentence is not the sort of entity
which can 'correspond' to anything other than another sentence" (Munz
1993, p. 212). If we think of truth as approximation to the true conditions
of the environment, then the better adapted, the more fit, would also
be the "verisimilitudinously true" (Munz 1993, p. 205). This, Munz
argues, makes his evolutionary theory of knowledge a type of realism:
"hypothetical realism."[37]

> We know that . . . knowledge would be different if the world
> were different; because if the world were different, it would have
> selected different embodied theories, and we would have had
> to select different disembodied organisms. But the selection
> process is not perfect and allows the survival of theories and
> organisms which are not a perfect fit. Hence we call this realism
> hypothetical realism in order to distinguish it from common or
> vulgar realism. (Munz 1993, p. 182)

Whether or not one is persuaded by Munz's argument, it does leave
the door open for a version of the invisible hand argument from economics. The reason is that the degree of adaptation depends on the
competition.

> If there is a great deal of competition, the organism can survive
> only if it is very minutely adapted to the environment. . . . But
> suppose an organism in an environment in which it has, for some
> reason or other, few or no competitors. In such a case compar-

---

[37] This is effectively the same as the fallibilist or conjectural realism discussed in the Popper
section of Chapter 3.

atively little adaptation is required for the organism to survive and it will be correspondingly difficult to think of it as a true embodied theory. In other words, the degree of fitness required for survival depends on the absence or presence of competitors. (Munz 1993, p. 161)

Carrying this argument over to the disembodied theories of science, the more competition the better the adaptation, the closer the fit, and, thus, the more verisimilitude associated with the theories that survive. As Munz put it in an earlier work:

> The final and perhaps greatest merit of the formula consists in the way in which ... explains that the growth of knowledge, through undetermined and unplanned and not designed, nevertheless, by the sheer accumulation of error eliminations, moves in the direction of truth. The strategy of the argument is perhaps not new. It is certainly reminiscent of the old argument of the invisible hand which, in the absence of conscious and willed design, nevertheless leads toward an optimization of economic returns. (Munz 1985, pp. 255–6)

This economic argument about competition and the invisible hand is prosecuted even more heavily in the Popperian evolutionary approach of W. W. Bartley and Gerard Radnitzky (Bartley 1984, 1990; Radnitzky and Bartley 1987; Wible 1998, Chs. 5 and 6). Evolutionary authors such as Campbell, Popper, and Munz are primarily concerned with explaining scientific knowledge (explaining the knowledge that we have) and then (secondarily) with relating this view of knowledge to traditional philosophical issues such as realism. Bartley and Radnitzky start from the same basic evolutionary approach of these authors, but their focus is less on explaining knowledge or answering traditional philosophical questions, and more on social reform: particularly the reform of our scientific and educational institutions. In other words, their focus, particularly Bartley (1990), is on the policy (science and educational policy) implications of the Popperian evolutionary approach to knowledge.

As Popper and Munz have argued, verisimilitude requires competition, and Bartley and Radnitzky make a direct extension of this argument to the competitive marketplace of scientific ideas. If the marketplace of ideas is competitive, if there are many alternative hypotheses competing in an open critical environment, then knowledge will emerge from this marketplace of ideas in the same way that efficiency emerges from a competitive market. On this view, the growth of knowledge does not require the collective control of a knowledge authority, nor does it require the "proper" scientific attitude on the part of scientists; it only requires an open and competitive environment. For Bartley, in particular, knowledge is a type of wealth, and the competitive marketplace of ideas generates this type of wealth in exactly the same way as the competitive market generates economic wealth.[38] He states this position quite baldly:

> As almost any thinker has experienced, the free and open competition of ideas does tend to lead, more directly than any other path, to the advancement of knowledge. And thus the institution known as the market, to the extent that it involves such competition, seems to be an appropriate model for trying to understand how knowledge, as well as other forms of wealth, increases. (Bartley 1990, p. 26)

Thus, it again seems that we have come full circle. We started with Quine's suggestion that there is "encouragement in Darwin" (1969c, p. 126) – a naturalized biological vision that was closely tied to the cognitive turn discussed in the first part of this chapter – and now here we are back at economics, with certain Popperian evolutionary epistemologists arguing for the competitive marketplace of scientific ideas as the most efficient industrial organization of our cognitive lives.[39] Is this philosophy, or biological science, or economics? Perhaps there is no answer; perhaps it is becoming clear that such watertight disciplinary distinctions are not phenomena that occur naturally within the literature of metascience. The boundary between economics and epistemology has repeatedly been shown to be neither crisp nor stable; it is, instead, an amorphous partition: fuzzy, fluid over time, and subject to constant renegotiation. Although it may be possible to discern a clear border at one particular point in time and for one particular group of discussants, the distinction quickly vanishes when exposed to either time series or cross-sectional variation. Perhaps rather than trying to erect and maintain such artificial barriers, it would be more fruitful to investigate the various multiple border crossings and interpenetrations that continually occur within the relevant discourse: a view that will be further kindled by the sociological approach discussed in the next chapter. Before moving on to that

---

[38] Bartley has direct connections with economics: he has always been a strong advocate of free market political philosophy, and was, until his death in 1990, the editor of Hayek's collected works. Because of this connection, Bartley's use of terms like market, competition, and equilibrium should be given an Austrian rather than a Walrasian reading.

[39] Chapter 8 will discuss many other, non-Popperian views, which employ economic argumentation in a related way.

topic, though, we have one more development in cognitive and biological naturalism to discuss.

4.4 Eliminative Materialism and the Philosophy of Mind

A number of different naturalisms have been discussed in this chapter and almost all of them, cognitive science-based and evolution-based alike, have been reformist in their epistemic spirit; they wanted to "fix" the problems of epistemology, to give new answers to the traditional epistemic questions. But epistemic reform is not the only possibility; not all naturalisms grounded in cognitive science and/or evolutionary biology approach epistemology from the perspective of the repairman, some would like to totally demolish it. There are certain contemporary naturalisms that seek to *eliminate* the traditional epistemological questions altogether; their goal is not to naturalize epistemology, but to naturalize it away. The philosophical program that I will discuss in this final section, *eliminative materialism*, is one such view.

Recall that knowledge has traditionally been defined as "justified true belief." Gettier-type examples questioned the "justified" part of the definition, and a number of authors have challenged the traditional notion of "truth," but no one thus far discussed in this (or any previous) chapter has explicitly questioned the notion that knowledge is a type of "belief." The debate has been about the exact specification of the special properties that beliefs must have in order to be called knowledge, not about whether knowledge was a special type of belief. Eliminative materialists challenge just this presumption. According to the strongest form of eliminative materialism, recent developments in neuroscience support the claim that "beliefs" *simply do not exist*, and, thus, all talk about beliefs should be eliminated from scientific discourse and replaced by talk about that which does exist: neurophysiological processes in the human brain. Of course, if beliefs do not exist, then it would seem rather futile to be searching for those justified and true beliefs that have traditionally been called knowledge; in other words, traditional epistemology is simply a waste of time. To see how the various parts of this eliminativist argument fit together it is useful to start with the concept of *folk psychology*.

Consider our commonsense explanations of human behavior: the way that we explain the behavior of our friends, family, colleagues, and even ourselves. Normally such explanations are not given in behaviorist terms (conditioned response), or Freudian terms (the struggle of ids and egos), or in neurophysiological terms (chemical processes in the brain); they are given in *intentional* terms – in terms of the *beliefs* and the *desires* of the individuals involved. Why did I just get up from the word processor? Well, I got up to get a cup of coffee – I had a desire for another cup of coffee; I had a belief that there was still some in the pot in the kitchen; and I got up to get a cup. Maybe conditioning was involved, perhaps even how I feel about my mother, and my physical movement was most certainly initiated by neural firings, but these are not the way that I *explain* what I did. I explain what I did in terms of my beliefs and desires. Such explanations are called *folk psychology* (FP), since they constitute our traditional (folk) explanatory schema (as well as the explanatory schemata of most social sciences).[40]

Despite the fact that FP plays such a significant part of our everyday lives,[41] it has recently come under harsh criticism as an empirical theory of human behavior. Authors like Stephen Stich (1983),[42] Patricia Churchland (1986, 1987) and Paul Churchland (1984, 1992) have argued aggressively that FP is *"at best* a highly superficial theory, a partial and unpenetrating gloss on a deeper and more complex reality" (Churchland 1992, p. 7) and that there is the serious "possibility that its principles are radically false and that its ontology is an illusion" (Churchland 1992, p. 6).[43] FP can not explain things like mental illness, sleep, memory, learning, or the ability to "catch a flyball on the run" (Churchland 1992, p. 7), and, perhaps even more important, it is exactly the same theory that was used to explain behavior by our ancient ancestors (including the behavior of the Greek gods) and as such it has not advanced in the last few thousand years.[44] Because folk physics, folk medicine, and folk astronomy were found to be false and replaced, why "is there any reason to think that ancient camel drivers would have greater insight or better luck when the subject at hand was the structure of their own minds rather

---

[40] Economists will quickly realize that microeconomic explanations, at least microeconomic explanations of *individual* behavior, are also of this type. Microeconomic explanations are a special class of folk psychological explanations, those where desires are restricted to things like utility (preference, profit, etc.) and beliefs are restricted to certain constraints (budget, cost, etc.) and parameters (prices, etc.). The important question of the relationship between economics and folk psychology will be deferred until Chapter 7.

[41] And even our moral and judicial codes: The difference between first-degree murder and a tragic accident is merely a question of intentionality.

[42] Stich no longer holds these views. His recent book explains how he awoke from his "dogmatic slumbers" (Stich 1996, p. 5).

[43] This argument was presented much earlier by Feyerabend (1963) and Rorty (1965, 1970). Although this eliminativism may seem surprising in light of these authors' later work, we will see (in Chapter 6) that at least for Rorty there is not necessarily anything incongruous about this position and his later philosophical attitude.

[44] "To use Imre Lakatos's terms, FP is a stagnant or degenerating research program and has been for millennia" (Churchland 1992, p. 8).

than the structure of matter or of the cosmos" (Stich 1983, pp. 229–30). As Paul Churchland summarizes the critique:

> FP suffers explanatory failures on an epic scale, that it has been stagnant for at least twenty-five centuries, and that its categories appear (so far) to be incommensurable with, or orthogonal to, the categories of the background physical science whose long term claim to explain human behavior seems undeniable. Any theory that meets this description must be allowed a serious candidate for outright *elimination*. (Churchland 1992, p. 9, emphasis added)

Now, if one wants to eliminate FP, because it is a bad theory of human behavior, then one must be able to show that FP actually is a *theory* of human behavior; poetry and fiction are ways of talking about human action, but no one is arguing that they should be eliminated and replaced by neurophysiology because they have failed as scientific theories. This is exactly the rather confusing position that eliminativists such as Patricia and Paul Churchland are in; they seem to be defending the empirical status of FP, but that is because they must first defend it *as* an empirical theory of human behavior before they can reject it for failing as such a theory.

So if we eliminate FP, what should replace it? According to eliminative materialism, it should be replaced by "matured neuroscience." Since neuroscience views all mental stuff as physical brain stuff, the resulting approach is, in addition to being eliminative of course, strictly physicalist or materialist. The argument, like the argument of all of the authors discussed in this chapter, is an argument for naturalization. In the case of eliminative materialism it is not naturalization on cognitive science *or* on evolutionary biology, it is naturalization on a *combination of the two*. For example, Patricia Churchland (1987) argues that a number of recent developments – technological change in the neurosciences; cheap, fast, computing that allows us to simulate neural networks; and many successful clinical and animal studies on the capacities of nervous systems – all contribute to a new understanding of how nervous systems function in the context of an organism's biological evolution. This is, according its supporters, naturalization on the very best recent work in both cognitive science and biology; it is (eliminative) naturalism based on our matured understanding of the biological processes that underlie the development, and thus govern the behavior, of the human nervous system and its cognitive capacities. The argument has much in common with both Goldman's cognitive approach and evolutionary epistemology.

> Looked at from an evolutionary point of view, the principal function of nervous systems is to enable the organism to move appropriately. Boiled down to essentials, a nervous system enables the organism to succeed in the four F's: feeding, fleeing, fighting, and reproducing. The principal chore of nervous systems is to get the body parts where they should be in order that the organism may survive. Insofar as representations serve that function, representations are a good thing.... a fancier style of representing is advantageous *so long as it is geared to the organism's way of life and enhances the organism's chances of survival.* (Churchland 1987, pp. 548–9, emphasis in original)

Although eliminative materialism combines cognitive and biological naturalization, it is still radically different from most of the views discussed above; it is revolutionary and eliminative about epistemology. Unlike the other approaches where cognitive science or biology could be used to answer traditional epistemic questions, eliminative materialism has abolished belief and all belief-couched questions, even those about the particular characteristics of those beliefs we call knowledge. So if this "mature neuroscience" that has replaced FP can not tell us which beliefs we ought to have (i.e., which are knowledge), then what epistemic work does such a theory do? How can one have a scientific philosophy that does not answer any questions about what is, or should be, knowledge?

The answer for eliminative materialists is to change the traditional set of questions. There is a physical world, and one can still ask how our theories or representations "hook up" to this world, but what one can not do is to frame the question in terms of having correct beliefs. The details are beyond the scope of the current discussion, but briefly the trick is to get away from thinking about theories (representations) as sentences (propositions). This, it is argued, will require that we adopt a new way of thinking about both truth (as representations will not be in sentence form) and explanation (as the D-N model is firmly grounded in the sentence view of scientific theories). Of course, these changes are all wrapped up with the original rejection of belief talk; without beliefs we lose "aboutness" and thus propositional attitudes, in turn the sentence characterization of theories, and finally truth and the D-N model of explanation. It is all tied up together, and according to eliminative materialism, it should all go out the window together.

> [I]t seems to me that the general frame of reference within which we might hope to discover how humans learn, understand, and

perceive is undergoing a major reconfiguration. Most of the questions which used to preoccupy us as graduate students and whose answers seemed necessary to advancing the general program in epistemology, now look either peripheral or misguided, and the general program itself looks troubled. . . . It is doubtful that knowledge in general is sentential; rather, representations are typically structures of a quite different sort. . . . And what of truth? If representational structures are not sentences (propositions), they are not truth-valuable; if they are to be evaluated, it must be in some other way. Consequently, the very concept of truth appears to be in for major reconsideration. (Churchland 1987, p. 545)

What is required to fill this (massive) breach is a way to "conceive of knowledge, and of explanatory understanding, in a systematically different way" (Churchland 1992, p. 121). The new approach is a family of theories called *connectionism* or *parallel distributed processing*.

If representational structures are not sentence-like, what are they? If computation is not logic-like, what is it like? Connectionism (also known as Parallel Distributed Processing, or PDP) is important, because it constitutes the beginnings of a genuine, systematic alternative to the "grand old paradigm." It appears to have the resources to provide neurobiologically plausible answers to these central questions. (Churchland 1987, p. 549)[45]

There is no question that connectionism has already brought about major changes in the way many cognitive scientists conceive of cognition. However, as we see it, what makes certain kinds of connectionist models genuinely revolutionary is the support they lend to a thoroughgoing eliminativism about some of the central posits of commonsense (or "folk") psychology. Our focus here is on beliefs or propositional memories, though the argument generalizes straightforwardly to all the other propositional attitudes. If we are right, the consequences of this kind of connectionism extends well beyond the confines of cognitive science, since these models, if successful, will require a radical reorientation in the way we think about ourselves. (Stich 1996, pp. 91–2)

---

[45] Part II of Churchland (1992) has a number of papers that describe connectionism and PDP (and their epistemic import) in detail. Also see Ch. 2 of Stich (1996).

This is radical and revolutionary naturalism. It starts with contemporary neuroscience as a naturalizing base and ends up by not only rejecting the Received View but essentially throwing out all of what is conventionally accepted about knowledge, explanation, and truth. It is an approach that is broadly consistent with Quine's naturalism (see the epigraph at the beginning of this chapter) and it also "appears to vindicate some central elements in Kuhn's perspective as well" (Churchland 1992, p. 159).

A viewpoint as radical as eliminative materialism will obviously not be without its critics. Although I will not attempt to survey the many criticisms that have been raised against eliminative materialism,[46] I would like to close this chapter by mentioning just one of the critical responses, because it involves a concept that also emerges in the recent literature on economic methodology. This is the concept of *supervenience*.

Eliminative materialism argues that since beliefs can not be reduced to physiological processes in the brain, they should be eliminated. But why? Even if we accept that mental activity is "ultimately" the result of (exclusively the result of) physical processes in the brain, must we accept the claim that one-to-one reduction of the mental to the physical, or the outright rejection of the mental, are the only two possibilities? What if mental activity is caused by physical processes in the brain but each mental event has (possibly) more than one physical instantiation? If two people had identical brains, identical in every single physical and chemical way, it seems reasonable to say that they would have the same thoughts (mental activity), but just because two people have the same thought, say hunger or lust, it need not imply that their brains are physically and chemically in exactly the same state. Two different people can think the same thought without having the same brain, but if they had the same brain, they would have the same thoughts. This idea is captured in the concept of supervenience.[47] Property A *supervenes* on property B if and only if fixing B fixes A, or in other words, if there can be no variation in A without variation in B. Thus, if the mental supervenes on the physical, it says that there can not be different thoughts without different physical processes; it leaves open the possibility of different physical processes producing the same thought. The supervenience of the mental on the physical allows one to maintain a commitment to a materialist ontology without requiring the reduction of mental kinds to physical kinds. There has been a protracted debate about whether such supervenience can be used to reconcile folk psychology and materialism (see

---

[46] Stich (1996) is a good guide to the critical literature, as he was once an outspoken advocate of eliminative materialism but has now been persuaded by its many critics.

[47] See Kim (1982, 1984) or Kincaid (1988, 1998).

Ch. 5 of Stich, 1996), and it is a debate that remains a long way from closure.

Although the concept of supervenience is most often associated with eliminative materialism and the philosophy of mind, it can also be applied to a number of traditional debates within the philosophy of social science (including economics[48]). First, consider the question of methodological individualism in social science. Although methodological individualism traditionally implies reductionism – reduce the social to the individual – supervenience allows for another possibility. If the social *supervenes* on the individual (or the sum of the individuals), then the same individual behavior would produce the same social behavior, but social behavior could not necessarily be reduced to the behavior of individual agents. In other words, "same individual" implies "same social," but "same social" need not imply "same individual." Similarly, supervenience also provides a different way of thinking about the relationship between micro- and macroeconomics. The standard way of thinking about "microfoundations" is reductionist – the macro needs to be reduced to the micro (usually a specific form of micro) and if it can not be reduced to micro then it needs to be eliminated – but if the macro simply supervenes on the micro, then it is possible to maintain that micro behavior is in some sense more basic (same micro implies same macro), but not require that macroeconomic features be reduced to microeconomic behavior (same macro need not imply same micro). These are just two of the many ways that the concept of supervenience has been applied to issues in the philosophy of social science, but they seem to be the two applications that have the most obvious relevance to economics. This final social twist on the supervenience story has carried a long way from the cognitive science and biological naturalism that have been the main focus of this chapter, but it does set the stage for the social turn that will be examined next.

---

[48] See Hoover (1995a), Jackson and Pettit (1992), Kincaid (1998), Nelson (1984), and Sensat (1988).

5

The Sociological Turn

Behind Every Fact is a theory and behind that an interest.
[Knight 1922, p. 479]

It is our contention, then, that the sociology of knowledge must concern itself with whatever passes for "knowledge" in a society.... And insofar as all human "knowledge" is developed, transmitted and maintained in social situations, the sociology of knowledge must seek to understand the processes by which this is done.... In other words, we contend that *the sociology of knowledge is concerned with the analysis of the social construction of reality.*
[Berger and Luckmann 1966, p. 3]

[U]pholding a strong distinction between origins and validity was emotionally rooted in the personal experiences of the founders of Logical Empiricism during the 1930s. For the founders of constructivist sociology of science, by contrast, the formative experiences were those of the 1960s. In Europe these experiences included not only the Vietnam war, but also Prague Spring and the student revolts. Here science was seen not as a savior, but a villain, part of the established authority to be resisted. The project became one of critique, indeed, of undermining the claims of the sciences to any special cognitive authority.
[Giere 1995, p. 7]

The naturalistic turn is not the only substantive turn in recent science theory. Another related but separable movement is the *sociological turn*

172

discussed in this chapter. It is clear from the work examined in the last two chapters that science is fundamentally social; Kuhn and others emphasized that science is a social activity, that science is done in communities, and that collectively held paradigms substantively influence what scientists do and do not "see." Since scientific theories and the other intellectual artifacts of science are (at least for most commentators) a type of belief, the social character of science means that scientific theories constitute a particular type of socially held belief. Now, if one were investigating any other type of social belief – say, the incest taboo or the relationship between inflationary expectations and monetary policy – one would consult the relevant social science. So why should this not also be the case for the beliefs of those within the scientific community? Why shouldn't scientific beliefs be explained by the same type of social factors that we use to explain the beliefs of any other social group? The answer for advocates of the sociological turn is that *they shouldn't*; scientific beliefs should in fact be explained in precisely the same way that we explain the beliefs held by any other social group.

Although the argument for explanatory symmetry between scientific and other social beliefs is just one particular aspect of the general sociological turn, it immediately raises questions about *which particular social theory* we should use in our explanatory schema. Do we explain the beliefs of scientists in functionalist, structuralist, behaviorist, Marxist, sociobiological, rational choice, or game theoretic terms? It seems that there are as many different sociological approaches to science as there are different approaches to social theory. One thing we will discover about the sociological turn, like the naturalistic turn, is that attitudes regarding the general approach are inexorably intertwined with attitudes about particular versions of it; supporters often praise the sociological approach in general when in fact they only support the application of one specific social theory, and similarly, critics attack the general approach when their target is really just one particular subprogram.

Another set of questions raised by the sociological approach involves the distinction between reformist and revolutionary naturalization discussed in the previous chapter. First, does a sociological approach to scientific belief usurp traditional epistemology and philosophy of science, or does it reinforce these more traditional views? And, second, if the sociological approach does replace philosophy, does it do so by providing its own (new and different) answer to the traditional epistemological questions, or does it simply change the subject? Although this last question is related to the normative versus descriptive distinction, the sociological turn puts a slightly different spin on it than either the cognitive or biological approaches discussed above. The difference is that for much of the sociological literature the lesson is *normative but negative*, that is, when sociologists go beyond mere description, they frequently make the case that scientific beliefs do *not* exhibit the epistemic virtues that science has traditionally been credited with. Thus, sociological approaches, like the work of Kuhn and others, are frequently viewed as supporting a relativist (specifically a socially relativist) perspective on scientific knowledge.

Finally, there is the issue of naturalism. To what extent is the socio-logical approach also naturalistic? In other words, is the sociology of sci-entific knowledge a type of naturalized epistemology? Although there is a certain amount of disagreement about the relationship between naturalism and the sociological approach, there does seem to be a clear majority opinion. The majority of commentators talk as if naturalism and sociology were *alternative approaches* to scientific knowledge; in fact, in the wake of the breakdown of the Received View, naturalism and soci-ology are often characterized as the two main contenders for the intel-lectual space once occupied by positivist-inspired philosophy of science. *I do not endorse this majority view.* I will present the sociological approach to scientific knowledge as one particular version of naturalism; on my reading, sociology is just one of the many different lanes that one can follow through the broad naturalistic turn.[1] While a more complete defense of this position will emerge in the pages below, I would like to make three points here in the beginning. First, like naturalism, these soci-ological approaches treat all phenomena – rocks, trees, stellar constella-tions, postpartum depression, the rate of interest on T-bills, and the beliefs of scientists – as legitimate subjects for scientific investigation. Second, like other naturalized epistemologists, sociologists of science are broadly empirical and eschew the traditional *a priorist* approach to the study of scientific knowledge; for such sociologists, epistemology is not autonomous or independent of theorizing in the special sciences (it is just that the relevant special science is sociology and not cognitive science or biology). Third, if one considers the main naturalistic question to be "what to naturalize on," then one could certainly naturalize on sociology just as easily as behavioral psychology, cognitive science, or evolutionary biology. Although the effectiveness of sociology as a nat-uralizing base is clearly undercut by the fact that it does not have the prestige of biology (or even cognitive science), there is nothing concep-

---

[1] Although this is not the standard reading of the relationship between the naturalistic and sociological turns, I am not alone in this interpretation (see Roth 1996 and Barnes 1991, for example). Of course, the degree to which this reading makes sense depends on *which* particular sociological approach one is considering. The naturalistic case is easiest to make for the Strong Program.

tually problematic about taking a social (rather than natural) theory as the relevant given for the naturalization of knowledge.

These are only a few of the issues raised by the sociological turn; many others will surface at various points later in the chapter. The presentation will proceed as follows: There are three sections. The first section provides the historical and philosophical background for the sociological turn. Section 2 discusses some of the many different research programs that constitute contemporary sociology of scientific knowledge (SSK). The third and final section examines one particular debate within the sociological literature and discusses some of its implications for economic science.

5.1 Society and Scientific Knowledge

5.1.1 Science and Society

The Received View characterized science as a set of propositions about the world, hopefully true propositions, but confirmed (or corroborated) and epistemologically justified propositions in any case. It was the job of the self-contained field of the philosophy of science to reflect, and legislate on, these propositions. The breakdown of the Received View changed all of this. Science is no longer sacrosanct; it is viewed as social and theory-laden, as underdetermined, as substantively heterogeneous, and as devoid of its previous crisp hierarchies (theoretical vs. empirical, theory vs. practice, discovery vs. justification, science vs. all other cultural activities, etc.). In Andrew Pickering's apt phrase, science has come to be "seen as fragmented, disunified, and scrappy" (Pickering 1995a, p. 3).

The literature on the sociology of scientific knowledge (SSK) beginning in the 1970s was clearly influenced by these changes in science theory. The sociological literature focused on the social and cultural aspects of science, and, as discussed above, on the fact that science could be understood in the same terms that one would understand any other type of social behavior or belief.

> The great achievement of SSK was to bring the human and social dimensions of science to the fore. SSK, one can say, thematized the role of *human agency* in science. It thus partially displaced the representational idiom by seeing the production, evaluation, and use of scientific knowledge as structured by the interests and constraints upon real agents. Scientific beliefs, according to SSK, are to be sociologically accounted for in just those terms. (Pickering 1995a, p. 9)

Important though it was, the Breakdown of the Received View was not the only (nor for some even the most important) factor contributing to the rise of SSK. Certain influences from earlier traditions in the social study of science also helped to shape the character of the post-Kuhnian sociological turn. The two most influential earlier approaches were the Marxist-inspired historical studies associated with the work of John Desmond Bernal, and the functionalist program associated with the work of Robert K. Merton.[2] I will spend some time on each of these two earlier approaches: the Marxist view will be discussed in Section 5.1.2, and the Mertonian school in Section 5.1.3.

Although the Bernalist and Mertonian approaches represent the immediate precursors to SSK, there are actually three different phases to the sociological study of science during the twentieth century. In addition to precursors, it is possible to identify two different phases within the SSK literature: the work of the first generation and then a more recent literature that has responded to it. The Strong Program and social constructivism constituted the first generation of SSK – inspired by Kuhn and the breakdown of the Received View as well as by earlier sociological approaches – and this first generation was followed by a more recent (second-generation) literature that has focused on certain weaknesses of the two original programs. Some of these weaknesses became apparent as the result of attacks from outside of SSK (particularly from philosophers), whereas others emerged as the result of critical discussions within the field. Section 5.2 will examine both phases of the SSK literature: the two versions of first generation – the Strong Program (in 5.2.1) and social constructivism (in 5.2.2) – and also a few of the program's more recent developments (in 5.2.3). The discussion is of course not intended to be exhaustive; here, as elsewhere, the guiding principle is to focus on those approaches that have (or will have) the closest connection to economics and economic methodology.

As we examine these specific programs, it is important to keep in mind a few recurrent themes. The first is the question of *social construction* and the related issue of *relativism*. To what degree do these various approaches to SSK consider science to be (merely) a social construction? In other words, to what extent do the various programs within SSK endorse the view that the objects and theories of science are completely constituted by human and social factors, leaving no role for objective

---

[2] These two traditions are not mutually exclusive, nor do they exhaust the sociological literature on science prior to the rise of SSK. Shapin (1982) discusses the earlier literature in detail.

nature in the determination of scientific beliefs?[3] We will discover that various programs within SSK offer quite different answers to these, and other, questions. Another issue is the question of *reflexivity*. If the beliefs of scientists are determined by their social context, then why shouldn't social context also determine the beliefs of the social scientists doing SSK? Should, or must not, the sociological approach also be applicable to sociology, and if so, doesn't it undermine (particularly the critical aspects of) the project itself? This, we will see, has been a very important issue in the history of the sociological approach and it is key to understanding many of the various moves that appear in the more recent literature. Finally, but most importantly for the task at hand, there are issues about economics and economic methodology. Many of these sociological approaches sound much like what an economist might say about the behavior of economic agents who happen to be scientists, and this raises important questions about which particular social science it is that we apply to the social study of science.

5.1.2 The Marxist Tradition in Science Studies

The first few pages of the Preface to Karl Marx's *A Contribution to the Critique of Political Economy* contain the classic statement of the materialist theory of history.

> In the social production of their existence, men inevitably enter into definite relations, which are independent of their will, namely *relations of production* appropriate to a given stage in the development of their material *forces of production*. . . . At a certain stage of development, *the material productive forces of society come into conflict with the existing relations of production*. . . . From forms of development of the productive forces these relations turn into their *fetters*. Then begins an era of social *revolution*. (Marx 1859, pp. 21–2, emphasis added)

Although Marx himself said very little about the contribution of science or scientific knowledge to the forces of production, it would seem to be perfectly reasonable, and wholly within the spirit of historical materialism, to explicitly include scientific knowledge among the material forces of production. If one makes this friendly amendment to Marx's theory of history, then it would mean that capitalist relations of production were initially "appropriate to" the productive forces of science, but as capitalism developed, the growth of the productive forces of scientific

---

[3] In other words, was Kuhn correct in his characterization of certain sociological approaches: that "Nature itself whatever that may be, has seemed to have no part in the development of beliefs about it" (Kuhn 1992, p. 8)?

knowledge would eventually "come into conflict with" capitalist relations of production. According to this version of historical materialism, science and capitalism grew up together – capitalism accommodated the scientific revolution – but then "at a certain stage" bourgeois property relations became a "fetter" on the further development of the productive forces of science. The full development of science, like the full development of the forces of production in general, requires a radical change in the dominant relations of production and, thus, necessitates the revolutionary transformation of capitalist society. This deterministic reading of historical materialism and its inescapable implications for the relationship between the development of capitalism and the growth of scientific knowledge became the key organizing insight for a group of British Marxist historians of science during the 1930s.[4]

The main figure in this Marxist-inspired literature was the practicing scientist (crystallographer) and historian of science J. D. Bernal (1939, 1953). Bernal's major works were directly influenced by Boris Hessen's (1931) early paper on the social and economic roots of Newton's *Principia*. Hessian, Bukharin, and a number of other Soviet intellectuals had attended the International Congress of the History of Science and Technology in London in the summer of 1931 and their papers, published as *Science at the Crossroads* (Bukharin et al. 1931), became the seminal contribution to the literature on the materialist historiography of science.[5] Simon Schaffer summarizes Hessen's argument.

> Hessen displayed Newton's greatest achievement as a response to the technical needs of the bourgeoise, and as conditioned by the ideological conflicts of the revolutions of the mid-seventeenth century. He went on to couple this analysis with enthusiastic advocacy of Soviet science policy, and of the promise offered by socialism for scientific development: "only in a socialist society will science become the genuine possession of all mankind." (Schaffe 1984, p. 23)[6]

[4] This interpretation also became the official Soviet-Stalinist party line about the relationship between capitalism and science (see McGucken 1984 and Werskey 1988).

[5] The fascinating story of the Soviet participation in the 1931 meetings and the eventual publication of Bukharin's volume is told by Wersky (1988, esp. 138–49). Wersky also provides a detailed discussion of the impact of Bernalism on the British scientific left and British science policy in general. McGucken (1984) also examines the impact of Bernalism on British science policy in the 1930s and 1940s.

[6] Schaffer argues that Hessen's Marxism was not as vulgar as it is presented in the secondary literature; economic relations matter, but the relationship is far more complex (and subtle) than the simple inclusion of science into the forces of production. This reading of Hessen brings his work much closer to some of the more recent literature in SSK: particularly Shapin and Schaffer (1985).

Bernal and his British associates employed this basic Marxist historical narrative to produce studies of many other episodes in the history of
science, as well as to promote a more popular movement in support of
the collective planning of science. Bernal's work equated eighteenth- and
nineteenth-century science and technology with the process of industri-
alization and capital accumulation; this explained the simultaneous rise
of modern science and the development of industrial capitalism, but it
also provided an intellectual foundation for the development of a new
socialist science that would be more responsive to real human needs and
less supportive of the forces of exploitation and capital accumulation.
For Bernal, like Hessen, the liberation of science from its capitalist servi-
tude would require a political revolution.

> We now see that though capitalism was essential to the early
> development of science, giving it, for the first time, a practical
> value, the human importance of science transcends in every way
> that of capitalism, and, indeed, the full development of science
> in the service of humanity is incompatible with the continuance
> of capitalism. (Bernal 1939, p. 409)

Although Bernal and the members of his school were not the only
contributors to early twentieth-century history and sociology of science
who were influenced by Marxist ideas, they were certainly the group that
had the most direct impact on later developments within SSK.[7] The next
major influence was the (primarily American) Mertonian school in the
sociology of science, discussed in the next section, but Merton's work, at
least in its initial phase, was partially motivated by the Marxist literature
of Hessen and others.

I have two final comments before leaving the topic of Marxian scholarship in the history and sociology of science. First, this literature seems
(as was the case for some of the psychological literature in Chapter 4)
to reverse the traditional relationship between natural and social science.
Instead of natural science being the source of knowledge that is carried,
via philosophy, to the social sciences that follow the scientific method, a
social theory (Marxism) is the source of knowledge about the nature and
significance of scientific activity.

> The relevance of Marxism to science is that it removes it from
> its imagined position of complete detachment and shows it as a

---

[7] Karl Mannheim (1936) was one of many others influenced by Marxist ideas. A few of the
surveys of the sociological literature that emphasize the Marxist connection include:
Collins and Restivo (1983), Restivo (1995), and Shapin (1992). For a very critical commentary regarding the Marxist connection to SSK, see Bunge (1991).

part, but a critically important part, of economic and social development. In doing so it can serve to separate off the metaphysical elements which throughout the whole course of its history have penetrated scientific thought. It is to Marxism that we owe the consciousness of the hitherto unanalysed driving force of scientific advance, and it will be through the practical achievements of Marxism that this consciousness can become embodied in the organization of science for the benefit of humanity. (Bernal 1939, p. 415)

Although there clearly is an element of the natural-social reversal in this literature, it should not be overemphasized. Hessen, Bernal, and other Marxist historians of science did emphasize the impact of the capitalist mode of production (and its elimination) on the rate and direction of science, but they did not go so far as to claim that social/economic conditions determine (wholly or even principally) the actual *content* of science. Science was for these authors basically true and objective; its speed, direction, and application were socially conditioned but not its content. For these authors, Marxism constituted the paradigm case of scientific knowledge, but this fact did not usurp the cognitive virtues of the natural sciences; "despite their effort to link scientific development to its historical conditions, they were definitely not critics of knowledge; they were critics of the economic system that thwarted its full development" (Aronowitz 1996, p. 209). This separation of context and content is generally not maintained by those writing in SSK.

Second, this Marxist literature could just as well (or perhaps more correctly) be called a type of *economics of science* as a version of the sociology of science. Marxism, particularly the deterministic brand of Marxism accepted by Hessen and Bernal, is an economic theory of history; it contains what might be considered a purely sociological component, but this social element is always subservient to the economic forces. We will discover that some of the later sociological literature also has the feel of, or could appropriately be defined as, the economics, rather than the sociology, of science.

5.1.3 The Mertonian Tradition in Science Studies

Robert K. Merton's 1935 doctoral dissertation (Merton 1970) focused on the rise of natural science in seventeenth-century England, and it was written in part as a response to the early Marxist histories of the subject. Like Max Weber's *Protestant Ethic*, Merton argued that the *ideas*, the norms and values, of ascetic Protestantism (not capitalist relations of production) created the proper cultural preconditions for the development of modern science. Merton's focus, like that of Hessen and Bernal, was on the external factors that determine the force, direction, and perhaps even complexion of science (not its actual content); the difference is that for Merton the relevant factors were sociological, like norms and cultural values, rather than economic forces like the Marxian law of value.[8]

The question of why science developed in seventeenth-century England seems to lead naturally to the question of science's general cognitive ascendancy. Science not only appeared, it never disappeared; it shifted the locus of cultural authority from God (through the clergy) to nature (through science), and vanquished all other forms of knowledge acquisition. The task of finding the cultural preconditions for science seems to entail isolating the unique cultural characteristics of science: characteristics that allowed it to ascend initially and then maintain its cognitive hegemony. The ultimate Mertonian question was: What makes science unique among cultural institutions, and how do those characteristics function to legitimize and maintain science's position in society? Notice the functionalism implicit in this question; identify the relevant cultural characteristics and then show how they *function* to maintain the social institution of science. Merton was a major figure in functionalist sociology, and this perspective is clearly reflected in his version of the sociology of science.

Merton identified four such cultural values that, when taken together, uniquely characterize the ethos of science.

- *Universalism*: The criteria for scientific evaluation are not specific to any particular individual or group. Scientific standards are independent of the author and applicable to all.
- *Communism*: Science is an intellectual commune. Scientists share their results and data with the wider scientific community.
- *Disinterestedness*: Scientists (qua scientist) are disinterested in the impact of their research. They do not seek political or financial rewards for their work and, thus, can follow the argument where it leads.
- *Skepticism*: No scientific result is accepted without careful scrutiny by empirical and logical criteria. Scientists refuse to believe any result until it has been demonstrated by scientific standards.

---

[8] Shapin (1988) traces Merton's alternative to Marxism to the influence of Pareto's sociology and the influence of the Harvard Pareto circle in the 1930s.

According to Merton, these four norms function in concert to sustain and validate the community of science. They allow the scientific community to function autonomously (or at least quasi-autonomously) from the wider culture in which it is embedded, and they provide the proper social context for the production of reliable scientific knowledge. It is important to note that Merton viewed these four institutional imperatives as normative as well as descriptive. They were clearly norms for the proper conduct of scientific inquiry; they represented ideal standards that scientific communities "ought" to strive for, but Merton also seemed to believe that they correctly described the cultural values exhibited by the most successful scientists.

> The ethos of science is that affectively toned complex of values and norms which is held to be binding on the man of science. The norms are expressed in the form of prescriptions, proscriptions, preferences, and permissions. They are legitimatized in terms of institutional values. They are imperatives, transmitted by precept and example and reinforced by sanctions are in varying degrees internalized by the scientist, thus fashioning his scientific conscience. (Merton 1973, pp. 268–9)

In an important sense Merton's four norms simply *replace* the (more) *a priori* standards provided by traditional philosophy of science. The confirmationism of the logical empiricists, or the Popperian falsificationist demarcation criterion, are also norms for the proper conduct of science; they constitute the distinctive and defining features of science; and they are norms that (at least their philosophical authors thought) could be observed in the best scientific practice. This seems to be exactly the same type of argument that Merton is making, except that the onus falls on *social norms* rather than *rules for individual behavior*. As Larry Laudan summarizes the relationship:

> What should be clear, however, is that both sociologists and philosophers of that era were inclined to think that agreement among scientists about the "facts of the matter" was the natural state of affairs and were disposed to explain such factual agreement by insisting that it was the direct result of agreement among scientists at a "deeper" level – at the level of procedures and methods (as the philosophers would put it) or at the level of norms and standards, incorporated into an institutional reward system (as the sociologists would have it). (Laudan 1984, p. 11)

The sociologist Thomas Gieryn makes a similar point but links it directly to Popper.

> His [Merton's] argument is as essentialist as Popper's, with the institutionalized ethos of science replacing falsifiability as a criterion for demarcating science from non-science. . . . In effect, the four social norms of science save the autonomy of science from external political or cultural interferences by arguing that such intrusions compromise the necessary moral conditions, which in turn make possible the extension of certified knowledge. . . . If the norms are read as demarcation criteria, then knowledge-producing activities not ensconced in that institutionalized moral frame must be nonscientific. (Gieryn 1995, pp. 398–9)

This desire for a (shared social norms) version of demarcation, a desire to find something *universal and distinctive* about science – whether the scientific "method" of Popper or Logical Positivism, or the institutional "norms" of Merton – is present in Merton's sociology of science, but we will find that it is absent from most of contemporary SSK. Much of the contemporary literature considers even the content of science to be socially constituted and contingent (thus neither universal nor distinctive). For this reason, I will employ the distinction between the *sociology of science* and the *sociology of scientific knowledge* (SSK). The idea is that the sociology of science does not really question the objective validity of science; like Merton, such sociologists generally assume that science provides reliable knowledge about the objective world and focus exclusively on characterizing the social and cultural context that allows the scientific enterprise to succeed.[9] For the sociology of science, only the context, not the content, of science is social. Most of the literature discussed in the rest of this chapter does not endorse this separation; it is the sociology of scientific *knowledge*. For these authors, the content, as well as the context, of science is inexorably social. Although it is useful to maintain the distinction between sociology of science and SSK (and I will do so throughout), I must also admit that the distinction

---

[9] It also would be possible for the sociology of science to simply suspend any judgment whatsoever on the question of scientific "knowledge." One could consider science just, purely and absolutely, as a culture to be studied, and like someone studying native religion, simply never ask (implicitly or explicitly) whether the gods (the scientific laws) are real or have the powers the shamans (or scientists) say they do. Although this does seem to be the goal of certain contemporary studies (Traweek, 1988, for example), it is very difficult to execute; the problem has to do with the dominance of (and thus embeddedness of the investigator in) scientific culture and the problem of reflexivity.

is not as crisp as it initially sounds and it can be difficult to apply in specific cases. One problem is that these attitudes fall along a continuum and often do not fit comfortably into either one of these two distinct groups; another problem is that there is frequently a lot of slippage on this issue within a particular text or between an author's works at two different points in time. As I said, it is a useful, but imperfect, conceptual tool.

Although Merton's reputation in the sociology of science was established primarily on the basis of his four norms of science and the surrounding literature, he is also known for a number of other contributions to the field that were more narrowly focused and more empirical.[10] On the empirical side, Merton was basically the founder of the American empirical school in the sociology of science. Merton, his students, and others in the school, employed a number of different statistical techniques in the investigation of "the interplay between social formations of scientists and cognitive developments in a field of science" (Merton 1977, p. 23). Empirical approaches such as citation analysis, content analysis, and a type of historical analysis that Merton called "prosopography" were applied to a myriad of different questions pertaining to the structure of science. These studies played much the same role that applied econometrics played in post-World War II economics; the theoretical frame of Mertonian functionalism (like the neoclassical synthesis) posed a multiplicity of empirical puzzles, and those puzzles in turn provided fodder for a barrage of different studies that combined some particular theoretical twist in the functionalist program, with a particular data set, and a slightly new statistical tool. The difference between this work and most applied econometrics during the same period was that in sociology generating the data was considered to be the main contribution and the statistical techniques were less important, whereas in economics the data was usually provided by the government (or central bank) and the econometric technique was considered to be the main contribution.

---

[10] In fact, there was a time during the 1970s, before the explosion of the post-Kuhnian literature, when Merton's later and more narrow work was considered to be much more important than his earlier investigations into the scientific ethos. Jonathan Cole and Harriet Zuckerman described the situation in the following way.

> [S]ociologists of science found in Merton's later work . . . greater "potential for elaboration" and a reasonably clear program of research. . . . Close inspection of the papers by newcomers to the field who appear on the list of most cited authors in the 1960s and 1970s shows that much of their empirical work begins with a problem posed in one or another of Merton's later papers. (Cole and Zuckerman 1975, p. 157)

In addition to parenting this empirical work in the sociology of science, Merton also introduced a number of (sometimes paradoxical) ideas that have become standard in the literature. Merton (1936, 1948) popularized the idea of a "self-fulfilling prophecy" in social science: the idea that in social science, unlike natural science, one can make a prediction that changes behavior in such a way that the prediction becomes true, even though it would not have been true had the prediction not been made. Economic examples of this phenomenon range from the story of the late-night talk show host who created a shortage of toilet paper by predicting it on a popular television show, to the more technical question of asymmetric expectations in New Classical macro models (Hands 1990a; Sent 1998a). Merton was also responsible for introducing the "Matthew Effect" (Merton 1968): the idea that scientists with established reputations are more likely to get things published (or get things credited to them) than lesser-known scientists, even if the work of the relatively unknown author is in fact superior. The term "Matthew Effect" now seems to have become an accepted part of contemporary academic culture.[11] A third Mertonian contribution pertained to "multiples" – the role of independent and multiple discoveries in the history of science (Merton 1961) – an idea that later appeared in the work of Kuhn and others.[12]

Whether we are considering Merton's four norms of the scientific ethos, the empirical work of the Merton school, or these interesting little insights into scientific culture, Merton's work leaves science safely on the high ground. Although Merton's orientation is quite different from (and perhaps even diametrically opposed to) that of Bernal and the Marxist school, he too never really challenges the natural scientists' right to the epistemic *terra altus*. To exploit David Edge's (1995, pp. 12–15) notion of a recurrent tension between the "technocratic" and the "critical" impulse in the sociology of science, the work of both Bernal and Merton fall squarely on the technocratic side. Bernal was a critic of capitalism, but not really a critic of natural science, and Merton was not particularly critical of either. This congeniality will disappear as we move forward into the post-Kuhnian SSK literature; there is a critical rumble by the first

---

[11] This includes economics. For example, Georgescu-Rogen (1992) uses it to explain why Samuelson's name, rather than his own, was attached to the substitution theorem, and Tollison (1986) used it to explain why Keynes got credit for the multiplier. There are certainly many other examples.

[12] Again Merton's idea has been applied to economics. See, for example, Patinkin (1983), Stigler (1982), and Niehans (1995a), who provides a list of forty such "multiples" in economic theory. See De Marchi (1995), Mirowski (1995a), Niehans (1995b), and Roncaglia (1995), for a critical discussion of Niehans's examples.

group, the Strong Program, which turns into a roar from many of those who follow.

5.2 The Sociology of Scientific Knowledge

Of course, the sociological turn was not initiated by Bernal or Merton; it came after the breakdown of the Received View and the general acceptance of theory and social-ladenness, underdetermination, and the other insights of historians and philosophers like Kuhn and Quine. As we will see, this later sociological wave (the first wave of SSK) contains an extremely wide range of different views, but there also is some minimal common ground. All of these different approaches are "united by a shared refusal of philosophical apriorism coupled with a sensitivity to the social dimensions of science" (Pickering 1992, p. 2). Because the stage was set for SSK earlier in this chapter, let us move directly to the first major research program: the Strong Program.

5.2.1 The Strong Program

More than any other approach in post-Kuhnian sociology of science, the *Strong Program* has been self-conscious about its function and goals; other programs are held together by vaguely shared strategies and commitments, but the Strong Program has *members*. This cohesiveness is enhanced by the fact that many of the program's early works were programmatic, laying out the basic research strategy and contrasting it to other perspectives in the philosophy and sociology of science. Although this self-consciousness contributed to the program's cohesiveness, its methodological candor also made it an easy target for (particularly philosophical) critics. The Strong Program provided a novel approach to understanding science, but the defense of that approach was offered in the same intellectual idiom familiar to philosophers – "here is the way that one ought to study science and here is exactly what you will gain by doing it this way." Comfortable on their home field, philosophers and historians of science have been quick to attack.[13]

---

[13] It is much more difficult for philosophers to get a solid bead on later programs in SSK (and the later the slipperier). The other three programs discussed in this chapter, for instance, are much less likely to lay out their methodological approach in advance and are much more likely to intermingle what they are doing with the act of doing it. The difference is in part that the Strong Program was on the cusp of a sea change in science theory; the message of Kuhn and others had been received but the accepted idiom was still foundationalist and analytical. Later authors were more likely to be influenced by postmodern and neopragmatist ideas (discussed in Chapter 6) and more likely to view their own approach, like the science they were studying, as contingent and socially conditioned.

The Strong Program, or Edinburgh School, formed around the work of Barry Barnes (1974, 1977, 1982), David Bloor (1976/1991, 1983), Donald MacKenzie (1990), Steven Shapin (1982), and others. Despite the program's relative cohesiveness, differences still remain among the various authors in the group. An official manifesto was never written, but the book that comes closest is probably Bloor's *Knowledge and Social Imagery* (1976/1991). Bloor makes the Strong Program's case systematically and with the type of methodological self-consciousness mentioned above. More recently Barnes, Bloor, and Henry (1996) have attempted to reassert (and clarify) the Strong Program's methodological stance in response to many of the early criticisms from both inside and outside SSK.

The Strong Program, unlike the Mertonian school, is concerned with the content of scientific knowledge; Bloor argued that earlier views left "untouched the nature of the knowledge thus created" (Bloor 1991, p. 3). The approach is naturalistic, specifically the generic naturalism discussed in Chapter 4; the Strong Program "is concerned with knowledge, including scientific knowledge, purely as a natural phenomenon" (Bloor 1991, p. 5). "In delineating the strong programme in the sociology of knowledge I have tried to capture what I think sociologists actually do when they unselfconsciously adopt the naturalistic stance of their discipline" (Bloor 1991, p. 157).

Bloor's project is not only naturalist, it is empirical; "knowledge" under consideration is not some special certified-as-privileged-by-a-philosopher knowledge, it is what the relevant scientists say is knowledge. "Instead of defining it as true belief – or perhaps, justified true belief – knowledge for the sociologist is whatever people take to be knowledge" (Bloor 1991, p. 5). This starting point, although radically different from the philosophy of science, would seem to be a straightforward approach to studying scientific knowledge as a *social* phenomena. For Bloor, "scientific knowledge" is stuff that occurs naturally within the community of scientists and it, like all natural and empirical phenomena, is subject to scientific explanation. The goal is simply to apply (social) science to the scientific investigation of a particular type of social phenomenon: scientific knowledge. For Bloor, the Strong Program just does science; it is a particular type of science (social) aimed at a particular domain of inquiry (scientific knowledge), but it is just science.

> Throughout the argument I have taken for granted and endorsed what I think is the standpoint of most contemporary science. . . . The overall strategy has been to link the social sciences as closely as possible with the methods of other empirical

sciences. In a very orthodox way I have said: only proceed as the other sciences proceed and all will be well. (Bloor 1991, p. 157)

But doesn't the application of the method of science to any topic (including scientific knowledge) require that one know what the scientific method *is* before one can apply it, and doesn't that carry us immediately out of the purely naturalistic world and back into the hands of traditional philosophers of science who legislate what science is rather than practicing it? No, not really, according to Bloor.

> The student of the piano may not be able to say what features are unique to the playing of his teacher, but he can certainly attempt to emulate them. In the same way we acquire habits of thought through exposure to current examples of scientific practice and transfer them to other areas. . . . My suggestion is simply that we transfer the instincts we have acquired in the laboratory to the study of knowledge itself. (Bloor 1984, p. 83)

So Bloor considers the Strong Program to be just successful (social) science, and it is possible to practice such science by rote or induction and it is never necessary to abandon the basic naturalistic stance. If this is the meta-method, then what is the method; what are the details of his approach? In other words, exactly how does one do Strong Program sociology?

Bloor presents *four methodological tenets* for the Strong Program, and these four tenets effectively *define* the program (Bloor 1991, p. 7).

- *Causality*: Seek the causal conditions that bring about the beliefs of scientists.
- *Impartiality*: Be impartial between true and false, or rational and irrational, beliefs.
- *Symmetry*: The same type of cause should be used to explain both true and false beliefs.
- *Reflexivity*: The explanations offered should also be applicable to the sociology of science.

The four tenets constitute the methodological heart of the Strong Program and they have generated a massive critical literature. Rather than trying to discuss this critical literature, or the Strong Program's response to these criticisms, I will just mention one of the issues that is particularly relevant to the later literature in SSK and/ or economics.

The main issue that needs to be considered is the controversial question of the role of *interests* in the Strong Program. Bloor's four tenets do not necessarily mandate exactly *how* one should go about explaining scientist's beliefs as long as one seeks: (1) the cause of those beliefs, (2) is impartial and symmetric about the truth or falsity of those beliefs, and (3) is willing to apply the same causal arguments to one's own work. Suppose, just for the sake of argument, that one makes the psychological claim that scientists hold beliefs about universal laws of nature because they are unconsciously seeking to (re)gain control over the universe of their childhood. It seems this argument could be made in such a way that it was consistent with Bloor's four tenets; it is a causal story, it could be applied to a scientist's beliefs about a theory whether the theory is true or false, and it could be applied to sociologists seeking general laws as well.

Of course, I am not seriously proposing this psychological story; the point is simply that the four tenets do not really mandate that any particular type of social/human science be used to explain scientists' beliefs, as long as whatever story is employed complies with the four tenets. This might lead one to suppose that the Strong Program employs a wide range of different social/human science theories in its efforts to explain the beliefs of scientists, but that supposition would be incorrect. The Strong Program relies almost exclusively on *one specific approach* to explaining scientific beliefs; such beliefs are explained on the basis of the *social interests* of the scientists. These interests are based on, and emerge from, the scientists' particular place in the overall pattern of social relationships; therefore, at any particular point in time, the relevant interests could take a variety of different forms – personal, group, professional, class, national, or others – but regardless of the specific form, the Strong Program's story always reduces to the argument that certain beliefs were in the "interests" of the relevant scientists and that such interests explain (causally, impartially, symmetrically, and reflexively) why the scientists have the beliefs that they have. This is not the only social/human science approach that could be used (consistent with the four tenets), but it is the main approach that *is* used. The use of social interests to explain scientist's beliefs has become *the key identifying characteristic of the Strong Program.*[14]

Of course, the role of interest explanations is just one of the many controversial issues raised by the literature of the Strong Program; many others will surface at later points in the discussion of the sociological turn. Since the Strong Program was the first of the post-Kuhnian programs, and because its supporters were so explicit about its

---

[14] Although interest explanations have become an identifying characteristic of the Strong Program, not every member of the program remains as interest-centered as Bloor. For example, the work by Mackenzie (1990) and Shapin (1994), although still broadly within the spirit of the Strong Program, shows far less commitment to interest explanations.

methodology, we will find that the Strong Program serves as both a point of reference and a point of departure for much of the later work in SSK.

5.2.2 Social Constructivism

The first round of SSK consisted of two, related but separable, programs: the Strong Program and *social constructivism*. In recent years, constructivism has received more attention than the Strong Program, even though it is far less easy to pin down exactly what it is that constructivism asserts. If the Strong Program is viewed as a relatively cohesive school with members, then social constructivism should be viewed as an amalgam of various authors who share a strong Wittgensteinian family resemblance. Major (early) works in the constructivist program would include: Collins (1985), Knorr Cetina (1981), and Latour and Woolgar (1979/1986).

Because there are many different versions of constructivist SSK – and, unlike the Strong Program, no particular text that might serve as a methodological handbook – it is very difficult to provide a "summary" of the constructivist view of science. Nonetheless, it seems useful to try. What I will do in the next few paragraphs is discuss six of the family characteristics shared by all (or at least most) of the different constructivist approaches. Although the list does not capture all of the family resemblances, and while many contributors would protest the inclusion of certain items on the list, it does convey the general spirit of the constructivist project. These six points will be followed by a more careful look at one particular version of the general approach: Harry Collins's work on replication in science. Collins is a good choice for a number of reasons. First, because all six of these characteristics are visible in his work (Collins 1985). Second, he has applied his approach to economics (Collins 1991). And third, he has more recently become a critic of some of the more radical versions of the constructivist program (Collins and Yearley 1992a and 1992b).

The first and perhaps most visible characteristic of the constructivist literature is that most of the research contains detailed *studies* of scientific practice. If there is methodological or programmatic discussion, it is usually secondary to the presentation of actual case studies (from either the history of science or from sites of current scientific practice) and these studies constitute the primary contribution of the work. Unlike the Strong Program where the early focus was often methodological, the emphasis in constructivist research has been less on *how* to do such work and more on providing examples *of what such studies actually look like*. In other words, constructivists generally get right to it. Perhaps we should call this the *hands on* aspect of constructionist SSK.

Second, constructionist studies tend to be very local, very specific, and situated at one particular site of knowledge production. There is less concern with scientific revolutions or general research programs; the focus tends be much more *micro*: one lab, one instrument, one result. This localness and microfocus blends in with the third feature of such studies: the emphasis on fieldwork, ethnographic inquiry, and participant observation. The social science that undergirds constructivist studies is more likely to be anthropological fieldwork than general social theories like those of Marx or Weber. The term "social construction" was popularized by Berger and Luckmann (1966), but contemporary authors put constructivist ideas to work in the context of specific, detailed, and richly textured case studies far more effectively than the constructivists of an earlier generation. Unlike the Marxism of Bernal, the functionalism of Merton, or the interests of sociology of the Strong Program, constructionist studies *do not generally start from tight priors*; the theoretical framework of the sociologist, like that of the scientists being studied, tends to be negotiated, contingent, and context-sensitive. Science is viewed as a process involving real agents doing real work in real time – pursuing goals, interacting, utilizing resources, producing scientific artifacts – and the sociologist conducting the study is seen to be doing many of these same things.

The fourth and fifth features of constructivist studies are also closely related. The fourth is that social constructivists view *very little as fixed and almost everything as up for grabs (or at least open to negotiation)*. Scientific knowledge is the product of an ongoing, continuous, and radically contingent negotiation among scientists, their agents, and institutions. This social negotiation not only determines what is legitimately "an electron" or "a gene," it also extends to social categories like "member of the research group" or the "interest of the scientific community." The fifth feature of constructivist studies is a spin-off of the negotiative flexibility, and it is perhaps the feature that is most unsettling to critics: *nature plays little or no role in scientific knowledge.* As a critical philosopher put it, "inputs from the nature are impotent" (Kitcher 1993, p. 164) The world that practicing scientists and traditional philosophers of science viewed as "discovered" by science, is, for constructivist SSK, "constructed" rather than discovered; scientists "make" knowledge they do not "find" it. As Knorr Cetina summarized the constructivist position.

> Since we constructivists believe that the world as it is is a *consequence* rather than a *cause* of what goes on in science, we have reverted the arrow between the scientific account and the world, considering the latter as a consequence rather than a cause of

> the former. The focus of attention has shifted to *what goes on in science when it produces these accounts.* . . . [scientific findings] are not just *found*, as the notion suggests, but are *fabricated* – the Latin root of the word fact is *facere*, "to make something." When you observe scientists in the laboratory, you find processes of *negotiation* at work, processes of decision making, which influence what the scientific findings are going to look like. In a sense, the scientific finding is construed in the laboratory by virtue of the decisions and the negotiations it incorporates. (Knorr Cetina in Callebaut 1993, p. 180, emphasis in original)

Now, it is important to point out the construction of scientific facts, findings, and artifacts does *not* necessarily entail an idealist ontology. Most constructivists would accept that there exists an independent material world, even one that influences the activities and beliefs of scientists by offering up various resistances to/within the knowledge production process, but what they would reject is the claim that the world described by science is the way that it is merely, or simply, because of the way the world (really) is. Again, Knorr Cetina:

> All of us constructivists, I think, are what they call *ontological realists*: We believe in the existence of the material world "out there," and we believe in the fact that this material world offers resistance when we act upon it. It will resist; we can't just do everything with it. So in that sense we are all realists. . . . Negotiating, for example, when they can stop the measurement, at what point they've got enough data, and at what degree or position they can say, "Now it is real!" . . . This *interpretative flexibility*, . . . prompts me to doubt that you can ever get at the real world as it really is. You can get *resistances* in the laboratory; but in order for these resistances to make sense, they have to be interpreted. The very moment you interpret them, you enter the realm of the social world. (Knorr Cetina in Callebaut 1993, pp. 184–5, emphasis in original)

Finally, all of these features add up to a *debunking* of science, or at least a debunking of the unique and universal cognitive privilege of science endorsed by traditional philosophy of science, most practicing scientists, and our (modern Western) popular culture. Science, these laboratory studies claim, is a social environment in which agents work, interact, negotiate, and ultimately constitute the world of scientific knowledge. This claim is not, for many constructivists, presented in a particularly pejorative way – it is exactly the same thing that goes on in any other artifact-producing site of human social activity – but, given the cognitive status of science, it is almost always *taken* to be pejorative.

Although these six features – hands on, micro, no tight priors, everything negotiable, impotence of nature, and the debunking of the traditional view of scientific knowledge – are present in most constructivist studies, I would like to focus on one particular work: Harry Collins's *Changing Order* (1985). Collins is concerned with the issue of *replication* in science, in particular the question of whether replication does, or the extent to which it does, perform the demarcational function that has traditionally been attributed to it by philosophers of science. According to the traditional view (and scientists' own stories) the fact that a particular result can be replicated (at least potentially) is an important factor in granting it scientific status. In Collins's words:

> Replicability, in a manner of speaking, is the Supreme Court of the scientific system. In the scientific value system replicability symbolizes the indifference of science to race, creed, class, color, and so forth. It corresponds to what the sociologist Robert Merton . . . called the "norm of universality." Anybody, irrespective of who or what they are, in principle ought to be able to check for themselves through their own experiments that a scientific claim is valid. (Collins 1985, p. 19)

Collins examined three specific cases of replication: the TEA-laser, detection of gravity waves, and parapsychological research on the emotional life of plants. If the last example seems to be outside the realm of traditional science, it is by design; if replication plays such an important role in science, it should play a substantially different role in pseudo-science. What Collins found was that there was no transcontextual way to decide what was and was not a legitimate replication. The factors that entered into scientists' decisions about the authenticity of a replication or potential replication were contextual and open to ongoing negotiation. Most replications were simply not done. If, as the result of negotiation, it was determined that the original observation was legitimate then there was no need to replicate; alternatively, if negotiations suggested that the observations were not legitimate, then there was no reason to reproduce a result that the scientific community had already agreed was without scientific importance. Collins coined the term *experimenter's regress* for the version of the underdetermination problem related to replication. As he described the situation in the study of gravity waves:

> What the correct outcome is depends upon whether there are gravity waves hitting the Earth in detectable fluxes. To find this

out we won't know if we have built a good detector until we
have tried it and obtained the correct outcome! But we don't
know what the correct outcome is until . . . and so on *ad infini-
tum*. (Collins 1985, p. 84)

In economics, the problems of replication and experimenter's regress
emerge most clearly in applied econometrics (see Mirowski 1995c,
1995d). It occurs in econometrics because successful empirical results can
only be obtained by using the appropriate econometric techniques, but
the only way to tell if the econometric techniques are appropriate is to
see if they provide successful empirical results. In general, experimenter's
regress means there is no natural (or data-given) stopping point in
empirical science; replication, like all other aspects of the knowledge
production process, is contingent, context-dependent, and negotiated. In
Collins's own words: "It is not the regularity of the world that imposes
itself on our senses but the regularity of our institutionalized beliefs that
imposes itself on the world" (Collins 1985, p. 148). Thus, Collins's work
on replication, like most constructivist research, is based on detailed case
studies of individual sites/episodes in science, depicts science as deeply
contingent and fundamentally socially constructed, characterizes nature
as relatively impotent, and tends to debunk the cognitive significance of
the scientific endeavor. "There is no realm of ideal scientific behaviour
. . . the canonical model of science – exists only in our imaginations"
(Collins 1985, p. 143).

5.2.3 Contemporary Developments

Given the general tone and what the first-generation SSK literature said about science, it should not come as any great surprise that
the program has been attacked by a dizzying array of critics. SSK has
drawn fire from the scientific community itself (Gross and Levitt 1994;
Gross, Levitt, and Lewis 1996); it has been criticized by philosophers who
want to replace the Received View with their own version of naturalized
epistemology (Goldman 1986; Kitcher 1993; Munz 1993); it has been
attacked for its "insinuating, exposé style" (Susser 1989, p. 248); it has
been criticized for its reading of Kuhn, Wittgenstein, and others (Friedman 1998); it has ostensibly been "refuted" by scientific discovery programs (Slezak 1989); it has been called both "voodoo epistemology"
(Roth 1987) and "voodoo sociology" (Cole 1996); it has been severely
criticized by a bevy of philosophers of social science (Hollis 1982;
Kincaid 1996; Rosenberg 1985a; Roth 1996); and, finally, it has been
called "deconstruction gone mad" by Thomas Kuhn himself (1992, p. 9).
And the list could go on and on.

Rather than try to deal with any of these criticisms directly, I will consider them indirectly by examining a few of the more recent developments within SSK. Because many of these developments (second-generation approaches) are actually efforts to solve, or circumvent what the authors perceive to be problems with the first-generation literature, these later developments are, in a sense, responses to many of the above criticisms. The two most recognized problems are the two issues mentioned above in Section 5.1.1: *reflexivity and relativism.* In fact, much of the second-generation SSK literature has focused rather directly on trying to answer, or fix, or circumvent in some way, these two problems. It is fair to say that the way in which various authors and programs have dealt with these particular issues is frequently the most important factor differentiating one second-generation program from another.

One of the most controversial approaches in the second-generation SSK literature is the *reflexivity school* (or as it is sometimes called, the hyperreflexivity school), a brand of SSK that evolved during the 1980s out of certain strains of the social constructivist program, particularly Latour and Woolgar (1979/1986). The most visible representatives of this perspective are Malcolm Ashmore (1989) and Steve Woolgar (1988, 1992). For the hyperreflexive school, *reflexivity is the most important thing about SSK.* The bottom line for such authors is that reflexivity – the "problem" associated with the application of SSK's debunking idiom to itself – is not a problem at all, but simply an opportunity. It is an opportunity to cast off our old, tired, representational ways; to upset our existing discursive strategies and to radically interrogate the language of representation; and to explore the critical "dynamic of iterative reconceptualization" (Woolgar 1992, p. 333). As Woolgar explains the reflexive opportunity:

> Reflexivity asks us to problematize the assumption that the analyst (author, self) stands in a disengaged relationship to the world (subjects, objects, scientists, things). It asks us to push symmetry one stage further, to explore the consequences of challenging the assumption that the analyst enjoys a privileged position vis-à-vis the subjects and objects which come under the authorial gaze. It does so, needless to say, in recognition that its own privilege is temporary. (Woolgar 1992, p. 334)

This is one of the most radical views[15] within SSK and authors often push the deprivileging theme so far as to deconstruct the standard

---

[15] Actually, the radicalness of hyperreflexivity is a point of contention. As we will see below, some critics argue that since hyperreflexivity erodes every position on which one might stand to critically engage science or the philosophy of science, it is not radical at all, but rather quite conservative.

conventions of academic discourse. Academic argumentation is recon-
ceptualized as art, literature, or entertainment, and the entire enterprise
of "studying science" is transformed into an exercise in reflexivity, irony,
and aporia. Although they are primarily concerned with reflexivity,
the hyperreflexive authors treat relativism in a similar way, and their
program could just as well be called hyperrelativism as hyperreflexivity.
Although their main focus is SSK, they also argue that once the reflexive fulcrum is put to work, its reconceptualizing power can be extended
to other (perhaps all other) aspects of intellectual life.

A very different approach to the concerns about reflexivity and relativism is presented by another contributor to the early constructivist
literature: Bruno Latour. Latour (1990, 1992, 1993, 1999), Michel Callon
(1986), and others (Callon, Law, and Rip, 1986) have popularized a
view of scientific knowledge called *Actor Network theory* (ANT).[16]
Latour, like Collins, was a producer of early laboratory studies; in fact
Latour and Woolgar's *Laboratory Life* (1979) is perhaps the most famous
of all such studies. But in recent years, the research programs of
Latour and Woolgar have diverged rather significantly. Latour is also
concerned with the issues of reflexivity and relativism, but he is quite
critical of the hyperreflexivity of his former coauthor; in his more recent
work, he has been trying to forge a new conception that does not reduce
to either constructivism or realism (or even a stable compound of these
two views).

Latour's basic approach is to think of science as a field for the interaction of human and nonhuman agency – with no particular priority
assigned to either set of actors on the field. This is a seemingly even more
radical form of the Strong Program's symmetry thesis; not only are true
and false theories treated in a symmetric way, human and nonhuman
actors/agents are treated symmetrically as well. This approach allows, for
example, nonhuman agents like the scallops of St. Brieuc Bay to actively
negotiate with (human) research scientists about their anchorage
(Callon 1986). The argument is that science is coproduced by the interaction of these two classifications of "actants" (any entity that has the
ability to act); it is the product of the interdependency and negotiations
of these two forms of agency, but cannot be reduced to either one.[17] In
a certain sense, Latour wants to preserve the intuitions behind *both* the
traditional view of science and the social constructivism of SSK – to
simultaneously incorporate the concept of agency endemic to each of

---

[16] Like social constructivism(s), there are multiple ANTs (see McClellan 1996).

[17] For a good example of what Latour means by "actant," see his discussion of nonhuman
"guns" and human "people" in the U.S. debate over firearm legislation involving the
National Rifle Association (Latour 1999, pp. 176–80).

these two ways of thinking about science into a single vision – but without assigning priority to either dimension. The traditional story about science is that "nature did it" – nature was the actor that had its way, that etched its will on the beliefs of scientists (and the rest of us in scientific culture) – by contrast, most of SSK supports the view that "society did it" – society, social interests and/or social structures have their way and etch their will on the beliefs of scientists. Latour wants to preserve both types of agency, but neither side needs (or gets) to be privileged or even ontologically nailed down. The natural and the social are constantly shifting and being renegotiated, so that, in the end, science emerges from the field of play of these two types of agency, but as the game is played the membership of each team, who is on which side as well as the total numbers, are constantly renegotiated on the field.

Supporters of ANT generally argue that their approach is just good empirical practice; both the traditional view and other versions of SSK rely on unobservables, things that are "behind" the observed – "nature" for the traditional view, and "social factors" for SSK – but ANT requires neither.

> We never see either social relations or things. We may only document the circulation of network-tracing tokens, statements, and skills. This is so important that one of us made it the first principle of science studies (Latour 1987, Ch. 1). . . . It is the basis of our empirical methods. (Callon and Latour 1992, p. 351)

Although this approach may have a certain postmodern flair with all its talk about shifting agency loci and actant renegotiation, Latour does not view it in that way; it is simply amodern (Latour 1990, 1992, 1993, 1999). Postmodern is where hyperreflexivity gets you, which for Latour is a dead end; amodern simply denies that either nature or society are fixed points for understanding or existing in the world.

> We did not come to this position for the fun of it or to play the deadly game of chicken, as we have been accused of doing, but because the field is cornered in a dead end from which we want to escape. . . . This debate occurs in social studies of science and technology and only there, since this is about the only place in social science where the number of border cases between "nature" and "society" is so great that it breaks the divide apart. Classical social theory, or philosophy of science, never faced this problem, since they ignored either the things or the society. (Callon and Latour 1992, p. 351)

The final approach that I would like to discuss in this section is Andrew Pickering's "Mangle of Practice" (1994, 1995a). Pickering's work owes much to ANT, but he is also interested in questions about the relationship between realism (in his terms "the material world") and SSK. Pickering's "Mangle" builds on his earlier work emphasizing the role of material "resistances" – what he calls the "dialectic of resistance and accommodation" (Pickering 1990, p. 702) – in the social construction of scientific knowledge. The dialectic of resistance and accommodation captures the complex interaction that takes place between the constructive efforts of the scientific community and the resistances that the material world offers to those constructive efforts. Knowledge is socially constructed, but the construction takes place within a context of material resistances that must be accommodated.

> This dialectic of resistance and accommodation in material practice surely justifies calling the resulting picture of scientific practice a realist one. But, I repeat, "realist" here means something different from "realist" as it appears in the standard realism debate. It points to a constitutive role for "reality" – the material world – in the production of knowledge, but it carries no necessary connotation of correspondence (or lack of correspondence) for the knowledge produced. (Pickering 1990, p. 706)

Although the "Mangle" expands the concept of resistance and accommodation in a number of different ways, the general emphasis on the social construction of scientific knowledge with a role for the material world remains the same. Although Pickering uses "mangle" in the British sense – as a clothes wringer – the more common American usage, as a verb, seems to work just as well.

> The . . . dialectic of resistance and accommodation is . . . a general feature of scientific practice. And it is . . . what I call *the mangle of practice*, or just the mangle. I find "mangle" a convenient and suggestive shorthand for the dialectic because . . . it conjures up the image of the unpredictable transformations worked upon whatever gets fed into the old-fashioned device of the same name used to squeeze the water out of washing. It draws attention to the emergently intertwined delineation and reconfiguration of machinic captures and human intentions, practices, and so on. (Pickering 1995a, pp. 22–3, emphasis in original)

Pickering argues that the mangle effectively avoids the problems associated with relativism and reflexivity because it focuses on performance and practice rather than representation; the entire mangle story is couched in the "performative idiom" (1995a, p. 7). The result may be some type of relativism – in fact he calls it "hyperrelativism" (1995a, p. 207) – but it is not the traditional relativism of SSK. Pickering follows the ANT theorists in avoiding both "the social" and "nature" (or anything else) as fixed points; not everything changes (gets mangled) at any particular instant of time, but no general pattern can be discerned regarding what aspects of the scientific culture will or will not change over time. His approach to reflexivity is much the same; he considers reflexivity as it is commonly discussed in the literature on SSK to be "an intensification of the representational idiom in science studies" (1995a, p. 11, note 17) and as such is not a real concern for the mangle view of science.

Although this concludes our quick tour of recent developments in the SSK literature, aspects of these three views – hyperreflexivity, ANT, and Pickering's mangle – will appear again in the next two sections, including the final section on economics. Before we (finally) get to economics, though, it is useful to have one more go at the issues of reflexivity and relativism. Disagreement on these two issues has led to a debate among a number of influential contributors to SSK – the so-called chicken debate – the topic to which I now turn.

5.3 Nature, Society, SSK, and Economics

The debate over issues such as relativism and reflexivity, and the seriousness of the responses of some authors to these issues, has led a number of those working in SSK to start talking about the field being in "crisis." While a majority seem to agree that some type of a crisis exists, there is a rather vociferous debate about just exactly what the nature of the crisis is and how it came to be. In the midst of this debate, one paper seems to have crystallized the discussion around a few key, and relatively clear, points of contention. The paper is "Epistemological Chicken" by Harry Collins and Steven Yearley (1992a). In this paper, Collins and Yearley accuse two separate groups – the hyperreflexivists and what they call the "French school" (ANT) – of pursuing research strategies that will ultimately lead to the destruction of SSK. The original Collins and Yearley paper was published with critical comments by ANT-theorists Callon and Latour (1992) and reflexivist Steve Woolgar (1992), as well as the authors' own reply (1992b). Since the opening exchange, the "chicken debate" has become a frequent point of departure for alternative approaches within science studies. Andrew Pickering (1995a) refers to the debate as part of the intellectual background for the development of his own mangle view of science, and supporters of the Strong Program have used it as a reference point for the recent clarification of their own views (Barnes, Bloor, and Henry 1996; Bloor 1999).[18]

There are a variety of reasons for paying attention to the chicken debate. First, the controversy so effectively highlights the main points of contention within contemporary SSK that it represents a useful microcosm of the current state of the field in general. Second, the debate raises a number of independently interesting issues in the philosophy of social science: issues that connect up with many of the more traditional philosophical questions discussed elsewhere in this book (realism vs. relativism, individualism vs. holism, etc.). Finally, the chicken debate raises some questions that are particularly relevant to economics and the economic methodology.

5.3.1 Epistemological Chicken: The Debate

Collins and Yearley (1992a) argue that second-generation programs like the reflexivity school and ANT have severely undermined the effectiveness and significance of SSK. The problem is that each new development in the field seems to be more relativist, and it has now reached a point where the entire program is threatened; each step has led to "an escalation of skepticism which we liken to the game of chicken; in this case the game is epistemological chicken" (Collins and Yearley 1992a, p. 302). Although the authors of these second-generation programs view themselves as being quite radical – and much more radical than first-generation SSK – Collins and Yearley argue that the real impact of their work is not radical at all but rather quite conservative. The problem is that these programs have enervated the sociological approach; they have pushed relativism and skepticism to the point where SSK has "nothing to say" (Collins and Yearly 1992a, p. 302). Rather than being able to challenge philosophy of science or the scientific community with respect to the fundamental question of why one theory comes to be accepted rather than another, the extreme relativist stance now renders SSK effectively mute. First-generation SSK – and for that matter the Bernalists and Mertonians – provided explanations for the success of particular scientific theories (and science in general). Although these explanations were couched in terms of social agency (social interests and social construction), and not the natural agency of philosophers or the scientific community, they systematically addressed the same key issues about the success of certain scientific theories, and thereby offered an important alternative to these establishment views. According to Collins and Yearley, this is the greatest contribution of SSK, and it is a

---

[18] Others discussing the debate include Friedman (1998) and Fuller (1996).

contribution that has been radically undermined by second-generation relativist views. Reflexivity and ANT are ostensibly sociological approaches to scientific knowledge that can "not tell us why only some actors have been able to get away with enforcing their view of the world" (Collins and Yearley 1992a, p. 323). Since these newer sociological approaches cannot answer this (the) fundamental question of science theory, the reigning philosophical stories remain firmly in place and therefore, according to Collins and Yearley, SSK has dropped the ball.

Collins and Yearley argue for *social realism* as an alternative to the relativism they find in the second-generation literature. SSK is a sociological inquiry and the explanations provided by those engaged in SSK should be based on social things (social structures, forces, interests, functions, etc.). This is not what philosophers and scientists do of course, but they are not doing SSK; those who are should be social realists. There are reasons why particular scientific theories come to be dominant and the explanation is to be found in the social forces at work within the scientific community.

> Our world is populated, we admit, by philosophically insecure objects, such as states of society and participant's comprehension. . . . But all worlds are built on shifting sands. We provide a prescription: stand on social things – be social realists – in order to explain natural things. The world is an agonistic field (to borrow a phrase from Latour); others will be standing on natural things to explain social things. That is all there is to it. (Collins and Yearley 1992b, p. 382)

In response to this argument for social realism, and in defense of ANT, Callon and Latour (1992) argued that Collins and Yearley were still stuck in the "nature pole" versus "social pole" dichotomy that actant network theory was designed to overcome. The natural realism of scientists and philosophers of science (where nature explains why people agree about the objects of nature), is diametrically opposed to the social pole (where society explains why people agree about the objects of nature), but this diametric opposition is precisely what the constantly shifting and continuously renegotiated agency of actants steadfastly avoids. According to Callon and Latour, there are two different ways that one can engage in reactionary science studies: one based on pure nature (the stories told by philosophers of science) and one based on pure society (the stories of Collins and Yearley, the Strong Program, and much of social constructivism); they argue that ANT offers a progressive alternative to both of these reactionary approaches. ANT focuses on the mutual coproduction of society and nature and does not rely on either pole as the fixed point for explanatory reference.

According to Callon and Latour, ANT offers many advantages over the social realism of Collins and Yearley. For one thing, scientists themselves are not the naive realists that Collins and Yearley suppose; scientists themselves have relatively flexible ontologies. Another reason for preferring ANT involves the observational status of the entities employed in the two different approaches to science studies. Callon and Latour insist that their approach is more empirically observable; social realism relies on unobservables like social structure and social interests (much like the stories told by scientists themselves rely on the agency of unobservables in nature), whereas ANT restricts itself purely to "the circulation of network-tracing tokens, statements, and skills" (Callon and Latour 1992, p. 351). Finally, and perhaps most importantly, they argue that social realism retains a form of epistemic privilege that has quite reactionary implications. For the social realists, it is pure society (society is privileged) and for scientists and philosophers of science it is pure nature (nature is privileged), but for Callon and Latour the point is to deconstruct epistemic privilege altogether by transcending both of these poles. To do otherwise is not only old-fashioned and reactionary, it is doomed to backfire on SSK; if any notion of epistemic privilege is retained, natural scientists will ultimately be able to wield it more effectively than sociologists. These arguments against social realism are not offered casually; SSK is in crisis and if not reformed in the direction of ANT the germinal insights of first-generation SSK will be lost. Recalling Callon and Latour's remarks quoted in the previous section:

> We did not come to this position for the fun of it or to play the deadly game of chicken, as we have been accused of doing, but because the field is cornered in a dead end from which we want to escape. (Callon and Latour 1992, p. 351)

Woolgar's response to Collins and Yearley is also critical, but his approach is quite different. For Woolgar, Collins and Yearly are philosophically out of touch and seem to long for the prepostmodernist days when things like "choosing a framework" and "ontological posits" made sense; they "still yearn for a metanarrative" (Woolgar 1992, p. 329). According to Woolgar, "Once we recognize the constitutive function of language," it becomes clear that the choice of "an epistemological stance is ludicrous" (Woolgar 1992, p. 331). We do not have an epistemological stance; an epistemological stance has us. Woolgar finds this particularly troubling, as SSK has made such a contribution to the rise of contemporary perspectivism, and that perspectivism is precisely what Woolgar claims Collins and Yearley ignore. For Woolgar, SSK's most important insight remains reflexivity, and, in particular, reflexivity's ability to disrupt and reconfigure our epistemic vision. To do anything other than revel in reflexivity – in particular, to engage in the causal old-speak of social realism – is to step backward and subvert the most important insight of SSK.

> Reflexivity asks us to problematize the assumption that the analyst (author, self) stands in a disengaged relationship to the world (subjects, objects, scientists, things). It asks us to push symmetry one stage further, to explore the consequences of challenging the assumption that the analyst enjoys a privileged position vis-à-vis the subjects and objects which come under the authorial gaze. (Woolgar 1992, p. 334)

Although Pickering edited the volume that contained the opening exchange between Collins and Yearley and their critics, his contribution to the debate came later in the presentation of his own mangle (1994, 1995a) view of science. As mentioned above, Pickering's mangle borrows heavily from the second-generation literature, particularly ANT, but his main focus is on the relationship between the "material world" and SSK. As he explains in the Preface to *The Mangle*, he began with an interest in the philosophical question of how knowledge relates to the world, but ultimately became more interested with the less philosophical, but still materialistic, question of how "the disciplined, industrialized, and militarized, technoscientific world in which I have lived my life, and how it ever got to be this way" (1995a, p. xii). Recall that Pickering emphasizes various material "resistances" to scientists' performances and the associated "dialectic of resistance and accommodation." This dialectic, although firmly denying the traditional representational view of scientific knowledge, is broadly realist in its metaphysical focus; scientists engage the material world and construct knowledge, but the material world resists in various ways, frustrating the scientists' intentions, and these resistances must be accommodated.

The mangle is similar to ANT in that it does not emphasize just one form of agency: "The mangle and the actor-network insist on the constitutive intertwining and reciprocal interdefinition of human and material agency" (Pickering 1995a, pp. 25–6). The main difference, according to Pickering, is that, whereas ANT remains squarely within the (traditional) representative idiom, the mangle emphasizes the performative aspects of the conceptual structures that emerge within the social context of science: these structures are representational, but they must also support various human practices and performances. Resistances are encountered and material agency emerges in the context of (and only in the context of) these performances. Science is "doing things," but it is not just human scientists that are doing things (have agency), nature is also doing things (has agency) by offering various resistances that scientists must accommodate. Pickering thus allows for material agency in a way that he argues many social realists do not, without giving nature the kind of free reign that is has in the accounts of philosophers of science and the scientists themselves.

> My argument is that we need to recognize that material agency is irreducible to human agency if we are to understand scientific practice. Nevertheless, I need to stress that the trajectory of emergence of material agency is bound up with that of human agency. Material agency does not force itself upon scientists. There is, to put it another way, no such thing as a perfect tuning of machines dictated by material agency as the thing-in-itself; scientists, to put it yet another way, never grasp the pure essence of material agency. Instead, material agency emerges via an inherently *impure* dynamics that couples the material agency and human realms. (1995a, pp. 53–4, emphasis in original)

Recently certain defenders of the Strong Program have offered their own, very different, response to the issues raised by the chicken debate (Barnes, Bloor, and Henry 1996; Bloor 1999). They also are concerned with the role of nature in sociological explanations of scientific knowledge, but their philosophical focus (and associated idiom) is much more traditional; they are concerned with the role played by "objective reality" in the determination of scientific belief. They criticize sociologists who practice what they call "methodological idealism," acting as if "the natural world, and our experience of it, played no significant role in the production of knowledge" (Barnes, Bloor, and Henry 1996, p. 13), and repeatedly cite Collins's social realism as a primary example of such methodological idealism (1996, pp. 14–15, 73–7). Barnes, Bloor and Henry simply assert that "methodological idealism is wrong" (1996, p. 13), in particular because it denies any checks or controls (or in Pickering's terms "resistances") on the cultural production of scientific representations.

> Methodological idealism does not give us a genuine technique for exposing the social element in knowledge: it only provides a means for expressing our prior assumptions on the matter. It has the disadvantage that it invites us to make unchecked suppositions about the scope and role of social factors, without providing any genuine controls on them. (Barnes, Bloor, and Henry 1996, p. 15)

The antidote to such idealism is, of course, some form of realism, and the defenders of the Strong Program argue that such an antidote is exactly what their approach provides.[19] The Strong Program "is part of a naturalistic and causal enterprise" (Bloor 1999, p. 87) and adheres to a relatively traditional epistemological position that prevents it from falling prey to the idealism that is present in so many other forms of SSK.

> No plausible sociology of knowledge could deny a role for such basic, material and causal factors in the process of belief formation: sometimes theories work, and we are impressed by this. To deny this would be to adopt a form of *idealism* in which the world is understood as an emanation of our beliefs, rather than as a cause of them. (Barnes, Bloor, and Henry 1996, p. 32, emphasis in original)

Although it is easy to claim that the Strong program allows for natural agency (avoids idealism) and maintains a traditional epistemological stance, this claim seems hard to reconcile with the program's original four methodological tenets: causality, impartiality, symmetry, and reflexivity. In fact, such a claim seems difficult to reconcile with any sociological analysis of scientific knowledge. After all, wasn't it one of the main points of the Kuhnian revolution that helped to precipitate the social turn, that traditional empiricist notions of causality and the relationship between knower and knowee no longer represented an adequate starting point for the study of scientific knowledge? So, how do these recent defenders of the Strong Program manage to walk the tightrope between traditional epistemology and sociology? The answer lies in the Strong Program's version of *empiricism*: a version that, for want of a better term, I will call *social empiricism*.[20] They start from a position that sounds much

---

[19] There is, of course, an issue about whether natural agency has always been part of the Strong Program, or whether it is a reinterpretation of the program in light of recent controversies such as the chicken debate. The argument in Barnes, Bloor, and Henry (1996) is that the Strong Program always allowed for nature to play a substantive role (it was never methodologically idealist) and those who have suggested otherwise (this includes most who have ever discussed the Strong Program) have simply misread the program's foundational works. My own view is that they have put a materialistic spin on the Strong Program, and although that spin may not be inconsistent with the foundational works, it does in fact push the argument in a very different direction than the early literature. This move seems entirely explicable now that the competition is from more radically social (they would say idealistic) versions of SSK, rather than from mainstream philosophy of science as it was during the first generation of literature.

[20] A social empiricism that does not seem to be much different than the social empiricism advocated by Miriam Solomon (1994a, 1994b), even though she presents her version as an alternative to SSK.

like (biologically or psychologically) naturalized epistemology: arguing that humans, like other animals, have developed "reasonably reliable and tolerably non-frustrating routines for interacting with the environment" (Barnes, Bloor, and Henry 1996, p. 32). The difference is, the Strong Programmers emphasize that in humans this information-processing ability has a fundamentally social component. Our empirical processing method requires *social calibration*; it only produces reliable knowledge when it is certified by coherence with the observations made by other members of the relevant epistemic community. Since a "social criterion" must be satisfied for an observation to be genuine and reliable, the door is left open for sociologists to explain why a particular social criterion is in effect and what social function, or interests, or structure, it serves. This social empiricism allows the Strong Program to be epistemologically rather traditional (at least relative to second-generation programs such as hyperreflexivity and ANT) and yet retain a fundamentally sociological theory of scientific knowledge.

Turning to another traditional theme: The recent defenders consider the Strong Program to be a *realist* approach, although again, not the realism associated with mainstream philosophy of science. Their empiricism leads them to a *descriptive realism* about science; they observe scientists acting *as if* the objects of scientific inquiry were independent of the scientist's investigation. In other words, actual scientists employ realist strategies in the activity of science, leading the Strong Program to endorse realism "as a feature of the behavior of scientists" (Barnes, Bloor, and Henry 1996, p. 83). The argument is that realism is not an ontological assumption (or at least need not be), rather it is an empirically identified phenomena (observed in the behavior of scientists) that needs to be sociologically explained. Such realism is not, of course, a unique feature of science – as the authors point out, all cultures, not just scientific cultures, are realist about their ontological posits – nonetheless this realism remains a significant feature of scientific life that requires explanation by SSK.

In summary, then, both Pickering and the recent reinterpreters (or clarifiers) of the Strong Program have, pace Collins and Yearley, tried in very different ways to let nature back into the sociological analysis of science without destroying the social aspect of the sociological inquiry. Pickering relies on the dialectic of resistance and accommodation associated with the (potentially frustrating) performative aspect of scientific culture, whereas Barnes, Bloor, and Henry rely on a type of social empiricism. It is not clear how these two attempts to respond to the issues raised in the chicken debate will pan out relative to social realism, the reflexivists, ANT, or even other approaches that I have not discussed, but it is clear that reflexivity has come full circle. The concern over the proper conduct of sociological inquiry in the study of science has now being reflected back onto the proper conduct of sociological inquiry into science. What I mean by this is that in an effort to promote SSK – against the philosophers of science and against the scientists' own representations of their actions – those in SSK turned to the defense and advocacy of particular approaches within sociology and to core (and sometimes quite traditional) questions about how sociological inquiry ought to be done. In the words of Collins and Yearley "epistemological problems are not resolved by empirical discoveries" (Collins and Yearley 1992a, p. 303). The result is that SSK now seems to be back to the point of trying to decide on epistemological and methodological issues so that *the inquiry*, that is SSK, can proceed most effectively and not lose ground to philosophers' and scientists' renditions of scientific knowledge.

5.3.2 SSK and Economics

In this final section, I will examine a few of the many contact points between SSK and economics, and in particular how these contact points impact economic methodology. Three of these relationships will be discussed, but before I start it is useful to point out two other bodies of literature – in fact, important and rapidly growing bodies of literature – that will not be considered at this point even though they also represent (at least indirect) contact points between economics and SSK. These two bodies of literature are both subsets of what I call the "economics of scientific knowledge" (ESK) in Chapter 8; they are the literature where economists are applying economic models to the study of science and scientific knowledge, and the research on what might be called "economically naturalized epistemology" (where philosophers of science are employing economics as a resource for the philosophical study of science). These are both extremely important and rapidly growing fields that have connections to SSK, but their examination will be deferred until Chapter 8, where they constitute the main topic of discussion. This section will examine three points of contact between SSK and economic methodology, *other than* ESK.

The first point of contact is the one that seems most obvious from the discussion in the last three chapters: *SSK has helped to undermine traditional philosophy of science and thereby the traditional approach to economic methodology.* We have seen that for most of the twentieth century, economists writing on methodology simply accepted *the shelf of scientific philosophy*: take items off the philosophical shelf and apply them to economics without too much reflection or reconfiguration. We have also seen that this approach has become extremely problematic now that philosophy of science is in such disarray: *and SSK has clearly contributed to that disarray*. Of course, SSK is not alone in contributing to the problems of the philosophy of science (Chapters 3 and 4 discussed many other contributors), but it has played a very important role. The most disquieting implications of the social turn of Kuhn and others seem to emanate from SSK. After all, if one takes the job of economic methodology to be its traditional normative task of finding the proper economic method – the search for a relatively small set of epistemically justified rules governing the conduct of proper scientific inquiry in economics – then *SSK tells us to give up on such methodology*. SSK says there basically are no such rules; the Legend is dead; quit doing philosophy of science and start doing something more sociological. Of course, this opens up a number of questions associated with using social science as a resource for the investigation of social science, but it represents a major change in methodological inquiry that was initiated, at least in part, by SSK.

The second point of contact is that *many studies in SSK look much like what an economist would write about science or the behavior of scientist agents*. Sometimes the "economics" being applied is heterodox (Marx in particular) and sometimes the arguments sound more like what a mainstream microeconomist would say about the behavior of rational agents (who just happen to be scientists). On the Marxist side, there is, of course, the early literature of Hessen and Bernal, but that literature is not the only case where Marxist political economy enters the sociological study of scientific knowledge. A number of commentators have noted (Callon 1995, p. 38; Hands 1994b, pp. 82–3; Mäki 1992a, pp. 79–81) that Latour and Woolgar's (1979/1986) model of credibility accumulation among scientists looks a lot like the Marxist model of capital accumulation. Perhaps a better example of Marxist influence is Pickering's "mangle of practice." Pickering talks a lot about the shop floor as the site for the mangle: the factory is the "double surface of emergence" of science and society (Pickering 1995a, p. 232), Taylorite management techniques represent an intensification of the "sociocyborg of production" (Pickering 1995a, p. 161), and efforts to computerize production are an attempt "to try even harder to squeeze the human out of the cyborg of production" (Pickering 1995a, p. 166). He explains that his performative approach is closely related to the Marxist historiography of Bernal and others but there also are significant differences; for Bernal, the content of scientific knowledge was independent of the social, the social forms were fixed at any particular point in time, and those forms were (teleologically) destined to evolve in a particular way (Pickering 1995a, pp. 251–2). For Pickering, the economic process of industrial production is a major factor in the mangle, but it affects the content as well as speed of science, and the relevant social forms are much more complex and dynamic than those envisioned by Marx's basic modes of production.

> A performative big picture of the history of science would be one in which Karl Marx, Boris Hessen and John Desmond Bernal basically got it right. . . . the only sense, I think, in which the Marxist tradition has tended to get it wrong is in thinking that the base somehow determines the superstructure. (Pickering 1995b, p. 418)

If we turn to mainstream economics, the list of contact points grows even larger. As Mäki notes:

> It is interesting from our point of view that much of recent sociology of science is built upon analogies drawn from economics. In these suggestions science is viewed as analogous to a capitalist market economy in which agents are maximizing producers who competitively and greedily pursue their self-interest. (Mäki 1992a, p. 79)

One example is Latour and Woolgar (1979/1986); their discussion of scientists' attempt to compete for credibility, and the development of a market for such credibility, can be read as a microeconomic argument as well as one from Marxian economics.

> Let us suppose that scientists are investors of credibility. The result is the creation of a *market*. Information now has value because, . . . it allows other investigators to produce information which facilitates the return of invested capital. There is a *demand* from investors for information . . . and there is a *supply* of information from other investors. The forces of supply and demand create the *value* of the commodity, which fluctuates constantly depending on supply, demand, the number of investigators, and the equipment of the producers. (Latour and Woolgar 1986, p. 206, emphasis in original)

Another constructivist author that seems to employ economic argumentation is Karin Knorr Cetina. She discusses two research strategies in particle physics: the "framing" strategy and the "exchange" strategy. The exchange strategy sounds like a group of scientists engaging in cost-benefit analysis to maximize the utility of their group research efforts.

> I have defined contingency in terms of a negative relationship
> of dependence between two desired goals, or research utilities,
> such that one utility can only be obtained or optimized at the
> cost of the other. In this situation particle physicists resort to a
> strategy of commerce and exchange: they balance research ben-
> efits against each other, and then "sell off" those which they
> think that, on balance, they may not be able to afford. (Knorr
> Cetina 1991, pp. 112–13)[21]

Yet another sociological approach that seems to carry a lot of economic baggage is the ANT of Latour and others. Chris McClellan (1996)
has argued that as ANT evolved out of Latour and Woolgar's *Laboratory Life* (1979/1986) and Latour's *Science in Action* (1987), it brought
with it a strong dose of the market analogy, an analogy that has been a
source of continual tension within the program. For some within ANT,
the scientist should be seen as an entrepreneur who builds a network
by enrolling actants through efficient investment of scarce resources;
success is market success and knowledge, like capital, is accumulated in
the process. Others involved in ANT accept some aspects of this market
story but consider it to be primarily a critique of the encroachment
of market rationality into every aspect of human life (including science).
Thus, as McClellan explains, elements of ANT pull in both directions of
"the great divide which separates *homo sociologicus* and *homo eco-
nomicus*" (McClellan 1996, p. 203). It is interesting to note that in a paper
presenting "Four Models for the Dynamics of Science," Callon (1995)
implicates economics (either Marxist or neoclassical) in two out of the
four views he discusses, but does not mention economics directly in
the "extended translation" approach that includes ANT. Nonetheless, at
the end of the paper, he lists two general areas for future research: The
first involves the application of ideas from industrial organization theory
such as "barriers to entry, differentiated return on investments, imperfect competition, diversification and differentiation strategies" (Callon
1995, p. 61), and the second concerns the links between technology and
economics: "The economics of technical change whose recent results
show a remarkable convergence with those of the sociology of science"
(Callon 1995, p. 61).

The third point of contact concerns the involvement of SSK in the
recent literature on the history of economic thought. A number of recent
authors have *applied SSK directly to the study of contemporary eco-*

---

[21] Pels (1997) makes the interesting argument (using the work of Knorr Cetina and others)
that much of early SSK focused on economics, but that the economic element has actually
decreased over time.

nomics and/or various topics in the discipline's history. In a few cases, economics has been studied by sociologists or historians influenced by SSK (e.g., Ashmore, Mulkay, and Pinch 1989; Collins 1991; Evans 1999; Pickering 1997; Poovey 1998; and Yonay 1994, 1998),[22] but in most cases economists are the ones employing SSK as a resource in the history of economic thought. The literature written by economists takes a number of different forms and covers a wide range of different subjects. There is some research that discusses the question of SSK and economics at a fairly general level: works such as Coats (1993a, 1993b), Hands (1994b, 1997a, 1999), Mäki (1992a, 1993b), and Sent (1997c). There are also economic studies that apply the work of one particular sociologist or sociological school; in addition to Mertonian-inspired studies such as Niehans (1995a), Patinkin (1983), and Tollison (1986), there are also economic applications of specific versions of contemporary SSK (Davis 1997a; Hands 1994c; and Sent 1998a, for example). Finally, there are a growing number of works in the history of economic thought that are broadly informed by SSK but do not apply any one particular school or approach: Bogaard (1999), Hands and Mirowski (1998), Henderson (1996), Klein (1997), Leonard (1994a, 1994b, 1995a, 1995b, 1997, 1998), Mirowski (1992, 1994, 1997a, 1999), Sent (1997a), Mirowski and Hands (1998), Weintraub (1988a, 1991a, 1991b, 1997), Weintraub and Mirowski (1994), and White (1994a, 1994b) are a few examples.[23] Although these recent SSK-inspired studies range widely over various topics in the history of economic thought, and exhibit different degrees of commitment to SSK, such studies have been fairly well received among historians of economic thought, and there seems to be a growing opinion that such approaches provide a richer understanding of their historical subjects than previous "reconstructions" in the history of economic thought based on positivist or Popperian philosophy of science (see Chapter 7). These SSK-inspired histories, of course, also raise various issues that are not present in more rules-based approaches, such as reflexivity and relativism, but the early

---

[22] Callon (1998) presents an interesting case, but one that is difficult to classify. The papers in the volume employ ANT-inspired analysis to the subject of markets (and their laws), but markets are not perceived wholly as a thing (in the economy) or as a construction of the community of economists (in economics); rather, the laws of markets are jointly coproduced by the movement of the economy and economics (see Callon's "Introduction" in particular). Is this ANT-inspired science studies applied to an economic subject, or the subject of economics? Perhaps both and neither, since such a distinction doesn't make much sense from the perspective of ANT.

[23] The relationship is less direct, but one also might consider some of the classic texts in the history of economic thought where the economic ideas are presented as emerging from a particular social context – say, Mitchell, 1967 – as an example of SSK-type ideas in the history of economic thought.

returns seem to suggest that the additional costs are small relative to the benefits.[24] Although a number of positive things can be said about this recent historical literature, we really haven't developed all of the background material that is necessary to examine it in any serious way. The problem is that much of this recent work in the history of economic thought is not only informed by SSK, it is also informed by a number of other recent developments within philosophy and science theory: in particular, the postmodernist, neopragmatist, and rhetorical literature discussed in the next chapter. Thus, while it has been important to examine the literature of the sociological turn, it is not the final step in our quest to explore the various aspects of science theory that are relevant to our story. The next chapter expands the search in a number of additional directions.

[24] For an alternative reading of the costs and benefits, see Backhouse (1992a, 1992b, 1997a) or Blaug (1994b). I examine the historiographical issues raised by such SSK-inspired studies in more detail in Hands (1997a).

6

Pragmatism, Discourse, and Situatedness

Philosophers, after all, are like everyone else; they want people who don't do what they do to believe that what they do is universally enabling. They want us to believe that the only good king is a philosopher king, and that the only good judge is a philosopher judge, and the only good baseball player is a philosopher baseball player. Well, I don't know about you, but I hope that my kings, if I should ever have any, are good at being kings, and that my judges are good at being judges, and that the players on my team throw strikes and keep 'em off the bases.

[Fish 1987, p. 1800]

Compared with other schools of economics the neoclassicals are notably butch. They are a motorcycle gang among economists, strutting about the camp with clattering matrices and rigorously fixed points, sheathed in leather, repelling affection. They are not going to like being told that they should be more feminine.

[McCloskey 1993, p. 76]

The last three chapters have focused on various contemporary developments within the philosophy of science and science studies. Although these two areas constitute much of contemporary science theory, they do not exhaust it, and more important, they do not exhaust the work that is relevant to the changing face of economic methodology. For one thing, despite the impact of logical positivism, not all philosophy is philosophy of science, and more general developments within disciplinary philosophy also impact debates about scientific and economic knowledge. The more general philosophical approach that will receive the most attention in this chapter is *pragmatism*. Classical pragmatism was the most influential philosophical school in late nineteenth- and early twentieth-century America, but the program was eclipsed by positivist-inspired philosophical analysis during the interwar period. In recent years, pragmatism has returned – in its classical form, as well as in a number of neopragmatist guises – and it now represents, if not the most influential, at least one of the fastest growing philosophical frameworks on the intellectual landscape. Section 6.1 examines classical pragmatism, whereas the first part of Section 6.2 discusses the neopragmatism of philosophers like Richard Rorty.

Not only do philosophical ideas from outside the philosophy of science influence how we think about scientific knowledge; intellectual ideas originating from outside the strict confines of disciplinary philosophy often have a similar (or even more pronounced) effect. One such intellectual development, and one that has been alluded to several times in previous chapters, is *postmodernism*. Postmodernism certainly isn't a "philosophical position" in the sense that logical positivism or utilitarianism are philosophical positions – it is simultaneously wider and deeper than such positions – but it is an influential constellation of ideas that has profoundly influenced contemporary intellectual culture including the discipline of philosophy (and certain areas within economic methodology). A second intellectual development – related to both postmodernism and pragmatism – is the *discursive turn*; the notion that what is most important about intellectual discourse in all fields is not the specific content of the discussion but the fact that it is *a discussion*. A third influential development is *feminism*; feminist perspectives cut across every aspect of contemporary culture including all of the various academic disciplines. There are feminist literatures, feminist histories, feminist ethics, feminist artistic movements, and feminist contributions to almost every other field of inquiry or aspect of culture, but most relevant to the discussion at hand, there are feminist approaches to epistemology, science studies, and economics. In response to these extrametascientific developments, the second half of this chapter will offer a brief foray into the literature of postmodernism, discourse analysis, and feminism, in an effort to elucidate some of the many (and growing) contact points between these movements and the field of economic methodology. Although I have started almost every chapter with a disclaimer to the effect that "this is not a comprehensive survey but only an attempt to point out some of the ways that this literature bears on (or might bear on) economic methodology"; such a warning is particularly pertinent to the discussion in this chapter.

6.1 The Pragmatic Turn

Pragmatism is back, and back in a pretty big way. Consider a few of the following examples. Quine's influential philosophical position has always been informed by pragmatic ideas (Quine 1981); so, too, for the work of Donald Davidson (1980), although he is less likely to use the term. A number of prominent philosophers who once endorsed scientific realism have now adopted a variant of the pragmatic stance; the most dramatic example being Hilary Putnam's (1995) evolution from scientific realism, to internal realism, to pragmatic realism. Many of the recent contributors to the philosophy of language take a pragmatic position (Brandom 1994, for example). Many philosophers who find experimental practice to be the key to understanding science – either its stability (Galison 1987) or its realism (Cartwright 1983; Hacking 1983) – have also been influenced by pragmatic ideas (see Lenoir 1988). The German philosophers of the Frankfurt school who once drew their inspiration from Marx and Freud now seem to be following Charles Sanders Peirce's pragmatic philosophy (Apel 1981; Habermas 1971 and 1992). Pragmatist ideas also seem to have a growing influence on the sociological side of science theory (see Lenoir 1992, or Barbara Herrnstein Smith 1997); among those discussed above, Andrew Pickering (1990, 1995a), in particular, uses pragmatic realism to undergird his postconstructivist vision of the sociological approach to scientific knowledge. And, finally, many of the philosophers who attempt to synthesize the best from both the naturalist and sociological turns seem to have much in common with classical pragmatism (Haack 1993 and Solomon 1995a for instance). And the list could go on and on.[1]

So how did this happen? As the question was posed in the introduction to a recent pragmatist reader:

> How is it that a philosophy so vibrant and promising at the turn of the twentieth century and so depleted at midcentury should revive now at the end: after positivism, phenomenology, logical analysis, naturalized epistemology, and deconstruction? (Goodman 1995, p. 1)

[1] A recent paper by Thomas Uebel (1996) is an interesting case in point. It argues that the positions of both Carnap and Schlick were quite close to the pragmatism of Charles S. Peirce. Whether or not one is persuaded by Uebel's argument, it is interesting that pragmatism has moved so demonstratively to center stage, that individual positivists are now being judged on the basis of how much their work conforms to pragmatic ideas.

Although a more substantive answer to this question will emerge in the next few sections, it seems useful at this point to make a few preliminary suggestions about how the argument will go. I will mention four issues at this point; others will surface in the following discussion.

First, pragmatism seems to provide a way out of what has become the major dilemma in contemporary metascience: the dilemma of being stuck between foundationalist philosophy, on the one hand and radical relativism, on the other. It seems that either science conforms to the narrow guidelines of some particular foundationalist-inspired philosophy of science, or we must conclude that science is nothing special at all (just social interests, just discourse, etc.). Pragmatism gives us another alternative; it is antifoundationalist – aggressively antifoundationalist – while retaining the notion that science is in fact rather special. All aspects of culture, at least for classical pragmatism, are not the same, and science is indeed a particularly beneficial form of life. The keys for (classical) pragmatism are: first, that while science has special, and desirable, properties, these special properties do not emerge because science provides a unique pathway to some sacred domain (the Truth, the Good, the Perfect), and second, these properties are quite general and are not based on narrow rules set down by some specific demarcation criterion that excludes all but the most cognitively pristine scientific activities. Pragmatism is proscience without being prophilosophy of science or eliminatively scientistic. As Charles Morris put it many years ago:

> [T]here is still an important difference between the pragmatists' conception of philosophy and that of the logical empiricists. The pragmatists have, without exception I believe, wished philosophy to become as scientific as possible, but have not limited philosophy to the philosophy of science. A scientific philosophy need not be a philosophy of science. (Morris 1963, pp. 96–7)

For pragmatism, science is special, but it is special because it helps us get on in (rather than get beyond) the mundane world, and because it is general enough that it can be applied to social, ethical, and other questions involving judgments of value in addition to those questions that are narrowly scientific. Again Charles Morris:

> It has been a central tenet of the pragmatists, no matter how great their other differences, that judgments of value are empirical in nature, and so have a cognitive or theoretical character amenable in principle to control by scientific methods. Stated in

another way, the pragmatists have believed that judgments of value as well as the statements of science conform to the pragmatic maxim and are meaningful in the same sense. (Morris 1963, p. 94)

A second motivation for the increased popularity of pragmatic philosophy – closely related to the fact that pragmatism is scientific without being scientistic – is that pragmatism blurs the relationship between theory and practice. Whether it is the experimental realism of Hacking (1983) and Cartwright (1983), the practice-centered view of Galison (1987, 1997), or the ethnography of scientific practice that characterizes much of SSK, practice has been elevated in recent science studies and the Received View's rigid hierarchy between "theory" and "practice" (among others) has been discredited. For pragmatism, there never was a meaningful distinction between the two – it lacked a rigid distinction between "knowing" and "doing" – thus allowing it to sit quite comfortably with the results from recent practice-centered approaches to the study of science.

A third reason for the resurgence of pragmatic ideas is that pragmatism is fundamentally *social*; for pragmatism science is social, human life is social, and the most important properties of human inquiry and human action emerge from our sociality. Because pragmatism does not start from the traditional epistemological question of how individual beliefs come to accurately reflect the properties of the objective world, the ostensive failure of all the traditional answers to this epistemic question has left pragmatism effectively unscathed. Not only is pragmatism safe from the criticisms that have plagued traditional approaches to epistemology and philosophy of science, it also has benefited from the fact that it has always endorsed the social perspective that has increasingly become the mainstay of post-Kuhnian metascience. In other words, pragmatism gains credibility from the problems of the Received View because it was never committed to the class of questions the Received View failed to answer, and it has always focused on the same (social) issues that emerged within the critical literature.

Finally, pragmatists have always been aware of the problems of theory-ladenness and underdetermination. Pragmatic philosophers have never insisted that empirical facts exist independently of the theory-, social-, and interest-laden context of human practice, or that the confrontation between theory and evidence should, or even could, be restricted to the formulaic testing procedure explicated by the Received View. For pragmatism, human knowledge is much messier, and far more interesting, than how it appears in traditional philosophy of science.

6.1.1 Peirce, Dewey, and Classical Pragmatism

The story goes that pragmatism was born in 1898 when William James first used the term during a philosophical address at the University of California. James attributed the term to Charles S. Peirce who had employed it twenty years earlier in two papers – "The Fixation of Belief" (1877) and "How to Make Our Ideas Clear" (1878) – published in the *Popular Science Monthly*. Peirce himself claimed that the term originally came from Kant, and that he had initially borrowed it in 1871 for a presentation at the Cambridge Metaphysical Club (Apel 1981, p. 16). Regardless of where the term first appeared, James's attribution of the term to Peirce brought distinction to the elder philosopher – an unexpected distinction, as Peirce had essentially retired from academic life after his dismissal from Johns Hopkins in 1884 and was, by the late 1880s, living in relative isolation in Milford, Pennsylvania. The additional attention provoked Peirce to reexamine his position: particularly as it compared to James's own, quite popular, and rather different, version of pragmatism. As a result of this reexamination, Peirce revised his earlier pragmatic position and by 1905 had renamed it "pragmaticism": a term that he felt was "ugly enough to be safe from kidnappers" (Peirce 1905a, 186).[2]

Although the differences between James and Peirce are significant, these differences do not exhaust the variation within classical pragmatism. At the turn of the century, the American philosophical scene seemed to be littered with pragmatisms – James's own *Pragmatism* (1907) mentions six different approaches, whereas Arthur Lovejoy's famous paper (1908) examines thirteen different versions of the general pragmatic perspective. Although most of these pragmatisms originated from within academic philosophy, a few were products of the more general popular culture. Given that our ultimate interest remains economic methodology, I will only examine two of the many versions of classical pragmatism – those of Peirce and Dewey – and offer only the précis version of each of these.

Peirce's original statements (1877, 1878) focused on the question of belief determination. According to Peirce, humans find doubt to be inherently unpleasant and consistently endeavor to avoid it. He argued

---

[2] Apel (1981) argues that there were actually four distinct periods in Peirce's philosophical development with pragmaticism being the final phase. Even if the phases were not distinct, it is clear Peirce's thought evolved over time, and, as a result, there are a number of different interpretations of his work within the contemporary literature (there are even authors who make Peirce into a simple falsificationist; Sullivan, 1991, criticizes this view). There has recently been a spate of interesting and entertaining biographical works on Peirce (Brent 1993, 1996; Ketner 1998).

that historically we have used basically four different methods to facilitate the fixation of belief (avoidance of doubt): the method of tenacity, the method of authority, the *a priori* method, and the scientific method. Tenacity involves forming a belief and sticking with it come what may: principally by systematically avoiding doubt-creating situations. Once doubt intervenes, the historically prevalent response has been the method of authority: relying on the officially sanctioned views of the church, state, or other social authority to eliminate doubt. The third, *a priori*, method is the method of rational and idealistic philosophy – Peirce refers specifically to Plato, Kant, and Hegel – and even though such philosophical positions are less popular today, they were common methods of doubt elimination among Peirce's intellectual cohort. Peirce's preferred approach to fixing belief is the fourth method: the method of science. As a practicing scientist, Peirce had participated in the scientific method and was deeply committed to extending the scientific approach into other areas of belief fixation.[3]

According to Peirce, the most troublesome characteristic of both the rationalist and empiricist traditions was their commitment to *foundationalism* and the search for certainty. The advocates of both of these traditional epistemological positions sought a methodological guarantee: a method that could guarantee, absolute, apodictic certainty. But for Peirce, such certainty was unattainable. All one could do was to conduct philosophy in the same manner as scientists have traditionally conducted scientific inquiry: proceed systematically, investigate empirically, be open to criticism, and respect the fallibilism of the investigative process. Above all, science was a social community, and the values of science – the axiological framework for the scientific approach to the fixation of belief – were community values. Scientific inquiry was a continuous and self-correcting process of critical appraisal by those within the scientific community: those who shared its values. Science was not legitimated by the words of philosophers – the spell of logic, the appeal to foundations, or the rhetoric of certainty – but by its contribution to the enhancement of human life; all of those things that philosophers proffered as grounding science, as the indubitable foundations for human knowledge, were in fact far less certain than the reliable daily output of the scientific community. To contrast this view with some of the views discussed in previous chapters, particularly positivism, it is useful to briefly examine Peirce's position on a number of specific issues.

---

[3] Backhouse (1994b) uses Peirce's four notions of belief fixation to explain why economists disagree. His bottom line is that economists disagree because they do not pay sufficient attention to empirical evidence. This use of Peirce seems to make him into a naive empiricist, which, as we will see, he certainly was not.

First, the perennial issue of truth. For Peirce, like so many others, science pursues truth, but what, for Peirce, is the truth that science pursues? Truth for Peirce is a property of certain beliefs, the beliefs that the scientific community would eventually converge to if inquiry were to continue indefinitely into the future. As science advances, certain beliefs become fixed and are not revised during the further progress of science; these beliefs, the beliefs that would be held by the scientific community at the end of inquiry, constitute truth. In Peirce's own words from one of his later works:

> But no doubt what is meant is that the objectivity of truth really consists in the fact that, in the end, every sincere inquirer will be led to embrace it ... I hold that truth's independence of individual opinion is due (so far as there is any "truth") to its being the predestined result to which sufficient inquiry *would* ultimately lead. (Peirce 1906, p. 288)

Notice that Peirce's concept of truth involves something *objective* (in the sense that it is a property of beliefs that exists independently of the beliefs of any particular individual); it is something *social* (it is a property of certain beliefs of the scientific community); and it is something that *would be* at the end of inquiry (opposed to what is now, or might be if certain procedures were followed). Also notice that nothing in the Peircean notion limits us to beliefs about "physical" processes or other things that we usually think of as amenable to "science"; truth as the ideal limit of a process of inquiry by a community of scientific inquirers could apply just as well to various inquiries outside the traditional domain of natural science. Finally, and relevant to any economic theory influenced by his pragmatism, Peirce's rather aggressive anti-individualism is clearly manifested in his notion of truth. Not only is scientific inquiry, and the truth that would emerge from it, a social and public affair, the beliefs of any individual are necessarily in error unless they happen to comply with what the community would believe in the limit.[4] As Habermas characterizes Peirce's view of the individual:

> This becomes apparent in Peirce's concept of the person, in which everything that makes a person into an individual is defined negatively, in terms of its difference from what is general – namely, in terms of the distance separating error from the truth and of that dividing the egoist from the community. The individual is something merely subjective and egoistic. (Habermas 1992, p. 108)

---

[4] For this reason Apel (1981, p. 92) refers to Peirce's position as "logical socialism"; perhaps cognitive socialism would be a better description.

In his early pragmatic essays, Peirce defined "the real" in terms of his notion of truth. For example, in "How to Make Our Ideas Clear," he characterized reality in the following way:

> The opinion which is fated to be ultimately agreed to by all who investigate, is what we mean by the truth, and the object represented in this opinion is the real. That is the way that I would explain reality. (Peirce 1978, p. 133)

This makes Peirce a scientific realist, but a scientific realist of a rather unusual sort. Instead of the traditional realism where scientific theories correctly represent the properties of the objective world, Peirce defines truth as that which the scientific community would believe at the end of inquiry, and then characterizes reality in terms of this truth; it is a realism that associates reality with possible knowledge. In Habermas's words, Peirce has a "cognizability" (1971, p. 98) notion of the real; a concept of reality that is based on his "methodological concept of truth" (1971, p. 99). Of course, because Peirce's notion of reality is based on his concept of truth, and his conception of truth is fundamentally social, Peirce ends up with social characterization of reality. Reality is established as what a particular community of inquirers would eventually believe. The social nature of reality is quite clear in the following remarks from one of Peirce's early works.

> And what do we mean by the real? . . . The real, then, is that which, sooner or later, information and reasoning would finally result in, and which is therefore independent of the vagaries of me and you. Thus, the very origin of the conception of reality shows that this conception essentially involves the notion of a COMMUNITY, without definite limits, and capable of a definite increase of knowledge. And so those two series of cognitions – the real and the unreal – consist of those which, at a time sufficiently future, the community will always continue to re-affirm; and these which, under the same conditions, will ever after be denied. (Peirce 1868, pp. 247–8, capitalization in original)

It is easy to see why the Peircean concepts of truth and reality – as a temporally emergent stable set in the belief space of a certain idealized community of inquirers – might harmonize with voices from post-Kuhnian philosophy of science and science studies. In addition, Peirce achieves this harmony while being consistently proscience, antifoundationalist, and naturalistic. By contrast, it also should be clear why many find Peirce's ideas to be rather controversial and why there is a tendency for contemporary authors to skim off a few aspects of his philosophical program without adopting it in toto.

Before turning to Dewey's version of classical pragmatism, it is useful to briefly mention two other aspects of Peirce's philosophical program that are relevant to the task at hand: his pragmatic maxim and abductive inference.[5] The pragmatic maxim plays somewhat the same role in Peirce's philosophical program as the verifiability criterion of meaningfulness plays in positivism: it serves to differentiate meaningful from meaningless discourse and places traditional metaphysics on the meaningless side of the line.[6] The classic statement of what later came to be called the pragmatic maxim is contained in "How to Make Our Ideas Clear."

> The essence of belief is the establishment of a habit; and different beliefs are distinguished by the different modes of action to which they give rise. If beliefs do not differ in this respect, if they appease the same doubt by producing the same rule of action, then no mere differences in the manner of consciousness of them can make them different beliefs, any more than playing a tune in different keys is playing different tunes. (Peirce 1878, p. 121)

Or as he put it more succinctly in a later work.

> [T]he rational purport of a word or other expression, lies exclusively in its conceivable bearing upon the conduct of life. (Peirce 1905a, p. 183)

To modify an old adage, Peirce's pragmatic maxim seems to say that "meaningful is as meaningful does"; statements have meaning if they can be translated into actions and two statements have the same meaning if they imply the same action. There has been a protracted debate, starting in Peirce's own time and continuing into the contemporary literature, about exactly how this pragmatic maxim is different, or if it is different, from some sort of operationalist or behaviorist maxim about the meaningfulness of empirical statements. If the pragmatic maxim reduces to a type of observability or verifiability criterion, then it would seem that Peirce's pragmatism has little to distinguish it from logical empiricism. In fact, some pragmatic philosophers sympathetic to positivism (Charles Morris 1963, for example) see the two criteria as essentially identical; the only difference being that pragmatism also was concerned with prac-

---

[5] One other important aspect of Peirce's work that will not be examined is his semiotics (theory of signs). For Peirce's own comments on the subject collected from a number of different works, see Peirce (1940), and for a contemporary discussion, see Habermas (1992, pp. 88–112).

[6] Peirce did significant work on metaphysics – his concepts of firstness, secondness, and thirdness – but he was insistent about dismissing traditional metaphysical programs. For a discussion of Peirce's metaphysical views and their relationship to his general philosophy, see Ketner (1998) and Ch. 2 of Lewis and Smith (1980).

tical matters – adding a criterion of theory choice that involved the practical usefulness of the theory – but it is just an add-on (recall the discussion of van Fraassen in Chapter 3). Other authors want to stress that since Peirce emphasized the experimentally actionable implications, his notion of experiment was much more robust than the foundationalist-inspired notion of observational implications at work in late positivism. For Peirce, the "method of ascertaining the meanings of words and concepts is no other than that experimental method by which all the successful sciences . . . have reached the degrees of certainty that are severally proper to them today; this experimental method being itself nothing but a particular application of the older logical rule, 'By their fruits ye shall know them'" (Peirce 1906, p. 271). On this more naturalistic reading, meaningful is just what science does, rather than the statements of a scientific theory being meaningful because they are in compliance with some empiricist (as opposed to merely empirical) criterion of meaning. Needless to say, we are not going to settle the debate over the pragmatic maxim at this point – nor do we need to – but it is an important issue, particularly as it relates to situating Peirce's pragmatism with respect to the contemporary naturalistic turn.

Finally, there is the issue of Peirce's notion of abduction. For Peirce, there were three forms of logical reasoning: deduction, induction, and abduction. These modes of inference are extremely important for Peirce, since he sees the *process of science*, the actual application of these forms of inference, as the most significant factor in knowledge production (remember, he has no indubitable first principles or foundations to fall back on). Although Peirce's views about deduction and induction were relatively standard (for the late nineteenth century), his concept of abduction was an important contribution. Abduction is the process of going from a fact to the theory that supports it. It is the process of seeing the connection between a fact, particularly a surprising fact, and the theory that would cover or explain it. Because abduction involves positing a hypothesis, Peirce sometimes referred to the abductive method as the method of "hypothesis" (Ketner 1998, pp. 294–8). An abductive "argument" thus takes the form:

> The surprising fact, C, is observed:
> But if A were true, C would be matter of course,
> Hence, there is reason to suspect A is true.
> (Peirce quoted by Hoover 1994, p. 301)[7]

---

[7] Niiniluto (1999) provides a detailed discussion of Peirce's notion of abduction and argues that this version was more general than his original formulation. Needless to say, it is possible to find more than one concept of abduction is Peirce's writings.

Abductive inferences seem to be the main "stuff" of good science. They represent the explanatory hunches and the creative insights that are the mainstay of successful scientific practice, and for Peirce they correspond to what is truly novel and knowledge expanding about human inquiry. Of course, one could respond that abduction is the stuff of all insight, and that it is just as easy to abduce a metaphysical explanation as a scientific one; to this, Peirce would probably respond that abduction is necessary, and not sufficient, for scientific knowledge.[8]

Because abduction is a relatively loose notion of inference, it received little attention during the heyday of the Received View where the focus was on deduction and the type of formulaic inductive inference that could be used to narrow rather than broaden the field of legitimate scientific activity. Now, of course, things have changed, and the question of ferreting out the differences among the various types of abductive inference that appear in different fields of inquiry seems to be a worthwhile project. Perhaps one could say that "neoclassical abduction" is an apt characterization of the pedagogical goal of economists who say they want their students to "think like an economist." Maybe such things could be said for other fields as well.

As a final point, it is important to note that even though Peirce was proscience and naturalistic, he did not (unlike some contemporary authors) want to replace philosophical discourse with a radically narrower set of questions. In the language of Chapter 4, he was a reformist, not revolutionary, naturalist. The goal was to apply the principles of scientific inquiry to the broad class of issues that had traditionally been the purview of philosophy, and not to eliminate most (some perhaps, but not most) of these questions from our reasoned investigation. The purpose was to change the scope of philosophy, not to replace it entirely. As Peirce says in the opening pages of "A Guess at the Riddle":

> The undertaking which this volume inaugurates is to make a philosophy like that of Aristotle, that is to say, to outline a theory so comprehensive that, for a long time to come, the entire work of human reason, in philosophy of every school and kind, in mathematics, in psychology, in physical science, in history, in sociology, and in whatever other department there may be, shall appear as the filling up of its details. The first step toward this is to find simple concepts applicable to every subject. (Peirce 1887–8, p. 247)

---

[8] Hintikka (1998) offers an interesting strategic (game-theoretic) interpretation of abductive inference.

Although Peirce's work has received a considerable amount of attention in recent years, the name that remains most closely associated with pragmatic philosophy is John Dewey, not Peirce. John Dewey represented "America's philosopher" to a greater degree than any other professional philosopher in the nation's history. For many years, Dewey was not only the country's most influential philosopher, he was one of its most influential intellectuals, and touched in some way almost every aspect of American social discourse and public debate. Although Dewey was a graduate student at Johns Hopkins during the time that Peirce was on the faculty, he was not initially influenced by Peirce. In the early years, Dewey was under the influence of Hegelian idealism, and it was only later after his own pragmatic turn that Dewey started to appreciate significant aspects of Peirce's work. Although Dewey shared the broad pragmatic theme of Peirce's program, there were considerable differences between the two men: in public persona as well as substantive philosophy.

Dewey was reacting first and foremost to the epistemologicalization of philosophy: the tendency, since at least Descartes, to think of all philosophical problems in terms of accurate representation of some ultimate reality. Whether this ultimate reality was considered to be something that humans themselves created, or whether it was something objective to be discovered, the core epistemological questions remained the same. How do our thoughts accurately reflect, or mirror, or represent, this ultimate reality? How do our thoughts correspond (or how could they possibly correspond) to the way the world really is? *Dewey rejected this entire philosophical framework.* According to Dewey, this framework originated in premodern, particularly slave, societies, where the pure and the ultimate were the exclusive domain of the few and the privileged; the ultimate reality became the sacred domain of the dominant class at the expense of the more practical and mundane, which were normally associated with the lower classes. There was a cultivated separation between *knowing* (a lofty, higher, privileged, goal of reflecting the ultimate) and *doing* (the lowly and mundane affairs of human practice and instrumental action). Dewey wanted to dissolve this separation and reaffirm a guiding role for practical affairs; he believed the key to modernism and the scientific form of life lie in just this reaffirmation. But he also felt that the institution of science created a great rift in Western life. If the ultimates – the true, the good, and the beautiful – were privileged and sacred, then science, this great engine of practical expediency and technical advance, was at odds with all that was sacred and revered. The terror of modernism was that really special human things, from poetry to metaphysical insight, appeared to be the antithesis of the mechanical and practical focus of science. Philosophers from Descartes through Kant and on to logical positivism, sought to reconcile these two tendencies in human culture, while continuing to maintain their separateness. For Dewey, such reconciliation efforts were fundamentally wrongheaded. One of Dewey's problems with the traditional approach was that it left moral and social questions on the other (nonscience) side of culture, thereby denying these areas the potential for the type of progress that has been experienced in the scientific fields. Ethics and values are privileged, but in an effort to stay free of the contamination of the more base science, they are unable to benefit from the progressive methodology that characterized science.

These and the other problems associated with the traditional approach all stem back to the Enlightenment's epistemological turn: to what Dewey calls the "spectator theory of knowledge."

> We tend to think of it after the model of a spectator viewing a finished picture rather than after that of the artist producing a painting. . . . these questions all spring from the assumption of a merely beholding mind on one side and a foreign and remote object to be viewed and noted on the other. They ask how a mind and world, subject and object, so separated and independent can by any possibility come into such relationship to each other as to make true knowledge possible. If knowing were habitually conceived of as active and operative, after the analogy of experiment guided by hypothesis, or of invention guided by the imagination of some possibility, it is not too much to say that the first effect would be to emancipate philosophy from all the epistemological puzzles which now perplex it. For these all arise from a conception of the relation of mind and world, subject and object in knowing, which assumes that to know is to seize upon what is already in existence. (Dewey 1948, pp. 122–3)

The main goal of Dewey's work was to break the "intellectual lockjaw called epistemology" (Dewey, quoted by Westbrook 1991, p. 137) by bringing the scientific method into all domains of inquiry. Although Dewey clearly endorsed the scientific method, the method he endorsed was a very general, perhaps even generic, approach to inquiry: the method of "analytic, experimental observation, mathematical formulation and deduction, constant and elaborate check and test" (Dewey 1927, p. 164). For Dewey the "scientific method is not confined to those who are called scientists" (Dewey 1970, p. 29); it was simply "an elaboration, often a highly technical one, of everyday operations" (1970, p. 29). To use

Robert Westbrook's felicitous term, Dewey had a "latitudinarian" view of science (Westbrook 1991, p. 142). But while the scientific method was quite general, it was also profoundly important; it was the single most reliable approach to the discovery of the type of practical truth that was most useful in making sense of human experience and guiding social action. Dewey did not endorse the scientific method, because it gave us "knowledge" in the traditional sense – correspondence to an ultimate reality that existed outside of human experience – but because it was the most effective tool in accommodating human experience.[9] As Westbrook characterized Dewey's vision of science:

> Although his conception of scientific method did set definite limits on what could count as "science," it was a most liberal formulation. It was so liberal that Dewey often comfortably used science as a synonym for reason, intelligence, and reflective thought, a practice that did not manifest, . . . an unduly narrow notion of the latter terms but rather a willingness to offer relatively relaxed entrance requirements to the house of science. (Westbrook 1991, p. 141)

For Dewey, as for Peirce, scientists (and others) do pursue truth, but the truth they pursue is not the standard notion of truth as a correspondence with an ultimate reality. For Dewey, truth is what works in the solution of concrete problems and furthers or enhances human life. This is an *instrumental* notion of truth[10] that sees truth as an effective instrument for the engagement of human life with material existence. It is an *active*, not a passive or reflective, notion of truth.

---

[9] Dewey's notion of "experience" is fundamental to his critique of traditional epistemology. His use of the term seems to resonate more with contemporary evolutionary epistemology than with the way the term is used within empiricist-inspired philosophy of science.

> Dewey's analysis . . . pointed to his larger critique of the concept of experience at the heart of traditional epistemology and to a different conception of experience, one congruent with the findings of evolutionary biology and functional psychology and evident in his own logical theory. This alternative conception of experience, which Dewey termed variously "immediate empiricism" or "naive realism," held that experience was not, ubiquitously, a knowledge-affair but rather "an affair of the intercourse of a living being with its physical and social environment" in which that living being was, in the first instance, not a knower but an "agent-patient, doer, sufferer, and enjoyer." (Westbrook 1991, p. 126)

[10] Dewey's instrumentalism should not be confused with the "instrumentalist" interpretation of theories associated with the Received View. The next section will examine a particular case in economic methodology – Friedman's methodology – where there has been some debate about these two different interpretations of instrumentalism.

If ideas, meanings, conceptions, notions, theories, systems are instrumental to an active reorganization of the given environment, to a removal of some specific trouble and perplexity, then the test of their validity and value lies in accomplishing this work. If they succeed in their office, they are reliable, sound, valid, good, true. If they increase confusion, uncertainty and evil when they are acted upon, then they are false. . . . Handsome is that handsome does. By their fruits shall ye *know* them. . . . The hypothesis that works is the *true* one; and *truth* is an abstract noun applied to the collection of cases, actual, foreseen and desired, that receive confirmation in their works and consequences. (Dewey 1948, pp. 156–7)

Notice that Dewey's instrumentalism is not (as he is often accused) simply the idea of choosing the most efficient means for achieving any particular (arbitrarily given) end or goal. For Dewey, knowledge shapes ends as well as the means for achieving them.

By one of those curious distortions so over-frequent in philosophical discussions, my use of the word "instrumental" in previous writings has been often represented as criticized as if it signified that "knowing" must be limited to some *predetermined specific end*. What I have said, time and again, is precisely to the opposite effect. It is that *scientific* knowing is the only *general* way in our possession of getting free from customary ends and of opening up vistas of new and freer ends. (Dewey from *The Later Works*, quoted in Seigfried 1996, p. 174)

Dewey argued that the reason why this pragmatic notion of truth seems so alien is the grip of our traditional epistemological vision.

In just the degree in which existence is divided into two realms, a higher one of perfect being and a lower one of seeming, phenomenal, deficient reality, truth and falsity are thought of as fixed, ready-made static properties of things themselves. Supreme Reality is true Being, inferior and imperfect Reality is false being. . . . Such a notion lies at the back of the head of every one who has, in however an indirect way, been a recipient of the ancient and medieval tradition. This view is radically challenged by the pragmatic conception of truth. (Dewey 1948, pp. 158–9)

Dewey's instrumentalist notion of truth combined with his latitudinarian view of science – a combination he called "empirical naturalism"

(Dewey 1929) – allowed for truth-seeking inquiry to extend broadly into politics, ethics, and other value-directed inquiries. Although the desire to integrate axiological inquiry was common to all pragmatists – all wanted values to be subject to the same type of rational examination that characterizes science – the issue was particularly poignant for Dewey because of his deep concern for social policy and axiological inquiry (Manicas 1998). It was ultimately the application of his quite liberal notion of scientific inquiry to other aspects of culture, particularly those involving the formation of values, that provided the driving force behind his work. In his own words:

> To frame a theory of knowledge which makes it necessary to deny the validity of moral ideas, or else to refer them to some other and separate kind of universe from that of common sense and science, is both provincial and arbitrary. The pragmatist has at least tried to face, and not to dodge, the question of how it is that moral and scientific "knowledge" can both hold of one and the same world. And whatever the difficulties in his proffered solution, the conception that scientific judgments are to be assimilated to moral is closer to common sense than is the theory that validity is to be denied of moral judgments because they do not square with a preconceived theory of the nature of the world to which scientific judgments must refer. (Dewey 1908, p. 83)

Dewey was concerned with social and ethical issues, and he maintained a view of science that would allow scientific inquiry to accommodate such topics, but it was *not just* that science could be *applied to* such fields. In a sense, science was coextensive with these fields. It was not a matter of science, out there and removed, being brought *to* the domain of axiological inquiry; rather, there was just one – instrumental, means-ends, matter-of-fact, intelligent – method of inquiry, and it had always been a part of human social existence. It is just that since the Enlightenment, the method had become markedly successful in the one particular domain we call science. The problem was, according to Dewey, that the process had not been allowed to come to fruition; its more general (and quite natural) extension to all aspects of human culture had been sabotaged by pressure, particularly philosophical pressure, for separation and purification. It should have been one continuous and many faceted application of intelligence to human experience; it just became arrested along the way.

This method, the method of intelligent inquiry, congeals effectively within the scientific fields because of the particular social structure of the scientific community. Science and knowledge are fundamentally social, and Dewey repeatedly criticized traditional epistemology for missing this point.

> But current philosophy held that ideas and knowledge were functions of a mind or consciousness which originated in individuals by means of isolated contact with objects. But in fact, knowledge is a function of association and communication; it depends upon tradition, upon tools and methods socially transmitted, developed and sanctioned. Faculties of effectual observation, reflection and desire are habits acquired under the influence of the culture and institutions of society, not ready-made inherent powers. (Dewey 1927, p. 158)

Not only is science social; it has a particular social structure that facilitates the process of intelligent inquiry. According to Dewey, the culture of science is critical, and yet open, cooperative, nonhierarchical, and maintains social consensus as the ultimate source of stability. For Dewey, science is *democratic* and therein lies the key to its intelligence and success. Science is simply an exemplar of the democratic problem solving and the extension of this democratic process to other aspects of culture will allow for the wider application of intelligence and the discovery of (instrumental) truth to those other aspects of culture. Democracy is ultimately *the* key to human knowledge.

> What Dewey is concerned to argue, early and late, is that democracy is the precondition for the application of intelligence to the solution of social problems. We need the method of intelligence ("the scientific method") to find out what our ends-in-view should be, as well as to find what means are to be used. And democracy is a precondition for the use of the method of intelligence in social life. (Putnam and Putnam 1990, p. 427)

Dewey was profoundly influential and had a wide-ranging, comprehensive, and continually evolving philosophical vision; in addition to these things, he lived a very long life and was intellectually productive during almost all of it. I have barely scratched the surface of Dewey's work. Nonetheless, I have tried to summarize the main themes of his instrumentalist pragmatism in a way that differentiates his position from that of other classical pragmatists such as Peirce, as well as from neo-pragmatists like Richard Rorty (discussed below). I have also set the stage for the next section that discusses, among other things, Dewey's impact on certain areas of economics.

6.1.2 Classical Pragmatism and Economics

The previous section discussed the classical pragmatism of Peirce and Dewey without any reference to economics; this section will examine some of the many points of contact between these two bodies of literature. I will discuss three, very different, examples of such contact: they occur at different points in time and involve entirely different aspects of economic theory. The first is the influence of Deweyan pragmatism on institutionalist economics (particularly the economics of Clarence Ayres). Although Ayresian institutionalism is certainly not a mainstream economic topic, it is relevant in this context, because it is a non-Marxist heterodox program that has explicit and rather pronounced links to classical pragmatism. Second, I will discuss the thesis defended by Abraham Hirsch and Neil De Marchi (1990) that Milton Friedman's methodology of positive economics is best understood as a version of Deweyan instrumentalism. Finally, and on a slightly different note, I will consider Peirce's own "Note on the Theory of the Economy of Research" (1879), a paper where the philosopher himself applied a relatively contemporary-looking economic model to the question of the optimal choice of scientific research projects. These are three very different types of cross-fertilization, but they provide a good sense of the diversity of the contact.

It is almost cliché that any discussion of American Institutionalism must include a reference to the "impact" of pragmatic philosophy. Like Hegel's influence on Marxian economics, or the impact of Bentham's utilitarianism on Mill's version of the classical program, pragmatism is automatically linked to institutional economic theory.[11] There are many different ways that one might approach the relationship between institutionalism and pragmatism; for example, one could examine Peirce's impact on institutional economics, or the way that Dewey's instrumentalism affected the work of Thorstein Veblen, or Dewey's impact on later institutionalists such as Wesley Clair Mitchell.[12] Rather than pursuing any of these, rather controversial, connections, I will focus on a case

---

[11] When I refer to "institutional" economics in this chapter, I mean the "old" institutionalism of Thorstein Veblen, John R. Commons, and those who were directly influenced by their work, and not the more recent, and perhaps more mainstream, economics of the "new" institutionalist school (sometimes called the "CDAWN" school after the names of its most influential contributors: Ronald Coase, Harold Demsetz, Armen Alchian, Oliver Williamson, and Douglass North). For various comparisons of the old and the new institutionalism, see Hodgson (1989, 1994, 1998a), Langlois (1986, 1989), Mayhew (1989), and Rutherford (1989, 1994).

[12] Bush (1989), Dyer (1986), Liebhafsky (1993), Mirowski (1987a), and Rutherford (1990) offer differing views on the Peirce-institutionalism connection and Tilman (1998) provides a recent discussion of Dewey and Veblen.

where the relationship between pragmatism and institutionalism is less contentious, where the impact is direct and well established within the literature: the relationship between Dewey's instrumentalism and the economics of Clarence Ayres.

Clarence E. Ayres received his Ph.D. in philosophy from the University of Chicago in 1917 but didn't begin his work on economic theory until thirteen years later. During the next twenty-five years, Ayres elaborated a theory of economic development and cultural change that rivaled Marx's materialism in historical scope. The theory provided an explanatory schema that encompassed both the development of the material forces of economic production as well as the corresponding evolution of social and cultural institutions. The theory, like Marx's historical materialism, provided a very general explanation of social and economic change applicable to all societies in all places and at all times, but it could be (and was) directed primarily, again like Marx, at the evolution of modern capitalist society. While Ayres was quite explicit about the intellectual origins of his theory – it came from the direct combination of Dewey's instrumentalism and Thorstein Veblen's institutionalist economics (particularly Veblen 1904 and 1923) – many commentators consider Dewey to be the more important influence.

> Although he has taken from Veblen his general approach and some of Veblen's interpretation of the evolving economic system, it is in Dewey's work that Ayres found the inspiration to go beyond Veblen. This is especially the case in connection with the problem of value. Ayres technological or instrumental theory of value, which is his main contribution in the field of economic theorizing, owes more to Dewey than to Veblen. (Gruchy 1972, pp. 89–90)

The core concept in Ayres's theory of economic development (1952, 1961, 1962) was the so-called Veblenian dichotomy of "technology" and "institutions." Expanding on Veblen's distinction between "business" (or salesmanship) and "industry" (or workmanship), Ayres maintained that every human culture was an uneasy combination of two basic and contradictory forces: the forward-looking, dynamic, and progressive forces of technology and instrumental value, and the backward-looking, static, and impeding forces of institutions and ceremonial value. These two forces, while always intertwined, in fact represent two distinct cultural poles, and the relative magnitude of their respective influences provides an explanation for the observed characteristics of any particular society.

> For Ayres, as for Dewey, means and ends form a continuum that arises from within the process of experience. There is, in this view, no dualistic separation between means conceived as experiential in origin and ends conceived in exclusively metaphysical terms. Thus Ayres made a clear distinction between genuine values, which are the technological stuff of experience, and ceremonial values, which are the product of cultural mores and institutionalized rank, status, and authority. (Hickerson 1987, p. 1129)

Because technology develops spontaneously as a result of the recombination of existing tools, and since institutions are inherently static, particular institutional configurations can never cause technological change, but they can impede or accommodate it. Certain institutions are relatively permissive of technological change, while others are relatively nonpermissive.[13] The basic rule for successful economic development is to promote institutional patterns that are permissive of technological progress and to eliminate those that resist or sabotage it.

> The history of the human race is that of a perpetual opposition of these forces, the dynamic force of technology continually making for change, and the static force of ceremony – status, mores, and legendary belief – opposing change. (Ayres 1962, p. 176)

As Ayres tells the story of Western economic development (1962), Roman invasion of Northern and central Europe brought Mediterranean technology, while destroying the existing institutional structures, but when the Romans withdrew Roman ceremonial patterns withdrew with them, leaving an institutional vacuum that was quite permissive of technological change: permissive enough to accommodate the industrial revolution.

Ayres's notion of technology is the cornerstone of his entire analysis and it comes directly from Dewey's instrumentalism.

> It was from John Dewey that I first learned what that way of knowing is. It is what Dewey called the "instrumental" process. This, as Dewey clearly realized, is identical with what Veblen was calling the "technological" process. Both of these great pioneers recognized this process as (in Veblen's words) "the life process"

---

[13] Ayres's work has undergone further elaboration by later institutionalists such as Louis Junker (1962), Marc Tool (1985), and others. A number of more recent discussions emphasize the Deweyan connection: Bush (1994) and Hickerson (1987), for example.

of mankind, a process that runs in unbroken continuity through the activities of all societies and has the same meaning for all, so that a good charitable bequest, or a good peace treaty, or a good system of regulation of the flights of airplanes, is good in exactly the same sense that a cave man's striking stone was good: good in the sense of bringing home the bacon. (Ayres 1961, p. 29)

Not only is Ayres's notion of technology derived from Dewey's pragmatism, his theory of value – and, because economics is fundamentally about valuing and choice, his entire economic theory – is based on Dewey's instrumental theory of valuation (Dewey 1939). Humans must resolve certain problems in their engagement with nature, and for Dewey, the solutions to these problems come about as a result of an instrumental process of trial and error: so, too, for economic problems and their solution. In our economic lives, we must find effective ways of provisioning, and the means for such provisioning are uncovered through the same instrumental process that typifies scientific knowledge acquisition for Dewey. To make economic decisions requires valuation – value must be assigned to the various options – and the method by which that valuation occurs is the same method of inquiry that occurs in science; the proper valuation is the instrumentally warranted valuation.[14]

Although there is more to Ayresian institutionalism than the Veblenian dichotomy and his theory of social valuation, this brief introduction is sufficient to drive home the point about the program's relationship to Dewey's pragmatism. Whether or not one thinks the Ayresian program

---

[14] Dewey and Ayres both made interesting comments about the terms "institutional," "technological," and "instrumental." It seems that Ayres considered calling his theory instrumental (rather than institutional) economics, whereas Dewey considered calling his philosophy "technological" (rather than instrumental) pragmatism.

> As a designation of a way of thinking in economics the term "Institutionalism" is singularly unfortunate, since it points only at that from which an escape is being sought. . . . As a designation of the way of thinking which recognizes the decisive part played by technology in economic life the term "instrumentalism" is far more satisfactory. (Ayres 1962, pp. 155–6, note 1)

> While a number of writers have brought forward the facts which are involved in this view, Dr. Clarence Ayres, as far as I am aware, was the first one explicitly to call science a mode of technology. It is probable that I might avoided a considerable amount of misunderstanding if I had systematically used "technology" instead of "instrumentalism" in connection with the view I put forth regarding the distinctive quality of science as knowledge. (Dewey, quoted by Junker 1962, p. 68, note 5)

was, or is, a reasonable theory of economic development, it is clear that he derived the key concept of technology directly from Dewey's instrumental theory of scientific knowledge. Ayres sought, as Dewey did, a concept of instrumental valuation that was explicitly normative – and, thus, antirelativist – while still being general enough that it did not eliminate every type of human inquiry that could not be forced into the Procrustean bed of the physical sciences, or (worse yet) the traditional foundationalist characterization of those sciences. For Ayres, as for Dewey and other pragmatists, the key to science was not that it transcended all other forms of culture, or as Ayres put it, not that it was not "a cult" (1962, pp. 278–9), but that it is a very special cult, with quite special, though practical, qualities: "the decisive difference between science and superstition is that the operational efficiency of scientific 'beliefs' is rather more apparent than that of other 'cults'" (1962, p. 279). Science doesn't touch god, but it does touch home.

The second point of contact between pragmatism and economics that I will examine concerns a more mainstream methodological topic – Milton Friedman's methodology of positive economics – but before embarking on that discussion, it is useful to clear up a potential confusion that arises because of the variety of ways the term "instrumentalism" is used within the methodological literature. While philosophers use the term in many different ways (see Mäki 1998a), it is not necessary for us to survey all of these possibilities. There are, though, *three different ways* that the term is used in contemporary economic methodology, and individuating these three uses should go a long way toward eliminating a potential source of considerable confusion. Because two of these are relevant to the previous discussion of institutionalism, and two are relevant to the following discussion of Friedman's methodology, this seems to be an opportune time to ferret out these various possibilities. The three uses are:

- Instrumentalism as it is used in the philosophy of science.
- Instrumentalism in Dewey's sense.
- Instrumental rationality as an attribute of the most efficient means to achieving given ends.

The first of these, instrumentalism within the philosophy of science, was examined in Chapter 3 in the section on Logical Empiricism. According to this interpretation of instrumentalism – commonly associated with Pierre Duhem (1954) – scientific theories are merely tools for prediction; they are merely "instruments" to facilitate the prediction of empirical observations, and do not in any sense (nor should they be expected to) explain the way the world really is. The second usage of the term, Deweyan instrumentalism, was discussed in detail in the previous section of this chapter. Mixing these two meanings of the term instrumentalism seems to be common in the methodological literature and it is potentially a source of much disagreement.

The second potential confusion relates to the second and third of the above uses. There is a growing contemporary literature (Hargreaves Heap 1989 and Stewart 1995, for example) that *criticizes* mainstream neoclassical economics *because it is instrumentalist*. The argument is that neoclassical economics involves (only) an *instrumental theory of rationality*. According to this instrumental view, "rationality" is solely a property of the relationship between means and ends – being rational simply involves choosing the most efficient means for achieving any given end – and has nothing to do with the nature of the end itself. Thus, one can just as rationally decide how to commit mass murder as how to spend one's fixed income on various bundles of consumption goods. Critics argue that there is significantly more to the concept of rationality than just this instrumental notion and that economics would benefit greatly from a more sophisticated concept: particularly one that allows for the rationality of goals as well as the means for achieving them. The irony is that, whereas this critique is one that most institutionalists would wholeheartedly endorse, those institutionalists would say that the problem is that *mainstream economics does not have* (rather than has) *an instrumentalist* theory of rationality. According to the (Veblen-Ayres-Dewey) instrumental theory of valuation, goals as well as means have instrumental value – not only means, but certain goals as well, are consistent with the human life process and are, thus, associated with instrumentally rational (i.e., good) social decision making. Both groups agree about the problem with mainstream economics: but those writing in contemporary philosophy of economics say the problem is because the mainstream *is* instrumentalist, whereas institutionalists say that the problem is because it *is not* instrumentalist. Perhaps identifying subscripts are in order – instrumental$_D$ for the Deweyan use of the term and instrumental$_R$ for the notion of instrumental rationality – or perhaps we should just remember that the words instrumental and instrumentalism are used in a variety of different ways and be careful not to mix them.

Milton Friedman's essay on positive economics (1953) was discussed in Chapter 2 along with the "F-twist" and the "assumptions" controversies that comprise the first round of methodological debate about Friedman's essay. A second round of debate opened up in 1979, with the publication of Larry Boland's "Critique of Friedman's Critics" (also

Boland, 1982).[15] Boland argued that the most consistent way to interpret Friedman's essay was to view it as an argument in favor of an instrumentalist approach to economic methodology. The type of "instrumentalism" that Boland accused Friedman of endorsing was the first (philosophy of science) type of instrumentalism on the above list – scientific theories are just predictive instruments – and, while Boland was not the first to interpret Friedman in this way (Wong 1973 and 1978, for example), the paper was widely read and set off a protracted (and continuing) debate.[16]

Hirsch and De Marchi (1990) changed the debate substantially by arguing that, while Friedman in fact advocated an instrumentalist position, a careful examination of his life and work suggests his instrumentalism is of a Deweyan, not a Duhemian, kind.[17] Their argument focused (unlike most of the work on Friedman's methodology) on his implicit working methodology – the method that can be discerned from his actual theoretical and empirical practice – rather than just examining what he wrote in the 1953 essay. They presented evidence that Friedman's Marshallian microeconomics, his monetary theory, his work on the permanent income hypothesis, his critique of Keynesian economics, as well as a number of his less-well-known projects (such as his study of professional incomes) could all be understood best as economic inquiries in the Deweyan instrumentalist mode.

> Thus, Friedman rejects the *logic* of economic theory, as formulated by the economic methodologists . . . just as Dewey does. And he seems to have a notion of what the appropriate logic should be, which is essentially the logic that Dewey formulated. . . . It is Friedman's position, as it was Dewey's, that 'the concepts involved [should be] regarded as hypotheses to be employed in observing and ordering of phenomena, and hence . . . [should] be tested by the consequences produced by acting upon them.' Theory should be judged according to how helpful it is when one uses it to try to understand past economic experience and to

---

[15] For an entertaining rendition of the events leading up to the publication of Boland (1979), see Ch. 1 of Boland (1997); Chs. 3 and 4 of the same book discuss the aftermath of the paper.

[16] A partial list would include: Boland (1980, 1981, 1987), Dennis (1986), Fels (1981), Frazer and Boland (1983), Hoover (1984), Lagueux (1994), Mäki (1986, 1992b), Rotwein (1980), and Wible (1984), as well as Ch. 4 of Blaug (1980/1992), Ch. 8 of Caldwell (1982/1994), and pp. 162–9 of Hausman (1992).

[17] A version of this thesis was also offered in Wible (1984).

predict future occurrences, and especially, by whether it leads to new insights as the process of further inquiry proceeds. (Hirsch and De Marchi 1990, p. 54)

In addition to examining Friedman's essay on methodology and his economic practice, Hirsch and De Marchi also trace the influence of his teacher and National Bureau of Economic Research (NBER) colleague Wesley Clair Mitchell. As Hirsch and De Marchi put it: There were "interesting traces of Mitchell's heterodoxy in Friedman's views about methodology" (1990, p. 2). Of course Mitchell is not Dewey, but Mitchell was pragmatically inclined (though clearly on the empiricist end of the pragmatic continuum); he was Veblen's student; his early work on *Business Cycles* (1913) was an attempt to empirically corroborate Veblen's theoretical insights from *The Theory of Business Enterprise* (1904); and he was one of the main representatives (along with Veblen) of what Dorothy Ross calls the scientistic version of American liberal exceptionalism (Ross 1991, Ch. 10). These are not philosophical or political connections that one would expect to find lurking in the background of Friedman's free market economics, but therein lies the rub. According to Hirsch and De Marchi, Friedman's positive economics (method and practice) is broadly instrumentalist in the Deweyan sense, but his free market political economy is not; his political economy was more influenced by Frank Knight. Now, although it is clear that Knight was also influenced by American pragmatism (Emmett 1990; Hammond 1991; Hands 1997b), he was quite hostile to Dewey's particular version of the pragmatic tradition – in part because he felt that it was too close to positivism and behaviorism (according to Knight the most pernicious of philosophical doctrines) – and he also advocated a political economy that was quite different from that of Dewey (or Veblen, or Mitchell) and much closer to that of Friedman. Although Hirsch and De Marchi uncover this tension between Friedman's (Deweyan) positive methodology and his (Knightian) political economy, they offer little in the way of rapprochement. They end their study of Friedman by insisting that his political economy was not a "substantive contribution" (1990, p. 292).

Whether or not one is entirely persuaded by Hirsch and De Marchi's argument, it is clear that they have provided an interesting new interpretation of Friedman's methodology and managed to connect Deweyan instrumentalism to a type of economics that is radically different from the American Institutionalism that is usually associated with pragmatic philosophy. Their work, along with recent work on Knight, also raises interesting questions about the general relationship between pragmatism and the early Chicago School of economics. The metascience most commonly associated with the Chicago School seems to be the self-conscious positivism of George Stigler, but perhaps that perception is more a product of the rhetorical success of the Received View than with the philosophical predilections (or practice) of the founders of the Chicago School. In any case, the fact that Friedman's instrumentalism is automatically associated with Duhemian instrumentalism – or, for that matter, the fact that Knight's methodological position is associated with *a priorism* – is clear evidence that the philosophy of science (particularly Received View philosophy of science) *set the terms of the debate* in mid-twentieth-century economic methodology. To be doing "science" has (up until very recently) meant to be doing empiricist-foundationalist science of either the logical empiricist or falsificationist sort; to do otherwise – for instance, to engage in scientific inquiry in a pragmatic way – was simply not to be doing science at all. Since Friedman's work was extremely successful and influential within the profession, the implication would seem to be that he must have been doing something that was in compliance with the tenets of (at least some part of) the Received View; Knight, because he insisted on defying the positivist party line, must have been supporting *a priorism*. Of course, the main message of the pragmatic turn is that these two options are no longer the only games in town.

The final example of the connection between classical pragmatism and economics takes us back to Peirce, in fact a paper published by Peirce in 1879. The paper, "A Note on the Theory of the Economy of Research," was essentially an application of cost-benefit analysis – in this case, cognitive cost-benefit analysis – to the problem of choosing among scientific research projects. A number of recent authors have taken note of the paper (Delaney 1992; Rescher 1976 and 1978; Stewart 1991; Wible 1994a, 1994b, and 1998), and some make the argument that "Peirce's interest in political economy exerted a strong influence on his theory of science" (Stewart 1991, p. 505).[18] The paper addresses a relatively straightforward problem in cost-benefit analysis: How should the scientific community allocate its resources to achieve the most epistemic efficiency?

> Peirce saw as one of the most fundamental problems of the scientific community the rational determination of "how, with a given expenditure of money, time and energy, to obtain the most valuable addition to our knowledge." ... In response to

---

[18] Although this 1879 paper is undoubtedly Peirce's most significant contribution to economics, it is certainly not his only contribution; Wible (1999) gives a complete list of his writings related to economics.

this problem, he worked out specific criteria in an area he called "The Economy of Research" that would function in the rational assessment on a cost-benefit basis of proposed research programs so as to optimize the allocation of limited resources in its pursuit of long-range goals. It was his conviction that if these or criteria like them were to be adopted by the funding arm of the scientific community, judgments otherwise unprincipled would come under the purview of rational criteria designed with long-range success in mind. (Delaney 1991, p. 34)

Peirce's approach to the problem was to maximize the difference between the total utility and total cost of various projects and the efficient solution was expressed in terms of the marginal conditions (ratios of marginal benefits and costs) familiar from contemporary microeconomics. If marginal benefit is greater than marginal cost for a particular project, increase the number of resources going to that project; if marginal cost is greater than marginal benefit, reduce the resource commitment. This, according to Peirce, provides a framework for analyzing the allocation of scientific resources and, thus, the division of cognitive labor between various research projects. It offers a solution to the problem of underdetermination, because it provides (cost-benefit) criteria for deciding among various scientific research programs when the data alone does not afford a clear choice. His paper is an early example of what might be termed the "economic approach" to the problem of scientific resource allocation and it presents us with a totally different type of connection between economics and pragmatic philosophy.[19]

Although Peirce's paper looks a bit like some of the recent "economics of science" that will be discussed in Chapter 8, there is an important difference. As we will see in Chapter 8, much of the recent literature on the economics of science focuses on invisible hand-type results: where epistemic efficiency emerges (or could emerge) as the result of the rational self-interested actions of individual scientists. Peirce would not endorse such a view of science. Peirce was radically anti-individualist and viewed science as cooperative and relatively selfless; his economics of research is about how the *scientific community* could efficiently allocate its resources. Peirce uses marginal analysis, but it is to discuss a planner's problem (epistemic planning by the scientific community) and not how cognitive efficiency would emerge from the self-interested actions of individualist scientist-agents.

[19] It is not entirely clear how much of the argument was original to Peirce and how much came from the economics literature. Stewart (1991) claims that Peirce was influenced by Ricardo – and more relevant to this particular paper – Cournot.

This brings us to one final, but important, point about the relationship(s) between classical pragmatism and economics. For pragmatists of all stripes, there is an "inseparable connection between rational cognition and rational purpose" (Peirce 1905a, p. 184) and as "purpose" necessarily involves doing things – putting things to work, producing and distributing – pragmatism necessarily connects cognition and economic activity. Pragmatism is not just a philosophy of knowledge that can be "applied" to economics like methodologists have tried to apply positivism and Popperian falsificationism; *it is a philosophy of knowledge that is inexorably tied up with economic life.* Dewey attributed the framework of classical epistemology to the class structure of the society from which that framework emerged; he also explicitly sought a characterization of scientific inquiry that would accommodate the moral and social sciences, while simultaneously maintaining democracy as the most important characteristic of such inquiries; finally Peirce, aggressively anti-individualist, and yet using what is now standard microeconomics to decide among various scientific research projects. These are not just cases of philosophers applying their ideas to economics, or of proffering ideas that can easily be picked up by economists; these are more cases of the inseparable intermeshing of philosophical and economic ideas.

6.2 Neopragmatism and the Discursive Turn

Although pragmatism is clearly back on the philosophical scene, there are reasons for its revival that are independent of any of the issues discussed in the previous section. In fact, there are reasons for the resurgence of pragmatic ideas that are totally independent of the philosophical problem-situation of classical pragmatists such as Peirce and Dewey. One such reason is the development of a neopragmatist philosophical perspective – particularly through the work of Richard Rorty (1979, 1982, 1989, 1991a, 1991b) – that manages to meld elements of classical pragmatism with aspects of postmodernism. Given Rorty's philosophical impact, and the fact that his work has influenced the literature on economic methodology, a brief summary of his position is clearly in order. But before embarking on the discussion Rorty's particular contribution, it will be useful to briefly broach the vexing and tangled question of *postmodernism*.

6.2.1 *Rorty, Neopragmatism, and Science as Discourse*

Although postmodernism has touched almost every aspect of contemporary intellectual life, it is not a philosophical "position" that can be summarized in the way that I have tried to summarize other aspects of contemporary science theory.[20] Perhaps the best method is to follow Allan Megill's (1989) lead in his discussion of postmodernism and approach the topic from Wittgenstein's "family resemblance" point of view; while postmodernism has no single defining characteristic, certain authors and certain texts bear a family resemblance that identifies them with the postmodernist perspective. The family resemblance seems to be most clear when we focus on what postmodernism *is against* – what it *opposes* – rather that what it advocates. Most important, postmodernism *contests modernism*. It challenges the entire intellectual and cultural inheritance of the Enlightenment; it contests reason-centered universalism and, thus, challenges traditional views of rationality in both science and society; it opposes not only conventional rationality but the necessity and authority of all universalist perspectives. A recurrent theme in postmodern discourse is that the project of the Enlightenment has simply run out of gas; the rationalist discourse that has provided the backdrop for, and the legitimization of, almost every aspect of our post-Enlightenment intellectual (and much of our practical) life, has been radically *delegitimized*.

One way to view the process of coming into postmodernism is to think about the historical evolution of the three main topics of classical philosophy: the true, the good, and the beautiful. Epistemology investigated the true, ethics the good, and aesthetics the beautiful. Originally all three were considered absolutes; all existed as universals independent of the particularities of time, place, culture, or individual perspective. Aesthetics was the first to give up its universality, the first to be situated, particularized, dependent on culture and perspective. Then came ethics. By the Enlightenment, there were many different ways of thinking about ethical matters – some religious-based, some thoroughly secular, none with a universal obeisance – and although these views could be discussed rationally, the absolutism of the good faded farther and farther into our collective philosophical memory. But truth held its ground. In fact, a main feature of the Enlightenment was to extend the method of truth finding – the method of science – into many of the domains that had once been occupied by other aspects of culture. Logical positivism is, thus, in a sense, philosophical high modernism; for strict positivism both aesthetics and ethics are purely perspectival – they depend on the perspective of the individual and have no objective meaning – meaningfulness and truth are reserved for science and logic alone. Megill (1985) thus refers to post-

---

[20] Nonetheless, at least one philosopher has the audacity to give it a birthday: "The dynamiting, at 3:32 P.M. on 15 July 1972, of the (Le Corbusier-based) Pruitt-Igoe housing development in St. Louis" (Bhaskar 1991, p. 139).

modernism as "aestheticizing knowledge" – basically doing to knowledge what modernism did to aesthetics. One implication of this aestheticization is a general suspicion of "theory" – after all, theories are attempts to corral contingency, to contain the particular within the universal and the absolute. Thus, postmodernism is, in Lyotard's much quoted phrase: "incredulity toward metanarratives" (Lyotard 1987, p. 74). All stories about necessity – in science, in society, in history, in ethics – are to be contested. Science is deconstructed, but then so are the other touchstones of modern life: progress, efficiency, justice; you name it.

Postmodernism, of course, comes in a variety of different hues, from the most radical to the relatively complaisant. On the extreme end, there are postmodernist authors who totally disavow any effort to find a "solution" to the postmodernist dilemma; they seem, instead, to simply revel in the abyss. But such extreme views are quite rare among those sympathetic to postmodernism. For most authors, being informed by postmodernist ideas simply means maintaining a deep suspicion about traditional modernist stories – be they stories about truth, necessity, justice, or anything else – and the more the stories seem to be endorsed by the powers that be, the more suspicious they are. Perhaps we can find a new postmodernist place to stand, but the assumption is that we are not going to find it by looking at the same old maps and asking the same old people. In this sense, many of the views discussed in previous chapters, those that have undermined and offered replacements for the Received View, seem to bear a faint postmodernist family resemblance. It is sometimes barely detectable, and many of the authors would vehemently deny it, but on close examination one can in fact make it out.

So if Kuhn and SSK are only remotely related to postmodernism, what names are associated with more extreme versions of the postmodernist view? Well, there is no definitive list, but names that often appear include: Friedrich Nietzsche from the end of the nineteenth century; Martin Heidegger from the first half of the twentieth century; and Michel Foucault, Jacques Derrida, and Jean-Francois Lyotard more recently. Nietzsche was perhaps the first to inaugurate this style of thought and although many aspects of his philosophy show traces of postmodernism, his perspectivist concept of truth – that all truth is partial, provisional, situated, and relative to the context of the knower, or as he put it, that truth is "a mobile army of metaphors, metonyms, and anthromorphisms" (Nietzsche 1954, p. 46) – is perhaps the most revealing. But even for Nietzsche, as with much of postmodernism, the nihilism that follows from aestheticizing (particularly) knowledge, is active, not a passive nihilism.

Nietzsche prescribes this nihilism as the appropriate attitude for modern, and postmodern, existence. Instead of drawing back from the void, we dance upon it. Instead of lamenting the absence of a world suited to our being, we invent one. We become the artists of our own existence, untrammeled by natural constraints and limitations. (Megill 1985, p. 34)

So there are a few philosophical names on the postmodernist list, but what about pragmatism? The short answer is that it is not entirely clear; the overlap between postmodernism and classical pragmatism is currently contested ground. Certainly classical pragmatists were anti-foundationalist and anti-quest-for-certainty – they emphasized that knowledge was always situated in practice and human interests; they stressed that science was social, theory-laden, and underdetermined; and they questioned the representational or mirroring aspect of traditional epistemology – all things consistent with postmodernism. As Kai Nielsen summarizes the relationship:

> What is on the mark in postmodernism is their rejection of grand meta-narratives purporting to give us "ultimate truth," . . . Postmodernists claim as well and rightly that there are neither privileged epistemic structures securing "final truth" nor a foundational knowledge more secure than anything achievable by sciences or in everyday life and free from the contingencies of time and place. If to say there is no truth or knowledge is to say that there is no *such* truth or *such* knowledge then such a claim is not absurd but arguably true and perfectly in accord with pragmatism. (Nielsen 1993, p. 548, emphasis in original)

By contrast, Peirce and Dewey had an optimism (about practical life, if not about philosophy) and a scientism (though latitudinarian) that seem to be wholly at odds with the spirit of postmodernism. As John Patrick Diggins remarks about Dewey:

> Dewey could agree with the postmodernist that philosophy has been trying futilely to prove what is not there; but while the postmodernist seems to delight in exposing the illusions of thinking, Dewey had long been convinced that the classical questions of philosophy have no practical bearing in daily life. (Diggins 1994, p. 8)

While there is no philosophical consensus regarding the relationship between pragmatism and postmodernism, there is certainly one influential philosopher who has argued consistently that classical pragmatism (particularly Dewey) and postmodernism have much in common; that philosopher is Richard Rorty, the "red-white-and-blue Nietzsche" (Westbrook 1991, p. 539).

> I have argued in the past that Deweyan pragmatism, . . . gives you all that is politically useful in the Nietzsche-Heidegger-Derrida-Foucault tradition. Pragmatism, I claim offers all the dialectical advantages of postmodernism while avoiding the self-contradictory postmodernist rhetoric of unmasking. (Rorty 1995, p. 130)

Although Rorty has written on a wide range of philosophical topics, the book that most clearly established his reputation was *Philosophy and the Mirror of Nature* (PMN) in 1979. PMN was a work that was as radical as it was influential; it amounted to an all-out attack on what Rorty considers to be the central dogma of the Western philosophical tradition. This central dogma is the "mirror metaphor," the core notion that the human mind "mirrors" the world. A corollary of the mirror metaphor is that "knowledge" amounts to a special class of representations: representations that are accurate or privileged.

> The next stage is to think that to understand how to know better is to understand how to improve the activity of a quasi-visual faculty, the Mirror of Nature, and thus to think of knowledge as an assemblage of accurate representations. Then comes the idea that the way to have accurate representations is to find, within the Mirror, a special privileged class of representations so compelling that their accuracy cannot be doubted. These privileged foundations will be the foundations of knowledge, and the discipline which directs us toward them – the theory of knowledge – will be the foundation of culture. (Rorty 1979, p. 163)

This traditional perspective on mind and knowledge makes philosophy into a kind of intellectual "usher," as the mother-discipline that "grounds" or provides "foundations" for the other parts of human culture like science, art, and ethics. This ushering role is particularly pronounced in positivist-inspired philosophy of science where the Received View attempted to provide standards for what was, and what was not, legitimate scientific (and thus for them, effectively all) knowledge. Abandoning the mirror metaphor would fundamentally alter the role of philosophy in our intellectual culture. In Rorty's own words:

> If there are no privileged representations in the mirror, then it will no longer answer to the need for a touch stone for choice

between justified and unjustified claims upon our belief. Unless some other such framework can be found, the abandonment of the image of the Mirror leads us to abandon the notion of philosophy as a discipline which adjudicates the claims of science and religion, mathematics and poetry, reason and sentiment, allocating an appropriate place to each. (Rorty 1979, p. 212)[21]

Rorty's attack on the mirror metaphor is two-pronged; he engages in a direct assault on the philosophical mainstream, while simultaneously trying to charm the disenfranchised with his own alternative view. The direct assault is based on the repeated failure of the project of philosophy-as-epistemology to succeed on its own terms; quite simply, the discipline of philosophy has never been able to do that which it claims it has the right (and the responsibility) to do. The allies that Rorty recruits for this assault on disciplinary philosophy include many of the names associated with postmodernism – such as Nietzsche and Heidegger – but also more mainstream critics of traditional epistemology and philosophy of science – Quine, Feyerabend, Kuhn, and various authors from SSK. His own alternative view was called "hermeneutics" in PMN, but he has consistently used the term "pragmatism" in later work.[22] I will use the term "neopragmatism" to distinguish Rorty's work (and the work of others who attempt to combine pragmatism and postmodernism) from classical pragmatism. The classical pragmatist that Rorty cites most frequently is John Dewey (Rorty 1994), and, although there are significant differences between Rorty and Dewey, it is also clear that the differences between Rorty and Peirce are even greater. In fact, Rorty is sometimes characterized as "pragmatism-without-Peirce."[23]

For Rorty (like many others), inquirers are inevitably situated and contextual; there is no transcendent philosophical position from which to judge all other positions. Criticism is possible under such conditions, but it is always criticism from within a particular situated perspective, and the resulting change will be piecemeal and relative to the local interests of those involved in the critical conversation. According to Rorty,

---

[21] Recall the discussion of intentionality and folk psychology (FP) from Chapter 4. Notice that since intentionality is closely related to representation – intentional states are "about," "stand for," or "represent" other things – Rorty's early (1965, 1970) eliminative materialism is not necessarily in conflict with the antirepresentationalism of his later neopragmatist position.

[22] He also calls it "left-wing Kuhnianism" as well as the "new fuzziness" (Rorty 1987, p. 41).

[23] See Hoover (1994), pp. 306–10, or Kimball (1995), pp. 53–4.

we look for new and better ways of talking and acting, new and better ways of redescription, but these are never "foundational"; they do not represent a "ground" or "starting point" prior to, or outside of, all cultural traditions. Rorty shares with classical pragmatism the rejection of science as a method for acquiring true representations, as well as its commitment to science as a means for practical engagement – "modern science does not enable us to cope because it corresponds, it just plain enables us to cope" (1982, p. xvii) – but stops (way) short of classical pragmatism in other areas. In particular, he shares the postmodernist vision about how we reached our current impasse.

> The idea . . . to have foundations was a result of Enlightenment scientism, which was in turn a survival of the religious need to have human projects underwritten by a nonhuman authority. . . . But unfortunately the Enlightenment wove much of its political rhetoric around a picture of the scientist as a sort of priest, someone who achieved contact with nonhuman truth by being "logical," "methodical," and "objective." This was a useful tactic in its day, but it is less useful nowadays. For . . . historians of science have made it clear how little this picture of the scientist has to do with actual scientific achievement, how pointless it is to try to isolate something called "the scientific method." (Rorty 1989, p. 52)

In the end, Rorty undermines philosophy, or at least the standard notion of philosophy as an intellectual underlaborer; he encourages us to "drop the notion of the philosopher as knowing something about knowing which nobody else knows so well" and to drop the notion that the philosophical "voice always has an overriding claim on the attention of the other participants in the conversation" (1979, p. 392).

Rorty's position has implications that go far beyond the study of scientific knowledge; it strikes at the intellectual foundations of our basic Western democratic institutions. Our long-cherished notions of freedom and democracy are undermined by the same forces that undermine our ideas about scientific knowledge. If there is no place to stand outside of culture in order to evaluate it, if all inquiry is situated and perspectival, and if natural science makes truth rather than discovers it, then on what grounds is it possible to endorse our social, political, and cognitive institutions? This problem, the problem of defending liberal social and political values in a world without a "first philosophy" or objective "foundations," is a problem that Rorty addresses in *Contingency, Irony, and Solidarity* (1989), his autobiographical essay (1993), and elsewhere.

He argues that neopragmatism in fact extends the values of the Enlightenment more effectively than a mainstream approach of philosophy-as-epistemology. Mainstream philosophy, particularly positivist philosophy of science, failed to go all the way with the message of the Enlightenment; the message was to do without god, but positivism didn't eliminate god, it simply substituted a new scientific one for the old theological one; "positivism preserved a god in its notion of Science (and its notion of 'scientific philosophy'), the notion of a portion of culture where we touched something not ourselves, where we found Truth naked, relative to no description" (1982, p. xliii). Rorty's position is that we should "try to get to the point where we no longer worship *anything*, where we treat *nothing* as a quasi-divinity, where we treat *everything* – our language, our conscience, or community – as a product of time and chance" (1989, p. 22, emphasis in original).

Another aspect of Rorty's answer to the question of liberal values involves the separation of the private and the public self. His radical epistemological position is characterized by "irony" and irony seems to be "inherently a private matter" (1989, p. 87); as Rorty himself admits, even he "cannot imagine a culture which socialized its youth in such a way as to make them continually dubious about their own process of socialization" (1989, p. 87). Rorty advocates both private irony and liberal hope: private irony in accepting that one's final vocabulary is not any closer to the Truth than the final vocabulary of others, and liberal hope that such private recognition will bring about a social world that is less cruel and more consistent with our liberal values. For Rorty, the fundamental premise "is that a belief can still regulate action, can still be thought worth dying for, among people who are quite aware that this belief is caused by nothing deeper than contingent historical circumstances" (1989, p. 189).

Given the radical nature of Rorty's position, it is hardly surprising that his work has generated a number of critical responses. It is fair to say that the philosophical community has taken Rorty to task on almost every aspect of his position.[24] Much of the criticism has focused on Rorty's interpretation of other philosophical positions: either major schools (like pragmatism and hermeneutics) or particular figures in the history of philosophy (particularly Heidegger and Dewey). His political

---

[24] The critical literature is massive, but a good starting place is the discussion in Hall (1994) and the papers in Malachowski (1990). The tone of the critical literature is captured nicely by Daniel Dennett's introduction of the "Rorty Factor": that we take "whatever Rorty says about anyone's views and multiply it by .742" (Dennett 1982, p. 349).

philosophy has also come under attack from a number of different directions and it has generated at least one book-length criticism (Bhaskar 1991). Despite this critical literature, Rorty remains an influential philosophical voice, and a voice that is heard outside of the academy as well as within disciplinary philosophy. In certain respects, Rorty is the late-twentieth-century philosopher who has come the closest to usurping the Deweyan title of America's foremost public philosopher. Rorty's version of neopragmatism also informs the philosophical positions of a number of other influential and publicly visible contemporary intellectuals – Stanley Fish (1980, 1989) and Cornel West (1987, 1993) for example – another factor contributing to his overall impact on the philosophical landscape. Perhaps Rorty is not a philosopher's philosopher – like, say, Quine – but he has contributed to the revival of pragmatic ideas and has attempted to reconcile those ideas with what many consider to be the postmodern moment; his pragmatism is not exactly Dewey's, but in his effort to bring pragmatism to bear on a significant (or at least potentially significant) ideational crisis, his historical role is much the same.

Rorty's work provides a convenient segue into one of the areas within science studies that has thus far slipped through the net extended by the discussion in this and previous chapters. The area is the study of *science as discourse*, or *the rhetoric of science*, and while it overlaps to a certain extent with the sociological literature examined in Chapter 5, and is often identified with recent postmodernist trends, it also has much in common with Rorty's neopragmatism. Rorty in effect opens the door to the study of science as discourse or rhetoric by focusing on human *conversation*; his claim that "there are no constraints on inquiry save conversational ones – no wholesale constraints derived from the nature of the objects, or of the mind, or of language, but only those retail constraints provided by the remarks of our fellow-inquirers" (Rorty 1982, p. 165). For Rorty, scientific knowledge is not the result of an attempt to mirror nature but rather the outcome of a particular type of social conversation: the scientific conversation. From here, it is but a short step to the explicit study of science as discourse or rhetoric: the view that science is best understood as a type of persuasion – a particular type of persuasion – but one that should be examined by employing the tools of rhetorical analysis. In its strongest form, the rhetoric of science not only asserts that science has an inexorable rhetorical component, but that it is *rhetorical all the way down*; that science can be reduced to "rhetoric without remainder" (Gross 1990, p. 33).

Although there are many different brands of rhetorical analysis within science studies,[25] they all seem to share the same basic insight about the discursive nature of scientific inquiry. This basic insight is summarized nicely in the following remarks by Allen Harris.

> What scientists do is interpret the empirical domain. What rhetors do is influence one another. What scientists do as rhetors is influence one another about interpretations of the empirical domain. In two easygoing definitions: *science* is the study of natural phenomena; *rhetoric* is the study of suasion. Both definitions will surely find opponents, but both are sufficiently general and sufficiently representative that we can proceed with a minimum of controversy: *rhetoric of science* is the study of suasion in the interpretation of nature. (Harris 1991, p. 282)

Although it is easy to connect the rhetoric of science with Rorty's neo-pragmatism, most of the discussion has been less concerned with Rorty than with the relationship between rhetoric and SSK. While it is quite clear that some contributors to the rhetorical literature see it as an *alternative* to the sociological studies of science – in particular an approach that avoids privileging the "authorial voice of the sociologist" (Fuhrman and Oehler 1986) – others see the two fields as effectively coextensive. One rhetorician that supports the convergence thesis is Alan Gross.

> [R]hetorical analysis is central to the sociology of science. Science becomes a literary activity, its operations producing a variety of "texts" – graphs, meter readings, laboratory conversations, lectures, papers, review articles, press conferences. Each must be interpreted, when interpretations differ, there is but one means of settlement: persuasion, the art of rhetoric. A strong constructivism makes rhetorical analysis methodologically imperative. (Gross 1991, p. 284)

Although the question of the relationship between the rhetoric of science and SSK – or perhaps the rhetorics of science and various SSKs – is an independently interesting question we will not pursue it here. The rhetoric of science has a clear analog in the study of economic science –

---

[25] While the various brands are all closely related, it is possible to differentiate at least *three* separate projects. The first is what might be termed the pure rhetoric of science (Campbell 1987; Gross 1990 and 1991; and Gross and Keith 1997, for example), whereas a second focuses on science as a form of social discourse (Gilbert and Mulkay 1984; Mulkay 1981 and 1985; and Mulkay and Gilbert 1982, for instance), and the third involves the application of Garfinkel's (1967) ethnomethodology to scientific work (Lynch 1985 and 1992, for example).

the *rhetoric of economics* – and that literature is one of the topics in the next section.

6.2.2 Economics, Neopragmatism, and Rhetoric

Because both neopragmatism and discourse analysis are touched by postmodernism, one place to start the examination of how these two sets of ideas have influenced recent debates about economics would be to look at the literature that explicitly examines "postmodernism and economics." Given postmodernism's overall impact on contemporary intellectual life, and the other social sciences in particular (Rosenau 1992), it is rather surprising how little direct impact the "aestheticization of knowledge" has had on the discipline of economics (or discourse regarding the discipline of economics).[26] With a few exceptions (e.g., Samuels 1996), most of the discussion about "postmodernism and economics" has occurred within the heterodox literature. This is most evident in Marxist economics[27] – since postmodernism was in many ways an explicit reaction to the ideas and institutions associated with mechanistic/scientistic Marxism – but other heterodox approaches also have engaged the postmodernist turn.[28] It should also be noted that, whereas most mainstream economists have been resistant to postmodernist ideas, this has not been the case for every historian of mainstream economics; Weintraub (1988a, 1989, 1991a, 1997) in particular, takes an approach to the history of mathematical economics that is informed by postmodernism and neopragmatism as well as SSK.[29]

While there does exist a small literature on postmodernism and economics, this work does not constitute the best-known or most discussed commingling of disciplinary economics and the literature

---

[26] There is an incipient literature that critiques postmodernism in economic methodology (Backhouse 1997a, for example), but postmodernism is defined very broadly in these critiques. It includes much of SSK and constructivist literature discussed in Chapter 5, Rorty-based neopragmatism, as well as the rhetoric of economics discussed below.

[27] One Marxist response is the "overdeterminationist" school of Resnick and Wolff (1987) and others (see, for example, Amariglio 1998; Amariglio, Resnick, and Wolff 1993; Amariglio and Ruccio 1994; Callari, Cullenberg, and Biewener 1995; Resnick and Wolff 1988; and the criticism in Backhouse 1998d).

[28] A special issue of the *Journal of Post Keynesian Economics* in 1991 contained a number of papers of postmodernism and economics including Mirowski (1991), Ruccio (1991), Samuels (1991), and Weintraub (1991b). Institutionalist discussions include Brown (1991, 1992), Hoksbergen (1994), Klein (1998), and others discussed below. On the other side of the political fence, Burczak (1994) has identified postmodernist themes in the work of certain Austrian economists.

[29] Weintraub's approach has been criticized by Backhouse (1992a, 1992b, 1997a) and Mäki (1994a).

examined in the previous section; that honor clearly goes to the *rhetoric of economics*. In simplest terms, the rhetoric of economics is *discourse analysis applied to economics*, although that is seldom the way it is characterized. To characterize the rhetoric of economics in this way seems a bit disparaging – making it just the "application" of the work of one small subfield of contemporary science studies to various topics within the discipline of economics – when in fact the rhetoric of economics is currently a main contender within (or perhaps replacement for) the methodology of economics. The reason for this is, not surprisingly, contingent and context-dependent; in science theory, as in science, individual personalities and social interests play a significant role in the determination of what becomes the dominant discourse. Just as a particular contingent constellation of forces made Popperian philosophy more important in economic methodology than in the philosophy of science more generally, so did such contingencies make rhetorical analysis relatively more influential in the study of economics than elsewhere within science studies.

While the rhetoric of economics is undoubtedly the best-known point of contact between economics and fields like neopragmatist philosophy and discourse analysis, it is not the first juncture that I will examine. Before turning to the rhetoric of economics, I would like to briefly continue the discussion in Section 6.1.2 by considering a debate over "cultural relativism" that has taken place recently within the literature of institutionalist economics. Although the debate concerns nonmainstream economics and may seem to be a bit off the beaten path, it in fact represents useful excursion, because it helps to illuminate (actually represents a microcosm of) a more general tension that has emerged within contemporary pragmatic philosophy; all sides of this institutionalist controversy endorse pragmatism, but for some it is the classical pragmatism of John Dewey, whereas for others it is a neopragmatism that owes much to Richard Rorty. It might be possible to draw out this tension by examining recent debates in other heterodox fields – Marxist, Austrian, Post-Keynesian, and others – but it is particularly clear in the institutionalist literature.

Recall that Clarence Ayres's theory of institutional change combined the so-called Veblenian dichotomy with John Dewey's theory of instrumental valuation. For Ayres, a change in social institutions was progressive if it was permissive of technological change – if it furthered technological values – where technological values were characterized in terms of Dewey's theory of instrumental valuation. Later institutionalists, particularly Marc Tool (1985, 1990), enhanced the normative bite of the Ayresian framework by explicitly endorsing a "Social Value Principle":

> Act or judge in a manner to provide for the continuity of human life and noninvidious recreation of community through the instrumental use of knowledge (quoted in Hoksbergen 1994, p. 692)

Or, as it is often put more aphoristically, it is a theory of social valuation based on the fact that "no society prefers square wheels to round wheels" (Waller and Robertson 1991, p. 1033).

This principle would provide institutionalists with a standard (an instrumental standard) for the appraisal of particular values, cultural forms, or institutions. It provides a standard by which it is possible to pass judgment on particular social values, structures, and policies – it is grounded in the antifoundational pragmatism of Veblen and Dewey – and yet it provides an explicit standard for the normative evaluation of different cultures. Those who endorse Tool's social value principle as a framework for social policy often cite Dewey in its defense.

> Dewey clearly believed that science as a system of values provides intelligence in the guidance of human action. Accordingly, institutional economics would fail in its *scientific mission* if it did not provide guidance in the area of policy formation. (Bush 1994, p. 654)

Many institutionalists find the social value principle to be problematic. It allows the social scientist to say that some cultural values are (at least relatively) "bad," whereas others are (relatively) "good" – those promoting instrumental values are good and those promoting ceremonial values are bad – and these normative evaluations are apparently transcultural. The principle exhibits a lack of cultural relativism that many find disconcerting, and the issue has opened up a fairly substantial debate within the institutionalist literature. On one side are defenders of the social value principle, the instrumentalist hard line,[30] and on the other side are various defenders of cultural relativism. Although the critics vary widely (much wider than among the defenders), it is possible to divide them into two, very rough, groups. The first group seems to defend cultural relativism by means of epistemic foundationalism.[31] The argument is effectively that since *science* is value free, and since institutionalism strives to be good science (and is in fact much better in this respect than mainstream economics), institutionalism must remain value free; which, in this context, means not passing judgment on the values of different

---

[30] These authors include Bush (1994), Hickerson (1987), and Tool (1985, 1990), among others.

[31] Examples are Gordon (1990) and Mayhew (1987).

cultures. Unlike this first group of value-free hard-liners, the arguments of second group of critics are informed by postmodernist and neopragmatist ideas. None of these critics suggest a nihilistic version of postmodernism – that there are absolutely no standards, even contingent, contextual, or discursive ones, by which cultures and/or values might be appraised – but all of them appeal to various standards for evaluation that have been influenced by the literatures discussed in the previous section. For Samuels (1990a), the emphasis is on the self-referentiality in Veblen's work and Veblen's recognition that instrumental, matter-of-fact knowledge, is not a universal category of evaluation, but a construction of one particular (our) form of life; for Waller and Robertson (1991), the answer is in discourse (values can only be evaluated dialectically in the context of community discussion and debate); for Brown (1991), the key is the debunking or critical aspect of postmodernism; for Mirowski (1987a), institutional economics became sidetracked into a scientistic instrumentalism by Dewey and Ayres (a better guiding insight would have come from Peirce's hermeneutics); and there are undoubtedly other variations as well. The point is simply that all of these responses try to recover an aspect of institutionalism that allows for its pragmatic instinct to travel more comfortably with contemporary perspectivism. These projects mirror, in the context of institutional economics, the recovery project that informs most of neopragmatist philosophy and related literatures. In fact, Rorty himself admits to the philosophical "split" that is reflected in the institutionalist debate. In Rorty (1994), he admits that his view of Dewey is not the majority view, and that the standard interpretation is more instrumentalist than his own Nietzschean or aestheticizing reading; the cultural relativism debate in institutionalism clearly mirrors this split within pragmatic philosophy.

The *rhetoric of economics* represents a very different contact point between economics and the triad of postmodernism, neopragmatism, and discourse analysis. The rhetorical turn in economics began with the publication of D. McCloskey's "The Rhetoric of Economics" in the *Journal of Economic Literature* in 1983. This is not to say that others were not thinking along similar lines, it is just that the publication of this substantial and forcefully written paper, in one of the American Economics Association's official journals, by someone who was already a distinguished economist, gave the project a rather grand grand-opening. Although the initial controversy has died down in recent years, it is not because the project has failed but rather because of its success; it is now one of the established approaches to the study of the scientific culture of economics and it has successfully blended in with a number of other projects in the history and philosophy of economics.

McCloskey starts by recounting how various "Methodological" approaches (positivist and Popperian) have failed to help us understand the professional activities of economists. The argument is that all these official Methodologies – big M methodologies – are rooted in modernism, and modernism has failed massively as a general framework for intellectual life. Small *m* methodologies – the workaday methodological practices of economists on the shop floor – serve a useful purpose, as does the higher order *Sprachethik* – the conversational norms of civilized discourse – but not Methodology as it has traditionally been practiced.

> Between the top and the bottom, a middle manager in a green suit, below the cool majesty of sprachethik and above the workaday utility of method with a small *m*, stands Methodology. Because it cannot claim the specificity of practical advice to economists, or to the lovelorn, it is not method. Because it does not claim the generality of how to speak well in our culture, or in economics, it is not sprachethik. It claims instead to be a universalization from particular sciences to a science of science in general. (McCloskey 1985a, p. 25)

For McCloskey, Methodology is an intellectual dead horse, but the problem is that it "can still deliver vicious kicks" (McCloskey 1994, p. 298).

Most of McCloskey's arguments for this massive failure are familiar from this and previous chapters. The Legend is dead; scientific theories are underdetermined and observations are theory-laden; science is social, interest-laden, situated, contextual, and contingent; *a priori* philosophical speculation does not capture, and cannot capture, the actual practice of successful science; language and discourse matter to every aspect of human culture including science; none of the traditional philosophical dichotomies – theory versus observation, discovery versus justification, positive versus normative, *a priori* versus *a posteriori*, or any others – constitute rigid or translocal designators; the significant things that have been said about science and knowledge were said by the likes of Kuhn, Quine, Rorty, and those in SSK, not Popper or logical positivists; and so on and so on. One unique McCloskeyan twist (and an audience sensitive twist, it might be noted) is the analogy between philosophers of science as methodological rule-makers and the meddling interference of governmental bureaucrats.

> The maker of rules for economic science has, of course, the noblest intentions. Like the man from the government, he is here to help you. But economists like to remark of similar cases of

> interference in the spontaneous order that noble intentions are no defense against laughable results. (McCloskey 1994, p. 20)

Clearly:

> It is a market argument. There is no need for philosophical law-making or methodological regulation to keep the economy of intellect running just fine. (McCloskey 1994, p. 28)

But even given all of the well-known problems with the Received View, and given the inability of any other program within the philosophy of science to come up with a generally accepted story about why/how science has made the achievements that it has, surely real scientists pursue, and often discover, the Truth. Not so, argues McCloskey. Lower case truths may be discovered, like "the temperature in Iowa City" (McCloskey 1994, p. 46), but not capital-T Truth, truth "in the mind of God" (McCloskey 1994, p. 47). The former is the stuff of human investigation; the latter is the mantra of philosophers.

> The very idea of Truth – with a capital T, something beyond what is merely persuasive to all concerned – is a fifth wheel, inoperative except that it occasionally comes loose and hits a bystander. If we decide that the quantity theory of money or the marginal productivity theory of distribution is persuasive, interesting, useful, reasonable, appealing, acceptable, we do not also need to know that it is True. (McCloskey 1994, pp. 46–7)

The key issue for McCloskey is persuasion; that which is persuasive is worthy of our attention, and that which is not, is not. The things that should interest us according to philosophers – or other self-appointed intellectual ushers – are of interest if and only if we are so persuaded; there was a time, in the halcyon days of brash modernism, that things like Methodology and Truth were interesting – we were persuaded – but we got over it and we moved on. Because the study of what persuades is *rhetoric*, the study of what persuades economists is the *rhetoric of economics*: the study of suasion in the disciplinary interpretation of the economy.

> Rhetoric does not deal with Truth directly; it deals with conversation. It is, crudely put, a literary way of examining conversation, the conversation of economists and mathematicians as much as of poets and novelists. . . . The word "rhetoric" here does not mean a verbal shell game, as in "empty rhetoric" or "mere rhetoric" (although form is not trivial either, and even empty rhetoric is full). Rhetoric is the art of speaking. More

broadly, it is the study of how people persuade. (McCloskey 1994, pp. 28–9)

McCloskey thus wants to replace the study of capital-M Methodology with the rhetoric of economics; the $3'' \times 5''$ card philosophy of economic science should be replaced by, among other things, ferreting out the master-tropes of metaphor, metonymy, synecdoche, and irony in economic discourse.[32] It is a new set of questions. How does the science of economics persuade? How does a particular economic paper, argument, theorem, or author persuade? How do economists persuade students, governments, and each other? How is economic authority conveyed and maintained? How does the social structure of disciplinary economics contribute to and reinforce the persuasive power of the economics profession? There are many other such questions and the rhetoric of economics queries them all.

The last decade has witnessed an explosion of work on the rhetoric of economics.[33] The range of specific economic topics that have been examined is staggering. Those taking (variants of) the rhetorical approach have examined: Samuelson, Muth, and Fogel (McCloskey 1985a), significance tests, standard errors, and econometrics (McCloskey 1985a, 1985b,

---

[32] It should be noted that, while McCloskey has consistently advocated the *rhetoric of economics*, in recent years the focus has shifted in the direction of a more liberal definition of what constitutes "rhetorical analysis." In early work, McCloskey employed a wide range of literatures – Kuhn, postmodernism, Rorty, Quine, SSK, and so on – in a critical fashion (to attack modernist Methodology), but stuck pretty close to classical rhetorical analysis as the proper replacement for the vanquished Method. Everybody could join in on the critique, but it was mostly departments of Rhetoric and Literature that were supposed to supply the alternative framework. In more recent work, the label is still rhetoric, but the number of things that count as rhetorical approaches seems to have expanded (see McCloskey 1994, pp. 102–5). For example, both Kuhn and SSK (all versions) now count as rhetorical approaches.

> The new sociologists and historians and rhetoricians of science call themselves "the children of Thomas Kuhn." Science studies have thrived since Kuhn spoke out in 1962, and the charge can be summarized in one word: rhetoric. . . . the "Social Studies of Knowledge" undertaken by British sociologists such as Harry Collins, Trevor Pinch, Michael Mulkay, Barry Barnes, Malcolm Ashmore, Steve Woolgar – rhetoric of science by another name. (McCloskey 1997, p. 102)

This appears in stark contrast to the attitude of those actually doing SSK, who generally seem to argue for the strict separation of sociological and discursive approaches (and the superiority of the former over the latter). Collins, for example, argues that "discourse analysis has been largely abandoned within SSK" (Collins and Yearley 1992a, p. 305).

[33] In addition to McCloskey's major books (1985a, 1990a, 1994, 1996, 1998) and papers too numerous to list, there also are a number of anthologies (Nelson, Megill, and McCloskey 1987; Klamer, McCloskey, and Solow 1988; Samuels 1990b; and Henderson, Dudley-Evans, and Backhouse 1993). Also see the Backhouse (1998e) Handbook entry on the subject.

1994, 1996; McCloskey and Zilak 1996, and elsewhere), prediction and expertise in economics (McCloskey 1985a, 1988, 1990a, and elsewhere), Chicago economics (McCloskey 1985a, 1989, 1994, and elsewhere), the nature of economic storytelling (McCloskey 1985a, 1990b, and elsewhere), blackboard economics (McCloskey 1994, 1996, and elsewhere), general equilibrium theory (McCloskey 1994, and elsewhere), New Classical Macro (Klamer 1984, and elsewhere), the rationality assumption (Klamer 1987), Samuelson's Principles Text (Klamer 1990), the relationship between economics and accounting (Klamer and McCloskey 1992), capital gains taxation policy (Chordes, Klamer, and Leonard 1993), the paradox of value (Swales 1993), Adam Smith (Brown 1993, 1994a), international trade theory and policy (Milberg 1996), higgling (Brown 1994b), Marxist economics (Milberg and Pietrykowski 1994), Keynesian economics (Gerrard 1991, and various papers in Marzola and Silva 1994), Friedman's quantity theory (Mayer 1997), feminist economics (Robertson 1996), Robert Lucas (Rossetti 1990), and this is at best only a partial listing.

Although the rhetorical turn has generated a substantial amount of criticism,[34] and the criticism has come from a variety of different directions, McCloskey has tried to respond to most of the main points (particularly in 1994). While it is impossible to examine a significant portion of this critical literature, or McCloskey's response, I would like to briefly consider two of the recurrent issues that arise within the debate. The first is what might be called the problem of *rhetoric and irrationalism*, and the second is the *so what?* question. Both of these issues are related to previous discussions about contemporary science theory.

It is pretty obvious why McCloskey gets branded an irrationalist. The rhetorical project abandons both Truth and Methodology: the sacred standards for demarcating that which is scientific and rational from that which is mere opinion and irrational whim. Aren't we left with anything goes? Doesn't this leave us vulnerable to the barbarians at the gates? Well, no, not really, according to McCloskey.

> Of course, some arguments are better than others. Anything does not go. Recognizing that nonetheless they are all arguments does not entail slipping into a hot tub of "relativism" as defined by conservative philosophers of science. One does not give up the ability to distinguish between the Ajax Kitchen Cleanser jingle and Gödel's Proof by noting that both are designed with

---

[34] Including Backhouse (1995a, 1997a, 1998c), Boylan and O'Gorman (1995, Ch. 2), Butos (1987), Caldwell and Coats (1984), Davis (1990b), Dyer (1988), Mäki (1988a, 1988b, 1993a, 1995), Mirowski (1987b), Rappaport (1995, 1998), and Rosenberg (1988a, 1988b, 1992).

an audience in mind, with a perlocutionary force, with patterns of repetition, . . . and all the rest. (McCloskey 1994, p. 290)

McCloskey's defense against the charge of irrationalism seems to be three-quarters neopragmatism and one-quarter economics. First the neopragmatism. Giving up on Methodology does in fact mean giving up on universal/absolute standards, but it does not mean giving up on local/contingent standards. Small-m methodology is quite useful. Following Rorty and Fish, McCloskey only claims that there does not exist a standard that is independent of the institutional circumstances – no standard independent of the local, contextual, contingent, situation on the ground at the site in question – and not that we do not have any way to evaluate at all; "saying that there is no standard independent of the institutions, is not the same as saying there is no standard" (McCloskey 1994, p. 305). There certainly are local practical standards for all kinds of things (including science) and we use them everyday. To use one of Stanley Fish's examples, there is no universal theory of baseball, but there is certainly the eminently practical advice to "throw strikes and keep'em off the bases" (Fish 1987). For a more McCloskeyan example, there is no economic Methodology, but there is the useful and practical methodological advice to "clean up the way you use statistical significance in econometric analysis." These standards are not universal, absolute, or transcendent, and that, as the pragmatic tradition tells us, is just fine.

> But only children and Platonists need transcendence. . . . Communities of adults, by contrast, have in practice no difficulty recognizing that their standards are not God's own, not transcendent and not ahistorical, while affirming that the standards are nonetheless worth enforcing. (McCloskey 1994, p. 311)

So how is this an economic argument? Well, it is back to philosophers as the men from the government. According to McCloskey, Methodology is like central planning, both in the sense that it comes from on high by those who believe they have the right to usher (economic resources in the Soviet case, cognitive resources in the case of the philosophy of science), and in the sense that what actually gets done has nothing at all to do with what the plan says (see the history of centrally planned economies on one hand, and Kuhn and Feyerabend on the other). But the failure of central planning (capital-P Planning, if you will) does not mean that the system was devoid of rationality on the shop floor (small-p planning). There can be, and generally will be, efficient and inefficient ways of doing various specific tasks at specific points in time in particular factories (and at particular scientific sites); the failure of central planning (or of logical positivism) does not imply that we must do without local standards of economic (or cognitive) efficiency.

Finally there is the "so what?" question. Suppose that we quit doing Methodology and start doing the rhetoric of economics; what will be gained by doing so? The answer to this question constitutes the closing chapters of both of McCloskey's main books on the rhetoric of economics (1985a, 1994). The last chapter of the 1985 book lists five separate (good) things that the rhetoric of economics can do. It can improve economic prose, improve teaching, improve economists' relations with other disciplines, improve economic argumentation, and improve the temper of economists. Although none of these five claims were abandoned in the final chapter of the 1994 book, the emphasis seems to shift to other concerns. One of the arguments in the later book is that rhetoric will make economics more human; it will help diminish the autism of disciplinary economics. Economists will be less concerned with formalistic navel-gazing and more concerned with participating in the wider conversation of humankind.

> To put the point another way, a rhetorical approach to economics fits better with being human. This is not to say that the Method of Science is inhuman. The problem is that it is only one tiny part of being human. (McCloskey 1994, p. 383)

Another theme is that rhetoric helps economists actually appreciate their discipline more; it makes economics a much better story. Modernist Methodology does not capture the great insights of economics – the brilliance of a Smith, a Ricardo, a Marx, or a Keynes – to understand why the rhetoric of these individuals was persuasive one needs to understand their context, their audience, and thus to understand and appreciate their work better. Lastly, McCloskey argues that rhetoric actually helps produce better economic science. One is forced to openly face the argument, to ferret out the assumptions, to find the common ground, to discover the nature of disagreement; rhetoric increases argumentative standards and, thereby, raises the quality of economic discourse. If this seems like a lot of good stuff, it certainly would be if it all came to pass. The Rhetoric of economics is work in progress; a substantial amount of research has already been done and more is on its way. Only time will tell whether McCloskey's optimism about the many benefits that will be garnered from such rhetorical investigations will eventually be realized.

6.3 Feminist Epistemology and Economics

As with earlier topics, the concerns of this final section are not independent of initiatives revealed elsewhere in this chapter. Feminism, like postmodernism, or pragmatism, is an active voice in contemporary intellectual and social life, and like these other movements, it affects our attitudes about science, knowledge, and economics. There are many sources of inspiration for feminist economic methodology,[35] but one of the most significant is the recent literature on feminist science theory. Although feminists have always considered science to be an important source of androcentric authority in contemporary culture, the science question has never been cut-and-dried in feminist thought; feminist analysis of science and scientific institutions has always involved a fair amount of tension. On the one hand, science is predominantly male and the technological products associated with science play an important role in the reproduction of the androcentric authority. On the other hand, the feminist social critique is rooted in the same Enlightenment notions of knowledge and truth that ostensibly provide the philosophical foundations for (and liberating power of) the scientific enterprise. This tension has generated various responses within the feminist literature; most significantly for the current project, efforts to resolve this tension have shifted recent feminist epistemology in a different direction than the path pursued by the first generation of modern feminist scholars. Sandra Harding (1986) has characterized this change as the change from "the woman question in science" to "the science question in feminism."

In the early feminist literature, discussion about science focused primarily on the number of women scientists and the way that females were depicted in various scientific theories: how to get women into the male-dominated scientific professions and how particular scientific disciplines (especially biology) function to reproduce male domination. The shift to "the science question in feminism" represented a significant and philosophically radical change in the locus of feminist attention regarding science. Feminists began to argue that the relevant issues were not just getting women into science or getting the gender-bias out of various scientific theories, but rather to focus the feminist critique on the nature, particularly the gendered-nature, of scientific knowledge itself. Feminism has always been concerned with social and political power, but the change focused increased attention on the connection between having knowledge – and having access to the means of knowing – and the maintenance of

---

[35] One source is actually McCloskey's most recent work on the rhetoric of economics where postwar mainstream economics is characterized as a sandbox game for boys.

> It is the essential sadness of boy's games. Unlike the games of girls, which so often have a human point, the boy's games in the sandbox are pointless, except perhaps as preparation for real earthmoving as adults. . . . The sad, unspeakably sad fact about the enterprise of modern economics is that much of what it claims to have accomplished since 1945 is a game in the sandbox. (McCloskey 1996, p. 14)

such power. In one sense, access to knowledge is a means to empower-ment, but more radically, the vehicle for the legitimization of knowledge claims is the vehicle for exclusion of those deemed epistemically sullied. In brief, the "science question in feminism" is where the feminist critique of science turned epistemological. In the words of Helen Longino:

> The feminist demonstration of masculine partiality and bias in well-established fields of inquiry has shaken our faith in con-ventional knowledge. How deeply must our skepticism reach? Is rationality itself only an instrument of male domination? Is objectivity a masculine illusion? If we answer here affirmatively, what is left as ground for our own feminist claims? These ques-tions attain their most threatening dimensions when we bring feminist analytic tools to bear on the natural sciences. (Longino 1988, p. 561)

Although there are a variety of different frameworks currently competing within the literature on feminist epistemology, I would like to focus primarily on two main approaches: *standpoint epistemology* and *contextual empiricism*. These two approaches have received the most attention within the philosophical literature and they seem to be the most relevant to the current work in feminist economic method-ology. Although there are many different versions of standpoint theory, my discussion will draw most heavily on the person who seems to be the best-known representative of this point of view: Sandra Harding (1991, 1993, 1995). Helen Longino (1990, 1992, 1994) will be enlisted as the main source for my discussion of feminist-inspired contextual (or social) empiricism.

While these two approaches seem to be the most influential inter-pretations of science that have originated from within the feminist literature, there are two other approaches that also receive substantial attention within feminist science studies: *feminist postmodernism* and *feminist empiricism*.[36] Although these two views are important, they require less elaboration, since they are feminist adaptations of views that have already been discussed. For example, feminist postmodernism is primarily the application of postmodernist ideas to questions about the gendered nature of scientific knowledge; the central problematic for such an exercise is a feminist version of the familiar postmodernist critique of universalizing discourse. Feminist empiricism, although not a new view about scientific knowledge derived from feminist inquiry, is in fact a

---

[36] There is also a small, but growing, literature on feminist pragmatism (see, for example, Code 1998; Moen 1997; Seigfried 1996, 1998).

perspective that plays an important (if often unrecognized) role in the literature on feminist economics. The term "feminist empiricism" was coined by Harding; it is "the argument that the sexist and androcentric claims to which the researcher objects are just the result of 'bad science'" (Harding 1991, p. 111).[37] For the feminist empiricist, there is nothing wrong with (even positivist) philosophy of science – the proper way to do science is clearly specified by the (objective and empirical) scientific method – the problem is that scientists *do not actually practice* the method of science. They allow their own sexist ideology to bias their results. According to feminist empiricism, the philosophy of science is fine; it is the practice of science that needs to be cleaned up. Like feminist postmodernism, this view is more of an application of philosophical ideas originating elsewhere than a new feminist epistemology. Nonetheless, feminist empiricism is particularly relevant to economics, as it captures the way that many economic methodologists – feminists and nonfeminists alike – feel about the practice of economics; critical economists often write as if the methodological norms provided by the philosophy of science are just fine, it is simply that economists do not live up to those standards. We will return to this issue at the end of this section; for now, let us turn to standpoint theory and contextual empiricism.

All *standpoint theories* (including feminist standpoint theories) are based in the idea that certain "standpoints" are (or can be) better than others for the pursuit of knowledge. In its most traditional or foundationalist form, standpoint theory asserts that certain standpoints are epistemically privileged: that people in certain social situations are more able to see the truth than people in other social situations. In its more pragmatic or constructivist form, standpoint theory simply claims that particular standpoints may – in certain contexts, and relative to a specific class of questions – have a significant perspectival advantage over other standpoints. Many standpoint theories have roots in Marxism – the idea that the proletarian perspective is privileged – that capitalists' understanding of the nature of capitalism will always be blocked because of blinders imposed by their own economic/class interests, whereas the proletariat is devoid of such ideological blinkers and can see the true nature of capitalist production.[38] The standpoint theme is not only in Marx, and Lukacs, it was also defended by Karl Mannheim (1936), one of the

---

[37] She calls it "spontaneous feminist empiricism" in more recent work (Harding 1993).
[38] Apparently, Marx was not alone among economists who privileged the standpoint of particular groups. Veblen (1934), it seems, placed particular weight on the standpoint of the European Jew (see Bush 1989, p. 1162).

precursors to contemporary SSK. Mannheim argued that it was the intelligentsia who were epistemically privileged because of their insulation from the entire structure of economic and class interests.

Harding's version of feminist standpoint epistemology starts from the familiar theme that all scientific beliefs are socially situated – theory, society, and interest-laden – but this situatedness does not lead to relativism. All beliefs are socially situated – we cannot evoke the view from nowhere, the "god-trick" (Haraway 1991, p. 189) – some situations are just better than others. In particular, the lives of women and other marginalized people provide a uniquely effectual starting point for the pursuit of knowledge. Harding (1991, pp. 121–33) offers eight separate reasons for privileging the standpoint of women. These range from the Mannheim-like claim that women "are valuable 'strangers'" (p. 124), to women's "oppression gives them fewer interests in ignorance" (p. 125), to women's lives orient them more toward the "production process" of transforming "natural" objects into "cultural" ones (p. 131), to this "is the right time in history" for the women's standpoint (p. 132). In later work, Harding has also added other arguments to defend her version of standpoint theory. One of these is that other, more standard, views within the philosophy of science also represent "standpoint" theories; empiricism in particular, privileges a specific standpoint – the dispassionate, disinterested, individual – as the ideal knowledge receptor (Harding 1993, p. 66). Harding calls the objectivity obtained by starting from the standpoint of women "strong objectivity." Previous objectivity was at best only "weak objectivity" – objectivity that could never achieve what it thought necessary to achieve (the view from nowhere) – now that we not only accept situatedness, but are willing to exploit the epistemic advantages of certain situations, our notion of objectivity is thereby strengthened. As she summarizes her view:

> [T]he notion of objectivity not only can but should be separated from its shameful and damaging history. Research is socially situated, and it can be more objectively conducted without claiming to be value-free. The requirements for achieving strong objectivity permit one to abandon notions of perfect, mirror like representations of the world, the self as a defended fortress, and the "truly scientific" as disinterested with regard to morals and politics, yet still apply rational standards to sorting less from more partial and distorted belief. Indeed, my argument is that these standards are more rational and more effective at producing maximally objective results than the ones associated with what I have called weak objectivity. (Harding 1991, p. 159)

As one might guess, the work of Harding and other standpoint theorists has elicited a wide range of critical responses. From within feminist science studies, postmodernist feminists accuse standpoint theorists of not being radical enough and endorsing a version of old-fashioned foundationalism (situational foundationism), while contextual empiricists (discussed below) accuse the standpoint theorists of throwing the scientific baby out with the positivist bathwater and of not being social enough in their epistemic stance. From outside of feminism, the critics are legion and highly diverse. There are a number of female philosophers of science who are critical of all (or any) attempt to provide a distinctly feminist epistemology, and since Harding's work is the best-known such project, it is a frequent target (Haack 1993; Koertge 1996; and Pinnick 1994, for example). There are critics from within mainstream philosophy of science (Kitcher 1994, for example) as well as from the sociology of science (Gieryn 1994, for example), but probably the most acerbic come from practicing scientists (ostensibly disinterested scientists) upset by the entire notion of situated knowledge (Gross and Levitt 1994).[39]

Before leaving standpoint theory, it is useful to point out that Harding endorses the standpoint approach for all "knowledge projects," particularly the natural sciences. Standpoint theory would, of course, be less controversial if it were restricted to the study of women in society, or even to the social sciences more generally. In fact, a standard criticism of the standpoint approach is that it is really a story about social science – how certain social standpoints are less encumbered when it comes to understanding the relevant social forces – but then this social science-based argument gets extended to the natural sciences where the underlying motivation regarding the social embeddedness of the relevant agents seems to be less compelling. While some would undoubtedly find standpoint theory to be problematic even if it were only an argument for privileging the starting point of women's lives in *the social sciences*, many others would find it to be far less controversial in this limited context; and remember it is only this less controversial case that is relevant to economics.

Although standpoint theory is the version of feminist epistemology that seems to get the most publicity, it is not the approach that has most influenced the philosophy of science. The feminist-inspired perspective that has more significantly piqued the interest of the philosophical mainstream is *contextual (or social) empiricism*. Although I will focus on the contextual empiricism of Helen Longino, related approaches – also

---

[39] Evidently, Harding once characterized Newton's *Principia Mathematica* as a "rape manual"; Gross and Levitt seem to be particularly incensed by such remarks.

called "feminist naturalism" – have been endorsed by Jane Duran (1998), Lynn Hankinson Nelson (1990, 1995), Miriam Solomon (1994a, 1994b) and Alison Wylie (1995).

Like standpoint theory (and almost every other view discussed in the last few chapters), contextual empiricism starts from the position that facts are social/theory-laden and that science is fundamentally social. Longino's twist on these givens is in one way more radical and in another way more traditional than what is derived from standpoint theory. On the radical side, Longino is very aggressive about prosecuting the social aspect of science and she is more sustained in her critique of epistemic individualism; on the traditional side, Longino has a view of science that is strongly antirelativist and much closer to the naturalists discussed in Chapter 4 than SSK or most of the authors examined in this chapter. For Longino, science is social, but this in no way implies that we must abandon the distinction between knowledge and opinion, or the idea that science is objective and based on confronting our theoretical conjectures with the empirical data.

Longino is a traditional empiricist in that sense experience remains the fundamental arbitrator and legitimator of all knowledge claims, but she takes the issues of theory-ladenness, underdetermination, and the sociality of science very seriously. So how does one remain steadfast to the notion that scientific theories are ultimately legitimated by sense data, while also recognizing that sense experiences are always local and contextual, processed through the minds of individuals who are in, and conditioned by, their social situations?

Longino's answer is that the particular social structure of science allows it (at least ideally) to exploit the multiplicity of the various conditioning social situations: in science "difference as a resource, not a failure" (Longino 1995, p. 388). Because social context conditions the facts available to a particular individual, the best way to empower the empirical domain is to have representation from a wide range of different social perspectives: wider representation means the involvement of more social situations, which in turn means the availability of a wider range of sense experiences.

> Because background assumptions can be and most frequently are invisible to the members of the scientific community for which they are background, and because unreflective acceptance of such assumptions can come to define what it is to be a member of such a community (thus making criticism impossible), effective criticism of background assumptions requires the presence

and expression of alternative points of view. (Longino 1991, p. 670)[40]

Of course, while diversity may be necessary for the growth of knowledge, it is not sufficient; the social organization of science must also be such that it allows for (ideally maximizes) the type of *critical engagement* that will stabilize the potential cacophony of these disparate voices. This critical environment is the key; it must be open to all, be devoid of *a priori* privileging of any particular stance, and be sensitive to "demonstrable evidential relevance" (Longino 1992, p. 209). The community of science is, thus, an "idealized epistemic community" (Longino 1994, p. 145) that satisfies the following four criteria (Longino 1992, p. 209, and elsewhere):

1. there are recognized avenues for the criticism of evidence, of methods, and of assumptions of reasoning;
2. the community as a whole responds to such criticism;
3. there exist shared standards that critics can invoke;
4. intellectual authority is shared equally among qualified practitioners.

Notice that these four criteria are *norms* for scientific inquiry. Longino is not offering descriptive sociology or relativistic deconstruction; she is endorsing a particular normative philosophy of science, offering criteria about how science *ought* to be organized in order to best contribute to the growth of knowledge. Not everything counts as knowledge; there is a right (or at least better) way and a wrong (or at least worse) way to conduct scientific inquiry. By contrast, although her approach is normative it is not individualistic; it does not specify (a la falsificationism or positivism) how the individual scientist must behave in order to properly do science. Longino's program is socially normative, not individually normative; there is a way to organize science so that it better serves our cognitive goals (the growth of knowledge) but the "ought" resides primarily in the social organization, not in the behavior of individual scientists.

> Taking these criteria as measures of objectivity, objectivity is dependent upon the depth and scope of the transformative interrogation which occurs in any given scientific community.

---

[40] Longino's position on this issue seems to be reminiscent of Feyerabend's early arguments about epistemic diversity (Feyerabend 1968) and certain aspects of Popperian critical rationalism (discussed in Chapter 7).

> . . . Knowledge and objectivity, on this view, are identified as the outcomes of social interactions, and hence, located not in individuals but in communities. (Longino 1992, p. 211)

The cognitive key to the social organization of science lies in its ability to foster effective *criticism*, and for "such criticism to be effective in promoting objectivity or knowledge rather than the world view of a privileged class, inquiring communities must grant equality of intellectual authority to all qualified participants in the dialogue" (Longino 1993, p. 167), "ideally as many as are available" (Longino 1995, p. 384). Diversity is necessary, but through the proper social organization this diversity promotes objectivity not chaos or relativism. The four norms provide the "conditions of effective criticism"; their "satisfaction assures that theories and hypotheses accepted in the community will not incorporate the idiosyncratic biases (heuristic or social) of an individual of subgroup" (Longino 1994, p. 145).

According to Longino, her approach simultaneously solves *the* problem in contemporary science studies – how to endorse the unique cognitive virtues of science and still admit its ladenness and sociality – as well as the particular problems facing feminist science studies. The feminist project turns on constructivism – how social factors condition, or even constitute our view of the world (including our scientific view) – but it also requires the critical bite of objective science. Longino and others see feminist science studies as tenuously poised on a kind of knife-edge. On one side lies the traditional notion of science that denies the constitutive power of the social context and, thus, denies that feminist epistemology has anything significant to say about knowledge; on the other side lies a kind of postmodernist relativism that makes everything discursive and subjective (domination, misogyny, and rape are disconnected from their objective referents). Longino believes that her account substantially flattens this knife-edge and gives feminist science studies "an account that can ground both the critical and the constructive projects of feminism" (Longino 1992, p. 212).

Concurrent with these developments in feminist epistemology, certain economists have recently begun an investigation into feminist economics that also includes various discussions of feminist economic methodology.[41]

---

[41] Feminist economists with a particularly methodological focus include Nancy Folbre (1993), Julie Nelson (1993, 1995, 1996), Janet Seiz (1993, 1995), Dianna Strassmann (1993a, 1994), and a number of the contributors to the Ferber and Nelson edited volume *Beyond Economic Man* (1993). Klamer (1991) and McCloskey (1993) combine feminism and rhetoric to indict mainstream economics. It also should be noted that both Harding (1995) and Longino (1993) have written about economics.

Most of this work takes the form of a disciplinary-focused feminist critique of mainstream economics – either as an economic version of feminist empiricism (not questioning the traditional story about scientific standards, but questioning whether male-dominated economics lives up to those standards) or in a more content-specific way by focusing on the gendered character of rational economic man – but there is also a literature that focuses on the gendered character of scientific knowledge in general (including, but not limited to, economics); this latter work is directly related to the literature on feminist epistemology.

The most common methodological position among economists working in the field of feminist economics is undoubtedly feminist empiricism.[42] The reasons for this seem to be similar to the reasons Harding suggested for the popularity of feminist empiricism within the natural sciences. It leaves intact much of scientists' "conventional understanding of the principles of adequate scientific research" (Harding 1991, p. 113); it "conserves, preserves, and saves understandings of scientific inquiry that have been intellectually and politically powerful" (Harding 1991, p. 113); and it is perhaps the most robust strategy "that many scientists can manage and still maintain the disciplinary respect necessary for their continuing access to funding and to teaching and laboratory appointments" (Harding 1991, p. 114). In other words, life in a male-dominated profession is difficult enough without openly questioning the epistemological backdrop that most practicing economists, including those who make hiring and tenure decisions, take for granted. Finally, it seems reasonable to add to Harding's list the plain fact that most feminist economists sincerely believe a version of the positivist story about science, in part for the reasons that Harding suggests – like its political power and persuasiveness – but in part just because of how deeply this vision of scientific knowledge has seeped into the professional psyche of those trained in the social sciences during the last hundred years. It is certainly much easier to question the assumption of maximizing behavior, or the realisticness of perfect competition, or the unstated implication that the only activities with an economic value are market activities, than it is to question the Legend story about the nature of scientific knowledge.

Despite the statistical majority of feminist empiricists among feminist economists, such empiricism will not be the focus of this section. Like the work of the (much smaller) band of feminist postmodernists, feminist empiricism does not endorse a uniquely feminist contribution to our

---

[42] One feminist empiricist response to some of the issues raised by feminist economics is given by Rebecca Blank (1993).

understanding of scientific (or economic) knowledge. Feminist economists may employ positivist ideas quite effectively in the critique of
mainstream economics – more effectively it seems than other heterodox
economists with similar critical intent – but it is the employment of a
preexisting, and more importantly prefeminist, philosophical position.
Such work is important to the feminist project in economics; it just lies
outside the scope of our current methodological inquiry. The two feminist methodological positions that will be examined below both involve
cases where feminist economists have attempted to integrate ideas from
recent feminist epistemology (Harding and Longino, in particular) into
their critique of mainstream economics. The first case is the recent work
of Julie Nelson (1993, 1995, 1996) and the second is Diana Strassmann's
(1993a, 1993b) translation of Longino's work into a economic argument
about (cognitive) price distortions.

Julie Nelson is one of the most methodologically concerned among
the recent contributors to feminist economics. Her collection *Feminism,
Objectivity and Economics* (1996) consistently examines a number of
different issues within contemporary economics through the lens of her
own particular feminist methodological perspective. Her methodological
vision starts, like all of the feminist epistemologies discussed above, with
a socially situated notion of objectivity. Following Harding's lead, Nelson
argues that our old – disinterested and individualistic – notion of objectivity is obsolete; it was always a delusion, though one with particular
persuasive (and political) power, and we are much better off getting
beyond it to a definition of objectivity that is "in line with a notion of
science as socially constructed, and scientists as social beings" (Nelson
1996, p. 39). Although Nelson endorses Harding's situated version
of "strong objectivity," she does not go so far as to endorse Harding's
feminist standpoint epistemology. Her methodological position seems
to blend Harding's situated view with Longino's feminist naturalism.
Nelson does not argue for a particular feminist way of knowing, or even
that feminist economics would necessarily produce something totally different than what is available from the economic mainstream. The point
is more that the current (androcentric) view is too narrow and over-
focused on things that (while important) are not the whole story about
economic life. For Nelson, feminist economics should broaden, diversify,
and thus improve, economic theorizing, not throw out everything that
has come before.

A good example of Nelson's approach is her discussion of Gary
Becker's (1981) work on the economics of the family (Nelson 1996, Ch.
5). Becker derives a number of the stylized facts about family life – such
as the sexual division of labor and various factors that influence the

demand for children – as comparative statics results from a model of household utility maximization. The household utility function – usually interpreted to be the utility function of the (altruistic) patriarch – is maximized subject to the family's budget constraint involving time and commodities: where commodities (Z_is) are produced in the household using market goods, household goods, time, and various types of human capital. In particular, Becker derives the sexual division of labor (one person engages solely in market activities while the other person engages entirely in household production) as a complete specialization result from international trade theory, with household utility (rather than world welfare) being maximized. He initially (1981, Ch. 2) derives complete specialization from a model where both agents in the household are completely identical (but one just happens to invest in household rather than market human capital), but then goes on to assert (much to the chagrin of many readers) that one sex naturally has more household human capital than the other and, thus, is naturally better suited for specialization in household production.[43] Nelson criticizes a number of different aspects of Becker's model. Although admitting that game theoretic bargaining models (such as McElroy and Horney 1981) where family characteristics emerge as Nash equilibria in a game between two players each having their own utility functions (and threat points) is an improvement on the Becker household utility model, she does not feel that such bargaining models go far enough. All these formal models seem to be more interested in exhibiting the power of microeconomic theory than in actually gaining any knowledge about marriage or the family. A more effective way to understand the family would be to start with a much more general economic concept – the notion of "provisioning" – and then proceed to an analysis that recognizes that families consist of "persons-in-relation" and that family decision making involves a "process" that is not amenable to choice-theoretic analysis. The resulting feminist economic analysis would involve less "epistemological machismo" (Nelson 1996, p. 66), but it would provide a much richer and a more in-depth understanding of the actual processes at work in family life. The standard approach to the economics of the family is obsessed with formalism, but provides no real understanding of the social forces (even economic forces) that undergird the institution of the family; feminist economics could provide an understanding of those forces.

---

[43] Needless to say (and not surprisingly), Becker's "new home economics" has been a frequent target for feminist writers. England (1993), McCloskey (1993), Strassmann (1993b), and Woolley (1993) are a few of the many examples. Becker also has methodological critics from outside of the feminist literature (Blaug 1992, Ch. 14, for example).

> Instead of using such richer models, economists have tended to focus on marriage and families only to the extent that they can be captured within a choice-theoretic model. The axioms of maximization and the methods of mathematical derivation are allowed to direct the development of analysis. Such procedure opens, not closes, the door to muddy thinking, misspecification, and poor analytical procedure. (Nelson 1996, p. 74)

Whether the topic is the economics of the family or one of the many other areas of economic inquiry that she examines, Nelson maintains that the standard choice-theoretic-based practice of the discipline is less informative, and in fact less objective, than what would be offered by an economics that was more sensitive to the issues raised by the feminist literature.

> Feminism does indeed have something to say about the objectivity of economics. By adopting a cultural value system that puts undue emphasis on masculine-associated traits and experiences, a concern for objectivity has been allowed to degenerate into a rigid objectivism, and a concern for reliable explanations of human behavior has been allowed to collapse into a dogmatic focus on constrained maximization. The feminist interpretation . . . does not depend on a world view that sees current economic practitioners as individually malicious, or sees sexism behind every tree, or sees formalism as a source of pure evil. It does not argue for a feminine economics, or for a new economics to be practiced only by females. What it argues for is a change in the value system of economics, so that economics can become flexible as well as hard, contextual as well as logical, human as well as scientific, and rich as well as precise. (Nelson 1996, p. 150)

Dianna Strassmann also endorses a richer feminist economics informed by developments in feminist epistemology as well as female experiences in social and economic life. Strassmann (1993b) translates Longino's contextual empiricism into an economic argument that criticizes the standard disciplinary practice in mainstream economics. Her argument provides an alternative way of thinking about the marketplace of scientific (or economic) ideas.

The claim is often made that science (or some particular science) involves the "marketplace of ideas," and, so the argument goes, if this marketplace is left to its own (competitive) devices it will produce (as if by an invisible hand) the most cognitively efficient outcome possible.[44]

---

[44] Such arguments were introduced in Chapter 4 in the section on Popperian evolutionary epistemology, and they will be examined in more detail in Chapter 8.

If one applies such an argument to the discipline of economics, then the marketplace of economic ideas should produce the best economic science; or, looked at alternatively, current economics must be the best possible (or at least best available) economics, because it has survived in the competitive marketplace of economic ideas. Strassmann contests just this claim. She argues that if one applies the marketplace of ideas to the discipline of economics one finds that the "marketplace" is one that is *imperfectly (not perfectly) competitive.*[45] Only certain forms of economic argumentation are officially sanctioned by the élite economists who control the most prestigious journals and graduate programs, and (not coincidentally) that which gets approved is that which reproduces their professional position. There is neither free entry nor perfect information in the marketplace for economic ideas and the result is exactly what one would expect from an imperfectly competitive environment: rent seeking, inefficiency, and price distortions. Strassmann argues that such imperfectly competitive behavior generates precisely the opposite type of social environment than what is required for scientific objectivity according to Longino's contextual empiricism.

> Helen Longino (1990) claims that objectivity within a discipline is enhanced when qualified practitioners share intellectual authority. Her arguments translate easily into the language of economics. The absence of free entry into the marketplace of economic ideas distorts the relative valuations of ideas in this arena, giving market power to dominant practitioners. The dominant practitioners may protect their intellectual stronghold with exclusionary practices. As any economist would agree, barriers to entry create price distortions. (Strassmann 1993b, p. 57)

Strassmann goes on to argue that price distortions are merely the tip of the iceberg, and, like Nelson, that a much richer feminist approach to economics would provide substantially more insight into economic life. Strassmann and Nelson are just two examples of economists who have recently combined feminist economic ideas with insights from feminist epistemology to produce a wide-ranging critique of the neoclassical mainstream as well as delineating a program that provides a less-gendered, and they argue substantially more objective, version of economic science.

---

[45] A similar point (without the feminist connection) is made by Mayer (1993).

7

Recent Developments in Economic Methodology

This leads to the writing of books of varying character and size, which one suspects are more interesting ... to their authors than they are to any considerable number of readers. ... this may be a comforting thought, since it means that books on methodology probably do not do much damage. The chief reservation would be that they are most likely to be read and taken seriously by the young.

[Knight 1940, p. 151]

Modern economists frequently preach falsificationism ... but they rarely practice it: their working philosophy of science is aptly described as "innocuous falsificationism."

[Blaug 1992, p, 111]

If one accepts the terminology of logical positivism and especially of Popper, a theory or hypothesis is "unscientific" if *in principle* it cannot be refuted by experience. Consequently, all apriori theories, including mathematics and praxeology, are "unscientific." This is merely a verbal quibble. No serious man wastes his time in discussing such a terminological question. Praxeology and economics will retain their paramount significance for human life and action however people may classify and describe them.

[Mises 1978, p. 70]

[I]f French chefs resembled neoclassical economists, French cuisine would be more monotonous, for the chefs would use very few ingredients. They would also strenuously insist that food containing any other ingredients was not French.

[Hausman 1992, p. 260]

The previous four chapters have examined a large portion of contemporary science theory, and, whereas I made a systematic effort to connect this work to various topics within economics, the main theme was in fact *science theory* rather than economics or economic methodology. Readers whose interest in science theory is derived from, and secondary to, their interest in economics, may be relieved by this chapter's explicit return to economic methodology. Of course, the previous chapters accomplished quite a lot; in particular, we discovered some (rather starkly apparent) common themes within the vast literature of science theory. Science is more disunified; underdetermined; theory-, metaphysics-, context-, and interest-laden; inherently social; fundamentally complex – and, well, scruffy – than what the Legend had led us to believe. By the same token, very few authors we examined wanted to abandon the scientific enterprise, or even to give up entirely on the project of philosophically delineating the exact nature of science's particular cognitive virtues. The bottom line was that most authors – not all, but most – were trying to find a new, more comfortable, middle ground somewhere between relativism and the Received View. Finally, we discovered that epistemology and political economy have consistently interacted at a much deeper level than generally recognized by those writing on economic methodology; substantive views about the epistemic order are not (and never have been) independent of views about the economic order.

The literature on economic methodology has exploded during the last thirty years and this chapter will examine many of these recent developments. Like the literature in Chapter 2, the work considered here is self-consciously methodological; the main difference is that this recent work comes after, and in most cases explicitly addresses itself to, developments in post-Legend metascience. The first section examines Popperian economic methodology, and Section 2 discusses recent developments within the Millian tradition. The third part looks at various contact points between economics and contemporary realism, while the final section discusses various cognitive and semantic themes.

7.1 The Popperian Tradition

Karl Popper clearly had a greater impact on postwar economic methodology than any other single philosopher (or philosophical school). As mentioned in Chapter 3, it seems ironic that his influence among economists is actually greater than his influence among philosophers of science in general. There seem to be several reasons for his impact on economic methodology. One appears to be the common perception that Popper's philosophy is relatively straightforward and easy to apply; his prose is clear and unpretentious, and the falsificationist program seems to offer a relatively simple demarcation criterion as well as a set of easily implemented methodological rules for the proper conduct of scientific inquiry (i.e., it makes good $3'' \times 5''$ card philosophy of science). Another motivation may involve Popper's own intellectual interests and concerns. Popper was originally motivated by questions about the scientific status of particular social sciences – specifically by the desire to use his demarcation criterion to eliminate Freudian psychology and Marxist social theory from the domain of legitimate scientific inquiry (Popper 1976b) – this, combined with his own preferences in the area of political philosophy, made Popper an obvious choice for those interested in economic science. A final reason for his influence – related to, but separable from, his interest in the social sciences – concerns his personal and professional connections (particularly at LSE) to a number of influential methodologically inclined economists: Friedrich Hayek (Caldwell 1992a, 1992b; Hutchison 1981, 1988), Richard Lipsey (De Marchi 1988a) and Mark Blaug (Blaug 1994a).[1]

Although it is clear that Popper had a significant impact on economic methodology, it is decidedly less clear just exactly what the nature of his contribution has been. The difficulty evaluating Popperian economic methodology can be traced to various *problems and tensions within the Popperian philosophical tradition*. First, there are tensions within Popper's own philosophy of natural science; second, there are tensions that arise because of perceived differences between Popper's philosophy of natural science and what he said/wrote about the social sciences; and, finally, tensions are created by the multiplicity of different views (particularly about what is most important in Popper's work) offered by various members of the "Popperian school." The next few sections will examine how these various tensions have manifested themselves within the literature on economic methodology.

7.1.1 Tensions within Popperian Methodology

Since Popperian *falsificationism* was introduced during the discussion of Hutchison in Chapter 2, and examined in detail in Chapter 3,

---

[1] It should be noted that Popper has also been influential among certain nonacademic writers on economic issues, particularly Soros (1998), who, among other things, used Popperian philosophy of science to develop a nonequilibrium theory of financial markets.

it will not be necessary to rehash the basic argument at this point. It should be noted though, that while Popper wrote on many different philosophical subjects, falsificationist philosophy of science – originally presented in *Logik der Forschung* (1934) – clearly remains the philosophical position that is most readily identified with his name. Ask almost any philosopher about Karl Popper's work and one will inevitably receive a recitation about bold conjectures and severe tests; and, I would add, one would get essentially the same lecture from any economist who recognized the name. Falsificationism is what most philosophers mean by "Popperian" philosophy of science, and falsificationism is what most economists mean by "Popperian" economic methodology. Popper's influence is as great as it is precisely because a number of influential methodologically inclined economists have *endorsed falsificationism as the proper methodology for economic science*. In addition to Terence Hutchison (1938) – the person who introduced falsificationist ideas into economics – long-time advocates of falsificationism include Richard Lipsey (1966), Mark Blaug (1980/1992, 1990a) and J. J. Klant (1984, 1988, 1994). In addition to these relatively mainstream economists writing explicitly about economic methodology, there are a number of heterodox economists who have, over the years, used falsificationist standards to critique mainstream economics (Robinson 1977 and Eichner 1983, for example) and others who have used falsificationism to defend their own particular heterodox program (Moseley 1995).

Although falsificationists in economics come in a variety of different hues, the common methodological message is that economists *should practice falsificationism*, but in fact *they almost never do*. The argument is that falsificationism lays out the rules for the proper conduct of scientific inquiry, and although many economists claim to follow its strictures – they *preach* falsificationism – they in fact almost *never practice it*. As Mark Blaug, perhaps the most vociferous of the "unrepentant" Popperians (Blaug 1994b), explains this position in the preface to the second edition of his survey of economic methodology.

> I argue in favor of *falsificationism*, defined as a methodological standpoint that regards theories and hypotheses as scientific if and only if their predictions are at least in principle falsifiable, that is, if they forbid certain acts/states/events from occurring. ... In addition, I claim that modern economists do in fact subscribe to the methodology of falsificationism: ... I also argue, however, that economists fail consistently to practice what they preach: their working philosophy of science is aptly characterized as "innocuous falsificationism." (Blaug 1992, p. xiii)

While Blaug is fairly outspoken on the matter, he is certainly not alone in his falsificationist critique of mainstream economic practice.[2] The standard falsificationist message is that *economics needs to clean up its act*; Popper has delineated the proper method for the conduct of scientific inquiry – the falsificationist method – and economists should, but do not, follow this scientific method. Economists, of course, engage in empirical research, but "much of it is like *playing tennis with the net down*: instead of attempting to refute testable predictions, modern economists all too frequently are satisfied to demonstrate that the real world conforms to their predictions, thus replacing falsificationism, which is difficult, with verification, which is easy" (Blaug 1992, p. 241, emphasis added). Falsificationists generally believe that it is time (actually past time) to raise the net.

It is certainly clear why falsificationism has such a strong appeal to those who believe that much of modern economics is on the wrong track because economists are not doing real (empirical) science. Given the traditional view of economic methodology – as providing a set of rules for the proper conduct of economic science – falsificationism seems to provide rules that are simultaneously stern and straightforward; a theory must be falsifiable by at least one empirical basic statement in order to be scientific at all, and the theory that has survived the most severe tests is the one that has the most support and is most preferred. Since this is *not* what economists generally do – "No extensive historiographical research is required to reveal that the development of economic analysis would look a dismal affair through falsificationist spectacles" (Latsis 1976b, p. 8) – falsificationism implies that the discipline of economics is in need of major repair, and tough methodological rules are needed to guide those repairs. Spare the rod, spoil the science.

Although it may be clear why falsificationism has such appeal for many economists – and why many practicing economists feel compelled to pay lip service to it even though they do not actually live up to its strictures – it is equally clear that such a methodology has a number of problems. The philosophical literature criticizing falsificationism is massive, and although many of these criticisms are relevant to the question of whether falsificationism is right for economics, I will limit my

---

[2] For Blaug, this criticism applies to both mainstream and heterodox economics. The second half of Blaug (1992) contains a number of case studies from within mainstream economics including demand theory, general equilibrium theory, international trade theory, human capital theory, the economics of the family, and a variety of others. He finds all of these fields to be wanting (to various degrees). In Blaug (1990a), he performs a similar exercise for a number of different areas within heterodox economics: Marxian, Radical, and others.

discussion to issues raised explicitly within the literature on economic methodology (and, even here, not all of the possible concerns). The discussion will focus on four general problem areas. These areas are quite broad, but they represent an ongoing source of critical tension within the Popperian approach to economic methodology.[3]

The *first* difficulty with falsificationism comes from the Duhem-Quine (underdetermination) problem discussed in Chapter 3. The problem is that no scientific theory is ever tested in isolation. A negative test shows that at least one element of the *test system* (theory plus auxiliary hypotheses) is in conflict with the evidence; it does not necessarily imply that the scientific theory is the problem. Of course, Popper was fully aware of the underdetermination problem and offered a rather simple solution: consider all of the auxiliary hypotheses to be part of the (assumed) unproblematic background knowledge and blame the refutation on the theory. This makes falsificationism into a type of conventionalist philosophy – accepting the background knowledge as unproblematic by convention – and when applied to a particular refutation the result is what Hausman calls a "*conventional* falsification" (1996, p. 214, emphasis in original). For this reason Lakatos referred to Popperian falsificationism as a "revolutionary conventionalist" (Lakatos 1970, p. 106) philosophical approach; observation statements are accepted by *decision*, and although one may still refer to these conventionally accepted statements as "observational," it is "only a manner of speech" (1970, pp. 106–7). This conventionalism is also Popper's response to the problems of theory-ladenness and the fallibility of the scientific empirical basis; deciding to accept observations as unproblematic is effectively a decision to (conventionally) accept one type of theory – the theories impregnating the data – and question another (the theory being tested). Theories are everywhere and there is no place to stand that is free of them all (no foundations), but Popper's (conventional) rule regarding the empirical basis allows us to test various aspects of the theoretical system while the whole ship remains afloat.

Popper's conventionalism about the empirical basis certainly creates difficulties for falsificationism (really severe difficulties for those who see falsificationism as a version of empiricist foundationalism), but let us, for the time being, just accept this (conventionalist) answer to the issues of underdetermination and theory-ladenness. Even so, there is still a

---

[3] Rather than trying to attribute these four concerns to any particular author let me just cite Caldwell (1982/1994a, 1984a, 1991a, 1991b, 1994b), Hands (1979, 1984a, 1985b, 1991a, 1991b, 1992), Hausman (1985, 1988, 1992, 1996), Latsis (1972, 1976b, 1983), Redman (1991), and Salanti (1987) as a few of the many places where these issues have been raised within the methodological literature.

problem with the falsificationist approach. The problem, emphasized by Daniel Hausman (1992, pp. 184–5; 1996, pp. 214–15) is that the exact same conventionalist procedure will work for confirmation as well as falsification; thus *undermining the entire falsificationist project* of replacing verification with refutation. In Hausman's words:

> Regardless of the basis for the decision to rely on some propositions to falsify others, such decisions are unavoidable. But, if it is permissible to include background knowledge among one's premises in order to make conventional *falsifications* possible, then one also makes conventional *verifications* possible. The conventional asymmetry thesis fails, and Popper has failed to defend his claim that scientists should seek falsifications only. (Hausman 1992, p. 185, emphasis in original)

The *second* important tension is related to Popper's *recognition* of issues like underdetermination and theory-ladenness; this recognition seems to leave falsificationism stuck between the Scylla of discredited foundationalism and the Charybdis of radical relativism. The problem is that most "Popperian" economic methodologists see falsificationism as a particular type of *empiricist foundationalism* – the good old-fashioned rule-making of the early positivists without the problem of induction – and it is this perceived foundationalism that generates most of the program's charm. Most falsificationists, of course, pay *lip service to fallibilism* – when philosophically pushed they admit that Popper is more than a modus tollens positivist – but that recognition seems to have little or no impact on their methodological recommendations or even *why* they support those recommendations. The economic methodologists who are most vocal in their support of Popper thus seem to practice what could aptly be called *innocuous fallibilism*; they preach fallibilism (if forced), but they almost never practice it. Now, whereas it is quite clear that Popper was never an empirical foundationalist, his release from this indictment generates at least two different types of problems. In economics, it means that *most falsificationists are Popperians for the wrong reason*. Alternatively, if most Popperian economists were to read Popper in a more contemporary way they wouldn't remain Popperians, since sophisticated falsificationism doesn't really do what these economists want methodology to do: chase the barbarians from the gates of scientific economics. But it gets worse. On the one hand, there are economists (and no doubt others) who support falsificationism for the wrong reasons, whereas on the other hand, there are a number of philosophers who recognize that Popper was sensitive to issues like theory-ladenness and underdetermination but therefore *conclude that he was a relativist*.

Most famous is perhaps D. C. Stove, who claimed in *Popper and After* that *LSD*[4] was instrumental in the "irrationalist revolution in the historiography and philosophy of science" (1982, p. 13). Although Stove's position is considered extreme, there are many others who also paint Popper with a relativist brush. Susan Haack, for instance, considers Popper a "closet sceptic" who does not consider science to be "even negatively under the control of experience" (1993, pp. 97–8), whereas Larry Laudan deems Popperian philosophy to be "through-and-through relativist in character" (1989, p. 370). So which is worse; to be supported because you missed the main lessons of the last fifty years of science theory; or to be denounced because you recognized these lessons and tried to develop a position that accommodated them? Neither answer puts falsificationism in a very comfortable position.

This brings us to the *third* tension within Popperian philosophy: the difficulties surrounding the notion of truth and the grounds for Popper's version of scientific realism. Popper's original 1934 position in *LSD* was methodological without being epistemological; the falsificationist methodology of bold conjecture and severe test provided a set of rules for the game of science without providing an ultimate aim or purpose for playing the game. As Lakatos characterized Popper's position: "The rules of the game, the methodology, stand on their own feet; but these feet dangle in the air without philosophical support" (Lakatos 1978, p. 154). Popper clearly recognized this gap and sought to fill it in later work.

> Since publishing the *Logik der Forschung* (that is since 1934) I have developed a more systematic treatment of the problem of scientific method: I have tried to start with some suggestions about the aims of scientific activity, and to derive most of what I have to say about the methods of science . . . from this suggestion. (Popper 1983, p. 131)

Popper's main suggestion, introduced in 1959 or 1960, was that science is a "search for truth."[5] Popper had always preferred scientific realism and wanted to characterize science as the search for truth, but in the early 1930s the correspondence theory of truth was in such philosophical disrepute that he strategically chose to "avoid the topic" (Popper 1965, p. 223). It was not until he became familiar with Alfred Tarski's theory that Popper lost his "uneasiness concerning the notion of truth" (Popper 1972, p. 320) and officially endorsed truth as the aim of science. But,

[4] Recall (from Chapter 3) that the English translation of *Logik der Forschung* (1934) was *The Logic of Scientific Discovery* (1968).

[5] Popper (1965; 1972, pp. 44–84 and pp. 319–35; 1976b, p. 150; 1983, pp. 24–7 and elsewhere).

whereas the turn toward truth may have made Popperian philosophy more epistemologically satisfactory, it also generated additional difficulties. The most obvious problem was that *falsificationist practice doesn't necessarily generate true theories*. Although the method of bold conjecture and severe test may discover falsity, it does not discover truth. Popper is a fallibilist – the scientific theory that has successfully passed a number of severe tests (is corroborated) may be preferred – but we do not know that it is true. Truth is a regulative idea, it is not something we are ever certain we have.

Popper's response to the problem of fallibilist truth was his theory of *truthlikeness* or *verisimilitude*. The concept of verisimilitude, Popper believed, would allow him to be able to say "that some theory T_1 is superseded by some new theory, say T_2, because T_2 is more like the truth than T_1" (Popper 1972, p. 57). Verisimilitude would allow Popper to defend falsificationism as a method that gets us closer to the truth – consistent with his scientific realism – while at the same time avoiding what he considered to be the essentialist pitfall of claiming that we actually have the truth. If the concept of verisimilitude could be worked out, and if the case could be made that falsificationist methodological rules are a good way of achieving it, then falsificationism would certainly be standing on solid epistemological ground; we would have good reason to believe that a theory that has passed severe tests will perform equally well in any future test. Unfortunately, it never worked; the Popperian approach to verisimilitude systematically unraveled starting with two papers by Tichy (1974) and Miller (1974). Ian Hacking refers to verisimilitude as "Popper's hokum" (1979, p. 387), and Graham Oddie, an advocate of a non-Popperian version of verisimilitude, claims that the Popperian literature has produced "embarrassing results" (1986, p. 164). Many Popperians are equally critical; Joseph Agassi calls it simply "a boo boo" (Agassi 1988, p. 473), John Worrall considers Popper's formal notion to be "unsound" (1982, p. 228), and David Miller argues that there is "a serious problem here, the problem of whether our intuitive judgments of truthlikeness or verisimilitude are in fact judgments of anything objective at all" (Miller 1994, pp. 197–8). Although Popper never abandoned the general concept of verisimilitude, or its importance, he did ultimately consider his attempt to formalize it an "admitted failure" (Popper 1983, p. xxxv).[6]

---

[6] I discuss verisimilitude and its importance to the Popperian program in greater detail in Hands (1991b). For an alternative view of verisimilitude and economics, see Zamora Bonilla (1999b). There also exists a substantial body of non-Popperian literature on verisimilitude and truth-likeness: see Niiniluoto (1998).

The bottom line is that with the failure of the project of verisimilitude the falsificationist tradition lost its hook to the truth; there simply does not exist a persuasive Popperian story about why following the falsificationist method of bold conjecture and severe test will give us theories that are closer to the truth. Of course, different Popperians express different opinions about the significance of this rather unsettling result – from Lakatos's plea for a "whiff of inductivism" (Lakatos 1978, p. 159) to John Watkins's (1984) effort to replace verisimilitude entirely with a corroborationist program – but the problem is universally recognized. "Popper has always been a scientific realist but he has never been able to show that his rules of method are guaranteed to yield truths about the world" (Nola 1987, p. 468). These problems, of course, do not bode well for falsificationist methodology in economics. If Popper can not explain how severely tested but nonfalsified theories are closer to the truth in natural science, then there certainly isn't any reason to believe that falsificationism will provide a successful technique for finding truth in economics.

The *final* tension within Popperian philosophy, and perhaps the most important for economics, is that while falsificationism is the standard interpretation of the Popperian position within economics, it is a reading of his philosophy that seems to be *at odds with the methodology that Popper actually endorsed when writing about the social sciences*. Popper did not write extensively about the methodology of social science, but what he did write emphasized the essential role of the "rationality principle" (hereafter RP) and "situational analysis" (hereafter SA) in the explanation of human behavior. Neither RP nor SA sit very comfortably with falsificationism.

Popper's comments about social science and SA were scattered about in a number of different places in his papers and books (1961, pp. 149–52; 1966, pp. 96–8; 1967; 1976a; 1976b, pp. 117–18 for example), but this situation has changed with the publication of "Models, Instruments, and Truth: The Status of the Rationality Principle in the Social Sciences" in Popper (1994). A version of this paper was originally presented to the Harvard Economics Department in 1963, and it represents the most extensive discussion of SA and the RP available in any of Popper's published works.[7]

According to Popper's SA, explanations of human behavior always take the following form. One starts with the "problem situation" of a

---

[7] An extract of this paper was published in French (Popper 1967), and a translation of that extract was published in a volume edited by Miller (Popper 1985), but these versions only contain about one-third of the original material. See Hands (1996) for more details.

particular agent; this problem situation includes the beliefs, goals, and desires of the individual, as well as the constraints the individual faces in trying to achieve these goals and desires. One "explains" the action of an individual by deducing that action from the individual's particular problem situation. The "animating law" for such an explanation is the RP, which states that the individual acted "adequately, or appropriately" (Popper 1994, p. 169) given the situation they were in. Following Koertge (1975, p. 440; 1979, p. 87), an SA explanation of why agent A did act X can be given in the following schematic form.

Description of the situation:	Agent A was in situation S.
Analysis of the situation:	In situation S the appropriate (rational) thing to do is X.
The Rationality Principle (RP):	Agents always act appropriately (rationally) given their situation.
Explanandum:	Therefore: A did X.

It should be clear that most microeconomic explanations of *individual* (or firm) behavior are a special case of this general explanatory schema; in the case of economics such explanations involve only certain kinds of goals (utility or profit for instance), certain kinds of constraints (budget or cost for instance), and certain ways of defining "appropriate" action (i.e. maximization or minimization), but the framework is clearly of the SA form.[8] Not only do many microeconomic explanations fit the general SA form, Popper admits that economics was the original inspiration for this approach.

> My views on the methodology of the social sciences are the result of my admiration for economic theory: I began to develop them, some twenty-five years ago, by trying to generalize the method of theoretical economics. (Popper 1994, p. 154)

One obvious difficulty with SA explanations is that they are extremely hard to reconcile with falsificationism; social science based on SA and the RP does not seem to be "science" at all on the basis of Popper's own (falsificationist) demarcation criterion.[9] There are a number of problems here (and not sufficient space to discuss them all), but the most obvious

---

[8] Evidently the SA-economics connection was well known in Popperian circles from the early 1960s (recall that Popper's presentation to the Harvard economics department was in 1963), but the first published paper to emphasize the connection was Latsis (1972).

[9] This tension has been recognized by a wide range of different authors (Caldwell 1991a, 1991b; Curtis 1989; Farr 1983; Hands 1985b, 1991a; Koertge 1975, 1979; Latsis 1972, 1976b, 1983; Nadeau 1993; Redman 1991; and Stokes 1997, among others); see Boland (1997, p. 162) for a contrary view.

difficulty concerns the status of the RP itself; the RP is the animating law in an (ostensibly) scientific explanation and yet it is immunized against potential falsification in Popper's methodological scheme. When an explanation involving the RP is tested and found faulty Popper asserts that it is "sound methodological policy to decide not to make the rationality principle, but the rest of the theory – that is, the model – accountable" (Popper 1994, p. 177). Such a defensive/ad hoc strategy hardly seems to be consistent with the falsificationist policy of sticking one's neck out, that is, the method of bold conjecture and severe test. Even Mark Blaug, a staunch defender of the falsificationist reading of Popper, admits that "Popper's defense of rational choice models will not wash in terms of the methodology of falsificationism" (Blaug 1994b, p. 113). Recognition of this tension led to the introduction of the distinction between Popper$_n$ (the falsificationist philosopher of natural science)[10] and Popper$_s$ (the SA philosopher of social science) in Hands (1985b). It should be noted that this issue is not just a concern for economics or the philosophy of social science; it is also a fundamental issue for the entire Popperian philosophical program. Remember that Popper explicitly developed his demarcation criteria to demarcate scientific theories from those that he considered to be pseudoscience: Marx and Freud in particular. How can these theories be criticized for failing to do that which even the best social science (in Popper's view) does not do either?

The following diagram may help in diagnosing the various difficulties with falsificationism, RP, and economics.

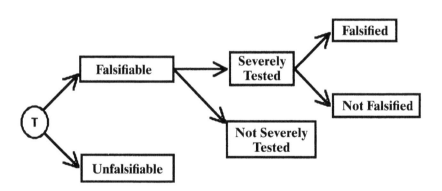

Starting from the far left-hand side consider a particular economic theory involving the RP. As Popper admits (1994, pp. 177–8) the

---

[10] With hindsight, Popper$_f$ (for falsificationist) would have been a better choice.

principle may be either false or unfalsifiable. If "appropriately" is defined in a very weak way (as say, whatever people do) then no one could ever violate the RP and, thus, an economic theory involving the principle would be unfalsifiable (and, thus, unscientific). If the RP is defined more strictly – so that some observable behavior is in fact "inappropriate" – then the principle is falsifiable, but it also is false, because people are likely to violate any/every standard of appropriate behavior, meaning that we end up in the far northeast corner of the diagram. Because Popper provides no way of choosing among falsified theories – falsified theories are just out – there is no way to decide (on falsificationist grounds) whether we should hold on to a particular economic theory involving the (false) RP. Finally, suppose that we do find a way to retain the RP so it is falsifiable but not falsified, then we are in the lower box on the far right-hand side with a severely tested and yet unfalsified theory, but then we are confronted with the *problem of verisimilitude*. We have no reason to believe that such a theory is true, or even that it is closer to the truth than any other theory that also has survived such severe tests. Economic theory involving the RP seems to end up in one of three rather unpleasant categories. Either it is unfalsifiable (not scientific), or it is false (and out), or if it does somehow manage to survive severe tests, then we still do not know that it is true, or even any closer to the truth, or better than any other theory that has survived similar tests.

Taken together, *these four tensions add up to some serious difficulties for falsificationist philosophy of science* in general and falsificationist economic methodology in particular. When the conventional element is added to give falsification some bite, the same bite is transferred to induction; falsificationism seems to be interpreted as either old-fashioned foundationalism or radical relativism; there does not exist any systematic connection between the practice of falsificationist methodology and the truthlikeness of the theories that have been tested according to its rules; and, finally, falsificationism seems to be radically at odds with what Popper has actually written about social science and economics. No wonder Hausman concluded his chapter on Popperian philosophy with the simple statement that "Popper's philosophy of science does not permit one to pose the central problems of theory appraisal in economics and does not help to resolve them" (Hausman 1992, p. 191).

7.1.2 The Lakatosian Turn

Lakatos's methodology of scientific research programs (MSRP) was also discussed in Chapter 3 and those wanting to refresh their memory about the notion of "progress," the importance of "novel facts," or the "pornographic metaphors" (Hacking 1979, p. 398) of "hard core" and "protective belt," should review Section 3.3.1. Unlike most philosophical approaches that make their way into economics third-or-more-hand, and frequently with dubious fidelity, Lakatos's impact was immediate, direct, and initiated by people who were quite knowledgeable about his work. The two authors most responsible for bringing Lakatos into economics were Spiro Latsis and Mark Blaug. Latsis was a graduate student and friend of Lakatos's who published the first philosophy paper applying the MSRP to economics (Latsis 1972) and also edited the first major collection of papers on the subject (Latsis 1976a).[11] Blaug authored the first Lakatosian paper published in an economics journal (Blaug 1975), shepherded the debate into the history of economic thought, and has been a consistent and outspoken advocate of Lakatos's philosophy.[12]

The literature on Lakatos and economics has become enormous. In addition to various general discussions (for example: Archibald 1979; Backhouse 1994a, 1997a; Blaug 1980/1992, 1991a, 1994b; Boylan and O'Gorman 1995; Caldwell 1982/1994, 1991a, 1991b; De Marchi 1991; Fulton 1984; Glass and Johnson 1989; Hands 1979, 1992; Hausman 1992, 1994; Hutchison 1976; Pheby 1988; Redman 1991; Remenyi 1979; Robbins 1979; and Shearmur 1991), there are Lakatosian case studies on almost every conceivable area of economic thought. A (nonexhaustive) list of these case studies includes: the theory of the firm (Ahonen 1990; Latsis 1972, 1976b; Nightingale 1994), the psychological foundations of economics (Coats 1976), Keynesian economics (Ahonen 1989; Blaug 1975, 1976, 1991b; Hands 1985a, 1990b; Leijonhufvud 1976; and

---

[11] Latsis was also responsible in another way, as the Latsis Foundation helped to fund the two conferences that generated a substantial portion of the work on the subject of Lakatos and economics – the first Lakatos conference (the Nafplion Colloquium on Research Programmes in Physics and Economics) held in Nafplion, Greece, in 1974 and the second Lakatos conference held in Capri, Italy, in 1989. These conferences produced the two volumes, Latsis (1976a) and De Marchi and Blaug (1991a), that have formed the backbone of the extensive literature on Lakatos and economics. While I can personally vouch for the intellectual vitality of the (2nd) Capri conference, the original Nafplion conference must have been even better, given the glowing remarks made by methodologists as diverse as Mark Blaug: "the conference of a lifetime" (Blaug 1994a, p. 24), and Lionel Robbins: "I personally found more stimulating than any other conference I have ever attended" (Robbins 1979, p. 996).

[12] Although Blaug has consistently defended Lakatosian methodology, it should also be noted that his interpretation of Lakatos's MSRP and his interpretation of Popperian falsificationism are sufficiently similar that his Lakatosian advocacy is often indistinguishable from his advocacy of falsificationism. This view, of course, differs from Popper himself who considered Lakatos to be an "unreliable and misleading" (Popper 1974, p. 999) interpreter of his work.

McGovern 1995), Post-Keynesian economics (Brown 1981), the Leontief Paradox (De Marchi 1976), general equilibrium theory (Backhouse 1993; Diamond 1988a; Rosenberg 1986; Salanti 1991, 1993a, 1993b; Toruno 1988; and Weintraub 1979, 1985a, 1985b, 1988b), new classical macro (Backhouse 1991, 1998b; Cross 1982; Hoover 1991; Maddock 1984, 1991; McMahon 1984), new economic growth theory (Foss 1998), hysteresis (Cross 1987, 1991), Sraffian economics (Backhouse 1995b; Steedman 1991, 1995), Austrian economics (Lavoie 1991a; Rizzo 1982), job search theory (Kim 1991), demand theory (Gilbert 1991), game theory (Bianachi and Moulin 1991), experimental economics (Smith, McCabe, and Rassenti 1991; Smith 1989), radical economics (Blaug 1990b; Reich 1995), Marxian economics (Blaug 1990c; Moseley 1995), the marginal revolution (Fisher 1986), Adam Smith's economics (O'Brien 1976), microfoundations (Janssen 1991; Weintraub 1979), evolutionary economics (Nightingale 1994), capital theory (Birner 1990), Henry George (Petrella 1988), financial economics (Schmidt 1982), and even the rhetoric of economics (Maloney 1994).

As discussed in Chapter 3, Lakatos's approach was quasi-historical; it attempted to meld various elements from Popper's normative philosophy of science with various elements from Kuhn-inspired historical inquiry. Lakatos's program deviated from Popperian falsificationism on at least three different levels: the methodological, the epistemological, and the meta-methodological. The most significant (or at least best known) of Lakatos's deviations from Popper occur at the *methodological* level. The most noticeable is that Lakatos switched the unit of analysis from scientific theories to scientific *research programs*. Although Lakatos, unlike Popper, admitted that all scientific research programs were "born refuted" (1970, pp. 120–21; 1971, p. 114), this fact does not, according to Lakatos, prevent these programs from being theoretically, or even empirically, progressive. A research program need not be abandoned even if it is degenerating; Lakatos (again unlike Popper) did not conflate appraisal and advice. The MSRP, thus, accommodates the actual history of science (Kuhn) while still providing a way to appraise the scientific progressiveness of any particular theoretical change (Popper). Lakatos stuck with Popper's notion of empirical content (the number of potential falsifiers), the conventional nature of the empirical basis, and Popper's notion of "independent testability" or "novel facts"; he diverged from Popper by focusing on research programs, shifting the notion of progress from falsification (which it was pretty clear from Kuhn and others that scientists almost never attempted) to *corroboration* of novel facts; and he separated appraisal and advice.

On the *epistemological* level, Lakatos tried to circumvent Popper's difficulties with truth and verisimilitude by appealing directly for a "whiff of inductivism" (Lakatos 1978). Unlike Popper, who argued that "We cannot justify our theories, or the belief that they are true; nor can we justify the belief that they are near to the truth" (Popper 1983, p. 61), Lakatos wanted to provide a way to "*recognize* progress" (Lakatos 1978, p. 156, emphasis in original) and to make the epistemological link between progressive problemshifts and getting closer to the truth. The link is forged, according to Lakatos, by "an inductive principle which connects realist metaphysics with methodological appraisals, verisimilitude with corroboration, which reinterprets the rules of the 'scientific game' as a-conjectural-theory about the *signs* of the growth of knowledge, that is, about the signs of *growing verisimilitude of our scientific theories*" (Lakatos 1978, p. 156, emphasis in original). Lakatos argued that without such an inductive principle methodological proposals were condemned to being conventions without any epistemological bite.

> Without this principle Popper's "corroborations" or "refutations" and my "progress" or "degeneration" would remain mere honorific titles awarded in a pure game. With a *positive* solution of the problem of induction, however thin, methodological theories of demarcation can be turned from arbitrary conventions into rational metaphysics. (Lakatos 1978, p. 165, emphasis in original)[13]

Finally, at the level of *meta-methodology* (choosing among scientific methodologies) Lakatos abandoned the *a priori* philosophical approach of both Popper and the logical positivists to embrace a quasi-historical framework for appraising methodologies that owes much to Kuhn. Lakatos's meta-method – the methodology of historical research programs (MHRP) – used the "best gambits" from the history of science to test various methodological proposals. According to MHRP "a general definition of science . . . must reconstruct the acknowledgedly best gambits as 'scientific': if it fails to do so, it has to be rejected" (Lakatos 1971, p. 111). Thus, a methodology – a view about the nature of scientific rationality – is preferred if it can rationalize a larger portion of the actual history of science. How are the best gambits determined? They are determined by the scientific élite itself: "if a demarcation criterion is inconsistent with the 'basic' appraisals of the scientific elite, it should be

---

[13] Although Lakatos clearly wanted more epistemological bite, it is not clear he ever really provided any. As one recent commentator put it, Lakatos's inductive principle was "supported not by argument but by pious hope" (Larvor 1998, p. 102).

rejected" (Lakatos 1971, p. 111). The argument is that whereas the general rules of scientific method may be open to debate, scientists generally know the scientific standing of any specific research program. Once the history of a particular scientific research program is reconstructed on the basis of the methodology that most adequately rationalizes the best gambits, any deviations of the actual history from the reconstruction can be delegated to *footnotes* (Lakatos 1971, p. 105).

Although various authors applying Lakatos to economics have emphasized different aspects of his approach, most of the literature has focused exclusively on *methodological* (rather than epistemological or meta-methodological) issues.[14] The two main methodological features that have received the most attention in economics are the *structure* and *appraisal* of particular research programs. Economists have tried to identify the *structure* of various research programs in economics by identifying the hard core, positive heuristic, negative heuristic, and so on, and as the above list suggests, an extremely diverse range of economic research programs have been subjected to such structural analysis. Once the various parts of the Lakatosian structure have been identified, the next step is usually to *appraise* the research program with respect to its theoretical and/or empirical progressivity. This means ascertaining whether the program has, or has not, generated any *novel facts* (theoretical progress) and/or whether any of these novel facts have actually been confirmed (empirical progress).

Rather than trying to sample a variety of the many Lakatosian case studies available in the economics literature, I will focus my attention on just one particular case: Roy Weintraub's (1985a) study of General Equilibrium Theory. This study is particularly significant for a number of reasons. It is one of only two book-length Lakatosian case studies; it focuses on an area of economics that is an established and highly respected part of the professional mainstream (and formed the backbone of post-World War II graduate education in economics); it employs not only the MSRP but also Lakatos's work on the growth of mathematical knowledge; and finally, as we will see, it seems to have caused a rather ironic interruption of the Lakatosian literature.

Although the subject of Weintraub's investigation is Walrasian general equilibrium theory, he actually argues that general equilibrium analysis isn't in fact an economic "theory," or even an economic "research

---

[14] One of the exceptions to this methodological focus is the (meta-methodological) debate over whether the paucity of novel facts in Keynes's *General Theory* should lead us to reject Lakatos's MSRP as the proper approach to the methodology of economics. See Blaug 1975/1976, 1990d, 1991b, and Hands 1985a, 1990b; McGovern 1995 summarizes the debate. Some of the epistemological issues are also examined in Hands (1991b).

program," at all. The relevant research program is *Neo-Walrasian eco-nomics*, and the work that goes on in what the profession calls Walrasian general equilibrium theory, is contained in the *hard core* of this Neo-Walrasian program. This hard core, like all Lakatosian hard cores, is insulated from contact with the empirical evidence by the theories and auxiliary assumptions in the program's protective belt. The more applied, more econometrically estimable, and less mathematical theories within the protective belt of the Neo-Walrasian program – from human capital theory, to the economics of the family, to international trade theory – represent contact points between the postulates of the hard core and the empirical evidence.

The Neo-Walrasian program is organized around the following six hard core propositions.

> HC1. There exist economic agents.
> HC2. Agents have preferences over outcomes.
> HC3. Agents independently optimize subject to constraints.
> HC4. Choices are made in interrelated markets.
> HC5. Agents have full relevant knowledge.
> HC6. Observable economic outcomes are coordinated, so they must be discussed with reference to equilibrium states.
>
> (Weintraub 1985a, p. 109)

The positive heuristic of the Neo-Walrasian program includes impera-tives to construct theories "in which agents optimize" and "that make predictions about changes in equilibrium states," whereas the negative heuristic implores us to avoid theories in which "irrational behavior plays any role" or in which "equilibrium has no meaning," and of course, not to "test the hardcore propositions" (Weintraub 1985a, p. 109).

One of Weintraub's main points is that the hard core did not "emerge fully armed like Athene from the head of Zeus" (Lakatos 1970, p. 133); it takes time for a hard core to harden. In particular, the sequence of papers on the existence of the equilibrium price vector in a Walrasian general equilibrium model – the sequence starting from the work of Abraham Wald and Karl Schlesinger (in Karl Menger's Vienna seminar in the early 1930s) and ending with the canonical presentation of the Arrow-Debreu-McKenzie (ADM) model in Arrow and Hahn (1971) – represented the *hardening of the hard core of the Neo-Walrasian model*. This story "makes sense of the historical record in a way no other expla-nation offered so far has" (Weintraub 1985a, p. 112).

Weintraub raises two main points about the mathematics involved in the research on the existence of general equilibrium. First of all, because the hardening process involves the systematic refinement of how the (fixed) hardcore propositions are interpreted – how they come to be interpreted in a consistent way – the hardening process *"requires mathematization of the program"* (Weintraub 1985a, p. 141). Second, and more relevant to the appraisal of the Neo-Walrasian program, the hardening process – since it is essentially mathematical – should be *appraised as mathematics*. In particular, Lakatos's philosophy of mathematics from *Proofs and Refutations* (1976)[15] should provide the standards for evaluating whether a particular problem shift within the hard core was progressive or degenerating (not the MSRP).[16] Of course, the standards for theoretical and empirical progressivity offered by Lakatos's MSRP *do* matter for the appraisal of the Neo-Walrasian program, but they matter for the appraisal of the applied theories in the protective belt. There are two (Lakatosian) standards of appraisal that are relevant to the Neo-Walrasian program: the (mathematical) standards of *Proofs and Refutations* for activity in the hard core, and the (empirical) standards of MSRP for the applied theories in the protective belt. As Weintraub summarizes his argument:

> Hence we have two separate criteria for appraising general equilibrium analysis: First, we use criteria appropriate for gauging mathematical progress to measure the growth of knowledge associated with the hardening of the core of the neo-Walrasian program. Second, we use traditional . . . appraisal techniques to evaluate the work in the belts of that hard core. These derived theories – such as demand theory, human capital theory, and the theory of effective protection – must indeed be tested and corroborated. . . . *To ask about the falsifiability of the Arrow-Debreu-McKenzie model is not to be hard-headed, positivistic, or rigorous. It is to be confused.* (Weintraub 1985a, p. 119, emphasis in original)

[15] *Proofs and Refutations* was based on Lakatos's 1961 Ph.D. thesis and a series of papers published in the *British Journal for the Philosophy of Science* in 1963–4; it was edited (posthumously) by John Worrall and Elie Zahar. There seems to be some debate about the editors' interpretative liberties; Larvor (1998, Ch. 2) argues that Lakatos himself would have made it less Popperian and more Hegelian.

[16] Weintraub is not alone in the recommendation that economists look to Lakatos's work on the philosophy of mathematics. For instance, Leijonhufvud commented:

> It is not surprising, then, that much of the work in pure economic theory is better described by Lakatos's "Proof and Refutations" than by his later MSRP. (Leijonhufvud 1976, p. 81)

Birner (1990, pp. 187–90) also combines Lakatos's philosophy of mathematics with the MSRP in his evaluation of certain areas of economic theory.

Not only are there two separate tests: Weintraub insists that Neo-Walrasian theory has successfully passed both of them. The progressivity of the hard core (mathematical) portion of the Neo-Walrasian program is defended in Weintraub (1985a), whereas the empirical progressiveness of certain theories in the protective belt is supported in Weintraub (1988b). Thus, it seems that mainstream Neo-Walrasian economics is just fine; mathematical general equilibrium theory has evolved in a way that demonstrates mathematical progress – progress necessary for the development of the overall program – and the myriad of subprograms in the protective belt are exhibiting sufficient empirical progress that the whole kit and caboodle gets an affirmative Lakatosian nod.

There have been numerous criticisms of Weintraub's story – Backhouse (1993), Blaug (1992, Ch. 8), Diamond (1988), Rosenberg (1986), Salanti (1991, 1993a, 1993b), Vilks (1992) – although perhaps not as many as one would expect given the importance of the relevant economic theory. The placement of Walrasian economics within the hardcore (as opposed to it being one of the many possible subprograms contained in the protective belt of a "neoclassical" hardcore) has been questioned; the (Lakatosian) notion of mathematical progress has been challenged, both as a philosophy of mathematics and as an accurate description of what occurred in the history of mathematical general equilibrium theory; the argument has been made that the (more empirical) theories in the protective belt do not connect up *at all* with the hardcore propositions; it has been suggested that the professional prestige accorded to general equilibrium theory/theorists has negative implications for the long run development of testable empirical theories within the protective belt; and, finally, the argument has been made that Weintraub's notion of empirical progress could just as well be positivist or falsificationist, as it has almost nothing to do with Lakatos's notion of novel facts.

Although I will leave it to the interested reader to assess the validity of (any of) these various accusations, I would like to point out a rather ironic implication of Weintraub's work. The irony is that while his inquiry is arguably the most significant work in the field of Lakatos and economics – in terms of the detail, the number of pages, and the prestige of the relevant program – it actually appears to have had a chilling effect on the further development of the field. There seem to be two main reasons for this negative impact. First, Weintraub himself has moved on. Without ever explicitly denouncing his Lakatosian work, Weintraub has redirected his study of general equilibrium theory and is now involved in a more self-consciously historical (and less methodological) investigation that attempts to weave together a number of different explanatory threads into a single historical narrative on twentieth-century economic thought. To the degree that his later work (Weintraub 1988a, 1989, 1991, 1997; Weintraub and Mirowski 1994) is informed by contemporary science theory, it is more the constructivist SSK discussed in Chapter 5, and the neopragmatism and other ideas discussed in Chapter 6, than Lakatos's work (MSRP, MHRP, or *Proofs and Refutations*). This historical-sociological turn is surely troubling for many economists sympathetic to the Lakatosian approach. Many supporters of Lakatos see the MSRP as a demarcationist tool: as providing a set of relatively strict rules that will constrain, and hopefully cleanse, the empirical practice of economists. For these authors, the problem with economics lies in its lack of empirical discipline – falsificationism is a little too strict in practice, but its empirical spirit is right – Lakatos is desirable because his approach allows us to keep much of modern economics (which a strict application of falsificationism would force us to condemn as unscientific), while still providing tough empirical rules for scientific progress in economics (see the introduction to Backhouse 1998a or Blaug 1992, 1994b). Given these objectives, Weintraub's movement in the direction of SSK and neopragmatism is a real problem; the person who authored the most significant Lakatosian case study now seems to be cavorting with the dark (or at least soft) side.

But there is a second problem with Weintraub's work that may be even worse (for Lakatosians) than his moving off into SSK – Weintraub demonstrates that general equilibrium theory is scientifically *just fine*. For most methodologists sympathetic to Lakatos, *general equilibrium theory is the paradigm case of what is wrong with contemporary economics*.

> Enormous intellectual resources have been invested in its endless refinements, none of which has even provided a fruitful starting point from which to approach a substantive explanation of the workings of an economic system. Its leading characteristic has been the endless formalization of purely logical problems without the slightest regard for the production of falsifiable theorems about actual economic behavior, which, we insist, remains the fundamental task of economics. The widespread belief that every economic theory must be fitted into the GE mold if it is to qualify as rigorous science has perhaps been more responsible than any other intellectual force for the purely abstract and nonempirical character of so much of modern economic reasoning. (Blaug 1992, p. 169)

If one is looking for Lakatos to provide tough empirical rules then one is going to be very troubled by Weintraub's endorsement of the progressivity of general equilibrium analysis. The problem is that if Walrasian general equilibrium theory – the least empirical aspect of modern economics – is scientifically progressive (or at least it is contained in the hardcore of an empirically progressive research program), then Lakatos's MSRP has no real methodological bite (it reduces to "anything goes" as Feyerabend [1975] originally claimed). In other words, if general equilibrium theory can slip through the Lakatosian net, then what good is the net? The bottom line is that Weintraub has demonstrated that Lakatos is not an effective methodological tool for doing what most economists who endorse Lakatos want his methodology to do – impose tougher empirical standards and depreciate abstract mathematical theorizing – and as a result it has (however inadvertently) taken the wind out of the Lakatosian sails. Weintraub's historical-sociological turn just adds insult to injury.

Finally, and quite independently of Weintraub's study, there is a whole controversy surrounding the Lakatosian notion of a *novel fact*. As Chapter 3 made clear, the concept of a novel fact is a troublesome philosophical notion. There are multiple (some partially overlapping and some contradictory) definitions of novel facts in the philosophical (even Lakatosian) literature; the idea of novelty has a long and controversial history in philosophy that seems to raise more questions than answers about the significance of the concept to the truth, usefulness, meaningfulness, or reliability of a scientific theory; and many contemporary philosophers doubt that novelty (under any of the available definitions) is relevant to the appraisal of scientific theories or research programs.[17] Even if one wants to argue that the correct prediction of a novel fact – assuming it is accepted by the relevant scientific community *as* a novel fact – serves as a type of "clincher" in a scientific debate, it still does not mean that it should be the sole, necessary, criterion for scientific progress. One can understand (and perhaps even sympathize with) how Popper arrived at his concept of non-ad-hocness, the notion of independent testability, and finally the importance of novel facts; one can also understand (and perhaps even sympathize with) how Lakatos extended Popper's ideas and gave novel facts even more weight, how later Lakatosians modified the definition of novel facts in order to improve the historical track record of the MSRP, and, finally, how we got into the

---

[17] Stephen Brush's remark on the subject is telling.

> The predictivist thesis gains little empirical support from the history of science. Any attempt to rescue it by redefining novelty in terms of what the theorist knew, when he knew it, and what he did or could have done with the information puts the philosopher in the position of a Watergate investigator without Deep Throat. (Brush 1995, p. 141)

current mess regarding novelty;[18] but that understanding should tell us *to stay away from novelty-based standards*, not make it our sole criterion for scientific progress.

Although all of this seems quite critical of Lakatos and economics, it need not be. The problem with novel facts, the definition or the actual identification, is an issue about using the MSRP as a tool for *the appraisal* of various research programs within economics, and appraisal is not the only way that the MSRP can be used to discuss economics. As many authors have suggested (De Marchi 1991; Hausman 1994), Lakatos's MSRP may be useful for understanding the *structure* of economics (or a particular economic theory), even if it is not a good tool for *assessment*. Economic theories do seem to have hardcores, protective belts, positive and negative heuristics, and so on. Identifying these characteristics and how they evolve over the history of a particular research program has generated some interesting historical studies. There is a notion of theoretical progress that seems to be at work in the history of economic thought and a better understanding of that notion would certainly provide us with valuable insights into the nature of economic inquiry. There is clearly a notion of empirical progress at work in economics as well. Although that notion of empirical progress undoubtedly has little or nothing to do with the Popper-based Lakatosian notion of a novel fact, the topic certainly seems to be worthy of investigation. Lakatos also provides a useful tool for *comparing* research programs. Two examples of such comparisons are the studies of the theory of the firm offered in Latsis's first paper (Latsis 1972) and in Nightingale's (1994) more recent extension. Both papers compare the neoclassical theory of the firm – with Popper's RP as a hardcore proposition – with other theories of economic organization such as the behavioral and evolutionary theories of the firm. In such cases, the Lakatosian framework can be a useful analytical tool, and if one stays away from narrow definitions of novel facts, one can actually compare various types of empirical progress. These are just two of many other possible examples.

The bottom line is that if one wants the MSRP to serve demarcationist ends – to provide strict methodological rules for demarcating good/scientific economics from bad/nonscientific economics – then it fails in its task; of course as the last four chapters have explained in detail, nothing else in contemporary science theory does the job either. By contrast, if one wants to use the MSRP for more doable jobs, that are local in character, primarily historical, less arrogant, and perhaps more interesting, then it may still have something to offer.

---

[18] I discuss this sequence in detail in Hands (1985a, 1988, 1991b, and 1991c).

7.1.3 Critical Rationalism and Economics

Although falsificationism is the most common reading of Karl Popper's philosophy, it is not the only interpretation of his work. An alternative reading of Popper's philosophy is *critical rationalism*. This interpretation of his central thesis is associated with a number of Popperian philosophers: Joseph Agassi, W. W. Bartley, Ian Jarvie, Gerard Radnitzky, and others.[19] These authors are less concerned with demarcating science from nonscience and more concerned with characterizing the social context necessary for the growth of scientific knowledge. The argument is that Popper's *Logik der Forschung* was a specific response to the particular problem situation in which Popper found himself in the early 1930s. According to this interpretation, falsificationism is *not* inconsistent with Popper's more general philosophy, but it *is* just one particular application of his general thesis; falsificationism is simply critical rationalism applied to the particular class of philosophical problems that concerned the logical positivists (and Popper) in the 1930s. The argument in that while Popper's philosophy solves these problems, it solves many other philosophical problems as well, and to focus on this one class of concerns, basically the problem of demarcation, is to ignore the more important general (and critical) message in his work.

Critical rationalism is more aggressively antifoundationalist than falsificationism,[20] but the rejection of foundationalism does not imply that critical rationalism reduces to relativism, descriptivism, or sociology. Critical rationalism is normative *without providing any strict rules* for the conduct of scientific inquiry. The program asserts that there are *rational reasons* for believing in one theory rather than another, but these reasons are based on systematic *criticism* – criticism that in turn depends on the proper critical environment rather than on following any particular

---

[19] Perhaps I should say "the other most popular reading of Popper's philosophy is critical rationalism," since there are perhaps as many different readings of Popper's philosophy as there are Popperians. In addition to Lakatos: Bartley (1984, 1990), Gellner (1974), Miller (1994), Musgrave (1993), and Watkins (1984) represent but a smattering of the available options. For an account – as the author says, a "melancholy account" – of the many disagreements (personal and philosophical) within the Popperian school, see Agassi (1993). Similar, though less melancholy, remarks can also be found in Feyerabend (1995).

[20] Many Popperians would use the term "antijustificationist" rather than antifoundationalist, but this term leads to more confusion than clarity. Popperians use the term "justified" in a variety of different ways: sometimes as firmly "grounded" or given firm "foundations," other times as "proven to be certain," and still other times as "supported by rational arguments." Because foundationalism is an established philosophical term that has an unambiguous extra-Popperian meaning, I will talk about foundationalism and not justificationism.

narrow set of methodological rules. Rationality is saved from relativism by hinging it on criticism rather than empirical foundations.

> We can often give reasons for regarding one theory as prefer-
> able to another. They consist in pointing out that, and how, one
> theory has hitherto withstood criticism better than another.
> (Popper 1983, p. 20)

Critical rationalism does not reject the falsificationist method of bold conjectures and severe test, it simply subsumes it as a special case of the more general critical method; falsificationism is the special method of *empirical criticism*. Falsificationism is not a theory of knowledge; it is simply the answer to the question of how one goes about exposing scientific theories to the maximum empirical criticism when the empirical basis is uncontested (by convention). In Popper's own words, "The *only* function which my theory of method assigns to observations, experiments, and measurements is the modest although important one of assisting criticism" (Popper 1994, p. 162, emphasis added).

The methodological problem for critical rationalism is neither the problem of demarcation nor the problem of finding rules for the practice of science that will transmit truth from empirical observations to scientific theories; the problem for critical rationalism is the question of *how to organize our scientific and educational institutions in a way that maximizes productive criticism*. For most critical rationalists, the important questions are not positivist or foundationalist questions, but questions about social epistemology and *the industrial organization of our cognitive lives*. This means that critical rationalist philosophy of science is a version of social epistemology: a version guided by the central notion of the role of criticism in the growth of knowledge. Although Popper clearly *identified* this problem – the problem of cognitive industrial organization – it is also fairly clear that he never really provided any solution to it. In works such as *Open Society*, Popper identified various forces opposed to criticism and the growth of knowledge, but stopped short of specifying in any detail a positive characterization of the requisite social institutions.

> What then are the institutions that encourage the critical
> approach which is so vital to science and how efficient are they?
> How do these institutions operate within the academy – in
> science as well as in fields of study not quite within the domain
> of science (such as the history of ideas)? These questions he
> never studied. Popper never asked, who are the guardians of the
> critical attitude and to whom can we complain that the job of

guarding it is not as well attended to as it should? (Agassi 1993, p. 224)

Different interpretations of critical rationalism have filled the "proper social institutions" gap in different ways. One version of critical rationalism, that of Bartley and Radnitzky (Bartley 1984, 1990; Radnitzky 1986, 1991; Radnitzky and Bartley 1987), fills the gap with an argument from the economic theory of competitive markets. This interpretation of critical rationalism was examined above in Chapter 4 in the section on evolutionary epistemology. For Bartley and Radnitzky, the proper industrial organization of our cognitive lives is the competitive marketplace of scientific (and other) ideas. If there are many alternative hypotheses competing in an open and critical environment, then knowledge will emerge from this marketplace of ideas in precisely the same way that economic efficiency emerges from a system of competitive markets. This version of critical rationalism – knowledge as a self-organizing web of belief – is a version of evolutionary epistemology that owes as much to economics as to biology. Other versions of critical rationalism (Agassi, for instance) owe much more to the Socratic dialectic, or Socratic *elenchos*, than to either evolutionary epistemology or economics. These Socratic variants (perhaps not surprisingly) often suggest a very different view of the political economy of science. Agassi (1993, pp. 224–41), for example, sees a much greater role for government/social intervention than Bartley and Radnitzky, and stresses the importance of the guiding hand of responsible leadership for the growth of scientific knowledge. It seems that in the Popperian tradition, as elsewhere in social epistemology, one's views about the epistemic order and one's views about the economic order are closely intertwined.

Although there are many versions of Popperian critical rationalism,[21] none fully articulated, and each with potential problems (see Hands 1993, pp. 184–6 for a few examples), they all retain the core argument that a proper *critical environment* is the key to basic questions about scientific knowledge. This argument – even in its current protean form – makes contact with a number of the views examined in previous chapters: evolutionary epistemology certainly, but also aspects of the

---

[21] Popper was extremely suggestive on these matters, but it was left to his students to develop more systematic versions of his suggestions. In addition to Bartley and Radnitzky's evolutionary epistemology and economics-inspired view, and Agassi's Socratic approach, there are also others: Miller (1994), for instance, who proffers a version of critical rationalism that is not easily distinguished from falsificationism, and Nola (1987), who views critical rationalism solely as a meta-method. Also remember there are later "Popperian" views that do not regularly employ the term critical rationalism: Musgrave (1983) and Watkins (1984), for instance.

sociology of science and SSK, Goldman's social epistemology, Peirce, and even Longino's social empiricism. If one is comparing Popperian views – falsificationism versus critical rationalism – then it is clear that critical rationalism is *a much more contemporary philosophical position than falsificationism*. First of all, although any version of falsificationism ever endorsed by Popper recognized the main lessons of contemporary science theory – underdetermination, theory-ladenness, and so on – critical rationalism seems to do so in a more sustained (and less-easily-ignored) way. Second, in addition to being more aggressively fallibilist and antifoundationalist than falsificationism, critical rationalism is also more naturalistic and less *a priori* in its general approach. Third, to the extent that critical rationalism is realist, it is realist by way of evolutionary epistemology and "fittingness" rather than mirroring or representation. Finally, and perhaps most important, critical rationalism focuses its main attention on the social organization of science and thereby turns questions of normative philosophy of science into questions about social epistemology.

> I stressed that the objectivity of natural and social science is not based on an impartial state of mind in the scientists, but merely on the fact of the public and competitive character of the scientific enterprise and thus on certain social aspects of it. This is why I wrote: "*what the 'sociology of knowledge' overlooks is just the sociology of knowledge* – the social and public character of science." Objectivity is based, in brief, upon *mutual rational criticism*, upon the critical approach, the critical tradition. (Popper 1994, pp. 69–70, emphasis in original)

So critical rationalism is more consistent with contemporary science theory than falsificationism, so what different implications does it have for economic methodology? There are many, but the most significant is that critical rationalism fits much more comfortably with *both* the practice of mainstream economics, *and* Popper's own recommendations regarding the social sciences (SA), than (even sophisticated) falsificationism. Many economic explanations are based on SA and there is substantially less tension (perhaps not any tension) between SA and critical rationalism than between SA and falsificationism. If Popper's real message is simply rational criticism, rather than falsificationist rules, then the method of SA seems to be quite fine (Caldwell 1991a). In his discussion of SA, Popper explains in detail how to modify a particular SA explanation when it seems to be in conflict with the empirical data, internally inconsistent, or in conflict with our more fundamental beliefs and/or more corroborated theories; if what we "call the objectivity of science, and the *rationality of science*, are merely aspects of the *critical discussion* of scientific theories" (Popper 1994, pp. 159, emphasis in original), then social science based on SA would seem to be an acceptable source of knowledge about human and social behavior. If there are many paths to effective criticism, then preserving the RP and modifying the rest of the SA could be a perfectly reasonable (and knowledge increasing) response. The critical rationalist reading of Popper's philosophy thus *releases the tension* between scientific rationality and SA social science (and still solves the Freud/Marx problem, since one could argue that such theories are not open to rational criticism) and it does so within a framework that is both more contemporary than, and devoid of many of the problems of, strict falsificationism.

Critical rationalism was introduced into economic methodology by Kurt Klappholz and Joseph Agassi in 1959 (Klappholz and Agassi 1959). The Klappholz/Agassi paper was ostensibly a review of two recent books on economic methodology, but it ended up criticizing, from a critical rationalist perspective, almost all of the reigning methodological interpretations in the literature: Robbins, Friedman, Samuelson, and (particularly) Hutchison. The argument for criticism rather than methodological rules was clear from the opening paragraph.

> [T]he impatience appears to give rise to the belief that, if only economists adopted this or that methodological rule, the road ahead would be at least cleared (and possibly the traffic would move briskly along it). Our view, on the contrary, is that there is only one generally applicable methodological rule, and that is the exhortation to be critical and always ready to subject one's hypothesis to critical scrutiny. (Klappholz and Agassi 1959, p. 60)

The problem for Klappholz and Agassi, like the problem for many critical rationalists, is that falsificationism, or any other narrow methodological *rule*, is simply too strict and rules out of court many important (particularly metaphysical) ideas that are essential for the growth of scientific knowledge. Empirical testing *is* important – it is *one* very important type of criticism – but it "is a cardinal mistake to lay down the rule that empirical testing against observable phenomena should be the *only* acceptable method of criticism" (Klappholz and Agassi 1959, p. 66, emphasis added). Criticism is a wide-ranging and many-faceted concept; it should not be – and can not be if it is to remain effective – restricted to one, particularly, quite narrow, dimension. The proper methodological stance is simply to "advocate the critical attitude, by trying to demonstrate its fruitfulness or by arguing against different approaches," but

"Above all . . . it is important to guard against the illusion that there can exist in any science methodological rules the mere adoption of which will hasten its progress" (Klappholz and Agassi 1959, p. 74).

Among those currently writing in the field of economic methodology, Lawrence Boland (1982, 1986, 1989, 1991, 1994, 1997) has undoubtedly been the most consistent advocate of the critical rationalist approach.[22] Boland studied under Agassi and came to economic methodology in the 1970s with a self-consciously (Socratic) critical rationalist perspective, a view inveterately reflected in his methodological work over the last thirty years. As he recently summarized his position:

> There is a very different view of Popper's theory of science that is not well known in economics. In this alternative view, falsifiability plays a very minor role. . . . Briefly stated, science for Popper is a special case of Socratic dialogue, namely, one where we learn with the elimination of error in response to empirical criticism. Rationality is critical debate – with the emphasis on debate. Popper sometimes calls this Critical Rationalism. Given its emphasis on Socratic dialectics, I will call this view the Socratic Popper. (Boland 1997, p. 263)

In the 1980s, when the main topic of debate seemed to be methodological rules based on "Popperian falsificationism *or* something else (positivism, Kuhn, Lakatos, etc.)," Boland consistently rejected the claim that advocates of Popperian falsificationism (Blaug, Hutchison, etc.) were endorsing a Popperian position *at all*. If Popper was for criticism and against methodological rules, how could his position be précised into the narrow set of falsificationist rules endorsed by methodological falsificationists? Boland, like his teacher Agassi, attributed this misinterpretation of Popper to the influence of Imre Lakatos:

> I repeatedly complained that they did not understand Popper if they thought his views can be fairly characterized as "falsificationist methodology." I told them that were confusing Popper with Imre Lakatos and that if they really understood Popper they would see that his view of science is Socratic, based on learning through criticism. A fair characterization would be that

[22] Although Boland has been the most sustained critical rationalist, he is not the only economic methodologist advocating a version of this position. Bruce Caldwell's *critical pluralism* is explicitly critical rationalist (Caldwell 1991a, 1991b, 1994) and J. J. Klant's *plausibilism* (Klant 1988, p. 108) is also related. The single best discussion of the whole debate about falsificationism and critical rationalism in economics is contained in three papers: Blaug (1994b), Boland (1994), and Caldwell (1994b).

Popper advocates what he calls "critical rationalism." (Boland 1997, p. 153)[23]

One problem Boland has tried to face in his methodological writings is the question of "So what does critical rationalist methodology look like"? In a sense, the rule makers, falsificationist or otherwise, have the advantage of a clear message; economics doesn't comply with the rules and it needs to clean up its act. That message has, as discussed above, a wide appeal. So what would Boland put in the place of such rules? The answer sounds more like science studies than methodological appraisal.

> The practice of a Popperian methodologist who follows the notion that science is Socratic debate will differ considerably from the activities of those methodologists who see themselves as Popperian falsificationists. Methodologists who follow the Socratic Popper will devote most of their time to fostering and encouraging criticism. . . . Using situational analysis, they will provide explanations of existing criticism and critiques, usually by identifying a problem for which existing solutions are inadequate or are in dispute. If there is an appraisal activity, it will be limited to the effectiveness of existing lines of criticism. (Boland 1997, p. 265)

Although Boland has undertaken a number of such studies himself (Boland 1982, 1986, 1989), perhaps the best example is the work of one of his students: Stanley Wong's (1978) definitive study of Samuelson's revealed preference theory.

The bottom line for Boland's methodological studies, despite the radically different focus, may not be too far from what most falsificationists conclude about mainstream economic practice.

> All needling aside, I find it an interesting dilemma for Popperian methodologists. Since Popper says that "science" is characterized primarily by its critical attitude, neoclassical economists seem unwilling to entertain methodology and its inherently methodological criticism of neoclassical theory. It is all too easy to argue that neoclassical economists are cowards. But, more important from my Socratic-Popper perspective, unwillingness

---

[23] Latsis (1972, 1976b, 1983) provides some interesting evidence for this claim. On the one hand, Latsis (like Boland) did not equate Popper and falsificationism – in fact Latsis attributed falsificationism to Hutchison and discussed Popper's view entirely in terms of SA and RP (again supporting Boland) – but, on the other hand, Latsis *was a student of Lakatos*. If the source of the misinformation was Lakatos, then why didn't Latsis fall victim to the ruse?

to tolerate methodological criticism may simply demonstrate that neoclassical economists are "unscientific." (Boland 1997, p. 286)

7.2 The Millian Tradition

Although Chapter 2 made it quite clear that the Millian tradition dominated economic methodology prior to the 1930s, it also made it clear that the Millian tradition actually encompasses a fairly wide range of different approaches including John Stuart Mill himself, but also Cairnes (1875), Neville Keynes (1917), and Robbins (1952). This section will examine two recent interpretations of the Millian view: Daniel Hausman (1992) and Nancy Cartwright (1989a). While these two projects both involve Mill's methodology and economics, their focus is substantially different. Hausman is clearly doing economic methodology; he is presenting a way of philosophically understanding (and appraising) the theoretical activity of modern economics. Hausman's view of economics is to be contrasted with other methodological positions: Friedman, falsificationism, Lakatos's MSRP, and even the rhetoric of economics. Cartwright also involves Mill's view of the method of political economy, but her project is significantly more general. Cartwright exploits what Mill says about economics to develop a general view of scientific theories. Cartwright reverses the traditional "shelf of scientific philosophy" view, by using Mill's philosophy of economics to help develop a more general framework for understanding scientific knowledge. Hausman will be considered first, since his approach is most easily juxtaposed to the previous Popperian views.

7.2.1 The Inexact and Separate Science of Economics

Daniel Hausman is a philosopher who has devoted most of his professional life to the study of economics. In addition to the main topic of this section – his interpretation of economics as an "inexact and separate science" (Hausman 1992) – he has also written a book-length case study of capital theory (Hausman 1981a) as well as making a substantial contribution to the literature on ethics and economics (Hausman and McPherson 1996).

Hausman starts from the position that none of the most popular approaches to economic methodology – falsificationism or Lakatos's MSRP in particular – provides an adequate framework for understanding "the structure and strategy of contemporary economics" (Hausman 1994, p. 205). The view that comes closest to *describing* the theoretical practice of contemporary economists – at least contemporary microeconomists[24] – is that of John Stuart Mill. Hausman is not entirely content with Mill's view as a *justification* of economic practice – although, for the most part, he thinks such a justification can be provided – but he does argue that Mill offers the best description of what economists do when they do economics. For this reason, it is fair to label Hausman's position a Millian view, even though he is critical of certain aspects of (and certain readings of) Mill's approach.

Hausman supports his evaluation of economics with a number of case studies from various areas within contemporary economic theory (Hausman 1981, 1992; Hausman and Mongin 1998). These studies provide evidence for the version of naturalism that Hausman attributes to his general approach. As he characterized the problem situation in one of his earliest papers:

> Although philosophers of science have always been interested in the actual work of scientists, there has been a strong turn in the last generation away from prescribing how science ought ideally to proceed and toward studying more carefully how science has proceeded. . . . In part this change reflects a general scepticism about the possibility of doing traditional foundationalist epistemology. Such scepticism is itself a reaction to the failure of the foundationalist program of the logical empiricists. The contemporary turn toward careful empirical science, which I shall call "empirical philosophy of science" or "the empirical approach to the philosophy of science." (Hausman 1980, p. 353)

Later in this paper, Hausman addresses the naturalistic theme even more but also notes an important difference between empirical philosophy of economics and similar exercises within the philosophy of natural science. This difference partially undercuts his commitment naturalism (at least regarding economics).

> It would help if we could begin with solid and well-confirmed philosophical theses. But no philosopher of science can now begin with these, since they are unavailable. A philosopher of

[24] Hausman focuses exclusively on what he calls "equilibrium theorizing," which includes microeconomic theory, general equilibrium theory, new classical macroeconomics, and much of game theory. What is left out, in addition to all of heterodox economics, is Keynesian-based macroeconomics, most economic forecasting, industry studies, most of what economists in government and industry do on a day-to-day basis (cost-benefit analysis, economic impact statements, cost studies, etc.), and all of pure (and much of applied) econometrics.

economics studying economic theory is in the same philosophical position as any empirical philosopher of science seeking knowledge about the sciences. The only important difference is that philosophers of physics, for example can begin with fewer doubts about the worth of the physics they study. (Hausman 1980, p. 358)

Such comments give us a clear view of the task that Hausman has set for himself; to understand the theoretical activities of mainstream equilibrium theorists in a way that is descriptively accurate, while still allowing space for the critical evaluation of that practice on the basis of a philosophy of science that is broadly (but weakly) naturalistic and avoids the problems of discredited foundationalism.

Hausman starts with Mill's deductive characterization of economics, emphasizing that economics is an *inexact* and *separate* science: inexact because the tendency laws available in economics do not (given disturbing factors) allow for exact empirical predictions of economic phenomena, and separate because unique causal factors undergird all of the phenomena within its domain (pursuit of wealth for Mill, or scarce means and unlimited wants for Robbins). According to Hausman, inexactness and separateness combine to give equilibrium theorizing its distinctive character. This character is captured in the following four properties, which provide an exemplar of the Millian *a priori* method *and* also accurately describe the practice of contemporary economic theorizing.

1. Economics is defined in terms of the casual factors with which it is concerned, not in terms of a domain.
2. Economics has a distinct domain, in which its causal factors predominate.
3. The "laws" of the predominating causal factors are already reasonably well known.
4. Economic theory, which employs these laws, provides a unified, complete, but inexact account of its domain. (Hausman 1992, pp. 90–1)[25]

As discussed in Chapter 2, since, according to Mill and his followers, the fundamental "laws" are already *known* – demonstrated by introspection and/or everyday experience – there is no reason to try to falsify them, search for other basic laws, or attempt to deal with phenomena that can not be subsumed under their causal influence. In Hausman's words: "Agents seeking their own material welfare is what makes economics run, and theories which dethrone this motive cease to be eco-

---

[25] Also Hausman (1994, p. 205, and 1996, p. 209).

nomics" (Hausman 1992, p. 95). One does, in Millian applied economics, deduce particular observations from a combination of these basic laws, initial conditions, *ceteris paribus* conditions, simplifying assumptions, and so on, but if the empirical predictions fail, it is never the basic laws that are rejected. First, these laws are "known" and thus are not subject to refutation; second, they are only tendency laws subject to disturbing forces that make them empirically "inexact" at best; third, to reject the basic laws would mean to quit doing economics, since they define the separate science of economics; and, finally, the test is never a test of the laws themselves (for all the reasons already stated) but only a test of whether the particular application exhibits the laws.

Although Hausman agrees with Mill about the role of inexact (tendency) laws in economics, he parts company with the classical economist when it comes to the philosophical justification of such laws. The issue really revolves around the question of what one means by an *inexact law*. According to the standard characterization – coming down from the Received View – scientific *laws* are true universal statements about empirical regularities. A "law-like" statement is a statement that would be a law if it were true; such law-like statements need to be distinguished from mere "accidental generalizations." As I write this: "all the coffee cups on my desk are empty" is a true statement, but it is merely an accidental generalization about the two cups on my desk and not a universal law. One way to distinguish between a law and an accidental generalization is that laws support counterfactual conditionals; the law that all Xs are Ys supports the counterfactual conditional that *if* this particular z is an X then it will also be a Y, while the same accidental generalization does not support such conditionals. Notice that the accidental generalization that "all the coffee cups on my desk are empty" does not support the counterfactual conditional that "if a coffee cup is on my desk then it will be empty." So how does all this translate into the inexact laws of economics?

According to Hausman (and Mill), the causal factors at work in economics give rise to *tendencies*; these tendencies may in fact manifest themselves in observable regularities, but sometimes they do not. There are many "disturbing factors" that can interfere with a particular tendency being observed in any specific case. To use one of Nancy Cartwright's (1989a) examples: Aspirins have the tendency to relieve headaches, but as anyone with frequent headaches knows, there can be disturbing factors that prevent this tendency from manifesting itself in any particular case (headache). For a simple economic example: an increase in the price of a substitute for a particular good has a tendency to increase the price of that good, and yet, as a brief back-of-the-envelope supply and demand exercise will demonstrate, many offsetting factors could easily interfere and prevent the price increase from being observed. Given that the empirical effects of these tendencies may or may not appear, depending on the relevant countervailing forces, the resulting laws are *inexact*. As Hausman uses these terms, "Tendencies are the causal powers underlying the genuine regularities that inexact laws express" (Hausman 1992, p. 127). This, of course, raises a serious question about the justification of such laws. Because they are inexact, they do not express true universal generalizations – sometimes they are true and sometimes they are not – and, thus, they are not, at least on the traditional definition, genuine scientific laws. When are we justified in accepting such inexact laws?

Hausman discusses four different (though not mutually exclusive[26]) ways of thinking about the notion of an inexact (or tendency) law.

1. Inexact laws are approximate. They are true within some margin of error.
2. Inexact laws are probabilistic or statistical. Instead of stating how human beings always behave, economic laws state how they usually behave.
3. Inexact laws make counterfactual assertions about how things *would be* in the absence of interferences.
4. Inexact laws are qualified with vague *ceteris paribus* clauses. (Hausman 1992, p. 128, emphasis in original)

Hausman argues that only the last two of these interpretations – the counterfactual or modal view, and the vague qualification or vague *ceteris paribus* view – are consistent with both Mill's writings and how equilibrium theorists actually view the laws of economics. In our earlier discussion of Mill in Chapter 2, the original Millian view was taken to be the modal view (following De Marchi 1986, and others), but the exegetical issue is irrelevant at this point, since Hausman claims that the *vague qualification* view is the proper way to think about inexact laws in economics, and he has very specific proposals (here parting ways with Mill) for assessing whether such claims are justified or not. As he puts it: "Not all appeals to *ceteris paribus* qualifications to explain away apparent disconfirmations are legitimate: it is certainly not the case that, *ceteris paribus*, we are all immortal or that dogs have six legs" (Hausman 1992, p. 133).

Hausman suggests four criteria for evaluating whether a vaguely qualified inexact law is justified; "one is justified in regarding a counterfac-

---

[26] And, as we will see below, these four are not exhaustive either.

tual claim with a vague antecedent or a statement with a vague *ceteris paribus* clause as a law only when four necessary conditions (lawlikeness, reliability, refinability, and excusability) are met" (Hausman 1992, pp. 139–40). Although we could explore each of these four conditions it is not really necessary; the main point is simply that, unlike Mill, Hausman specifies some relatively tough standards for justifying the type of inexact laws that are at work in economics. The "laws" of economics are very inexact – they are often empirically refuted (recall Blaug's remarks about not practicing falsificationism) – and while for Hausman this does *not* automatically mean the laws are inadequate for inclusion into legitimate economic science, he does require some additional, quite stringent, standards for when such (inexactly) refuted laws should be retained. "In my view, one may regard a generalization as a law even though it would, but for its qualifications, face disconfirmation, only if it is lawlike, reliable, refinable, and excusable" (Hausman 1992, p. 141). These standards allow him to argue that it *is possible to justify* the equilibrium theorizing of economists (even though Mill's defense was inadequate), while simultaneously arguing that *not everything* that goes on in economics is scientifically legitimate. Some moves by the economics profession – for example, disregarding the spate of recent psychological critiques of utility theory[27] – are not appropriate and methodological criticism is in order. Although equilibrium theorizing is generally okay, and the dogmatism of economists is generally justified, economists sometimes get carried away and engage in dogmatic behavior that can not be philosophically defended. A related view of inexactness and tendencies will be discussed in the next section on Cartwright, and Lawson's realist reading of tendency laws will be presented in Section 7.3.

A substantial critical literature has developed around Hausman's methodological views: including, Backhouse (1995c, 1997b), Hoover (1995b), Hutchison (1998), Mäki (1996a, 1998c, 2000b), and Reuten (1996, 1997).[28] Although it is not necessary to go into any of this literature in detail, it is useful to mention a few of main critical points. First of all, almost every critic has emphasized that there is more to economics than the mainstream, and more to the mainstream than equilibrium theorizing. Hausman has responded that although this is undoubtedly true, it really doesn't matter very much; what makes economics unique, what the profession identifies as the best work, and what constitutes the

---

[27] Hausman discusses one particular criticism – the case of preference reversals – in detail in Chapter 13 of 1992.

[28] Hausman (1996, 1997, 1998a, and 2000) provide responses to some of these criticisms. There is also an exegetical literature that focuses on Hausman's reading of Mill (De Marchi 1986; Hausman 1981b and 1995, for example).

core of graduate education, is in fact equilibrium theorizing. Hausman has also been criticized because he is too forgiving – too soft, not falsificationist enough – about the dogmatic (empirical) practice of the economics profession (Backhouse 1995c, 1997b; Hutchison 1998; and Reuten 1996, 1997, for instance). These critics basically push the falsificationist party line that inexactness is no excuse; if economic laws are falsified they should be abandoned; inexactness, separateness, and countervailing forces do not constitute an excuse for dogmatism. While these first two criticisms approach Hausman's project from the outside (from other economics and/or other methodological approaches), Mäki (1996a, 1998c) attacks the key supposition that inexactness and separateness are two independent aspects of economic theorizing that can/should be separately evaluated. Mäki argues that although Hausman presumes such independence, he provides no reasonable philosophical grounds for such a presupposition. Yet another criticism (Backhouse 1995c; Mäki 1998c, and others) is that Hausman is much better at description than prescription. If one accepts Hausman's claim about the importance of equilibrium theorizing, then it does seem to be the case that Mill's deductive *a priori* method does a reasonably good job describing the important behavior of economists (certainly better than say, falsificationism). The problem is that Hausman wants prescription as well as description, and he clearly seems to be less convincing in (and has dedicated far fewer pages to) his prescriptive efforts. Some (particularly falsificationists) simply disagree with Hausman's entire story about the justification of inexact laws, while others (Mäki 1998c, for example) argue that the problem is that Hausman never really provides any detailed philosophical justification for his prescriptive views (that there is no epistemic meat on the prescriptive bones). A final criticism is one that connects up nicely with issues raised repeatedly in earlier chapters. Mäki (1998c) argues that methodological "rules" – Hausman's or otherwise – may have less to do with what goes on (descriptively) in economics than the social organization of the discipline. Perhaps if one wants to describe the behavior of economists, one should look less to philosophy and more to social science.

Before leaving the discussion of *The Inexact and Separate Science*, it is useful to examine the particular view of scientific theories that Hausman employs in his analysis. This interpretation of scientific theories helps him (among other things) explain much of the abstract mathematical theorizing that goes on in economics without compromising his basic empiricist view of science. It is a view of theories that is also endorsed by a number of others writing in the philosophy of economics. Hausman endorses what is called the *semantic view of theories*. Although there are many specific versions of the semantic view,[29] Hausman seems to prefer Giere's (1984, 1988, 1999) less formal, model-theoretic, view.

Perhaps the easiest way to understand this version of the semantic view is to contrast it with the standard, *statement*, view of scientific theories. According to the standard view, scientific theories are simply sets of statements; they may be true or false, or corroborated or falsified on the basis of other statements about the empirical data, but they are statements in any case. According to this version of the *semantic* view a scientific theory merely *defines a predicate*.[30] For example, Newtonian mechanics defines the predicate "is a Newtonian system," whereas Keynesian economics defines the predicate "is a Keynesian economy." Such predicates "cannot be true or false or provide any predictions" (Hausman 1992, p. 74). The way that empirical claims *are* generated from such scientific theories is to formulate an "empirical hypothesis" that "x is an example of the scientific theory T." Thus, "our solar system is a Newtonian system" is an empirical hypothesis associated with Newtonian mechanics, whereas "the U.S. economy in 1933 was a Keynesian economy" is an empirical hypothesis associated with Keynesian economics. Empirical hypotheses, unlike scientific theories, can be true or false. In Hausman's case, neoclassical economics defines a predicate "is an economic equilibrium system," and an "actual economy is an economic equilibrium system if and only if the laws of consumer choice theory and of the theory of the firm are true of it, and equilibrium obtains" (Hausman 1992, p. 74).

Giere uses the analogy of a *map* to clarify the semantic view's distinction between a scientific theory and the empirical hypotheses generated from it.

> There are two things going on. Let me use an analogy. You draw maps of the world; you *create* maps. Now a map does not say anything; a map makes no statements. . . . The way you give it empirical content is to go out in the world and say, "Aha, that part of the world is like my map! My map represents it, my map

---

[29] There are basically four different versions of the semantic view of theories: the *model-theoretic* (Giere 1984, 1988, 1999), the *phase-space* (Suppe 1977, 1988, 1989), the *state-space* (Lloyd 1984, 1988; van Fraassen 1970, 1980), and the *set-theoretic or structuralist* (Balzer and Moulines 1996; Balzer, Moulines, and Sneed 1987; Sneed 1971; Stegmüller 1976, 1979; Suppes 1961, 1967, 1977). Morrison and Morgan (1999a) provide a useful discussion of some of these different views. Since the structuralist interpretation has been applied directly to economics, it will be examined in more detail in Section 7.4.2.

[30] It is important to note that not all versions of the semantic view of theories define scientific theories in this way. See Cartwright (1999a) for a discussion of how this (Giere) version differs from other versions of the semantic view.

is a good map! It represents that part of the world!" And then you say how and why it fits. There are two separate things: there are maps and there are the claims you make using the maps. (Giere in Callebaut 1993, p. 224, emphasis in original)

Since Hausman tries to use terms in the way they are used by practicing economists, he makes a few terminological modifications to the model-theoretic view. What the semantic view generally calls a "theory," Hausman calls a *model*. He also refers to the hypothesis that the model applies to some particular part of the world a *theoretical hypothesis*. Thus, Hausman would say the Keynesian *model* defines the predicate "is a Keynesian economy" and the claim that the U.S. economy in 1933 was a Keynesian economy would be a *theoretical hypothesis* associated with the Keynesian model. So what, for Hausman, then is a scientific theory? Well, a scientific theory is the combination of a model and the hypothesis that it is true of something in the world. As Hausman puts it: "A model plus a *general* theoretical hypothesis asserting that the assumptions of the model are true of some portion of the world results in a theory" (1992, p. 77, emphasis in original). So the Keynesian economic *theory*, according to Hausman's terminology, would be a combination of the Keynesian model and the claim that some economy satisfies (or satisfied) the assumptions of the model.

This version of the semantic view of theories allows Hausman to do many things, but perhaps the most important is to separate the purely theoretical (usually mathematical) work of model-building and model-elaborating from the empirical project of applying the model to some part of the economic world. Most of what economists do when they are doing "economic theory" is independent of whatever theoretical/empirical hypotheses might be involved in applying the model to the world; on Hausman's view this is a perfectly appropriate type of "theoretical activity." Abstract mathematical theorizing like general equilibrium theory, that seems so troublesome for many other methodological views (especially falsificationism) is perfectly explicable on Hausman's version of the semantic view of theories (and one does need to tie themselves all up in hard cores, protective belts, and novel facts).

> They are merely constructing concepts and employing mathematics and logic to explore further properties which are implied by the definitions they have offered. Such model building and theorem proving does not presuppose that one believes that the particular model is of any use in understanding the world. . . . In so far as one is only working with a model, one can dismiss any questions about the realism of the assumptions one makes. But

remember that the reason is that one is saying *nothing* about the world. ... Empirical assessment is out of order simply because there is nothing to assess: no empirical claims have been made. (Hausman 1992, p. 79, emphasis in original)

Not only is purely mathematical theorizing appropriate, it is an integral part of the equilibrium theorizing of economists that can, for Hausman, be justified along empiricist, yet relatively naturalistic, lines.

7.2.2 Economics, Capacities, and Tendencies

Nancy Cartwright's philosophy of science has evolved over the years since the publication of her influential book on *How the Laws of Physics Lie* (1983). She has continued to endorse a version of scientific *realism*, but it is no longer just the entity realism (Hacking 1983) of her earlier work.[31] Cartwright's approach is generally *naturalist*, but it is a generic naturalism and not one of the specific – pick something to naturalize on – naturalisms discussed in Chapter 4. The general vision owes more to Neurath (Cartwright, Cat, Fleck, and Uebel 1996) than to evolutionary epistemology; the argument is simply that the final court of appeal for philosophical debates about science is the actual practice of science. This naturalism allows Cartwright to be quite comfortable – again like Neurath – with the *disunity* of science. Different sciences involving different entities and different causal mechanisms actually exist – thus knowledge is disunified – period. Finally, Cartwright is *antifoundationalist*, and extremely sensitive to both theory-ladenness and underdetermination, while staying safely away from the slippery slope of relativism. There is objective knowledge; it is just local, disunified, and quite different from what was proffered by the Received View.

Cartwright's approach is broadly empirical and, yet, she is openly hostile to the (foundationalist) tradition of Humean empiricism. From a Humean, or radical empiricist, point of view, causality is simply a matter of the constant conjunction of empirical events: event A causes event B, if and only if A happens before B, and events of type A regularly occur in conjunction with events of type B. According to this view, scientific (causal) laws are simply universal statements about such empirical event regularities. As noted in previous chapters, this Humean view of scientific laws is literally the stuff of Legend; it was present in early logical

---

[31] Hacking's (1983) phrase was: "If you can spray them, they exist." Cartwright would now modify this phrase in the constructivist direction: "*When* you can spray them, they exist" (Cartwright 1994a, p. 292, emphasis in original).

positivism and it has continued to exert a significant influence within mainstream philosophy of science.

As previous chapters have copiously documented, there are a myriad of problems with the Humean tradition, but the one issue that receives the brunt of Cartwright's critical attention is the empiricist injunction to eschew all "behind the scenes" forces or "occult" concepts such as causal powers, underlying forces, or essential natures. In what amounts to a fairly aggressive counter-eschewal, Cartwright (1989a, 1992, 1994a, 1994b) has reintroduced the essentialist vocabulary of natures, necessities, and capacities into the philosophy of natural science. The motivation for the reintroduction is consistently naturalist. Such concepts are, she maintains, absolutely fundamental to our understanding of science, because they are absolutely fundamental to the way that scientists themselves understand science. Those involved in the actual practice of science presuppose the existence of relatively enduring and stable natures, or capacities, in the systems they study – and since these stable capacities, not Humean event regularities, are responsible for the causal claims of science – our understanding of science depends on our understanding the role of these capacities.

> The generic causal claims of science are not reports of regularities but rather ascriptions of capacities, capacities to make things happen, case by case. "Aspirins relieve headaches." This does not say that aspirins always relieve headaches, or always do so if the rest of the world is arranged in a particularly felicitous way or that they relieve headaches most of the time, or more often than not. Rather it says that aspirins have the capacity to relieve headaches, a relatively enduring and stable capacity that they carry with them from situation to situation; a capacity which may if circumstances are right reveal itself by producing a regularity, but which is just as surely seen in one good single case. (Cartwright 1989a, pp. 2–3)

This emphasis on capacities drastically reduces the importance of laws (causal laws in the traditional Humean sense) in scientific activity. The capacities of the system regulate the causal laws that operate within it, and these causal laws, in turn, are responsible for whatever explanatory power or empirical properties the system might have. As Cartwright explains:

> It is not the laws that are fundamental, but rather the capacities. Nature selects the capacities that different factors shall have and sets bounds on how they can interplay. Whatever associations occur in nature arise as a consequence of the actions of these

> more fundamental capacities. In a sense, there are no laws of association at all. They are epiphenomena. (Cartwright 1989a, p. 181)

Notice that Cartwright's position is based on a type of "naturalist" or "practical" empiricism; she accepts observations about what practicing scientists do as evidence about what science is, but these observations do not support the claim that real scientists employ, have access to, or believe in, the pristine theory-neutral observations of radical empiricism. This naturalistic version of empiricism is a long way from the incorrigible empirical basis of Hume or the early logical positivists. In fact, from this naturalistic perspective, the traditional view about empirical observation seems to be entirely metaphysical, a dogma of (radical) empiricism.

> But what about this decontaminated data base? Where is it in our experience? It is a philosophical construction, a piece of metaphysics, a way to interpret the world. . . . this construction is far more removed from our everyday experience of the world as we interact with it and describe it to others than are homely truths about triggering mechanisms, precipitating factors, impediments, and the like which mark out the domain of natures. (Cartwright 1992, pp. 60–1)

Notice how Cartwright's argument for capacities interacts with her commitment to naturalistic empiricism. First, what science is must be regulated by the practice of science, and she argues repeatedly that real practicing scientists actually do presuppose that capacities and causal powers exist in the systems they study. Second, given the problems of theory-ladenness and underdetermination, there is no reason to feel any more confident about the "observations" of traditional empiricists, than there is to be confident about capacities and causal powers. In fact, given that scientists actually believe in, and intervene with, such capacities, and scientists do not employ the observational base of the traditional view, there is *more* reason to believe in capacities than in a theory-neutral observation domain of empiricist foundationalism.

> My experiences are of people and houses and pinchings and aspirins, all things which I understand, in large part, in terms of their nature. I do not have any raw experience of a house as a patchwork of colors. . . . Sense data, or *the given*, are metaphysical constructs which, unlike natures, play no role in testable scientific claims. (Cartwright 1992, pp. 60–1, emphasis in the original)

Okay, so Cartwright's philosophy of natural science challenges empiricist foundationalism, does so in an almost essentialist way, and seems to be consistent with both the naturalistic turn and the actual practice of science. So what does her approach have to do with, or say about, economics? Well, economics actually enters into Cartwright's argument in *two different*, but rather substantive, ways. First of all, at the level of evidence, econometrics, or at least one kind of econometrics,[32] is offered as an example of how capacities show up in the work of practicing scientists. Cartwright's use of economics stands in stark contrast to the modus operandi of every other philosopher of natural science we have discussed; she looks at the practice of (a part of) *economics to see how scientists actually do science.* Although the use of "econometrics as exemplar" is unusual within the philosophy of science, it is probably less important to the overall program than her second foray into the realm of economics. The second ingress occurs because the philosophical model for Cartwright's view of capacities – the case from the history of philosophy, where another philosopher of science characterized causal mechanisms in the same way that Cartwright characterizes such mechanisms – is *John Stuart Mill's analysis of tendency laws in economics.* These two uses of economics are very different and warrant separate examination. I will start with the use of econometrics.

Recall that, according to Cartwright, scientists presuppose capacities when their work posits stable causal mechanisms that are fundamental, that is, causal mechanisms that remain constant as the system passes through various transformations. She argues that such capacities are found in the way that economists use econometrics: "I am going to concentrate on one tiny corner of modern science – econometrics – where I hope I can show what it is we do in science that commits us to capacities" (Cartwright 1989b, p. 190).

The main argument about econometrics is presented in terms of the simple demand equation:

$$q = \alpha p + u$$

---

[32] Particularly the econometrics of the Cowles Commission in the 1930s and the earlier econometrics of Haavelmo and Frisch. More specifically, she does not find such capacities in the recent econometric work of Leamer (1983) or Hendry (1980). Cartwright (1989b) argues that Leamer's approach avoids inference altogether, whereas Hendry's approach, lacking a commitment to stable structure, is fundamentally instrumentalist: "Hendry's work, while it has much in common with Cowles, is not committed to capacities; whereas, I maintain, the Cowles commission was" (Cartwright 1989b, p. 193). Econometrics is also discussed in (1991, 1995b, and 1998) and other economic examples in (1994b, 1995a, and 1997).

where "q represents quantity demanded, and p, price; u is supposed to represent some kind of random shock which turns the deterministic relationship into a probabilistic one" (Cartwright 1989a, p. 149). The estimated parameter α, which represents the relationship between price and quantity, is, according to Cartwright, a *stable capacity*. This parameter "measures the strength of price's capacity to produce (or inhibit) demand" (Cartwright 1989b, p. 195); it represents a presumed causal relationship between the variables p and q, and it is a relationship that remains intact across variation in the other factors that can change the quantity demanded – shifts in the demand curve caused by changes in u. To Cartwright, the commitment to such relationships demonstrates that econometricians are committed to a view of nature, or the economy, that includes stable causal capacities.

> That, in general, is just what is reflected in econometric method. Parameters are estimated in one context, and those values are assumed to obtain in entirely different contexts. Couple that with the observation I made earlier that these parameters connect causes and effects, and you see why I talk here about stable causal tendencies. (Cartwright 1989a, p. 153)[33]

It should be noted that while Cartwright offers econometrics as one exemplar of scientific commitment to capacities, she is careful to point out that she is not necessarily committed to the particular capacities that economists discuss. Physicists are also committed to such capacities, and there Cartwright seems to be more sanguine about the capacities involved.

> Econometrics is a notoriously uncertain science, with a spotty record for predictive success. . . . One principal claim I make here is, not that the phenomena of economic life are governed by capacities, but rather that the methods of econometrics presuppose this, . . . But the claim is more far-reaching than that. . . . What I claim for econometrics will be equally true in any field that uses conventional statistical methods to make inferences about causes. . . . I will argue that the same is true of the methods of physics; and, whatever is the case in economics, in physics these methods work, and the capacities that justify them are scarcely to be rejected. (Cartwright 1989a, p. 158)

---

[33] Sent (1996) challenges Cartwright's reading of economics in general, and Cowles econometrics in particular. Hoover (1997) also criticizes Cartwright's view of econometrics.

Using econometrics as scientific exemplar is certainly unique among philosophers of science, but the second way that Cartwright involves economics is even more important to her overall position – her model for a philosopher of science who properly recognized the role of capacities in science is John Stuart Mill: not J. S. Mill writing about physics, but J. S. Mill writing about the method of political economy. Recall that Mill's main difference between economics and physics was that in the physical world causal forces act separately (or additively) so that the nature of the causes can be inferred from the empirical behavior of the system in question. In economics, things are not that simple; the social world is quite complex and economic causes are almost never isolated or act alone (nor are they additive). The result is that in economics it is not possible to conduct empirical studies that are capable of isolating any of the various, and constantly changing, causes.

> In a situation like this, the conventional methods of induction will be insufficient. For Mill, they must be augmented by principles we can glean from our general knowledge of human nature. This "mixed method of induction and ratiocination" is what he calls "a priori." (Cartwright 1989a, p. 183)

The solution for Mill was to focus on the underlying causal "tendencies" at work in the economic system, rather than the (Humean) laws associated with event regularities; for "John Stuart Mill the basic laws of economics are laws about enduring 'tendencies' and not laws about what happens; that is, laws about capacities and not just about the sequence of events" (Cartwright 1989a, p. 183). These tendencies, or their immediate effects, are seldom directly observed in economics because of the ubiquitous presence of countervailing forces. As discussed in the section on Mill, the paradigm case of a tendency law is the falling rate of profit in classical economics – the essential nature of capitalist production generates a tendency for the rate of profit to fall, even though countervailing forces and disturbing causes may (almost always) prevent this tendency from being empirically observed.

Analysis of such laws about tendencies requires a particularly strong type of "abstraction," an abstraction that strips away all of the disturbing factors in order to isolate the relevant causal tendency. This type of causal force, or tendency, and the way that one attempts to isolate it is precisely the type of activity that Cartwright finds in the practice of modern physical science (and Cowles econometrics). Cartwright's capacities are just a particular version of Mill's tendency laws.

> What *is* an ideal situation for studying a particular factor? It is a situation in which all other "disturbing" factors are missing.

> ... *When all other disturbances are absent, the factor manifests its power explicitly in its behaviour.* ... This tells you something about what will happen in very different, mixed circumstances – but only if you assume that the factor has a fixed capacity that it carries with it from situation to situation.
>
> The argument is structurally identical to my arguments ... that our standard ways of identifying, and then applying, causal models make sense only if one presupposes that there are capacities, stable capacities that remain the same even when they are removed from the context in which they are measured. ... And John Stuart Mill has taught us that to reason in that way is to presuppose that there are stable tendencies, or capacities, at work in nature. (Cartwright 1989a, pp. 190–1, emphasis in original)

One question to ask about Cartwright's use of Mill and tendency laws is how her interpretation differs (if it differs) from Hausman's interpretation. Recall that Hausman provided four different interpretations of "inexact" tendency laws – (1) approximation, (2) probabilistic, (3) counterfactual/modal, and (4) vague *ceteris paribus* qualification – and chose the fourth as most philosophically defensible as well as most consistent with the practice of equilibrium economics. Perhaps the best way to think about Cartwright's view is to take her *problem* to be the same as Hausman's (and Mill's, and Robbins's) – the problem of justifying the use of economic laws that are simply not (universally) true – but to provide a slightly different, and less empiricist, *answer*. Cartwright basically adds a fifth interpretation to Hausman's list:

> 5. Inexact laws are statements about capacities. They describe, not what happens when a certain cause is present, but rather what the cause has the tendency, or capacity, to do.

This is a less empiricist reading of "law" and "cause" than any of Hausman's four interpretations. For Hausman, even inexact laws link causes and their associated effects; for Cartwright inexact laws link cause and the effects they *tend to have*. For example, consider the inexact law that "A has a tendency to cause B." For Hausman, this law says that "Given a number of (perhaps vague) *ceteris paribus* assumptions, A will be (observationally) associated with B"; at least inexactly, or *ceteris paribus*, A appears with B. For Cartwright, the same inexact law could be read as "It is in the nature of A to be (observationally) associated with B"; notice that A need not appear (even *ceteris paribus*) with B for the law to hold. For Cartwright, a causal law is not about what something *does* (as with Hume), but it is also not about the nature of its *being or essence* (as with Aristotle); it is about *what is in its nature to do*. As she compares her own view of the laws of Newtonian mechanics with the *ceteris paribus* view:

> If the laws of mechanics are not universal, but nevertheless true, there are at least two options for them. They could be pure *ceteris paribus* laws: laws that hold only in circumscribed conditions or so long as no factors relevant to the effect besides those specified occur. . . . Presumably this option is too weak for our example of Newtonian mechanics. . . . For cases like this, the older language of *natures* is appropriate. It is in the nature of a force to produce an acceleration of the requisite size. That means that *ceteris paribus*, it *will* produce that acceleration. But even when other causes are at work, it will "try" to do so. The idea is familiar in the case of forces: *trying* to produce an acceleration. . . . In general what counts as "trying" will differ from one kind of cause to another. To ascribe a behaviour to the nature of a feature is to claim that that behaviour is exportable beyond the strict confines of the *ceteris paribus* conditions, although usually only as a "tendency" or a "trying." (Cartwright 1994a, pp. 285–6, emphasis in original)

Although the jury is clearly still out on Cartwright's general capacities view of science, it is equally clear that her approach relies on economics in a much more substantive way than most philosophies of natural science. Economics is one of the sciences consulted in the naturalistic inquiry and Mill's economic method is the key philosophical insight that undergirds the entire approach. No other philosopher discussed so far involves economics in such a substantive way – even those (like Neurath, Popper, and others) where economic and epistemic concerns were deeply interwoven – and all this takes place within the confines of a philosophical view that combines the most recent naturalistic trends with a talk about natures that would do Aristotle proud.

7.3 Realist Themes

The argument was made in Chapter 3 that certain brands of scientific realism appear to have benefited from the problems associated with (empiricist) foundationalism. This section will examine how some of these contemporary realisms have made their way into the literature on economic methodology. The first section will examine critical realism, a position derived from Bhaskarian transcendental realism. Critical realism is an expanding program and has, in recent years, gained a number of economic devotees. Tony Lawson has been the most prolific of these critical realists, and his work will be the main focus of the first section. The second section will examine another version of realism – that of Uskali Mäki – as well as providing a rather quick look at how van Fraassen's antirealism has influenced the literature on economic methodology.

7.3.1 Critical Realism

Roy Bhaskar's *transcendental realism* was discussed briefly in Chapter 3. At that point, the main focus was how Bhaskar and other realist philosophers have parlayed the troubles of empiricist foundationalism into arguments supporting various realist interpretations of scientific inquiry. Although Bhaskar's approach is realist, it is not simply the scientific realism associated with Richard Boyd or the realist wing of the Received View; Bhaskar's position is essentially (perhaps essentialistically) ontological. He argues, contrary to the empiricist tradition, that the goal of science is to uncover the intransitive causal mechanisms that underlie, and ultimately generate, the transitive event regularities that have traditionally been the focus of philosophers of science. Like Cartwright, Bhaskar argues that such realism about underlying causal capacities is absolutely necessary to make sense of the actual practice of successful science; the difference is that Cartwright's work reflects a generic naturalism – the discussion of knowledge begins and ends with scientific practice – whereas Bhaskar draws more on transcendental philosophy – an inquiry into the question of what the world would need to be like in order to make possible the generalized practice of science. The distinction is subtle; it is essentially the difference between the features of nature that are implicit in scientific practice, and the features of nature that are necessary for scientific practice. Bhaskar's view of laws, causal mechanisms, tendencies, and capacities is actually quite close to Cartwright's; the main difference is the philosophical emphasis. Both deny that causal laws are about what things *do* (as with empiricism), but Bhaskar emphasizes being – what *is* the essential nature of things – whereas Cartwright is concerned with what *it is in the nature of things to do* (note: *do*, not is or be).

Bhaskar's transcendental realism has recently received a lot of attention from economists and others interested in social theory. One of the most important reasons for this attention has been the work of Tony Lawson: his own writings, the writings of his students, and others influenced by his research. In a long series of papers (including Lawson 1989a, 1989b, 1994a, 1995, 1996, and 1997b) and the book *Economics*

and Reality (1997a), Lawson has systematically explicated a philosophical approach to economics called *critical realism*.[34] Critical
realism is derived from Bhaskar's transcendental realism, but it extends Bhaskar's approach by articulating a general realist framework
(underlaboring) for the social sciences; a framework that simultaneously: (1) imposes some broad constraints on the project of social
theorizing, and (2) provides a vehicle for the philosophical critique of
mainstream economics.

Lawson starts from the Bhaskarian insight that social systems are fundamentally open – lacking, in particular, the experimental closure of the
laboratory – and as such are particularly ill-suited to the empiricist-
inspired scientific methodology of seeking event regularities of the form
"whenever event x then event y" (Lawson 1997a, p. 17). For Lawson, the
goal of social science is the identification of the *deep structures* and
underlying causal powers that give rise to the general pattern of observed
events; the goal is causal explanation – causal in the Bhaskarian, not the
Humean, sense – and not the discovery of laws formulated in terms of
constant conjunctions of empirical events. The wrong approach to social
explanation – the approach that, according to Lawson, has guided most
of the work in mainstream economics – is *deductivist*. The deductivist
approach characterizes science as the search for explanations that
involve subsumption under general covering laws that can be couched
in terms of empirical event regularities. Thus, recalling the discussion of
the Received View in Chapter 3, the deductivist approach to science
seeks scientific explanations of the *deductive-nomological* (D-N) form,
where the covering laws involved in these explanations are consistent
with a Humean (or radical empiricist) notion of scientific laws. In other
words for Lawson: deductivism = the D-N *form* of explanation + the
Humean notion of a *scientific law*.

> Now my central claim with respect to contemporary mainstream
> economics is that it is most accurately characterized as deduc-
> tivist. By deductivism I understand a mode of explanation which
> involves deducing the explanandum from a set of initial condi-
> tions plus regularities that take the *form* "whenever this event

[34] Because the term "critical realism" is/has been used in a number of ways that are quite
different from Lawson's use of the term, it is helpful to mention a few of these alternatives. Lawson's critical realism should *not* be confused with Musgrave's (1983) version of
Popperian critical rationalism, which he calls critical realism; the "critical realist" response
to American pragmatism and idealism in the 1930s (Montague 1937); or the critical
"realist" approach to political science and international relations (and there are undoubtedly other uses as well).

or state of affairs then that event or state of affairs." (Lawson 1997b, p. 88, emphasis in original)[35]

Systems where such constant conjunctions do arise – systems where deductivism will work – are *closed* systems; laboratories are attempts to create such closed systems, but such systems effectively never occur in economics or the other social sciences. Social science demands that we abandon deductivism in favor of transcendental realism; look for the deep underlying mechanisms, powers, and *tendencies* that are ultimately responsible for the general pattern of observed events. These underlying tendencies are deeper, more essentialist/Aristotelian, and, consequently, less empiricist, than even the tendencies that emerge from Cartwright's interpretation of science.

> Because actual events or states of affairs may be codetermined by numerous, often countervailing, mechanisms the action of any one mechanism, though real and perhaps expressing necessity in nature, may not be directly manifest or "actualized." Character-istic ways of acting or effects of mechanisms which may not be actualized because of the openness of the relevant system are conceptualised here as *tendencies*. . . . Tendencies, in short, are potentialities which may be exercised or in play without being directly realised or manifest in any particular outcome. (Lawson 1997a, pp. 22–3, emphasis in original)

Since the connection between these underlying causal powers and their associated tendencies are only weakly related to – and in the pres-ence of sufficiently powerful countervailing forces, totally disconnected from – their empirical manifestations, it is not possible to "discover" these causal forces by straightforward empirical means (positivist, Popperian, or any other approach). The appropriate investigative tool is *retroduction*. Similar to Peirce's abduction, retroduction moves directly

---

[35] It is useful to point out that Lawson's use of the term "deductivism" – as a combination of the D-N form of explanation and a (rather radically) empiricist characterization of sci-entific laws – is different from the way the term is generally used within the philosophical literature. There is an extensive philosophical literature on the "limits of deductivism" (Grünbaum and Salmon, 1988, for example), but it focuses exclusively on the first part of Lawson's definition (the D-N model). Bhaskar also uses the term "deductivism," but he seems to emphasize the latter (Humean law) part as the target of his critique (Bhaskar 1994, p. 19, for example). These are in fact *two separate issues* – the deductive form of expla-nation and the Humean conception of laws – and it would probably be useful to keep them separate in a way that Lawson fails to do. This two-part definition of deductivism is par-ticularly problematic in the analysis of neoclassical economics where the elaborate use of mathematics suggests a deductive mode of explanation, but the relevant "laws" seem to be radically at odds with the Humean conception of event regularities.

from the phenomenal level to relevant causal mechanisms that underlie the phenomena.

> [T]he central mode of inference is neither deduction or induction. Rather it is retroduction. The aim is not to cover a phenomenon under a generalisation . . . but to identify a factor responsible for it, that helped produce, or at least facilitated it. The goal is to posit a mechanism . . . which, if it existed and acted in the postulated manner, could account for the phenomenon singled out for explanation. (Lawson 1997a, p. 212)

Thus far, the discussion of Lawson's critical realism has focused on the features it shares with Bhaskar's transcendental realism. Lawson's own contribution (in addition to applying critical realism to mainstream economics) is the addition of a particular *social ontology*; in fact, critical realism = transcendental realism + a "specific theory of social ontology" (Lawson 1997a, p. 157). Bhaskar emphasized the importance of ontology; Lawson tries to tell us what an appropriate social ontology should look like.

Although there are many facets to Lawson's social ontology, the one that seems most important for the analysis of economics is his emphasis on human *choice* and *intentionality*. If the subject is human social behavior, then, according to Lawson, one must allow for the possibility of intentional human *agency*. This characterization of agency – based on intentionality and admitting reasons as causes – was discussed in Chapter 4.

> By human *agency* I mean the specific powers and capabilities of human beings. By human acts or *action* I understand the intentional exercise of human agency, i.e. intentional human doings. By ascribing *intentionality* to actors I understand actions to be those human doings that are caused by reason(s), where reasons, in turn, are beliefs grounded in the practical interests of life. . . . Finally, I take the notion of *choice* to denote a power possessed by each individual whereby, in any situation, he or she could really have acted other than he or she did. (Lawson 1997a, p. 174)

Lawson argues that on this notion of choice, *neoclassical economics does not actually involve choice at all*. Despite the sustained rhetoric of choice and decision, mainstream economists impose (because of their commitment to deductivism) an implicit ontology on economic agents that denies them any real choice; neoclassical agents can not do other than maximize, or they cease to be economic agents. If economic agents actually *chose*, then it would be possible for them to do otherwise and their actions would not be subject to general laws of the form "whenever event of type x then event of type y."

> In the formal "models" found in mainstream journals and books, human choice is ultimately denied. For if real choice means anything it is that any individual could always have acted otherwise. And this is precisely what contemporary "theorists" are unable to allow in their formalistic modelling. . . . Instead, individuals are represented in such a way that, relative to their situations, there is almost always but one preferred or rational course of action and this is always followed. (Lawson 1997a, p. 9)

Now, although intentionality and choice are important – actually necessary – they are clearly not the whole story about human action or society (remember Bhaskar). Critical realism does not reduce to folk psychology. In addition to individual intentionality, there are also deep social structures and underlying causal mechanisms that influence the events on the surface of social life. Similar to Anthony Giddens's theory of structuration (Giddens 1973, 1986), the critical realist approach to social explanation requires *both* individual intentional action *and* deep social structures and relationships. The *social* and the *individual* both matter, but neither is the prime mover; individual intentional actions reproduce social structures and social relationships – and, in this sense, the social is a consequence of individual action – but social structures and social relationships also condition, and at certain junctures even determine, the actions of individual agents. "Both polar conceptions must be rejected as untenable" (Lawson 1997a, p. 167); the proper ontological framework for social inquiry is a middle ground between "voluntaristic idealism" and "mechanical determinism" (Lawson 1997a, p. 168). The result is an economic science that is less pristine, but one that is also less autistic, and much more like the messy and contingent knowledge production process familiar from contemporary science theory.

> Economic analysis as conceived here, then, will usually be a complicated and messy affair. Unlike the simplistic positivistic conception of science as elaborating event regularities, the process of uncovering and explaining significant causal structures and mechanisms, . . . will usually be a painstaking, laborious, and time-consuming, transformative activity, one that gives rise to results that will always be partial and contingent (and usually contested). . . . But if, in economics, such complications are unavoidable, in this respect as in many others, I repeat yet

once more, the situation is just as in any other science. (Lawson 1997a, pp. 270–1)

Although Lawson obviously believes that mainstream economics is *not* consistent with critical realism, it is equally clear that he believes there are many other theoretical programs in economics – currently as well as historically – that do sustain ontological outlooks consistent with critical realism. Lawson himself has examined the critical realist elements in the work of a number of different economic theories – including Menger (Lawson 1996), Hayek (Lawson 1994b, 1997d), Post-Keynesian economics (Lawson 1994d), Paul David's (1985, 1994) work on path-dependence (Lawson 1997a), and his own earlier work (Kilpatrick and Lawson 1980) on Britain's productivity slowdown (Lawson 1997a) – while others sympathetic to critical realism have added Marshall (Pratten 1998), transactions cost economics (Pratten 1997), Marxian economics (Pratten 1993), evolutionary economics (Foss 1994), and economic education (Emami and Riordau 1998), as well as participating in the discussion about Menger (Clive Lawson 1996), Hayek (Fleetwood 1996; Peacock 1993), and Post-Keynesianism (Pratten 1996; Rotheim 1998).[36] In addition to these efforts to uncover critical realist influences in various economic theories, there is also a growing critical realist literature that addresses more traditional methodological issues; for example, Lawson (1994c, 1997c) considers the general role of economic methodology, Runde (1996) discusses Popper's propensity interpretation of probabilities, Lawson (1992) analyzes Friedman's methodology, and van Eeghen (1996) uses critical realism to help reconcile Popper$_n$ and Popper$_s$.

A literature is starting to develop that criticizes Lawson and the other critical realists, although at this point it is relatively new and it is not yet clear how successful supporters will be in gainsaying these criticisms.[37] Rather than trying to sort out the various sides of this ongoing debate, I will just close the discussion of critical realism by briefly mentioning a few (actually four) of the criticisms that have been raised.

The first set of criticisms concerns the role of *transcendental* philosophy (Boylan and O'Gorman 1997a; Parsons 1997a, 1999). Questions have been raised about the details of Lawson's particular (Bhaskarian) transcendental approach, as well as the entire issue of trying to do "tran-

---

[36] This list is only a small portion of the literature that has applied critical realism to various topics within economics (and other social sciences). More extensive lists can be found in Lawson (1996, p. 405, note 3), Lawson (1997a, p. 300, note 20), and Fleetwood (1997, p. 5, note 2).

[37] Lawson (1997b, 1998, 1999) responds to many of these issues.

scendental" analysis in the context of our contemporary, philosophically modest, intellectual environment. Doesn't the entire project of resolutely asserting what *must* be the case seem to have a certain philosophical arrogance about it? Related to the issue of transcendental analysis, but a bit more general, is the second criticism that Bhaskar's realism does not actually respond to developments within contemporary science theory (Baert 1996). Bhaskar's approach – termed "philosophical Leninism" by one critic (Aronowitz 1996, p. 212) – while gesturing in the direction of the constructivism, social-ladenness, and the historical situatedness of scientific knowledge, ultimately leaves nature firmly in control of the scientific throttle; we must always admit the possibility of being wrong (fallibilism), but it is correspondence with the intransitive way things "really are" that ultimately differentiates science from all other human activities. Because Lawson's critical realism is explicitly concerned with social life, it may be more sensitive to the social context, but these issues need careful consideration. Third, and more specific to Lawson, is the issue of *mainstream economics* (Backhouse 1997c; Hands 1997c; Hausman 1998b, 1999; Parsons 1999; Viskovatoff 1998). A credible argument can be made that neither mainstream neoclassical theory nor modern econometrics fits Lawson's "deductivist" description. In fact, even though he clearly wants to critique mainstream economics, Lawson's reading of it (as empirical realism) may actually turn him into the mainstream's epistemological defender; he accuses economics of precisely the type of empiricism that influential twentieth-century economic theorists have consistently *claimed* to be engaged in (despite the denial of almost every other methodological commentator). Echoing Uncle Remus's Brer Rabbit from nineteenth-century American literature, the mainstream should be saying: "Oh please Dr. Lawson, don't throw me into the empiricist briar patch." Finally, and perhaps most important, is the problem of what might be called *endearing structures*. Critical realists want to identify – and believe science can identify – the enduring and intransitive causal structures that lie behind the surface phenomena of social life, and yet they offer *no unique method*, no particular approach, or technique, that gives us privileged access to those enduring structures. What prevents *endearing* structures from masquerading as enduring structures? Despite the problems associated with positivism and Popperian falsificationism, isn't validating the endearing precisely what such empiricist methodologies were designed to avoid? In Ricardian economics, the endearing things claimed to be enduring were the Malthusian law of population and the Ricardian law of rents, for Marx it was the law of value and the law of the tendency of the rate of profit to fall, perhaps for post-War Walrasian economics it was that every economic agent is endowed with a twice differentiable strictly quasi-concave utility function defined over the commodity choice space. It is just not clear how opening the door to such an ontological minefield provides an adequate response to the well-known problems of empiricist foundationalism, or more important, how it helps us to better understand economic life.

7.3.2 Realism and Anti-Realism in Economics

Tony Lawson is not the only recent author who has written extensively on the relationship between philosophical realism and economic theory. This section will examine the work of Uskali Mäki, the other main contributor to the recent literature on "realism and economics." This section also contains a brief discussion of the van Fraassen-inspired antirealist methodological approach of Thomas A. Boylan and Paschal O'Gorman.

Although both Lawson and Mäki have written extensively on the subject of realism and economics, their approaches are quite different. Lawson is clearly engaged in *prescriptive metaphysics*;[38] he wants economists to change the way they think about necessity and being. According to Lawson, there is a right ontological approach (critical realism), and a wrong ontological approach (empirical realism), and he wants to convince economists to move from the latter to the former. Mäki, although generally sympathetic to philosophical realism, seems to be less concerned with promoting, or finding converts to, any specific ontological framework (at least any that is currently available). His project, while retaining long-run normative aspirations, is more immediately descriptive and less narrowly focused on changing the ontological framework of mainstream economic theory. A main concern is to uncover the types of realism that are implicit in the work of various economists, and to ferret out the possible implications (consistencies, inconsistencies, unrecognized connections, etc.) of those realist influences. A critique may emerge from such studies, but it would not be the ontological critique of prescriptive metaphysics; it is more likely to involve a specific inconsistency or opacity emerging from the investigation of a particular economist or economic theory. Mäki describes his own approach as *bottom-up*, and contrasts it to the *top-down* approach that describes critical realists such as Lawson.

How does scientific realism fit with economics? At this point it is important to see that we can approach examining the rela-

---

[38] Alvin Goldman (1993, p. 113) uses this term to describe certain approaches within the philosophy of mind and cognitive science.

tionship between economics and realism from two points of view. One may adopt a top-down approach: Fix a version of scientific realism as the right one; check whether economics fits; if it does, say "hooray!"; if it fails to fit, blame economics and insist on its revision so as to improve the fit. One may also adopt a bottom-up approach; identify a set of generic key features of economics as a science; check this set against a large variety of realist ideas; depending on the outcome, make such realist ideas subject to rejection, adjustment, or replacement by new realist ideas, so as to improve the fit. . . . The bulk of my own work has been in the spirit of the bottom-up line. (Mäki 1998e, p. 302)

One of Mäki's earliest contributions involved clarifying the distinction between the terms *realism and realisticness* (Mäki 1989, 1998d). Economists often talk about the "realism of the assumptions," but the term "realism" is rather ambiguous in this context. The "assumptions" controversy could be clarified by using the term "realisticness" (or unrealisticness) – to describe the relationship between the assumptions of an economic theory or model and the features of the world that it is supposed to represent – rather than realism. Realism is a philosophical thesis – it characterizes a particular class of meta-theoretical views – whereas realisticness is a property of particular theories, models, and/or representations. There is not any necessary relationship between these two features; a particular economic theory could provide an accurate description of a certain class of economic phenomena (be realistic) and yet be consistent with an instrumentalist (non-realist) view of scientific theories, whereas another theory that claimed to uncover the real causal forces behind some particular aspect of economic life (be realist) might be descriptively inaccurate. Realism and realisticness are both important, but they are quite different issues.

The difference between realism and realisticness is just one of the various tools that Mäki has used to disambiguate the complex relationship between philosophical realism and economic science. He has examined the work of a number of different economic theorists and theories – including Austrian economics (Mäki 1990a, 1990b, 1992c, 1997), Friedman's methodology (Mäki 1986, 1989, 1992b, 2000a), and Ronald Coase's transactions cost economics (Mäki 1998f, 1998g, 1998h, 1998i, 1999b) – as well as the difference between realism in economics and realism in the physical sciences (Mäki 1989, 1996b, 1998e, 2000b), the role of isolation and abstraction in economics (Mäki 1992d, 1994b, 1998f), and a number of other issues. I will discuss two of these topics in this section – Mäki's argument about the main difference between realism in economics and realism in physics, and his recent work on Coase's methodology – and save his (closely related) work isolation until the final section of this chapter (where similar work by other authors is examined).

Mäki has argued repeatedly that economics is immune to an entire line of debate – perhaps *the* major line of debate – about the question of scientific realism in physical science. He argues that debates about realism versus antirealism in physics often hinge on the ontological status of the theoretical entities postulated by theoretical physics – electron, quarks, photons, and so on – particularly the question of whether such entities are *real* in the sense that commonsense physical objects such as tables and chairs are real.

> The science of physics hypothesizes an entirely different realm of objects, composed of configurations of subatomic particles, gravitational and electromagnetic fields, black holes, curved space-time. This theoretical realm of scientific objects radically transcends the boundaries of ordinary common sense experience. The issue of scientific realism about physics is one of the reality of the scientific realm and the truth of statements about it. (Mäki 1996b, pp. 433–4)

Mäki argues that this issue – the reality of these new theoretical entities – which is so important in natural science *does not emerge in economics*, and once we understand the difference it becomes much more clear why the language of the realism/antirealism debates from the philosophy of physics maps so poorly onto the interests/concerns of economic methodologists. His argument[39] is that the "theoretical terms" of economics – firms, consumers, prices, quantities, profit, interest rates, investment, and such – do not refer to an entirely different realm of objects, but are in fact quite familiar from commonsense experience.

> In economics, the situation seems to be drastically different. The constituents of the worlds hypothesized in economic theories appear to be more or less the same as those inhabiting the realm of our ordinary conceptualized experience. No radical gap seems to prevail between the scientific realm and the ordinary realm. Economic theories speak about objects that are confronted in our ordinary experience about economic matters – business

---

[39] Mäki's defense of this claim involves his notion of "isolation," which will be discussed below.

firms and households, their aims and expectations, money and goods and their prices, land and labor and capital, wages and profits and taxes. Therefore, the existence of the objects of the scientific realm should not be a major issue in economics. (Mäki 1996b, p. 434)[40]

The issue for economics is not the existence of the entities, but the way they are *arranged*. Scientific economics and commonsense economics (and different research programs within scientific economics) arrange these objects in very different ways and, therefore, include/exclude very different factors into/from their causal stories about economic relationships. The debate about realism and economics is not about the existence of the entities discussed but about whether the essential causal mechanisms have or have not been included into the relevant theory. Realist economic science should identify significant truths about the way the world works (www) and different economic theories highlight different causal structures as essential for the www (Mäki 1998e, 1999a). The search for such causal processes is consistent with a substantial amount of unrealisticness – as well as rhetoric, social construction, and other issues raised by contemporary science theory – and still remain a *realist* economic inquiry.[41]

Mäki argues that a proper understanding of these issues can help us to better understand – and sometimes even critique – particular research programs and/or the work of individual economists. One example is his recent work on Ronald Coase (Mäki 1998f, 1998g, 1998h, 1998i, 1999b). Coase won the 1991 Nobel Prize in economics (Coase 1992); he is well-known for the "Coase theorem" (Coase 1960) and his theory of the firm (Coase 1937), as well as providing theoretical ingredients for the body of literature known as "transactions cost economics." Although he arrived at the University of Chicago relatively late in his career

---

[40] It is interesting that Hausman (1998b) makes a similar point, but considers it to be a *criticism* of Mäki's (and Lawson's) view.

[41] Although this is not the place for a general critique of Mäki's argument, it should be noted that his claims about the "commonsense" nature of the entities discussed by economic theory is certainly open to question. The fact that one is surrounded by "consumers" in the grocery store, and that "consumers" appear in formal economic theory (like Arrow and Hahn 1971 or Mas-Colell, Whinston, and Green 1995), may have much more to do with our choice of *words* than with the ontic identity of those flesh and blood people standing beside you at the checkout counter and the consumption set ($X_h \subseteq \mathbb{R}^n$) and preference relation ($\succeq_h$) combinations that characterize "consumers" in modern economic theory. Anyone who has taught undergraduate economics must surely be skeptical about the claim that the theoretical entities of economics are essentially the same as the entities the words identify in everyday life: consider "investment" or "profit," for example (Lawson 1999, pp. 276–7 makes a similar argument in response to Hausman 1998b).

(Medema 1994, p. 6), Coase is generally associated with a certain brand of "Chicago school" economics, particularly in the area of law and economics. What is perhaps less well known is that Coase has been an outspoken critic of the methodological practice of mainstream neoclassical economics – what he often calls "blackboard economics" – as well as the "methodology of positive economics" endorsed by his colleague Milton Friedman (Coase 1978, 1988). Mäki's investigation of Coase's methodological and theoretical writings reveals a sustained commitment to *both* the *realisticness* of the assumptions of economic theories, and a generally *realist* approach to economic theory. Mäki contrasts this to Milton Friedman who endorses the *unrealisticness* of the assumptions and a *Friedmanian mixture* of realist and instrumentalist views on the nature of economic theory (Mäki 1992b, p. 181).

Although Coase's methodological arguments and the practice of his transactions cost economics seem to be generally consistent, Mäki does uncover an interesting methodological tension in Coase's work. The tension surfaces between Coase's critique of mainstream "blackboard" economics and his *economics of economics* (Mäki 1998g, 1999b). When Coase is criticizing blackboard economics, he is endorsing a particular type of *prescriptive* methodology: "He urges economists to change their habits of operating with unrealistic blackboard theories and to pursue realistic theories instead, using case studies as an empirical basis for theorizing" (Mäki 1998g, p. 255). This amounts to a "type of methodological regulationism" (Mäki 1998g, p. 260). By contrast in other work (particularly Coase 1988), Coase suggests that the discipline of economics constitutes a *free market for economic ideas* – a market that operates efficiently in the absence of methodological regulation. In attempting to sort out the various issues involved in this tension, Mäki also uncovers an additional problem; Coase's economic investigation of the economics profession does *not* involve transactions cost economics. In fact, if one *were* to investigate the discipline of economics from the perspective of transactions cost economics, one might find that blackboard economics is a relatively efficient way of organizing the discipline.

> [T]he current dominance of a highly formalized one "paradigm" is highly efficient in reducing transactions costs because it brings about a lot of standardization. Formalized standardization helps decrease search and monitoring costs, it facilitates communication and assessment of research outcomes. One might even go as far as arguing that blackboard economics is the best sort of economics one can hope for, since it is free from the costs that

are generated by the complications of empirical field work, the results of which are usually subject to a lot of uncertainty and multiple and rival interpretations. (Mäki 1998g, p. 265)

Such arguments not only lead us to a better understanding of "realism and economics"; they also make it clear that reflexivity and irony are not restricted to those employing constructivist and/or rhetorical approaches.

Although Mäki and Lawson have been the strongest defenders of realism in recent economic methodology, they are not the only recent authors to discuss this subject. Thomas Boylan and Paschal O'Gorman (1995, 1996, 1997a, 1997b, 1998) have articulated a methodological position called *causal holism* that is antipodal to the realist approaches of both Lawson and Mäki. Causal holism combines a rather radical empiricism – and the associated ontophobia – with an unabashed recognition of the problems of theory-ladenness underdetermination; it melds van Fraassen's constructive empiricism with Quine's holism (both discussed in Chapter 3). Like van Fraassen, the aim of science is to furnish accurate *descriptions* – to save the phenomena – and although scientific theories may also explain, their explanatory role is epistemically sterile; scientific explanations play a purely pragmatic (or constructivist or rhetorical) role and have nothing to do with the cognitive or epistemic virtues of the theories involved in such explanations. *Pure* economic theory must be assessed on the basis of its descriptive adequacy – an epistemological assessment – while explanation is relegated to *applied* economics and has nothing to do with the empirical adequacy of the relevant theory. Like Quine, their empiricism is naturalist and antifoundationalist; there is no first philosophy, and the meaning of a particular statement is determined by how it hangs together with other statements in our overall web of belief. It is an empiricism – in fact, a rather radical empiricism – and yet it accepts most of contemporary criticisms of empiricist foundationalism.

Boylan and O'Gorman have put causal holism to work, not only by criticizing other approaches to economic methodology – Lawson and Mäki on one side, and McCloskey on the other – but also by using it to help unpack certain existing critiques of mainstream economic theory: particularly that of Nicholas Kaldor (Boylan and O'Gorman 1995, 1997b).[42] It remains to be seen whether causal holism will be useful in the analysis of other topics within economic methodology or whether it will be effective in gaining other adherents. For now, it seems to be a

---

[42] Lagueux (1994) has used similar arguments from van Fraassen's constructive empiricism to criticize Friedman's instrumentalism.

two-author show, but it is a show that demonstrates that a version of genteel empiricism may be able survive the antifoundationalist storm and offer something to postfoundationalist economic methodology.

7.4 Cognitive and Semantic Themes

This final section will discuss two subfields of contemporary methodology that do not fit comfortably under any of the previous labels. The first of these is the work of Alexander Rosenberg who has turned the critique of folk psychology (discussed at the end of Chapter 4) into a systematic critique of microeconomics and rational choice theory. The second section discusses a literature that is substantially more amorphous; it concerns various efforts to analyze the notion of an economic model and/or how such models relate to the concepts of idealization and abstraction.

7.4.1 Intentionality, Folk Psychology, and Economics

Like Daniel Hausman, Alexander Rosenberg is a philosopher who has spent a good portion of his professional life trying to understand the theoretical activity of academic economists. His first book – *Microeconomic Laws* (1976) – investigated the cognitive status of microeconomic theory, but his signature argument was not presented until later work. This signature argument – Rosenberg's basic claim regarding *the key philosophical problem* with economic theory – was presented in the late 1970s and early 1980s (Rosenberg 1980a, 1980b, 1983, and elsewhere) and has been articulated and elaborated in numerous later works (1989, 1992, 1994b, 1995a, 1995b, 1998, and elsewhere). While Rosenberg has often changed his mind regarding the immediate implications and/or the significance of this core difficulty, his basic characterization of the problem has remained unchanged. Although Rosenberg has also written extensively on the philosophy of biology (Rosenberg 1985b, 1994a) – and even though other philosophers see economics and biology as sharing many of the same cognitive virtues and/or foibles – his appraisal of these two fields has remained separate, and in many ways antithetical.

Rosenberg's philosophical framework, unlike most of the authors discussed in this chapter, is basically a contemporary version of the Received View. His notion of scientific laws and causality are empiricist in the Humean tradition; scientific explanations involve subsumption under covering laws in the manner specified by the D-N model; and although there are clearly difficulties associated with theory-ladenness, underdetermination, and such, these problems are nowhere near significant enough for us to abandon, or even consider, a major revision of, the philosophical framework that has provided the backbone for the modern rational-scientific form of life. Mainstream philosophy of science has an adequate (or at least serviceable) characterization of science – one that is consistent with what goes on in most natural sciences – the relevant questions for the philosophy of economics are simply whether economics lives up to this characterization, and if not, then why not.[43]

Rosenberg answers the first question negatively; *economics has not demonstrated* the type of *empirical progress* that characterizes the natural sciences. The empirical predictions of economists are few in number, never very specific, and not very accurate (economics is "predictively weak," Rosenberg 1992, p. 56); economic predictions are too generic and/or qualitative (it is "condemned to generic predictions at best," Rosenberg 1992, p. 69); the theory is incapable of providing a reliable basis for social policy ("it was the increasing dissatisfaction of policy makers with the reliability of microeconomic and macroeconomic forecasting that led to a perception of economic theory in 'crisis'," Rosenberg 1992, p. 87); and, most importantly for Rosenberg, the empirical predictions of economists have *not exhibited systematic improvement* though time (it does not have "enough" predictive power and "it never seems to acquire any more than it had at he hands of say, Marshall," Rosenberg 1992, p. 67). Rosenberg adds a bit of a naturalist twist by suggesting that he is only following economists themselves who "have a commitment to an empiricist epistemology" (Rosenberg 1992, p. 18), but despite this disclaimer his position remains generally within the mainstream (philosopher as usher) tradition. He combines the normative philosophical claim that "long-term improvement in predictive success is a necessary accomplishment of any discipline that claims to provide knowledge" (Rosenberg 1992, p. 56) with the empirical argument that economics has radically failed to live up to this standard.

Although the argument that economics fails to make the type of accurate empirical predictions required for successful science is a common indictment of economics – this is one way to read both the falsificationist critique (Blaug and others) and the arguments about inexactness (Hausman) – Rosenberg offers a unique explanation for why this is the case. Rosenberg attributes the failure of economics to a feature that it shares with most other social sciences: *the commitment to the intentional explanatory framework of belief, action, and desire.* Economic

---

[43] While Rosenberg's more recent work often recognizes that "in the philosophy of science there is no longer any conviction about the existence of a litmus test that will indicate the cognitive status of a theory" (Rosenberg 1994b, p. 217), this recognition doesn't seem to have substantially altered his view of either science or economics.

explanations are based on the argument that economic agents have beliefs (about prices, income, costs, expectations, and other constraints), and they have desires (utility, profit, etc.), and that their actions (behavior) can be explained as the result of rationally attempting to satisfy (usually maximize) their desires subject to the constraints they face. In this explanatory schema *reasons are causes*; the intentional framework of belief and desire provides the agent with reasons for the action, and those reasons in turn are used to generate a causal explanation for the agent's action. Such *belief, action, desire* (hereafter BAD) explanations were discussed in the section on *folk psychology* (Chapter 4), and according to Rosenberg, they form the backbone of all economic explanations as well the explanations of many other social sciences; "the claim that economic agents act so as to attain their most preferred available alternative is pretty clearly a straightforward variant on this folk-psychological principle" (Rosenberg 1995a, p. 119).

A simple version of this BAD explanatory schema is given by Rosenberg's [L]:

> [L] If any agent, x, wants d, and x believes that a is a means to attain d under the circumstances, then x does a. (Rosenberg 1995a, p. 31)

Notice that [L] is essentially identical to Popper's SA framework for social science explanations involving the RP. In both frameworks, there is an appropriate action given the desires and beliefs about how to satisfy those desires, and explanation relies on the "covering law" that all agents act appropriately; that x does what is a (or perhaps, the best) "means to attain d under the circumstances."[44] Even if one doubts Rosenberg's claim that such a scheme captures all economic explanations, it certainly captures the basic explanatory framework employed in many *microeconomic* explanations of *individual* behavior, and it ostensibly undergirds any explanation of aggregated phenomena that relies on such micro-foundations. Clearly, this is the way that many economists explain, and equally clearly – as was apparent from the discussion of both eliminative materialism and Popperian SA – there are many problems associated with such an explanatory framework. Rosenberg discusses a myriad of such problems; I will just mention the four that seem to be most important.

---

[44] It is ironic that there exists such a massive philosophical literature surrounding folk psychology and [L] explanations, and there also exists an essentially parallel (smaller, but equally spirited) literature in the Popperian tradition surrounding SA and the RP, and yet these two literatures seem to exist in hermetic (supercilious?) isolation from each other.

First, is the *regress* or circularity problem. In order to employ [L], one needs to know what people believe. The obvious way to find out what they believe is to ask them, but this opens the door to a potentially infinite regress. In order to connect what people say their beliefs are with their "real beliefs" one must presuppose a scheme like [L] – they desire to tell us their real beliefs; they believe that the best way to fulfill this desire is to tell the truth; so they truthfully tell us what they believe. Because we normally interpret speech acts in terms of [L], any effort to test the schema seems to presuppose it; the result is a potentially vicious regress problem for [L] as a framework for scientific explanation.

> In order to explain an action, we need to identify the beliefs and desires that produced it, in accordance with [L]. In order to identify those beliefs and desires with any precision, we need to know more about further beliefs and desires. If to do that, we need to know about still further desires and beliefs, the original problem faces us all over again. We have made little progress in answering the challenge to our original explanation. (Rosenberg 1995a, p. 39)

The second problem concerns the logical relationship between *reasons and causes*. Within the confines of the covering law framework, reasons are only explanatory if they bring about actions, but many times agents have perfectly good reasons for their actions and yet those reasons are patently not the cause of what they end up doing. One of the examples that (Rosenberg 1995a, pp. 34–5) gives is the jogger who runs ten kilometers a day. The reason she runs is that it is "good for her" – a perfectly good reason that she believes and expresses honestly – and yet suppose the "real reason" is physiological; she is addicted to the endorphins released during the process of running. She has good reasons, but they are not the cause of the action. Whereas this example may seem far removed from economics, it illustrates an important point; giving reasons, even good reasons, is not the same as delineating causes. Even if we grant that certain types of reasons *may* be causes – they can be shown to bring about actions in a lawlike way – there is not any necessary relationship between giving reasons and identifying real causal factors.

The third problem was discussed above in the section on Popper's RP: the "law" that people act appropriately – in the way that they believe is the means to attain their goal – is extremely problematic. As the general law in a covering law explanation, it seems to be *either false or unfalsifiable*. If "appropriate" is narrowly defined – for example, maximizing a Cobb-Douglas Utility function – then it will be false as a general law (there will always be people who falsify such a general law). By contrast, if it is defined very broadly – for example in a way that "seems satisfactory" to the agent – then it is unfalsifiable (as one could define any and all behavior in such a way). These difficulties are, of course, in addition to all of the standard underdetermination problems associated with the empirical testing of any general scientific law.

The fourth point draws on the eliminative materialist critique of folk psychology discussed at the end of Chapter 4; *the intentional vocabulary of belief and desire simply do not identify scientifically significant features of the world*; they do not "cut nature at the joints."[45] Like folk astronomy and folk physics – and unlike the vocabulary of mature neuroscience – they should be condemned to the dustbin of history along with the rest of our prescientific concepts.

> The real source of trouble for economists' attempts to find *improvable* laws of economic behaviour is something that has only become clear in the philosophy of psychology's attempts to understand the intentional variables of commonsense and cognitive philosophy. "Beliefs" and "desires" – the terms in which ordinary thought and the social sciences describe the causes and effects of human action – do not describe "natural kinds." They do not divide nature at the joints. . . . Because of the character of our intentional variables, we cannot expect to improve our intentional explanations of action beyond their present levels of predictive power. But the level of predictive power of our intentional theory is no higher than Plato's. (Rosenberg 1994b, p. 224)

The bottom line for Rosenberg is that commitment to the BAD explanatory schema is the ultimate source of the economics profession's ongoing cognitive difficulties and it explains why it has not demonstrated a very good, or systematically improving, empirical track record. Eco-

---

[45] Another reading of the difficulty with intentional explanations comes from Davidson (1980). For Davidson, beliefs always involve a *normative* element. If it is raining, and you have an umbrella, and you want to stay dry, then you *ought* to open it. This is what rationality is all about; rational conduct is that which is warranted by the relevant intentional states. In this case a rationality assumption is just the assumption that the agent does in fact act in the way that is rational. In this way a causal intentional explanation – Rosenberg's [L] or Popper's SA – is just a combination of a normative interpretation (something is rational and thus ought to be done) and a rationality assumption (that the person does what is rational). Thus, for Davidson intentional explanations are irreducibly normative, and therefore fundamentally different from the descriptive explanations in the natural sciences.

nomics relies on explanations of the [L] form and it is a framework for the scientific explanation of human action that is plagued by insuperable difficulties. So, of course, economics fails as a predictive science. How could it possibly succeed given the inadequacies of its basic explanatory scheme?

> Now, at any rate, we have an explanation for why the assumptions of economic theory about individual action have not been improved, corrected, sharpened, specified, or conditioned in ways that would improve the predictive power of the theory. None of these things have been done by economists because they cannot be done. The intentional nature of the fundamental explanatory variables of economic theory prohibits such improvement. (Rosenberg 1992, p. 149)

Although Rosenberg has consistently maintained his critical position on [L] and economics, he has in fact offered a number of different conjectures regarding what economic theory *does* do (given that it fails as improvable empirical science). Or as he put it in the title of one paper: "If economics isn't science, what is it?" (1983). His two main answers have been "applied mathematics" and "contractarian political philosophy." The applied math appellation is certainly not unique to Rosenberg; many others have also suggested that economics seems to be just an exercise in deducing all of the possible mathematical implications of a particular abstract definition of rationality. The contractarian political philosophy label is less familiar, though. Rosenberg's argument is that in recent years so many political philosophers have adopted the analytical framework of Walrasian general equilibrium theory that it now represents a part of the "best contractarian argument for the adoption of the market as a social institution" (Rosenberg 1992, p. 220). Thus economic theory has now become "one important component in the research program of contractarian political philosophy . . . an exercise in the formal development of a solution to the problem of what economic institutions will be agreed upon by agents who must enter into a contract to establish them" (Rosenberg 1992, p. 220). Needless to say, one can find Rosenberg's critical remarks about [L] and economics quite insightful without accepting (either of) his stories about what economics actually *is* (and in all fairness to Rosenberg, he himself seems much more committed to the critical aspect of his analysis than to either of these descriptive stories).

While space considerations preclude a detailed discussion of the many criticisms that have been leveled against various aspects of Rosenberg's analysis of the plight of economics and the reason for its pitiful condition,[46] I will close this section by just mentioning a few of the issues that have been raised.[47] For one thing, Rosenberg's story seems most convincing when applied to *microeconomic* explanations of *individual* behavior. The problem is, of course, that much of economics is macro, and even in the micro domain, the relevant behavior of interest often involves (exclusively) aggregated *market* phenomena. When one adds to this the fact that much of the scientific activity of economists is actually econometrics and/or descriptive statistical analysis, Rosenberg's general argument about economics starts to break down even if one agrees with him about individual microeconomic behavior. Another issue involves empirical prediction; Rosenberg essentially starts with the fact of predictive failure. If one defines economics broadly as what professional economists do rather than what appears in the "best" theory journals, then the "failure" may not be as great as Rosenberg suggests. Of course, even if applied economists have a better predictive track record than Rosenberg assumes, there is still a serious question about the relationship between such applied work and the technical literature of economic theory. A third difficulty, and perhaps the most relevant to the views discussed in previous chapters, is Rosenberg's traditional philosophical framework. The interest seems to be philosophical legislation, and legislation that ignores most of the developments of contemporary science theory. For Rosenberg, there seems to be nothing essentially wrong with the mainstream philosophy of science view of laws, causality, testing, explanation, and such; the problem is with economics (or [L] social science generally). In addition to considering a more radical view of knowledge – naturalist, neopragmatist, constructivist, or whatever – there also are some less radical options that would allow Rosenberg to retain much of his epistemological scaffolding without being painted into the corner where [L] explanations are unscientific; there are many alternative ways of thinking about *scientific explanation* that are more flexible than the covering law model, and yet do not entail jumping onto a relativist slippery slope.[48] Finally, there are the various existing responses to the critique of folk psychology: supervenience (discussed in Chapter 4) and the instrumentalist response (for instance, Dennett 1978).[49] There

---

[46] These include Cottrell (1995), Hands (1984b; 1993, pp. 171–83), Hausman (1989), Hudson (1997), Kincaid (1996, pp. 200–6), Mäki (1996a), Nelson (1986, 1990), Rappaport (1995, 1998), and Ross (1995).

[47] Rosenberg's response to these (and other) criticisms are scattered throughout his work (1989, 1992, 1995a, 1995b, 1995c, and elsewhere).

[48] Some of these alternative explanatory schemes are cited in Hands (1998).

[49] Rosenberg has given significant attention to both of these, particularly the instrumentalist response, but he considers them irrelevant to the debate about economics. Superve-

is a lot of literature on folk psychology and only a very small part is eliminitativist; any defense of the scientific adequacy of BAD explanations, becomes, via Rosenberg's own argument, a defense of microeconomic explanations of individual behavior.

Despite all of these (and other) criticisms, it remains quite clear that Rosenberg has struck a significant chord regarding the difficulties of economic science (at least about economics as a theory of individual behavior). He has also lashed his critique of economics to the ongoing debates within the philosophy of psychology and philosophy of social science more generally in a way that facilitates the interaction among these fields and economic methodology. Although Rosenberg clearly poses a challenge to certain other positions within recent economic methodology,[50] at this point it is not entirely clear how his work will impact the methodological literature more generally. What does seem clear is that a significant door has been opened; a door that not only allows ideas from the philosophy of psychology to flow into economic methodology but also alters the role that economics plays in the debates in psychology, decision theory, political theory, political philosophy, and a host of other fields.

7.4.2 Abstraction, Isolation, and Model Theory

This has been a very long chapter, and in this final section, I would just like to indicate some of the recent work that examines the role of abstraction, isolation, and models, in economics. It is only the tip of the iceberg, but I will discuss just three of the available views: the so-called structuralist (and the associated Poznan) approach, Mäki's work on isolation, and Mary Morgan's recent work on economic models. Readers will need to dig into the references for other perspectives, or for a more in-depth examination of these three views.

Although the *structuralist view of scientific theories* originated in Pat Suppes (1957, 1961) "west coast" model theory (Diederich 1996, p. 15), the program is generally associated with Continental, particularly German, philosophy of science. The early program-defining works were Joseph Sneed's *The Logical Structure of Mathematical Physics* (1971)

---

nience is inconsistent with economists' own commitment to microfoundations and methodological individualism, whereas an instrumentalist approach fails, since economics fails to be a good predictor. These debates obviously remain open.

[50] For example, Rosenberg's position seems to stand as a prima facie refutation of most of what Tony Lawson says about "deductivism" and "empirical realism" in economics. Rosenberg basically says that economics fails to be precisely the same kind of science that Lawson asserts it is (but should not be). Cottrell (1998) criticizes Lawson from the perspective of recent debates within the philosophy of mind.

and Wolfgang Stegmüller's *The Structure and Dynamics of Theories* (1976). Other important contributions to the structuralist program include Stegmüller (1979), Balzer, Moulines, and Sneed (1987), and Balzer and Moulines (1996).[51] Unlike many other approaches to the philosophy of science, Sneed-Stegmüller structuralists have, almost from the beginning, exhibited a profound interest in applying their program to economics. In part, this seems to come as the result of a sincere interest in the foundations of economic theory, but one also suspects that it is motivated by the fact that economics is particularly well-suited to the structuralist approach; as we will see, structuralism involves the set-theoretic "reconstruction" of the logical structure of scientific theories, and the mathematical framework of modern economics (Walrasian general equilibrium theory as well as formal Marxian-Sraffian models) makes it particularly well suited to such reconstructions. A nonexhaustive list of structuralist applications to economics would include: the sixteen papers in Stegmüller, Balzer, and Sophn (1982), most of the contributions to Balzer and Hamminga (1989), a few of the papers in Hamminga and De Marchi (1994), Balzer (1982, 1985), De la Sienra (1992), Hamminga (1983, 1990), Händler (1980a, 1980b, 1982), Hands (1985c, 1985d), Haslinger (1983), Kuokkanen (1993), Leinfellner (1983), Pearce and Tucci (1982), Requate (1991), and Vilks (1992).[52]

[51] Diederich, Ibarra, and Mormann (1994) provide an extensive bibliography of structuralist writings during the 1989–94 period and reference bibliographic works on the earlier literature.

[52] The term *structuralism* is used to identify a wide range of different approaches within philosophy and social science – including Piaget's developmental psychology, Lévi-Strauss' anthropology, Saussure's linguistics, certain brands of Marxism, and many others – and although it may be possible to uncover relationships between Sneed-Stegmüller structuralism and some of these other forms of structuralism, I will act as if set-theoretic structuralism is a free-standing philosophical position. There is one exception to this rule though, and that is the *Bourbaki* structuralist program in the foundations of mathematics. The Sneed-Stegmüller program is directly indebted to Bourbakism – it is "an extension of the 'Bourbaki Program' in mathematics to theories of empirical science" (Diederich 1996, p. 15) – and most Sneed-Stegmüller structuralists consider Bourbaki to be an antecedent to their approach.

> Other schools of thought have been described as "structuralistic." We find "structuralisms" in the social sciences (psychology, linguistics, ethnology), in (French) philosophy, and in the foundations of mathematics (mainly the Bourbaki program). Only the latter can we say that it has a substantial connection with "our" structuralism. With respect to the other uses of the term, the relationships are quite remote, if present at all. (Moulines 1996, p. 1)

It is interesting to note that since Bourbaki had such an important impact on Debreu (1959) and many other post-World War II (particularly Cowles) mathematical economists (Hands 1985c; Mirowski 1999, Ch. 6; Weintraub and Mirowski 1994), those doing Sneed-

The structuralist program is one variant of the *semantic* (or model-theoretic) view of theories discussed in Section 7.2.1. Like Hausman's version of the semantic view, structuralists do not regard scientific theories as statements, but rather as defining predicates; the difference is that for the structuralists these predicates are exclusively *set-theoretic*. Structuralists view scientific theories as *structures* rather than statements: structures that are related to their empirical claims by certain systematic logical relationships. Specifying these logical relationships – reconstructing the theory in such a way as to uncover these relationships – is one of the main goals of the structuralist approach. These relationships are clarified by axiomatization of the theory, in particular by *set-theoretic* axiomatization, and the predicates defined by (reconstructed) scientific theories are set-theoretic entities. On the structuralist interpretation, if the Keynesian theory (KT) defines the predicate "is a Keynesian economy," (hereafter "is a K") then the sentence "A is a K" either is or is not true of the set A.

The members of the class of entities for which the predicate "is a K" is true are the *models* for the theory KT. Thus, if some economy A satisfies the axioms of KT – if "A is a K" is true – then *A is a model for KT*.[53] The next important bit of structuralist language is the notion of a *potential (or possible) model*. Possible models (or potential models) for the theory KT are things for which it makes some sense to attempt to apply the theory: things for which "is a K" could conceivably be true. Potential models are things that have at least enough structural similarity to the theory in question to qualify as "possibly" being models. To continue the Keynesian example, "the U.S. economy in 1960" is a *potential model* for KT – the statement may or may not be true, but there is enough structural similarity that it makes sense to ask the question – by contrast, "my coffee cup" or "the computer software industry" are not potential models for KT. More formally, potential models are set-theoretic entities that can be characterized in the language of the theory: things that could conceivably be models. Of course, not all potential models actually are models. Thus, if the set of all models for a theory T is given by $M(T)$, and the set of potential (or possible) models by $M_p(T)$, then we have the relationship $M(T) \subseteq M_p(T)$. In general, scientists

Stegmüller reconstructions in mathematical economics could, strangely enough, be considered to be the legitimate heirs to the Cowles-Bourbaki tradition in mathematical economics.

[53] This use of "model" comes from mathematical logic and is not the way that economists normally use the term. Recall that Hausman replaced the term "theory" with "model" – thus, Hausman (and most economists) would say "the Keynesian *model* defines the predicate 'is a K'" – and use the term "theoretical hypothesis" for claims such as "A is a K."

working in a particular theory T would only concern themselves with elements of $M_p(T)$, and the empirical activity of these scientists would consist of checking to see if various elements of $M_p(T)$ are also elements of $M(T)$.

Notice that neither $M(T)$ or $M_p(T)$ necessarily involves any non-mathematical element; the theory, its potential models (and thus models) could all contain/refer to purely mathematical entities. Surely something more must be added if we are to characterize *scientific* theories and "not just their mathematical skeletons" (Stegmüller 1979, p. 13) – or to put it another way, if we are to get beyond Bourbaki to structuralist philosophy of science. The jump to science is accommodated by the concept of a *partial potential (or possible) model.* A partial potential model is a potential model with the *theoretical terms removed*, a concept that is introduced to solve the structuralist version of the theory-ladenness problem: the *problem of theoretical terms* (Sneed 1971, p. 38; Stegmüller 1978, p. 43; 1979, p. 21). The structuralists provide a particular definition of "T-theoreticity" and then derive the set of *partial potential models* (M_{pp}) from the set of *potential models* (M_p) by "throwing out" (Stegmüller 1979, p. 22), or "lopping off" (Sneed 1971, p. 166; Stegmüller p. 25), the T-theoretical terms from the descriptions of the elements of M_p. Thus, each element of M_{pp} (each $x \in M_{pp}$) is something that could conceivably be a model for the theory and can be described without using any T-theoretical terms. This concept of a partial potential model gets us closer to the empirical target of a scientific theory, but we are not quite there. A particular x could in fact be an element of the set $M_{pp}(T)$ – and thus have sufficient structural similarities to be a potential model for T, and also be devoid of T-theoretical terms – and yet still be an abstract mathematical object (like a system of equations). The final scientific link is forged by the *set of intended applications*. The set of intended applications (I) is simply the set of concrete (as opposed to purely mathematical) entities that the theory is about or is supposed to refer to. Every scientific theory thus contains "a set I of *intended applications* containing those real systems to which the theory's practitioners intend to apply the theory" (Balzer 1998, p. 450). The set "I is assumed to be a subset of M_{pp}" (Balzer 1998, p. 45); in other words, it is assumed that the elements of I must have the same structure as the elements of M_{pp} (i.e., that $I \subseteq M_{pp}$). The concrete entities in I – things such as firms, consumers, real domestic product, and interest rates, for economic theories – must be configured (usually reconfigured) into the non-T-theoretical vocabulary of M_{pp}. Without a set of intended applications one simply has an abstract set-theoretical structure; with it, the structuralists argue, one has a set-theoretical reconstruction of a scientific theory.

So putting all the parts together, a scientific theory T is an ordered pair $\langle\langle C,I\rangle\rangle$ where C is the *core* of the scientific theory and I is the set of intended applications. Because the core consists of the set of models, potential models, and partial potential models, the final characterization is

$$T = \langle\langle C, I\rangle\rangle = \langle\langle M, M_p, M_{pp}, I\rangle\rangle.$$

The sets M, M_p and M_{pp} capture the *essential structural* characteristics of the theory T and define the fundamental predicate "x is a P" (where P is the predicate defined by T). The core C is related to the set of intended applications I by $I \subseteq M_{pp}$.[54]

Thus, we can now state explicitly the structuralist view of the relationship between the logical structure of a scientific theory and its empirical claims. The theory $T = \langle\langle C, I\rangle\rangle$ makes empirical claims in the following way. For any $x \in I$, we say that "x is a P" (where P is the predicate defined by T) if and only if there exist T-theoretical terms which can be added to the description of x in such a way that x becomes a model for T. Recall that since $I \subseteq M_{pp}$, we have $x \in M_{pp}$ for each $x \in I$, but as each element of M_{pp} was defined by "lopping off" the theoretical terms from an element of M_p, if we could "add back" the theoretical terms (theoretically enrich x), we would obtain an x^* such that $x^* \in M_p$. Of course, $M \subseteq M_p$, so it *may* be that $x^* \in M$; it may be that the theoretically enriched element of I is actually a model for the theory. If such an enrichment is possible so $x^* \in M$, then we say the empirical claim "x is a P" is true, and x constitutes a concrete application of the scientific theory T. Structuralists go on to discuss the *dynamics* of evolutionary and revolutionary theory change (Kuhn 1976; Stegmüller 1978, 1979), but this is enough to give us the basic notion of a structuralist set-theoretic reconstruction of a scientific theory.[55]

To get a feel for what a structuralist reconstruction of an economic theory might look like it is probably easiest to consider a particular example. The example I will present is my own – from Hands (1985d) – and although I make no claims about it being a particularly great structuralist reconstruction, it should be sufficient for illustrative purposes.[56]

[54] This is, of course, an abbreviated presentation of the structuralist approach. For more detail and the definitions of many other components of the structuralist characterization, the reader should examine the original sources (Sneed 1971; Stegmüller 1976, 1979; Balzer, Moulines, and Sneed 1987; Balzer and Moulines 1996). Balzer (1998) provides a relatively detailed discussion of the structuralist approach in just a few pages.

[55] I discuss some of the structuralist dynamical notions in Hands (1985c, pp. 312–15).

[56] This is one of many structuralist reconstructions of a pure exchange Walrasian general equilibrium system. While I focus on aggregate excess demand functions, other

Consider a Walrasian pure exchange economy (PEE) with n goods and H individuals (or households), where the goods are indexed by $i = 1, 2, \ldots, n$ and the individuals by $h = 1, 2, \ldots, H$. Each individual h maximizes a well-behaved utility function $U^h: \mathbb{R}^n_+ \to \mathbb{R}$ subject to the budget set $B^h(p) = \{x \in \mathbb{R}^n_+ | \, p^T x \geq p^T \omega^h\}$ where $\omega^h = (\omega^h_1, \omega^h_2, \ldots \omega^h_n) \in \mathbb{R}^n_{++}$ is h's initial endowment and $p = (p_1, p_2, \ldots, p_n) \in \mathbb{R}^n_{++}$ is the price vector. Utility maximization generates individual h's demand function,

$$x^h(p, \omega^h) = (x^h_1(p, \omega^h), x^h_2(p, \omega^h), \ldots, x^h_n(p, \omega^h)).$$

Suppressing the endowment parameters in the demand functions and summing over all individuals, we have the market excess demand z for the ith good given by:

$$z_i(p) = x_i(p) - \omega_i = \sum_{h=1}^{H} x^h_i(p) - \sum_{h=1}^{H} \omega^h_i(p),$$

with the aggregate excess demand function given by $z(p) = (z_1(p), z_2(p), \ldots, z_n(p))$. A strictly positive general equilibrium price vector is a $p^* \in \mathbb{R}^n_{++}$ such that $z_i(p^*) = 0$ for all $i = 1, 2, \ldots, n$.

If we take the market excess demand function as the primitive concept then we have the following definition for the set of potential model (M_p) for PEE.

Definition D1: x is a *potential model* of PEE $(x \in M_p)$ if there exists a structure consisting of an n, N, z, p, and D such that

    1. $x = \langle\langle n, N, z, p, D \rangle\rangle$,
    2. $N = \{1, 2, \ldots, n\}$ and n is a positive integer,
    3. $D \subseteq \mathbb{R}^n_{++}$,
    4. $p \in D$,
    5. $z: D \to \mathbb{R}^n$ where z is a continuous function.

Recall that according to the structuralist view of scientific theories the potential models are the things for which the theory *might* be true. The models of the theory, on the other hand, are the structures which actually satisfy the axioms of the theory. PEE has two such axioms. These are given in the following definition.

---

reconstructions emphasize utility, preferences, or individual demands. Other Walrasian reconstructions include Balzer (1982, 1985), Haslinger (1983), Janssen and Kuipers (1989), Requate (1991), and Vilks (1992).

Definition D2: x is a *model* of PEE (x ∈ M) if there exists a structure consisting of an n, N, z, p, and D such that

1. x ∈ M_p,
2. z(p) = z(λp) for all p ∈ D and for all λ > 0,
3. $p^T z(p) = 0$ for all p ∈ D.

Condition (2) requires excess demand functions to be homogeneous of degree zero, and condition (3) is Walras's Law; the former says that only relative prices matter and the latter says that the total value of all excess demands sum to zero for all price vectors (not just p*). Notice that M ⊆ M_p as required by the structuralist approach.

Although neither D1 nor D2 mention utility or utility maximization, the results in Debreu (1974) guarantee that if x ∈ M then there will always exist a set of n individual traders, each with a well-behaved utility function, such that the utility maximizing choices of these traders add up to the excess demand function z. This can be stated as a theorem.

Theorem T1: For all x ∈ M there exists a set of n traders whose maximization of a well-behaved utility function generates z.

Proof: Debreu (1974).

Of course the existence of a general equilibrium price vector is the most important theorem of PEE. This is a second theorem.

Theorem T2: For all x ∈ M there exists a p* such that z(p*) = 0.

Proof: This is a standard existence result (for example, Arrow and Hahn, 1971, p. 28).

Of course, we could go on generating additional theorems and relating this particular structuralist reconstruction with various models from the heyday of general equilibrium theory (1950–75),[57] but the purpose was just to give an example of the structuralist approach applied to a particular economic theory. It should be clear that reconstructing mathematical economic theories along structuralist lines is a quite practicable task. As the many different reconstructions of PEE attest, the mathematical nature of many economic theories make them fertile ground for structuralist exercises.

This reconstruction of PEE does elucidate one of the major problems associated with the structuralist approach to economic theory.[58] The problem is that what makes a set-theoretical reconstruction a piece of structuralist philosophy of science (rather than merely a piece of

---

[57] See Hands (1985d) for such exercises.
[58] Other criticisms are discussed in Hands (1985c).

Bourbakian mathematics) is the set of intended applications (I), and yet *it is not at all clear that such sets exist* for highly mathematical economic theories. For example, the above reconstruction does not even mention the set I, or, for that matter, the set of possible potential models (M_{pp}) that I is supposed to be a subset of. One might suggest that the set I includes such things as the "New York Stock Exchange" and the "Pike Place market in downtown Seattle," but this is an extremely difficult case to make given the structuralist definition of I. Recall that $I \subseteq M_{pp}$ and that M_{pp} is defined by "lopping off" the PEE-theoretical term from the potential models defined in D1. Because excess demand functions are PEE-theoretical, it is not at all clear what might be left of M_p after it is detheoreticalized, and it is even less clear how things such as the New York Stock Exchange or Seattle's Pike Place market could conceivably have enough structure in common with the lopped subset M_{pp} to be contained within any subset of it. This problem is in no way unique to this particular reconstruction, or even general equilibrium theory;[59] it is a general problem that has produced a substantial amount of skepticism on the part of structuralist authors. For example, Balzer asserted that "in economics we cannot point out a single real, concrete system which is commonly accepted by economists to be a standard example of PEE" (Balzer 1982, p. 41) and Händler claimed that many economic theories were pure theories, where a "pure theory does not intend to speak about reality" it is just a "picture of a possible world which does not actually exist" (Händler 1982, p. 75).

One way to view the problem of intended applications involves recognizing that economic theories involve *idealizations*. Economic theories describe the objects within their intended domain (things that would be included among the intended applications on a less formal definition of "intended applications") at best only inexactly or approximately, and thus the theory and its intended applications do not have the reductive set-theoretic relationship required by the structuralist view.[60] Recognizing the importance of idealization helped to motivate the turn toward the so-called *Poznan approach to idealization*, particularly the work of the Polish scholar Lezek Nowak.[61] Nowak (1980, 1994) not

---

[59] Hamminga (1990) found the same problem in Marxian economics.

[60] Of course, inexactness is also the focus of Hausman's semantic approach, but since he has not bound himself to the set-theoretic formalism, the problem takes a different form.

[61] Hamminga (1998a) provides a short but concise summary of the Poznan approach. The Hamminga and De Marchi (1994) volume contains a number of different economic applications of the Poznan method, while Hamminga (1989) compares Sneed and Nowak directly on the subject of Marxian value theory. Poznan idealization is indirectly related to the "plausibility" approach of Hamminga (1983), Klant (1984), and Nooteboom (1986); see Hamminga (1998b).

only approached the question of the role of idealization in science in a way that was generally amenable to the structuralist framework, his analysis focused on idealization in a particular economic theory: Marx's *Capital*.

While there is not room to examine Poznan idealization in any great detail, it is fairly easy to state the main argument. According to Nowak and others, scientific theories idealize systematically away from (messy/realistic) concrete examples in an effort to isolate the essential features of the relevant scientific law (such as Marx's labor theory of value in Volume I of *Capital*) and then, just as systematically, drop the various idealizing conditions in order to obtain more and more concretized versions of the basic theory (like Marx in Volume III).

> Roughly speaking, Nowak (1980) argues that the sciences start with simple models that abstract (Nowak uses the term *idealize*) from counteracting forces. Subsequent steps involve introducing more and more realistic assumptions that replace the abstractions one has started with. Nowak employs the term *concretization* for replacing *idealizational statements* by conditions that obtain in nature. When all idealizational statements are removed a fully concretized model is obtained. (Janssen 1994, p. 101, emphasis in original)

Although it clearly remains an open question whether economic theories can ever obtain a "fully concretized model," it is certainly clear that some type of idealization occurs in economics and perhaps this framework can provide some (or a new) handle on this important aspect of economic practice. It is also fairly clear how the Poznan approach fits comfortably with the general structuralist project of reconstructing economic theory.

> From this viewpoint, reconstruction of a theory means, first, to find the relevant idealizing conditions, second, to study the way in which scientists "concretize" their laws by successively dropping their idealizing conditions, and third, to study the relationship between the ideal, nonexisting objects for which the scientist believes his theory would hold, and the real objects that the theory is ultimately intended to describe. (Balzer and Hamminga 1989, p. 2)

One person who insists that processes like idealization are extremely important to understanding economics, but who disagrees with the details of the Poznan approach is Uskali Mäki (1992d, 1994b, 1996b,

1998e). For Mäki, the really important concept is *isolation* not idealization. Isolation is roughly the process of separation, dividing the relevant
universe into two separate subsets or fields.

> In an *isolation*, something, a set X of entities, is "sealed off" from
> the involvement or influence of everything else, a set Y of
> entities; together X and Y comprise the universe. The isolation
> of X from Y typically involves a representation of the interrela-
> tionships among the elements of X. Let us call X the *isolated
> field* and Y the *excluded field*. (Mäki 1992d, p. 321, emphasis
> in original)

On Mäki's view, *abstraction* is a particular type of isolation. When "a
universal or quasi-universal is isolated from particular exemplifications"
(Mäki 1992d, p. 322), then an abstraction, or abstracting isolation, has
occurred. For example, talking about "the competitive market" rather
than a particular case like "the domestic market for Iowa wheat
last year" involves abstraction. Isolations that do not involve such a
change in level – isolations where "the level of abstraction remains
unchanged" (Mäki 1992d, p. 322–3) – are called *horizontal isolations*,
whereas those that do involve a change in the level of abstraction are
called *vertical isolations*. Idealizations are one particular way of bringing
about a horizontal isolation. *Idealizations* are horizontal isolations
brought about by setting the value of some parameter to 0 or ∞; economic examples include things such as the infinite divisibility of commodities, the perfectly elastic marginal revenue curve of a competitive
firm, and zero transactions cost. The reverse of abstraction, the process
of moving to a lower level of abstraction is called *concretization*; increasing abstraction (vertical isolation) is the same as decreasing concreteness, while decreasing abstraction (vertical deisolation) is the same as
increasing concreteness. The following noneconomic example helps to
clarify these ideas.

> Consider your table on which lie two books, one blue, the other
> yellow, a pencil, and a piece of paper. Horizontal isolation takes
> place if you focus on – include in your "model" – the blue book
> and the pencil only, to the exclusion of the other two items.
> Horizontal de-isolation takes place if you then add the piece
> of paper or the yellow book or both in your model. Vertical iso-
> lation is an operation whereby you move from the particular
> items on your table to colors and pencils in general and from
> your two books to bookhood; in short, from concrete to abstract,
> from tokens to types of various generality, in some cases from
> particulars to universals. The reverse operation is vertical de-
> isolation. (Mäki 1998f, p. 8)

As discussed above (in Section 7.3.2), Mäki claims that the *entities* involved in scientific economics do not differ from the entities found in common everyday business life – what he calls "commonsensibles" (Mäki 1998e, p. 307) – the difference concerns how these things are *arranged*. Another way to put this is that economics is concerned with *isolation*. Isolation, either vertical or horizontal, doesn't introduce new stuff, it merely rearranges, or perhaps abstracts (in the case of vertical isolation), that which one started with. Consider the quote in the previous paragraph. Even the vertical movement (abstraction) from the pencils on the desk to "pencils in general," or from the books on the desk to "bookhood" in general, *does not* introduce some new kind of thing in the way that moving from those same pencils and books to the "electrons" that physicists tell us they are composed of *does* introduce a new kind of thing. As economists are mostly engaged in various sorts of isolative strategies, they do not, Mäki argues, open themselves up to the same class of realist philosophical controversies that have traditionally concerned philosophers of physics.

> Many of the posits of physical theories are based on postulating theoretical, non-observational entities such as electrons, photons and quarks. Many others are based on modifying entities by way of abstraction and idealization – such as mass points and frictionless planes. Most, virtually all, posits, of economic theories are of the latter kind rather than the former. . . . The theoretical isolations of economics are mainly among commonsensibles rather than the sort of unobservables encountered in physical science. (Mäki 1998e, p. 308–9)

This, of course, leaves economists with questions about whether particular economic theories capture the essential aspects of the economic world – *the way the world works* (www) as a constraint on economic theorizing (Mäki 1998e, 1998f, 1999a, 2000b) – but these questions are substantially different than the questions raised by the concept of "idealization" within the Poznan approach or the set of possible potential models (M_{pp}) of the structuralist view.

Before closing this chapter, it is useful to discuss one other critical tack on the Poznan and structuralist views: Mary Morgan's work on economic models (Morgan 1988, 1996, 1997, 1998, 1999a, 1999b). Morgan does not suggest that Poznan idealization and Sneed-Stegmüller reconstruction do not tell us anything about scientific models; it is just that such formal analysis – or for that matter the positivist-inspired work on scientific models (e.g., Nagel 1961) – do not tell the whole story about the role of models in science: particularly in economics. The *role of models in economics* is a complex story and must be investigated by examining the actual modeling *practice* of economists, and not just by looking at the role of models in physics or mathematical logic, or by armchair philosophizing. The existing philosophical literature on models – including all of the approaches discussed above – "do not properly address the problem of why economists might use or need the things they call 'models'" (Morgan 1998, p. 316).

Morgan makes two main claims about economic models. The first, following Margaret Morrison and their collaborative research (Morrison 1998, 1999; Morrison and Morgan 1999b), is that models act as *mediators*. Models mediate between theories and data, and to mediate effectively they must maintain a certain degree of autonomy from both the theory and the data. Think of a mediator in a legal dispute. In order to be effective, the mediator's actions can not be determined solely by either the plaintiff or the defendant; mediators must take account of, and be sensitive to, both parties, but they also must maintain a certain degree of independence. So, too, for models in economics (and elsewhere in science). Morgan's second main point is that economic models *tell stories*. Models are not passive; they need to be questioned in order to set off their dynamics, and the model's dynamics almost always involve a story (Morgan 1999a). What would even a supply and demand model, or the IS-LM model, or the Solow growth model, be without its associated story? Morgan argues, following both Hesse (1966) and the literature on the rhetoric of economics, that models involve metaphors, but metaphors (such as structural relations, abstraction, or isolation) are not all there is to a model. The metaphor and the story are mutually co-constraining; "The metaphor introduces the model ... but also constrains the story that can be told within it, while the story the economist wants to tell in turn limits the interpretation of the metaphor" (Morgan 1998, p. 320). The intuitive appeal of this "story" story is supported by the case study of Irving Fisher's monetary theory (Morgan 1997, 1999b) as well as her earlier work on empirical models in econometrics (Morgan 1988, 1990). Although Morgan's work on models is still in the early stages, and whereas it is certainly not the only alternative to the structuralist and Poznan views,[62] it does seem to provide some important first steps toward a better understanding of the role of models in economics, and it is an understanding that combines the formal approaches discussed in this section with the more rhetorical and constructivist approaches discussed earlier.

---

[62] Other interpretations of the role of models in economics include Boumans (1999), Cartwright (1997), Gibbard and Varian (1978), Reuten (1999), Bogaard (1999), and Walsh (1987).

8

The Economic Turn

Life is both acquisition of information, i.e., a cognitive process, and economic enterprise (one is almost tempted to call it commercial). An increase in knowledge about the outside world produces economic advantages; these then exert the selection pressure which causes the mechanisms that acquire and store information to develop further.

[Lorenz 1977, p. 28]

The central concern of that branch of philosophy known as epistemology or the theory of knowledge should be the growth of knowledge. This means that the theory of knowledge is a branch of economics.

[Bartley 1990, p. 89]

The production of knowledge is an economic activity, an industry, if you like. Economists have analyzed agriculture, mining, iron and steel production, ... and the production of all sorts of goods and services, but they have neglected to analyze the production of knowledge. This is surprising because there are a good many reasons why an economic analysis of the production of knowledge seems to be particularly interesting and promising of new insights.

[Machlup 1962, p. 9]

[T]he attempt to constitute a thriving "economics of science" ... is not calculated to win friends and converts to the project, nor will it achieve its intended effect of recommending economic analysis to the denizens of science studies, but will

rather simply confirm . . . pre-existing prejudices about economists being incorrigibly imperialistically aggressive, preter-
naturally surly, hopelessly tin-eared when it comes to listening
to the actors, lumpenly lead-footed when trespassing on other
disciplines, and woefully ignorant.

[Mirowski 1996a, pp. 72–3]

Previous chapters have emphasized the broad range of interactions that
have occurred (and are occurring) along the shifting frontier between
economics and science theory. This chapter will continue this theme but
shift the focus in a substantially different direction. For a variety of
reasons discussed below, economics recently has become actively
involved in the general study of scientific knowledge; science theory has
begun to take an *economic turn*. Much like cognitive psychology
(Chapter 4), evolutionary biology (Chapter 4), and sociological theory
(Chapter 5), economics is no longer just a *subject for* science theory, it
has now become an important resource *to be used in* science theory. The
previous two chapters focused primarily on the flow of ideas from philosophy and science studies into economics; this chapter will examine the
flow of ideas in the opposite direction: from economics into contemporary science theory. This counterflow was mentioned at various points in
earlier chapters, but now it becomes the main focus.

The first section will discuss some of the factors that have contributed
to the economic turn; many of these issues will be familiar from previous chapters, while others will take us into entirely new areas of inquiry.
The second section briefly examines some of the earlier (1960s and
1970s) literature on the "economics of science." The third section turns
to the recent literature where economics is employed as a resource for
science theory – what I call the *economics of scientific knowledge* (ESK)
– this is the most substantive section and the one that relates most clearly
to the rest of the book. The discussion of ESK is subdivided into three
parts: work by philosophers, work by economists, and alternative (nonmainstream) approaches. The final section will close with some general
reflections about the economic turn and its relationship to the issues
raised in previous chapters.

8.1 The Economic Turn in Contemporary Science Theory

I suspect that for many readers the most natural connection
between economics and scientific knowledge has nothing whatsoever to
do with the arguments in the previous seven chapters. The most obvious

way to connect economics and science seems to be through *the economy*. Improvements in scientific knowledge lead to research and development, which in turn leads to new technology, which manifests itself in improved goods and services, and these improvements ultimately increase the overall level of economic activity. In other words, science is important to economists because it contributes to economic growth. Although the subject of economic growth is undoubtedly responsible for some of the interest in the economics of science, it doesn't seem to be a motivation that involves any of the philosophical issues discussed above. How have developments within contemporary science theory contributed to the economic turn? Well, contemporary science theory suggests that practicing scientists follow their own (or group) interests and not necessarily the methodological rules laid down by philosophers of science. If that is the case, then why not employ economics – the social science that is most concerned with the collective consequences of self-interested behavior – to help explain the activity of these scientific agents?

So which is it? Is the economic turn motivated by concerns over economic growth and economic policy, or is it a result of various members of the science theory community attempting to reconcile the interest-ladenness of scientific activity with the cognitive virtues of science? The answer is *both and many other things*. The remainder of this section will discuss six separate (often related, but separable) developments that have contributed to the economic turn in recent science theory. All are important, but none should be considered to be anything like "the cause" of the economic turn (although each one may be the main reason why a particular scholar, or a particular group of scholars, turned to economics). I will begin with influences that seem to be the farthest away from economic methodology and science theory, and then slowly make my way back to the themes of previous chapters.

1. *Growth Theory:* Although economic growth has been the subject of economic analysis since at least Adam Smith, particular developments taking place within growth theory since the late 1950s have systematically directed economists' attention toward the role of science and scientific knowledge. Although the original Solow (1956) growth model did not include "science" or "knowledge" or even "information" in any systematic way – technology was exogenous – the empirical articulation of the model that occurred during the theory's first two decades led economists to ask serious questions about the role of this particular exogenous factor. Solow employed an aggregate version of the standard neoclassical production function $Y = F(K,N)$ where Y = aggregate real output, K = capital, and N = labor. Given this production function, changes in real output will obviously come about as the result of changes

in K and/or L, but there doesn't seem to be any systematic endogenous way of talking about the impact of technological change. One can certainly argue that technological change will *shift* the production function so that more output can be obtained from any particular combination of capital and labor – one can write $Y = AF(K,N)$ with $A > 0$ as the technology "shift parameter" – but the source of any ΔA would be exogenous to the economic model. Although technology and science were strictly outside the model, efforts to empirically measure the contribution of changes in the endogenous variables (ΔK and ΔL) to changes in real output (ΔY) kept coming up with a large residual – the "Solow residual" – that could not be explained by changes in the quantity of either capital or labor (Denison 1967, 1979; Solow 1957). The controversy surrounding the Solow residual led a number of economists to begin investigating the role of knowledge acquisition and the impact of technological change (Arrow 1962a; Uzawa 1965). An even more significant step was made in the late 1980s and early 1990s with the "new" or "endogenous" growth theory of Paul Romer (1986, 1990, 1994) and others (Lucas 1988). The growth models that emerge from this literature provide an endogenous theory of technological change by combining elements of the earlier growth theory with the assumption of increasing returns (an idea that goes back to at least Young 1928); elements of imperfect competition; and some of the microeconomic research on science, R&D, and technological change discussed below. This is an important and growing theoretical literature that has undoubtedly had an impact on economists' interest in scientific knowledge.

2. *The Microeconomics of Science Policy:* There have been at least three major debates over science policy in the English-speaking world during the twentieth century. The first was the British debate over the social control of science in the 1930s involving, among others, J. D. Bernal and the philosopher Michael Polanyi. Bernal argued for more direct social control of scientific activity, while Polanyi argued that the scientific community should retain substantial autonomy from governmental involvement.[1] The second controversy was the U.S. debate over government funding of basic science in the period immediately following World War II. One of the most influential documents of this debate was Vannevar Bush's *Science – The Endless Frontier* (1945). Bush was wartime director of the Office of Scientific Research and Development and became the first director of the National Science Foundation in 1950;

---

[1] J. D. Bernal was discussed in Chapter 5 and Polanyi's most famous work on the subject was "The Republic of Science" (1962). See Brooks (1996), Mirowski (1997b), or Werskey (1988) for a general discussion of the debate.

the launch of Sputnik in October 1957 effectively ended the debate in Bush's favor. This early Cold War controversy over science policy prompted much of the economics of science literature that will be discussed below in Section 8.2. We are still in the midst of the third debate. The end of the Cold War and increased public concern regarding the size of the government sector (and its deficit) has intensified an ongoing debate regarding national "Science Policy" in the United States and elsewhere. How much, and in what specific ways, should the government be involved in basic research? Are there new institutional structures emerging within the knowledge industry that should be encouraged or discouraged by the public sector? What is the proper relationship between higher education and scientific research? If research money is scarce shouldn't the relevant funding agencies have an effective economic tool for properly evaluating the costs and benefits of various projects? Such questions have clearly contributed to the growing interest in the economics of scientific knowledge (ESK).

3. *Extending the Explanatory Reach of Microeconomics:* One reason that microeconomists have turned their formidable modelling skills in the direction of science is simply because it provides an excellent opportunity for extending the theoretical reach of economics. Like public choice theory or the economics of the family – where economists sometimes seem more concerned with demonstrating the breadth of economic analysis than with making new discoveries about the behavior of elected representatives or family life – the literature on the economics of science sometimes seems to be driven more by the desire to extend the explanatory reach of economics than by the desire to make new discoveries about the behavior of scientists or the character of scientific knowledge. While extending the reach of economics is always appealing, the appeal is enhanced if the most recent theoretical tools can be employed in the analysis, and the economics of science seems to score here, too. Many of the theoretical concepts employed in the economics of science – game theory, path dependency, transactions cost economics, complexity theory, and so forth – are of relatively recent vintage. This is clearly another feature that adds to the overall professional viability of the research project. The combination of these two features – the desire to extend the tools of economics into new explanatory domains and the ability to employ recent developments in economic theory while doing so – certainly helps to explain why the study of scientific behavior has recently piqued the interest of economic theorists.

4. *Can Science be both Social and Rational?* Finally we have reached a topic that draws on the discussion from previous chapters. The breakdown of the Received View and related developments raise a number of

important questions. How can (or can) science be epistemically privileged, given that it is underdetermined, theory-laden, socially conditioned, and practiced by individuals who appear to systematically violate all of the rules that philosophers of science have laid down as guidelines for the proper conduct of scientific inquiry? Is there a way to save some kind of scientific rationality from the creeping relativism of recent science theory? These are difficult questions, but they also seem to be questions where economics might be able to provide some useful guidance; in fact, economics would appear to be the social science that is best suited to address this particular class of problems. For over two hundred years, economists have focused on the question of how individually self-interested agents can, within the context of certain institutional structures, bring about a result that is simultaneously (1) socially desirable and (2) not the intention of any individual agent or group of agents. Not only have economists analyzed institutions (such as the competitive market) that channel self-interested behavior into socially desirable consequences, they have also spent a great amount of time and effort studying the conditions under which such an optimal result may fail to occur (market failure) and how such failures might be rectified. Now shift this argument over to the context of science. One of the main points of Kuhn, SSK, and others is that scientists do not in fact obey the (epistemically proper) rules of scientific method; they are, in Philip Kitcher's apt phrase, "epistemically sullied" agents (Kitcher 1993, p. 364). But now (following the argument from economics), suppose that it could be shown that individual scientists *do not need* to follow the rules of scientific method *in order for* cognitively optimal results to emerge from the social context of the scientific community. Presto, the relativist threat is disarmed; *epistemically sullied agents might still give us the cognitive right stuff* (and if not, economics might be able to help with the problem of how to tweak the scientific institutions in such a way that the right stuff does emerge). Defusing relativism in this way is one of the major motivations for the philosophers that have recently turned to economics for insights into the production of scientific knowledge.

5. *Economics as a Naturalizing Base:* In Chapter 4, it was argued that if one is going to use the special sciences as a resource for the general study of scientific knowledge, one needs to decide *which* science will be taken as the starting point; one needs to choose a *naturalizing base* (or bases). Evolutionary biology and cognitive psychology have served as the naturalizing base for most of the naturalist-inspired philosophical literature of the last few decades. Although the sociological literature is often contrasted with naturalism, I argued in Chapter 5 that one way to think of SSK is to view it as a version of naturalism that takes social

science as the naturalizing base. So why not economics? Why not start with economics as the naturalizing base for the general study of scientific knowledge? Evolutionary biology certainly has more epistemic clout than economics, but that is not necessarily the case for psychology or sociology. Economics would seem to be just as legitimate a scientific "given" as either one of these two other human sciences. Now, of course, economics may not work; it may not provide as much insight into scientific activity as sociology or cognitive psychology, but there doesn't seem to be any *a priori* reason not to try it (and given [4] above, there seem to be a number of very good reasons why it might be successful). Although I am not aware of any philosopher who admits to starting with economics as a naturalizing base, it seems that for most of the philosophers discussed below in Section 8.3.1 that is exactly what they are doing.

6. *Economics and Epistemology are Deeply Intertwined:* One of the repeated themes in previous chapters was how intertwined the way we think about the economy is with the way we think about scientific knowledge. There is not some pristine "shelf of philosophy" that economists can take ideas from in order to "apply" them in the domain of economic science. The stuff on the philosophical shelf is in part (and always has been) conditioned by political economic context and economic ideas – Neurath's positivism was motivated in part by his Marxist social theory; Popper wanted to exclude Marxism but include microeconomics; developments in cognitive science had origins in Simon's critique of neoclassical theory; invisible hands and steady states in evolutionary epistemology look like invisible hands and steady states in economics, pragmatism affirms the economically grounded craftsman over the esoteric seeker of abstract truth; standpoint epistemology has its roots in the economic relations of production; and the list goes on and on. In one sense, the economic turn just makes this interpenetration explicit by being clear about the particular economic ideas that are being elicited and how they enter into the analysis. Economics was always there; the only difference is that now with ESK we actually get to see the rabbit go into the hat.

Although these six things certainly do not exhaust the factors that have contributed to the economic turn, they capture much of what has motivated the recent literature. As one becomes familiar with the different tacks that economists and philosophers have taken through the economic turn, it will become fairly clear which of the six factors has been most significant for specific authors and groups of authors. Before actually turning to this recent literature, I would like to make few remarks about why the material is subdivided in the way that it is.

Chapter 5 emphasized the distinction between the sociology of science and the sociology of scientific knowledge (SSK), with Merton being the paradigm case of the former and the Strong Program and social constructivism being instances of the latter. The distinction between these two fields focused on the *content* of science. For SSK, the content of science is conditioned by the social context of the knowledge production process – there is an epistemic component – and, thus, the analysis has potential implications (usually negative) for the cognitive content of science. For Merton and other sociologists of science, the analysis has no such epistemic component. It is *presumed* that science produces legitimate knowledge, but the sociological factors that Merton examines are independent of the cognitive content of the science being examined. This is, of course, consistent with the Received View's perspective on the proper division of intellectual labor between sociologists of science and philosophers of science; sociologists analyze only the social structure and function of science (only the pipes), whereas philosophers handle the (implicitly more important) job of evaluating the cognitive quality of product flow. SSK, of course, blurs both of these distinctions; there is no useful distinction between the conduit and the scientific theory that flows through it, both are merely aspects of the social character of science, and there is no rigid distinction between the job of philosophers and the job of sociologists. As I said in Chapter 5, I think the difference between the sociology of science and SSK is a useful distinction – it seems to cut up a massive amount of literature in a reasonably useful way – but it is imperfect, quite flexible, and may not be the right tool for others with different purposes.

Now we turn to the economics of science: in a certain sense, substituting "economics" for "sociology" for the task of analyzing the activity and products of science. I would like to employ a similar distinction between the *economics of science* and the *economics of scientific knowledge* (ESK). The basic argument is that the economics of science analyzes (explains and/or predicts) the behavior of scientists in the same way that an economist might analyze (explain and/or predict) the behavior of firms or consumers. Like the Mertonian school of sociology, the economics of science almost always *presumes* that science produces products of high cognitive quality, but investigating whether it "really" does so is not considered to be the proper subject for economic analysis (it would be like an economist investigating whether the products of a firm "really" satisfy consumer wants). By contrast, ESK, like SSK, would address the question of whether the epistemologically right stuff is being produced in the economy of science; ESK mixes economics and normative science theory. The distinction between the economics of science and

ESK mirrors not only the difference between sociology of science and SSK, but also the traditional distinction between microeconomics and welfare economics. Microeconomics, it is usually argued, predicts and/or explains the behavior of economic agents, whereas welfare economics focuses on the question of whether the social configuration produced as a result of the actions of these agents is "optimal" or "efficient." Now, the standards for efficiency in welfare economics have traditionally been rooted in the utility of the agents themselves – and, thus, is grounded (at least at its core) in ethics, not epistemology – but it is a relatively short jump to ESK, where the question is whether the behavior of the scientific agents brings about a social configuration that is epistemically "optimal" or "efficient." The economics of science predicts and/or explains the behavior of scientists and scientific institutions, whereas ESK adds the question of whether those actions and institutions produce scientific products that are cognitively efficient or optimal (or if they are not optimal, how the institutions might be changed in order to improve epistemic efficiency).

While the distinction between the economics of science and ESK owes much to the distinction between the sociology of science and SSK, the barrier separating the economics of science from ESK is even more permeable than the one separating the sociology of science from SSK. This said, I still find the distinction useful and will try to stick to it as far as it goes in the following sections.

With this warning, let us now turn to the brief examination of the economics of science in Section 8.2. There are two main reasons why this section is relatively brief. First, the economics of science has a much weaker link to economic methodology and contemporary science theory than the ESK discussed in Section 8.3, and second, there are a number of recent surveys that do an excellent job covering this material (Diamond 1996; Mirowski and Sent 2000; Sent 1999; Stephan 1996; Zamora Bonilla 2000).[2]

8.2 The Economics of Science

The combination of Solow growth theory and the early Cold War debate over science policy combined to produce a flurry of intellectual activity on the subject of the economics of science and technology in the late 1950s and early 1960s. Dasgupta and David (1994), major figures in what has been called the "new economics of science" (one

---

[2] The Diamond (1996) survey was published with comments by more than thirty authors; these comments reflect both the current interest in, and wide range of divergent views about, the economics of science.

version of ESK), refer to this postwar literature as the *old economics of science*. Two of the most influential papers in this literature were Arrow (1962b) and Nelson (1959). The main contribution of these and similar papers was to apply the standard tools of welfare economics, particularly cost-benefit analysis and the theory of externalities and public goods, to the question of the "optimal" level of basic scientific research.

Although the economic theory employed in these papers will be familiar to most readers, a quick review still seems useful, since the argument forms the backdrop for most of the later work in the economics of science (and ESK). According to the standard argument the *socially optimal* (or efficient) quantity of any particular good is given by the quantity that maximizes the *net social benefit* (NSB), where the net social benefit is the difference between the total social benefit (SB) and the total social cost (SC) associated with the consumption and production of the good. The solution to finding the socially optimal quantity (Q) of any particular good is thus given by the optimization problem

$$\underset{\{Q\}}{\text{Max}}\ \text{NSB}(Q) = \text{SB}(Q) - \text{SC}(Q).$$

The first-order condition for this maximization problem requires the marginal social benefit (MSB) to be equal to the marginal social cost (MSC). Thus, if we make the standard assumptions – the social benefit is simply the sum of all the private benefits; the social cost is simply the sum of all of the private costs; the marginal private benefit to each individual decreases as more of the good is consumed; and the good is produced under short-run conditions of diminishing marginal returns (and, thus, increasing marginal private costs) – the social optimal quantity (Q_{so}) will be given at the intersection of MSB and MSC, as shown in Figure 8.1.

Of course, for most goods in a market economy, the problem is not determining the quantity Q_{so}, but rather determining the *relationship* between Q_{so} and quantity of the good produced by a competitive market (Q^*). Competitive markets will produce goods where supply is equal to demand (Figure 8.2), while the socially optimal output is Q_{so}. The relevant question for social welfare is under what circumstances will $Q_{so} = Q^*$? In other words, under what conditions will the competitive market produce the right (socially optimal) quantity of the good? A related question is of course the issue of *market failure*: the conditions under which the market "fails" to produce the socially optimal quantity of the good ($Q_{so} \neq Q^*$). The standard argument is that if there are no *externalities* – no positive externalities (if the only benefits accrue to the buyers of the good so that MSB = D) and no negative externalities (if the only

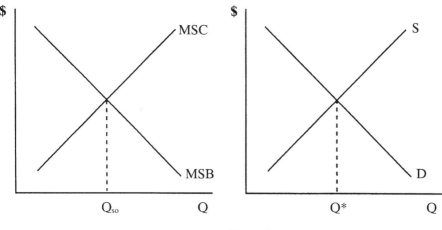

Figure 8.1   Figure 8.2

costs associated with the production of the good accrue to the individual producers so that MSC = S) – then the competitive market will produce the right quantity of the good. If there are positive externalities (MSB > D) or negative externalities (MSC > S), then there will be market failure ($Q_{so} \neq Q^*$); in particular, positive externalities alone cause the good to be underproduced ($Q^* < Q_{so}$) and negative externalities alone cause the good to be overproduced ($Q^* > Q_{so}$).

So how were these concepts of social optimality and externalities employed in "old" economics of science? Well, there were a variety of different views, but the bottom line for most authors was that basic scientific research has substantial *positive* externalities and is therefore *underproduced* by the competitive market. Some argued that science was in fact a *pure public* good, as the stock of knowledge is not diminished by any individual's "consumption" of it, whereas others simply argued for a (often large) positive externality (as depicted in Figure 8.3). The main policy implication was that basic science, like education and other goods with positive externalities, needs to be subsidized, perhaps massively subsidized, by the government.[3] Another policy suggestion

---

[3] Although the argument that science involves positive externalities and, thus, needs to be subsidized by the government has undoubtedly been the majority view among economists working in the field, not everyone who has employed this cost-benefit framework has come to this conclusion. Johnson (1972) and Rottenberg (1981), for example, are critical of the subsidy argument (primarily because of the government's inability to compute the costs and/or benefits of science), whereas Kealy (1996, 1998) advocates complete laissez-faire.

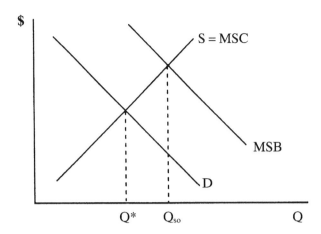

Figure 8.3

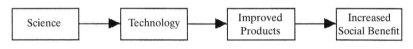

Figure 8.4

involved the use of patents and other property right guarantees to the scientific producer so they might be better able to recover some of the social benefits that accrue to others.

The argument for the positive externality associated with scientific research was grounded in part on the so-called *linear model* of the relationship between research in basic science and the resulting social benefits. In its simplest form, the linear model argued that scientific research led to technological change, which in turn led to the development of new goods and services and thus increased individual (and thus social) benefits (Figure 8.4). Although the linear model is now regarded as overly simplistic by most researchers in the field, it still seems to play an important (if implicit) role in popular debates about the role of science in society.

The application of the tools of welfare economics to the question of the efficient output of scientific research was not the only approach to the (old) economics of science. There also were a number of industrial organization economists – the most influential being Edwin Mansfield

$(1966, 1972, 1991, 1996)^4$ – who produced studies of the impact of science, technology, and R&D on (and in) a number of specific industries. Following in the wake of the debate over the Solow residual, and motivated in part by governmental (particularly military) concerns regarding the pay-off from pure science, Mansfield and others approached the question of the relationship between scientific knowledge and commercial product innovation from an entirely different (microdisaggregated) point of view and produced a number of empirical case studies of the knowledge-innovation nexus within specific U.S. industries. These studies often provided valuable information about particular industries and product lines, but the results proved difficult to generalize across (or among) various industrial sectors.

While the applied welfare economics and industry studies constitute a large portion of the existing (and ongoing) work on the economics of science, these two approaches do not exhaust the wide-ranging and diverse literature that might legitimately be called the "economics of science." There have been efforts to integrate certain sociological insights and economics into a comprehensive theory of scientific reputation seeking (Stephan 1996; Ziman 1994; and others); there have been various empirical studies of the importance of place, time, and location in science (Stephan and Levin 1992, for example); a number of economists have analyzed scientific behavior in terms of human capital theory (discussed in Stephan 1996); there have also been efforts to redefine the traditional notions of rival and nonrival goods to better accommodate recent changes in the industrial structure of contemporary knowledge production (see Nelson and Romer 1996); as well as numerous other theoretical and empirical twists and turns. Science clearly has an economic impact that can be, and has been, examined from a number of different economic perspectives. This literature is not only growing rapidly, it is also being taken more and more seriously by those who are in the position of making science policy decisions. It is important and interesting, but not as directly relevant to (even broadly defined) economic methodology as the subject of the next section: the economics of scientific knowledge.

8.3 The Economics of Scientific Knowledge (ESK)

The next three subsections will examine three different approaches to ESK: philosophers applying various aspects of economic theory to science; economists studying science with an eye toward the growth knowledge; and, finally, a brief discussion of some of the ways that nonmainstream economics has (and could be) involved in the study

---

[4] Diamond (1999) provides a detailed discussion (and complete bibliography) of Mansfield's contribution to the economics of science and technology.

of scientific knowledge. In each of these cases, I will focus on relatively recent work and try as much as possible to tie the arguments up with the literature considered in previous chapters.

8.3.1 Philosophers and ESK

We have seen many examples where philosophers (and others) employed economic concepts and argumentation in the service of science theory. Although the list of examples is fairly long, I would like to add a few additional items that have thus far escaped attention. C. A. Hooker (1995) could certainly be added to the roster of those who actively employ economic argumentation in their evolutionary approach to scientific knowledge. Nicholas Rescher is a prolific contributor to the philosophical literature who frequently characterizes the growth of scientific knowledge in economic terms (Rescher 1989, 1996; Wible 1994b, 1998). Alvin Goldman, whose cognitive science and reliabilism were discussed in detail in Chapter 4, has explicitly employed economics in a number of different philosophical projects involving the production and distribution of knowledge (Goldman and Shaked 1991; Cox and Goldman 1994; Goldman and Cox 1996; Sent 1997b).[5] Michel Blais (1987) has applied the theory of repeated games to epistemological questions; Joseph Sneed (1989) has put his own brand of set-theoretic structuralism to work on the economics of science; Steve Fuller (1991) has examined the proprietary grounds of knowledge; Zamora Bonilla (1999a, 1999b) has even applied economic argumentation to certain questions in economic methodology; and there are undoubtedly many others that could be added to the list. Finally, it is useful to note that there have been philosophers who used terms such as the "economics of science," even though they do not really employ any ideas from economic theory; for instance Mach (1893, 1898) where "economic" meant roughly "simplest."

Although many more examples could certainly be listed, the goal of this section is not to catalogue all of the philosophers who have, in one way or another, employed economic reasoning in their characterization of scientific knowledge. Rather than trying to say a little something about all the

---

[5] Goldman is certainly a good example to make the point that not all philosophers who employ economics in science theory come up with the same answer to the same question. For example, on the question of the "free marketplace of scientific ideas," we saw in Chapter 4 that Bartley and other Popperians made an invisible hand argument for cognitive efficiency of laissez-faire. On this same subject, Goldman and Cox (1996) argue for the benefits of an adversarial system (rather than a marketplace); whereas Kitcher (1997) takes the position that sometimes the free market works and sometimes it doesn't.

various contributions, I would like to focus on just one contemporary philosopher – Philip Kitcher – and try to unpack his particular research project in some detail. Kitcher is an excellent choice, because his work represents the most influential and most self-conscious attempt by a philosopher of science to enlist economics in an effort to salvage scientific rationality and normative epistemology from the threat of relativism and social constructivism. Kitcher certainly wants to save (at least some of the) old-fashioned epistemic virtues (Kitcher 1993, p. 127) from the philosophical problems of Chapters 3–6, and he sees social epistemology grounded in an economic model of individual agency and social coordination as the most viable solution to the problem. While Kitcher admits that normative philosophy of science is under duress, he wants to show that "reports of its demise are greatly exaggerated" (Kitcher 1992, p. 114), and to do so in such a way that is relatively naturalist and also recognizes, though does not surrender to, the social aspects of the scientific endeavor. The goal is to "provide a philosophical framework for the study of science which combines the insights of Legend with the insights of its critics" (Kitcher 1993, p. 390): to find a new middle ground that will "replace both sleepy complacency and Luddite rage" (1993, p. 391).

Kitcher's road to economics starts with the *reliabilism* of Goldman and others discussed in Chapter 4. Recall that knowledge has traditionally meant "justified true belief," and that beliefs are generally considered to reside within individual human beings; individuals have traditionally been (and remain for Kitcher) the subject of knowledge. Kitcher's twist – which concedes a major point to Kuhn and the sociologists – is that what counts as a "justification," the standards of reliability, must be *social* standards. What matters is the reliability of the social process that affects the beliefs of individuals; in fact, it is not really important whether any particular individual has reliable beliefs or not; instead, what is most important to the epistemic community is the *distribution* of reliable beliefs within that community. We want to encourage social processes and the supporting institutions that increase the ratio of reliable beliefs to total beliefs within the population. The relevant issue is, thus, *social epistemology*, or, to translate the project into the language of economics, it's a study in (epistemic) industrial organization: the industrial organization of our cognitive lives. Economists are interested in finding out the arrangement of our social institutions that is most conducive to economic efficiency; Kitcher's normative philosophical project is to find out the arrangement of our cognitive institutions that is most conducive to epistemic efficiency (that best encourages the formation of reliable beliefs). Knowledge still resides in individuals (not society), but the important questions are about the (epistemic) efficiency of our social institutions.[6]

> [T]he main social epistemological project consists in the inves-
> tigation of the reliability of various types of social processes.
> Once we have recognized that individuals form beliefs by relying
> on information supplied by others, there are serious issues
> about the conditions that should be met if the community is to
> form a consensus on a particular issue – questions about the divi-
> sion of opinion and of cognitive effort within the community,
> and issues about the proper attribution of authority. I shall refer
> to the field of problems just outlined as *the study of the organi-
> zation of cognitive labor.* . . . To the extent that we can make
> realistic presuppositions about human cognitive capacities and
> about the social relations found in actual communities of inquir-
> ers, we can explain, appraise, and *in principle* improve our col-
> lective epistemic performance. (Kitcher 1994, p. 114, emphasis in
> original)

According to Kitcher, the key to the growth of knowledge – and here he borrows from biology – is diversity: in this case cognitive diversity. Institutions and social processes that increase the distribution of reliable knowledge in society are those which encourage a *cognitive division of labor* (Kitcher 1990, 1993, 1994). As Kitcher put it in Chapter 8 of *The Advancement of Science*:

> At various points . . . I have suggested that there are advantages
> for a scientific community in cognitive diversity. Intuitively, a
> community that is prepared to hedge its bets when the situation
> is unclear is likely to do better than a community that moves
> quickly to a state of uniform opinion. Much of the rest of this
> chapter will be devoted to exploring this intuitive idea and trying
> to understand the kinds of social arrangements that might foster
> welcome diversity. (Kitcher 1993, p. 344)

Now, since knowledge is promoted by cognitive *diversity*, it is fairly easy to see why Kitcher does not see the growth of knowledge to be threatened by the sullied behavior emphasized by Kuhn and the con-structivists. If real scientists do not follow the rules, if they do not always obey the methodological norms, it might actually be a good thing; if

---

[6] Kitcher's characterization of the social has frequently been a source of criticism for his approach; see Fuller (1994), Hands (1995), Kincaid (1997), Mirowski (1995b, 1996b), and Solomon (1995b), for example.

everyone followed the same set of rules, there would be cognitive *uniformity* and not (knowledge promoting) cognitive diversity. It is also fairly easy to see how economics comes into play. What better discipline than economics to explain how individual (in this case scientist) agents acting in sullied and self-interested ways could bring about a division of (in this case cognitive) labor? Sociologists and philosophers might think that there is necessarily a tension between the socially optimal division of cognitive labor and the sullied behavior of individual scientists – between Q_{so} and Q^* – but economists know (and seem to have mathematical models to prove) that it need not always be the case. It is possible for self-interested behavior to have good collective, even epistemic, consequences.

> Much thinking about the growth of science is permeated by the thought that once scientists are shown to be motivated by various types of social concerns, something epistemically dreadful has been established. On the contrary, as I shall repeatedly emphasize, particular kinds of social arrangements make good epistemic use of the grubbiest motives. (Kitcher 1993, p. 305)[7]

Kitcher's most intensive use of economics – such as the game-theoretic models he employs in Chapter 8 of *Advancement* – are essentially "how possibly" results; that is, the models are designed to demonstrate how it is possible that egotistical motives could lead to a division of cognitive labor. How it is possible that "sullied scientists will do better than the epistemically pure" (Kitcher 1993, p. 310), or how it is possible that "motives often dismissed as beyond the pale of scientific decision making can, under a wide range of conditions, play a constructive role in the community's epistemic enterprise" (1993, p. 245). Now it is important to note that Kitcher is not, unlike certain other philosophers (for instance, Bartley), making an argument for complete laissez-faire. Kitcher is not saying that sullied self-interested behavior always leads

---

[7] It is useful to point out an important difference between the way that economists use certain terms and the way they are used by Kitcher and others (even SSK). For those in science theory, the good motives are generally considered to be *individual* (look for the truth; be objective; test your theories), whereas the grubby or sullied motives are *social* (get promoted, get tenure, attain status). By contrast, economists usually think about these issues in the reverse way; the good motives are generally *social* (help the poor; act in the social interest) and the sullied motives are *individual* (maximize your utility; act in your own self-interest). This means that when those in science studies characterize the invisible hand, it is something that brings about good unintended consequences from grubby social motives, whereas economists, of course, think of it as bringing about good unintended consequences from grubby individual motives.

(as if by an invisible hand[8]) to a socially optimal division of cognitive labor; he is saying, more consistent with mainstream economics, that it is possible to have such unintended optimality, but that specific instances will need to be considered on a case-by-case basis (and, in certain cases, collective intervention may be required).

The best way to see how Kitcher uses economics is to actually work through a part of one of the many formal models that he presents in Chapter 8 of *Advancement*. The one I will examine provides the basic argument for the (possibility of the) cognitive division of labor. The division of labor result is derived as a property of the noncooperative (Nash) equilibrium of a single-prize lottery game played by N self-interested scientists. I will follow the (notationally much tidier) presentation of the argument provided by Roorda (1997).

Let there be two possible theories that scientists might work on: T_1 and T_2. There are N scientists (N > 0) and each scientist works on (is devoted to) one and only one theory. Thus, if we let n be the number devoted to T_1, then N – n will be devoted to T_2. Let A_1 be the assertion that T_1 will ultimately come to be the accepted theory and A_2 the assertion that T_2 will come to be accepted. Because one of the two theories will ultimately come to be accepted we have the following conditional probability relation:

$$P(A_1 | n) + P(A_2 | n) = 1 \quad \text{for all } n \leq N.$$

We also make the reasonable assumption that if no one works on a theory it will never come to be accepted, so:

$$P(A_1 | 0) = P(A_2 | N) = 0.$$

Each scientist will maximize their own expected utility and each knows that the other N – 1 scientists are also maximizing their own expected utility. To simplify the analysis, assume that the scientists are competing for a prize of 1 unit of utility and that prizes in this (lottery) game are allocated in the following way. Once it is known whether T_1 or T_2 wins (comes to be accepted) the scientists who worked on the losing theory get nothing (a payoff of zero utility). Those who worked on the winning theory get their names thrown into a hat and the (1 unit of utility) winner is selected at random; the others working on the winning theory also get nothing. Thus, if n scientists are working on T_1, the expected utility of any

---

[8] In fact, the term "invisible hand" is conspicuously absent in Kitcher, 1993. Although most reviewers – philosophers (Fuller, 1994; Solomon, 1995b) as well as economists (Hands 1995; Mirowski 1995, 1996b) – see Kitcher as making an invisible-hand-type argument, he does not actually use the term.

one of these n scientists is given by EU_1 and the expected utility of any one of the scientists working on T_2 is given by EU_2, where:

$$EU_1 = [1 \cdot P(A_1 | n)]/n \quad \text{and} \quad EU_2 = [1 \cdot P(A_2 | n)]/N - n.$$

The equilibrium concept for the lottery game is a *Nash* equilibrium. A group of n scientists working on T_1 and $N - n$ working on T_2 is a Nash equilibrium if no scientist would defect (change the theory they are working on) given the play of the other scientists. The distribution n will be such a Nash equilibrium if it is both stable upwards and stable downwards; *stable upwards* means that no one will move from T_2 to T_1 (n will not get bigger), whereas *stable downwards* means that no one will move from T_1 to T_2 (n will not get smaller). Thus, the Nash equilibrium distribution n* is characterized by the following two conditions:

$$\frac{1 \cdot P(A_1 | n^* + 1)}{n^* + 1} \leq \frac{1 \cdot P(A_2 | n^*)}{N - n^*} \quad (n^* \text{ is stable upwards})$$

$$\frac{1 \cdot P(A_2 | n^* - 1)}{N - n^* + 1} \leq \frac{1 \cdot P(A_1 | n^*)}{n^*} \quad (n^* \text{ is stable downwards})$$

The Nash equilibrium will exhibit the *cognitive division of labor* if some scientists are working on T_1 and some scientists are working on T_2. Thus, we can say that the equilibrium distribution n* supports the cognitive division of labor if $n^* \neq 0$ and $n^* \neq N$. Notice that $n^* \neq 0$ if $n = 0$ is *not stable upwards* (that is if someone will start working on T_1 whenever $n = 0$) and that $n^* \neq N$ if $n = N$ is *not stable downwards* (that is if some one will quit working on T_1 whenever $n = N$). Thus, the Nash equilibrium distribution n* supports the cognitive division of labor when the following two conditions hold:

$$\frac{P(A_1 | 1)}{1} > \frac{P(A_2 | 0)}{N} \Rightarrow P(A_1 | 1) > \frac{1}{N} \tag{1}$$

$$\frac{P(A_2 | N - 1)}{1} > \frac{P(A_1 | N)}{N} \Rightarrow P(A_2 | N - 1) > \frac{1}{N} \tag{2}$$

The fact that the two conditions on the right-hand side are relatively easy to satisfy thus completes the argument that sullied scientists could (acting noncooperatively) bring about a cognitive division of labor. The Nash equilibrium for Kitcher's model of sullied scientific behavior is consistent with a cognitive division of labor; it shows that such a sullied equilibrium of cognitive labor is possible. This "how possibly" result provides useful information for the idealized epistemic planner – the "philosopher-monarch" who is "organizing the scientific work force so as to promote the collective achievement of significant truth" (Kitcher 1993, p. 305).

While this is certainly not Kitcher's only result, nor is Kitcher the only philosopher employing such arguments in contemporary science theory, this one example gives us a good sense of how these types of arguments generally go. As Kitcher admits, such models involve "toy scientists" in "toy communities" (1993, p. 305), but this is exactly the way that game-theoretic economic models are employed in the analysis of economic problems and policies. Because there are many ways such a game might be specified and the behavior of the individual scientists characterized; there are many different (noncooperative) solution concepts, the possi-bility of mixed strategies, cooperation and coalition formation, dynam-ics, comparative statics; and opportunity to specify higher order games with their own solution concepts (say perfect subgame equilibrium); the possibilities for such models of scientific behavior are effectively un-limited. Now, if a few economists were producing such models, it would be a relatively uninteresting curiosity from the viewpoint of the general theory of knowledge, but Kitcher and others doing this research are influ-ential mainstream philosophers of science. This is not just a curiosity; it is becoming an increasingly popular approach in contemporary philoso-phy of science and (social) epistemology. Such models employ arguments borrowed from economics to salvage normative (particularly scientific realist) philosophy of science from the criticism and potential relativism of the social turn.

> Given his emphasis on the epistemic virtues of diversity, Kitcher's game-theoretic analysis can be assimilated to his larger project of articulating a post-positivist version of scientific realism: by demonstrating that the social forces which affect scientific theory choice can serve to maintain an environment conducive to pro-gress, Kitcher seeks to disarm the potent arguments leveled against realism by social constructivists. (Roorda 1997, p. 217)

Although such models certainly raise a number of difficulties,[9] the point here is just to note that such work clearly involves economics in

---

[9] I examined some of these problems in Hands (1997d). Fuller (1994), Kincaid (1997), Mirowski (1995b, 1996b), Roorda (1997), Solomon (1995b), and Wray (2000) also discuss a number of difficulties with Kitcher's approach. The ESK literature by Kitcher and other philosophers certainly represents fertile ground for further investigation by those working in economic methodology; even though it comes *from philosophers* and directly *employs economics*, the authors seem to be totally unaware (perhaps conveniently unaware) of the literature on the philosophy of economics and economic methodology.

the study of scientific methodology, and as such it is economic methodology under the broader characterization that I have been suggesting.
This work exists because of the issues raised in Chapters 3–6, and it is
considered to be some of the most sophisticated philosophical responses
to those issues. Unlike earlier, more idiosyncratic, attempts by philosophers to employ economic argumentation in the study of scientific
knowledge, these models are being promoted by influential mainstream
philosophers of science and they employ the idiom as well as the ideas
of contemporary economics. These are models in the sense that economists create and use models. Start with a game theoretic model from
industrial organization theory; change firms or players to "scientists"; add
the adjective "epistemic"; make a few more technical changes, and sud-
denly you have a philosophical model of scientific knowledge (and a
philosophically respectable model at that).

8.3.2 Economists and ESK

Although economists are generally motivated by different issues
than philosophers such as Kitcher (Numbers 1–3 on the earlier list of six
for economists, and 4–7 for philosophers) the economics profession
is also engaged in the production of its own version(s) of ESK: the so-
called *new economics of science*. The economists actually involved in
the research employ the adjective "new" primarily to differentiate their
own theoretical approaches – which involve game theory, bounded
rationality, transactions costs, and more attention to institutions – from
the earlier economics of science, but this literature is also "new" in
another sense as well; it is much more explicit about normative epistemology and the cognitive evaluation of the various scientific institutions
it considers. In other words, it is ESK and not just the (old) economics
of science.

Although the field has expanded rapidly in the last few years (Brock
and Durlauf 1999; Dasgupta and David 1994; David 1998; Durlauf 1997;
Leonard 1997; and Wible 1991, 1992, 1998, for example), it is not entirely
new; there actually exists a rather long, if sporadic, tradition of (relatively) mainstream economists discussing the growth of scientific knowledge. In some sense, Hayek (1937) made an early contribution to the
subject, as well as Machlup (1962) and Tullock (1966). This earlier work
is certainly different than the recent literature – in particular, it employs
substantially different theoretical tools – but the underlying questions
are very much the same. Although more recent contributions are often
(though not always) more formal, they are certainly not homogeneous
with respect to their underlying theoretical framework. In addition to
those cited above, one could add Boland (1971, 1989), Diamond (1988b),

and Kahn, Landsburg, and Stockman (1992, 1996) to the list of economic contributions to ESK (and there are undoubtedly others). Economists writing on ESK during the last few decades have clearly reflected a wide range of theoretical perspectives and economic tools (and, for that matter, science policy recommendations).

As in the previous section on the philosophical literature, I will not attempt to summarize the arguments offered by all (or most) of these different economists. Rather, I would like to focus on two specific approaches that seem to be particularly useful in illuminating the range of work that is available within the recent economic literature. These are also two theoretical approaches that provide an effective contrast to both the earlier research by economists and also the work of Kitcher and other philosophers. The first paper I will examine is probably the best-known economic contribution to ESK, and it is the paper that defined the entire field of the *new* economics of science: Partha Dasgupta and Paul David (1994). The second paper is one of James Wible's many contributions to the field, in this case his work on the economic organization of science, the firm, and the marketplace (Wible 1995, and Ch. 9 of 1998).

Dasgupta and David are less interested in providing a formal "model" of scientific activity than in characterizing a broad general framework for research in the new economics of science. Their approach draws on a wide range of resources from within both science theory and economics: earlier research on the economics of science, the Mertonian tradition in the sociology of science, the work of Michael Polanyi (and to a lesser extent Kuhn), evolutionary epistemology, Paul David's earlier research on path-dependency and other topics in economic history (David 1985, 1994, etc.), information theory, and game theory (particularly the theory of dynamic games). The general framework they offer can serve (and in some sense was designed to serve as) a template for a broad range of research activities including: specific formal models of scientific behavior and/or institutions, empirical assessment of particular institutional configurations within science, and the evaluation of various science policies (past or present).

Dasgupta and David start from the position, endorsed by Merton and others, that although science is in fact epistemically special, its specialness is (exclusively) the result of its particularly unique form of social organization and does not, as philosophers have traditionally argued, depend on the cognitive chastity of individual scientists: the "accumulation of reliable knowledge is an essentially social process" (David 1998, p. 16). This particular reliability-producing form of social organization is called *open science*, and the best exemplar of this organization is modern collegiate science: "Activities supported by state funding and the patronage of private foundations and carried on today in universities and public (not-for-profit) institutions" (David 1998, p. 15). The most important distinguishing characteristic of open science is, perhaps not surprisingly, its openness (what Merton called Communism); results are made public as quickly as possible and are generally available for all to see/use/criticize. Open science, thus, contrasts sharply with both "the older secretive hunting of nature's secrets" (David 1998, p. 16) and the more proprietary applied science that characterizes the world of contemporary industrial and military research.

The key to the success and continued reproduction of open science lies in the way that its organizational structure channels individual self-interest into open behavior. The vehicle for this transmission is the *reward system* of open science, and in particular its emphasis on the *priority* of scientific discoveries (another Mertonian concept). One can not receive priority (and, thus, credit) for a particular discovery unless that discovery is made public. The desire for priority thus pulls in two different (but both ultimately virtuous) directions. On the one hand, one does not want to "go public" with results that will be overturned by others – remember, anyone can criticize and/or replicate – and so one has an incentive to conduct extensive empirical tests and/or to engage in any other type of activity that is necessary to verify that results are actually reliable before public disclosure. On the other hand, one gets no credit for being the second person to discover the same thing – the issue is priority – and so one also has an incentive to make discoveries public as quickly as possible. Open science is thus a social organization where the individual's own interest is best served by making reliable results, and only reliable results, public as quickly as possible. The scientific community is a unique type of social organization that monitors and maintains a winner-take-all game among individual scientists, the outcome of which is the production and public disclosure of reliable scientific knowledge.

> In brief, the norm of openness is incentive-compatible with a collegiate reputational reward system based upon accepted claims to priority; it also is conducive to individual strategy choices whose collective outcome reduces excess duplication of research efforts and enlarges the domain of informational complementaries. This brings socially beneficial spillovers among research programs and abets rapid replication and swift validation of novel discoveries. (David 1998, p. 17)

Dasgupta and David's characterization of open science has (industrial organization) implications for the design of an optimal incentive structure for the scientific community. Since the big payoff should go to the winners of key winner-take-games, this "suggests the desirability of a payment schedule which consists of something like a flat salary for entering science, supplemented by rewards to winners of scientific competitions, with the proviso that the better is the performance, the higher will be the reward" (Dasgupta and David 1994, p. 499). This makes open science particularly well suited for universities where teaching compensation covers a portion, or perhaps all, of the flat salary component of scientists' total income.

Although the social organization of collegiate science is responsible for the origin and dissemination of reliable scientific knowledge, the system of open science does not exhaust the totality of the "scientific community." In addition to collegiate science, there exists a parallel system of applied science and technology that is housed primarily in research facilities of specific industries and the military sector. These two different parts of the overall scientific community are complementary and mutually reinforcing, but they have very different social structures. Once scientific knowledge has been publicly disclosed by open science, it becomes *codified information*: "knowledge reduced and converted into messages that can be easily communicated among decision agents" (Dasgupta and David, p. 493). As information, it becomes a nonrival good (use by one individual does not reduce the availability or utility of the good to other individuals) and is thus subject to different kinds of institutional structures and economic reward mechanisms. Given the nonrival character of codified information, proprietary behavior is not necessarily at odds with a requirement of openness and public disclosure as it is in the case of (generally less codified and more tacit) scientific "knowledge"; in other words, once knowledge becomes information it can be allocated efficiently by competitive markets like any other good. Scientific knowledge thus has significant spillovers on the output of goods and services, but the unique social structure of open science and its specific reputation-based reward system is not necessary for the efficient allocation of information (publicly disclosed knowledge) as it is for scientific knowledge itself.

It is important to note that whereas Dasgupta and David discuss the structure of industrial science, that (relatively standard economic story) is not their main point or contribution. They are much more interested in why open science *needs the special and nonmarket institutional structure of collegiate science*, than why applied science and technology does not need such a structure. Although their argument is different, Dasgupta and David's policy implications are more consistent with those of Michael Polanyi than any of the authors discussed above; in particular, their position is quite contrary to the argument for the competitive marketplace of scientific ideas offered by philosophers like Bartley and Radnitzky. Their bottom line is that the institutional structure of science is running *just fine* and is not in need of any major institutional reform, but it is *not* just fine because open science is a competitive market. Rather, science is just fine because open science has a unique institutional structure and reward system that is managed *by the scientific community itself.* Of course, this special community produces and discloses knowledge that (as information) gets picked up and used by the market system to produce new goods and services and thus increase social welfare and economic growth, but the market only starts to work effectively at the second stage. The first stage is the exclusive domain of, and production of reliable knowledge is dependent on, the unique social reward structure of collegiate science.

The political message that emerges from Dasgupta and David's new economics of science is the defense of the *autonomy* of (open) science. The ability of science to produce and disclose reliable knowledge is highly sensitive to changes in the underlying reward structure of science; radical changes – whether they be well-intentioned changes by representative governments attempting to increase the social productivity of science, or the self-interested penetrations of corporate capital and management strategies into the scientific republic – are very likely to upset the delicate balance of individual incentives and reliable collective outcomes that constitute successful open science. Because there are economic benefits from the spillovers into industrial technology, science should continue to be subsidized, but these subsidies, Dasgupta and David would argue, should not come with governmental strings attached; science is a unique social configuration, the management of which should be left essentially to those within the republic of science. The production of scientific knowledge requires an extremely delicate configuration of particular social conditions; leave it alone if you want it to continue working (continue the subsidy, but leave it alone).

> Now, in addition to the benefits that individual scientists may enjoy in being left freer from the vexations of strict supervision, especially from attempts at strict control by inexpert authorities, the exercise of autonomy in the sense of the scientific community's self-governance and control over the research agenda carries some obvious benefits for a society that values the growth of knowledge. (Dasgupta and David, p. 505)

Of course, while the overall policy message is in favor of scientific autonomy, Dasgupta and David would also argue that one of the benefits of a well-worked-out new economics of science would be that it would be able to provide an effective set of tools for the evaluation of various types of incremental adjustments and thereby improve the cognitive efficiency of science. The argument against radical change is certainly not an argument against economically informed institutional tweaking at the margin. It is just that the new economics of science is relatively new and the only clear message at this point is that science is something that is best left to the experts: the scientists themselves.

James Wible has made a number of contributions to the ESK litera-ture,[10] but I will focus on just one specific example; his discussion of the "complements" approach to the economics of science (Wible 1995 and Ch. 9 of 1998). Like Dasgupta and David (and for that matter Kitcher), Wible is interested in using economic analysis to understand how the particular social structure of science produces, or at least facilitates, the growth of scientific knowledge, and, once the mechanism is understood, be able to better evaluate various suggestions for improving the cogni-tive efficiency of science. Also, like the other authors discussed in this section, Wible does much more than simply apply the notion of the invis-ible hand to the marketplace of scientific ideas; in fact, Wible insists even more strongly than other authors, that the simple transposition of argu-ments about the efficiency of competitive markets into the scientific domain is not the right approach to, or the best way to learn from, ESK.

Wible begins with a relatively straightforward, and by now rather familiar, definition of science.

> Science is an array of organizations and processes for producing fundamental knowledge about the nature of the World. The institutions and organizations of science are unique. They are different than anything else observed in either the private or public sector of the economy. (Wible 1998, p. 159)

Science is social, but unlike the characterization offered by many in SSK, science is both unique and exceptional; it gives us "fundamental knowledge about the nature of the World."

Although Wible quickly dismisses the suggestion that science is just a competitive market, he does examine two different economic theories of science: a *substitutes* view and his own *complements* view. The substitutes approach is a general framework for thinking about science that includes a wide range of literature on the economics of science and ESK. Wible elaborates one particular rather sophisticated version of the substitutes

---

[10] Including Wible (1991, 1992, 1994a, 1994b, and 1995). Most of his work on the subject is reprinted in revised form in Wible (1998).

approach and argues that although it does give us some useful insights into the production of scientific knowledge, it does not go far enough. This version of the substitutes approach then becomes the foil for the presentation of his own complements approach.

What Wible calls the substitutes approach to economic questions is the basic notion that nonmarket institutions (government, nonprofits, etc.) serve as *substitutes* for markets. Within this (standard) framework competitive markets and their associated efficiency is the point of departure; when markets fail, then an institutional *substitute* must be found (usually involving government) for the specific market failure. This substitutes framework was clearly reflected in the economics of science literature discussed in Section 8.2. "What the substitutes argumentative structure of economics presents is an ahistorical, evolutionary story regarding the efficiency of competition and attempts to correct the side effects of free markets with government intervention" (Wible 1998, p. 161).

One particular twist on the basic substitutes approach, Wible argues, is the "New Institutionalist" or "transactions cost" literature associated with the work of Armen Alchian and Harold Demsetz (1972), Ronald Coase (1937, 1960), Oliver Williamson (1975, 1985), and others.[11] One of the main theoretical contributions of this literature is the explanation of business *firms* in terms of market failure. The problem of the firm – the question of Why do firms exist? – is answered by arguing that transactions costs prevent markets from working efficiently in the production goods and services. This is a *substitutes theory of institutions* that makes the firm (and other nonmarket institutions like the government) institutional structures that "come into existence to compensate for the inadequacies of markets" (Wible 1998, p. 163).

Although the application of New Institutionalism to the economics of science is relatively new,[12] Wible encourages this substitutes approach as a useful (if incomplete) tool for the economic analysis of scientific knowledge. Instead of asking: Why do firms exist? This approach would ask the question: Why does Science exist? The answer would, of course, be that the institutional structure of science exists in order to minimize the transactions cost that would be associated with the production of scientific knowledge in competitive markets; the institutions of science exist in order "to reduce the transactions cost of pursuing science" (Wible 1998, p. 171). Wible contends that while this is a useful insight – no doubt

---

[11] See note 11 in Chapter 6. Coase's work was also discussed in Chapter 7.
[12] At least two recent dissertations have applied aspects of the New Institutional economics to the study of science: one in economics (Thomas Leonard 1997) and one in philosophy (Shi 2000).

science does have something to do with lowering transactions cost – it is not, as a substitutes theory of scientific institutions would suggest, the entire story.

As an alternative, Wible proposes his own *complements* approach to economic institutions. The complements view, perhaps not surprisingly, sees nonmarket institutions like the government, the firm, and science, as complements to, rather than substitutes for, the competitive market.

> The complements position is broadly characterized by the following propositions: that many institutions may be necessary for a more complete view of economic activity (institutional pluralism) and that no institution plays a preeminent role surpassing that of all other institutions. While the market and the firm are among the most significant institutions of society, neither is primary. (Wible 1998, p. 172)

Although the complementarity of market and nonmarket institutions is important to Wible, it is only one aspect of his overall view of science and scientific knowledge. He argues also, drawing on a wide range of philosophical ideas – Popper, Peirce, Rescher, Hayek, and others – argues that there is a fundamental problem that both types of institutions must solve; it is simultaneously an epistemic problem and an economic problem (actually an epistemic problem that leads to an economic problem). The epistemic problem is that humans face fundamental *epistemic uncertainty* – knowledge is always fallible, uncertain, tenuous, and constantly being revised – this uncertainty leads to the economic (resource allocation) problem of *epistemic scarcity*.

> In an indeterministic world and economy, there exists the continuous creation, destruction, and annihilation of knowledge. The epistemic structure of society and the economy is quite fragile. Fundamental uncertainty exists. A situation of epistemic scarcity is created. (Wible 1998, p. 173)

The solution to the fundamental problem of epistemic scarcity lies in *diversity* (again a familiar theme). The conditions of knowledge acquisition require flexibility and the ability to respond to changing conditions in a variety of different ways. A single institutional structure is too risky when it comes to the production of knowledge; we need institutional portfolio diversification.

> In the complements view, a variety of qualitatively differentiated organizations are essential for resolving epistemic scarcity.

> Humanity cannot depend on just one institution like the market
> or even the primacy of one institution among others. We cannot
> put all of our organizational "eggs" into one institutional basket.
> (Wible 1998, pp. 174–5)

Wible, like others, also emphasizes the *dual* nature of the scientific enterprise. What he calls *primary science* involves a "unique nonmarket structure" (Wible 1998, p. 177) and although he does not provide much detail, it seems that what he has in mind is similar to Dasgupta and David's (or Merton's) characterization of open science. This primary science is contrasted with *secondary science* where there is a more extensive "reliance on markets" (Wible 1998, p. 177). What Wible has in mind regarding a competitive aspect of science seems to be the same industrial and military research discussed by Dasgupta and David. For Wible, nonmarket institutions such as primary science and market-dominated institutions such as secondary science are complements that both serve in their own way to solve the problem of epistemic scarcity; they play different roles, but both are important and neither one should be considered more essential than, or to be a substitute for, the other. Markets matter, but they are only one part of the story, and the other part – primary science – is not just here because of transactions cost or some other source of market failure prevent the market from working in this one particular area. Science is economic – it uses resources and deals with the problem of epistemic scarcity – and it can (and should) be analyzed with the help of contemporary economic theory, but it is not just another example of *either* the free market at work *or* an institution that substitutes for the free market when it fails in particular ways (public goods, externalities, transactions cost, . . .).

Of course, serious criticisms could be raised about various aspects of Wible's analysis. But like the framework of Dasgupta and David, or Kitcher's toy scientists, the issue for us is not the pros or cons of the particular details, but the overarching recognition that there is a substantial amount of work being done in ESK. It is work that begins from the proposition that science is fundamentally social and that the philosophical problems discussed in previous chapters require a serious response; it explicitly characterizes the production and dissemination of scientific knowledge in economic terms; it applies concepts from contemporary economic theory like noncooperative game theory, information theory, and the New Institutionalist economics; and, perhaps most importantly for the literature on economic methodology, completely reverses the arrow that previously ran from science theory to economics.

8.3.3 Alternative Visions of ESK

While the previous sections examined a number of different views, they were all essentially *mainstream* views: mainstream philosophy of science and mainstream economics. Of course, some approaches might be considered more mainstream than others – for instance, one could question whether the New Institutionalism employed by Wible and others is really mainstream economics – but compared to Marxian economics, or (old) institutionalism, or von Mises's version of the Austrian program, all of the ESK discussed thus far (even that written by philosophers) has employed relatively mainstream economics. In fact, one could argue that Kitcher's argument is doubly mainstream; he employs mainstream economics in the immediate service of mainstream philosophy of science.[13]

Although there exists a critical literature that directly challenges the entire project of applying mainstream economics to the study of scientific knowledge,[14] that literature will not be the subject of this section. This section will focus on what might be called an indirect challenge to mainstream-based ESK; the use of relatively nonmainstream economic ideas in the study of scientific knowledge. Granted, the distinction between mainstream and nonmainstream economic ideas is rather fuzzy, but it still can serve as a useful, if imperfect, demarcation line between the literature in this section and work such as that of Kitcher, Wible, and Dasgupta and David. I will first begin with a brief sampling of the existing literature that might be placed within the category of nonmainstream-based ESK, and, second, I will engage in some (perhaps wild) speculation about various projects that could be (or perhaps even are being, undertaken) in this broad area.

One body of literature that involves nonmainstream economics in the study of science is of course the Marxist literature in the history and philosophy of science: Karl Mannheim (1936), the Marxist historians of science discussed in Chapter 5 (Bernal 1939, 1953; Hessen 1931), more recent New Left renditions of the Bernal view (Rose 1994, for example), versions of social epistemology that involve some type of epistemic central planning (Fuller 1988, 1992, for example), and the sociological literature that involves aspects of Marxist theory (Pickering, early Latour

---

[13] At one point, I referred to Kitcher's position as "neoclassically naturalized epistemology" (Hands 1995, p. 615), but that opens the whole debate about whether noncooperative game theory is "really" neoclassical economics. The term "mainstream" should avoid such controversy; noncooperative game theory is (now) clearly part of mainstream economics.

[14] Davis (1997b), Hands (1995, 1997d), Mirowski (1995, 1996b, 1996a), O'Neill (1990), and Sent (1996, 1997b, 1999), for example.

and Woolgar, parts of Actor Network Theory, etc.). Much of this literature has already been discussed in previous chapters.

Another body of literature on scientific knowledge that involves
economic ideas, but not ideas from mainstream economics, are social
exchange models of science that draw on sociological or anthropological
concepts of "exchange," such as gift-giving, that are totally alien to the
way that exchange has traditionally been (and continues to be) characterized within economics. This literature is rather extensive and overlaps
with the sociological literature discussed in Chapter 5, but two influential examples are W. O. Hagstrom (1965 and elsewhere) and P. Bourdieu
(1975 and elsewhere). Although these and similar approaches (particularly Bourdieu) have generated a substantial literature involving
"exchange" theories of knowledge, they seldom appear in economists'
work on science or in the mainstream philosophy of science literature
that involves economics (Mäki 1992a is an exception); one suspects their
absence is primarily a reflection of the radically different theoretical
concepts involved in such approaches.

Yet another relevant literature is the portion of economic history that
considers the "economic conditions" necessary (or at least sufficient) for
the growth of the scientific community. Although some of this literature
is also Marxist in origin, and other parts could be considered "mainstream" economic history, there is also a significant body of historical literature that is neither Marxist nor mainstream and yet it grounds the
capacity to produce scientific knowledge in requisite economic "conditions." An example of such work that is Marxist in orientation, but makes
a very different argument than Hessen and other Bernalists, is Hadden
(1994). Hadden focuses more on the "relations of production," and
argues that the rise of commodity exchange and the associated calcula-
tion of abstract values (prices) in the social domain contributed to the
rise of the mechanistic worldview in the natural domain. A different economic origins story is provided by Poovey (1998). She draws on a wide
range of different perspectives – SSK, recent history of science, elements
of postmodernism, and others – to weave a detailed historical narrative
that forges a relationship between the rise of modern science (particularly the modern concept of a fact) and certain institutions of early
capitalism (particularly double-entry bookkeeping). Poovey provides an
extremely rich history with an extensive discussion of a number of important figures in the history of economic thought, but she is certainly not
the only SSK-inspired author to connect the social configuration of the
scientific community with the achievement of a certain level of economic
development. Shapin (1994), for example, repeatedly emphasizes the
link between "economic ease" and the development of the idea of

"disinterestedness." He argues in effect that economic development pro-vided economic foundations – conditions *in* the economy of production and distribution – for the emergence of Merton's norms within one (ini-tially) small segment of society.[15] Although this topic certainly deserves much more attention than just mentioning a few examples, the point should be quite clear from this brief sampling. There exists a vast body of literature that grounds science in particular *economic conditions* – generally the conditions of surplus-creating capitalism – and while these arguments need not be inconsistent with more mainstream research involving game theory and/or the utility maximizing behavior of indi-vidual scientists, it is actually a separate body of literature (and one that seems to fit quite comfortably with heterodox economics).[16]

Although these three different literatures (and no doubt others) relat-ing economics or visions of the economy to scientific knowledge cur-rently exist, there seems to be a significant unrealized potential in this area. What follows in the remainder of this section is a short list of poten-tial research projects in nonmainstream-based ESK. In certain cases, work on these topics is already underway; in other cases, they are merely research proposals (at least I am not aware that such work is forthcom-ing); in either case, they are all clearly fertile fields for further investiga-tion. Of course, many of these approaches could also be (and have been) combined with game theory or some other more formal modeling strat-egy from contemporary mainstream economics. This list is only sugges-tive of a few of the many possibilities, and the items are not presented in any particular order.

- *Evolutionary Economics*: The body of literature that could rea-sonably be classified as "evolutionary economics" is both enor-mous and extremely diverse.[17] The field overlaps with both institutionalism (going back to at least Veblen 1919) and Aus-trian economics (particularly Hayek and Schumpeter), and it also has a number of contemporary strains that are fairly close to mainstream economics in both emphasis and theoretical tools

---

[15] It is interesting to note that David (1998) discusses the historical conditions for the emer-gence of science but does not link it directly to economic conditions. David offers an eco-nomic analysis of scientific institutions but characterizes the historical emergence of those institutions in essentially social terms.

[16] One could include the growing literature on Big-Science and Cold War technoscience and its relationship to the particular political-economic conditions of the post-World War II era as other examples of this general genre of literature (Mirowski 1999, for example).

[17] See Geoffrey Hodgson's writings on the subject (1993, 1997, or 1998b, for example) for evidence of both the vastness and diversity of the field.

(Alchian 1950; Nelson and Winter 1982; and others). Of course, many economists doing research in ESK have been influenced by (and view their work as an extension of) these contemporary strains of evolutionary economics. But in addition to these established approaches, there also exists a relatively new and rapidly growing literature on evolutionary economics that does not take the standard microreductionist strict-Darwinian approach to evolutionary change (Eldredge 1997). Rather than starting from the individualistic focus of genetic reductionism, this literature grounds its evolutionary economics in macro-oriented evolutionary biology such as the punctuated equilibrium theory of Stephen Jay Gould, Niles Eldredge, and others. While this approach is relatively new (although it does share a family resemblance with institutionalist models of economic change that involve institutions or other collectivities as the units of selection) it does offer the prospect for combining evolutionary epistemology and economics into a version of ESK that (unlike most of the existing literature) does not assume methodological individualism as one of its initial presuppositions. A research program in ESK built on this type of nonreductionist evolutionary economics would not only reflect recent changes in evolutionary biology and connect up with certain heterodox traditions in economics, it might also be capable of taking advantage of recent developments in computational mathematics and dynamical modeling.

- *(Old) Institutionalist ESK*: Related to the literature on nonreductionist evolutionary economics and also Wible's version of ESK, but focusing more on philosophical questions and less on modeling might be a version of old institutionalist ESK that combines Veblenian (or Veblen-Ayres) economics with contemporary neopragmatism. Recall from Chapter 6 that neopragmatists like Rorty are often seen by the philosophical community to be closer to postmodernism and radical relativism than to classical pragmatists like Peirce and Dewey. The main reason for this seems to be that neopragmatists like Rorty insist on keeping their (instrumentalist) evaluation criterion extremely local and contingent; the only way in which the sentence "A is good (or true)" makes any neopragmatist sense is with the addition of something like "in this particular context" or "under these specific contingent conditions." This means that such evaluations are always "relative to" the particular conditions, and, thus, many philosophers consider them to be more relativist-nihilist than pragmatic-useful. Enter (actually reenter) institutionalist economics; recall from the discussion of Ayres's theory of economic development in Chapter 6 that one of the goals of the Veblen-Ayres tradition in institutionalist theory was to put some practical economic meat on Dewey's instrumentalist bones (an effort supported by Dewey). Although it would certainly be a formidable task, it might be possible to reconfigure the Veblen-Ayres economic tradition into a version of ESK that is compatible with (and somewhat derelativizes) contemporary neopragmatism.

- *Hayekian ESK*: Although Hayek's name appears frequently in the ESK literature (in Wible's work, some of the evolutionary economics discussed immediately above, the evolutionary epistemology of philosophers such as Bartley and Radnitzky, etc.), there is certainly room for additional research on a Hayekian version of ESK. Like many working on ESK, "Hayek proposed that we examine the role of various institutions in assisting the creation, discovery, use, conveyance, and conservation of *knowledge*" (Caldwell 1997, p. 1885, emphasis in original), but his perspective has a number of unique features that make it potentially fruitful for additional work in ESK. For one thing, Hayek viewed human behavior as self-interested, and yet he also developed a complex theory of social rule-following that was consistent with this individual rationality (see Vanberg 1994, 1998). Hayek's way of reconciling individual rationality and rule-following might provide some useful insights into the complex relationship between the actions of sullied scientists and the rules of proper scientific method. The Hayekian approach also seems to be consistent with recent developments in the theory of complex adaptive systems. Another important feature of Hayek's approach is that he developed a detailed philosophy of mind/psychology (Hayek 1952) consistent with his view of economics and knowledge. This link between human cognition and ESK does exist in the work of philosophers such as Kitcher and Goldman, but seems to be absent from most of what economists have written on the subject; Hayek's work might be able to provide some missing links.

- *Bounded Rationality in ESK*: There are many different versions of "bounded rationality" being bantered about in contemporary economics (see Conlisk 1996; Rubinstein 1998; Sargent 1993; Sent 1997a, 1998b), many of which bear little resemblance to Simon's original concept (discussed in Chapter 4), but any (or all) of these might be useful in talking about the "rationality" of scientists. In some sense, much of ESK (written by both economists and philosophers) is an attempt to employ the standard *economic* notion of rationality (utility maximization) in the investigation of *scientific* rationality (discovering knowledge). But, if Simon and others are correct, real human rationality is not the same as economic rationality – real humans have limitations on both the amount of information they have available and their computational ability to process that information – they are therefore (at best) only boundedly rational. This leads to an obvious question: If we want to replace methodological rule-following with the rational action of individual scientists, why not model the individual scientists as boundedly rational human beings instead of treating them as fully informed neoclassical economic agents? Of course, there are as many different ways of thinking about how boundedly rational scientists might or might not produce scientific knowledge as there are different conceptualizations of bounded rationality, but it seems that any of them would be a good place to begin a serious research program in ESK.

- *Economic Sociology and ESK*: Finally, there exists an elaborate body of literature on economic sociology (Granovetter and Swedberg 1992; Smelser and Swedberg 1994; Swedberg 1987, 1998, etc.) that could be directed toward the scientific community and scientific knowledge. From the definition of economic sociology – "the application of the frames of reference, variables, and explanatory models of sociology to that complex of activities concerned with the production, distribution, exchange, and consumption of scarce goods and services" (Smelser and Swedberg 1994, p. 3) – the Economic Sociology of Scientific Knowledge would simply need to replace "scarce goods and services" with "scientific knowledge." Now, because economic sociology originated in the work of the sociological big-three – Weber, Marx, and Durkheim – there are assuredly aspects of this approach already embedded in some of the sociological literature on scientific knowledge. And since certain Austrians (Schumpeter) and institutionalists (Veblen) are also cited as progenitors, it could be argued that this approach is subsumed by some of the research areas already suggested. Nonetheless, given that an extensive recent literature exists; it focuses on socially situated actors and the meaningful behavior of those actors; it emphasizes institutions and institutional change as well as production and distribution; and it is often presented as a sociological alternative to New Institutionalist economics; it seems to be an obvious candidate for application in ESK.

8.4 Some Final Thoughts on the Economic Turn

Well, this chapter has covered a lot of ground – from the motivations for the economic turn, to a detailed discussion of some examples from the philosophical and economic literature, to some speculation about a number of nonmainstream research programs that might be undertaken within ESK. Not only has a lot of ground been covered, it is entirely *new ground* for a book on economic methodology. Until very recently no one would have considered including a discussion of the economics of science in a volume on economic methodology (and perhaps some readers still think it is a bad idea), but if one defines economic methodology broadly as any literature connecting economics and the study of scientific knowledge, then such economic studies of the production and distribution of scientific knowledge (particularly those attempting to make normative claims about good and bad knowledge) clearly counts as one (growing) aspect of economic methodology. This chapter also has demonstrated the extent of the existing (and potential) economic penetration into contemporary science theory; there has been an extraordinarily large amount of highly diverse work done in the field, and hopefully the chapter has also demonstrated that there is still a vast amount of work to do and a variety of perspectives to do it from.

All this said, the economic turn does pose a number of issues and concerns for both science studies and the traditional field of economic methodology. Some of these concerns are practical in orientation – who wins and who loses by various moves on the field of science theory – whereas others are more related to traditional philosophical questions. In the last few pages of this chapter I will discuss a few (actually three) of these issues and concerns. Of course these three represent but a small sample of the many questions raised by the economic turn.

Once one opens the study of science to the question of interests and incentives – as opposed to the approach of traditional philosophy of science that assumed that there was a cognitively right thing to do and that scientists would automatically do it – one raises the question of *whose interests are served* by various moves within the field of science theory. In particular, we can ask the question of who might gain or lose from the economic turn. Of course, because the payoffs to winners and losers will depend on which particular version of the vast array of ESKs we are talking about, let's just pick one and focus the discussion on the interests that might be served by that particular version (I leave it to readers to do the exercise with other versions). Let's pick Kitcher's *Advancement* program. Whose interests might be served by the success of this project?

Obviously traditional philosophers of science who are attempting to defuse the epistemically corrosive implications of Kuhn, SSK, and others, and the associated fall of the Legend, would be served by Kitcher's success. His program is sensitive to the social character of science and accepts many of the points raised by the critical literature, and yet saves both the privilege of science and a version of scientific realism. He also accomplishes this in such a way that generally reaffirms the legitimacy of the philosophy of science as an independent epistemic usher. It is equally clear that the scientific community would be served by the success of Kitcher's program. It hasn't been discussed much in previous chapters, but there is currently a Science War going on (Gross and Levitt 1994; Gross, Levitt, and Lewis 1996; Ross 1996; Sokal and Bricmon 1998); funds are scarce and sociologists who debunk the cognitive status of science threaten the livelihood of individual scientists and perhaps ultimately the entire culture of open science. In the words of one sociologist:

> It seems that the "old" positivistic image of science, as an abstract, timeless search for irrefutable facts – ending the pain of uncertainty, the burden of dilemma and choice, separable from "society," and leading inexorably to technical innovations for the good of all – exhibits an apparently puzzling tenacity. But it should not surprise us that this is so. . . . So long as the state remains the main provider of research finance, scientists themselves will hold fast to the old picture, as it has earned them, in times past, access to the political arena and the resources that they need. (Edge 1995, p. 18)

Refuting the relativist claims of many of the sociologists and rhetoricians of science would certain be an advantage to the scientific community's side in the Science Wars.

So it seems that philosophers of science and natural scientists would generally gain from the success of a Kitcher-like program (and that radical debunkers of all stripes would lose), but what about the economics profession? Well, one can tell a winner story or a loser story, but it is not clear which ultimately outweighs the other. The benefits are pretty easy to see. Economists have a wide range of models that can be applied to Kitcher-like projects; papers can be published and dissertations written. Because these arguments will also make their way into the seats of power in contemporary science policy (Congressional subcommittees, NSF, etc.), economists would have the benefit of having an impact on the allocation of scientific resources (as well the total allocation of resources to science versus other things). This all sounds quite good for the economics profession, but there is one problem. The problem is that economics is generally seen as the most "scientific" of the social sciences; economics has the mathematics, the econometrics, the Nobel Prize, and economics courses are taught from textbooks just like the natural sciences. Economics, more than any other social science, has gained from the Legend. Now, of course, a Kitcher-like project intends to save a portion of the Legend, but it does so in what is at best a round-about way (invisible hands, Nash equilibria, and epistemically well-designed incentive schemes). It may be that economics is better served by the traditional view than any substitute for it (even one that economists have a hand in designing). Perhaps simply continuing to endorse the Legend would do much more to serve the interests of economists than whatever contribution the profession might make to ESK.

A second concern is the issue of *reflexivity*. In what sense can economists use a conception of scientific knowledge based on ideas from economics to evaluate the scientific standing of economics or a particular economic theory? Recall (from Chapter 5) how the reflexivity problem emerges within SSK. If the beliefs of scientists are constituted by their social context and not the objective world "out there," then shouldn't this also be true for social scientists doing SSK? If so, in what sense should we believe what these sociologists say about what goes on in natural science "out there"? If all science is a product of the social context in which it is produced, then this must also be true for SSK. The process of debunking undercuts the case for being in the position to debunk. As clear from the earlier discussion of SSK, this is a problem that has been a major concern within the sociological literature, and it is a problem that does not have any easy solution.

Economists doing ESK will certainly run into a similar problem. If scientists are pursuing their own self-interest (reputation, promotion, etc.) then economic scientists must be pursuing their own self-interest as well. Even if one can make the case – via the invisible hand or a story about the epistemic efficiency of the Nash equilibrium within the community of economists – that such self-interested behavior still leads to the right (true, verisimilitudinous, reliable, . . .) results, serious problems remain. First is the simple empirical fact that most economists neither claim, nor believe, that what they are doing is acting in their own narrow self-interest; most economists claim (and believe) they are trying to discover the way things really are in the portion of the economy they are investigating. This empirical fact is a concern, but one can get around it in a number of ways, just like economists can get around the "fact" that managers do not say (or believe) that they set marginal revenue equal to marginal cost. More significantly, the argument that economists are pursuing their own self-interest and not truth or any other epistemic goal, must also apply to the economists writing ESK. Now, one might not initially see that this is a problem, because the same invisible hand (or other optimality producing result) might support true meta-theories about the actions of economists, even though the economists proposing those meta-theories were acting in their own self-interest and not intending to discover the (meta-theoretical) truth, but this leads to an infinite regress. There must now be a meta-meta-theorist that can show how the self-interested behavior of the meta-theorist leads to the meta-theoretical truth in the same way that the meta-theorist demonstrated that the self-interested behavior of economists leads to the truth about economic agents, and so on and so on.[18]

The simple fact is that if one want to "evaluate" something (good or bad, true or false, easy or difficult, . . .), then one needs a standard of evaluation that is based on something other than the thing being evaluated. This is not to suggest that reflexivity is some crippling problem that emerges when economists do ESK and not elsewhere in our intellectual life. All I am saying is that if one believes that a notion of good and bad science derived from ESK can be snapped easily into the traditional normative methodological framework in the same way that say falsificationism or Lakatos's MSRP snapped into it, then they will be sorely surprised. ESK is no worse than any other naturalism in this sense – evolutionary epistemology has difficulty evaluating biological theories; Goldman's reliabilism would have difficulty evaluating theories within cognitive science – but it does raise a whole troublesome class of issues that did not need to be faced when philosophy was clearly on a different (higher) level than the sciences that it was supposed to evaluate.[19]

The final issue is one that actually seems to come down in favor of ESK. As we have seen, all forms of naturalism have difficulty when it comes to normative philosophy of science. We might be able to *describe*

[18] One way out is to break the chain by arguing that economists are not scientists. ESK investigates science and if economics isn't science, then reflexivity never becomes an issue. A more subtle version of this would argue that although economics might be *a type* of science, it is a *different* type than those studied by ESK. This is essentially the argument offered in Stephan and Levin (1996). They argue that their economic analysis of science is not relevant to economics because (1) science is done in teams and economics isn't, (2) grants are not as important in economics as natural science, and (3) priority is assigned differently in economics than natural science. Although it is not clear that Stephan and Levin offer these arguments to get around the problem of reflexivity, that is, nonetheless, the result of their argument.

[19] See Mäki (1999b) for the most detailed examination of the reflexivity issue in the economics of economic knowledge.

scientific behavior in scientific (naturalistic) terms, but how can we make a normative evaluation in such terms? Recall that it is essentially an epistemic version of Hume's guillotine; we cannot deduce an epistemic ought from an "is" any more than we can deduce an ethical ought from an "is." ESK actually puts an interesting twist on this issue: not really a clear solution, but perhaps a less problematic way of thinking about it. An economic view of rules or norms is less alienated from the behavior of the agents that it is applied to than the view of norms inherited from philosophy. In economics, the interesting question about norms involves how they persist, that is, get reproduced: the mechanism by which it is that the agents come to play by this particular set of rules. The general philosophical perspective on norms (ethical or epistemic) is essentially an usher's or a central planner's view; the problem is to find the right rules so agents who play by them will produce the right stuff (the good or the true). For economists, the perspective is different. The question is more about emergence and sustainability; the problem is to understand what the agents must be like so that these particular norms emerge and are sustained as the social outcome of the actions of the relevant agents. Why do people sign contracts: even epistemic ones?

So the characterization of norms and rules is different, what does this have to do with ESK and the traditional problem of extracting norms from naturalistic philosophical programs? Well, two things. First, the economist's notion of norms seems to generate less tension with naturalism than the philosophical concept. On the economist's account, one is not deducing ought from is, one is deducing "this rule emerged" from "no one intended it to happen." Granted, the latter also has its problems, but it seems at least to be a different set of problems than the traditional philosophical issue. Second, and this may be a rather bold empirical claim, but *there never was an epistemic central planning authority.* Whatever rules that scientists have chosen to play by, those rules have emerged from within the context of scientific play. Science was not started by an epistemological philosopher-king who worked out the rules in advance so that when the game was played the epistemically right behavior emerged and we all ended up with antibiotics, satellite TV, and air conditioning. First, there was human activity and then, somehow, the rules of science emerged out of it and were sustained. Perhaps ESK has some real advantages with respect to this particular aspect of post-Legendary science theory.

9

Conclusion

> To think that people trained in logic and philosophy should actually contribute to the solution of major theoretical problems in the sciences sounds presumptuous. Mainly it was naive. The enterprise assumes, quite mistakenly, that one can extract the theories of a science from their disciplinary culture and analyze them in the abstract. Later analytic philosophers of science were thus victims of an assumption they adopted uncritically from their logical empiricist elders. The typical result has been the creation of relatively isolated subdisciplines populated by philosophers and a few scientific sympathizers. The sciences in question have continued to develop following their own dynamics.
>
> [Giere 1999, p. 16]

The previous eight chapters have covered a vast amount of ground and it is now time to take stock and reflect more generally on the overall project. Although the previous chapters have surveyed science theory and economic methodology, and systematically examined various relationships between the two, the title was not "Surveying Methodology and the Literature Relevant to It." The title is *Reflection without Rules*, and that title was designed to convey a two-pronged assertion about the recent methodological literature: (1) that simple rules-based economic methodology has quietly and unceremoniously passed from the scene, and (2) that its disappearance need not be, and has not been, the death knell for philosophical and science-theoretical reflection on, and involvement with, the discipline of economics. In fact, the passage has actually facilitated an extremely fertile harvest of new and interesting reflections on a wide array of broadly methodological topics. The new literature has developed in part because of the space opened up by the failure of rules-seeking methodology, but there are also many other factors. One of these factors is undoubtedly a change in personnel. There is now an entirely new generation of authors on the scene, a generation brought up on postlegendary philosophical perspectives, more willingly inter- and multidisciplinary, and more sensitive to wider intellectual developments. Of course, it is also clear that the upheaval of the 1930s and 1940s, and the reactions it engendered regarding the role of science, philosophy, economics, and rational thought in general, has systematically faded from our collective consciousness. No doubt many of the rule-makers believed they were keeping the barbarians from the gates (Hutchison, for example, has been explicit about this) and their intellectual tone and posture were a response to this role. Perhaps their work was a necessary job well done; perhaps it was the story needed by the powers that be in order to remain the powers that be; and perhaps (my choice) the desire for rules-seeking methodology should be described and understood, not judged. In any case, it is a new century and the intellectual world has changed. A much broader type of economic methodology is thriving despite the failure to find the narrow set of rules that seemed to be the single-minded task of mid-twentieth-century methodological discourse.

Given the quiet demise of rules-based methodology, and given the explosion of work documented in Chapters 7 and 8 (and scattered about in the "economic connections" discussions in Chapters 3–6), one option would be to retain a narrow definition of economic methodology and simply declare the field to be *dead*; the recent research could then be divided up and classified under existing categories: sociology of science, philosophy of science, rhetorical studies, history of economic thought, social epistemology, or whatever. I obviously do not endorse this position. My argument is that we simply abandon the narrow rules-based definition of economic methodology and redefine the field to be any literature that *substantively involves both economics and science theory*; on this definition economic methodology is not only alive, but alive and well. Although I have not thus far introduced a new name for this broader field of methodological inquiry, I would like to do so here in the conclusion. I will refer to this newly expanded field as *the new economic methodology*. I must admit to feeling somewhat uneasy about the introduction of a new appellation. Touting "the new X" raises some obvious questions. So why the name change? Who cares what it is called? Let's just get on with doing it. In a sense I agree. When philosophers of science use economic arguments in their investigations of scientific knowledge, or those in SSK employ economic argumentation in the sociological study of scientific knowledge, nothing is gained by insisting that they are "really doing the new economic methodology." No, this is not my goal. My motivation is, I think, both less presumptuous and far simpler.

There are basically three reasons for talking about the new economic methodology. The first reason is by far the simplest and most straightforward. I simply *need a term for* all of the literature discussed above. There is a massive, growing, and extremely interesting literature that involves both economics and contemporary science theory, and it would be nice to have a single term to refer to it all. The new economic methodology seems to be such a term. Second, I think the term "new economic methodology" draws our attention to the passing of the old[1] methodology and I personally think that is a useful thing. As someone who spent many years trying to knock down individual rules-based approaches one shot at a time, it is a relief to know that the background machinery that kept pumping out potential targets has finally broken down. But I realize this is too personal. The point is really that the old narrow methodology was quite uninteresting to almost everyone other than a relatively small set of economists. A broader approach will be (is) far more appealing to a much wider range of scholars and the name change will help signal that it's not the same old game. Finally, and most significantly, the name change alerts all the different authors, writing to different audiences, and trained in different fields, that perhaps something common is going on: something that warrants investigation. Consider, for example, philosophers of science such as Kitcher and others who are employing economics in their philosophical work. These authors write as if philosophical questions have never been raised about the scientific standing of economic theory; it is one thing when economists fail to ask such questions – it is often frustrating to methodologists, but at least it is understandable – it is much less understandable when philosophers of science seem to be oblivious to two hundred years of methodological debate. Perhaps connecting all of these disparate, but related, domains of inquiry under a single new rubric will contribute to the mutual recognition of related efforts and thus help to facilitate effective cross-fertilization. Perhaps this is too much to ask, but I do not see how a name change could possibly hinder such efforts.

---

[1] One needs to be careful with the use of the adjective "old" in this context. As I emphasized in the discussion of Millian methodology in Chapter 2, and I will elaborate in more detail below, shelf-based methodology is primarily a mid-twentieth-century phenomenon and, thus, in many ways the "new" methodology actually has much more in common with the prepositivist methodological "tradition" than with its immediate predecessor.

So I am going to call it the new economic methodology; it is up to
readers to decide if the label sticks (and/or does any useful work). In this
concluding section I will simply reflect a bit on two aspects of the overall
project of the new economic methodology. First, I would like to highlight
a few of the many "lessons" learned from the new literature and the
events leading up to it. The following section provides a rather long
list of some of these lessons. Many of the items on the list were stated
explicitly (and often) in preceding chapters, whereas others were perhaps
implicit in the previous discussion but not expressly delineated. The list
emphasizes broad general features of contemporary science theory and
the new economic methodology, rather than specific positions or particular views, and I have not included references in the list (both specifics
and references are copiously provided in the previous eight chapters).
These "lessons" are not presented in order of importance, or in order of
appearance in previous chapters. The only order – and it is a weak order-
ing at best – is to start with items that should be relatively noncontro-
versial (at least after the preceding chapters) and then slowly move into
areas where there is less consensus. The final section will try to respond
to a few of the new literature's potential critics and to shine some light
on the road ahead. The road to the new methodology is not without
(fresh) potholes, and it seems useful to illuminate them as quickly and
clearly as possible.

9.1 Lessons from the New Economic Methodology

- The Received View and the Legend are gone. They are
  not available to be used as economic methodologists have
  attempted to use them in the past. There is nothing serviceable
  on the shelf. This means that a certain type of rules-based
  methodology – that which relied on the shelf of scientific philosophy – is no longer available. This is not an argument that we
  "should" or "ought" to do something different; should and ought
  suggest that a choice is involved, and we have no choice in this
  matter; the cupboard is bare. Of course, there are many other
  choices – many choices about what to do now that the shelf is
  empty – but this one particular version of rules-based methodology is no longer available.
- The search for a few narrow methodological rules that will definitively differentiate good scientific economics from other stuff
  (nonscience, nonsense, noncognitively-meaningful discourse,
  muck, or whatever) has faded away and is no longer the main
  subject of methodological writing. This is not to say that it has
  totally disappeared, or that it has been definitively "over-

thrown"; this is not how changes take place in such fields. Patricia Churchland's remark that opened Chapter 4 – "Paradigms rarely fall with decisive refutations; rather, they become enfeebled and slowly lose adherents. . . . But many of us sense that working within 'the grand old paradigm' is not very rewarding" (1987, p. 546) – applies to the grand old paradigm of economic methodology as well. This change is, of course, related to the first lesson – the empty shelf – but it is a separate issue. The loss of the shelf means that *one particular source* of rules is no longer available, this second lesson is about *a more general loss of interest* in finding narrow rules (whatever their source).

- Not only has the search for a few simple rules faded from the methodological literature, it is reasonably clear from the discussion of the Millian tradition in Chapter 2, and elsewhere, that the narrow rules-based view of economic methodology was itself somewhat of an historical aberration. The "traditional" rules-based view of economic methodology was not really the traditional view in a wider sense – it wasn't Mill's view, or Cairnes's, or Neville Keynes's, or, for that matter, Robbins's or Hayek's. It was a particular way of thinking about economic methodology that emerged in the middle of the twentieth century; this change was of course related to the impact of positivism and the Received View but also a number of other factors and conditions, including the social experiences of the interwar period, as well as the stabilization of economic science around the twin towers of Walrasian neoclassicism and Keynesian macroeconomics.

- The Legend is gone and no replacement seems to be anywhere in sight, but there are some identifiable general features that emerge from within the diverse literature of contemporary science theory. In general science theory is antifoundationalist, naturalistic, sensitive to issues of theory-ladenness and underdetermination, and acutely attuned to the social character of science. These things of course have had, and will continue to have, a major influence on the literature of the new economic methodology.

- The studies that make their way into the new methodological literature are much more careful about the details of the economics being examined, whether it be in the history of economic thought or studies of contemporary practice. Following the approach of constructivist SSK and contemporary history of science, those studying various areas of economics with an eye toward philosophical or methodological insight are increasingly likely to look very carefully at one particular episode, or set of results, or paper, or research team. There are fewer studies of the "neoclassical revolution" or "the Keynesian revolution" and more emphasis on detailed investigations of particular sites of economic knowledge production. The resulting history seems to be simultaneously deeper and richer. This is not to say that historians of economic thought have not traditionally engaged in careful and detailed historical work; they have. The point is more about the *kind* of studies that were used to exhibit methodological insights; those were often fairly quick fly-overs of the relevant history. The problem was that whereas certain historians of economic thought were producing thick histories – histories that emphasized complexity, contingency, and the importance of a wide range of different factors and influences – such histories were far too messy to be of any help to those pursuing the (old) methodological goal of finding a few neat and tidy rules for the proper conduct of economic science. The change in methodological focus has effectively dissolved this tension between thick history and methodological inquiry.

- Of course, not having the Received View's shelf of scientific philosophy does not in any way mean that disciplinary philosophy is off limits to those trying to make sense of economic science. Philosophy has not entirely left the stage: just one particular narrow brand of philosophy of science. As the discussion of pragmatism, postmodernism, and feminist epistemology in Chapter 6 made clear, as well as much of the recent methodological work examined in Chapter 7, philosophical ideas continue to play an important role in the new economic methodology. It is just that a much wider range of philosophical ideas are now (again) available for consideration. In addition to involving a wider range of philosophical ideas, those ideas are used more selectively, and are more likely to be reconfigured for a particular problem or concern. This is much closer to the role that philosophy played in nineteenth-century methodological debates than the role it played during the heyday of the Received View.

- The use of a wider range of philosophical resources also reintroduces a number of philosophical ideas that were considered to be off limits in methodology just a few decades ago.

- Metaphysics matters: Metaphysics and ontology can now be seriously discussed within economic methodology without the accompaniment of positivist finger wagging. This is particularly clear from the discussion of naturalism in Chapter 4 and the examination of various version of realism in Chapter 7, but metaphysics surfaced elsewhere as well.

- Pragmatism is back; positivist-inspired philosophy is no longer the only game in town when it comes to "scientific" philosophy. As Chapter 6 argued, this has a number of effects on contemporary science theory and the associated work in economic methodology. The revival of pragmatism also has affected methodological discourse in ways that are much more subtle; most important, there has been a change in general philosophical tone. When the Received View was in sole possession of the epistemic high ground, the only options seemed to be the binary choice of Received View *or* relativism (or a slippery slope toward relativism). Now there are other options; unwillingness to accept the Legend does not mean giving up on science as a unique (and uniquely useful) social organization or method of belief determination.

- Ethics also has reentered the discussion of how philosophy and economics interact. Because the focus has been science theory, the recent literature on ethics and economics was not given any serious attention in the preceding chapters, but it is clearly a growing field and it is also clear that the revival is due, at least in part, to the loosening of the positivist grip. It is not surprising that economics was viewed as (or asserted to be) totally disconnected from ethics in a philosophical environment where ethical discourse was deemed "meaningless." Naturalist and pragmatic moves, along with the general erosion of the "science" versus "nonsense" bifurcation, has opened new space for the philosophy of ethics, which not only seems to be alive and well, but busy cross-breeding with economics in creative ways.

- Philosophy of mind matters to discussions about economics in ways that it hasn't in years. Mill was certainly aware of the importance of the philosophy of mind to economics, and struggled to make the various parts of his intellectual vision – epistemology, psychology, and economics – fit together, as did Robbins, Hayek, Simon, and others (with varying degrees of success). As the research examined in

Chapter 4, Rosenberg's discussion of folk psychology, the explicit attention to the role of intentionality in Lawson's critical realism, and a number of other topics all suggest, these issues are clearly back on the methodological table.

■ Philosophy of mathematics matters to the relationship between mathematics and economic theory. There was a time in methodological debate when there seemed to be just two sides: the group claiming there was "too much" mathematics in economics, and those who thought that the discipline's scientific status was monotonically increasing in the use of mathematics. As Weintraub's discussion of Lakatos's philosophy of mathematics, the structuralists' set theoretic reconstructions of economic theories, various historical papers on the role of Bourbakian mathematics in the evolution of general equilibrium theory, and many other works emphasize, it is not just a question of more or less. The role that mathematics plays in any particular area of economics depends on the kind of mathematics it is, the historical context and interests involved in its promotion, as well as the philosophical notions that undergird the specific mathematical project.

• In addition to all of this philosophical diversity within the methodological literature, there is also an increased tendency to just go it alone with respect to philosophy. As many of the examples from the end of Chapter 7 attest, those writing in the new economic methodology often deny that much help can be found in what philosophers (or even historians or sociologists) have written about science theory. There is a massive literature on scientific realism, but Mäki and others argue that such literature provides very little help in making sense of realism in economics. So, too, for recent work on "models"; there is an extensive literature analyzing the role of models in natural science, but Morgan and others argue that it misses the way that models work (particularly mediate) in economics. In these cases, the authors are not rejecting the importance of philosophical issues and concerns, but they are rejecting the claim that methodologists can effectively use philosophers' (or others') answers to these issues and concerns in any prepackaged way. Those doing economic methodology need to look very carefully at what goes on in economics and not try to force the discipline into the procrustean bed of science theory that was initially concerned with natural science. This is, of course, true of Legend philosophy of science, but the point is wider than just the rejection of the shelf of scientific philosophy. The point is that those looking at economics are increasingly likely to find their own answers to questions about economics (even "philosophical" questions about economics) rather that borrowing from *any* existing approach to scientific knowledge.

- The tendency of economic methodologists to go it alone is consistent with recent trends within the philosophy of science; not only is the Received View gone, the whole idea of *a single* scientific method has increasingly been displaced. The current themes within even mainstream philosophy of natural science are disunity, pluralism, and diversity. Naturalism shifts the focus from a single foundation for all science to a variety of relatively stable portions of our overall web of belief. Of course, as suggested by the discussion of Neurath in Chapter 3, elements of such pluralism and naturalism existed within positivism, but these elements were not the aspects of positivism that had a significant impact on the literature in economic methodology.

- The idea that science is social, from Kuhn, to SSK, to social epistemology, also introduces a fundamental change in the relationship between philosophy of science and the social sciences. There was a time during the high tide of the Received View when the philosophy of social science (any social science) was relegated to the status of second-class philosophical citizen. But, if the particular epistemic properties of scientific knowledge are not a result of individual scientists following narrow methodological rules but rather come about as a result of the social structure and characteristics of scientific communities, then the best handle for understanding scientific knowledge in general would seem to come from the social sciences. The social sciences, thus, change from being the epistemic underclass to playing a key role in the explanation of how scientific knowledge comes to exist at all. This role reversal seems to be an obvious point and yet it also seems to elude most of the philosophers of science who employ economics, as well as (and this is even a bigger surprise) most of the philosophers working in the field known as the "philosophy of the social sciences."

- The relationship between "science" and "society" is far more complex than the Legend would have us believe. Science is fundamentally social, but it goes deeper than that; scientific knowledge is not one thing, and human interests something else. From Kuhn, to SSK, to pragmatism, to feminist epistemology: knowledge and interests are deeply intertwined; or to put it alternatively, "interests" are not separate from "knowledge-producing interests." So, too, when the relevant interests are economic. As I have repeatedly emphasized, the relationship between political economy and epistemology is a much more complex relationship than once thought (or we were willing to admit). In case after case, philosophers have characterized scientific knowledge in ways that accommodates their particular social, political, and political economic commitments; whereas views about the character of scientific knowledge come to predominate in part because of how they fit with various social, political, and economic forces. In Shapin and Shaffer's apt phrase: "Solutions to the problem of knowledge are solutions to the problem of the social order" (1985, p. 332). Or, to put it more in terms of the shelf of scientific philosophy: there never was a pristine shelf out there for economists to use; it was always, at least partially, in here.

9.2 A Few Issues of Concern

In this final section, I would like to respond to a couple of the most obvious concerns about the new economic methodology. These remarks can be viewed as an effort to preempt potential criticism and/or as an effort to illuminate a few of the potential potholes that lie in the road immediately ahead. As the previous list (or for that matter the whole book) should make clear, I am optimistic about most of the existing work within the new economic methodology as well as the potential for future research. There is a whole new world of interesting possibilities and I hope that in some small way this book will help recruit participants for this exciting new methodological endeavor. Nonetheless, despite my global optimism, I also think there will be groups that are opposed, and that it is useful to point out a few of the problems that might lie ahead: forewarned is forearmed.

- First is the question of whose interest is served (or rather not served) by the new economic methodology? Although it seems to be a bandwagon that many could join with benefit to all, I believe there are two groups of economists who may be (and in certain cases have been) resistant to a broader methodological turn. These groups are important because their work taken together represents the preponderance of the methodological literature since World War II; in a sense, they were the ones who kept "methodology" alive in the dark days between the 1930s and the recent revival. The two groups are *heterodox economists* and the *rules-seeking methodologists* (particularly falsification-ists) who have been critical of mainstream practice. Although these two groups represent a wide range of different views about the kind of theorizing that economists *should do*, they share a very common vision regarding the *critical importance of economic methodology for identifying problems* in the practice of mainstream economic science. It is quite likely that both groups will have the same problem identifying with, and participating in, the new economic methodology. The problem is that the new methodology does not seem to provide a position from which to *criticize* the practice of economists; the new methodology appears to have lost its prescriptive bite. Since the old economic methodology provided strict rules – particularly rules gleaned from positivist or falsificationist philosophy of science – it could be used prescriptively to critique the practice of mainstream economists. The new methodology seems much less willing to be enrolled in this critical task. These two groups warrant a separate response; I will start with heterodox economists.

■ There are a number of responses to heterodox economists who might resist the new economic methodology. First, it is clear that the old methodology didn't really work very well for the economic heterodoxy. It didn't work for a variety of reasons, but one of the most important is that heterodox approaches do not generally stand up any better to a positivist or falsificationist critique than mainstream economics. Of course, as the last forty years of science theory from Kuhn, to SSK, to the naturalist turn, all demonstrate, *no science lives up to such standards*, but that is not the point. The point is that falsificationism (for example) doesn't serve the interests of heterodox economists because the same tough standards can be used to indict heterodox theory. Second, turning to the benefits of the new economic methodology, one has only to leaf through the last eight chapters to find a myriad of connections between the new approach and heterodox economics. The new methodology does not freeze out heterodox theory; in fact, it opens the possibility to a widely expanded role. Heterodox influences have been shown in several different aspects of contemporary science theory: Marxist economics in SSK and ESK; Simon's bounded rationality and cognitive science; institutionalism and pragmatism; feminist epistemology and economics; and on and on. There is certainly not any reason for heterodox economists to fear the new economic methodology; the old methodology was a powerful weapon, but one that was just as likely to blow up in the user's face as to hit the intended target, and the new methodology represents fertile ground with numerous opportunities for heterodox involvement.

■ The response to the critical rules-seeking methodologists is more difficult. On the one hand, this group is responsible for tilling the ground that has made available the new methodological harvest; on the other hand, the new methodology suggests that such efforts are no longer needed. Thanks, but step aside, doesn't seem to be the best basis for rapprochement. The key argument of this traditional position has been that mainstream economics needs to "clean up its act"; it needs to do more serious empirical testing and engage in less abstract mathematical modeling. If rules-seeking methodologists have a replacement in mind, it is less likely to be a radical new economic theory than simply a change in emphasis more in the direction of applied and empirically testable economic theories (often more Marshallian micro and more Keynesian macro). The first response to this group is a question that is pretty obvious but doesn't sound very conciliatory: "So what do you have to lose"? Even the research of these same methodologists suggest that despite all of the *strict rules* offered by falsificationist and positivist philosophy of science the economics profession hasn't paid any attention to, and essentially doesn't give a whit about, such rules. As Ron Giere put it in the quote that opened this chapter: "The sciences in question have continued to develop following their own dynamics" (1999, p. 16). One suspects that if somehow an alien time traveler could remove all traces of "falsificationism" from the historical record – exorcise it completely from our minds and documents – *economics would look exactly the same.* The prescriptive methodological "bite" seems to be more of an imperceptible nibble. But this impactive failure is just one side of the coin; the other is to suppose economists did respond; suppose they did reject all theories that were empirically falsified or did not consistently predict Lakatosian novel facts. *Nothing would be left standing*; there would be no economics. Of course, contemporary science theory clearly demonstrates that no science would be left standing if judged by such methodological rules. Strict rules such as falsificationism draw a clear line in the sand; the problem is that every science that has ever existed natural or social ends up on the nonscience side. How is it that strict methodological rules can be used to keep the barbarians from the gates, when the rules do not allow you make *any* meaningful distinction between the very best science and the activities of the worst barbarians? Let it go; however well intended it was, this whole strict-rules project just hasn't done what those who embraced it wanted it to do. Although these remarks seem rather negative – why the old methodology didn't work – there are also many positive things about the new economic methodology. Although certain parts of the new methodological literature eschew any discussion of normative methodological appraisal, that is certainly not the case for all authors and all approaches. Many of the naturalistic projects, various versions of realism, constructive empiricism, certain projects within ESK, Mertonian approaches to the sociology of science, certain brands of feminist epistemology, and others, allow for some type of normative or prescriptive evaluation of the scientific endeavor. In fact, trying to preserve an element of normative advice within the context of a post-Legend, socially sensitive, naturalistic framework has been *the main research goal of philosophers of science* during the last few decades. The general attitude of philosophers of science has been: "Okay, positivism is dead, but we do not accept relativism as the only alternative; so let's put our shoulder to the wheel and figure out what a reasonable middle ground might look like." It would be nice to see economic methodologists of the critical rules-seeking persuasion follow this lead.

• Although certain contributors to recent science theory, including almost all of the philosophers of science involved, are seeking a kind of middle ground that will recover (or salvage) some aspect of normative epistemology, those working in the new economic methodology need to be aware of how difficult this task will be. One approach to the question has been to retain the basic idea of normative philosophy of science, but to weaken the notion of normativity involved in the analysis; another approach, and the one that is most likely to involve economics, is to move to a social epistemology that continues to make epistemically normative evaluations but makes them on the social structures and organizations involved in science, rather than on the behavior (rule-guided or otherwise) of individual scientists. Both of these approaches recognize the sociality of science and, thus, both approaches potentially involve interaction with, and perhaps even the direct employment of, ideas from economics, but there are a number of issues that emerge from these research projects that did not exist in the earlier approaches to normative philosophy of science. One issue is reflexivity. If economics is directly involved in our understanding of the general nature of scientific knowledge then how could such scientific understanding play a role in the normative evaluation of economic science. As my remarks at the end of Chapter 8 suggest, this is not a problem that is necessarily any worse for economics than for sociology, cognitive science, evolutionary biology, or any other discipline involved in naturalized epistemology, but it is a problem that surfaces in the application of any new normative philosophy of science (however weak or social it might be) to economics, and it is a problem that did not exist with earlier approaches. A second issue is the interpretation of "the social." One of the issues that separates various views within the sociology of science and SSK is the question of the social – how it is defined, characterized, the role it plays, whether it can be reduced or not, how (or if) it operates causally, and so on (recall the chicken debate in Chapter 5) – this issue also separates SSK from various ESKs, and differentiates various approaches within ESK. The problem is, of course, that once one starts to talk about the role of the social in the production of anything, including scientific knowledge, then one opens up three hundred years of debate within social science and the philosophy of social science regarding the nature, role, character, and reduction of the social (and, correspondingly, the individual). Again, this is no more an issue in the discussion of economics within the new methodology, or the employment of economics within contemporary science theory, than elsewhere, but it is a whole new set of controversies that didn't seem to be on the table in the earlier framework. These are important problems; they are not the only problems, and they are hopefully not insurmountable problems, but they are good things to keep in mind as we move forward down the new methodological road.

There are, of course, many more issues raised by the new economic methodology, and many other responses to various critics, but this seems to be sufficient for the purpose at hand. In the above chapters, I have tried to provide both a detailed survey and a better understanding of the complexity of economic methodology and contemporary science theory. I have also argued for changing the subject; or, to be more accurate, I have argued that the subject has been changed and I have admitted being pleased about that change. In the spirit of contemporary naturalism, I have attempted to convince the reader that certain processes are successfully at work in methodological discourse (as in science) and that our understanding of the process in general is best when conditioned by an understanding of those specific processes.

REFERENCES

Achinstein, Peter and Barker, Stephen F., eds. 1969. *The Legacy of Logical Positivism.* Baltimore, MD: Johns Hopkins University Press.

Agassi, Joseph. 1988. *The Gentle Art of Philosophical Polemics.* La Salle, IL: Open Court.

Agassi, Joseph. 1993. *A Philosopher's Apprentice: In Karl Popper's Workshop.* Amsterdam: Rodopi.

Agassi, Joseph. 1998. "To Salvage Neurath." *Philosophy of the Social Sciences* 28: 83–101.

Ahonen, Guy. 1989. "On the Empirical Content of Keynes' *General Theory*." *Ricerche Economiche* 43: 256–67.

Ahonen, Guy. 1990. "A 'Growth of Knowledge' Explanation to the Response to Chamberlin's Theory of Monopolistic Competition." *Research in the History of Economic Thought and Methodology* 7: 87–103.

Alchian, Armen. 1950. "Uncertainty, Evolution and Economic Theory." *Journal of Political Economy* 58: 211–22.

Alchian, Armen A. and Demsetz, Harold. 1972. "Production, Information Costs, and Economic Organization." *American Economic Review* 62: 777–95.

Amariglio, Jack. 1998. "Poststructuralism." In *The Handbook of Economic Methodology*, ed. J. B. Davis, D. W. Hands, and U. Mäki, 382–8. Cheltenham: Edward Elgar.

Amariglio, Jack and Ruccio, David. 1994. "Postmodernism, Marxism, and the Critique of Modern Economics." *Rethinking Marxism* 7: 7–35.

Amariglio, Jack, Resnick, Stephen, and Wolff, Richard D. 1993. "Division and Difference in the 'Discipline' of Economics." In *Knowledges: Historical and Critical Studies in Disciplinarity*, ed. E. Messer-Davidow, D. R. Shumway, and D. J. Sylvan, 150–84. Charlottesville: University Press of Virginia.

Apel, Karl-Otto. 1981. *Charles S. Peirce: From Pragmatism to Pragmaticism.* Atlantic Highlands, NJ: Humanities Press.

Archibald, G. C. 1979. "Method and Appraisal in Economics." *Philosophy of the Social Sciences* 9: 304–15.

Ariew, R. 1984. "The Duhem Thesis." *British Journal for the Philosophy of Science* 35: 313–25.

Aronowitz, Stanley. 1996. "The Politics of the Science Wars." In *Science Wars*, ed. A. Ross, 202–25. Durham, NC: Duke University Press.

Arrow, Kenneth J. 1962a. "The Economic Implications of Learning by Doing." *Review of Economic Studies* 29: 155–73.

Arrow, Kenneth J. 1962b. "Economic Welfare and the Allocation of Resources for Invention." In *The Rate and Direction of Inventive Activity*, ed. R. R. Nelson, 609–26. Princeton, NJ: Princeton University Press.

Arrow, Kenneth J. and Debreu, Gerard. 1954. "Existence of an Equilibrium for a Competitive Economy." *Econometrica* 22: 265–90.

Arrow, Kenneth J. and Hahn, Frank H. 1971. *General Competitive Analysis*. San Francisco: Holden-Day.

Ashmore, Malcolm. 1989. *The Reflexive Thesis: Wrighting the Sociology of Knowledge*. Chicago: University of Chicago Press.

Ashmore, Malcolm, Mulkay, Michael, and Pinch, Trevor. 1989. *Health and Efficiency: A Sociology of Health Economics*. Milton Keynes: Open University Press.

Ayer, A. J. 1946. *Language, Truth, and Logic*, 2nd ed. New York: Dover.

Ayer, A. J. 1967. "Man as a Subject for Science." In *Philosophy, Politics, and Society*, 3rd series, ed. P. Laslett and W. G. Runciman, 6–24. New York: Barnes & Noble.

Ayer, A. J. 1990. *The Meaning of Life*. New York: Charles Scribner's Sons.

Ayer, A. J., ed., 1959. *Logical Positivism*. New York: Free Press.

Ayres, Clarence E. 1952. *The Industrial Economy: Its Technological Basis and Institutional Destiny*. Boston: Houghton Mifflin.

Ayres, Clarence E. 1961. *Toward A Reasonable Society*. Austin, TX: University of Texas Press.

Ayres, Clarence E. 1962. *The Theory of Economic Progress: A Study of the Fundamentals of Economic Development and Cultural Change*, 2nd ed. New York: Schocken Books.

Baars, Bernard J. 1986. *The Cognitive Revolution in Psychology*. New York: The Guilford Press.

Bacharach, Michael. 1989. "The Role of 'Verstehen' in Economic Theory." *Ricerche Economiche* 43: 129–50.

Backhouse, Roger E. 1991. "The Neo-Walrasian Research Program in Macroeconomics." In *Appraising Economic Theories: Studies in the Methodology of Scientific Research Programs*, ed. M. Blaug and N. De Marchi, 403–26. Aldershot: Edward Elgar [reprinted as chapter 2 of Backhouse 1998a].

Backhouse, Roger E. 1992a. "The Constructivist Critique of Economic Methodology." *Methodus* 4: 65–82.

Backhouse, Roger E. 1992b. "Rejoinder: Why Methodology Matters." *Methodus* 4: 58–62.

Backhouse, Roger E. 1993. "Lakatosian Perspectives on General Equilibrium Theory." *Economics and Philosophy* 9: 271–82 [reprinted as chapter 4 of Backhouse 1998a].

Backhouse, Roger E. 1994a. "The Lakatosian Legacy in Economic Methodology." In *New Directions in Economic Methodology*, ed. R. Backhouse, 173–91. London: Routledge [reprinted as chapter 5 of Backhouse 1998a].

Backhouse, Roger E. 1994b. "The Fixation of Economic Beliefs." *Journal of Economic Methodology* 1: 33–42 [reprinted as chapter 15 of Backhouse 1998a].

Backhouse, Roger E. 1995a. "A Decade of Rhetoric." *Journal of Economic Methodology* 2: 293–311 [reprinted as chapter 8 of Backhouse 1998a].

Backhouse, Roger E. 1995b. "Comment on Steedman." In *Heterodox Economic Theories: True or False?*, ed. F. Moseley, 23–40. Aldershot: Edward Elgar.

Backhouse, Roger E. 1995c. "An Empirical Philosophy of Economic Theory." *British Journal for the Philosophy of Science* 46: 111–21 [reprinted as chapter 16 of Backhouse 1998a].

Backhouse, Roger E. 1997a. *Truth and Progress in Economic Methodology*. Cheltenham: Edward Elgar.

Backhouse, Roger E. 1997b. "An 'Inexact' Philosophy of Economics?" *Economics and Philosophy* 13: 25–37 [reprinted as chapter 17 of Backhouse 1998a].

Backhouse, Roger E. 1997c. "Critical Realism: A Critique." (forthcoming).

Backhouse, Roger E. 1998a. *Explorations in Economic Methodology: From Lakatos to Empirical Philosophy of Science.* London: Routledge.

Backhouse, Roger E. 1998b. "Lakatos and Economics." In *Explorations in Economic Methodology: From Lakatos to Empirical Philosophy of Science*, 39–55. London: Routledge.

Backhouse, Roger E. 1998c. "Rhetoric and Methodology." In *Explorations in Economic Methodology: From Lakatos to Empirical Philosophy of Science*, 103–19. London: Routledge.

Backhouse, Roger E. 1998d. "Should Economists Embrace Postmodernism?" In *Explorations in Economic Methodology: From Lakatos to Empirical Philosophy of Science*, 134–45. London: Routledge.

Backhouse, Roger E. 1998e. "Rhetoric." In *The Handbook of Economic Methodology*, ed. J. B. Davis, D. W. Hands, and U. Mäki, 419–22. Cheltenham: Edward Elgar.

Baert, Patrick. 1996. "Realist Philosophy of the Social Sciences and Economics: A Critique." *Cambridge Journal of Economics* 20: 513–522.

Balzer, Wolfgang. 1982. "A Logical Reconstruction of Pure Exchange Economics." *Erkenntnis* 17: 23–46.

Balzer, Wolfgang. 1985. "The Proper Reconstruction of PPE." *Erkenntnis* 23: 185–200.

Balzer, Wolfgang. 1998. "Set-Theoretic Structuralism." In *The Handbook of Economic Methodology*, ed. J. B. Davis, D. W. Hands, and U. Mäki, 448–52. Cheltenham: Edward Elgar.

Balzer, Wolfgang and Hamminga, Bert., eds. 1989. *Philosophy of Economics.* Dordrecht: Kluwer.

Balzer, Wolfgang and Moulines, C. Ulises, eds. 1996. *Structuralist Theory of Science.* Berlin: Walter de Gruyter.

Balzer, Wolfgang, Moulines, C. Ulises, and Sneed, Joseph D., eds. 1987. *An Architectonic For Science: The Structuralist Program.* Dordrecht: D. Reidel.

Barkai, Haim. 1996. "The Methodenstreit and the Emergence of Mathematical Economics." *Eastern Economic Journal* 22: 1–19.

Barnes, Barry. 1974. *Scientific Knowledge and Sociological Theory.* London: Routledge.

Barnes, Barry. 1977. *Interests and the Growth of Knowledge.* London: Routledge.

Barnes, Barry. 1982. *Thomas Kuhn and Social Science.* New York: Columbia University Press.

Barnes, Barry. 1991. "How Not to Do the Sociology of Knowledge." *Annals of Scholarship* 8: 321–35.

Barnes, Barry, Bloor, David, and Henry, John. 1996. *Scientific Knowledge: A Sociological Analysis.* Chicago: University of Chicago Press.

Barrotta, Pierluigi. 1996. "A neo-Kantian Critique of von Mises's Epistemology." *Economics and Philosophy* 12: 51–66.

Bartley, W. W. III. 1984. *The Retreat to Commitment*, 2nd ed. La Salle, IL: Open Court (1st edition 1962).

Bartley, William W. III. 1990. *Unfathomed Knowledge, Unmeasured Wealth.* La Salle, IL: Open Court.

Bear, D. V. T. and Orr, Daniel. 1967. "Friedman and Machlup on the Significance of Testing Economic Analysis." *Journal of Political Economy* 73: 37–60.

Becker, Gary. 1981. *A Treatise on the Family.* Cambridge, MA: Harvard University Press.

Berger, Peter L. and Luckmann, Thomas. 1966. *The Social Construction of Reality: A Treatise in the Sociology of Knowledge.* New York: Anchor Books.

Bernal, John Desmond. 1939. *The Social Function of Science*. London: Routledge.

Bernal, John Desmond. 1953. *Science and Industry in the Nineteenth Century*. London: Routledge.

Bhaskar, Roy. 1978. *A Realist Theory of Science*, 2nd ed. Brighton: Harvester.

Bhaskar, Roy. 1987. *Scientific Realism and Human Emancipation*. London: Verso.

Bhaskar, Roy. 1989. *Reclaiming Reality*. London: Verso.

Bhaskar, Roy. 1991. *Philosophy and the Idea of Freedom*. Oxford: Blackwell.

Bhaskar, Roy. 1994. *Plato Etc*. London: Verso.

Bianchi, Marina and Moulin, Hervé. 1991. "Strategic Interactions in Economics: the Game Theoretic Alternative." In *Appraising Economic Theories: Studies in the Methodology of Scientific Research Programs*, ed. M. Blaug and N. De Marchi, 179–96. Aldershot: Edward Elgar.

Birner, Jack. 1990. *Strategies and Programmes in Capital Theory: A Contribution to the Methodology of Theory Development*. Ph.D. Dissertation, University of Amsterdam.

Birner, Jack. 1999. "The Surprising Place of Cognitive Psychology in the Work of F. A. Hayek." *History of Economic Ideas* (1999).

Blais, Michel J. 1987. "Epistemic Tit for Tat." *Journal of Philosophy* 84: 363–75.

Blank, Rebecca M. 1993. "What Should Mainstream Economists Learn from Feminist Theory." In *Beyond Economic Man: Feminist Theory and Economics*, ed. M. A. Ferber and J. A. Nelson, 133–43. Chicago: University of Chicago Press.

Blaug, Mark. 1958. *Ricardian Economics: A Historical Study*. New Haven, CT: Yale University Press.

Blaug, Mark. 1975. "Kuhn versus Lakatos, or Paradigms versus Research Programmes in the History of Economics." *History of Political Economy* 7: 399–419 [reprinted with minor revisions as Blaug 1976].

Blaug, Mark. 1976. "Kuhn versus Lakatos, or Paradigms versus Research Programmes in the History of Economics." In *Method and Appraisal in Economics*, ed. S. J. Latsis, 149–80. Cambridge: Cambridge University Press.

Blaug, Mark. 1980. *The Methodology of Economics: Or How Economists Explain*. Cambridge: Cambridge University Press.

Blaug, Mark. 1990a. *Economic Theories, True or False? Essays in the History and Methodology of Economics*. Aldershot: Edward Elgar.

Blaug, Mark. 1990b. "A Methodological Appraisal of Radical Economics." In *Economic Theories, True or False? Essays in the History and Methodology of Economics*, 57–87. Aldershot: Edward Elgar.

Blaug, Mark. 1990c. "A Methodological Appraisal of Marxian Economics, Parts I and II." In *Economic Theories, True or False? Essays in the History and Methodology of Economics*, 17–56. Aldershot: Edward Elgar.

Blaug, Mark. 1990d. "Reply to D. Wade Hands' 'Second Thoughts on "Second Thoughts": Reconsidering the Lakatosian Progress of *The General Theory*.'" *Review of Political Economy* 2: 102–4.

Blaug, Mark. 1991a. "Afterword." In *Appraising Economic Theories: Studies in the Methodology of Scientific Research Programs*, ed. M. Blaug and N. De Marchi, 499–512. Aldershot: Edward Elgar.

Blaug, Mark. 1991b, "Second Thoughts on the Keynesian Revolution." *History of Political Economy* 23: 171–92.

Blaug, Mark. 1992. *The Methodology of Economics: Or How Economists Explain*, 2nd ed. Cambridge: Cambridge University Press.

Blaug, Mark. 1994a. "Not Only an Economist – Autobiographical Reflections of a Historian of Economic Thought." *The American Economist* 38: 12–27.

Blaug, Mark. 1994b. "Why I Am Not a Constructivist: Confessions of an Unrepentant Popperian." In *New Directions in Economic Methodology*, ed. R. Backhouse, 109–36. London: Routledge.

Blaug, Mark. 1998. "The Positive-Normative Distinction." In *The Handbook of Economic Methodology*, ed. J. B. Davis, D. W. Hands, and U. Mäki, 370–4. Cheltenham: Edward Elgar.

Block, Walter. 1980. "On Robert Nozick's 'On Austrian Methodology'." *Inquiry* 23: 397–444.

Bloor, David. 1976. *Knowledge and Social Imagery*. London: Routledge.

Bloor, David. 1983. *Wittgenstein: A Social Theory of Knowledge*. New York: Columbia University Press.

Bloor, David. 1984. "The Strengths of the Strong Programme." In *Scientific Rationality: The Sociological Turn*, ed. J. R. Brown, 75–94. Dordrecht: D. Reidel.

Bloor, David. 1991. *Knowledge and Social Imagery*, 2nd ed. Chicago: University of Chicago Press.

Bloor, David. 1992. "Left and Right Wittgensteinians." In *Science as Practice and Culture*, ed. A. Pickering, 266–82. Chicago: University of Chicago Press.

Bloor, David. 1999. "Anti-Latour." *Studies in History and Philosophy of Science* 30: 81–112.

Blumberg, Albert E. and Feigel, Herbert. 1931. "Logical Positivism: A New Movement in European Philosophy." *The Journal of Philosophy* 28: 281–296.

Boettke, Peter. 1998. "von Mises, Ludwig." In *The Handbook of Economic Methodology*, ed. J. B. Davis, D. W. Hands, and U. Mäki, 534–40. Cheltenham: Edward Elgar.

Bogaard, Adrienne van den. 1999. "Past Measurement and Future Prediction." In *Models as Mediators*, ed. M. S. Morgan and M. C. Morrison, 282–325. Cambridge: Cambridge University Press.

Boland, Lawrence A. 1971. "Methodology as an Exercise in Economic Analysis." *Philosophy of Science* 38: 105–17.

Boland, Lawrence A. 1979. "A Critique of Friedman's Critics." *Journal of Economic Literature* 17: 503–22 [reprinted with minor revisions as chapter 2 of Boland 1997].

Boland, Lawrence A. 1980. "Friedman's Methodology vs. Conventional Empiricism." *Journal of Economic Literature* 18: 1555–7.

Boland, Lawrence A. 1981. "Satisficing in Methodology: A Reply to Rendigs Fels." *Journal of Economic Literature* 19: 84–6.

Boland, Lawrence A. 1982. *The Foundations of Economic Method*. London: George Allen & Unwin.

Boland, Lawrence A. 1986. *Methodology for a New Microeconomics*. Boston: Allen & Unwin.

Boland, Lawrence A. 1987. "Boland on Friedman's Methodology: A Summation." *Journal of Economic Issues* 21: 380–8.

Boland, Lawrence A. 1989. *The Methodology of Economic Model Building*. London: Routledge.

Boland, Lawrence A. 1991. "The Theory and Practice of Economic Methodology." *Methodus* 3: 6–17 [reprinted with minor revisions as chapter 8 of Boland 1997].

Boland, Lawrence A. 1994. "Scientific Thinking Without Scientific Method: Two Views of Popper." In *New Directions in Economic Methodology*, ed. R. Backhouse, 154–72. London: Routledge [reprinted with minor revisions as chapter 20 of Boland 1997].

Boland, Lawrence A. 1997. *Critical Economic Methodology: A Personal Odyssey*. London: Routledge.

Bostaph, Samuel. 1978. "The Methodological Debate Between Carl Menger and the German Historicists." *Atlantic Economic Journal* 3–16.

Boumans, Marcel. 1999. "Built-In Justification." In *Models as Mediators*, ed. M. S. Morgan and M. C. Morrison, 66–96. Cambridge: Cambridge University Press.

Böhm-Bawerk, Eugen von. 1890. "The Historical vs. the Deductive Method in Political Economy." *Annals of the American Academy of Political and Social Science* 1: 244–71.

Bourdieu, Pierre 1975. "The Specificity of the Scientific Field and the Social Conditions of the Progress of Reason." *Social Science Information* 14: 19–47.

Boyd, Richard. 1973. "Realism, Underdetermination, and a Causal Theory of Evidence." *Nous* 8: 1–12.

Boyd, Richard. 1983. "On the Current Status of the Issue of Scientific Realism." *Erkenntnis* 19: 45–90.

Boyd, Richard. 1991. "Realism, Anti-foundationalism and the Enthusiasm for Natural Kinds." *Philosophical Studies* 61: 127–48.

Boyd, Richard. 1992. "Construction, Realism, and Philosophical Method." In *Inference, Explanation, and Other Frustrations: Essays in the Philosophy of Science*, ed. J. Earman, 131–98. Berkeley: University of California Press.

Boylan, Thomas A. and O'Gorman, Paschal F. 1995. *Beyond Rhetoric & Realism in Economics: Towards a Reformulation of Economic Methodology*. London: Routledge.

Boylan, Thomas A. and O'Gorman, Paschal F. 1996. "Empiricism without the Dogmas: A Causal Holist Perspective" [unpublished].

Boylan, Thomas A. and O'Gorman, Paschal F. 1997a. "Critical Realism and Economics: A Causal Holist Critique." *Ekonomia* 1: 9–21 [reprinted with minor revisions as chapter 8 of Fleetwood 1999].

Boylan, Thomas A. and O'Gorman, Paschal F. 1997b. "Kaldor on Method: A Challenge to Contemporary Methodology." *Cambridge Journal of Economics* 21: 503–17.

Boylan, Thomas A. and O'Gorman, Paschal F. 1998. "van Fraassen, Bas." In *The Handbook of Economic Methodology*, ed. J. B. Davis, D. W. Hands, and U. Mäki, 526–7. Cheltenham: Edward Elgar.

Bradie, Michael. 1986. "Assessing Evolutionary Epistemology." *Biology and Philosophy* 1: 401–59.

Bradie, Michael. 1998. "Evolutionary Epistemology." In *The Handbook of Economic Methodology*, ed. J. B. Davis, D. W. Hands, and U. Mäki, 167–71. Cheltenham: Edward Elgar.

Brandom, Robert B. 1994. *Making It Explicit: Reasoning, Representing, Discursive Commitment*. Cambridge, MA: Harvard University Press.

Brent, Joseph. 1993. *Charles Sanders Peirce: A Life*. Bloomington, IN: Indiana University Press.

Brent, Joseph. 1996. "Pursuing Peirce." *Synthese* 106: 301–22.

Bridgman, Percy W. 1927. *The Logic of Modern Physics*. N.Y.: Macmillan [ninth printing 1961].

Bridgman, Percy W. 1938. "Operational Analysis." *Philosophy of Science* 5: 114–31.

Brock, William A. and Durlauf, Steven N. 1999. "A Formal Model of Theory Choice in Science." *Economic Theory* 14: 113–30.

Bronfenbrenner, Martin. 1971. "The 'Structure of Revolutions' in Economic Thought." *History of Political Economy* 3: 136–51.

Brooks, Harvey. 1996. "The Evolution of U. S. Science Policy." In *Technology, R&D, and the Economy*, ed. B. L. R. Smith and C. E. Barfield, 15–48. Washington, DC: Brookings and AEI.

Brown, Doug. 1991. "An Institutionalist Look at Postmodernism." *Journal of Economic Issues* 25: 1089–1104.

Brown, Doug. 1992. "Institutionalism and the Postmodern Politics of Social Change." *Journal of Economic Issues* 26: 545–52.

Brown, E. K. 1981. "The Neoclassical and Post-Keynesian Research Programs: The Methodological Issues." *Review of Social Economy* 34: 111–32.

Brown, Vivienne. 1993. "Decanonizing Discourse: Textual Analysis and the History of Economic Thought." In *Economics and Language*, ed. W. Henderson, T. Dudley-Evans, and R. Backhouse, 64–84. London: Routledge.

Brown, Vivienne. 1994a. *Adam Smith's Discourse: Canonicity, Commerce, and Conscience.* London: Routledge.

Brown, Vivienne. 1994b. "Higgling: The Language of Markets in Economic Discourse." In *Higgling: Transactors and Their Markets in the History of Economics* [Supplement to *HOPE* vol. 26], ed. N. De Marchi and M. S. Morgan, 66–93. Durham, NC: Duke University Press.

Brush, Stephen G. 1993. "Prediction and Theory Evaluation: Cosmic Microwaves and the Revival of the Big Bang." *Perspectives on Science* 1: 565–602.

Brush, Stephen G. 1995. "Dynamics of Theory Change: The Role of Predictions." In *PSA 1994*, Vol. II, 133–45. East Lansing, MI: PSA.

Bukharin, Nikolai et al., eds. 1931. *Science at the Crossroads.* London: Frank Cass & Co.

Bunge, Mario. 1991. "A Critical Examination of the New Sociology of Science: Part I." *Philosophy of the Social Sciences* 21: 524–60.

Burns, Arthur F. and Mitchell, Wesley C. 1946. *Measuring Business Cycles.* New York: National Bureau of Economic Research.

Burzak, Theodore A. 1994. "The Postmodern Moments in F. A. Hayek's Economics." *Economics & Philosophy* 10: 31–58.

Bush, Paul D. 1989. "Institutionalist Methodology and Hermeneutics: A Comment on Mirowski." *Journal of Economic Issues* 23: 1159–72.

Bush, Paul D. 1994. "The Pragmatic Instrumentalist Perspective on the Theory of Institutionalist Change." *Journal of Economic Issues* 28: 647–57.

Bush, Vannevar. 1945. *Science – The Endless Frontier.* Washington, DC: U.S. Government Printing Office.

Butos, William. 1987. "Rhetoric and Rationality: A Review Essay of McCloskey's The Rhetoric of Economics." *Eastern Economic Journal* 13: 295–304.

Cairnes, John E. 1875. *The Character and Logical Method of Political Economy*, 2nd ed. New York: Harper and Brothers [1st edition 1857]

Caldwell, Bruce J. 1982. *Beyond Positivism: Economic Methodology in the Twentieth Century.* London: George Allen & Unwin.

Caldwell, Bruce J. 1984a. "Some Problems with Falsificationism in Economics." *Philosophy of the Social Sciences* 14: 489–95.

Caldwell, Bruce J. 1984b. "Praxeology and Its Critics: An Appraisal." *History of Political Economy* 16: 363–79.

Caldwell, Bruce J. 1988. "Hayek's Transformation." *History of Political Economy* 20: 513–41.

Caldwell, Bruce J., ed. 1990. *Carl Menger and His Legacy in Economics.* Durham, NC: Duke University Press.

Caldwell, Bruce J. 1991a. "Clarifying Popper." *Journal of Economic Literature* 29: 1–33.

Caldwell, Bruce J. 1991b. "The Methodology of Scientific Research Programmes in Economics: Criticisms and Conjectures." In *Economics, Culture and Education: Essays in Honour of Mark Blaug*, ed. G. K. Shaw, 95–107. Aldershot: Edward Elgar.

Caldwell, Bruce J. 1992a. "Hayek the Falsificationist? A Refutation." *Research in the History of Economic Thought and Methodology* 10: 1–15.

Caldwell, Bruce J. 1992b. "Hayek the Falsificationist: Reply to Hutchison." *Research in the History of Economic Thought and Methodology* 10: 33–42.

Caldwell, Bruce J., ed. 1993. *The Philosophy and Methodology of Economics*, Vols. I, II, and III. Aldershot: Edward Elgar.

Caldwell, Bruce J. 1994a. *Beyond Positivism: Economic Methodology in the Twentieth Century*, 2nd ed. London: Routledge.

Caldwell, Bruce J. 1994b. "Two Proposals for the Recovery of Economic Practice." In *New Directions in Economic Methodology*, ed. R. Backhouse, 137–53. London: Routledge.

Caldwell, Bruce J. 1997. "Hayek and Socialism." *Journal of Economic Literature* 35: 1856–90.

Caldwell, Bruce J. 1998a. "Hayek, Friedrich A." In *The Handbook of Economic Methodology*, ed. J. B. Davis, D. W. Hands, and U. Mäki, 220–26. Cheltenham: Edward Elgar.

Caldwell, Bruce J. 1998b. "Hutchison, Terence W." In *The Handbook of Economic Methodology*, ed. J. B. Davis, D. W. Hands, and U. Mäki, 232–35. Cheltenham: Edward Elgar.

Caldwell, Bruce J. and Coats, A. W. 1984. "The Rhetoric of Economics: A Comment on McCloskey." *Journal of Economic Literature* 22: 575–8.

Callari, Antonio, Cullenberg, Stephen, and Biewener, Carole, eds. 1995. *Marxism in the Postmodern Age: Confronting the New World Order*. New York: Guilford Press.

Callebaut, Werner. 1993. *Taking the Naturalistic Turn*. Chicago: University of Chicago Press.

Callon, Michel. 1986. "Some Elements of a Sociology of Translation: Domestication of the Scallops and the Fishermen of St Brieuc Bay." In *Power, Action, and Belief: A New Sociology of Knowledge*, ed. J. Law, 196–233. London: Routledge.

Callon, Michel. 1995. "Four Models for the Dynamics of Science." In *Handbook of Science and Technology Studies*, ed. S. Jasanoff, G. E. Markle, J. C. Petersen, and T. Pinch, 29–63. Thousand Oaks, CA: Sage.

Callon, Michel, ed. 1998. *The Laws of the Markets*. Oxford: Blackwell.

Callon, Michel and Latour, Bruno. 1992. "Don't Throw the Baby Out with the Bath School! A Reply to Collins and Yearley." In *Science as Practice and Culture*, ed. A. Pickering, 343–68. Chicago: University of Chicago Press.

Callon, Michael, Law, John, and Rip, Arie, eds. 1986. *Mapping the Dynamics of Science and Technology: Sociology of Science in the Real World*. London: Macmillian.

Campbell, Donald T. 1960. "Blind Variation and Selective Retention in Creative Thought as in Other Knowledge Processes." *Psychological Review* 67: 380–400.

Campbell, Donald T. 1974. "Evolutionary Epistemology." In *The Philosophy of Karl Popper Vol. I*, ed. P. A. Schlipp, 413–63. La Salle, IL: Open Court.

Campbell, Donald T. 1988. "The Author Responds: Popper and Selection Theory." *Social Epistemology* 2: 371–77.

Campbell, Donald T. 1990. "Levels of Organization, Downward Causation, and the Selection-Theory Approach to Evolutionary Epistemology." In *Theories of the Evolution of Knowing*, ed. G. Greenberg and E. T. Tobach, 1–17. Hillsdale, NJ: Lawrence Erlbaum Associates.

Campbell, Donald T. 1993. "Plausible Coselection of Belief by Referent: All the 'Objectivity' that is Possible." *Perspectives on Science* 1: 88–108.

Campbell, Donald T., Heyes, Cecilia M., and Callebaut, Werner. 1987. "Evolutionary Epistemology Bibliography." In *Evolutionary Epistemology: A Multi-paradigmatic Program*, ed. W. Callebaut and R. P. Pinxten, 405–31. Dordrecht, Holland: D. Reidel.

Campbell, John A. 1987. "Charles Darwin: Rhetorician of Science." In *the Rhetoric of the Human Sciences*, ed. J. Nelson, A. Megill, and D. N. McCloskey, 69–86. Madison: University of Wisconsin Press.

Carnap, Rudolf. 1928. *Der Logische Aufbau der Welt*. Berlin: Weltkreis-Verlag [translated as *The Logical Structure of the World*. Berkeley: University of California Press, 1969].

Carnap, Rudolf. 1963. "Intellectual Autobiography." In *The Philosophy of Rudolf Carnap*, ed. P. A. Schilpp, 3–84. LaSalle, IL: Open Court.

Carnap, Rudolf, Hahn, Hans, and Neurath, Otto. 1929. "The Scientific Conception of the World: The Vienna Circle (*Wissenschaftliche Weltauffassung, Der Wiener Kreis*)." 1973 reprint, Dordrecht, Holland: D. Reidel Publishing Co.

Cartwright, Nancy. 1983. *How the Laws of Physics Lie*. Oxford: Oxford University Press.

Cartwright, Nancy. 1989a. *Nature's Capacities and Their Measurement*. Oxford: Clarendon.

Cartwright, Nancy. 1989b. "A Case Study in Realism: Why Econometrics Is Committed to Capacities." In *PSA 1988 Vol. II*, ed. A. Fine and J. Leplin, 190–7. East Lansing, MI: Philosophy of Science Association.

Cartwright, Nancy. 1991. "Replicability, Reproducibility, and Robustness: Comments on Harry Collins." *History of Political Economy* 23: 143–55.

Cartwright, Nancy. 1992. "Aristotelian Natures and the Modern Experimental Method." In *Inference, Explanation, and Other Frustrations: Essays in the Philosophy of Science*, ed. J. Earman, 44–71. Berkeley: University of California Press.

Cartwright, Nancy. 1994a. "Fundamentalism vs. The Patchwork of Laws." *Proceedings of the Aristotelian Society* 94: 279–92.

Cartwright, Nancy. 1994b. "Mill and Menger: Ideal Elements and Stable Tendencies." In *Idealization VI: Idealization in Economics*, ed. B. Hamminga and N. De Marchi, 171–88. Amsterdam: Rodopi.

Cartwright, Nancy. 1995a. "*Ceteris Paribus* Laws and Socio-Economic Machines." *The Monist* 78: 276–94.

Cartwright, Nancy. 1995b. "Probabilities and Experiments." *Journal of Econometrics* 67: 47–59.

Cartwright, Nancy. 1997. "Models: Blueprints for Laws." *Philosophy of Science*, 64 (Proceedings): S292–S303.

Cartwright, Nancy. 1998. "Capacities." In *The Handbook of Economic Methodology*, ed. J. B. Davis, D. W. Hands, and U. Mäki, 45–8. Cheltenham: Edward Elgar.

Cartwright, Nancy. 1999a. "Models and the Limits of Theory: Quantum Hamiltonians and the BCS Model of Superconductivity." In *Models as Mediators*, ed. M. S. Morgan and M. C. Morrison, 241–81. Cambridge: Cambridge University Press.

Cartwright, Nancy. 1999b. *The Doppled World: A Study of the Boundaries of Science*. Cambridge: Cambridge University Press.

Cartwright, Nancy, Cat, Jordi, Fleck, Lola, and Uebel, Thomas. 1996. *Between Science and Politics: The Philosophy of Otto Neurath*. Cambridge: Cambridge University Press.

Cat, Jordi, Cartwright, Nancy, and Chang, Hasok. 1996. "Otto Neurath: Politics and the Unity of Science." In *The Disunity of Science: Boundaries, Contexts, and Power*, ed. P. Galison and D. J. Stump, 347–69. Stanford: Stanford University Press.

Chamberlin, Edward. 1933. *The Theory of Monopolistic Competition*. Cambridge, MA: Harvard University Press.

Chappell, V. C., ed. 1968. *Hume: A Collection of Critical Essays*. Notre Dame, IN: University of Notre Dame Press.

Chomsky, Noam. 1959. "Review of Verbal Behavior." *Language* 35: 26–58.

Chordes, Joseph, Klamer, Arjo, and Leonard, Thomas. 1993. "Academic Rhetoric in the Policy Arena: The Case of Capital Gains Taxation." *Eastern Economic Journal* 19: 459–79.

Churchland, Patricia S. 1986. *Neurophilosophy: Toward a Unified Science of the Mind-Brain*. Cambridge, MA: MIT Press.

Churchland, Patricia S. 1987. "Epistemology in the Age of Neuroscience." *The Journal of Philosophy* 84: 544–53.

Churchland, Patricia S. and Churchland, Paul M. 1983. "Stalking the Wild Epistemic Engine." *Nous* 17: 5–18.

Churchland, Paul M. 1984. *Matter and Consciousness*. Cambridge, MA: MIT Press.

Churchland, Paul M. 1992. *A Neurocomputational Perspective: The Nature of Mind and the Structure of Science*. Cambridge, MA: MIT Press.

Coase, Ronald H. 1937. "The Nature of the Firm." *Economica* 4: 386–405.

Coase, Ronald H. 1960. "The Problem of Social Cost." *Journal of Law and Economics* 3: 1–44.

Coase, Ronald H. 1978. "Economics and Contiguous Disciplines." *Journal of Legal Studies* 7: 201–11.

Coase, Ronald H. 1988. "How Should Economists Choose?" In *Ideas, Their Origins, and Their Consequences*, 63–79. Washington, DC: American Enterprise Institute.

Coase, Ronald H. 1992. "The Institutional Structure of Production." *American Economic Review* 82: 713–19.

Coats, A. W. 1969. "Is There a 'Structure of Scientific Revolutions' in Economics?" *Kyklos* 22: 289–95.

Coats, A. W. 1976. "Economics and Psychology: the Death and Resurrection of a Research Programme." In *Method and Appraisal in Economics*, ed. S. J. Latsis, 43–64. Cambridge: Cambridge University Press.

Coats, A. W. 1983a. "Half A Century of Methodological Controversy in Economics: As Reflected in the Writings of T. W. Hutchison." In *Methodological Controversy in Economics: Historical Essays in Honor of T. W. Hutchison*, ed. A. W. Coats, 1–42. Greenwich, CT: JAI Press.

Coats, A. W. 1983b. "Bibliography of Terence W. Hutchison's Writings." In *Methodological Controversy in Economics: Historical Essays in Honor of T. W. Hutchison*, ed. A. W. Coats, 265–9. Greenwich, CT: JAI Press.

Coats, A. W. 1992. "The Historicist Reaction in English Political Economy, 1870–90." In *On the History of Economic Thought: British & American Economic Essays*, Vol. I, 220–30. London: Routledge [originally published in 1954].

Coats, A. W. 1993a. "The Sociology of Knowledge and the History of Economics." In *The Sociology and Professionalization of Economics: British and American Economic Essays, Vol II*, 11–36. London: Routledge.

Coats, A. W. 1993b. "The Sociology of Science: Its Application to Economics." In *The Sociology and Professionalization of Economics: British and American Economic Essays, Vol II*, 37–57. London: Routledge.

Code, Lorraine. 1998. "Feminists and Pragmatists." *Radical Philosophy* 87: 22–30.

Coffa, J. Alberto. 1991. *The Semantic Tradition From Kant to Carnap: to the Vienna Station*. Cambridge: Cambridge University Press.

Cohen, Joshua. 1995. "Samuelson's Operationalist-Descriptivist Thesis." *Journal of Economic Methodology* 2: 53–78.

Cole, Jonathan R. and Zuckerman, Harriet. 1975. "The Emergence of A Scientific Specialty: The Self-Exemplifying Case of the Sociology of Science." In *The Idea of Social Structure: Papers in Honor of Robert K. Merton*, ed. L. A. Coser, 139–74. New York: Harcourt Brace Jovanovich.

Cole, Stephen. 1996. "Voodoo Sociology: Recent Developments in the Sociology of Science." In *The Flight from Science and Reason*, ed. P. R. Gross, N. Levitt, and M. W. Lewis, 274–87. Baltimore, MD: Johns Hopkins University Press.

Collier, Andrew. 1994. *Critical Realism: An Introduction to Roy Bhaskar's Philosophy of Science*. London: Verso.

Collins, Harry M. 1985. *Changing Order: Replication and Induction in Scientific Practice.* Beverly Hills, CA: Sage.

Collins, Harry M. 1991. "The Meaning of Replication and the Science of Economics." *History of Political Economy* 23: 123–42.

Collins, Harry M. 1995. "Science Studies and Machine Intelligence." In *Handbook of Science and Technology Studies*, ed. S. Jasanoff, G. F. Markle, J. C. Peterson, and T. Pinch, 286–301. Thousand Oaks, CA: Sage.

Collins, Harry M. and Yearley, Steven. 1992a. "Epistemological Chicken." In *Science as Practice and Culture*, ed. A. Pickering, 301–26. Chicago: University of Chicago Press.

Collins, Harry M. and Yearley, Steven. 1992b. "Journey into Space." In *Science as Practice and Culture*, ed. A. Pickering, 369–89. Chicago: University of Chicago Press.

Collins, Randall and Restivo, Sal. 1983. "Development, Diversity, and Conflict in the Sociology of Science." *The Sociological Quarterly* 24: 185–200.

Conslisk, John. 1996. "Why Bounded Rationality?" *Journal of Economic Literature* 34: 669–700.

Cooter, Robert and Rapoport, Peter. 1984. "Were the Ordinalists Wrong About Welfare Economics?" *Journal of Economic Literature* 22: 507–30.

Cottrell, Allin. 1995. "Intentionality and Economics." *Economics and Philosophy* 11: 159–76.

Cottrell, Allin. 1998. "Realism, Regularities, and Prediction." *Review of Social Economy* 56: 347–55.

Cox, James C. and Goldman, Alvin. 1994. "Accuracy in Journalism: An Economic Approach." In *Socializing Epistemology*, ed. F. F. Schmitt, 189–215. Lanham, MD: Roman & Littlefield.

Cross, Rod. 1982. "The Duhem-Quine Thesis, Lakatos and the Appraisal of Theories in Macroeconomics." *Economic Journal* 92: 320–40.

Cross, Rod. 1987. "Hysteresis and Instability in the Natural Rate of Unemployment." *The Scandinavian Journal of Economics* 89: 77–89.

Cross, Rod. 1991. "Alternative Accounts of Equilibrium Unemployment." In *Appraising Economic Theories: Studies in the Methodology of Scientific Research Programs*, ed. M. Blaug and N. De Marchi, 294–323. Aldershot: Edward Elgar.

Cross, Rod. 1998. "The Duhem-Quine Thesis." In *The Handbook of Economic Methodology*, ed. J. B. Davis, D. W. Hands, and U. Mäki, 107–10. Cheltenham: Edward Elgar.

Curtis, Ronald. 1989. "Institutional Individualism and the Emergence of Scientific Rationality." *Studies in History and Philosophy of Science* 20: 77–113.

Cziko, Gary A. and Campbell, Donald T. 1990. "Comprehensive Evolutionary Epistemology Bibliography." *Journal of Social and Biological Structures* 13: 41–82.

Danailov, Atanas and Tögel, Christfried. 1990. "Evolutionary Epistemology: Science Philosophy." In *Theories of the Evolution of Knowing*, ed. G. Greenberg and E. Tobach, 19–28. Hillsdale, NJ: Lawrence Erlbaum Associates.

Dasgupta, Partha and David, Paul A. 1994. "Toward A New Economics of Science." *Research Policy* 23: 487–521.

David, Paul A. 1985. "Clio and the Economics of QWERTY: The Necessity of History." *American Economic Review* 75: 332–7.

David, Paul A. 1994. "Why Are Institutions The 'Carriers of History': Path Dependence and the Evolution of Conventions, Organizations and Institutions." *Structural Change and Economic Dynamics* 5: 205–20.

David, Paul A. 1998. "Common Agency Contracting and the Emergence of 'Open Science' Institutions." *American Economic Review* 88: 15–21.

Davis, John B. 1988. "Sraffa, Wittgenstein and Neoclassical Economics." *Cambridge Journal of Economics* 12: 29–36.

Davis, John B. 1990a. "Cooter and Rapoport on the Normative." *Economics and Philosophy* 6: 139–46.

Davis, John B. 1990b. "Rorty's Contribution to McCloskey's Understanding of Conversation as the Methodology of Economics." *Research in the History of Economic Thought and Methodology* 7: 73–85.

Davis, John B. 1994. *Keynes's Philosophical Development*. Cambridge: Cambridge University Press.

Davis, John B. 1997a. "New Economics and Its History: A Pickeringian View." In *New Economics and Its History* [Supplement to *HOPE* vol. 29], ed. J. B. Davis, 289–302. Durham, NC: Duke University Press.

Davis, John B. 1997b. "The Fox and the Henhouses: the Economics of Scientific Knowledge." *History of Political Economy* 29: 741–46.

Davidson, Donald. 1980. *Essays on Actions and Events*. Oxford: Oxford University Press.

Day, Timothy and Kincaid, Harold. 1994. "Putting Inference to the Best Explanation in Its Place." *Synthese* 98: 271–95.

Deane, Phyllis. 1983. "The Scope and Method of Economic Science." *The Economic Journal* 93: 1–12.

Deaton, Angus and Muelbauer, John. 1980. *Economics and Consumer Behavior*. Cambridge: Cambridge University Press.

Debreu, Gerard. 1959. *Theory of Value*. New Haven, CT: Yale University Press.

Debreu, Gerard. 1974. "Excess Demand Functions." *Journal of Mathematical Economics* 1: 15–21.

Delaney, C. F. 1992. "Peirce on the Social and Historical Dimensions of Science." In *The Social Dimensions of Science*, ed. E. McMullin, 27–46. Notre Dame, IN: University of Notre Dame Press.

De la Sienra, Adolfo G. 1992. *The Logical Foundations of the Marxian Theory of Value*. Dordrecht: Kluwer.

De Marchi, Neil. 1970. "The Empirical Content and Longevity of Ricardian Economics." *Economica* 37: 257–76.

De Marchi, Neil. 1976. "Anomaly and the Development of Economics: the Case of the Leontief Paradox." In *Method and Appraisal in Economics*, ed. S. J. Latsis, 109–27. Cambridge: Cambridge University Press.

De Marchi, Neil. 1983. "The Case For James Mill." In *Methodological Controversy in Economics: Historical Essays in Honor of T. W. Hutchison*, ed. A. W. Coats, 155–84. Greenwich, CT: JAI Press.

De Marchi, Neil. 1986. "Discussion: Mill's Unrevised Philosophy of Economics: A Comment on Hausman." *Philosophy of Science* 53: 89–100.

De Marchi, Neil. 1988a. "Popper and the LSE Economists." *The Popperian Tradition in Economics and Beyond*, ed. N. De Marchi, 139–66. Cambridge: Cambridge University Press.

De Marchi, Neil. 1988b. "John Stuart Mill Interpretation Since Schumpeter." In *Classical Political Economy: A Survey of Recent Literature*, ed. W. O. Thweatt, 137–62. Boston: Kluwer.

De Marchi, Neil. 1991. "Introduction: Rethinking Lakatos." In *Appraising Economic Theories: Studies in the Methodology of Scientific Research Programs*, ed. M. Blaug and N. De Marchi, 1–30. Aldershot: Edward Elgar.

De Marchi, Neil. 1995. "Comments on Niehans, 'Multiple Discoveries'." *The European Journal of the History of Economic Thought* 2: 275–79.

De Marchi, Neil and Blaug, Mark, eds. 1991. *Appraising Economic Theories: Studies in the Methodology of Scientific Research Programs*. Aldershot: Edward Elgar.

De Marchi, Neil and Sturges, R. P. 1973. "Malthus and Ricardo's Inductivist Critics: Four Letters to William Whewell." *Economica* 40: 379–93.

Denison, Edward. 1967. *Why Growth Rates Differ: Postwar Experience in Nine Western Countries*. Washington, DC: Brookings.

Denison, Edward. 1979. *Accounting for Economic Growth*. Washington, DC: Brookings.

Dennett, Daniel. 1982. "Comments on Rorty." *Synthese* 53: 349–56.

Dennett, Daniel. 1987. *The Intentional Stance*. Cambridge, MA: MIT Press.

Dennis, Ken. 1986. "Boland on Friedman: A Rebuttal." *Journal of Economic Issues* 20: 633–64.

Dewey, John. 1908. "Does Reality Possess Practical Character?" In *Pragmatism: A Contemporary Reader*, ed. R. B. Goodman, 79–91. New York: Routledge [1995].

Dewey, John. 1927. *The Public and Its Problems*. Athens, Ohio: Swallow Press [1991].

Dewey, John. 1929. *Experience and Nature*, 2nd ed. New York: Dover [1958].

Dewey, John. 1939. *Theory of Valuation*. Chicago: University of Chicago Press.

Dewey, John. 1948. *Reconstruction in Philosophy*, Enlarged Edition. Boston: Beacon Press.

Dewey, John. 1970. "Unity of Science as a Social Problem." In *Foundations of the Unity of Science: Toward an International Encyclopedia of Unified Science*, Vol. 1, ed. O. Neurath, R. Carnap, and C. Morris, 29–38. Chicago: University of Chicago Press.

Diamond, Arthur M., Jr. 1988a. "The Empirical Progressiveness of the General Equilibrium Research Program." *History of Political Economy* 20: 119–35.

Diamond, Arthur M., Jr. 1988b. "Science as a Rational Enterprise." *Theory and Decision* 24: 147–67.

Diamond, Arthur M., Jr. 1996. "The Economics of Science." *Knowledge and Policy: The International Journal of Knowledge Transfer and Utilization* 9: 6–49.

Diamond, Arthur M., Jr. 1999. "Edwin Mansfield's Contribution to the Economics of Technology." Paper presented at the American Economics Association Annual meeting in January 1999 in New York.

Diederich, Werner. 1996. "Structuralism As Developed Within the Model-Theoretical Approach to the Philosophy of Science." In *Structuralist Theory of Science*, ed. W. Balzer and C. U. Moulines, 15–21. Berlin: Walter de Gruyter.

Diederich, Werner, Ibarra, Andoni, and Mormann, Thomas. 1994. "Bibliography of Structuralism II (1989–94 and Additions). *Erkenntnis* 41: 403–18.

Diggins, John Patrick. 1994. *The Promise of Pragmatism: Modernism and the Crisis of Knowledge and Authority*. Chicago: University of Chicago Press.

Doppelt, Gerald. 1990. "The Naturalist Conception of Methodological Standards in Science." *Philosophy of Science* 57: 1–19.

Duhem, Pierre. 1954. *The Aim and Structure of Physical Theory*. Translated by P. P. Wiener. Princeton: Princeton University Press [original published in French in 1906].

Duran, Jane. 1998. *Philosophies of Science/Feminist Theories*. Boulder, CO: Westview Press.

Durlauf, Steven N. 1997. "Limits to Science or Limits to Epistemology?" *Complexity* 2: 31–7.

Dyer, Alan W. 1986. "Veblen on Scientific Creativity: The Influence of Charles S. Peirce." *Journal of Economic Issues* 20: 21–41.

Dyer, Alan W. 1988. "Economic Theory as an Art Form." *Journal of Economic Issues* 22: 157–66.

Earman, John. 1993. "Carnap, Kuhn, and the Philosophy of Scientific Methodology." In *World Changes: Thomas Kuhn and the Nature of Science*, ed. P. Horwich, 9–36. Cambridge, MA: MIT Press.

Edge, David. 1995. "Reinventing the Wheel." In *Handbook of Science and Technology Studies*, ed. S. Jasanoff, G. E. Markle, J. C. Peterson, and T. Pinch, 3–23. Thousand Oaks, CA: Sage.

Eichner, A. S. 1983. "Why Economics is Not Yet a Science." *Journal of Economic Issues* 17: 507–20.

Eldredge, Niles. 1997. "Evolution in the Marketplace." *Structural Change and Economic Dynamics* 8: 385–98.

Emami, Zohreh and Riordau, Timothy. 1998. "Tony Lawson on Critical Realism: What's Teaching Got to Do With It?" *Review of Social Economy* 56: 311–23.

Emmett, Ross B. 1990. "The Economist as Philosopher: Frank H. Knight and American Social Science During the Twenties and Early Thirties." Ph.D. Dissertation, University of Manitoba.

England, Paula. 1993. "The Separative Self: Androcentric Bias in Neoclassical Assumptions." In *Beyond Economic Man: Feminist Theory and Economics*, ed. M. A. Ferber and J. A. Nelson, 37–53. Chicago: University of Chicago Press.

Evans, Robert. 1999. "Economic Models and Policy Advice: Theory Choice or Moral Choice?" *Science in Context* 12: 351–80.

Farr, James. 1983. "Popper's Hermeneutics." *Philosophy of the Social Sciences* 13: 157–76.

Favretti, Rema Rossini, Sandri, Giorgio, and Scazzieri, Roberto. 1999. *Incommensurability and Translation: Kuhnian Perspectives on Scientific Communication and Theory Change.* Cheltenham: Edward Elgar.

Fels, Rendigs. 1981. "Boland Ignores Simon: A Comment." *Journal of Economic Literature* 19: 83–4.

Ferber, Marianne A. and Nelson, Julie A., eds. 1993. *Beyond Economic Man: Feminist Theory and Economics.* Chicago: University of Chicago Press.

Feyerabend, Paul K. 1963. "Materialism and the Mind-Body Problem." *Review of Metaphysics* 17 [reprinted in Feyerabend 1981].

Feyerabend, Paul K. 1968. "How to be Good Empiricist – A Plea for Tolerance in Matters Epistemological." In *The Philosophy of Science*, ed. P. H. Nidditch, 12–39. Oxford: Oxford University Press.

Feyerabend, Paul K. 1975. *Against Method.* London: New Left Books.

Feyerabend, Paul K. 1995. *Killing Time.* Chicago: University of Chicago Press.

Fish, Stanley. 1980. *Is There a Text in This Class?* Cambridge, MA: Harvard University Press.

Fish, Stanley. 1987. "Dennis Martinez and the Uses of Theory." *The Yale Law Journal* 96: 1773–1800.

Fish, Stanley. 1989. *Doing What Comes Naturally: Change, Rhetoric, and the Practice of Theory in Literary and Legal Studies.* Durham, NC.: Duke University Press.

Fisher, Robert. 1986. *The Logic of Economic Discovery.* New York: New York University Press.

Fleetwood, Steve. 1996. "Order Without Equilibrium: A Critical Realist Interpretation of Hayek's Notion of Spontaneous Order." *Cambridge Journal of Economics* 20: 729–47.

Fleetwood, Steve. 1997. "Situating Critical Realism in Economics." *Ekonomia* 1: 1–8 [reprinted with minor revisions as chapter 7 of Fleetwood 1999].

Fleetwood, Steve, ed. 1999. *Critical Realism in Economics: Development and Debate.* London: Routledge.

Folbre, Nancy. 1993. "How Does She Know? Feminist Theories of Gender Bias in Economics." *History of Political Economy* 25: 167–84.

Foss, Nicolai J. 1994. "Realism and Evolutionary Economics." *Journal of Social and Evolutionary Systems* 17: 21–40.

Foss, Nicolai J. 1998. "The New Growth Theory: Some Intellectual Growth Accounting." *Journal of Economic Methodology* 5: 223–46.

Frazer W. J. and Boland, L. A. 1983. "An Essay on the Foundations of Friedman's Methodology." *American Economic Review* 73: 129–44.

Friedman, Michael. 1992. "Philosophy and the Exact Sciences: Logical Positivism as a Case Study." In *Inference, Explanation, and Other Frustrations: Essays in the Philosophy of Science*, ed. J. Earman, 84–98. Berkeley: University of California Press.

Friedman, Michael. 1993. "Remarks on the History of Science and the History of Philosophy." In *World Changes: Thomas Kuhn and the Nature of Science*, ed. P. Horwich, 37–54. Cambridge, MA: MIT Press.

Friedman, Michael. 1998. "On the Sociology of Scientific Knowledge and Its Philosophical Agenda." *Studies in History and Philosophy of Science* 29: 239–71.

Friedman, Michael. 1999. *Reconsidering Logical Positivism*. Cambridge: Cambridge University Press.

Friedman, Milton. 1946. "Lange on Price Flexibility and Employment: A Methodological Criticism." *American Economic Review* 36: 613–31.

Friedman, Milton. 1953. "The Methodology of Positive Economics." In *Essays in Positive Economics*, 3–43. Chicago: University of Chicago Press.

Friedman, Milton and Schwartz, Anna J. 1991. "Alternative Approaches to Analyzing Economic Data." *American Economic Review* 81: 39–49.

Frisby, David. 1976. "Introduction to the English Translation." In *The Positivist Dispute in German Sociology*, ed. T. W. Adorno et al., ix–xlix. New York: Harper Torchbooks.

Fuhrman, Ellsworth R. and Oehler, Kay. 1986. "Discourse Analysis and Reflexivity." *Social Studies of Science* 16: 293–307.

Fuller, Steve. 1988. *Social Epistemology*. Bloomington, IN: Indiana University Press.

Fuller, Steve. 1991. "Studying the Proprietary Grounds of Knowledge." *Journal of Social Behavior and Personality* 6: 105–28.

Fuller, Steve. 1992. "Social Epistemology and the Research Agenda of Science Studies." In *Science as Practice and Culture*, ed. A. Pickering, 327–428. Chicago: University of Chicago Press.

Fuller, Steve. 1994. "Mortgaging the Farm to Save the (Sacred) Cow." *Studies in History and Philosophy of Science* 25: 251–61.

Fuller, Steve. 1996. "Talking Metaphysical Turkey About Epistemological Chicken, and the Poop on Pidgins." In *The Disunity of Science: Boundries, Contexts, and Power*, ed. P. Galison and D. J. Stump, 170–86. Stanford, CA: Stanford University Press.

Fuller, Steve. 2000. *Thomas Kuhn: A Philosophical History of Our Times*. Chicago: University of Chicago Press.

Fulton, G. 1984. "Research Programmes in Economics." *History of Political Economy* 16: 187–205.

Galison, Peter. 1987. *How Experiments End*. Chicago: University of Chicago Press.

Galison, Peter. 1997. *Image & Logic: A Material Culture of Microphysics*. Chicago: University of Chicago Press.

Galison, Peter. 1998. "The Americanization of Unity." *Deadalus* 127: 45–71.

Garfinkel, Harold. 1967. *Studies in Ethnomethodology*. Englewood Cliffs, NJ: Prentice Hall.

Garnett, Robert F. Jr., ed. 1999. *What Do Economists Know? New Economics of Knowledge*. London: Routledge.

Gellner, Ernest. 1974. *Legitimation of Belief*. Cambridge: Cambridge University Press.

Georgescu-Roegen, Nicholas. 1992. "Nicholas Georgescu-Roegen About Himself." In *Eminent Economists*, ed. M. Szenberg, 128–59. Cambridge: Cambridge University Press.

Gerrard, B. 1991. "Keynes's *General Theory*: Interpreting the Interpretations." *Economic Journal* 101: 276–87.

Gettier, Edmund L. 1963. "Is Justified True Belief Knowledge?" *Analysis* 23: 121–3.

Gibbard, Alan and Varian, Hal R. 1978. "Economic Models." *The Journal of Philosophy* 75: 664–77.

Giddens, Anthony. 1973. *The Class Structure of Advanced Societies*. London: Hutchison.

Giddens, Anthony. 1986. *The Constitution of Society: Outline of the Theory of Structuration*. Berkeley: University of California Press.

Giere, Ronald N. 1984. *Understanding Scientific Reasoning*, 2nd ed. New York: Holt, Rinehart & Winston.

Giere, Ronald N. 1988. *Explaining Science: A Cognitive Approach*. Chicago: University of Chicago Press.

Giere, Ronald N. 1995. "Viewing Science." *PSA 1994*, Vol. II, 3–16. East Lansing, MI: PSA.

Giere, Ronald N., ed. 1992. *Cognitive Models of Science*. Minneapolis, MN: University of Minnesota Press.

Giere, Ronald N. 1999. *Science Without Laws*. Chicago: University of Chicago Press.

Gieryn, Thomas F. 1994. "Objectivity for These Times." *Perspectives on Science*, 324–49.

Gieryn, Thomas F. 1995. "Boundaries of Science." In *Handbook of Science and Technology Studies*, ed. S. Jasanoff, G. E. Markle, J. C. Peterson, and T. Pinch, 393–443. Thousand Oaks, CA: Sage.

Gilbert, Christopher L. 1991. "Do Economists Test Theories? Demand Analysis and Consumption Analysis as Tests of Theories of Economic Methodology." In *Appraising Economic Theories: Studies in the Methodology of Scientific Research Programs*, ed. M. Blaug and N. De Marchi, 137–68. Aldershot: Edward Elgar.

Gilbert, G. Nigel and Mulkay, Michael. 1984. *Opening Pandora's Box: A Sociological Analysis of Scientists' Discourse*. Cambridge: Cambridge University Press.

Glass, J. C. and Johnson, W. 1989. *Economics: Progression, Stagnation or Degeneration?* Hempstead UK: Harvester Wheatsheaf.

Glymour, Clark. 1980. *Theory and Evidence*. Princeton: Princeton University Press.

Goldman, Alvin. 1986. *Epistemology and Cognition*. Cambridge, MA: Harvard University Press.

Goldman, Alvin. 1987. "Foundations of Social Epistemics." *Synthese* 73: 109–44.

Goldman, Alvin. 1992. "In Defense of the Simulation Theory." *Mind and Language* 7: 104–19.

Goldman, Alvin. 1993. *Philosophical Applications of Cognitive Science*. Boulder, CO: Westview Press.

Goldman, Alvin. 1995. "Simulation and Interpersonal Utility." *Ethics* 105: 709–26.

Goldman, Alvin. 1999. *Knowledge in a Social World*. Oxford: Oxford University Press.

Goldman, Alvin and Cox, James C. 1996. "Speech, Truth, and the Free Market for Ideas." *Legal Theory* 2: 1–32.

Goldman, Alvin and Shaked, M. 1991. "An Economic Model of Scientific Activity and Truth Acquisition." *Philosophical Studies* 63: 31–55.

Goodman, Nelson. 1955. *Fact, Fiction, and Forecast*. Cambridge, MA: Harvard University Press.

Goodman, Russell B., ed. 1995. *Pragmatism: A Contemporary Reader*. New York: Routledge.

Gordon, Donald F. 1955. "Operational Propositions in Economic Theory." *Journal of Political Economy* 63: 150–61.

Gordon, Robert M. 1986. "Folk Psychology as Simulation." *Mind and Language* 1: 158–71.

Gordon, Robert M. 1992. "The Simulation Theory: Objections and Misconceptions." *Mind and Language* 7: 11–34.

Gordon, H. Scott. 1991. *The History and Philosophy of Social Science*. London: Routledge.

Gordon, Wendell. 1990. "The Role of Tool's Social Value Principle." *Journal of Economic Issues* 24: 879–86.

Granovetter, Mark and Swedberg, Richard, eds. 1992. *The Sociology of Economic Life*. Boulder, CO: Westview Press.

Green, Christopher D. 1992. "Of Immortal Mythological Beasts: Operationalism in Psychology." *Theory & Psychology* 2: 291–320.

Greenfield, Robert L. and Salerno, Joseph T. 1983. "Another Defense of Methodological Apriorism." *Eastern Economic Journal* 9: 45–56.

Gross, Alan G. 1990. *The Rhetoric of Science*. Cambridge, MA: Harvard University Press.

Gross, Alan G. 1991. "Rhetoric of Science Without Constraints." *Rhetorica* 9: 283–99.

Gross, Alan G. and Keith, William M., eds. 1997. *Rhetorical Hermeneutics: Invention and Interpretation in the Age of Science*. Albany: State University of New York Press.

Gross, Paul R. and Levitt, Norman. 1994. *Higher Superstition: the Academic Left and Its Quarrels with Science*. Baltimore, MD: Johns Hopkins University Press.

Gross, Paul R., Levitt, Norman, and Lewis, Martin W., eds. 1996. *The Flight From Science and Reason*. New York: New York Academy of Sciences.

Gruchy, Allen G. 1972. *Contemporary Economic Thought: The Contribution of Neo-Institutional Economics*. Clifton, NJ: Augustus M. Kelley.

Grünbaum, Adolf and Salmon, Wesley C., eds. 1988. *The Limitations of Deductivism*. Berkeley: University of California Press.

Gunn, Richard. 1989. "Marxism and Philosophy: A Critique of Critical Realism." *Capital and Class* 37: 87–116.

Gutting, Gary. ed. 1980. *Paradigms and Revolutions*. Notre Dame, IN: University of Notre Dame Press.

Haack, Susan. 1993. *Evidence and Inquiry: Towards Reconstruction in Epistemology*. Oxford: Blackwell.

Habermas, Jürgen. 1971. *Knowledge and Human Interests*. Boston: Beacon Press.

Habermas, Jürgen. 1987. "Philosophy as Stand-in and Interpreter." In *After Philosophy*, ed. K. Baynes, J. Bohman, and T. McCarthy, 296–315. Cambridge, MA: MIT Press.

Habermas, Jürgen. 1992. *Postmetaphysical Thinking: Philosophical Essays*. Boston: MIT Press.

Hacking, Ian. 1979. "Imre Lakatos's Philosophy of Science." *British Journal for the Philosophy of Science* 30: 381–410.

Hacking, Ian. 1983. *Representing and Intervening*. Cambridge: Cambridge University Press.

Hacking, Ian. 1996. "The Disunities of the Sciences." In *The Disunity of Science: Boundaries, Contexts, and Power*, ed. P. Galison and D. J. Stump, 37–74. Stanford, CA: Stanford University Press.

Hacking, Ian. 1999. *The Social Construction of What?* Cambridge, MA: Harvard University Press.

Hacohen, Malachi H. 1998. "Karl Popper, the Vienna Circle, and Red Vienna." *Journal of the History of Ideas* 59: 711–34.

Hadden, Richard W. 1994. *On the Shoulders of Merchants: Exchange and the Mathematical Conception of Nature in Early Modern Europe*. Albany: State University of New York.

Hagstrom, W. O. 1965. *The Scientific Community*. New York: Basic Books.

Hall, D. L. 1994. *Richard Rorty: Prophet and Poet of the New Pragmatism*. Albany: State University of New York Press.

Hall, R. and Hitch, C. 1939. "Price Theory and Business Behavior." *Oxford Economic Papers* 2: 12–45.

Hamminga, Bert. 1983. *Neoclassical Theory Structure and Theory Development.* New York: Springer-Verlag.

Hamminga, Bert. 1989. "Sneed versus Nowak: An Illustration In Economics." *Erkenntnis* 30: 247–65.

Hamminga, Bert. 1990. "The Structure of Six Transformations in Marx's Capital." *Poznan Studies in the Philosophy of Science and the Humanities* 16: 89–111.

Hamminga, Bert. 1998a. "The Poznan Approach." In *The Handbook of Economic Methodology*, ed. J. B. Davis, D. W. Hands, and U. Mäki, 388–90. Cheltenham: Edward Elgar.

Hamminga, Bert. 1998b. "Plausibility." In *The Handbook of Economic Methodology*, ed. J. B. Davis, D. W. Hands, and U. Mäki, 364–6. Cheltenham: Edward Elgar.

Hamminga, Bert and De Marchi, Neil., eds. 1994. *Idealization VI: Idealization in Economics.* Amsterdam: Editions Rodopi.

Hammond, J. Daniel. 1991. "Frank Knight's Antipositivism." *History of Political Economy* 23: 359–81.

Hammond, J. Daniel. 1993. "An Interview with Milton Friedman on Methodology." In *The Philosophy and Methodology of Economics Vol. I*, ed. B. J. Caldwell, 216–38. Aldershot: Edward Elgar [interview conducted in May 1988].

Händler, Ernst W. 1980a. "The Logical Structure of Modern Neoclassical Static Microeconomic Equilibrium Theory." *Erkenntnis* 15: 33–53.

Händler, Ernst W. 1980b. "The Role of Utility and of Statistical Concepts in Empirical Economics: The Empirical Claims of the Systems of Aggregate Market Supply and Demand Functions Approach." *Erkenntnis* 15: 129–57.

Händler, Ernst W. 1982. "The Evolution of Economic Theories: A Formal Approach." *Erkenntnis* 18: 65–96.

Hands, D. Wade. 1979. "The Methodology of Economic Research Programmes." *Philosophy of the Social Sciences* 9: 293–303 [reprinted with minor revisions as chapter 1 of Hands, 1993].

Hands, D. Wade. 1983. "'Testing' Perfect Competition: A Comment." *Economic Inquiry* 21: 588–90.

Hands, D. Wade. 1984a. "Blaug's Economic Methodology." *Philosophy of the Social Sciences* 14: 115–25 [reprinted with minor revisions as chapter 3 of Hands 1993].

Hands, D. Wade. 1984b. "What Economics is Not: An Economist's Response to Rosenberg." *Philosophy of Science* 51: 495–503.

Hands, D. Wade. 1985a. "Second Thoughts on Lakatos." *History of Political Economy* 17: 1–16 [reprinted with minor revisions as chapter 4 of Hands 1993].

Hands, D. Wade. 1985b. "Karl Popper and Economic Methodology: A New Look." *Economics and Philosophy* 1: 303–35 [reprinted with minor revisions as chapter 6 of Hands 1993].

Hands, D. Wade. 1985c. "The Structuralist View of Economic Theories: A Review Essay." *Economics and Philosophy* 1: 303–35.

Hands, D. Wade. 1985d. "The Logical Structure of Pure Exchange Economics: Another Alternative." *Theory and Decision* 19: 259–78.

Hands, D. Wade. 1988. "Ad Hocness in Economics and the Popperian Tradition." In *The Popperian Legacy in Economics*, ed. N. De Marchi, 121–37. Cambridge: Cambridge University Press [reprinted with minor revisions as chapter 7 of Hands 1993].

Hands, D. Wade. 1990a. "Grunberg and Modigliani, Public Predictions and the New Classical Macroeconomics." *Research in the History of Economic Thought and Methodology* 7: 207–23.

Hands, D. Wade. 1990b. "Second Thoughts on 'Second Thoughts': Reconsidering the Lakatosian Progress of *The General Theory*." *Review of Political Economy* 2: 69–81 [reprinted with minor revisions as chapter 5 of Hands 1993].

Hands, D. Wade. 1991a. "Popper, the Rationality Principle and Economic Explanation." In *Economics, Culture and Education: Essays in Honour of Mark Blaug*, ed. G. K. Shaw, 108–19. Aldershot: Edward Elgar.

Hands, D. Wade. 1991b. "The Problem of Excess Content: Economics, Novelty, and a Long Popperian Tale." In *Appraising Economic Theories: Studies in the Methodology of Scientific Research Programs*, ed. M. Blaug and N. De Marchi, 58–75. Aldershot: Edward Elgar [reprinted with minor revisions as chapter 9 of Hands 1993].

Hands, D. Wade. 1991c. "Reply to Hamminga and Mäki." In *Appraising Economic Theories: Studies in the Methodology of Scientific Research Programs*, ed. M. Blaug and N. De Marchi, 91–102. Aldershot: Edward Elgar.

Hands, D. Wade. 1992. "Falsification, Situational Analysis, and Scientific Research Programs: The Popperian Tradition in Economic Methodology." In *Post-Popperian Methodology of Economics*, ed. N. De Marchi, 19–53. Boston: Kluwer [reprinted with minor revisions as chapter 8 of Hands 1993].

Hands, D. Wade. 1993. *Testing, Rationality, and Progress: Essays on the Popperian Tradition in Economic Methodology*. Lanham, MD: Rowman & Littlefield.

Hands, D. Wade. 1994a. "Blurred Boundaries: Recent Changes in the Relationship Between Economics and the Philosophy of Natural Science." *Studies in History and Philosophy of Science* 25: 751–72.

Hands, D. Wade. 1994b. "The Sociology of Scientific Knowledge." In *New Directions in Economic Methodology*, ed. R. Backhouse, 75–106. London: Routledge.

Hands, D. Wade. 1994c. "Restabilizing Dynamics: Construction and Constraint in the History of Walrasian Stability Theory." *Economics and Philosophy* 10: 243–83.

Hands, D. Wade. 1995. "Social Epistemology Meets the Invisible Hand: Kitcher on the Advancement of Science." *Dialogue* 34: 605–21.

Hands, D. Wade. 1996. "Karl Popper on the Myth of the Framework: Lukewarm Popperians +1, Unrepentant Popperians −1." *Journal of Economic Methodology* 3: 317–47.

Hands, D. Wade. 1997a. "Conjectures and Reputations: The Sociology of Scientific Knowledge and the History of Economic Thought." *History of Political Economy* 29: 695–739.

Hands, D. Wade. 1997b. "Frank Knight's Pluralism." In *Pluralism in Economics*, ed. A. Salanti and E. Serepanti, 194–206. Aldershot: Edward Elgar.

Hands, D. Wade. 1997c. "Empirical Realism as Meta-Method: Tony Lawson on Neoclassical Economics." *Ekonomia* 1: 39–53 [reprinted with minor revisions as Chapter 10 of Fleetwood 1999].

Hands, D. Wade. 1997d. "Caveat Emptor: Economics and Contemporary Philosophy of Science." *Philosophy of Science* 64 (Proceedings): S107–S116.

Hands, D. Wade. 1998. "Scientific Explanation." In *The Handbook of Economic Methodology*, ed. J. B. Davis, D. W. Hands, and U. Mäki, 439–43. Cheltenham: Edward Elgar.

Hands, D. Wade and Mirowski, Philip. 1998. "Harold Hotelling and the Neoclassical Dream." In *Economics and Methodology: Crossing Boundaries*, ed. R. Backhouse, D. Hausman, U. Mäki, and A. Salanti, 322–97. London: Macmillan.

Hanson, N. R. 1958. *Patterns of Discovery*. Cambridge: Cambridge University Press.

Haraway, Donna J. 1991. *Simians, Cyborgs, and Women: The Reinvention of Nature*. New York: Routledge.

Harding, Sandra. 1986. *The Science Question in Feminism*. Ithaca, NY: Cornell University Press.

Harding, Sandra. 1991. *Whose Science? Whose Knowledge? Thinking from Women's Lives.* Ithaca, NY: Cornell University Press.

Harding, Sandra. 1993. "Rethinking Standpoint Epistemology: What Is 'Strong Objectivity'?" in *Feminist Epistemologies*, ed. L. Alcoff and E. Potter, 49–82. London: Routledge.

Harding, Sandra. 1995. "Can Feminist Thought Make Economics More Objective?" *Feminist Economics* 1: 7–32.

Hargreaves Heap, Shaun. 1989. *Rationality in Economics.* Oxford: Basil Blackwell.

Harré, Rom. 1986. *Varieties of Realism.* Oxford: Basil Blackwell.

Harris, Paul L. 1992. "From Simulation to Folk Psychology: The Case for Development." *Mind and Language* 7: 120–44.

Harris, R. Allen. 1991. "Rhetoric of Science." *College English* 53: 282–307.

Harsanyi, John C. 1955. "Cardinal Welfare, Individualistic Ethics and Interpersonal Comparisons of Utility." *Journal of Political Economy* 63: 309–21.

Haslinger, Franz. 1983. "A Logical Reconstruction of Pure Exchange Economics: An Alternative View." *Erkenntnis* 20: 115–29.

Hausman, Daniel M. 1980. "How to do the Philosophy of Economics." In *PSA 1980*, Vol. I, ed. P. D. Asquith and R. N. Giere, 353–62. East Lansing, MI: PSA.

Hausman, Daniel M. 1981a. *Capital, Profits, and Prices: An Essay in the Philosophy of Economics.* New York: Columbia University Press.

Hausman, Daniel M. 1981b. "John Stuart Mill's Philosophy of Economics." *Philosophy of Science* 48: 363–85.

Hausman, Daniel M. 1985. "Is Falsificationism Unpracticed or Unpracticable?" *Philosophy of the Social Sciences* 15: 313–19.

Hausman, Daniel M. 1988. "An Appraisal of Popperian Economic Methodology." In *The Popperian Legacy in Economics*, ed. N. De Marchi, 65–85. Cambridge: Cambridge University Press.

Hausman, Daniel M. 1989. "Explanatory Progress in Economics." *Social Research* 56: 361–81.

Hausman, Daniel M. 1992. *The Inexact and Separate Science of Economics.* Cambridge: Cambridge University Press.

Hausman, Daniel M. 1994. "Kuhn, Lakatos and the Character of Economics." In *New Directions in Economic Methodology*, ed. R. Backhouse, 195–215. London: Routledge.

Hausman, Daniel M. 1995. "The Composition of Economic Causes." *The Monist* 78: 295–307.

Hausman, Daniel M. 1996. "Economics as Separate and Inexact." *Economics and Philosophy* 12: 207–20.

Hausman, Daniel M. 1997. "Theory Appraisal in Neoclassical Economics." *Journal of Economic Methodology* 4: 289–96.

Hausman, Daniel M. 1998a. "Separateness, Inexactness and Economic Method: A Very Brief Response." *Journal of Economic Methodology* 5: 155–6.

Hausman, Daniel M. 1998b. "Problems with Realism in Economics." *Economics and Philosophy* 14: 185–213.

Hausman, Daniel M. 1999. "Ontology and Methodology in Economics." *Economics and Philosophy* 15: 283–8.

Hausman, Daniel M. 2000. "Realist Philosophy and Methodology of Economics: What Is It?" *Journal of Economic Methodology* 7: 127–33.

Hausman, Daniel M. and McPherson, Michael S. 1996. *Economic Analysis and Moral Philosophy.* Cambridge: Cambridge University Press.

Hausman, Daniel M. and Mongin, Philippe. 1998. "Economists' Responses to Anomalies: Full-Cost Pricing versus Preference Reversals." In *New Economics and Its History*, ed. J. B. Davis, 255–72. Durham, NC: Duke University Press.

Hayek, Friedrich A. 1934. "Carl Menger." *Economica* a: 393–420.

Hayek, Friedrich A. 1937. "Economics and Knowledge." *Economica* 4: 33–54.

Hayek, Friedrich A. 1952. *The Sensory Order: An Inquiry Into the Foundations of Theoretical Psychology*. Chicago: University of Chicago Press.

Hayek, Friedrich A. 1967a. "Degrees of Explanation." In *Studies in Philosophy, Politics and Economics*, 3–21. Chicago: University of Chicago Press [originally published in 1955].

Hayek, Friedrich A. 1967b. "The Theory of Complex Phenomena." In *Studies in Philosophy, Politics and Economics*, 22–24. Chicago: University of Chicago Press [originally published in 1964].

Hayek, Friedrich A. 1967c. "The Results of Human Action but Not of Human Design." In *Studies in Philosophy, Politics and Economics*, 96–105. Chicago: University of Chicago Press.

Hayek, Friedrich A. 1973. "The Place of Menger's *Grundsätze* in the History of Economic Thought." In *Carl Menger and the Austrian School of Economics*, ed. J. R. Hicks and W. Weber, 1–14. Oxford: Oxford University Press.

Hayek, Friedrich A. 1979. *The Counter-Revolution of Science*, 2nd ed. Indianapolis, IN: Liberty Press [1st edition 1952].

Hempel, Carl G. 1962. "Rational Action." *Proceedings and Addresses of the American Philosophical Association* 35: 5–23.

Hempel, Carl G. 1965. *Aspects of Scientific Explanation*. New York: The Free Press.

Hempel, Carl G. 1966. *Philosophy of Natural Science*. Englewood Cliffs, NJ: Prentice Hall.

Hempel, Carl G. 1969. "Logical Positivism and the Social Sciences." In *The Legacy of Logical Positivism*, ed. P. Achinstein and S. F. Barker, 163–94. Baltimore, MD: Johns Hopkins University Press.

Hempel, Carl G. and Oppenheim, Paul. 1948. "Studies in the Logic of Explanation." *Philosophy of Science* 15: 135–75 [reprinted (with postscript) as chapter 10 of Hempel 1965].

Henderson, James P. 1990. "Induction, Deduction, and the Role of Mathematics: The Whewell Group vs. The Ricardian Economists." *Research in the History of Economic Thought and Methodology* 7: 1–36.

Henderson, James P. 1996. *Early Mathematical Economics: William Whewell and the British Case*. Lanham, MD: Roman and Littlefield.

Henderson, James P. 1998. "Whewell, William." In *The Handbook of Economic Methodology*, ed. J. B. Davis, D. W. Hands, and U. Mäki, 547–9. Cheltenham: Edward Elgar.

Henderson, Willie, Dudley-Evans, Tony, and Backhouse, Roger., eds. 1993. *Economics and Language*. London: Routledge.

Hendry, David F. 1980. "Econometrics – Alchemy or Science?" *Economica* 47: 387–406.

Hesse, Mary. 1966. *Models and Analogies in Science*. Notre Dame, IN: University of Notre Dame Press.

Hessen, Boris. 1931. "The Social and Economic Roots of Newton's 'Principia'." In *Science at the Crossroads*, ed. N. Bukharin et al., 151–211. London: Frank Cass & Co.

Hickerson, Steven R. 1987. "Instrumental Valuation: The Normative Compass of Institutional Economics." *Journal of Economic Issues* 21: 1117–43.

Hintikka, Jaakko. 1998. "What is Abduction? The Fundamental Problem of Contemporary Epistemology." *Transactions of the Charles S. Peirce Society* 34: 503–33.

Hirsch, Abraham. 1992. "John Stuart Mill on Verification and the Business of Science." *History of Political Economy* 24: 843–66.

Hirsch, Abraham. 1995. "John Stuart Mill and the Problem of Induction." In *Monetarism and the Methodology of Economics: Essays in Honour of Thomas Mayer*, ed. K. D. Hoover and S. M. Sheffrin, 217–24. Aldershot: Edward Elgar.

Hirsch, Abraham and De Marchi, Neil. 1990. *Milton Friedman: Economics In Theory and Practice*. Ann Arbor: University of Michigan Press.

Hodgson, Geoffrey M. 1989. "Institutional Economic Theory: the Old versus the New." *Review of Political Economy* 1: 249–69.

Hodgson, Geoffrey M. 1993. *Economics and Evolution: Bringing Life Back Into Economics*. Ann Arbor: University of Michigan Press.

Hodgson, Geoffrey M. 1994. "The Return of Institutional Economics." In *The Handbook of Economic Sociology*, ed. N. J. Smelser and R. Swedberg, 58–76. Princeton, NJ: Princeton University Press.

Hodgson, Geoffrey M. 1997. "Economics and the Return to Mecca: The Recognition of Novelty and Emergence." *Structural Change and Economic Dynamics* 8: 399–412.

Hodgson, Geoffrey M. 1998a. "The Approach of Institutional Economics." *Journal of Economic Issues* 36: 166–92.

Hodgson, Geoffrey M. 1998b. "Evolutionary Economics." In *The Handbook of Economic Methodology*, ed. J. B. Davis, D. W. Hands, and U. Mäki, 160–7. Cheltenham: Edward Elgar.

Hoefer, Carl and Rosenberg, Alexander. 1994. "Empirical Equivalence, Underdetermination, and Systems of the World." *Philosophy of Science* 61: 592–607.

Hoksbergen, Roland. 1994. "Postmodernism and Institutionalism: Toward a Resolution of the Debate on Relativism." *Journal of Economic Issues* 28: 679–713.

Hollander, Samuel. 1983. "William Whewell and John Stuart Mill On the Methodology of Political Economy." *Studies in History and Philosophy of Science* 14: 127–68.

Hollander, Samuel. 1985. *The Economics of John Stuart Mill*, 2 Vols. Toronto: University of Toronto Press.

Hollander, Samuel and Peart, Sandra. 1999. "John Stuart Mill's Method in Principle and Practice: A Review of the Evidence." *Journal of the History of Economic Thought* 21: 369–97.

Hollis, Martin. 1982. "The Social Destruction of Reality." In *Rationality and Relativism*, ed. M. Hollis and S. Lukes, 67–86. Cambridge, MA: MIT Press.

Hollis, Martin and Nell, Edward J. 1975. *Rational Economic Man: A Philosophical Critique of Neo-Clasical Economics*. Cambridge: Cambridge University Press.

Hooker, C. A. 1995. *Reason, Regulation, and Realism*. Albany: State University of New York Press.

Hoover, Kevin D. 1984. "Methodology: A Comment on Frazer and Boland." *American Economic Review* 74: 789–92.

Hoover, Kevin D. 1991. "Scientific Research Program or Tribe? A Joint Appraisal of Lakatos and the New Classical Macroeconomics." In *Appraising Economic Theories: Studies in the Methodology of Scientific Research Programs*, ed. M. Blaug and N. De Marchi, 364–94. Aldershot: Edward Elgar.

Hoover, Kevin D. 1994. "Pragmatism, Pragmaticism and Economic Method." In *New Directions in Economic Methodology*, ed. R. Backhouse, 286–315. London: Routledge.

Hoover, Kevin D. 1995a. "Is Macro for Real?" *The Monist* 78: 235–57.

Hoover, Kevin D. 1995b. "Why Does Methodology Matter to Economics?" *Economic Journal* 105: 715–34.

Hoover, Kevin D. 1997. "Econometrics and Reality" (forthcoming).

Houthakker, Hendrik S. 1950. "Revealed Preference and the Utility Function." *Econometrica* 17: 159–74.

Houthakker, Hendrik S. 1983. "On Consumption Theory." In *Paul Samuelson and Modern Economics*, ed. E. C. Brown and R. M. Solow, 57–68. New York: McGraw Hill.

Hoyningen-Huene, Paul. 1993. *Reconstructing Scientific Revolutions: Thomas S. Kuhn's Philosophy of Science.* Trans. Alexander Levine. Chicago: University of Chicago Press.

Hudson, Richard. 1997. "Rosenberg, Intentionality, and Explanatory Strategies in Financial Economics" [paper presented at the History of Economics Society Meetings, Charleston, S.C., June 1997].

Hull, David. 1988. *An Evolutionary Account of the Social and Conceptual Development in Science.* Chicago: University of Chicago Press.

Hull, David. 1997. "What's Wrong with Invisible-Hand Explanation?" *Philosophy of Science* 64 (Proceedings): S117–S126.

Hume, David. 1888. *A Treatise of Human Nature*, Reprinted from the Original Edition in Three Volumes, ed. L. A. Selby-Bigge. Oxford: Oxford University Press [originally published in 1739].

Hutchison, Terence. 1938. *The Significance and Basic Postulates of Economic Theory.* London: Macmillan.

Hutchison, Terence. 1941. "The Significance and Basic Postulates of Economic Theory: A Reply to Professor Knight." *Journal of Political Economy* 49: 732–50.

Hutchison, Terence. 1960. *The Significance and Basic Postulates of Economic Theory.* New York: Augustus M. Kelly.

Hutchison, Terence. 1973. "Some Themes from *Investigations of Method*." In *Carl Menger and the Austrian School of Economics*, ed. J. R. Hicks and W. Weber, 16–37. Oxford: Oxford University Press.

Hutchison, Terence. 1976. "On the History and Philosophy of Science and Economics." In *Method and Appraisal in Economics*, ed. S. J. Latsis, 181–205. Cambridge: Cambridge University Press.

Hutchison, Terence. 1981. *The Politics and Philosophy of Economics.* New York: New York University Press.

Hutchison, Terence. 1988. "The Case for Falsificationism." In *The Popperian Legacy in Economics*, ed. N. De Marchi, 169–81. Cambridge: Cambridge University Press.

Hutchison, Terence. 1992a. "Hayek and 'Modern Austrian' Methodology: Comment on a Non-Refuting Refutation." *Research in the History of Economic Thought and Methodology* 10: 17–32.

Hutchison, Terence. 1992b. *Changing Aims in Economics.* Oxford: Blackwell.

Hutchison, Terence. 1996. "On the Relations Between Philosophy and Economics: Part I: Frontier Problems in an Era of Departmentalized and Internationalized 'Professionalism'." *Journal of Economic Methodology* 3: 187–213.

Hutchison, Terence. 1998. "Ultra-deductivism from Nassau Senior to Lionel Robbins and Daniel Hausman." *Journal of Economic Methodology* 5: 43–91.

Irzik, Gürol and Grünberg, Teo. 1995. "Carnap and Kuhn: Arch Enemies or Close Allies?" *British Journal for the Philosophy of Science* 46: 285–307.

Jackson, Frank and Pettit, Philip. 1992. "In Defense of Explanatory Ecumenism." *Economics and Philosophy* 8: 1–21.

Jackson, William A. 1995. "Naturalism in Economics." *Journal of Economic Issues* 39: 761–80.

Jaffé, William. 1976. "Menger, Jevons and Walras De-homogenized." *Economic Inquiry* 14: 511–24 [reprinted as Chapter 17 of Walker 1983].

James, William. 1907. *Pragmatism: A New Name for Some Old Ways of Thinking.* Cambridge, MA: Harvard University Press [1975].

Janssen, Maarten C. W. 1991. "What Is This Thing Called Microfoundations?" *History of Political Economy* 23: 687–712.

Janssen, Maarten C. W. 1994. "Economic Models and Their Application." In *Idealization VI: Idealization in Economics*, ed. B. Hamminga and N. De Marchi, 101–16. Amsterdam: Rodopi.

Janssen, Maarten C. W. and Kuipers, Theo A. F. 1989. "Stratification of General Equilibrium Theory: A Synthesis of Reconstructions." In *Philosophy of Economics*, ed. W. Balzer and B. Hamminga, 183–205. Dordrecht: Kluwer.

Jevons, William Stanley. 1877. *The Principles of Science.* London: Macmillan.

Jevons, William Stanley. 1879. *Theory of Political Economy*, 2nd ed. London: Macmillan [1st edition 1871, Augustus M. Kelley reprint 1957].

Johnson, Harry G. 1972. "Some Economic Aspects of Science." *Minerva* 10: 10–18.

Jolink, Albert. 1999. "T. W. Hutchison's Role in the Dissemination of Otto Neurath's Physicalism to Economics." Paper presented at the History of Economics Society Annual meeting in June 1999 at the University of North Carolina, Greensboro.

Junker, Louis J. 1962. "The Social and Economic Thought of Clarence Edwin Ayres." Ph.D. Dissertation. University of Wisconsin, Ann Arbor, MI: University Microfilms.

Kahn, James A., Landsburg, Steven E., and Stockman, Alan C. 1992. "On Novel Confirmation." *British Journal for the Philosophy of Science* 43: 503–16.

Kahn, James A., Landsburg, Steven E., and Stockman, Alan C. 1996. "The Positive Economics of Methodology." *Journal of Economic Theory* 68: 64–76.

Karsten, S. 1973. "Dialectics and the Evolution of Economic Thought." *History of Political Economy* 5: 399–419.

Kauder, Emil. 1957. "Intellectual and Political Roots of the Older Austrian School." *Zeitschrift für Nationalökonomie* 17: 411–25.

Kealey, Terence. 1996. *The Economic Laws of Scientific Research.* New York: St. Martin's.

Kealey, Terence. 1998. "Why Science is Endogenous: a Debate with Paul David and Ben Martin, Paul Romer, Chris Freeman, Luc Soete and Keith Pavitt." *Research Policy* 26: 897–923.

Ketner, Kenneth Laine. 1998. *His Glassy Essence: An Autobiography of Charles Sanders Peirce.* Nashville, TN: Vanderbilt University Press.

Keuzenkamp, Hugo A. 1994. "What if an Idealization is Problematic? The Case of the Homogeneity Condition in Consumer Demand." In *Idealization VI: Idealization in Economics*, ed. B. Hamminga and N. De Marchi, 243–54. Amsterdam: Rodopi.

Keynes, John Maynard. 1962. *A Treatise on Probability.* New York: Harper and Row [1st edition 1921].

Keynes, John Neville. 1917. *The Scope and Method of Political Economy*, 4th ed. London: Macmillan & Co. [1st edition 1890, Augustus M. Kelley reprint 1986].

Kilpatrick, A. and Lawson, Tony. 1980. "On the Nature of Industrial Decline in the UK." *Cambridge Journal of Economics* 4: 85–102.

Kim, Jaegwon. 1982. "Psychophysical Supervenience." *Philosophical Studies* 41: 51–70 [reprinted as chapter 10 of Kim 1993].

Kim, Jaegwon. 1984. "Concepts of Supervenience." *Philosophy and Phenomenological Research* 45: 155–76 [reprinted as chapter 4 of Kim 1993].

Kim, Jaegwon. 1988. "What is 'Naturalized Epistemology?'" *Philosophical Perspectives* 2: 381–405 [reprinted as chapter 12 of Kim 1993].

Kim, Jaegwon. 1993. *Supervenience and Mind*. Cambridge: Cambridge University Press.

Kim, Jinbang. 1991. "Testing in Modern Economics: the Case of Job Search Theory." In *Appraising Economic Theories: Studies in the Methodology of Scientific Research Programs*, ed. M. Blaug and N. De Marchi, 105–30. Aldershot: Edward Elgar.

Kimball, Bruce. 1995. *The Condition of American Education: Pragmatism and a Changing Condition*. New York: College Entrance Examination Board.

Kincaid, Harold. 1988. "Supervenience and Explanation." *Synthese* 77: 251–81.

Kincaid, Harold. 1996. *Philosophical Foundations of the Social Sciences*. Cambridge: Cambridge University Press.

Kincaid, Harold. 1997. "Individualism and Rationality." In *Individualism and the Unity of Science*, 119–42. Lanham, MD: Roman & Littlefield.

Kincaid, Harold. 1998. "Supervenience." In *The Handbook of Economic Methodology*, ed. J. B. Davis, D. W. Hands, and U. Mäki, 487–8. Cheltenham: Edward Elgar.

Kitcher, Philip. 1990. "The Division of Cognitive Labor." *The Journal of Philosophy* 87: 5–22.

Kitcher, Philip. 1992. "The Naturalists Return." *The Philosophical Review* 101: 53–114.

Kitcher, Philip. 1993. *The Advancement of Science: Science Without Legend, Objectivity Without Illusions*. Oxford: Oxford University Press.

Kitcher, Philip. 1994. "Contrasting Conceptions of Social Epistemology." In *Socializing Epistemology: The Social Dimensions of Knowledge*, ed. F. F. Schmitt, 111–34. Lanham, MD: Roman and Littlefield.

Kitcher, Philip. 1997. "An Argument About Free Inquiry." *Noûs* 31: 279–306.

Klamer, Arjo. 1984. "Levels of Discourse in New Classical Economics." *History of Political Economy* 16: 263–90.

Klamer, Arjo. 1987. "As If Economics and Their Subject Were Rational." In *The Rhetoric of the Human Sciences*, ed. J. S. Nelson, A. Megill, and D. N. McCloskey, 163–83. Madison: University of Wisconsin Press.

Klamer, Arjo. 1990. "The Textbook Presentation of Economic Discourse." In *Economics and Discourse: An Analysis of the Language of Economics*, ed. W. J. Samuels, 129–65. Boston: Kluwer.

Klamer, Arjo. 1991. "On Interpretative and Feminist Economics." In *Economics, Culture and Education: Essays in Honour of Mark Blaug*, ed. G. K. Shaw, 133–41. Aldershot: Edward Elgar.

Klamer, Arjo and McCloskey, D. N. 1992. "Accounting as the Master Metaphor of Economics." *The European Accounting Review* 1: 145–60.

Klamer, Arjo, McCloskey, D. N., and Solow, Robert M., eds. 1988. *The Consequences of Economic Rhetoric*. Cambridge: Cambridge University Press.

Klant, Johannes J. 1984. *The Rules of the Game*. Cambridge: Cambridge University Press.

Klant, Johannes J. 1988. "The Natural Order." In *The Popperian Legacy in Economics*, ed. N. De Marchi, 87–117. Cambridge: Cambridge University Press.

Klant, Johannes J. 1994. *The Nature of Economic Thought: Essays in Economic Methodology*. Trans. T. S. Preston. Aldershot: Edward Elgar.

Klappholz, Kurt and Agassi, Joseph. 1959. "Methodological Prescriptions in Economics." *Economica* 26: 60–74.

Klein, Judy L. 1997. *Statistical Visions in Time: A History of Time Series Analysis 1662–1938*. Cambridge: Cambridge University Press.

Klein, Philip A. 1998. "Is Postmodern Institutionalism the Wave of the Future? A Reply to Hoksbergen." *Journal of Economic Issues* 32: 833–43.

Knight, Frank H. 1922. "Ethics and Economic Interpretation." *Quarterly Journal of Economics* 36: 454–81.

Knight, Frank H. 1940. "'What is Truth' in Economics?" *Journal of Political Economy* 48 [reprinted as chapter 7 of Knight 1956, page references to reprint].

Knight, Frank H. 1956. *On the History and Method of Economics*. Chicago: University of Chicago Press.

Knorr Cetina, Karin. 1981. *The Manufacture of Knowledge: An Essay on the Constructivist and Contextual Nature of Science*. New York: Pergamon.

Knorr Cetina, Karin. 1991. "Epistemic Cultures: Forms of Reason in Science." *History of Political Economy* 23: 105–22.

Koch, Sigmund. 1992. "Psychology's Bridgman vs. Bridgman's Bridgman." *Theory & Psychology* 2: 261–90.

Koertge, Noretta. 1975. "Popper's Metaphysical Research Program for the Human Sciences." *Inquiry* 19: 437–62.

Koertge, Noretta. 1979. "The Methodological Status of Popper's Rationality Principle." *Theory and Decision* 10: 83–95.

Koertge, Noretta. 1996. "Feminist Epistemology: Stalking an Un-Dead Horse." In *The Flight from Science and Reason*, ed. P. R. Gross, N. Levitt, and M. W. Lewis, 413–19. Baltimore, MD: The Johns Hopkins University Press.

Koopmans, Tjalling C. 1947. "Measurement Without Theory." *The Review of Economics and Statistics* 29: 161–72.

Koopmans, Tjalling C. 1949. "A Reply." *The Review of Economics and Statistics* 31: 86–91.

Koopmans, Tjalling C. 1957. *Three Essays on the State of Economic Science*. New York: McGraw Hill.

Koot, Gerard M. 1987. *English Historical Economics. 1970–1926: The Rise of Economic History and NeoMercantilitsm*. Cambridge: Cambridge University Press.

Kornblith, Hilary. 1985a. "Introduction: What is Naturalistic Epistemology." In *Naturalizing Epistemology*, ed. H. Kornblith, 1–13. Cambridge, MA: MIT Press.

Kornblith, Hilary., ed. 1985b. *Naturalizing Epistemology*. Cambridge, MA: MIT Press.

Kuhn, Thomas S. 1962. *The Structure of Scientific Revolutions*, 1st ed. Chicago: University of Chicago Press.

Kuhn, Thomas S. 1970a. *The Structure of Scientific Revolutions*, 2nd ed. Chicago: University of Chicago Press.

Kuhn, Thomas S. 1970b. "Reflections on My Critics." In *Criticism and the Growth of Knowledge*, ed. I. Lakatos and A. Musgrave, 231–78. Cambridge: Cambridge University Press.

Kuhn, Thomas S. 1976. "Theory-Change as Structure-Change: Comments on the Sneed Formalism." *Erkenntnis* 10: 179–99.

Kuhn, Thomas S. 1977a. *The Essential Tension*. Chicago: University of Chicago Press.

Kuhn, Thomas S. 1977b. "Second Thoughts on Paradigms." In *The Structure of Scientific Theories*, 2nd ed., ed. F. Suppe, 459–82. Urbana, IL: University of Illinois Press.

Kuhn, Thomas S. 1992. *The Trouble with the Historical Philosophy of Science*. An Occasional Publication of the Department of History of Science, Harvard University, Cambridge, MA.

Kuhn, Thomas S. 1993. "Afterword." In *World Changes: Thomas Kuhn and the Nature of Science*, ed. P. Horwich, 311–41. Cambridge, MA: MIT Press.

Kulkarni, Deepak and Simon, Herbert. 1988. "The Process of Scientific Discovery: The Strategy of Experimentation." *Cognitive Science* 12: 139–75.

Kuokkanen, Martti. 1993. "On the Structuralist Constraints in Social Scientific Theorizing." *Theory and Decision* 35: 19–54.

Lagueux, M. 1994. "Friedman's 'Instrumentalism' and Constructive Empiricism in Economics." *Theory and Decision* 37: 147–74.

Lakatos, Imre. 1968. "Criticism and the Methodology of Scientific Research Programmes." *Proceedings of the Aristotelian Society* 69: 149–86.

Lakatos, Imre. 1970. "Falsification and the Methodology of Scientific Research Programmes." In *Criticism and the Growth of Knowledge*, ed. I. Lakatos and A. Musgrave, 91–196. Cambridge: Cambridge University Press.

Lakatos, Imre. 1971. "History of Science and Its Rational Reconstruction." In *Boston Studies in the Philosophy of Science*, ed. R. C. Buck and R. S. Cohen, 174–82. Dordrecht: D. Reidel.

Lakatos, Imre. 1976. *Proofs and Refutations*. Cambridge: Cambridge University Press.

Lakatos, Imre. 1978. "Popper on Demarcation and Induction." In *The Methodology of Scientific Research Programmes: Philosophical Papers, Vol. I*, 139–67. Cambridge: Cambridge University Press.

Langley, Pat, Simon, Herbert, Bradshaw, Gary, and Zytkow, Jan. 1987. *Scientific Discovery: Computational Explorations of the Creative Process*. Cambridge, MA: MIT Press.

Langlois, Richard N. 1989. "What Was Wrong with the Old Institutional Economics (and What is Still Wrong with the New)." *Review of Political Economy* 1: 270–98.

Langlois, Richard N., ed. 1986. *Economics as a Process: Essays in the New Institutional Economics*. New York: Cambridge University Press.

Larvor, Brendan. 1998. *Lakatos: An Introduction*. London: Routledge.

Latour, Bruno. 1987. *Science in Action*. Cambridge, MA: Harvard University Press.

Latour, Bruno. 1990. "Postmodern? No, Simply A Modern! Steps Toward an Anthropology of Science." *Studies in History and Philosophy of Science* 21: 145–71.

Latour, Bruno. 1992. "One More Turn After the Social Turn." In *The Social Dimensions of Science*, ed. E. McMullin, 272–94. Notre Dame, IN: University of Notre Dame Press.

Latour, Bruno. 1993. *We Have Never Been Modern*. Cambridge, MA: Harvard University Press.

Latour, Bruno. 1999. *Pandora's Hope: Essays on the Reality of Science Studies*. Cambridge, MA: Harvard University Press.

Latour, Bruno and Woolgar, Steve. 1979. *Laboratory Life: the Construction of Scientific Facts*. Beverly Hills, CA: Sage.

Latour, Bruno and Woolgar, Steve. 1986. *Laboratory Life: the Construction of Scientific Facts*, 2nd ed. Princeton, NJ: Princeton University Press.

Latsis, Spiro J. 1972. "Situational Determinism in Economics." *British Journal for the Philosophy of Science* 23: 207–45.

Latsis, Spiro J., ed. 1976a. *Method and Appraisal in Economics*. Cambridge: Cambridge University Press.

Latsis, Spiro J. 1976b. "A Research Programme in Economics." In *Method and Appraisal in Economics*, ed. S. J. Latsis, 1–41. Cambridge: Cambridge University Press.

Latsis, Spiro J. 1983. "The Role and Status of the Rationality Principle in the Social Sciences." In *Epistemology, Methodology, and the Social Sciences*, ed. R. S. Cohen and M. W. Wartofsky, 123–51. Dordrecht: D. Reidel.

Laudan, Larry. 1977. *Progress and Its Problems*. Berkeley: University of California Press.

Laudan, Larry. 1984. *Science and Values*. Berkeley: University of California Press.

Laudan, Larry. 1986. "Some Problems Facing Intuitionist Meta-Methodologies." *Synthese* 67: 115–29.

Laudan, Larry. 1989. "If It Ain't Broke, Don't Fix It." *British Journal for the Philosophy of Science* 40: 369–75.

Laudan, Larry. 1990. "Normative Naturalism." *Philosophy of Science* 57: 44–59.

Laudan, Larry et al. 1986. "Scientific Change: Philosophical Models and Historical Research." *Synthese* 69: 141–223.

Lavoie, Don. 1990. "Understanding Differently: Hermeneutics and the Spontaneous Order of Communicative Process." In *Carl Menger and His Legacy in Economics*, ed. B. J. Caldwell, 359–77. Durham, NC: Duke University Press.

Lavoie, Don. 1991a. "The Progress of Subjectivism." In *Appraising Economic Theories: Studies in the Methodology of Scientific Research Programs*, ed. M. Blaug and N. De Marchi, 470–86. Aldershot: Edward Elgar.

Lavoie, Don., ed. 1991b. *Hermeneutics and Economics*. London: Routledge.

Lawson, Clive. 1996. "Realism, Theory, and Individualism in the Work of Carl Menger." *Review of Social Economy* 54: 445–64 [reprinted with minor revisions as chapter 3 of Fleetwood 1999].

Lawson, Tony. 1985. "The Context of Prediction (and the Paradoxes of Confirmation)." *British Journal for the Philosophy of Science* 36: 393–407.

Lawson, Tony. 1989a. "Abstraction, Tendencies and Stylised Facts: A Realist Approach to Economic Analysis." *Cambridge Journal of Economics* 13: 59–78.

Lawson, Tony. 1989b. "Realism and Instrumentalism in the Development of Econometrics." *Oxford Economic Papers* 41: 236–58.

Lawson, Tony. 1992. "Realism, Closed Systems, and Friedman." *Research in the History of Economic Thought and Methodology* 10: 149–69.

Lawson, Tony. 1994a. "A Realist Theory for Economics." In *New Directions in Economic Methodology*, ed. R. Backhouse, 257–85. London: Routledge.

Lawson, Tony. 1994b. "Realism and Hayek: A Case of Continuing Transformation." In *Capitalism, Socialism and Knowledge: the Economics of F. A. Hayek*, Vol. I, ed. M. Colonna, H. Hagemann, and O. Hamouda, 131–59. Aldershot: Edward Elgar.

Lawson, Tony. 1994c. "Why Are So Many Economists so Opposed to Methodology?" *Journal of Economic Methodology* 1: 105–33.

Lawson, Tony. 1994d. "The Nature of Post-Keynesianism and Its Links to Other Traditions: A Realist Perspective." *Journal of Post-Keynesian Economics* 16: 503–38.

Lawson, Tony. 1995. "A Realist Perspective on Contemporary 'Economic Theory'." *Journal of Economic Issues* 29: 1–32.

Lawson, Tony. 1996. "Developments in Economics as Realist Social Theory." *Review of Social Economy* 54: 405–22 [reprinted with minor revisions as chapter 1 of Fleetwood 1999].

Lawson, Tony. 1997a. *Economics and Reality*. London: Routledge.

Lawson, Tony. 1997b. "Critical Issues in *Economics as Realist Social Theory*." *Ekonomia* 1: 75–117 [reprinted with minor revisions as chapter 12 of Fleetwood 1999].

Lawson, Tony. 1997c. "On Criticizing the Practices of Economists: A Case for Interventionist Methodology." In *Pluralism in Economics*, ed. A. Salanti and E. Serepanti, 13–36. Aldershot: Edward Elgar.

Lawson, Tony. 1997d. "Development in Hayek's Social Theorising." In *Hayek: Economist and Social Philosopher*, ed. S. F. Frowen, 125–47. New York: St. Martins.

Lawson, Tony. 1998. "Clarifying and Developing the *Economics and Reality* Project: Closed and Open Systems, Deductivism, Prediction, and Teaching." *Review of Social Economy* 56: 356–75.

Lawson, Tony. 1999. "What Has Realism Got To Do With It?" *Economics and Philosophy* 15: 269–82.

Leamer, Edward. 1983. "Let's Take the Con Out of Econometrics." *American Economic Review* 73: 31–64.

Leijonhufvud, Axel. 1976. "Schools, 'Revolutions,' and Research Programmes in Economic Theory." In *Method and Appraisal in Economics*, ed. S. J. Latsis, 65–108. Cambridge: Cambridge University Press.

Leinfellner, W. 1983. "Marxian Paradigms versus Microeconomic Structures." In *Epistemology, Methodology, and the Social Sciences*, ed. R. S. Cohen and M. W. Wartofsky, 153–201. Dordrecht: D. Reidel.

Lenoir, Timothy. 1988. "Practice, Reason, Context: The Dialogue Between Theory and Experiment." *Science in Context* 2: 3–22.

Lenoir, Timothy. 1992. "Practical Reason and the Construction of Knowledge." In *The Social Dimensions of Science*, ed. E. McMullin, 158–97. Notre Dame, IN: University of Notre Dame Press.

Leonard, Robert J. 1994a. "Laboratory Strife: Higgling as Experimental Science in Economics and Social Psychology." In *Higgling: Transactors and Their Markets in the History of Economics* [Supplement to *HOPE* vol. 26], ed. N. De Marchi and M. S. Morgan, 343–69. Durham, NC: Duke University Press.

Leonard, Robert J. 1994b. "Reading Cournot, Reading Nash: The Creation and Stabilisation of the Nash Equilibrium." *Economic Journal* 104: 492–511.

Leonard, Robert J. 1995a. "Social Signs, Social Science: The Vienna Circle, the Visual Arts, and Social Theory in the Interwar Period." Paper presented at the History of Economics Society Annual meeting in June 1995 at the University of Notre Dame.

Leonard, Robert J. 1995b. "From Parlor Games to Social Science: von Neumann, Morgenstern, and the Creation of Game Theory 1928–1944." *Journal of Economic Literature* 33: 730–61.

Leonard, Robert J. 1997. "Value, Sign and Social Structure: the 'Game' Metaphor and Modern Social Science." *The European Journal of the History of Economic Thought* 4: 299–326.

Leonard, Robert J. 1998. "Karl Menger and Social Science in Interwar Vienna." *Isis* 89: 1–26.

Leonard, Thomas Clark. 1997. "The Reason of Rules in the Intellectual Economy: The Economics of Science and the Science of Economics." George Washington University Ph.D. Dissertation.

Lester, Richard A. 1946. "Shortcomings of Marginal Analysis for Wage-Employment Problems." *American Economic Review* 36: 63–82.

Lewin, Shira B. 1996. "Economics and Psychology: Lessons for Our Own Day from the Early Twentieth Century." *Journal of Economic Literature* 34: 1293–1323.

Lewis, J. David and Smith, Richard L. 1980. *American Sociology and Pragmatism: Mead, Chicago Sociology, and Symbolic Interactionism*. Chicago: University of Chicago Press.

Liebhafsky, E. E. 1993. "The Influence of Charles Sanders Peirce on Institutional Economics." *Journal of Economic Issues* 27: 741–54.

Lipsey, Richard G. 1966. *An Introduction to Positive Economics*, 2nd. ed. London: Weidenfeld and Nicholson.

Lloyd, Elisabeth A. 1984. "A Semantic Approach to the Structure of Population Genetics." *Philosophy of Science* 51: 242–64.

Lloyd, Elisabeth A. 1988. *The Structure and Confirmation of Evolutionary Theory*. Westport, CT: Greenwood Press.

Longino, Helen E. 1988. "Review Essay: Science, Objectivity, and Feminist Values." *Feminist Studies* 14: 561–74.

Longino, Helen E. 1990. *Science as Social Knowledge: Values and Objectivity in Scientific Inquiry*. Princeton: Princeton University Press.

Longino, Helen E. 1991. "Multiplying Subjects and the Diffusion of Power." *The Journal of Philosophy* 8: 666–74.

Longino, Helen E. 1992. "Essential Tensions – Phase Two: Feminist, Philosophical, and Social Studies of Science." In *The Social Dimensions of Science*, ed. E. McMullin, 198–216. Notre Dame, IN: University of Notre Dame Press.

Longino, Helen E. 1993. "Economics for Whom?" In *Beyond Economic Man: Feminist Theory and Economics*, ed. M. A. Ferber and J. A. Nelson, 158–68. Chicago: University of Chicago Press.

Longino, Helen E. 1994. "The Fate of Knowledge in Social Theories of Science." In *Socializing Epistemology: The Social Dimensions of Knowledge*, ed. F. F. Schmitt, 135–57. Lanham, MD: Roman and Littlefield.

Longino, Helen E. 1995. "Gender, Politics, and the Theoretical Virtues." *Synthese* 104: 383–97.

Lorenz, Konrad. 1977. *Behind the Mirror: A Search for a Natural History of Human Knowledge*. Trans. R. Taylor. New York: Harcourt Brace Jovanovich.

Lovejoy, Arthur. 1908. "The Thirteen Pragmatisms." *Journal of Philosophy* 5: 5–12, 29–39.

Lovering, John. 1990. "Neither Fundamentalism nor 'New Realism': a Critical Realist Perspective on Current Divisions in Socialist Theory." *Capital and Class* 42: 30–54.

Lucas, Robert E. Jr. 1988. "On the Mechanics of Economic Development." *Journal of Monetary Economics* 22: 3–42.

Lynch, Michael. 1985. *Art and Artifact in Laboratory Science: A Study of Shop Work and Shop Talk in a Research Laboratory*. London: Routledge.

Lynch, Michael. 1992. "Extending Wittgenstein: The Pivotal Move from Epistemology to the Sociology of Science." In *Science as Practice and Culture*, ed. A. Pickering, 215–65. Chicago: University of Chicago Press.

Lyotard, Jean-Francois. 1987. "The Postmodern Condition." In *After Philosophy: End or Transformation?*, ed. K. Baynes, J. Bohman, and T. McCarthy, 73–94. Cambridge, MA: MIT Press.

Mach, Ernst 1893. "The Economy of Science." In *The Science of Mechanics*, trans. T. J. McCormak, 577–95. LaSalle, IL: Open Court [6th edition 1960].

Mach, Ernst. 1898. "The Economical Nature of Physical Inquiry." In *Popular Scientific Lectures*, trans. T. J. McCormak, 186–213. LaSalle, IL: Open Court.

Machlup, Fritz. 1946. "Marginal Analysis and Empirical Research." *American Economic Review* 36: 519–54.

Machlup, Fritz. 1955. "The Problem of Verification in Economics." *Southern Economic Journal* 22: 1–21.

Machlup, Fritz. 1962. *The Production and Distribution of Knowledge in the United States*. Princeton, NJ: Princeton University Press.

Machlup, Fritz. 1964. "Professor Samuelson on Theory and Realism." *American Economic Review* 54: 733–6.

Machlup, Fritz. 1966. "Operationalism and Pure Theory in Economics." In *The Structure of Economic Science, Essays on Methodology*, ed. S. R. Krupp, 53–67. Englewood Cliffs, NJ: Prentice Hall.

Machlup, Fritz. 1969. "Positive and Normative Economics: An Analysis of the Ideas." In *Economic Means and Social Ends: Essays in Political Economics*, ed. R. L. Heilbroner, 99–129. Englewood Cliffs, NJ: Prentice-Hall [reprinted as chapter 9 of Caldwell 1993, Vol. II].

MacKenzie, Donald. 1990. *Inventing Accuracy: A Historical Sociology of Nuclear Missile Guidance*. Cambridge, MA: MIT Press.

Maddock, Rodney. 1984. "Rational Expectations Macrotheory: A Lakatosian Case Study in Program Adjustment." *History of Political Economy* 16: 291–310.

Maddock, Rodney. 1991. "The Development of New Classical Macroeconomics: Lessons for Lakatos." In *Appraising Economic Theories: Studies in the Methodology of Scientific Research Programs*, ed. M. Blaug and N. De Marchi, 335–59. Aldershot: Edward Elgar.

Mäki, Uskali. 1986. "Rhetoric at the Expense of Coherence: A Reinterpretation of Milton Friedman's Methodology." *Research in the History of Economic Thought and Methodology* 4: 27–43.

Mäki, Uskali. 1988a. "How to Combine Rhetoric and Realism in the Methodology of Economics." *Economics and Philosophy* 4: 89–109.

Mäki, Uskali. 1988b. "Realism, Economics and Rhetoric: A Rejoinder to McCloskey." *Economics and Philosophy* 4: 167–9.

Mäki, Uskali. 1989. "On the Problem of Realism in Economics." *Ricerche Economiche* 43: 176–97.

Mäki, Uskali. 1990a. "Scientific Realism and Austrian Explanation." *Review of Political Economy* 2: 310–44.

Mäki, Uskali. 1990b. "Mengerian Economics in Realist Perspective." In *Carl Menger and His Legacy in Economics*, ed. B. J. Caldwell, 289–310. Durham, NC: Duke University Press.

Mäki, Uskali. 1992a. "Social Conditioning in Economics." In *Post-Popperian Methodology of Economics*, ed. N. De Marchi, 65–104. Boston: Kluwer.

Mäki, Uskali. 1992b. "Friedman and Realism." *Research in the History of Economic Thought and Methodology* 10: 171–95.

Mäki, Uskali. 1992c. "The Market as an Isolated Causal Process: A Metaphysical Ground for Realism." In *Austrian Economics: Tensions and New Directions*, ed. B. J. Caldwell and S. Boehm, 35–59. Boston: Kluwer.

Mäki, Uskali. 1992d. "On the Method of Isolation in Economics." *Poznan Studies in the Philosophy of the Sciences and the Humanities* 26: 317–51.

Mäki, Uskali. 1993a. "Two Philosophies of the Rhetoric of Economics." In *Economics and Language*, ed. W. Henderson, T. Dudley-Evans, and R. Backhouse, 23–50. London: Routledge.

Mäki, Uskali. 1993. "Social Theories of Science and the Fate of Institutionalism." In *Rationality, Institutions and Economic Methodology*, ed. U. Mäki, B. Gustafsson, C. Knudson, 76–109. London: Routledge.

Mäki, Uskali. 1994a. "Methodology Might Matter, But Weintraub's Meta-Methodology Shouldn't." *Journal of Economic Methodology* 1: 215–31.

Mäki, Uskali. 1994b. "Isolation, Idealization and Truth in Economics." In *Idealization VI: Idealization in Economics*, ed. B. Hamminga and N. De Marchi, 147–68. Amsterdam: Rodopi.

Mäki, Uskali. 1995. "Diagnosing McCloskey." *Journal of Economic Literature* 23: 1300–18.

Mäki, Uskali. 1996a. "Two Portraits of Economics." *Journal of Economic Methodology* 5: 1–38.

Mäki, Uskali. 1996b. "Scientific Realism and Some Peculiarities of Economics." In *Realism and Anti-Realism in the Philosophy of Science*, ed. R. S. Cohen, R. Hilpinen, and Q. Renzong, 427–47. Dordrecht: Kluwer.

Mäki, Uskali. 1997. "Universals and the *Methodenstreit*: a Re-examination of Carl Menger's Conception of Economics as an Exact Science." *Studies in History and Philosophy of Science* 28: 475–95.

Mäki, Uskali. 1998a. "Instrumentalism." In *The Handbook of Economic Methodology*, ed. J. B. Davis, D. W. Hands, and U. Mäki, 253–6. Cheltenham: Edward Elgar.

Mäki, Uskali. 1998b. "Realism." In *The Handbook of Economic Methodology*, ed. J. B. Davis, D. W. Hands, and U. Mäki, 404–9. Cheltenham: Edward Elgar.

Mäki, Uskali. 1998c. "Separateness, Inexactness, and Economic Method." *Journal of Economic Methodology* 5: 147–54.

Mäki, Uskali. 1998d. "Realisticness." In *The Handbook of Economic Methodology*, ed. J. B. Davis, D. W. Hands, and U. Mäki, 409–13. Cheltenham: Edward Elgar.

Mäki, Uskali. 1998e. "Aspects of Realism About Economics." *Theoria* 13: 301–19.

Mäki, Uskali. 1998f. "Is Coase a Realist?" *Philosophy of the Social Sciences* 28: 5–31.

Mäki, Uskali. 1998g. "The Problem of Social Coase: Between Regulation and Free Market in Economic Methodology." In *Coasean Economics: Law and Economics and the New Institutional Economics*, ed. S. G. Medema, 249–69. Boston: Kluwer.

Mäki, Uskali. 1998h. "Coase, R. H." In *The Handbook of Economic Methodology*, ed. J. B. Davis, D. W. Hands, and U. Mäki, 64–7. Cheltenham: Edward Elgar.

Mäki, Uskali. 1998i. "Against Posner Against Coase Against Theory." *Cambridge Journal of Economics* 22: 587–95.

Mäki, Uskali. 1999a. "The Way the World Works (www): An Ontological Constraint on Economic Theorizing." In *The Economic Realm: Studies in the Ontology of Economics*, ed. U. Mäki. Cambridge: Cambridge University Press.

Mäki, Uskali. 1999b. "Science as a Free Market: A Reflexivity Test in an Economics of Economics." *Perspectives on Science* 7: 486–509.

Mäki, Uskali. 2000a. "Kinds of Assumptions and Their Truth: Shaking an Untwisted F-twist." *Kyklos* 53: 303–22.

Mäki, Uskali. 2000b. "Reclaiming Relevant Realism." *Journal of Economic Methodology* 7: 109–25.

Malachowski, A., ed. 1990. *Reading Rorty*. Oxford: Blackwell.

Maloney, John. 1994. "Economic Method and Economic Rhetoric." *Journal of Economic Methodology* 1: 251–67.

Manicas, Peter T. 1998. "John Dewey and American Social Science." In *Reading Dewey: Interpretations for a Postmodern Generation*, ed. L. A. Hickman, 43–62. Bloomington: Indiana University Press.

Mannheim, Karl. 1936. *Ideology and Utopia: An Introduction to the Sociology of Knowledge*. San Diego, CA: Harcourt Brace Jovanovich.

Mansfield, Edwin. 1966. "National Science Policy: Issues and Problems." *American Economic Review* 56: 476–88.

Mansfield, Edwin. 1972. "Contribution of R&D to Economic Growth in the United States." *Science* 175: 477–86.

Mansfield, Edwin. 1991. "Academic Research and Industrial Innovation." *Research Policy* 20: 1–12.

Mansfield, Edwin. 1996. "Contributions of New Technology to the Economy." In *Technology, R&D, and the Economy*, ed. B. L. R. Smith and C. E. Barfield, 114–39. Washington, DC: Brookings and AEI.

Marshall, Alfred. 1949. *Principles of Economics*, 8th ed., New York: Macmillan [1st edition 1890].

Marx, Karl. 1859. *A Contribution to the Critique of Political Economy* [Moscow: Progress Publishers, 1970].

Marzola, Alessandra and Silva, Francesro, eds. 1994. *John Maynard Keynes: Language and Method*. Aldershot: Edward Elgar.

Mas-Colell, Andreu, Whinston, Michael D., and Green, Jerry D. 1995. *Microeconomic Theory*. Oxford: Oxford University Press.

Massey, Gerald J. 1965. "Professor Samuelson on Theory and Realism: A Comment." *American Economic Review* 55: 1155–64.

Masterman, Margaret. 1970. "The Nature of a Paradigm." In *Criticism and the Growth of Knowledge*, ed. I. Lakatos and A. Musgrave, 59–89. Cambridge: Cambridge University Press.

Mayer, Thomas. 1993. *Truth versus Precision in Economics*. Aldershot: Edward Elgar.

Mayer, Thomas. 1995. *Doing Economic Research: Essays on the Applied Methodology of Economics*. Aldershot: Edward Elgar.

Mayer, Thomas. 1997. "The Rhetoric of Friedman's Quantity Theory Manifesto." *Journal of Economic Methodology* 4: 199–220.

Mayhew, Anne. 1987. "Culture: Core Concept Under Attack." *Journal of Economic Issues* 21: 587–603.

Mayhew, Anne. 1989. "Contrasting Origins of the Two Institutionalisms: the Social Science Context." *Review of Political Economy* 1: 319–33.

McClellan, Chris. 1996. "The Economic Consequences of Bruno Latour." *Social Epistemology* 10: 193–208.

McCloskey, D. N. 1983. "The Rhetoric of Economics." *Journal of Economic Literature* 21: 481–517.

McCloskey, D. N. 1985a. *The Rhetoric of Economics*. Madison: University of Wisconsin Press.

McCloskey, D. N. 1985b. "The Loss Function Has Been Mislaid; The Rhetoric of Significance Tests." *American Economic Review* 75: 201–5.

McCloskey, D. N. 1988. "The Limits of Expertise: If You're So Smart, Why Ain't You Rich." *The American Scholar* 57: 393–406.

McCloskey, D. N. 1989. "Why I Am No Longer a Positivist." *Review of Social Economy* 47: 225–38.

McCloskey, D. N. 1990a. *If You're So Smart: The Narrative of Economic Expertise*. Chicago: University of Chicago Press.

McCloskey, D. N. 1990b. "Storytelling in Economics." In *Economics and Hermeneutics*, ed. D. Lavoie, 61–75. London: Routledge.

McCloskey, D. N. 1993. "Some Consequences of a Conjective Economics." In *Beyond Economic Man: Feminist Theory and Economics*, ed. M. A. Ferber and J. A. Nelson, 69–93. Chicago: University of Chicago Press.

McCloskey, D. N. 1994. *Knowledge and Persuasion in Economics*. Cambridge: Cambridge University Press.

McCloskey, D. N. 1996. *The Vices of Economists – The Virtues of the Bourgeoisie*. Amsterdam: Amsterdam University Press.

McCloskey, D. N. 1997. "Big Rhetoric, Little Rhetoric: Gaonkar on the Rhetoric of Science." In *Rhetorical Hermeneutics: Invention and Interpretation in the Age of Science*, ed. A. G. Gross and W. M. Keith, 101–12. Albany: State University of New York Press.

McCloskey, D. N. 1998. *The Rhetoric of Economics*, 2nd ed. Madison: University of Wisconsin Press.

McCloskey, D. N. and Zilak, Steven T. 1996. "The Standard Error of Regressions." *Journal of Economic Literature* 34: 97–114.

McElroy, Margorie B. and Horney, Mary Jean. 1981. "Nash Bargained Household Decisions: Toward a Generalization of the Theory of Demand." *International Economic Review* 22: 333–49.

McGucken, William. 1984. *Scientists, Society, and State: The Social Relations of Science Movement in Great Britain 1931–1947*. Columbus: Ohio State University Press.

McGovern, Siobhain. 1995. "On a Maze of Second Thoughts and On the Methodology of Economic Methodology." *Journal of Economic Methodology* 2: 223–37.

McMahon, Michael R. 1984. "An Appraisal of the New Classical Macroeconomics." *Journal of Macroeconomics* 6: 335–46.

Medema, Steven. 1994. *Ronald H. Coase*. New York: St. Martin's Press.

Megill, Allan. 1985. *Prophets of Extremity: Nietzsche, Heidegger, Foucault, Derrida*. Berkeley: University of California Press.

Megill, Allan. 1989. "What Does the Term 'Postmodern' Mean?" *Annals of Scholarship* 6: 125–51.

Melitz, Jack. 1965. "Friedman and Machlup on the Significance of Testing Economic Assumptions." *Journal of Political Economy* 73: 37–60.

Menger, Carl. 1963. *Problems of Economics and Sociology*. Trans. L. Schneider. Urbana: University of Illinois Press [1st edition 1883].

Menger, Carl. 1976. *Principles of Economics*. Trans. J. Dingwall and B. F. Hoselitz. New York: New York University Press [1st edition 1871].

Menger, Karl. 1973. "Austrian Marginalism and Mathematical Economics." In *Carl Menger and the Austrian School of Economics*, ed. J. R. Hicks and W. Weber, 38–60. Oxford: Oxford University Press.

Merton, Robert K. 1936. "The Unanticipated Consequences of Purposive Social Action." *American Sociological Review* 1: 894–904.

Merton, Robert K. 1948. "The Self-Fulfilling Prophecy." *The Antioch Review* 8: 193–210.

Merton, Robert K. 1961. "Singletons and Multiples in Scientific Discovery: A Chapter in the Sociology of Science." *Proceedings of the American Philosophical Society* 105: 470–86 [reprinted in Merton 1973]

Merton, Robert K. 1968. "The Matthew Effect in Science." *Science* 159: 56–63 [reprinted in Merton 1973].

Merton, Robert K. 1970. *Science, Technology and Society in Seventeenth-Century England*. New York: Harper & Row [originally published in *Osiris* in 1938].

Merton, Robert K. 1973. *The Sociology of Science: Theoretical and Empirical Investigations*. Chicago: University of Chicago Press.

Merton, Robert K. 1977. "The Sociology of Science: An Episodic Memoir." In *The Sociology of Science in Europe*, ed. R. K. Merton and J. Gaston, 3–141. Carbondale: Southern Illinois University Press.

Meyering, Theo C. 1989. *Historical Roots of Cognitive Science: The Rise of a Cognitive Theory of Perception from Antiquity to the Nineteenth Century*. Dordrecht: Kluwer Academic.

Milberg, William. 1996. "The Rhetoric of Policy Relevance in International Economics." *Journal of Economic Methodology* 3: 237–59.

Milberg, William and Pietrykowski, Bruce A. 1994. "Objectivism, Relativism and the Importance of Rhetoric for Marxist Economics." *Review of Radical Political Economics* 26: 85–109.

Mill, John Stuart. 1874. "On the Definition of Political Economy; and on the Method of investigation Proper To It." In *Essays on Some Unsettled Questions of Political Economy*, 2nd ed. London: Longmans, Green, Reader & Dyer [Augustus M. Kelley reprint 1968, 1st edition 1844].

Mill, John Stuart. 1884. *A System of Logic, Ratiocinative and Inductive: Being a Connected View of the Principles of Evidence and the Methods of Scientific Investigation*, 8th ed. New York: Harper & Brothers [1st edition 1843].

Mill, John Stuart. 1909. *Principles of Political Economy with Some of Their Applications to Social Economy*. New York: D. Appleton & Co. [from the 5th London edition, 1st edition 1848].

Mill, John Stuart. 1961. "Autobiography." In *Essential Works of John Stuart Mill*, ed. Max Lerner, 11–182. New York: Bantam Books [originally published in 1873].

Miller, David. 1974. "Popper's Qualitative Theory of Verisimilitude." *British Journal for the Philosophy of Science* 25: 166–77.

Miller, David. 1994. *Critical Rationalism*. La Salle, IL: Open Court.

Miller, Richard W. 1987. *Fact and Method*. Princeton, NJ: Princeton University Press.

Mirowski, Philip. 1987a. "The Philosophical Basis of Institutionalist Economics." *Journal of Economic Issues* 21: 1001–38.

Mirowski, Philip. 1987b. "Shall I Compare Thee to a Minkowski-Ricardo-Leontief Matrix of the Hicks-Mosak Type?" *Economics and Philosophy* 3: 67–96.

Mirowski, Philip. 1988. "Physics and the Marginal Revolution." In *Against Mechanism: Protecting Economics from Science*, 11–30. Lanham, MD: Rowman & Littlefield.

Mirowski, Philip. 1989a. *More Heat Than Light: Economics As Social Physics: Physics as Nature's Economics*. Cambridge: Cambridge University Press.

Mirowski, Philip. 1989b. "The Measurement Without Theory Controversy." *Economies et sociétés* 11: 65–87.

Mirowski, Philip. 1989c. "How to Do Things with Metaphors: Paul Samuelson and the Science of Neoclassical Economics." *Studies in History and Philosophy of Science* 20: 175–91.

Mirowski, Philip. 1991. "Postmodernism and the Social Theory of Value." *Journal of Post Keynesian Economics* 13: 565–82.

Mirowski, Philip. 1992. "Looking for Those Natural Numbers: Dimensionless Constants and the Idea of Natural Measurement." *Science in Context* 5: 165–188.

Mirowski, Philip. 1994. "A Visible Hand in the Marketplace of Ideas: Precision Measurement as Arbitrage." *Science in Context* 7: 563–89.

Mirowski, Philip. 1995a. "A Confederacy of Bunches: Comment Upon Niehans on 'Multiple Discoveries'." *The European Journal of the History of Economic Thought* 2: 279–89.

Mirowski, Philip. 1995b. "Philip Kitcher's *Advancement of Science*: A Review Article." *Review of Political Economy* 7: 227–41.

Mirowski, Philip. 1995c. "Three Ways to Think About Testing in Econometrics." *Journal of Econometrics* 76: 25–46.

Mirowski, Philip. 1995d. "Civilization and Its Discounts." *Dialogue* 34: 541–60.

Mirowski, Philip. 1996a. "Comments on Diamond Paper." *Knowledge and Policy* 9: 72–75.

Mirowski, Philip. 1996b. "The Economic Consequences of Philip Kitcher." *Social Epistemology* 10: 153–69.

Mirowski, Philip. 1997a. "The Attribution of Quantitative Error and the Erasure of Plural Interpretations in Various Sciences." In *Pluralism in Economics*, ed. A. Salanti and E. Screpanti, 260–77. Cheltenham: Edward Elgar.

Mirowski, Philip. 1997b. "On Playing the Economics Trump Card in the Philosophy of Science: Why It Did Not Work for Michael Polanyi." *Philosophy of Science* 64 (Proceedings): S127–S138.

Mirowski, Philip. 1998a. "Operationalism." In *The Handbook of Economic Methodology*, ed. J. B. Davis, D. W. Hands, and U. Mäki, 346–49. Cheltenham: Edward Elgar.

Mirowski, Philip. 1998b. "What Should be Bounded When It Comes to Bounded Rationality? or Automata vs. Simulacra" (forthcoming).

Mirowski, Philip. 1999. *Machine Dreams* (forthcoming).

Mirowski, Philip and Hands, D. Wade. 1998. "A Paradox of Budgets: The Postwar Stabilization of American Neoclassical Demand Theory." In *From Interwar Pluralism to Postwar Neoclassicism* [Supplement to *HOPE* vol. 30], ed. M. S. Morgan and M. Rutherford, 269–92. Durham, NC: Duke University Press.

Mirowski, Philip and Sent, Esther-Mirjam. 2000. "Introduction." In *Science Bought and Sold*, ed. P. Mirowski and E.-M. Sent (forthcoming).

Mises, Ludwig von. 1949. *Human Action*. New Haven, CT: Yale University Press.

Mises, Ludwig von. 1978. *The Ultimate Foundation of Economic Science*, 2nd ed. Mission, KA: Sheed Andrews and McMeel [1st edition published in 1961].

Mitchell, Wesley C. 1913. *Business Cycles*. Berkeley: University of California Press.

Mitchell, Wesley C. 1967. *Types of Economic Theory*, Vols. I and II. New York: Augustus M. Kelley.

Moen, Marcia K. 1997. "Peirce's Pragmatism as a Resource for Feminism." *Transactions of the Charles S. Peirce Society* 27: 435–50.

Montague, W. P. 1937. "The Story of American Realism." *Philosophy* 12: 140–61.

Moore, G. E. 1903. *Principia Ethica*. Cambridge: Cambridge University Press.

Morgan, Mary S. 1988. "Finding a Satisfactory Empirical Model." In *The Popperian Legacy in Economics*, ed. N. De Marchi, 199–211. Cambridge: Cambridge University Press.

Morgan, Mary S. 1990. *The History of Econometric Ideas*. Cambridge: Cambridge University Press.

Morgan, Mary S. 1996. "Idealization and Modeling: A Review of Bert Hamminga and Neil De Marchi (eds.) *Idealization in Economics*." *Journal of Economic Methodology* 3: 131–48.

Morgan, Mary S. 1997. "The Technology of Analogical Models: Irving Fisher's Monetary Worlds." *Philosophy of Science* 64 (Proceedings): S304–S314.

Morgan, Mary S. 1998. "Models." In *The Handbook of Economic Methodology*, ed. J. B. Davis, D. W. Hands, and U. Mäki, 316–21. Cheltenham: Edward Elgar.

Morgan, Mary S. 1999a. "Models, Stories and the Economic World." In *The Economic Realm: Studies in the Ontology of Economics*, ed. U. Mäki. Cambridge: Cambridge University Press.

Morgan, Mary S. 1999b. "Learning From Models." In *Models as Mediators*, ed. M. S. Morgan and M. C. Morrison, 347–88. Cambridge: Cambridge University Press.

Morris, Charles. 1963. "Pragmatism and Logical Empiricism." In *The Philosophy of Rudolf Carnap*, ed. P. A. Schilpp, 87–98. LaSalle, IL: Open Court.

Morrison, Margaret. 1998. "Modelling Nature Between Physics and the Physical World." *Philosophia Naturalis* 38: 65–85.

Morrison, Margaret. 1999. "Models as Autonomous Agents." In *Models as Mediators*, ed. M. S. Morgan and M. C. Morrison, 38–65. Cambridge: Cambridge University Press.

Morrison, Margaret and Morgan, Mary S. 1999a. "Introduction." In *Models as Mediators*, ed. M. S. Morgan and M. C. Morrison, 1–9. Cambridge: Cambridge University Press.

Morrison, Margaret and Morgan, Mary S. 1999b. "Models as Mediating Instruments." In *Models as Mediators*, ed. M. S. Morgan and M. C. Morrison, 10–37. Cambridge: Cambridge University Press.

Moseley, Fred. 1995. "Marx's Economic Theory: True or False? A Marxian Response to Blaug's Appraisal." In *Heterodox Economic Theories: True or False?*, ed. F. Moseley, 88–118. Aldershot: Edward Elgar.

Motterlini, Matteo, ed. 1999. *For And Against Method: Imre Lakatos and Paul Feyerabend*. Chicago: University of Chicago Press.

Moulines, C. Ulises. 1996. "Structuralism: The Basic Ideas." In *Structuralist Theory of Science*, ed. W. Balzer and C. U. Moulines, 1–13. Berlin: Walter de Gruyter.

Mulkay, Michael. 1981. "Action and Belief or Scientific Discourse? A Possible Way of Ending Intellectual Vassalage in Social Studies of Science." *Philosophy of the Social Sciences* 11: 163–71.

Mulkay, Michael. 1985. *Word and the World: Explorations in the Form of Sociological Analysis*. London: Routledge.

Mulkay, Michael and Gilbert, G. Nigel. 1982. "Joking Apart: Some Recommendations Concerning the Analysis of Scientific Culture." *Social Studies of Science* 12: 585–613.

Munz, Peter. 1985. *Our Knowledge of the Growth of Knowledge*. London: Routledge.

Munz, Peter. 1993. *Philosophical Darwinism: On the Origin of Knowledge by Means of Natural Selection*. London: Routledge.

Murphy, Nancy. 1989. "Another Look at Novel Facts." *Studies in History and Philosophy of Science* 20: 385–88.

Musgrave, Alan. 1981. "'Unreal Assumptions' in Economic Theory: The F-Twist Untwisted." *Kyklos* 34: 377–87.

Musgrave, Alan. 1988. "The Ultimate Argument for Scientific Realism." In *Relativism and Realism in Science*, ed. R. Nola, 229–52. Dordrecht: Kluwer Academic Publishers.

Musgrave, Alan. 1993. *Common Sense, Science and Scepticism*. Cambridge: Cambridge University Press.

Nadeau, R. 1993. "Confuting Popper on the Rationality Principle." *Philosophy of the Social Sciences* 23: 446–67.

Nagel, Ernest. 1961. *The Structure of Science: Problems in the Logic of Scientific Explanation*. New York: Harcourt, Brace & World.

Nagel, Ernest. 1963. "Assumptions in Economic Theory." *American Economic Review* 53: 211–19.

Nelson, Alan. 1984. "Some Issues Surrounding the Reduction of Macroeconomics to Microeconomics." *Philosophy of Science* 51: 573–94.

Nelson, Alan. 1986. "New Individualist Foundations for Economics." *Nous* 20: 469–90.

Nelson, Alan. 1990. "Social Science and the Mental." *Midwest Studies in Philosophy* 15: 194–209.

Nelson, J., Megill, A., and McCloskey, D. N., eds. 1987. *The Rhetoric of the Human Sciences*. Madison: University of Wisconsin Press.

Nelson, Julie A. 1993. "Value-Free or Valueless? Notes on the Pursuit of Detachment in Economics." *History of Political Economy* 25: 121–45.

Nelson, Julie A. 1995. "Feminism and Economics." *Journal of Economic Perspectives* 9: 131–48.

Nelson, Julie A. 1996. *Feminism, Objectivity and Economics*. London: Routledge.

Nelson, Lynn Hankinson. 1990. *Who Knows? From Quine to a Feminist Empiricism*. Philadelphia, PA: Temple University Press.

Nelson, Lynn Hankinson. 1995. "A Feminist Naturalized Philosophy of Science." *Synthese* 104: 399–421.

Nelson, Richard R. 1959. "The Simple Economics of Basic Research." *Journal of Political Economy* 67: 297–306.

Nelson, Richard R. and Winter, Sidney G. 1982. *An Evolutionary Theory of Economic Change*. Cambridge, MA: Harvard University Press.

Nelson, Richard R. and Romer, Paul M. 1996. "Science, Economic Growth, and Public Policy." In *Technology, R&D, and the Economy*, ed. B. L. R. Smith and C. E. Barfield, 49–74. Washington, DC: Brookings and AEI.

Neurath, Otto. 1937. "Unified Science and Its Encyclopaedia." *Philosophy of Science* 4: 265–77.

Newell, Allen and Simon, Herbert. 1972. *Human Problem Solving*. Englewood Cliffs, NJ: Prentice Hall.

Newton-Smith, W. H. 1995. "Popper, Science and Rationality." In *Karl Popper: Philosophy and Problems*, ed. A. O'Hear, 13–30. Cambridge: Cambridge University Press.

Nickles, Thomas. 1995. "Philosophy of Science and History of Science." *Osiris* 10: 139–63.

Niehans, Jürg. 1995a. "Multiple Discoveries in Economic Theory." *The European Journal of the History of Economic Thought* 2: 1–28.

Niehans, Jürg. 1995b. "Multiple Discoveries Defended: A Reply." *The European Journal of the History of Economic Thought* 2: 293–8.

Nielsen, Kai. 1993. "Peirce, Pragmatism and the Challenge of Postmodernism." *Transactions of the Charles S. Peirce Society* 29: 513–60.

Nietzsche, Friedrich. 1954. "On Truth and Lie in an Extra-Moral Sense." In *The Portable Nietzsche*, 42–7. Selected and Translated with an Introduction, Preface, and Notes by Walter Kaufmann. New York: Viking Penguin.

Nightingale, John. 1994. "Situational Determinism Revisited: Scientific Research Programmes in Economics Twenty Years On." *Journal of Economic Methodology* 1: 233–52.

Niiniluoto, Ilkka. 1998. "Verisimilitude: the Third Period." *British Journal for the Philosophy of Science* 49: 1–29.

Niiniluoto, Ilkka. 1999. "Defending Abduction." *Philosophy of Science* 66 (Proceedings): S436–S451.

Nola, Robert. 1987. "The Status of Popper's Theory of Scientific Method." *British Journal for the Philosophy of Science* 38: 441–80.

Nola, Robert. 1988. "Introduction: Some Issues Concerning Relativism and Realism in Science." In *Relativism and Realism*, ed. R. Nola, 1–35. Dordrecht: Kluwer Academic.

Nooteboom, Bart. 1986. "Plausibility in Economics." *Economics and Philosophy* 2: 197–224.

Nowak, Leszek. 1980. *The Structure of Idealization: Towards a Systematic Interpretation of the Marxian Idea of Science*. Dordrecht: D. Reidel.

Nowak, Leszek. 1994. "The Idealizational Methodology and Economics." In *Idealization VI: Idealization in Economics*, ed. B. Hamminga and N. De Marchi, 303–36. Amsterdam: Rodopi.

Nozick, Robert. 1977. "On Austrian Methodology." *Synthese* 36: 353–92 [reprinted as chapter 5 of Nozick 1993].

Nozick, Robert. 1981. *Philosophical Explanations*. Cambridge, MA: Harvard University Press.

Nozick, Robert. 1993. *Socratic Puzzles*. Cambridge, MA: Harvard University Press.

Oakley, Allen. 1994. *Classical Economic Man: Human Agency and Methodology in the Political Economy of Adam Smith and J. S. Mill*. Aldershot: Edward Elgar.

Oakley, Allen. 1997. *The Foundations of Austrian Economics From Menger to Mises*. Aldershot: Edward Elgar.

O'Brien, D. P. 1976. "The Longevity of Adam Smith's Vision: Paradigms, Research Programmes and Falsifiability in the History of Economic Thought." *Scottish Journal of Political Economy* 23: 133–51.

Oddie, Graham. 1986. "The Poverty of the Popperian Program for Truthlikeness." *Philosophy of Science* 53: 163–78.

O'Donnell, R. 1990. "The Epistemology of J. M. Keynes." *British Journal for the Philosophy of Science* 41: 333–50.

O'Hear, Anthony. 1987. "Has the Theory of Evolution Any Relevance to Philosophy?" *Ratio* 29: 16–35.

O'Neill, John. 1990. "Property in Science and the Market." *The Monist* 73: 601–15.

O'Neill, John. 1995. "In Partial Praise of a Positivist: The Work of Otto Neurath." *Radical Philosophy* 74: 29–38.

O'Neill, John. 1997. "Comment: Hayek and the Positivists." In *Hayek: Economist and Social Philosopher*, ed. S. F. Frowen, 152–3. New York: St. Martin's.

Papineau, David. 1993. *Philosophical Naturalism*. Oxford: Blackwell.

Parsons, Stephen D. 1997a. "Why the 'Transcendental' In Transcendental Realism?" *Ekonomia* 1: 22–38 [reprinted with minor revisions as chapter 9 of Fleetwood 1999].

Parsons, Stephen D. 1997b. "Mises, The A Priori, and the Foundations of Economics." *Economics and Philosophy* 13: 175–96.

Parsons, Stephen D. 1999. "Economics and Reality: A Philosophical Critiique of Transcendental Realism." *Review of Political Economy* 11: 455–66.

Patinkin, Don. 1983. "Multiple Discoveries and the Central Message." *American Journal of Sociology* 89: 306–23.

Peacock, Mark S. 1993. "Hayek, Realism and Spontaneous Order." *Journal for the Theory of Social Behaviour* 23: 249–64.

Pearce, David and Tucci, Michele. 1982. "On the Logical Structure of Some Value Systems of Classical Economics: Marx and Sraffa.' *Theory and Decision* 14: 155–75.

Pearce, Kerry A. and Hoover, Kevin D. 1995. "After the Revolution: Paul Samuelson and the Textbook Keynesian Model." In *New Perspectives on Keynes* [Supplement to *HOPE* vol. 27], ed. A. F. Cottrell and M. S. Lawlor, 183–216. Durham, NC: Duke University Press.

Peart, Sandra. 1995. " 'Disturbing Causes,' 'Noxious Errors,' and the Theory-Practice Distinction in the Economics of J. S. Mill and W. S. Jevons." *Canadian Journal of Economics* 28: 1194–1211.

Peirce, Charles S. 1868. "Some Consequences of Four Incapacities." In *Philosophical Writings of Peirce*, ed. J. Buchler, 228–50. New York: Dover [1955].

Peirce, Charles S. 1877. "The Fixation of Belief." In *Charles S. Peirce: Selected Writings*, ed. P. P. Weiner, 91–112. New York: Dover [1966].

Peirce, Charles S. 1878. "How to Make Our Ideas Clear." In *Charles S. Peirce: Selected Writings*, ed. P. P. Weiner, 113–36. New York: Dover [1966].

Peirce, Charles S. 1879. "A Note on the Theory of the Economy of Research." In *United States Coast Survey* for the fiscal year ending June 1876, U. S. Government Printing Office [reprinted in *Operations Research* 15, 1967, 642–8, and as an appendix to Wible 1994b].

Peirce, Charles S. 1887–8. "A Guess at the Riddle." In *The Essential Peirce: Selected Philosophical Writings, Vol. 1 (1867–1893)*, ed. N. Houser and C. Kloesel, 245–79. Bloomington, IN: Indiana University Press [1992].

Peirce, Charles S. 1905a. "What Pragmatism Is." In *Charles S. Peirce: Selected Writings*, ed. P. P. Weiner, 180–202. New York: Dover [1966].

Peirce, Charles S. 1905b. "Issues of Pragmaticism." In *Charles S. Peirce: Selected Writings*, ed. P. P. Weiner, 203–23. New York: Dover [1966].

Peirce, Charles S. 1906. "Pragmatism in Retrospect: A Last Formulation." In *Philosophical Writings of Peirce*, ed. J. Buchler, 269–89. New York: Dover [1955].

Peirce, Charles S. 1940. "Logic as Semiotic: The Theory of Signs." In *Philosophical Writings of Peirce*, ed. J. Buchler, 98–119. New York: Dover [1955].

Pels, Dick. 1997. "Mixing Metaphors: Politics or Economics of Knowledge?" *Theory and Society* 26: 685–717.

Petrella, F. 1988. "Henry George and the Classical Scientific Research Program: The Economics of Republican Millennialism." *American Journal of Economics and Sociology* 47: 239–56.

Pheby, John. 1988. *Methodology and Economics: A Critical Introduction*. London: Macmillan.

Pickering, Andrew. 1990. "Knowledge, Practice and Mere Construction." *Social Studies of Science* 20: 682–729.

Pickering, Andrew. 1992. "From Science as Knowledge to Science as Practice." In *Science as Practice and Culture*, ed. A. Pickering, 1–26. Chicago: University of Chicago Press.

Pickering, Andrew. 1994. "Objectivity and the Mangle of Practice." In *Rethinking Objectivity*, ed. A. Megill, 109–25. Durham, NC: Duke University Press.

Pickering, Andrew. 1995a. *The Mangle of Practice: Time, Agency, and Science*. Chicago: University of Chicago Press.

Pickering, Andrew. 1995b. "After Representation: Science Studies in the Performative Idiom." *PSA 1994*, Vol. 2, 413–19. East Lansing, MI: PSA.

Pickering, Andrew. 1997. "The History of Economics and the History of Agency." In *The State of the History of Economic Thought*, ed. J. P. Henderson, 6–18. London: Routledge.

Pinnick, Cassandra L. 1994. "Feminist Epistemology: Implications for Philosophy of Science." *Philosophy of Science* 61: 646–52.

Pitt, Joseph C. 1988. *Theories of Explanation*. Oxford: Oxford University Press.

Polanyi, Michael. 1958. *Personal Knowledge*. Chicago: University of Chicago Press.

Polanyi, Michael. 1962. "The Republic of Science." *Minerva* 1: 54–73.

Poovey, Mary. 1998. *A History of the Modern Fact: Problems of Knowledge in the Sciences of Wealth and Society*. Chicago: University of Chicago Press.

Popper, Karl R. 1934. *Logik der Forschung*. Vienna: Julius Springer Verlag [with the imprint "1935"].

Popper, Karl R. 1959. *The Logic of Scientific Discovery*. New York: Basic Books [translation of Popper 1934].

Popper, Karl R. 1961. *The Poverty of Historicism*, 3rd ed. New York: Harper and Row.

Popper, Karl R. 1965. *Conjectures and Refutations*, 2nd ed. New York: Harper and Row.

Popper, Karl R. 1966. *The Open Society and Its Enemies*, Vol. 2, 2nd ed. New York: Harper and Row.

Popper, Karl R. 1967. "La Rationalité et le Statut de Principe de Rationalité." In *Les Fondements Philosophiques des Systems Economiques*, ed. E. M. Classen, 142–50. Paris: Payot.

Popper, Karl R. 1968. *The Logic of Scientific Discovery*, 2nd ed. New York: Basic Books.

Popper, Karl R. 1972. *Objective Knowledge*. Oxford: Oxford University Press.

Popper, Karl R. 1974. "Replies to My Critics." In *The Philosophy of Karl Popper*, ed. P. A. Schilpp, 961–1197. LaSalle, IL: Open Court.

Popper, Karl R. 1976a. "The Logic of the Social Sciences." In *The Positivist Dispute in German Sociology*, ed. T. W. Adorno et al., 87–104. New York: Harper and Row.

Popper, Karl R. 1976b. *Unended Quest: An Intellectual Autobiography*. LaSalle, IL: Open Court.

Popper, Karl R. 1983. *Realism and the Aim of Science*. Totowa, NJ: Rowman and Littlefield.

Popper, Karl R. 1985. "The Rationality Principle." In *Popper Selections*, ed. D. Miller, 357–65. Princeton: Princeton University Press.

Popper, Karl R. 1994. *The Myth of the Framework: In Defense of Science and Rationality*. London: Routledge.

Pratten, Stephen. 1993. "Structure, Agency and Marx's Analysis of the Labour Process." *Review of Political Economy* 5: 403–26.

Pratten, Stephen. 1996. "The 'Closure' Assumptions as a First Step: Neo-Ricardian Economics and Post-Keynesianism." *Review of Social Economy* 54: 423–43 [reprinted with minor revisions as chapter 2 of Fleetwood 1999].

Pratten, Stephen. 1997. "The Nature of Transactions Cost Economics." *Journal of Economic Issues* 31: 781–803.

Pratten, Stephen. 1998. "Marshall on Tendencies, Equilibrium, and the Statical Method." *History of Political Economy* 30: 121–63.

Putnam, Hilary. 1975. *Mind, Language, and Reality*. Cambridge: Cambridge University Press.

Putnam, Hilary. 1983. *Realism and Reason*. Cambridge: Cambridge University Press.

Putnam, Hilary. 1994. *Words and Life*. Cambridge, MA: Harvard University Press.

Putnam, Hilary. 1995. *Pragmatism*. Oxford: Blackwell.

Putnam, Hilary and Putnam, Ruth Anna. 1990. "Epistemology as Hypothesis." *Transactions of the Charles S. Peirce Society* 26: 407–33.

Quine, W. V. O. 1951. "Two Dogmas of Empiricism." *Philosophical Review* 60: 20–43.

Quine, W. V. O. 1969a. "Ontological Relativity." In *Ontological Relativity & Other Essays*, 26–68. New York: Columbia University Press.

Quine, W. V. O. 1969b. "Epistemology Naturalized." In *Ontological Relativity & Other Essays*, 69–90. New York: Columbia University Press.

Quine, W. V. O. 1969c. "Natural Kinds." In *Ontological Relativity & Other Essays*, 114–38. New York: Columbia University Press.

Quine, W. V. O. 1975. "On Empirically Equivalent Systems of the World." *Erkenntnis* 9: 313–28.

Quine, W. V. O. 1980a. *From a Logical Point of View*, 2nd rev. ed. Cambridge, MA: Harvard University Press.

Quine, W. V. O. 1980b. "Two Dogmas of Empiricism." In *From a Logical Point of View*. 2nd rev. ed., 20–46. Cambridge, MA: Harvard University Press. [revised reprint of Quine 1951].

Quine, W. V. O. 1981. "The Pragmatists' Place in Empiricism." In *Pragmatism: Its Sources and Prospects*, ed. R. Mulvaney and P. M. Zeltner, 23–39. Columbia: University of South Carolina Press.

Quine, W. V. O. 1995. *From Stimulus to Science*. Cambridge, MA: Harvard University Press.

Radnitzky, Gerard. 1986. "Towards an 'Economic' Theory of Methodology." *Methodology and Science* 19: 124–47.

Radnitzky, Gerard. 1991. "Refined Falsificationism Meets the Challenge from the Relativist Philosophy of Science." *British Journal for the Philosophy of Science* 42: 273–84.

Radnitzky, Gerard and Bartley, William W. III, eds. 1987. *Evolutionary Epistemology, Rationality, and the Sociology of Knowledge*. LaSalle, IL: Open Court.

Rappaport, Steven. 1995. "Is Economics Empirical Knowledge?" *Economics and Philosophy* 11: 137–58.

Rappaport, Steven. 1998. *Models and Reality in Economics*. Cheltenham: Edward Elgar.

Redman, Deborah A. 1991. *Economics and the Philosophy of Science*. Oxford: Oxford University Press.

Redman, Deborah A. 1997. *The Rise of Political Economy as a Science*. Cambridge, MA: MIT Press.

Reich, Michael. 1995. "Radical Economics: Successes and Failures." In *Heterodox Economic Theories: True or False?*, ed. F. Moseley, 45–70. Aldershot: Edward Elgar.

Reisch, George A. 1991. "Did Kuhn Kill Logical Positivism?" *Philosophy of Science* 58: 264–77.

Reisch, George A. 1997a. "How Postmodern was Neurath's Idea of Unity of Science?" *Studies in History and Philosophy of Science* 28: 439–451.

Reisch, George A. 1997b. "Economist, Epistemologist . . . and Censor? On Otto Neurath's *Index Verborum Prohibitorum*." *Perspectives on Science* 5: 452–80.

Remenyi, J. V. 1979. "Core Demi-core Interaction: Towards a General Theory of Disciplinary and Subdisciplinary Growth." *History of Political Economy* 11: 30–63.

Requate, Till. 1991. "Once Again Pure Exchange Economies: A Critical View Towards the Structuralistic Reconstructions By Balzer and Stegmüller." *Erkenntnis* 34: 87–116.

Rescher, Nicholas. 1976. "Peirce and the Economy of Research." *Philosophy of Science* 43: 71–98.

Rescher, Nicholas. 1978. *Peirce's Philosophy of Science*. Notre Dame, IN: University of Notre Dame Press.

Rescher, Nicholas. 1989. *Cognitive Economy: The Economic Dimension of the Theory of Knowledge*. Pittsburgh, PA: University of Pittsburgh Press.

Rescher, Nicholas. 1996. *Priceless Knowledge: Natural Science in Economic Perspective*. Lanham, MD: Rowman and Littlefield.

Resnick, Stephen A. and Wolff, Richard D. 1987. *Knowledge and Class: A Marxian Critique of Political Economy*. Chicago: University of Chicago Press.

Resnick, Stephen A. and Wolff, Richard D. 1988. "Marxian Theory and the Rhetorics of Economics." In *The Consequences of Economic Rhetoric*, ed. A. Klamer, D. N. McCloskey, and R. M. Solow, 47–63. Cambridge: Cambridge University Press.

Restivo, Sal. 1995. "The Theory Landscape in Science Studies: Sociological Traditions." In *Handbook of Science and Technology Studies*, ed. S. Jasanoff, G. E. Markle, J. C. Peterson, and T. Pinch, 95–110. Thousand Oaks, CA: Sage.

Reuten, Geert. 1996. "A Revision of the Neoclassical Economics Methodology – Appraising Hausman's Mill-twist, Robbins-gist, Popper-whist." *Journal of Economic Methodology* 3: 39–68.

Reuten, Geert. 1997. "What About Falsifiability? Further Notes on Hausman's Revision of the Neoclassical Economic Methodology." *Journal of Economic Methodology* 4: 297–302.

Reuten, Geert. 1999. "Knife Edge Caricature Modelling: The Case of Marx's Reproduction Schema." In *Models as Mediators*, ed. M. S. Morgan and M. C. Morrison, 197–240. Cambridge: Cambridge University Press.

Ricardo, David. 1817. *On the Principles of Political Economy and Taxation*. Vol. I of *The Collected Works of David Ricardo*, ed. P. Sraffa and M. Dobb. Cambridge: Cambridge University Press [1951].

Rizzo, M. J. 1982. "Mises and Lakatos: A Reformulation of Austrian Methodology." In *Method, Process, and Austrian Economics*, ed. I. M. Kirzner, 53–72. Lexington, MA: Lexington Books.

Robbins, Lionel. 1932. *An Essay on the Nature & Significance of Economic Science*. London: Macmillan.

Robbins, Lionel. 1952. *An Essay on the Nature & Significance of Economic Science*, 2nd ed. London: Macmillan.

Robbins, Lionel. 1979. "On Latsis's *Method and Appraisal in Economics*: A Review Essay." *Journal of Economic Literature* 17: 996–1004.

Robertson, Linda R. 1996. "'Debating Markets': A Rhetorical Analysis of Economic Discourse." *Feminist Economics* 2: 98–113.

Robinson, Joan. 1933. *The Economics of Imperfect Competition*. London: Macmillan.

Robinson, Joan. 1977. "What Are the Questions?" *Journal of Economic Literature* 15: 1318–39.

Romer, Paul M. 1986. "Increasing Returns and Long Run Growth." *Journal of Political Economy* 94: 1002–37.

Romer, Paul M. 1990. "Endogenous Technological Change." *Journal of Political Economy* 98: 71–102.

Romer, Paul M. 1994. "The Origins of Endogenous Growth." *Journal of Economic Perspectives* 8: 3–22.

Roncaglia, Alessandro. 1995. "Multiple Discoveries: Quantitative Data and Ideological Biasees. A Comment on Niehans." *The European Journal of the History of Economic Thought* 2: 289–93.

Roorda, Jonathan. 1997. "Kitcher on Theory Choice." *Erkenntnis* 46: 215–39.

Rorty, Richard. 1965. "Mind-Body Identity, Privacy, and Categories." *Review of Metaphysics* 19: 24–54.

Rorty, Richard. 1970. "In Defense of Eliminative Materialism." *Review of Metaphysics* 24: 112–21.

Rorty, Richard. 1979. *Philosophy and the Mirror of Nature*. Princeton, NJ: Princeton University Press.

Rorty, Richard. 1982. *Consequences of Pragmatism*. Minneapolis: University of Minnesota Press.

Rorty, Richard. 1987. "Science as Solidarity." In *The Rhetoric of the Human Sciences*, ed. J. S. Nelson, A. Megill, and D. N. McCloskey, 38–52. Madison: University of Wisconsin Press.

Rorty, Richard. 1989. *Contingency, Irony, and Solidarity*. Cambridge: Cambridge University Press.

Rorty, Richard. 1991a. *Objectivity, Relativism, and Truth: Philosophical Papers Vol I.* Cambridge: Cambridge University Press.

Rorty, Richard. 1991b. *Essays on Heidegger and Others: Philosophical Papers Vol II.* Cambridge: Cambridge University Press.

Rorty, Richard. 1993. "Trotsky and the Wild Orchids." In *Wild Orchids and Trotsky: Messages from American Universities*, ed. M. Edmundson, 31–50. New York: Penguin.

Rorty, Richard. 1994. "Dewey Between Hegel and Darwin." In *Modernist Impulses in the Human Sciences 1870–1930*, ed. D. Ross, 54–68. Baltimore, MD: Johns Hopkins University Press.

Rorty, Richard. 1995. "Feminism and Pragmatism." In *Pragmatism: A Contemporary Reader*, ed. R. B. Goodman, 125–48. New York: Routledge.

Rose, Hilary. 1994. *Love, Power, and Knowledge: Towards a Feminist Transformation of the Sciences (Race, Gender, and Science)*. Bloomington: Indiana University Press.

Rosenau, Pauline M. 1992. *Post-modernism and the Social Sciences: Insights, Inroads, and Intrusions*. Princeton, NJ: Princeton University Press.

Rosenberg, Alexander. 1976. *Microeconomic Laws: A Philosophical Analysis*. Pittsburgh, PA: University of Pittsburgh Press.

Rosenberg, Alexander. 1980a. *Sociobiology and the Preemption of Social Science.* Baltimore, MD: Johns Hopkins University Press.

Rosenberg, Alexander. 1980b. "A Skeptical History of Economic Theory." *Theory and Decision* 12: 75–85.

Rosenberg, Alexander. 1983. "If Economics Isn't Science, What is it?" *Philosophical Forum* 14: 296–314.

Rosenberg, Alexander. 1985a. "Methodology, Theory, and the Philosophy of Science." *Pacific Philosophical Quarterly* 66: 377–93.

Rosenberg, Alexander. 1985b. *The Structure of Biological Science*. Cambridge: Cambridge University Press.

Rosenberg, Alexander. 1986. "Lakatosian Consolations for Economists." *Economics and Philosophy* 2: 127–39.

Rosenberg, Alexander. 1988a. "Rhetoric is Not Important Enough for Economists to Bother About." *Economics and Philosophy* 4: 173–6.

Rosenberg, Alexander. 1988b. "Economics is Too Important to be Left to the Rhetoricians." *Economics and Philosophy* 4: 129–49.

Rosenberg, Alexander. 1989. "Are Generic Predictions Enough?" *Erkenntnis* 30: 43–68.

Rosenberg, Alexander. 1992. *Economics – Mathematical Politics or Science of Diminishing Returns?* Chicago: University of Chicago Press.

Rosenberg, Alexander. 1994a. *Instrumental Biology or the Disunity of Science.* Chicago: University of Chicago Press.

Rosenberg, Alexander. 1994b. "What is the Cognitive Status of Economic Theory?" In *New Directions in Economic Methodology*, ed. R. Backhouse, 216–35. London: Routledge.

Rosenberg, Alexander. 1995a. *Philosophy of Social Science*, 2nd ed. Boulder, CO: Westview Press.

Rosenberg, Alexander. 1995b. "The Metaphysics of Microeconomics." *The Monist* 78: 352–67.

Rosenberg, Alexander. 1995c. "Laws, Damn Laws, and Ceteris Paribus Clauses." *The Southern Journal of Philosophy* 34: 183–204.

Rosenberg, Alexander. 1996. "A Field Guide to Recent Species of Naturalism." *British Journal for the Philosophy of Science* 47: 1–29.

Rosenberg, Alexander. 1998. "Folk Psychology." In *The Handbook of Economic Methodology*, ed. J. B. Davis, D. W. Hands, and U. Mäki, 195–7. Cheltenham: Edward Elgar.

Ross, Andrew, ed. 1996. *Science Wars.* Durham, NC: Duke University Press.

Ross, Don. 1995. "Real Patterns and the Ontological Foundations of Microeconomics." *Economics and Philosophy* 11: 113–36.

Ross, Dorothy. 1991. *The Origins of American Social Science.* Cambridge: Cambridge University Press.

Rossetti, Jane. 1990. "Deconstructing Robert Lucas." In *Economics and Discourse: An Analysis of the Language of Economics*, ed. W. J. Samuels, 225–43. Boston: Kluwer.

Roth, Paul A. 1987. *Meaning and Method in the Social Sciences.* Ithaca, NY: Cornell University Press.

Roth, Paul A. 1996. "Will the Real Scientists Please Stand Up? Dead Ends and Live Issues in the Explanation of Scientific Knowledge." *Studies in History and Philosophy of Science* 27: 43–68.

Rotheim, Roy J. 1998. "On Closed Systems and the Language of Economic Discourse." *Review of Social Economy* 56: 324–34.

Rottenberg, Simon. 1981. "The Economy of Science: The Proper Place of Government in the Growth of Science." *Minerva* 19: 43–71.

Rotwein, Eugene. 1959. "On 'The Methodology of Positive Economics'." *Quarterly Journal of Economics* 73: 554–75.

Rotwein, Eugene. 1980. "Friedman's Critics: A Critic's Reply to Boland." *Journal of Economic Literature* 18: 1553–5.

Rubinstein, Ariel. 1998. *Modeling Bounded Rationality.* Cambridge, MA: MIT Press.

Ruccio, David F. 1991. "Postmodernism and Economics." *Journal of Post Keynesian Economics* 13: 495–510.

Runde, Jochen. 1996. "On Popper, Probabilities, and Propensities." *Review of Social Economy* 54: 465–85 [reprinted with minor revisions as chapter 4 of Fleetwood 1999].

Rutherford, Malcolm. 1989. "What is Wrong with the New Institutionalist Economics (and What is Still Wrong with the Old)." *Review of Political Economy* 1: 299–318.

Rutherford, Malcolm. 1990. "Science, Self-Correction and Values: From Peirce to Institutionalism." In *Social Economics: Retrospect and Prospect*, ed. J. Lutz, 391–406. Boston: Kluwer Academic.

Rutherford, Malcolm. 1994. *Institutions in Economics: The Old and the New Institutionalism.* Cambridge: Cambridge University Press.

Salanti, Andrea. 1987. "Falsification and Fallibilism as Epistemic Foundations of Economics." *Kyklos* 40: 368–92.

Salanti, Andrea. 1991. "Roy Weintraub's *Studies in Appraisal*: Lakatosian Consolations or Something Else?" *Economics and Philosophy* 7: 221–34.

Salanti, Andrea. 1993a. "A Reply to Professor Weintraub." *Economics and Philosophy* 9: 139–144.

Salanti, Andrea. 1993b. "Lakatosian Perspectives on General Equilibrium Analysis: A Reply." *Economics and Philosophy* 9: 283–7.

Salmon, Wesley C. 1966. *The Foundations of Scientific Inference*. Pittsburgh, PA: University of Pittsburgh Press.

Salmon, Wesley C. 1989. "Four Decades of Scientific Explanation." In *Scientific Explanation*, ed. P. Kitcher and W. C. Salmon, 3–219. Minneapolis: University of Minnesota Press.

Samuels, Warren J. 1990a. "The Self-Referentiality of Veblen's Theory." *Journal of Economic Issues* 24: 695–718.

Samuels, Warren J. 1991. "'Truth' and 'Discourse' in the Social Construction of Economic Reality: An Essay on the Relation of Knowledge to Socioleconomic Policy." *Journal of Post Keynesian Economics* 13: 511–24.

Samuels, Warren J. 1996. "Postmodernism and Economics: A Middlebrow View." *Journal of Economic Methodology* 3: 113–20.

Samuels, Warren J., ed. 1990b. *Economics and Discourse: An Analysis of the Language of Economics*. Boston: Kluwer.

Samuelson, Paul A. 1938a. "A Note on the Pure Theory of Consumer's Behaviour." *Economica* 5: 61–71.

Samuelson, Paul A. 1938b. "The Empirical Implications of Utility Analysis." *Econometrica* 6: 344–56.

Samuelson, Paul A. 1938c. "A Note on the Pure Theory of Consumer's Behaviour: An Addendum." *Economica* 5: 353–4.

Samuelson, Paul A. 1947. *Foundations of Economic Analysis*. Cambridge, MA: Harvard University Press.

Samuelson, Paul A. 1948a. *Economics*. New York: McGraw Hill.

Samuelson, Paul A. 1948b. "Consumption Theory in Terms of Revealed Preference." *Economica* 15: 243–53.

Samuelson, Paul A. 1950. "The Problem of Integrability in Utility Theory." *Economica* 17: 355–85.

Samuelson, Paul A. 1953. "Consumption Theorems in Terms of Overcompensation Rather Than Indifference Comparisons." *Economica* 20: 1–9.

Samuelson, Paul A. 1963. "Problems of Methodology – Discussion." *American Economic Review* 53: 231–6.

Samuelson, Paul A. 1964. "Theory and Realism: A Reply." *American Economic Review* 54: 736–9.

Samuelson, Paul A. 1965. "Professor Samuelson on Theory and Realism: Reply." *American Economic Review* 55: 1164–72.

Samuelson, Paul A. 1972. "Maximum Principles in Analytical Economics." *American Economic Review* 62: 249–62.

Samuelson, Paul A. 1992. "My Life Philosophy: Policy Credos and Working Ways." In *Eminent Economists: Their Life Philosophies*, ed. M. Szenberg, 236–47. Cambridge: Cambridge University Press.

Sargent, Thomas. 1993. *Bounded Rationality in Macroeconomics*. Oxford: Oxford University Press.

Sawyer, K. R., Beed, Clive, and Sankey, H. 1997. "Undetermination in Economics: The Duhem-Quine Thesis." *Economics and Philosophy* 13: 1–23.

Schabas, Margaret. 1990. *A World Ruled by Number: William Stanley Jevons and the Rise of Mathematical Economics.* Princeton, NJ: Princeton University Press.

Schabas, Margaret. 1995. "John Stuart Mill and Concepts of Nature." *Dialogue* 34: 447–65.

Schaffer, Simon. 1984. "Newton at the Crossroads." *Radical Philosophy* 37: 23–8.

Schmidt, R. H. 1982. "Methodology and Finance." *Theory and Decision* 14: 391–413.

Schmitt, Frederick F. 1985. "Bibliography." In *Naturalizing Epistemology*, ed. H. Kornblith, 269–99. Cambridge, MA: MIT Press.

Schultz, Henry. 1938. *Theory and Measurement of Demand.* Chicago: University of Chicago Press.

Schwartz, Pedro. 1972. *The New Political Economy of J. S. Mill.* Durham, NC: Duke University Press.

Seigfried, Charlene Haddock. 1996. *Pragmatism and Feminism: Reweaving the Social Fabric.* Chicago: University of Chicago Press.

Seigfried, Charlene Haddock. 1998. "John Dewey's Pragmatist Feminism." In *Reading Dewey: Interpretations for a Postmodern Generation*, ed. L. A. Hickman, 187–216. Bloomington: Indiana University Press.

Seiz, Janet. 1993. "Feminism and the History of Economic Thought." *History of Political Economy* 25: 185–201.

Seiz, Janet. 1995. "Epistemology and the Tasks of Feminist Economics." *Feminist Economics* 1: 110–18.

Senior, Nassau W. 1836. *An Outline of the Science of Political Economy* [New York: Augustus M. Kelly reprint 1965].

Sensat, Julius. 1988. "Methodological Individualism and Marxism." *Economics and Philosophy* 4: 189–219.

Sent, Esther-Mirjam. 1996. "What an Economist Can Teach Nancy Cartwright." *Social Epistemology* 10: 171–92.

Sent, Esther-Mirjam. 1997a. "Sargent Versus Simon: Bounded Rationality Unbound." *Cambridge Journal of Economics* 21: 323–38.

Sent, Esther-Mirjam. 1997b. "An Economists' Glance at Goldman's Economics." *Philosophy of Science* 64 (Proceedings): S139–48.

Sent, Esther-Mirjam. 1997c. "STS: A Reflexive Review." *History of Political Economy* 29: 751–60.

Sent, Esther-Mirjam. 1998a. *The Evolving Rationality of Rational Expectations.* Cambridge: Cambridge University Press.

Sent, Esther-Mirjam. 1998b. "Bounded Rationality." In *The Handbook of Economic Methodology*, ed. J. B. Davis, D. W. Hands, and U. Mäki, 36–40. Cheltenham: Edward Elgar.

Sent, Esther-Mirjam. 1999. "Economics of Science: Survey and Suggestions." *Journal of Economic Methodology* 6: 95–124.

Shapin, Steven. 1982. "History of Science and Its Sociological Reconstructions." *History of Science* 20: 157–211.

Shapin, Steven. 1988. "Understanding the Merton Thesis." *Isis* 79: 594–605.

Shapin, Steven. 1992. "Discipline and Bounding: The History and Sociology of Science As Seen Through the Externalism-Internalism Debate." *History of Science* 30: 333–69.

Shapin, Steven. 1994. *A Social History of Truth: Civility and Science in Seventeenth-Century England.* Chicago: University of Chicago Press.

Shapin, Steven and Schaffer, Simon. 1985. *Leviathan and the Air-Pump: Hobbes, Boyle, and the Experimental Life.* Princeton, NJ: Princeton University Press.

Shearmur, Jeremy. 1991. "Popper, Lakatos and Theoretical Progress in Economics." In *Appraising Economic Theories: Studies in the Methodology of Scientific Research Programs*, ed. M. Blaug and N. De Marchi, 35–52. Aldershot: Edward Elgar.

Shi, Yanfei. 2000. "Economics of Scientific Knowledge: A Rational Choice Neo-Institutionalist Theory of Science." Ph.D. Dissertation, University of Newcastle.

Simon, Herbert. 1945. *Administrative Behavior*. New York: Macmillan.

Simon, Herbert. 1957a. *Administrative Behavior*, 2nd ed. New York: Macmillan.

Simon, Herbert. 1957b. *Models of Man*. New York: John Wiley.

Simon, Herbert. 1986. "Interview." In *The Cognitive Revolution in Psychology*, ed. B. J. Baars, 362–81. New York: The Guilford Press.

Simon, Herbert. 1991. *Models of My Life*. New York: Basic Books.

Simon, Herbert. 1992. "Scientific Discovery as Problem Solving." *International Studies in the Philosophy of Science* 6: 3–14.

Slezak, Peter. 1989. "Scientific Discovery by Computer as Empirical Refutation of the Strong Program." *Social Studies of Science* 19: 563–600.

Smelser, Neil J. and Swedberg, Richard. 1994. "The Sociological Perspective on the Economy." In *The Handbook of Economic Sociology*, ed. N. J. Smelser and R. Swedberg, 3–26. Princeton, NJ: Princeton University Press.

Smith, Barbara Herrnstein. 1997. *Belief and Resistance*. Cambridge, MA: Harvard University Press.

Smith, Barry. 1990. "Aristotle, Menger, Mises: An Essay in the Metaphysics of Economics." In *Carl Menger and His Legacy in Economics*, ed. B. J. Caldwell, 263–88. Durham, NC: Duke University Press.

Smith, Barry. 1997. "The Connectionist Mind: A Study of Hayekian Psychology." In *Hayek: Economist and Social Philosopher*, ed. S. F. Frowen, 9–29. New York: St. Martin's.

Smith, Vernon. 1989. "Theory, Experiment, and Economics." *Journal of Economic Perspectives* 3: 151–69.

Smith, Vernon, McCabe, Kevin A., and Rassenti, Stephen J. 1991. "Lakatos and Experimental Economics." In *Appraising Economic Theories: Studies in the Methodology of Scientific Research Programs*, ed. M. Blaug and N. De Marchi, 197–226. Aldershot: Edward Elgar.

Sneed, Joseph D. 1971. *The Logical Structure of Mathematical Physics*. Dordrecht: Reidel.

Sneed, Joseph D. 1989. "Micro-Economic Models of Problem Choice in Basic Science." *Erkenntnis* 30: 207–24.

Sokal, Alan and Bricmont, Jean. 1998. *Fashionable Nonsense: Postmodern Intellectuals' Abuse of Science*. New York: Picador.

Solomon, Miriam. 1994a. "Social Empiricism." *Noûs* 28: 325–43.

Solomon, Miriam. 1994b. "A More Social Epistemology." In *Socializing Epistemology*, ed. F. F. Schmitt, 217–33. Lanham, MD: Roman & Littlefield.

Solomon, Miriam. 1995a. "The Pragmatic Turn in Naturalistic Philosophy of Science." *Perspectives on Science* 3: 206–30.

Solomon, Miriam. 1995b. "Legend Naturalism and Scientific Progress: An Essay on Philip Kitcher's *The Advancement of Science*." *Studies in History and Philosophy of Science* 26: 205–18.

Solow, Robert M. 1956. "A Contribution to the Theory of Economic Growth." *Quarterly Journal of Economics* 70: 65–94.

Solow, Robert M. 1957. "Technical Change and the Aggregate Production Function." *Review of Economics and Statistics* 39: 312–20.

Soros, George. 1998. *The Crisis of Global Capitalism*. New York: Public Affairs Press.

Stanfield, Ron. 1974. "Kuhnian Scientific Revolutions and the Keynesian Revolution." *Journal of Economic Issues* 8: 97–109.

Steedman, Ian. 1991. "Negative and Positive Contributions: Appraising Sraffa and Lakatos." In *Appraising Economic Theories: Studies in the Methodology of Scientific Research Programs*, ed. M. Blaug and N. De Marchi, 435–50. Aldershot: Edward Elgar.

Steedman, Ian. 1995. "Sraffian Economics and the Capital Controversy." In *Heterodox Economic Theories: True or False?*, ed. F. Moseley, 1–22. Aldershot: Edward Elgar.

Stegmüller, Wolfgang. 1976. *The Structure and Dynamics of Theories*. New York: Springer-Verlag.

Stegmüller, Wolfgang. 1978. "A Combined Approach to the Dynamics of Theories." *Theory and Decision* 9: 39–75.

Stegmüller, Wolfgang. 1979. *The Structuralist View of Theories*. New York: Springer-Verlag.

Stegmüller, Wolfgang, Balzer, Wolfgang, and Sophn, Wolfgang, eds. 1982. *Philosophy of Economics*. New York: Springer-Verlag.

Stephan, Paula E. 1996. "The Economics of Science." *Journal of Economic Literature* 34: 1199–235.

Stephan, Paula E. and Levin, Sharon. 1992. *Striking the Mother Lode in Science: The Importance of Age, Place, and Time*. Oxford: Oxford University Press.

Stephan, Paula and Levin, Sharon. 1996. "Comment on Diamond Paper." *Knowledge & Policy* 9: 72–5.

Sterelny, Kim. 1993. "Science and Selection." *Biology and Philosophy* 9: 45–62.

Stevens, Stanley S. 1939. "Psychology and the Science of Science." *Psychological Bulletin* 36: 221–63.

Stewart, Hanish. 1995. "A Critique of Instrumental Reason in Economics." *Economics and Philosophy* 11: 57–83.

Stewart, W. Christopher. 1991. "Social and Economic Aspects of Peirce's Conception of Science." *Transactions of the Charles S. Peirce Society* 27: 501–26.

Stich, Stephen P. 1983. *From Folk Psychology to Cognitive Science*. Cambridge, MA: MIT Press.

Stich, Stephen P. 1996. *Deconstructing the Mind*. New York: Oxford University Press.

Stigler, George J. 1947. "Professor Lester and the Marginalists." *American Economic Review* 37: 154–7.

Stigler, George J. 1982. "Merton on Multiples, Denied and Affirmed." In *The Economist as Preacher and Other Essays*, 98–103. Chicago: University of Chicago Press.

Stokes, Geoff. 1997. "Karl Popper's Political Philosophy of Social Science." *Philosophy of the Social Sciences* 27: 56–79.

Stove, D. C. 1982. *Popper and After*. New York: Pergamon.

Strassmann, Dianna. 1993a. "The Stories of Economics and the Power of the Storyteller." *History of Political Economy* 25: 147–65.

Strassmann, Dianna. 1993b. "Not a Free Market: the Rhetoric of Disciplinary Authority in Economics." In *Beyond Economic Man: Feminist Theory and Economics*, ed. M. A. Ferber and J. A. Nelson, 54–68. Chicago: University of Chicago Press.

Strassmann, Dianna. 1994. "Feminist Thought and Economics; Or, What Do the Visigoths Know?" *American Economic Review* 84: 153–8.

Sullivan, Patrick F. 1991. "On Falsificationist Interpretations of Peirce." *Transactions of the Charles S. Peirce Society* 27: 197–219.

Suppe, Frederick. 1977. *The Structure of Scientific Theories*, 2nd ed. Urbana: University of Illinois Press.

Suppe, Frederick. 1988. "A Nondeductivist Approach to Theoretical Explanation." In *The Limitations of Deductivism*, ed. A. Grünbaum and W. C. Salmon, 128–66. Berkeley: University of California Press.

Suppe, Frederick. 1989. *The Semantic Conception of Theories and Scientific Realism*. Urbana: University of Illinois Press.

Suppes, Patrick. 1957. *Introduction to Logic*. New York: Van Nostrand.

Suppes, Patrick. 1961. "A Comparison of the Meaning and Uses of Model in Mathematics and the Empirical Sciences." In *The Concept and the Role of Models in Mathematics and Natural and Social Science*, ed. H. Freudenthal, 163–77. Dordrecht: Reidel.

Suppes, Patrick. 1967. "What Is a Scientific Theory?" In *Philosophy of Science Today*, ed. S. Morgenbesser, 55–67. New York: Basic Books.

Suppes, Patrick. 1977. "The Structure of Theories and the Analysis of Data." In *The Structure of Scientific Theories*, 2nd ed., ed. F. Suppe, 266–83. Urbana: University of Illinois Press.

Susser, Bernard. 1989. "The Sociology of Knowledge and Its Enemies." *Inquiry* 32: 254–60.

Swales, John M. 1993. "The Paradox of Value: Six Treatments in Search of the Reader." In *Economics and Language*, ed. W. Henderson, T. Dudley-Evans, and R. Backhouse, 223–39. London: Routledge.

Swedberg, Richard. 1987. "Economic Sociology: Past and Present." *Current Sociology* 35: 1–221.

Swedberg, Richard. 1998. "Economic Sociology." In *The Handbook of Economic Methodology*, ed. J. B. Davis, D. W. Hands, and U. Mäki, 134–8. Cheltenham: Edward Elgar.

Thagard, Paul. 1993. "Societies of Minds: Science as Distributed Computing." *Studies in History and Philosophy of Science* 24: 49–67.

Tichy, Pavel. 1974. "On Popper's Definitions of Verisimilitude." *British Journal for the Philosophy of Science* 25: 155–60.

Tilman, Rick. 1998. "John Dewey as User and Critic of Thorstein Veblen's Ideas." *Journal of the History of Economic Thought* 20: 145–60.

Tollison, R. D. 1986. "Economists as the Subject of Economic Theory." *Southern Economic Journal* 52: 909–22.

Tool, Marc R. 1985. *The Discretionary Economy: A Normative Theory of Political Economy*. Boulder, CO: Westview.

Tool, Marc R. 1990. "Culture Versus Social Value? A Response to Anne Mayhew." *Journal of Economic Issues* 24: 1122–33.

Toruno, Mayo C. 1988. "Appraisals and Rational Reconstructions of General Equilibrium Theory." *Journal of Economic Issues* 22: 127–55.

Traweek, Sharon. 1988. *Beamtimes and Lifetimes: the World of High Energy Physicists*. Cambridge, MA: Harvard University Press.

Tullock, Gordon. 1966. *The Organization of Inquiry*. Durham, NC: Duke University Press.

Uebel, Thomas E. 1992. *Overcoming Logical Positivism From Within: The Emergence of Neurath's Naturalism in the Vienna Circle's Protocol Sentence Debate*. Amsterdam: Editions Rodopi.

Uebel, Thomas E. 1996. "Anti-Foundationalism and the Vienna Circle's Revolution in Philosophy." *British Journal for the Philosophy of Science* 47: 415–40.

Uebel, Thomas E. 1998. "Neurath, Otto." In *The Handbook of Economic Methodology*, ed. J. B. Davis, D. W. Hands, and U. Mäki, 331–3. Cheltenham: Edward Elgar.

Uzawa, Hirofumi. 1965. "Optimum Technical Change in an Aggregate Model of Economic Growth." *International Economic Review* 6: 18–31.

Vanberg, Viktor J. 1994. *Rules and Choice in Economics*. London: Routledge.

Vanberg, Viktor J. 1998. "Rule Following." In *The Handbook of Economic Methodology*, ed. J. B. Davis, D. W. Hands, and U. Mäki, 432–5. Cheltenham: Edward Elgar.

van Eeghen, Piet-Hein. 1996. "Towards a Methodology of Tendencies." *Journal of Economic Methodology* 3: 261–84.

van Fraassen, Bas. 1970. "On the Extension of Beth's Semantics of Physical Theories." *Philosophy of Science* 37: 325–39.

van Fraassen, Bas. 1980. *The Scientific Image*. Oxford: Clarendon.

Veblen, Thorstein. 1904. *The Theory of Business Enterprise*. New York: Charles Scribner's Sons [New Brunswick, NJ: Transactions, 1978].

Veblen, Thorstein. 1919. *The Place of Science in Modern Civilization and Other Essays*. New York: Viking.

Veblen, Thorstein. 1923. *Absentee Ownership and Business Enterprise in Recent Times*. B. W. Huebsch [New York: Augustus M. Kelley reprint 1964].

Veblen, Thorstein. 1934. "The Intellectual Pre-eminence of Jews in Modern Europe." *Essays in Our Changing Order*. New York: Viking Press.

Vilks, Arnis. 1992. "A Set of Axioms for Neoclassical Economics and the Methodological Status of the Equilibrium Concept." *Economics and Philosophy* 8: 51–82.

Vining, Rutledge. 1949a. "Koopmans on the Choice of Variables to Be Studied and of Methods of Measurement." *The Review of Economics and Statistics* 31: 77–86.

Vining, Rutledge. 1949b. "A Rejoinder." *The Review of Economics and Statistics* 31: 91–4.

Viskovatoff, Alex. 1998. "Is Gerard Debreu a Deductivist? Commenting on Tony Lawson's *Economics and Reality*." *Review of Social Economy* 56: 335–46.

Vonnegut, Kurt. 1981. *Palm Sunday*. New York: Dell Books.

Wald, Abraham. 1951. "On Some Systems of Equations of Mathematical Economics." *Econometrica* 19: 368–403.

Walker, Donald A., ed. 1983. *William Jaffé's Essays on Walras*. Cambridge: Cambridge University Press.

Waller, William T., Jr. and Robertson, Linda R. 1991. "Valuation as Discourse and Process: Or, How We Got Out of a Methodological Quagmire On Our Way to Purposeful Institutionalist Analysis." *Journal of Economic Issues* 25: 1029–48.

Walras, Léon. 1954. *Elements of Pure Economics*. Trans. W. Jaffé from the 4th definitive edition, 1926. Homewood, IL: Richard D. Irwin [1st edition 1874, Augustus M. Kelley reprint 1977].

Walsh, Vivian. 1987. "Models and Theory." In *The New Palgrave: A Dictionary of Economics*, ed. J. Eatwell, M. Millgate, and P. Newman, 482–3. London: Macmillan.

Walsh, Vivian. 1996. *Rationality, Allocation, and Reproduction*. Oxford: Oxford University Press.

Watkins, John. 1984. *Science and Scepticism*. Princeton, NJ: Princeton University Press.

Weintraub, E. Roy. 1979. *Microfoundations*. Cambridge: Cambridge University Press.

Weintraub, E. Roy. 1982. "Review of *The Mathematical Experience* by P. J. Davis and R. Hersh." *Journal of Economic Literature* 20: 114–15.

Weintraub, E. Roy. 1983. "On the Existence of a Competitive Equilibrium, 1930–1954." *Journal of Economic Literature* 21: 1–39.

Weintraub, E. Roy. 1985a. *General Equilibrium Analysis: Studies in Appraisal*. Cambridge: Cambridge University Press.

Weintraub, E. Roy. 1985b. "Appraising General Equilibrium Analysis." *Economics and Philosophy* 1: 23–37.

Weintraub, E. Roy. 1988a. "On the Brittleness of the Orange Equilibrium." In *The Consequences of Economic Rhetoric*, ed. A. Klamer, D. N. McCloskey, and R. M. Solow, 146–62. Cambridge: Cambridge University Press.

Weintraub, E. Roy. 1988b. "The Neo-Walrasian Program is Empirically Progressive." In *The Popperian Legacy in Economics*, ed. N. De Marchi, 213–27. Cambridge: Cambridge University Press.

Weintraub, E. Roy. 1989. "Methodology Doesn't Matter, But the History of Thought Might." *Scandinavian Journal of Economics* 91: 477–93.

Weintraub, E. Roy. 1991a. *Stabilizing Dynamics: Constructing Economic Knowledge.* Cambridge: Cambridge University Press.

Weintraub, E. Roy. 1991b. "Surveying Dynamics." *Journal of Post Keynesian Economics* 13: 525–44.

Weintraub, E. Roy. 1997. "Is 'Is' a Precursor of' a Transitive Relation?" In *Pluralism in Economics*, ed. A. Salanti and E. Screpanti, 212–31. Cheltenham: Edward Elgar.

Weintraub, E. Roy and Mirowski, Philip. 1994. "The Pure and the Applied: Bourbakism Comes to Mathematical Economics." *Science in Context* 7: 245–72.

Werskey, Gary. 1988. *The Visible College: A Collective Biography of British Scientists and Socialists of the 1930s.* London: Free Association Books [originally published 1978].

West, Cornel. 1987. *The American Evasion of Philosophy: A Genealogy of Pragmatism.* Madison: University of Wisconsin Press.

West, Cornel. 1993. *Keeping Faith: Philosophy and Race in America.* New York: Routledge.

Westbrook, Robert. 1991. *John Dewey and American Democracy.* Ithaca, NY: Cornell University Press.

Whitaker, John K. 1975. "John Stuart Mill's Methodology." *Journal of Political Economy* 83: 1033–49.

White, Michael V. 1994a. " 'That God-Forgotten Thornton': Exorcising Higgling After *On Labour.*" In *Higgling: Transactors and Their Markets in the History of Economics* [Supplement to *HOPE* vol. 26], ed. N. De Marchi and M. S. Morgan, 149–83. Durham, NC: Duke University Press.

White, Michael V. 1994b. "Bridging the National and the Social: Science and Character in Jevons's Political Economy." *Economic Inquiry* 32: 429–44.

Wible, James R. 1984. "The Instrumentalism of Dewey and Friedman." *Journal of Economic Issues* 18: 1049–70.

Wible, James R. 1991. "Maximization, Replication, and the Economic Rationality of Positive Economic Science." *Review of Political Economy* 3: 164–86.

Wible, James R. 1992. "Fraud in Science: An Economic Approach." *Philosophy of the Social Sciences* 22: 5–27.

Wible, James R. 1994a. "Charles Sanders Peirce's Economy of Research." *Journal of Economic Methodology* 1: 135–60.

Wible, James R. 1994b. "Rescher's Economic Philosophy of Science." *Journal of Economic Methodology* 1: 314–29.

Wible, James R. 1995. "The Economic Organization of Science, the Firm, and the Marketplace." *Philosophy of the Social Sciences* 25: 39–68.

Wible, James R. 1998. *The Economics of Science: Methodology and Epistemology as if Economics Really Mattered.* London: Routledge.

Wible, James R. 1999. "The Economic Writings of C. S. Peirce and His Critique of Utilitarianism: Darwin, Dmesis, and *De Gustibus Non Est Disputandum.*" Paper presented at the History of Economics Society Annual meeting in June 1999 at the University of North Carolina, Greensboro.

Williamson, Oliver. 1975. *Markets and Hierarchies.* New York: Free Press.

Williamson, Oliver. 1985. *The Economic Institutions of Capitalism.* New York: Free Press.

Winch, Peter. 1990. *The Idea of a Social Science*, 2nd ed. London: Routledge [1st edition 1958].

Wittgenstein, Ludwig. 1922. *Tractatus Logico-Philosophicus.* London: Routledge and Kegan Paul.

Wittgenstein, Ludwig. 1953. *Philosophical Investigations.* Oxford: Blackwell.

Wong, Stanley. 1973. "The F-Twist and the Methodology of Paul Samuelson." *American Economic Review* 63: 312–25.

Wong, Stanley. 1978. *The Foundations of Paul Samuelson's Revealed Preference Theory.* Boston: Routledge Kegan Paul.

Woolgar, Steve. 1981. "Interests and Explanation in the Social Study of Science." *Social Studies of Science* 11: 365–94.

Woolgar, Steve. 1992. "Some Remarks about Positionism: A Reply to Collins and Yearley." In *Science as Practice and Culture*, ed. A. Pickering, 327–42. Chicago: University of Chicago Press.

Woolgar, Steve, ed. 1988. *Knowledge and Reflexivity.* London: Sage.

Woolley, Frances R. 1993. "The Feminist Challenge to Neoclassical Economics." *Cambridge Journal of Economics* 17: 485–500.

Worrall, John. 1982. "Scientific Realism and Scientific Change." *Philosophical Quarterly* 32: 99–124.

Worrall, John. 1989. "Structural Realism: The Best of Both Worlds?" *Dialectica* 43: 99–124.

Wray, K. Brad. 2000. "Invisible Hands and the Success of Science." *Philosophy at Science* 67: 163–75.

Wylie, Alison. 1995. "Doing Philosophy As a Feminist: Longino on the Search for a Feminist Epistemology." *Philosophical Topics* 23: 345–58.

Ylikoski, Petri. 1995. "The Invisible Hand and Science." *Science Studies* 8: 32–43.

Yonay, Youval P. 1994. "When Black Boxes Clash: Competing Ideas of What Science Is in Economics, 1924–39." *Social Studies of Science* 24: 39–80.

Yonay, Youval P. 1998. *The Struggle Over the Soul of Economics: Institutionalist and Neoclassical Economists in America Between the Wars.* Princeton, NJ: Princeton University Press.

Young, Allyn. 1928. "Increasing Returns and Economic Progress." *Economic Journal* 38: 527–42.

Zahar, E. G. 1995. "The Problem of the Empirical Basis." In *Karl Popper: Philosophy and Problems*, ed. A. O'Hear, 45–74. Cambridge: Cambridge University Press.

Ziman, John. 1994. *Prometheus Bound: Science in A Dynamic Steady State.* Cambridge: Cambridge University Press.

Zamora Bonilla, Jesus P. 1999a. "Elementary Economics of Scientific Consensus." *Theoria* 14: 461–88.

Zamora Bonilla, Jesus P. 1999b. "Verisimilitude and the Scientific Strategy of Economic Theory." *Journal of Economic Methodology* 6: 331–50.

Zamora Bonilla, Jesus P. 2000. "Economics, Economic Methodology and Methodonomics." Paper presented at the European Society for the History of Economic Thought Meetings in Graz, Austria, Feb. 25–7, 2000.

WEB SITES

The following Web sites contain a wealth of information about various topics discussed in the preceding chapters. All of these sites provide links that connect to a variety of related sites.

Economic Methodology and History of Economic Thought

History of Economics (links to sources on many figures and schools in this history of economic thought)
www.eh.net/HE/

History of Economics Society (HES)
www.eh.net/HE/HisEcSoc/

International Network for Economic Methodology
www.econmethodology.org/

A Mill Page
www.cpm.ll.ehime-u.ac.jp/AkamacHomePage/Akamac_E-text_Links/Mill.html

Center For Critical Realism
www.criticalrealism.demon.co.uk/index.html

Philosophy of Science

Institute Vienna Cirle
hhobel.phl.univie.ac.at/wk/

Karl Popper-Institute
hhobel.phl.univie.ac.at/wk/

History and Philosophy Working Group (HOPOS)
hhobel.phl.univie.ac.at/wk/

The Karl Popper Web
http://www.eeng.dcu.ie/~tkpw/

Naturalism and Cognitive Science

Resources in the Philosophy of Mind and Cognitive Science
www.hku.hk/philodep/www/mind.htm

On Evolutionary Epistemology
www.ed.uiuc.edu/facstaff/g-cziko/stb/

Principia Cybernetica Web
http://pespmc1.vub.ac.be/DEFAULT.html

Philosophy and the Neurosciences Online
www.artsci.wustl.edu/~pjmandik/philneur.html

Sociological Approaches

Sociology of Knowledge
www.cudenver.edu/~mryder/itc_data/soc_knowledge.html

Virtual STS
http://post.queensu.ca/~simonb/vstsmain.htm

Actor Network Resource
www.comp.lancs.ac.uk/sociology/antres.html

Pragmatism

The Pragmatism Cybrary
www.pragmatism.org/

Charles Sanders Peirce
www.door.net/arisbe/

The Center for Dewey Studies
www.siu.edu/~deweyctr/index2.html

Feminist Epistemology

Feminist Epistemology
www.cddc.vt.edu/feminism/epi.html

Postmodernism

Everything Postmodern
broquard.tilted.com/postmodern/episte.html

INDEX

For EU product safety concerns, contact us at Calle de José Abascal, 56–1°,
28003 Madrid, Spain or eugpsr@cambridge.org.

www.ingramcontent.com/pod-product-compliance
Ingram Content Group UK Ltd.
Pitfield, Milton Keynes, MK11 3LW, UK
UKHW012155180425
457623UK00007B/47